Why Do You Need this New Edition?

The digital age has revolutionized the public relations industry, and there have been many new developments since 2005 when the fifth edition was published. This new edition reflects today's practice by giving up-to-date practical information on how to write and produce public relations materials in multiple formats for traditional media and the "new media" that also includes social networking sites.

The textbook also remains well grounded in how to prepare publicity materials for traditional media such as newspapers, magazines, radio, and television. These "traditional" media are still widely used and have even extended their reach through online offerings. In sum, the "traditional" media and the "new media" are converging and today's public relations writer must understand how they reinforce each other in terms of reaching various publics.

The sixth edition builds upon the popularity of the previous editions by being the most comprehensive "how to" text on the market. It's written in plain English and contains clear, step-by-step guidelines for everything from how to write a blog to working with drive-time DJs and planning an event. It, unlike other textbooks, gives step-by-step procedures that include examples from award-winning campaigns. The text also provides the context of the entire public relations process—research, planning, communication, and evaluation. Some key features of this new edition include:

1. An entirely new chapter on using the Web and social networking sites.
2. Making e-mail pitches to journalists and bloggers to get publicity.
3. Using key words for search engine optimization (SEO).
4. Maximizing distribution via electronic newswires and feature-placement services.

5. How to get your client on the *Today* show or *David Letterman.*
6. The odds of getting Jennifer Lopez or Brad Pitt to attend your event.
7. When it's OK to send an e-vite to an event.
8. How to convert a television news release (VNR) to a YouTube video.
9. Composing a publicity photo that actually gets published.
10. The basics of how to work with journalists and bloggers.
11. Checklists in every chapter giving step-by-step guidelines for writing publicity materials.
12. New PR Casebooks that give detailed information on how an organization conducted an award-winning campaign.
13. New skill building activities at the end of every chapter to help you apply the basic concepts to real situations.
14. Pithy pull-out quotes from leading professionals about today's "real-world" practice.
15. Extensive references to websites in every chapter so you can do more exploring of ideas, programs, and concepts.
16. Revised chapters on how to plan an event, conduct a complete public relations campaign, and measure your success.
17. Summary of key points and concepts at the end of every chapter.
18. A glossary of key terms and their definitions.

In sum, this new edition is a virtual encyclopedia of how to prepare public relations materials in today's digital world. This book, more than any other comparable introductory writing text, tells you how to work in today's rapidly changing digital environment.

PEARSON

Public Relations Writing and Media Techniques

SIXTH EDITION

Dennis L. Wilcox
San Jose State University

PEARSON

Boston ▪ New York ▪ San Francisco
Mexico City ▪ Montreal ▪ Toronto ▪ London ▪ Madrid ▪ Munich ▪ Paris
Hong Kong ▪ Singapore ▪ Tokyo ▪ Cape Town ▪ Sydney

Acquisitions Editor: *Jeanne Zalesky*
Editorial Assistant: *Megan Lentz*
Marketing Manager: *Suzan Czajkowski*
Production Supervisor: *Roberta Sherman*
Editorial-Production Service: *Modern Graphics, Inc.*
Manufacturing Buyer: *Debbie Rossi*
Electronic Composition: *Modern Graphics, Inc.*
Interior Design: *Denise Hoffman*
Cover Administrator: *Kristina Mose-Libon*

For related titles and support materials, visit our online catalog at www.ablongman.com

Between the time website information is gathered and then published, it is not unusual for some sites to have closed. Also, the transcription of URLs can result in typographical errors. The publisher would appreciate notification where these errors occur so that they may be corrected in subsequent edition.

ISBN-13: 978-0-205-64828-3
ISBN-10: 0-205-64828-2

Cataloging-in-publication data unavailable at press time.

Printed in the United States of America

10 9 8 7 6 5 4 3 2 1   HAM   12 11 10 9 8

Credits appear on page 547, which constitutes an extension of the copyright page.

Contents

Preface   xix

▮PART 1 The Basics of Public Relations Writing

▮ CHAPTER 1 Getting Organized for Writing   1

The Framework of Public Relations Writing   1

Writing Is Only One Component   1   ▪   Writers as
Communication Technicians   2

TIPS FOR SUCCESS   Writing Is One of Five Skills   3

The Public Relations Writer   3

Objectives   3   ▪   Audiences   5   ▪   Channels   5

Preparation for Writing   6

Computers   6   ▪   Reference Sources   8

TIPS FOR SUCCESS   Useful Websites for Public Relations Writers   14

Research: The Prelude to Writing   16

Search Engines   17   ▪   Electronic Databases   18

Writing Guidelines   19

Outlining the Purpose   19

TIPS FOR SUCCESS   Need Information? Use a Database   20

Sentences   21   ▪   Paragraphs   22   ▪   Word Choice   22   ▪
Active Verbs and Present Tense   23

TIPS FOR SUCCESS   How to Improve Your Writing   24

Imagery   25

Errors to Avoid   26

Spelling   26   ▪   Gobbledygook and Jargon   26   ▪   Poor Sentence
Structure   27   ▪   Wrong Words   27   ▪   "Sound-alike" Words   28   ▪
Redundancies   28   ▪   Too Many Numbers   29   ▪   Hype   29   ▪
Bias and Stereotypes   29   ▪   Politically Incorrect Language   30

TIPS FOR SUCCESS   Devices for Achieving Clear Writing   29

Summary   31

Skill Building Activities   32

Suggested Readings   32

■ **CHAPTER 2 Becoming a Persuasive Writer   34**

Persuasion: As Old as Civilization   34

The Basics of Communication   35
Sender 35 ■ Message 35 ■ Channel 36 ■ Receiver 36

Theories of Communication   37
Media Uses and Gratification 37 ■ Cognitive Dissonance 38

TIPS FOR SUCCESS   A Persuasion Sampler   38
Framing 39 ■ Diffusion and Adoption 40 ■ Hierarchy of Needs 41

Factors in Persuasive Writing   42
Audience Analysis 42

TIPS FOR SUCCESS   How to Write Persuasive Messages   42
Source Credibility 43 ■ Appeal to Self-Interest 45

TIPS FOR SUCCESS   Appeals That Move People to Act   45
Clarity of the Message 46 ■ Timing and Context 46 ■ Symbols, Slogans, and Acronyms 46 ■ Semantics 47 ■ Suggestions for Action 48 ■ Content and Structure 48

TIPS FOR SUCCESS   Why Writing Fails to Persuade   50

PR CASEBOOK   Emotional Appeals Humanize an Issue   53

Persuasive Speaking   54

Persuasion and Propaganda   55

The Ethics of Persuasion   56

TIPS FOR SUCCESS   An Ethics Test for Public Relations Writers   57

Summary   58

Skill Building Activities   59

Suggested Readings   60

■ **CHAPTER 3 Avoiding Legal Hassles   61**

A Sampling of Legal Problems   61

Libel and Defamation   62
The Fair Comment Defense 64 ■ Avoiding Defamation Suits 65

Invasion of Privacy   65
Employee Newsletters 66 ■ Photo Releases 66 ■ Product Publicity and Advertising 67 ■ Media Inquiries about Employees 67 ■ Employee Blogs 68 ■ Virtual Online Communities 69

Copyright Law   69
Fair Use versus Infringement 70

TIPS FOR SUCCESS   Don't Plagiarize: It's Unethical   71

Photography and Artwork   72   ▪   Work for Hire   73

TIPS FOR SUCCESS   Guidelines for Using Copyrighted Material   74
Copyright Issues on the Internet   75

Trademark Law   76
The Protection of Trademarks   76   ▪   The Problem of Trademark Infringement   79

TIPS FOR SUCCESS   Trademarks Require a Capital Letter   79
Misappropriation of Personality   81

Regulatory Agencies   82
The Federal Trade Commission   82   ▪   The Securities and Exchange Commission   84

Other Federal Regulatory Agencies   86
The Federal Communications Commission   86   ▪   The Food and Drug Administration   87   ▪   Bureau of Alcohol, Tobacco, and Firearms   87

Working with Lawyers   88

Summary   89

Skill Building Activities   89

Suggested Readings   90

▪ CHAPTER 4 Finding and Making News   91

The Challenge of Making News   91

What Makes News   92
Timeliness   92   ▪   Prominence   94

TIPS FOR SUCCESS   If It's May, It's National Asparagus Month   95
Proximity   96   ▪   Significance   97   ▪   Unusualness   98   ▪   Human Interest   99   ▪   Conflict   100   ▪   Newness   101

How to Find News   101
Internal News Sources   101   ▪   External News Sources   102

How To Create News   103
Brainstorming   105   ▪   Special Events   105

TIPS FOR SUCCESS   32 Ways to Create News for Your Organization   106
Contests   108   ▪   Polls and Surveys   109   ▪   Top 10 Lists   110

TIPS FOR SUCCESS   How to Conduct a Credible Survey   111
Product Demonstrations   112   ▪   Stunts   112   ▪   Rallies and Protests   114   ▪   Personal Appearances   115   ▪   Awards   116

Summary   116

Skill Building Activities   117

Suggested Readings   117

PART 2 Writing for Mass Media

■ CHAPTER 5 Writing the News Release 118

The Backbone of Publicity Programs 118

The Value of News Releases 119

Planning a News Release 119
The Basic Questions 119 ■ Selection of Paper 120 ■ Spacing and Margins 120 ■ Use AP Style 122

Types of News Releases 122
Announcements 122 ■ Spot Announcements 122 ■ Reaction Releases 123 ■ Bad News 123 ■ Local News 124

Parts of a Traditional News Release 124
Letterhead 125 ■ Contacts 126 ■ Headline 126 ■ Dateline 127 ■ The Lead 128

TIPS FOR SUCCESS 10 Classic News Release Mistakes 129
Body of the Text 131 ■ Description of the Organization 133

Writing the E-mail News Release 134

TIPS FOR SUCCESS Rules for Writing a News Release 135

Preparing the Multimedia News Release 136

Summary 139

Skill Building Activities 139

Suggested Readings 140

■ CHAPTER 6 Preparing Fact Sheets, Advisories, Media Kits, and Pitches 141

Expanding the Publicity Tool Kit 141

Fact Sheets 141

Media Advisories 144

Media Kits 146
Compiling a Media Kit 147 ■ Electronic Media Kits 149

PR CASEBOOK Leapin' Lizards!!! CD Media Kit Makes Giant Lizard a Star 150

Pitching a Story 152

Researching the Publication   154

TIPS FOR SUCCESS   **How To Successfully Pitch Bloggers**   **155**

Preparing the Pitch   156

TIPS FOR SUCCESS   **Writing the "Perfect" Pitch**   **157**

TIPS FOR SUCCESS   **Guidelines for Pitching Stories by E-Mail**   **159**

Follow Up on Your Pitch   160

Summary   **161**

Skill Building Activities   **161**

Suggested Readings   **161**

■ **C H A P T E R 7 Creating News Features and Op-Ed**   **163**

The Value of Features   **163**

Planning a News Feature   **164**

Ways to Proceed   165

Types of Features   **168**

Case Study   168   ■   Application Study   169

TIPS FOR SUCCESS   **Writing a Case Study**   **169**

Research Study   170   ■   Backgrounder   171   ■   Personality
Profile   173   ■   Historical Piece   173

TIPS FOR SUCCESS   **Writing a Personality Profile**   **174**

Parts of a Feature   **175**

The Headline   175

TIPS FOR SUCCESS   **Writing a Great Feature Story**   **176**

The Lead   177   ■   The Body   178   ■   The Summary   179   ■   Photos
and Graphics   179

Placement Opportunities   **180**

Newspapers   180   ■   General Magazines   180   ■   Specialty/Trade
Magazines   180   ■   Internal Publications   181

Writing an Op-Ed   **181**

TIPS FOR SUCCESS   **Writing the "Perfect" Op-Ed**   **183**

Letters to the Editor   184

Summary   **186**

Skill Building Activities   **186**

Suggested Readings   **187**

■ **CHAPTER 8 Selecting Publicity Photos and Graphics   188**

The Importance of Publicity Photos   188

Components of a Good Photo   188
Technical Quality 189

TIPS FOR SUCCESS   How to Take Product Photos that Get Published   189
Subject Matter 190 ■ Composition 191 ■ Action 192 ■
Scale 193 ■ Camera Angle 193 ■ Lighting and Timing 194 ■
Color 196

Working with Photographers   196
Finding Photographers 197

TIPS FOR SUCCESS   Photo Advice from the Experts   197
Contracts 198 ■ The Photo Session 198 ■ Cropping and
Retouching 199 ■ Ethical Considerations 199

Writing Photo Captions   200

PR CASEBOOK   The Photo News Release   201

Creating Other Graphics   202
Charts 203 ■ Diagrams 204 ■ Renderings and Scale
Models 204 ■ Line Drawings and Clip Art 204

Maintaining Photo and Art Files   205

Distributing Photos and Artwork   205

Summary   206

Skill Building Activities   206

Suggested Readings   207

■ **CHAPTER 9 Writing for Radio and Television   208**

The Wide Reach of Broadcasting   208

Radio   208
Radio News Releases 209

TIPS FOR SUCCESS   How To Write a Radio News Release   212
Audio News Releases 212 ■ Public Service Announcements 215 ■
Radio Media Tours 222

Television   223
   Video News Releases   225

TIPS FOR SUCCESS   The Jargon of Writing for Video   229

PR CASEBOOK   Television B-Roll Is an Explosive Hit   230
   Public Service Announcements   233   ■   Satellite Media Tours   234

TIPS FOR SUCCESS   Guidelines for a Successful SMT   237

Personal Appearances and Product Placements   239
   Talk Shows   240

TIPS FOR SUCCESS   The Ideal Talk Show Guest   242
   Magazine Shows   242   ■   Product Placement   242   ■   Radio
   Promotions   244   ■   Community Calendars   245   ■   Documentary
   Videos   246

Summary   247

Skill Building Activities   247

Suggested Readings   248

■ **CHAPTER 10 Distributing News to the Media   249**

Reaching the Media   249
   Media Databases   249   ■   Editorial Calendars   252   ■
   Tip Sheets   253

Distribution of Materials   254
   E-Mail   254

TIPS FOR SUCCESS   Selecting a Distribution Channel   255
   Online Newsrooms   257   ■   Electronic Wire Services   259

**TIPS FOR SUCCESS   Maximizing Distribution of Online
                     News Releases   261**
   Feature Placement Firms   264

TIPS FOR SUCCESS   The Components of a Successful Food Feature   265
   Photo Placement Firms   267   ■   Mail   268   ■   Fax   269

Summary   270

Skill Building Activities   271

Suggested Readings   271

■ **CHAPTER 11 Getting Along with Journalists 272**

The Importance of Media Relations 272

The Media's Dependence on Public Relations 273

Public Relations' Dependence on the Media 274

Areas of Friction 275

Hype and News Release Spam 275

TIPS FOR SUCCESS Working with Bloggers 276

Name Calling 278 ■ Sloppy/Biased Reporting 279 ■ Tabloid Journalism 279

TIPS FOR SUCCESS Correcting Errors in News Stories 280

Advertising Influence 281

Working with Journalists 282

Media Interviews 282

TIPS FOR SUCCESS Alternatives to Saying "No Comment" 283

News Conferences 285 ■ Teleconferences and Webcasts 288 ■ Media Tours 289

PR CASEBOOK A Media Tour Pays Off 290

Previews and Parties 291 ■ Press Junkets 293 ■ Editorial Board Meetings 294

A Media Relations Checklist 297

Media Etiquette 298

Crisis Communication 300

Summary 302

Skill Building Activities 303

Suggested Readings 304

■ **PART 3 Writing for Other Media**

■ **CHAPTER 12 Tapping the Web and New Media 305**

The Internet: Pervasive in Our Lives 305

The World Wide Web 306

TIPS FOR SUCCESS Traditional Media versus New Media 307

Writing for the Web 310

TIPS FOR SUCCESS Writing for a Website 312

Building an Effective Website 313 ■ Making the Site Interactive 315 ■ Attracting Visitors to Your Site 316 ■ Tracking Site Visitors 318 ■ Return on Investment 319 ■ Who Controls the Site? 320

The Basics of Webcasting **321**

The Rise of Social Media **322**

TIPS FOR SUCCESS **Road Signs on the New Media Highway** **323**
Tapping into Usenet and Listservs 324 ▪ Using RSS to
Distribute and Manage Information 325

The Explosion of Blogs **326**

TIPS FOR SUCCESS **How to Write a Blog** **327**

TIPS FOR SUCCESS **IBM's Guidelines for Employee Blogs** **331**

TIPS FOR SUCCESS **Responding to Rogue Websites** **332**
Making Friends on MySpace and Facebook 333 ▪ YouTube:
King of Video Clips 334

PR CASEBOOK **Trojan Uses the Web and Social Media to Promote
Sexual Health** **336**
Flickr: Sharing Photos 338 ▪ Getting a Second Life 339 ▪
Texting, Twitter, and Wikis 340 ▪ Podcasts: The
Portable Medium 342 ▪ The Next Generation: Web 3.0 345

The Continuing Role of Traditional Media **345**

Summary **348**

Skill Building Activities **349**

Suggested Readings **349**

▪ **CHAPTER 13 Producing Newsletters and Brochures** **351**

The Value of Print Publications **351**

The Balancing Act of Editors **353**
A Mission Statement Gives Purpose 354 ▪ Editorial Plans 355

PR CASEBOOK **Magazine Puts a "Face" on Saving Children's Lives** **356**

Newsletters and Magazines **358**
Meeting Audience Interests 359 ▪ Design 360 ▪
Format 361 ▪ Layout 363

TIPS FOR SUCCESS **How to Create Great Publications** **364**
Photos and Illustrations 365 ▪ Headlines 365 ▪
Lead Sentences 367

Online Newsletters **368**

Brochures **369**
Planning 370 ▪ Writing 371

TIPS FOR SUCCESS **Basic Brochure Design 101** **372**
Format 373 ▪ Paper 373 ▪ Type Fonts 375 ▪
Ink and Color 376 ▪ Finding a Printer 377

TIPS FOR SUCCESS How Much Will It Cost? **378**

Annual Reports **378**

    Planning and Writing 380 ■ Trends in Content and Delivery 381

Desktop Publishing **382**

Summary **384**

Skill Building Activities **384**

Suggested Readings **385**

■ **CHAPTER 14** **Writing E-Mail, Memos, and, Proposals** **386**

The Challenge of Managing Communication Overload **386**

E-Mail **387**

    Purpose 388

TIPS FOR SUCCESS Avoid E-Mail Clutter: Use Voice Mail **389**

    Content 390

TIPS FOR SUCCESS Mind Your E-Mail Manners **391**

    Format 392

Memorandums **393**

    Purpose 393 ■ Content 394 ■ Format 394

Letters **395**

    Purpose 395

TIPS FOR SUCCESS How to Write Efficient Letters **396**

    Content 396 ■ Format 397

Proposals **398**

    Purpose 399 ■ Organization 399

TIPS FOR SUCCESS How to Write a Position Paper **400**

Summary **401**

Skill Building Activities **402**

Suggested Readings **402**

■ **CHAPTER 15** **Giving Speeches and Presentations** **403**

The Challenge of the Speaking Circuit **403**

The Basics of Speech Writing **403**

    Researching Audience and Speaker 403 ■ Laying the
    Groundwork 404

PR CASEBOOK A Systematic Approach to Speechwriting **405**

Writing the Speech   406

The Basics of Giving a Speech   409

TIPS FOR SUCCESS   How to Introduce a Speaker   409

Know Your Objective   410 ■ Structure the Message for the Ear   410 ■ Tailor Remarks to the Audience   411 ■ Give Specifics   411

TIPS FOR SUCCESS   Keep Your Audience in Mind   412

Keep It Timely and Short   412 ■ Gestures and Eye Contact   413

Visual Aids for Presentations   414

TIPS FOR SUCCESS   Nonverbal Communication Speaks Volumes   414

PowerPoint   415

Other Speech Formats   418

Panels   418

TIPS FOR SUCCESS   How to Improve a Speech   419

Debates   420

Speaker Training and Placement   420

Executive Training   420 ■ Speaker's Bureaus   421 ■ Placement of Speakers   422 ■ Publicity Opportunities   424

TIPS FOR SUCCESS   The Speech as News Release   425

Summary   425

Skill Building Activities   426

Suggested Readings   426

■ **CHAPTER 16   Using Direct Mail and Advertising   428**

The Basics of Direct Mail   428

Advantages of Direct Mail   429 ■ Disadvantages of Direct Mail   430

Creating A Direct Mail Package   430

Mailing Envelope   430 ■ The Letter   431

TIPS FOR SUCCESS   How to Write a Fund-Raising Letter   432

TIPS FOR SUCCESS   How to Do a Direct Mail Package   434

Brochures   434 ■ Reply Card   435 ■ Return Envelope   435 ■ Gifts   435

The Basics of Public Relations Advertising   436

Advantages of Advertising   437 ■ Disadvantages of Advertising   438

Types of Public Relations Advertising   **438**

Image Building   438   ■   Investor and Financial
Relations   441   ■   Public Service   441   ■
Advocacy/Issues   442   ■   Announcements   444

Creating a Print Ad   **444**

Headline   444   ■   Text   445   ■   Artwork   445   ■
Layout   445

TIPS FOR SUCCESS   **Effective Ad Elements**   **446**

Working with An Ad Agency   **446**

TIPS FOR SUCCESS   **Getting the Most from Your Ads**   **447**

Other Advertising Channels   **447**

Billboards   447   ■   Transit Panels   448   ■   Buttons and Bumper
Stickers   448   ■   Posters   448

PR CASEBOOK   **A PR/Advertising Campaign Fights Rape**   **449**

Sponsored Books   450   ■   T-Shirts   450   ■
Promotional Items   451

Summary   **451**

Skill Building Activities   **452**

Suggested Readings   **452**

■ PART 4 Managing Programs and Campaigns

■ CHAPTER 17 Organizing Meetings and Events   453

A World Filled with Meetings and Events   **453**

Staff and Committee Meetings   **454**

TIPS FOR SUCCESS   **How Good Are Your Meetings?**   **455**

Group Meetings   **456**

Planning   456

TIPS FOR SUCCESS   **How to Plan a Meeting**   **456**

Registration   459   ■   Program   460

Banquets   **461**

Working with Catering Managers   462

TIPS FOR SUCCESS   **Making a Budget for a Special Event**   **463**

Logistics and Timing   464

Receptions and Cocktail Parties   **465**

Open Houses and Plant Tours   466

TIPS FOR SUCCESS   How to Plan an Open House   469

Conventions   470
    Planning   470 ▪ Program   471

TIPS FOR SUCCESS   Making Reservations on the Web   473

Trade Shows   473
    Exhibit Booths   474 ▪ Press Rooms and Media Relations   475

Promotional Events   477

TIPS FOR SUCCESS   Corporate Sponsorships: Another Kind of Event   477
    Using Celebrities to Attract Attendance   478

PR CASEBOOK   When Going to the Restroom Is an Event   479
    Planning and Logistics   480

Summary   481

Skill Building Activities   482

Suggested Readings   482

▪ CHAPTER 18 Planning Programs and Campaigns   483

The Value of a Written Plan   483

Developing a Plan   484
    Gathering Information   484 ▪ Analyzing the Information   486

Elements of the Plan   486
    Situation   486

TIPS FOR SUCCESS   Components of a Public Relations Plan   487
    Objectives   488

PR CASEBOOK   Sunkist Turns Lemons into Lemonade for a Cause   490
    Audience   492 ▪ Strategy   492

TIPS FOR SUCCESS   How Public Relations Helps Fulfill Marketing Objectives   493
    Tactics   494 ▪ Calendar   494 ▪ Budget   497 ▪ Evaluation   498

Submitting a Plan for Approval   499

TIPS FOR SUCCESS   Do You Have a Winning Campaign?   500

Summary   500

Skill Building Activities   501

Suggested Readings   502

■ **CHAPTER 19 Measuring Success 503**

The Importance of Measurement 503

TIPS FOR SUCCESS Factors in Program Evaluation 505

Program Objectives 506

Measurement of Production/Distribution 507

Measurement of Message Exposure 507

Media Impressions 509 ■ Advertising Value Equivalency 509 ■
Systematic Tracking 511 ■ Monitoring the Internet 512 ■
Requests and 800 Numbers 514 ■ Cost per Person 515 ■
Event Attendance 515

Measurement of Audience Awareness 516

Measurement of Audience Attitudes 517

Measurement of Audience Action 518

Evaluation of Newsletters and Brochures 519

Content Analysis 519 ■ Readership Surveys 520 ■
Article Recall 521 ■ Readability 521 ■ Advisory Boards
and Focus Groups 522

Writing a Measurement Report 522

Summary 523

Skill Building Activities 524

Suggested Readings 524

Glossary 526
Index 531
Photo Credits 547

Preface

The sixth edition of *Public Relations Writing and Media Techniques* continues its widely acclaimed reputation for being the most comprehensive "how to" text on the market. It will give you a complete toolkit for writing and creating a full range of public relations materials for distribution through traditional media and what is now known as the "new media."

It is a user-friendly text written in plain English that contains clear, step-by-step guidelines illustrated by multiple examples from actual award-winning public relations programs conducted by many well-known organizations.

Although the emphasis is on the "nuts and bolts" of effective public relations writing and techniques, the text also provides the conceptual framework and broader context of how the tactics of public relations fit into the entire public relations process—research, planning, communication, and evaluation. The idea is to ensure that you not only know "how" to write public relations materials, but that you also understand "why" they are written from the standpoint of furthering organizational objectives.

The many updates, revisions, and additions to this new edition reflect today's work in public relations. Perhaps the most significant changes in this edition concern the digital revolution that has significantly changed how public relations writers think and work. News releases are now electronic, but so are media kits, newsletters, and brochures. The rise of blogs and other social media such as Facebook, MySpace, and YouTube have also challenged and given new opportunities for public relations practitioners. This edition, more than any other comparable introductory writing text, tells you how to work in the rapidly changing digital environment.

New in the Sixth Edition

The fundamentals of public relations writing remain the same, but how materials are formatted and distributed is constantly evolving. Many media techniques commonly used two or three years ago when the fifth edition was published are now considered out-of-date. Indeed, more than one public relations professional has pronounced that the traditional news release is now dead. This may be an exaggeration, but the fact does remain that today's multimedia news release in digital form is no longer a "trend," but actual practice.

New Chapter on the Internet and New Media

Chapter 12, "Tapping the Web and New Media," is a completely new chapter that tells you how public relations pros are now using the Web to bypass traditional media to reach audiences and engage them in dialogue. The basics of creating and maintaining a website are presented, as well as how to do Webcasts. You will learn about the power of blogs, how to write a blog, and how to work with bloggers to get publicity for your organization. The chapter also offers examples of how various public relations campaigns have used social networking sites such as Facebook, MySpace, and YouTube and virtual reality sites such as Second Life. Texting, Twitter, wikis, podcasts, and RSS feeds are also discussed from the standpoint of showing you how to use these new media in public relations. Numerous examples from the "real world" are given.

Other chapters integrate the Internet and the new media as appropriate. Chapter 5 discusses the format for a digital news release and the components of a multimedia news release. Chapter 6 explains how to prepare electronic media kits and pitch bloggers. Chapter 8 includes the mechanics of distributing publicity photos on the Internet. Chapter 9 is devoted to distribution methods, including the use of online newsrooms and electronic services such as Business Wire. Chapter 13 has information about online newsletters, and Chapter 14 reviews the do's and don'ts of e-mail.

Expanded Information on Key Aspects of Today's Public Relations Practice

The daily activities of public relations practitioners and how they work have changed since the fifth edition. The Internet is now an integral part of our lives, and the traditional and "new" media are converging. Public relations writers today must now master the characteristics of multiple media in order to use them effectively. This edition offers expanded treatment of various topics, offering more emphasis and information. Some examples include:

- The new capabilities of search engines such as Google, Yahoo!, and MSN (Chapter 1)
- Techniques for persuasive writing (Chapter 2)
- News release distribution via e-mail and the Internet (Chapter 5)
- Multimedia news releases (Chapter 5)
- E-mail pitches to journalists and bloggers (Chapter 5)
- Ghostwriting op-ed articles (Chapter 7)
- Video news releases (VNRs) on YouTube (Chapter 9)
- Online newsrooms as part of websites (Chapter 10)
- Electronic newswires such as Business Wire and PR Newswire (Chapter 10)
- Feature-placement firms such as Family Features (Chapter 10)
- News conferences and media tours (Chapter 11)
- The rise of blogs in influence and reach (Chapter 12)
- The popularity of social networking sites such as Facebook and MySpace (Chapter 12)

- Podcasts as "service" journalism (Chapter 12)
- Online newsletters on intranets (Chapter 13)
- PowerPoint presentations (Chapter 15)
- Trade shows as marketing events (Chapter 17)
- Writing a public relations proposal for approval (Chapter 18)
- The metrics of monitoring the Internet (Chapter 19)

How-To Checklists for the Aspiring Writer

Every chapter has new and revised "**TIPS FOR SUCCESS**" features that offer students checklists on how to write various materials and conduct basic media relations techniques. Such checklists provide step-by-step directions and help students grasp basic concepts that are discussed and elaborated upon in the chapter. Some examples:

- Useful websites for public relations writers (Chapter 1)
- An ethics test for public relations writers (Chapter 2)
- Guidelines for using copyrighted material (Chapter 3)
- How to publicize the results of a survey (Chapter 4)
- Rules for writing a news release (Chapter 5)
- How to pitch bloggers (Chapter 6)
- How to pitch stories by e-mail (Chapter 6)
- How to write the "perfect" op-ed (Chapter 7)
- Taking publicity photos that get published (Chapter 8)
- How to write a radio news release (Chapter 9)
- The ideal talk show guest (Chapter 9)
- Using keywords for search engine optimization (Chapter 10)
- How to work with bloggers (Chapter 11)
- Steps for writing a Web page (Chapter 12)
- How to write a blog (Chapter 12)
- Steps for writing and designing a brochure (Chapter 13)
- How to write e-mails that get opened (Chapter 14)
- How to introduce a speaker (Chapter 15)
- Factors that improve a speech (Chapter 15)
- How to write a fund-raising letter (Chapter 16)
- Using Web-based invitation systems (Chapter 17)
- Writing a public relations plan for approval (Chapter 18)
- How to evaluate a public relations campaign (Chapter 19)

New PR Casebooks to Stimulate Interest and Insight

A textbook filled with "how to" concepts can be somewhat boring if there are no practical examples from the "real world." The extensive use of "examples" is a highlight of this text in two ways. First, an example of how a concept was used in an actual situation is given throughout every chapter. Second, a more in-depth summary of a particular campaign is given in a boxed "PR Casebook" that helps students understand how various techniques complement each other in a campaign. Some new cases include the following:

- The "Think Outside the Bottle" campaign by environmental activist groups about the use of bottled water (Chapter 4)
- Using Dr. Seuss characters to launch the NEA's Read Across America campaign (Chapter 4)
- The roll-out of the Apple iPhone (Chapter 4)
- Planter's Peanuts 100th anniversary campaign (Chapter 6)
- Shedd Aquarium's promotion of a lizard exhibit (Chapter 6)
- Nintendo's CEO writes an op-ed for the LA Times (Chapter 7)
- Panasonic's publicity photo showing its new 150-inch plasma television (Chapter 8)
- A security firm's VNR featuring the blowing up of a transit bus (Chapter 9)
- Mattel's massive toy recall (Chapter 11)
- A Webcast by the U.S. Office of Engraving about the new $5 bill (Chapter 12)
- Trojan brand establishes a profile on Facebook to talk about sexual health (Chapter 12)
- Monterey Aquarium taps into Flickr, a photo-sharing site (Chapter 12)
- IBM's guidelines for employee blogs (Chapter 12)
- An award-winning feature story in St. Jude's Research Hospital's magazine (Chapter 13)
- An integrated campaign to inform young males about date rape (Chapter 16)
- Procter & Gamble's Charmin restrooms in New York's Times Square (Chapter 17)

New Skill Building Activities at the End of Each Chapter

Back by popular demand, skill building activities have again been placed at the end of each chapter instead of in the instructor's manual. The skill building activities provide students with practical assignments to reinforce the techniques they have learned in each chapter.

Quotes from Leading Professionals

Selected quotes from leading professionals are highlighted in each chapter. These short, pithy statements give the essence of a professional's insights and wisdom on a particular concept or technique. This approach is much more readable than a short narrative or Q&A with a professional that are featured in some texts.

Organization of the Book

The text is divided into four parts. It is organized in a way that makes it adaptable for either a semester or quarter course. In fact, some universities use the text for two courses in public relations writing. The first course usually covers the fundamentals of basic writing and how to prepare publicity materials for traditional media such as newspapers, magazines, radio, and television. The second course is then focused on controlled or sponsored media; preparing materials for newsletters, brochures, presentations, and websites. The text is written and organized so instructors can easily mix and match chapters that suit their students' needs. The four book sections are:

Part 1: The Basics of Public Relations Writing
Part 2: Writing for Mass Media
Part 3: Writing for Other Media
Part 4: Managing Programs and Campaigns

Part 1: The Basics of Public Relations Writing

This section introduces students to the basic framework of today's public relations practice and the role of the public relations writer. Chapter 1 reviews the basic concepts of good writing, errors to avoid, and what equipment is needed. Chapter 2 continues with the components of persuasive writing, provides a brief background of major communication theories, and ends with the ethical responsibilities of the public relations writer. Chapter 3 provides a legal framework for preparing materials. Attention is given to libel, privacy, copyright, trademarks, and governmental regulatory agencies. Chapter 4 helps students think strategically and creatively about what makes news. Traditional journalistic values are emphasized, but students are also briefed on how to generate news through special events, contests, and even stunts.

Part 2: Writing for Mass Media

The focus of this section is how to prepare basic materials for distribution to traditional mass media outlets. Chapter 5 thoroughly details the structure and format of the news release, which is the basic workhorse of public relations work. Attention is given to writing and formatting news releases, including multimedia ones, that are distributed via e-mail and electronic news services. Chapter 6 continues the process by detailing how to prepare fact sheets, media alerts, and media kits. Particularly valuable is a section on how to "pitch" journalists about a story. Chapter 7 focuses on the writing of news features, such as personality profiles and product-application stories. The writing of opinion pieces, such as op-eds, is also discussed. Chapter 8 examines the elements of good publicity photos and graphics, which often make a story more appealing to media outlets. It also offers suggestions on how to work with photographers and how to write photo captions. Chapter 9 is about writing for radio and television. Public service announcements (PSAs) are explored, as are the mechanics of producing video news releases (VNRs), booking guests on talk shows, and conducting satellite media tours. Chapter 10 is a detailed examination of how to use media databases and distribute public relations materials a number of ways, including via e-mail, online newsrooms, and wire services. The pros and cons of each method are discussed. Chapter 11 reviews the basics of effective media relations and how to work with journalists.

Part 3: Writing for Other Media

A great amount of public relations writing is for what is called "controlled" or "sponsored" media; in other words, media that don't have external gatekeepers that filter the organization's messages. Chapter 12 is about effectively using the Web and the new media. The construction and maintenance of websites are discussed. The chapter also examines webcasts, blogs, podcasts, and social networking sites, such as Facebook and YouTube, and explores how these new media are being used in public relations campaigns. Chapter 13 offers information on how to write and design print and online newsletters and brochures. The writing of annual reports also is discussed. Chapter 14 offers students a lesson in e-mail etiquette and details how to write e-mails to journalists that get opened. The writing of memos and proposals is also discussed. Chapter 15 is about how to write and give speeches and presentations. Guidelines for visual aids such as PowerPoint are provided. Chapter 16 is about preparing direct mail pieces and the key elements of public relations advertising.

Part 4: Planning Programs and Campaigns

This section gives students the broad picture and helps them understand that multiple tactics are used throughout a well-planned public relations campaign. Chapter 17 is focused on organizing meetings and events. Everything from how to hold committee meetings, organize a banquet, plan a convention, set up a trade show, and select a celebrity for a promotional event is discussed. Chapter 18 offers the essential elements of a public relations campaign, providing the information needed to integrate the various strategies and tactics into an effective campaign. Chapter 19 explores how to measure the success of a campaign, including the use of metrics.

Student Learning Tools

Each chapter of *Public Relations Writing and Media Techniques* includes several learning tools to help students better understand the concepts and give them the practice they need to apply what they have learned. In each chapter, you will find:

Chapter opening preview. ■ The preview shows the major sections and structure of the chapter.

"Tips for Success" boxed inserts. ■ These are checklists and guidelines that concisely give the essence of how to do various tactics and techniques discussed in the chapter.

Quotes from professionals. ■ Text boxes highlighting short quotes from professionals that emphasize a key concept in the text.

End-of-chapter summary. ■ The major themes and concepts are summarized in a series of brief sentences.

Skill Building Activities. ■ Several suggested assignments are offered to help students practice and apply what they have learned from the chapter.

Suggested Readings. ■ Readily accessible books and articles are suggested for additional reading.

Websites. ■ The websites for organizations mentioned in the text are provided so students can access more information about a particular program or campaign.

PR Casebook. ■ A summary of an actual public relations program, in many chapters, that illustrates and elaborates on a key topic.

■ Supplements

Instructors and students have a variety of tools available to them that will help make teaching and learning with *Public Relations Writing and Media Techniques* easier.

Instructor's Manual and Test Bank

The Instructor's Manual includes chapter outlines, sample syllabi, learning objectives, class activities, and discussion questions. The Test Bank includes several hundred multiple-choice and True/False questions. Available for download through our Instructor's Resource Center at www.pearsonhighered.com/irc (access code required).

Computerized Test Bank

The user-friendly interface enables instructors to view, edit, and add questions, transfer questions into tests, and print tests in a variety of fonts. Search and sort features allow instructors to locate questions quickly and arrange them in preferred order. Available for download through our Instructor's Resource Center at www.pearsonhighered/irc (access code required).

PowerPoint Slides

This text-specific comprehensive package consists of a collection of lecture outlines and graphic images keyed to every chapter in the text. The PowerPoint slides can be downloaded from our Instructor's Resource Center at www .pearsonhighered.com/irc (access code required).

MyCommunicationKit for Public Relations (Access Code Required)

MyCommunicationKit is an online supplement that offers book-specific learning objectives, chapter summaries, flashcards, and practice tests, as well as video clips and activities to aid student learning and comprehension. Also included in MyCommunicationKit are Research Navigator and weblinks, both of which provide assistance with and access to powerful and reliable research material. Please contact your local Pearson Allyn & Bacon representative for details or go to www.mycommunicationkit.com.

Public Relations Study Site

This website features public relations study materials for students, including flashcards and a complete set of practice tests for all major topics. Students will also find links to valuable sites for further exploration of major topics. The site can be accessed at www.abpublicrel.com.

Acknowledgments

I would like to thank those who reviewed the previous edition and made many suggestions that have been incorporated into this revision Claire Badaracco, Marquette University; Lora J. DeFore, Mississippi State University; Donn Silvis, California State University, Dominguez Hills; and Brenda J. Wrigley, Michigan State University. And a special thanks to the following educators who provided input for the sixth edition: Jeanne Allison, University of Missouri, St. Louis; Coy Callison, Texas Tech University; Kirk Hallahan, Colorado State University; Johnathan M. Marlow, Howard Payne University; Winston Mitchell, City University of New York, Medgar Evers College; Donnalyn Pompper, Temple University; and Erin E. Wilgenbusch, Iowa State University.

About the Author

Dennis L. Wilcox, Ph.D.

Dr. Wilcox is professor emeritus of public relations at San Jose State University and former director of the School of Journalism & Mass Communications. He is the lead author of *Public Relations Strategies and Tactics*, a popular introductory text, and coauthor of *Public Relations Today: Managing Competition and Conflict.*

He is an accredited (APR) member of the Public Relations Society of America (PRSA) and is also in the organization's College of Fellows recognizing his lifelong contributions to the profession. Wilcox is a former chair of the PRSA Educator's Academy and the public relations division of the Association for Education in Journalism & Mass Communications (AEJMC). Among his many awards is PRSA's "Educator of the Year" and the Xifra-Heras Award from the University of Girona (Spain) for contributions to international public relations education.

Wilcox is currently active in the International Public Relations Association (IPRA) and is a member of the Arthur W. Page Society, an organization of senior public relations executives. He now travels extensively giving university lectures and professional workshops in such diverse nations as Chile, Argentina, Latvia, Romania, Spain, Ukraine, Serbia, Kenya, India, Australia, and Thailand. His philosophy, to quote St. Augustine, is "The world is a book, and those who do not travel read only a page." He can be reached at denniswilcox@msn.com.

Getting Organized for Writing

1

TOPICS covered in this chapter include:

The Framework of Public
Relations Writing   1

The Public Relations Writer   3

Preparation for Writing   6

Research: The Prelude to Writing   16

Writing Guidelines   19

Errors to Avoid   26

The Framework of Public Relations Writing

The primary focus of this book is on one aspect of public relations practice—the writing and distribution of messages in a variety of formats and media channels. To the uninitiated, this activity is the sum and substance of public relations. For them, PR stands for "press releases." Because of this, it's necessary to first establish the framework in which public relations writing takes place.

Writing Is Only One Component

First, it is important to realize that the preparation of messages for distribution is only one part of the public relations process. Public relations is actually composed of four core components: **research, planning, communication,** and **evaluation.** Public relations writing is part of the communication component, which only occurs after research has been conducted and extensive planning to formulate the goals and objectives of a campaign have taken place. Planning also involves the selection of audiences to be reached, the key messages to be distributed, and the strategies that should be used to ensure the overall success of the program or campaign.

Strategies are statements of direction. A strategy, for example, might be to use multiple media outlets to reach women between the ages of 18 to 30 to make them aware of a new cosmetic on the market. In a public relations campaign, each strategy is made operational through a list of tactics. A tactic, for example, might entail the writing and placement of feature articles and "new product" reviews in appropriate women's magazines. Such a tactic might even be specified to the point of listing how many product news releases and features would be written and what "angle" would be used in each one. Another tactic might be the placement of a celebrity spokesperson on a particular television show that reaches women in the target audience.

Writers as Communication Technicians

Public relations writers and media placement specialists are responsible for implementing the tactics of a campaign or program. They, by definition, fulfill the "technician" roles. They are the "production" staff who write the news releases, formulate the feature stories, and contact the television show producer to make a "pitch" for the company's spokesperson to appear as a guest to talk about the product.

The role of writer and technician is the standard entry-level position in public relations, but some in the public relations field have been writers and media relations experts for most of their careers. This is because most positions in public relations at corporations or public relations firms are at the technician level. A speechwriter or an editor of an employee newsletter, for example, may be a skilled technician by definition, but he or she is also a highly prized professional who receives a good salary because of his or her expertise.

The concept of public relations roles is the result of research by Professors Glen Broom and David Dozier at San Diego State University. In their research, four roles emerged: (1) the *expert prescriber*—consultants to top management for strategic planning, (2) the *communication facilitator*—primarily the liaison between the organization and its public, (3) the *problem-solving facilitator*—works with management to solve current problems in a process-oriented way, and (4) the *communication technician*—practitioners who provide technical services such as news release writing, event planning, and graphic design.

Although the concept of four roles is interesting, further research by Dozier determined that it was more useful to simply distinguish between managers and technicians. Dozier says, "Managers make policy decisions and are held accountable for public relations outcomes," whereas "technicians carry out the low-level mechanics of generating communication products that implement policy decisions made by others."

This is not to say that professional practitioners don't fulfill both manager and technician roles. A professional may primarily be a manager but also be deeply involved in preparing a media kit or arranging a special event. By the same token, a public relations writer in an organization with limited staffing may primarily be a technician but also be involved in the planning of an entire campaign. The Tips for Success on page 3 outlines additional skills that a public relations writer should possess.

As you can see, the total framework of public relations is much more than just "press releases." Such materials are important, but they are only one highly visible manifestation of the entire public relations process. With this framework in mind, we begin our discussion about public relations writing and media techniques. At the end of the book, we will return to the managerial aspects of public relations with chapters on campaign planning and program evaluation.

Writing Is One of Five Skills

Fraser Seitel, a communications consultant and author of *The Practice of Public Relations*, agrees that knowledge of communications, and particularly writing skills, is a basic skill in public relations work. He says, "At best, PR practitioners are professional communicators. Communications is their skill. That means they must be the best writers, speakers, media experts, communication theorists, etc. in the organization."

He also offers four other basic skills that are necessary for success in public relations:

- **Knowledge of public relations.** Public relations practitioners must understand that they must communicate for understanding. He says, "PR is the opposite of confusing or distorting or obfuscating or, worst of all, lying. The essence of PR lies in acting credibly and telling the truth." Practitioners must "educate" management about the principles that form the foundation of proper public relations practice.

- **Knowledge of current events.** "PR people are called upon to cover the waterfront. . . ." That means the first thing public relations professionals must do is read the papers and be aware of current issues and personalities that are shaping the public agenda. "In the very best sense, the skilled PR person must be a Renaissance man or woman."

- **Knowledge of business.** Practitioners must have a knowledge of business and how the organization sustains itself. "Unless you can speak the 'language' of the organization, you'll have trouble being accepted as part of the team. . . ."

- **Knowledge of management.** Public relations practitioners must understand and appreciate how organizational policy is shaped and the pressures on management. "An essential part of the PR job is to 'interpret' the philosophy, policies and programs of management." ■

■ The Public Relations Writer

Although the public relations writer and the journalist share a number of common characteristics in their approach to writing, the public relations writer differs in objectives, audiences, and channels.

Objectives

A journalist is usually employed by a news organization to gather, process, and synthesize information for the primary purpose of providing news to the organization's subscribers, viewers, or listeners. A hallmark of professional reporting is to present information in an objective manner. A reporter's personal preference may affect the choice of words and the news angle but, in general, the reporter tries to maintain an attitude of neutrality.

The public relations writer, in contrast, is usually employed by an organization that wants to communicate with a variety of audiences, either through the news media or through other channels of communication. These organizations may include corporations, government agencies, environmental groups, labor unions, trade associations, or public relations firms that provide information on behalf of clients.

The writer's purpose is advocacy, not objectivity. The goal is not only to accurately inform, but also to persuade and motivate. Edward M. Stanton, former chairman of the Manning, Selvage & Lee public relations firm, once described public relations activity in *Public Relations Quarterly* as "working with clients on strategy and messages, and then delivering these messages to target audiences in order to persuade them to do something that is beneficial to the client."

Harold Burson, chairman emeritus of Burson-Marsteller and a longtime leader in the public relations profession, defines public relations activity, including writing, as "advancing information in the public forum for the purpose of contributing to public opinion." To be effective and credible, public relations messages must be based on facts. Burson continues:

> Nevertheless, we are advocates, and we need to remember that. We are advocates of a particular point of view—our client's or our employer's point of view. And while we recognize that serving the public interest best serves our client's interest, we are not journalists. That's not our job.

Professor Robert Heath, coauthor of *Rhetorical and Critical Approaches to Public Relations*, points out that the role of advocate is a time-honored one. It goes back 2,000 years to Aristotle, who conceptualized the term *rhetoric*—the ability to determine what needs to be said and how it should be said to achieve desired outcomes. Heath writes that rhetoric "entails the ability and obligation to demonstrate to an audience facts and arguments available to bring insight into an important issue."

Hence, all public relations writing should begin with the question, "How does this help the organization achieve its objectives?" For example, "Does the news release contain the key messages about the product and how it can benefit customers?"

The editor of a company employee newsletter must also consider company objectives when planning various articles. If the company wants to increase employee productivity, the editor may decide to (1) run several features about employees who have achieved high productivity in their jobs, (2) develop a regular column giving tips and advice about how to increase individual productivity, and (3) write some stories explaining how high productivity makes the company competitive and ensures job security.

A good example of how an employee publication supports corporate objectives is the *Philips Roving Reporter*, a video magazine directed to the 18,000 North American employees of Philips Electronics that is available via Philips' corporate intranet. The producers/editors used 2- to 3-minute video features to attract employee interest, excitement, and loyalty. News segments featured younger employees from the "middle ranks" rather than senior executives in dark suits just making pronouncements. The video magazine's objectives were to:

1. Increase understanding of the company's products and scope of business.
2. Educate employees to speak more intelligently and passionately about Philips in an effort to increase referrals of company products to their friends and families.

If an organizational newsletter is directed to consumers, the objectives may be quite different. Akron Children's Hospital, for example, started *Inside Children* as a way of reaching single-family households with children and family incomes of $30,000 or more within its 17-county service area. The objectives of the newsletter, published three times a year, were:

1. Generate business by building awareness for various departments and programs.
2. Recruit participants for various pediatric drug and clinical trials.
3. Generate requests for more information from the hospital's referral telephone line and the website.
4. Distribute various parenting and child health materials to interested parents.

Audiences

The traditional journalist writes for one audience—readers, listeners, or viewers of the medium for which he or she works. Newspapers, magazines, radio, and television are usually defined as "mass media," because the audience is numerous and anonymous and its members have little in common. A suburban daily newspaper, for example, circulates primarily among people who share a common residential area but have a broad range of backgrounds and interests. Such mass media, by definition, usually present material written at the fourth- to sixth-grade level and offer a wide variety of stories and features to satisfy almost any interest, be it sports, local news, or the daily horoscope.

In contrast, the readers of a special-interest magazine share a strong interest in only one subject—a particular hobby, a specific industry, or a highly specialized occupation. Reporters for such magazines write about just one subject for a limited and intensely interested audience.

The public relations writer, however, may write for numerous and radically different audiences—employees, community leaders, customers, teenagers, seniors, women, various ethnic and racial groups, travelers, governmental regulatory agencies, investors, farmers, and many others. Effective public relations writing requires careful definition of the audience and its composition so that information can be tailored to its interests and concerns. A public relations writer performs research constantly to determine the audience's needs, concerns, and interests. Armed with this information, the public relations writer can write a more persuasive message. The concepts of public opinion and persuasion are discussed in Chapter 2.

Channels

Journalists, by nature of their employment, primarily reach their audiences through one channel, the medium that publishes, broadcasts, or posts their work on websites. The public relations writer, with many specific audiences to reach, will probably use many channels. Indeed, public relations writers must not only determine the message, but they must also select the most effective channel of communication. In many cases, the channel might not be any of the traditional mass media. The most effective channel for the tailored message may be direct mail, a pamphlet, an organizational newsletter, a videotape, a poster, a special event, or even the Internet via online newsletters, chat groups, websites, blogs, podcasts, or even e-mail. In most cases, a combination of channels is selected to achieve maximum message penetration and understanding. This important concept is illustrated throughout this book by showing how organizations have used multiple media channels for a single project or campaign.

In this age of Internet-based communications, it is particularly important that today's public relations writer be prepared to provide information in a variety of media formats. A report on a seminar, sponsored by BusinessWire and West Glen Communications, summarized the beliefs of journalists and public relations professionals attending the meeting. It stated:

> It is clear . . . that no single news medium will be able to retain its audience. Media brands that intend to compete will be providing multimedia newscasts to give consumers immediacy, entertainment, interactivity, and choice in how to get their news. For PR practitioners, such news formats will require an in-depth understanding of not only each news brand and its respective audience, but also all of the components of the media mix, as they become more and more diverse in what information they present and how they present it.

Preparation for Writing

It is essential for the public relations writer to have a workspace that includes a computer and a printer, Internet access, and a reference library.

Computers

The most important piece of equipment in a public relations office is a computer. It may be a desktop computer or a more portable notebook (laptop) computer. Laptops are becoming more popular as faster technology, wireless networks, and lower prices enable users to log on almost anywhere and anytime. In fact, industry analysts estimated that laptops would account for the majority of U.S. computer sales by 2008 and worldwide sales by 2009.

Cheap, fast global communication, online commerce, the ability to find answers to almost any question on the Web using a search engine and the many wonders of the Internet are all underpinned by the widespread availability of inexpensive, powerful PCs. ■ The Economist

Public relations professionals spend much of their working day in front of a computer. One survey of independent public relations practitioners, many of whom work from home, found that they spend considerable amounts of time on the computer. Professors Vincent Hazelton of Radford University and Jay Rayburn of Florida State University conducted a study for the Public Relations Society of America (PRSA) and found that independent practitioners spend 25 percent of their time writing and another 16 percent of their time producing other communication tools. Another 6 percent of time is spent on research, and 23 percent is spent dealing with the media. In sum, about 70 percent of their time is tied directly or indirectly to working on a computer.

In addition, the USC Annenberg School Center for the Digital Future reported that the average U.S. Internet user spent 15.3 hours a week online in 2007, up from 8.9 hours in 2006. In other words, Americans are now spending as much time on the Internet as they spend watching television. Indeed, the *Economist*, in a 2006 article about the 25th anniversary of the personal computer (PC), noted, "Many office workers spend more time with their PCs than they do asleep or with their families."

The personal computer enables people to use sophisticated word processing software programs that permit maximum flexibility to write, edit, format, insert artwork, and merge information into a complete document. Word processing packages such as Microsoft Word or MacWrite have built-in dictionaries for checking spelling and grammar plus other features, such as a thesaurus, page preview, search and replace, word count, pagination, and editing functions. These tools substantially reduce the time needed for revisions and rewrites.

Microsoft Office is a popular package for public relations writers because it offers programs that make it possible to complete a variety of tasks. Most editions of Microsoft Office include the following: (1) Word, for creating and editing basic text documents; (2) Excel, for basic accounting and formatting of graphs and tables; (3) PowerPoint, for making presentations; (4) Publisher, for creating flyers and newsletters; and (5) Outlook, for sending and receiving e-mail. Many documents and graphics created in Microsoft Office programs can be converted into HTML for use on websites.

The type of computer you use is a matter of personal choice. The first decision is whether you want a desktop or a laptop. Public relations writers who are in the same office on a daily basis often prefer a desktop, because they can generally get more memory and hard disk space for less money than a comparable laptop. In addition, they like the idea of having larger monitors, currently 20 to 24 inches, than what can be found on a laptop.

Others, particularly students and professionals who travel frequently, prefer laptops because of their portability and flexibility. College bookstores, for example, report that more students are buying laptops because they can use them in the classroom, the campus library, and anywhere with wireless capability. In many cases, professionals have it both ways. They have a laptop that serves as a basic CPU (computer processing unit) that can go on the road with them, but they also use the laptop in the office, connecting it to a regular keyboard and a larger monitor. Figure 1.1 shows a product publicity photo showing a new laptop model.

The second choice is whether to buy an Apple or a PC. Both have their advocates. The PC crowd likes the idea that about 90 percent of the computers sold are PCs, and various software applications are more readily available because of this large market. PCs, in general, are also cheaper than Apple products and easier to repair, because many standardized components are common to all PC brands.

Apple devotees, however, remain undaunted. They cite product reviews that say Apple machines are faster, better, and far less prone to malicious software than Microsoft's Vista operating system. In addition, Apple's Leopard operating system has

▶ **FIGURE 1.1** **Computers for Today's Needs.** Laptops have overtaken desktops in terms of worldwide sales. In this product publicity photo distributed to the media via an electronic newswire, an employee of Dell Japan displays a new model during a press conference in Tokyo.

considerably narrowed the compatibility gap with PCs. Many people also like the slick, modern design of Apple products.

Computer manufacturers and software publishers, of course, are continually improving their products, making them even more powerful and versatile. It is now possible to get a good quality desktop computer and monitor for between $500 and $1,000. A good quality laptop costs between $800 to $1,200. That's the good news. The bad news is that the computer you buy today will be made obsolete by even more powerful operating systems and sophisticated hardware in 6 months.

Working professionals, recognizing the rapid pace at which new computer and software products come to market, often recommend that you buy the most powerful computer and collateral equipment you can possibly afford. A key consideration when buying a computer is whether it can be easily upgraded to add more memory, storage capacity, and processing speed as technology advances.

In 2008, experts were recommending that you buy a computer with a minimum 1 GB of memory and a 160 GB or larger hard drive. However, most experts recommend 2 GB of memory, because software programs, such as Adobe's *InDesign*, *Photoshop*, *Illustrator*, *Acrobat*, and *GoLive*, require a lot of memory to operate at maximum efficiency. In addition, experts recommended a machine with a DVD-ROM/CD-RW combo drive, multiple USB ports, a dual core processor, and a wireless card. Individuals interested in video editing and sophisticated gaming, of course, should purchase even more powerful computer hardware. As of mid-2008, some desktops were already offering 4 GB of memory and 700 GB hard drives.

Fortunately, printer technology does not change as rapidly as computers and software. You should buy a color inkjet or laser printer that produces high-quality, professional-looking documents and photos. Many public relations writers buy a combination printer, copier, scanner, and fax to conserve workspace. Although combination devices are cost-effective, some professionals complain that one machine trying to do multiple functions is more prone to breakdowns and mediocre performance. In 2008, a reasonably good printer with multiple functions cost between $100 and $150.

Reference Sources

A reference library is a must for any writer. Basic sources should be part of your book library, but they can also be in the format of a software program, a CD-ROM, a DVD, or an online resource. The key point is to have references that quickly give you instant access to a body of knowledge and enable you to confirm basic factual information.

Encyclopedias ■ The world's most popular reference source is now Wikipedia (www.wikipedia.org), which is regularly among the top 10 visited sites on the Internet. It recorded 52 million visitors in 2007. According to *The New York Times* in March 2008, "Close to one-third of the content appears in English—about 2,276,000 articles out of an approximate 7,500,000 total. The English articles contain more than 990 million words."

> **❝ Wikipedia already has more visitors than the online** *New York Times*, **CNN, and other mainstream sites. ❞** ■ *The Economist*

Wikipedia is unique in several ways. First, it is an online encyclopedia that is free to anyone with an Internet connection. Second, it is written by thousands of volunteers who post and edit entries. And anyone, including you, can edit an entry simply by clicking "edit this page." The idea is that another person, with more expertise, may also "edit" the entry, so there's a constant self-correcting process if an entry is factually incorrect. Traditionalists still express concern about the accuracy of information without the benefit of qualified experts certifying the entries, but Wikipedia has gained stature and greater acceptance as a legitimate source in recent years.

Another widely used source is the *Britannica Ultimate Reference Suite*, which is available on DVD and online at www.britannica.com. It is a comprehensive online resource that includes 65,000 articles and about 50 million words. It also features a dictionary, a thesaurus, an atlas, audio and video clips, and links to thousands of external links. It is available on an annual subscription basis, and the online edition claims that an article is updated every 20 minutes.

Another popular encyclopedia available on a subscription basis is Microsoft's *Encarta*. It's available on DVD and online (www.encarta.msn.com), and it has about 42,000 articles. *Encarta* features videos from the Discovery Channel, a colorful interface, a storehouse of famous quotations, translation dictionaries for international students, a dictionary and thesaurus, a world atlas, and the ability to download free updates every week.

Dictionary ■ The most common reference book is an up-to-date dictionary, and many writers keep a paperback version handy for a fast check instead of taking the time to log on to the Internet or bring up a software version.

The most extensive dictionary is the *Oxford English Dictionary* (OED), which contains more than 600,000 word definitions. But this number of words, in a 20-volume set, is probably more dictionary than anyone can absorb. Consequently, Oxford University offers a "compact" edition, the *Oxford Pocket Dictionary and Thesaurus*, which contains about 145,000 words and is available online for free word checking. A paperback version should be kept handy.

Most daily newspapers, including *The Wall Street Journal*, use *Webster's New World Dictionary*, college version. Another popular dictionary is Houghton Mifflin's *American Heritage Dictionary of the English Language*, known for its inclusion of up-to-date slang and regional expressions, its lively word histories, and its extensive use of photography.

Dictionaries are readily available as part of Microsoft Word, on CD-ROM and DVD, and even online. For example, one can purchase CD-ROM and DVD versions of *Webster's Electronic Dictionary* and the *American Heritage Electronic Dictionary*. These dictionaries are commonly used for spell checking, but they are also able to supply writers with words they don't even know. Type "Mexican" and "dog" and the dictionary gives you "Chihuahua."

Another approach is www.dictionary.com. It offers a dictionary and thesaurus as well as translation tools for Spanish, French, German, Italian, and Portuguese. Another good word site is www.yourdictionary.com, which provides links to 60 specialized glossaries in business, computing, law, and medicine.

Stylebook ■ A writer's reference library should contain several stylebooks. All writers, on occasion, puzzle over a matter of punctuation, subject–verb agreement, or the use of passive or active voice. Strunk and White's *The Elements of Style* has saved numerous writers from embarrassment over the years, but other grammar and style texts are also available. For example, *A Pocket Style Manual* by Diana Hacker (Bedford/St. Martin's Press) is a popular spiral-bound, pocket-sized paperback that gives the fundamentals of grammar, punctuation, and sentence structure. It also contains basic information about writing term papers. Another very readable style guide is *Please Don't Do That: The Pocket Guide to Good Writing* by John Schulz (Marquette Books).

In terms of journalistic writing, the most widely used stylebook is the *Associated Press Stylebook and Briefing on Media Law*. It is used by most weekly and daily newspapers in the United States, and it is updated and revised on a periodic basis. For example, in the most recent edition, the AP stylebook updated its spellings and capitalization for Internet terms. The following words are AP style:

BlackBerry: Capitalize the second B because it is a trademarked name.

blog: Lowercase.

CD-ROM: A compact disc acting as a read-only memory device. A CD *disc* is redundant.

cell phone: Two words; an exception to *Webster's Dictionary*.

disc: Use this spelling if you are using a term such as *videodisc*. However, a *hard disk* is located in your computer.

DSL: Acronym for *digital subscriber line*.

DVD: Acronym for *digital video disk* (or *digital versatile disk*).

e-mail: Electronic mail or message. Not capitalized. Also, hyphenate such words as *e-commerce* and *e-business*. The lowercase prefix is an exception to *Webster's* preference.

FAQ: Acronym for *frequently asked questions*, a format often used to summarize information on the Internet.

high-tech: Never *hi-tech*.

home page: This is two words and not capitalized.

Internet: First letter capitalized. *Net* can be used in later references.

intranet: A private network inside a company or an organization. Unlike Internet, it is lowercase.

IT: Acronym for *information technology*; spell it out in a story.

JPEG, JPG: Acronyms for *joint photographic experts group*. Common type of image compression used on the Internet.

online: Lowercase and one word.

podcast: Lowercase.

PowerPoint: one word with a capital P in the middle.

wiki: lowercase, but *Wikipedia* is a proper noun.

World Wide Web: The shorter term, "the Web," is acceptable.

The New York Times Stylebook is also widely used. Writers who cover business or prepare news releases about business topics often use *The Wall Street Journal Stylebook*.

These manuals enable you, as a public relations writer, to prepare materials in the writing style used by most newspapers. They cover such topics as capitalization, abbreviations, punctuation, titles, and general word usage. For example, there is a trend in the media to combine words that were once written separately or hyphenated; hence, the proper style is now *software*, *database*, *lifestyle*, *teenager*, *spreadsheet*, and *nonprofit*.

Media Directories ■ If you are in the business of contacting journalists and sending news releases to the media, it is important to have lists of publications, names of editors, and addresses readily available. Local directories of media outlets are often available from the chamber of commerce, the United Way, or other civic groups. Metropolitan, state, or regional directories also exist.

Media directories are available in print, CD-ROM, and online. The most popular are Web-based directories that are updated daily to reflect changes in media contact names and addresses.

Probably the most comprehensive media database is Bacon's (www.us.cision.com). It has three North American products: (1) *Newspaper/Magazine Directory*, (2) *Radio/TV/Cable Directory*, and the (3) *Internet Media Directory*. It also offers the *Metro California Media Directory* and the *New York Publicity Outlets Directory*. In 2008, each of these directories cost between $450 and $500, so it can be a major investment for a freelance public relations writer.

According to Bacon's, these directories list more than 100,000 media outlets and 900,000 editors, analysts, freelancers, syndicated columnists, broadcast journalists, and bloggers. It also advertises that it makes more than 10,000 updates every business day to ensure that contact information is always up-to-date.

Bacon's online media database allows a public relations writer to build targeted media lists by beat, market, demographics, media type, country, and audience. In addition, the company offers an editorial calendars database of over 5,000 magazine and newspaper editorial calendars. According to Bacon's, a public relations writer can use this database to find out when publications are planning special issues around a holiday, a specific industry, annual product roundups, or major tradeshows. Another service is profiles of influential contacts in specific industries in terms of their interests and how to approach them with a story idea. Figure 1.2 shows a sample online listing from Bacon's.

BurrellesLuce (www.burrellesluce.com) also has a comprehensive online media database that includes many of the same services as Bacon's. Its media database includes over 76,000 media outlets in North America and 380,000 staff listings with their contact preferences.

The major advantages of such online media databases is that they provide the ability to build a media distribution list, to print labels, and even to send news releases by e-mail. They also offer media monitoring, enabling practitioners to match actual news coverage against a distribution list so they can evaluate their efforts. Other firms, such as Vocus (www.vocus.com), offer similar services as well as the ability to track media clips generated by news releases.

Other directories include the *Gebbie Press All-in-One Directory* (www.gebbieinc.com) and the *National Pitch Book*, published by the *Bulldog Reporter* (www.bulldogreporter.com). Media directories are discussed at greater length in Chapter 10.

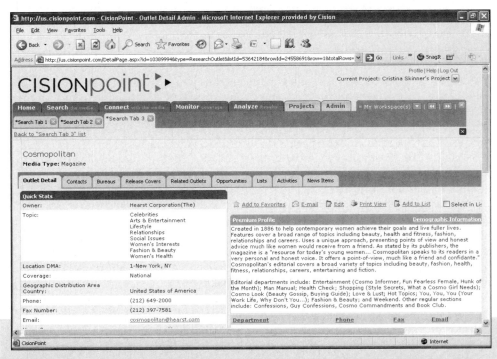

FIGURE 1.2 Online media databases provide extensive information about how to reach publications, broadcast outlets, and Internet sites. This example, showing the profile of *Cosmopolitan* magazine, comes from Bacon's (Cision), which has the largest database in the industry.

Professional Publications

■●Standard references should be supplemented with subscriptions to professional periodicals. It is important for the professional writer to keep up with developments in the field and to learn about new techniques that can improve the writing, production, and distribution of public relations material.

A number of publications cover the public relations field. Newsletters include *PR Reporter, PR News, Jack O'Dwyer's Newsletter,* the *Ragan Report, Bulldog Reporter,* and *Communication Briefings.* The last one is an excellent source of information about writing techniques. *PRWeek,* started in England and now with a U.S. edition, is a glossy, four-color tabloid that chronicles the public relations business, primarily the campaigns of various public relations firms. The Public Relations Society of America (PRSA) also produces a monthly tabloid newspaper, *Public Relations Tactics,* filled with many "how to" articles. Several of these publications are shown in Figures 1.3 through 1.5.

Magazines about the public relations field include the *Public Relations Strategist,* published by the PRSA, and *Communication World,* published by the International Association of Business Communicators (IABC). You can subscribe to these publications or receive them as part of your annual membership fees. Other magazines are *Public Relations Quarterly* and *O'Dwyer's PR Report.* See Figure 1.5 for *O'Dwyer's Daily Report,* available online. The two major scholarly publications in the field are *Public Relations Review* and the *Journal of Public Relations Research.* The websites of a number of publications are listed in the Tips for Success on page 14.

▶ **FIGURE 1.3** *PRWeek.* *PRWeek,* a glossy 24-page tabloid, has a European version and an American version. It covers the activities of public relations firms, campaigns, trends, and issues in the industry.

▶ **FIGURE 1.4** *Public Relations Tactics. PR Tactics* is a monthly tabloid published by the Public Relations Society of America (PRSA). Its focus is on professional development, practical tips for conducting public relations, and trends in the field.

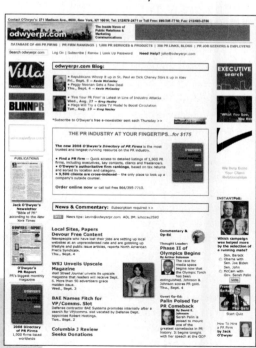

▶ **FIGURE 1.5** *O'Dwyer's Newsletter.* O'Dwyerpr.com is the online version of *O'Dwyer's Newsletter.* It has links to a large number of other sites and has an archive of public relations resources available to subscribers.

Useful Websites for Public Relations Writers

Public relations writing requires research and facts. Here's a sampling of sites on the Internet where you can find information.

General Information

www.elibrary.com Provides full-text articles from multiple sources, including newspapers, newswires, magazines, etc.

www.newsindex.com Access to hundreds of articles.

www.writersdigest.com/101sites/ Best Websites for writers, sites range from dictionaries to general reference sites and writer's organizations.

www.technorati.com Listings of blogs in every conceivable subject.

www.bartleby.com/people/strunk-w.html Strunk & White's *The Elements of Style* online.

www.pollingreport.com Compilation of findings from surveys regarding trends in public opinion.

www.thomas.loc.gov Site for the Library of Congress and the starting point for legislative and congressional information.

www.infoplease.com Online almanacs on various topics from business to history and sports.

www.biography.com Backgrounds on current and historical figures.

www.acronymfinder.com Definitions of acronyms, abbreviations, and initials.

www.howstuffworks.com Descriptions, diagrams, and photos explaining how devices work.

www.statistics.com Statistics from government and other sources on a range of subjects.

www.ipl.org University of Michigan site offering links to various sources, from dictionaries to writing guides and newspapers.

www.resourceshelf.freeprint.com A favorite among reference librarians.

www.salary.com Salaries in all fields, including public relations.

Public Relations

www.about.com Lists multiple guide sites. Public relations site offers articles, directories, forums, etc.

www.pr-education.org Aggregate of PR-related sites and services.

www.prplace.com Lists Internet addresses and hot links to PR organizations and how-to information in the public relations field.

www.prcentral.com Good list of case studies and a news release library.

www.businesswire.com News releases by company and industry.

www.prnewswire.com News releases by company and industry.

www.workinpr.com Job announcements, trends in employment, etc.

www.tsnn.com The Trade Show News Network.

Organizations

www.prfirms.org Council of Public Relations Firms

www.iabc.com International Association of Business Communicators (IABC)

www.prsa.org Public Relations Society of America (PRSA)

www.ipra.org International Public Relations Association (IPRA)

www.pac.org Public Affairs Council (PAC)

www.niri.org National Investor Relations Institute (NIRI)

www.instituteforpr.com Institute of Public Relations (IPR)

www.ifea.com International Festivals and Events Association (IFEA)

Publications

www.odwyerpr.com Daily update on public relations, plus archives and links to public relations articles.

www.brandweek.com *Brandweek*

www.ragan.com Ragan's newsletters and public relations resources

www.prsa.org/tactics *Public Relations Tactics*

www.prsa.org/strategist *The Strategist*

www.prweekus.com *PRWeek*

www.iabc.com/cw *Communication World*

www.combriefings.com *Communication Briefings*

In addition to articles about trends and issues in the field, these magazines also carry advertisements for companies that specialize in services such as news release distribution, media monitoring, photography, podcasts, and video news releases.

Many public relations professionals, especially those who specialize in media relations and placement, also read the journalism trade press. Such publications include *Editor & Publisher*, *Broadcasting & Cable*, *Advertising Age*, and *MediaWeek*. They provide a good overview of trends in the field and changes in executive jobs. For a more critical perspective of media performance and foibles, there are the *Columbia Journalism Review* and the *American Journalism Review*.

Internet Groups and Blogs ■ Up-to-date information on public relations and media techniques can also be gained via the Internet. A number of Usenet groups (a global system of discussion areas called *newsgroups*) and listservs (a software program for setting up and maintaining discussion groups through e-mail) are devoted to public relations. You can review the possibilities simply by doing a topic search on Google, Yahoo!, or MSN. Such groups may be sponsored by public relations firms, individuals, or public relations groups, such as PRSA and IABC, for its members.

The International Public Relations Association (IPRA), for example, has a forum for its global membership at ipra@yahoogroups.com. Members in such diverse nations as India, Australia, Canada, Poland, and the United States make queries, provide information, and generally give each other tips on how to handle various situations. One IPRA member, for example, asked the group for advice on how to set a strategic communications plan for the Kuwait Institute of Banking Studies and received a number of helpful suggestions from other professionals throughout the world.

Another listserv group open to anyone is prbytes@yahoogroups.com. In one message, for example, an individual asked for advice on how to find and negotiate with a celebrity to attend a local fund-raising event.

There also are any number of blogs about public relations and almost any other topic. Technorati (www.technorati.com) maintains a virtual catalog of blogs that numbers in the millions. As of mid-2008, almost 3,000 blogs are devoted to public relations alone. Some of the more popular are badpitch.blogspot.com, POPPR.blogspot.com, www.canuckflack.com, and www.mguerrilla.com. A number of public relations firms also operate blogs. Two examples are http://wagnercomm.blogspot.com and www.mlpr.com/blogworks. An excellent compilation of blogs, articles, and resources can be found at www.thenewpr.com/wiki/pmwiki.php.

As with everything else on the Internet, listservs and blogs come and go, so it's a good idea to check with some professionals in the field about current listservs or blogs focusing on public relations and marketing communications. They can also offer insight into what forums offer the most information and value.

Current Events and Trends ■ Writing often starts with a creative idea and a good understanding of the world around you. Many public relations employers screen job applicants by administering a current events quiz to ascertain the scope of an individual's interests and intellectual curiosity. Employers require outstanding writing skills, but they are also looking for a second dimension in a public relations writer: knowing what to write about.

Thus, aspiring public relations writers should make it a habit to read at least one weekly newsmagazine (e.g., *Time*, *Newsweek*, *U.S. News & World Report*, *The Economist*), a local daily newspaper, and a daily newspaper with national circulation, such as *The New York Times*, *The Wall Street Journal*, or even the *Financial Times*. All of these publications, of course, have their own websites that offer limited or full access to stories. Nationally syndicated public affairs programs on radio and television are also good sources of current event knowledge and interpretative analysis.

Current nonfiction best sellers should also be part of your reading program. A popular book is an indication of public interest, and often media interest, in a particular topic. Books about diet, health, personal growth, or wealth are perennial bestsellers. Couples expecting their first child have put *What to Expect When You're Expecting* on the bestseller list for several years. Another book of major public interest that also has been on the *New York Times* bestseller list for several years is Malcolm Gladwell's *The Tipping Point*, a study of how fads get started.

Many people get all their news and entertainment from television. You should know what is being presented to the public for several reasons. First, media coverage sets the agenda for people's thinking. Second, watching the national and local news will show you what kinds of stories are used and how they are handled. Other programs, especially talk shows, will teach you what sorts of stories get on the air and indicate the kind of audience that tends to watch such programs.

In sum, paying attention to current events and the thoughts of opinion leaders pays several dividends. First, it makes you a well-informed person, and hence more attractive to employers for public relations writing jobs. Second, knowing the public's concerns helps you construct more salient messages for your target audience. Third, current events and subjects of popular books often provide a "news hook" for obtaining media acceptance of your material.

A company making security locks for computer files, for example, was virtually ignored by the media until news stories about computer hackers breaking into national security systems made national headlines. And publicists for food products have long recognized that information about the health benefits of a product will attract more media attention. Using current public and media interests as a "news hook" for generating publicity is discussed further in Chapter 4.

■ Research: The Prelude to Writing

An essential first step to any public relations writing task is the gathering of relevant information. The process is called *research*, and it can take many forms.

In some cases, all the facts will be readily available from a client or employer. All you need to do is pick up some background materials, ask a few questions, and start writing. More often than not, however, the information you need to understand the subject thoroughly and write a well-crafted piece requires some digging.

Let's assume you are given the assignment of writing a news release about a new product. One of your first contacts, no doubt, will be the vice president of marketing, who will give you the general details about the price and availability of the product. In order to understand better the benefits or capabilities of the product, however, you may need to interview someone in the company's research and development (R&D) department who was responsible for developing the product.

You may stop there in your inquiries, or you may decide to do some research on the potential market for the product and how you might position the product against the competition. One way to do this is to research competing products on the market to determine why your product is different or better. You may also want to contact some experts in the field by e-mail or telephone to get their assessment. Their comments, if they give permission, could be included in your news release as a form of endorsement for the new product. On another level, you might talk with some consumers to find out what would convince them to try the product. Is it price, convenience, brand reputation, or reliability?

Public relations writers are constantly looking up information, whether for a news release or for background on what kinds of issues and trends might affect a current employer or prospective client. Fortunately, a virtual universe of information is available to you at the click of a mouse. Thanks to the information revolution, two valuable resources are available: Internet search engines and electronic databases.

Search Engines

Software programs called **browsers** enable you to view documents created specifically for the Internet's World Wide Web and other Internet services. The most commonly used browser is Microsoft's Internet Explorer.

Browsers work in tandem with powerful online **search engines,** which are essential to finding information about virtually any subject on the Internet and World Wide Web. They are essential because the World Wide Web is somewhat like walking into a vast library without the benefit of a floor plan or even a card catalog. According to Wikipedia, there were over 100 billion websites worldwide as of 2008.

Search engines make it possible for you to simply type in a keyword or two and click "Go." Within a few seconds, the computer screen shows all the links that the search engine has found relating to the topic. The hard part is checking out the promising links, because the search engine may have found several hundred possibilities.

Google, at this writing, is the most widely used online search engine. Of the 62 billion worldwide Internet searches conducted in December 2007, for example, Google was used for almost 50 percent of them. This, according to an Internet research firm, compares with 17 percent for Yahoo! and 13 percent for Microsoft. It's worth noting that the third most used search engine in the world is Baidu, which is based in Beijing. Its relative market share is almost 14 percent, and its use will continue to rise as China becomes even more Internet connected. A listing of useful websites for public relations writers is shown in the Tips for Success on page 14.

In general, it is a good idea to use several search engines, because all of them have different strengths and weaknesses. Peter Meyers, writing in *The Wall Street Journal*, assessed the most popular search engines. He thought Google was best for news, images, and general Web searches. He noted, "Google has the broadest range of solid tools and did the best job of distinguishing between ad-supported results and real ones."

Yahoo!, according to Meyers, excels in its Yellow Pages listings, particularly if you live in a major metropolitan market. MSN gets high ratings for its stem-searching tool and its automatic searches for all variations of a word. Yahoo! also gets good reviews for news searches that also look for audio and visual video clips.

The most important part of your search for information is choosing the right keywords. You should be as specific as possible to make sure you don't get a display listing hundreds of pages. Nouns make the best keywords.

The *Associated Press Stylebook* gives some additional tips for a search:

- Use uncommon words that identify your topic. Unusual proper or technical names are good. Avoid words with dual meanings.

- Use several keywords at a time, or even phrases. You can use two or three different phrases.

- Use synonyms. You might find different information with "attorney" instead of "lawyer."

- Use connecting words such as AND, OR, or NOT. Syntax varies with search engines, so check the help page if you are not sure how to structure these queries. Some search engines, for example, want you to put quotes around a phrase to limit a search. For example, a search for "site: apple.com iPod" will only provide links that appear on official Apple Web pages.

The editors of the *Associated Press Stylebook* make a final, cautionary point. They say, "Do not mistake the Web for an encyclopedia, and the search engine for a table of contents. The Web is a sprawling databank that's about one quarter wheat and three-quarters chaff. Any information you find should be assessed with the same care that you use for everything else."

Electronic Databases

The second valuable source of information, which is often more comprehensive than various websites, are electronic databases that provide in-depth information and full texts of published articles. Many of these databases, such as Lexis/Nexis, are available online, and many organizations subscribe to their services. Another approach is to simply use your local city or campus library; many libraries provide free access to multiple reference databases.

One popular database is *Academic Search Premier*, which provides the full text for almost 5,000 publications, including more than 3,600 academic journals. It is said to be the world's largest multidisciplinary database. The majority of full-text articles are available as searchable PDFs. Another favorite of public relations writers is *ProQuest Newsstand*, which is the full text of U.S. and international news sources in newspaper and periodical formats.

Advertising agencies, public relations firms, and marketing departments regularly consult another electronic database, *Simmons Study of Media and Markets*. It reports research data on lifestyles, media behavior, and brand preferences of the American consumer by gender, age, and household income.

In sum, if you need in-depth information about any topic—from the biography of a business executive to market conditions in Zambia—an electronic database is a good source. See the Tips for Success on page 20 for a listing of popular databases.

Writing Guidelines

The ability to write well is essential for work in public relations. Countless client surveys and interviews with public relations employers confirm that good writing is at the top of their list of expectations. John Beardsley, chairman and CEO of Padilla Speer Beardsley, is quoted in *The Strategist* as saying, "In our business, everything involves language, more so than almost any other activity."

J. Ronald Kelly, senior vice president of Cohn & Wolfe public relations, adds:

> The majority of our entry-level work requires good, basic writing skills. I simply do not have the time to teach grammar, spelling, punctuation, subject–verb agreement, and use of active verbs, lead writing, inverted pyramid style, etc. And as you know, time is money in an agency setting. Therefore, I seek graduates who can contribute to the bottom line from the first day. I need people who have good mastery of basic writing skills.

Outlining the Purpose

Before beginning any writing assignment, take the time to ask yourself some key questions. Public relations counselors Kerry Tucker and Doris Derelian suggest six basic questions:

1. What is the desired communication outcome? In other words, what do we want our audience to do or not do?
2. Who is our target audience? Defining your audience in terms of age, gender, and educational level helps set the framework of the message.
3. What are our target audience's needs, concerns, and interests?
4. What is our message? Do you want to inform or persuade?
5. What communication channel is most effective?
6. Who is our most believable spokesperson?

Answering these questions goes a long way toward helping you determine the content and structure of your message. Regarding questions 2 and 3, Julie Story Goldsborough, president of a Kansas public relations firm, says, "I try to delve into the minds of the readers. What is the main benefit to them? What do they want to know about the subject?"

The next step is to outline question 4 more fully—what is the message? Usually, an outline includes major topics, and minor topics within each

> **The use of fact and emotion in a story is critical— particularly in public relations. In a world cluttered with messages competing for audience time and attention, our messages and stories require both elements to be effective.**
>
> ■ Kevin Dugan, founder of the Bad Pitch Blog

Need Information? Use a Database

Although "Googling it" is a highly popular way of finding information, it's not always the best way to find in-depth information. Both students and professionals should take advantage of the many electronic databases that are available at the library. The following are a few databases that libraries commonly subscribe to that you may find useful:

Academic Search Premier.   Full text of more than 4,600 publications, including more than 3,600 academic journals. It's the world's largest multidisciplinary database.

Associations Unlimited.   Basic information on more than 455,000 associations and nonprofit groups at the international, national, state, and local levels.

Articles from Magazines, Journals, and Newspapers (Gale Power Research).   A one-stop source for newspaper, magazine, and journal articles on a wide range of topics.

Britannica Online.   The full text of the 32-volume *Encyclopedia Brittanica* and *Webster's New International Dictionary.* Over 130,000 links to websites.

Gale's Ready Reference Shelf.   Integrates 14 directories, including media directories for newspapers, magazines, broadcast outlets, and newsletters.

Merriam-Webster's Collegiate Dictionary and Thesaurus.   Includes definitions, pronunciation guides, and word histories for more than 75,000 words.

Oxford Dictionary of National Biography.   This full-text database features biographies of over 55,000 individuals.

AP Images.   Photos, images, and audio files from the Associated Press.

Alt-Press Watch.   Full text of newspapers, magazines, and journals of the alternative and independent press.

Ethnic NewsWatch.   Full-text database of newspapers, magazines, and journals of the ethnic and minority press.

Infotac OneFile.   A one-stop source for news and periodical articles on a wide range of topics.

Lexis/Nexis Academic.   Complete text of newspapers, magazines, newswires, TV transcripts, and trade publications.

Factiva.   General news as well as company, industry, and other business information from newspapers, newswires, magazines, and trade journals from 22 countries.

Global Market Information Database.   An online resource providing information on industries, countries, and consumers.

Simmons Study of Media and Markets.   Information and research on lifestyles, media behavior, and product preferences of U.S. consumers by gender, age, and household income.

CountryWatch.   Full-text reports on over 190 countries and contents of national newswires.

Ulrich's Periodicals Directory.   Basic information on periodicals, journals, and magazines around the globe.

World Factbook.   Basic information and statistics about countries. ■

major topic. One approach to outlining is to list the major message points as major topics. For example, you might have one to three key points that you want to communicate in a news release or a feature story. Under each of these headings, jot down a list of the facts, statistics, and examples you will give to support the major point.

Once the objectives and content of the message are determined, the next challenge is to compose a succinct, well-organized document that uses all of the rules of grammar, punctuation, and spelling correctly. Entire books are available that are devoted to composition, and you should refer to the list of additional resources at the end of the chapter. However, here are a few general guidelines you should keep in mind as you prepare to write public relations materials.

Sentences

Sentences should be clear and concise. Long, compound sentences slow the reader down and often are difficult to understand. In general, a sentence containing 25 to 30 words is difficult even for a college-educated audience. This does not mean that all sentences should be 8 to 10 words long; you should strive for a variety of lengths, with the average sentence being about 15 to 17 words.

In many cases, a complex sentence simply contains more words than necessary. Take this bloated sentence, for example: "They have assisted numerous companies in the development of a system that can be used in the monitoring of their customer service operations." Revised, this sentence is more concise and easier to understand: "They have helped many companies develop systems for monitoring their customer services operations."

Communication Briefings has compiled a list of word savers that can help keep sentences concise and on course. You should shorten the common wordy phrases on the left to the single words on the right when writing or editing copy:

a great number of	many
at this point in time	now
come to a realization	realize
despite the fact that	although
due to the fact that	because
for the purpose of	for, to
give approval of	approve
of the opinion that	believe
owing to the fact that	because
since the time when	since
take under consideration	consider
until such time as	until
with the exception of	except for
would appear that	seems
as to whether	whether

Paragraphs

Short paragraphs are better than long ones. A review of a daily newspaper shows that the journalistic style is short paragraphs averaging about six to eight typeset lines. Lead paragraphs in news stories are even shorter—about two or three lines.

Public relations writing should follow the same guidelines. Short paragraphs give the reader a chance to catch a breath, so to speak, and continue reading. Long paragraphs not only tax the reader's concentration but also encourage the reader to "tune out."

Remember that the paragraph on your computer screen is even longer when set in a newspaper column only 2 inches wide. Your 8 lines become 12 lines in a newspaper or magazine. A typical paragraph contains only one basic idea. When another idea is introduced, it is time for a new paragraph.

Short, punchy paragraphs are particularly important for online news releases and newsletters. According to a study by Sun Microsystems, it takes 50 percent more time for an individual to read material on a computer screen. Consequently, according to Michael Butzgy, owner of a New York communications firm, people need key information in short, digestible chunks.

Word Choice

College-educated writers often forget that words common to their vocabulary are not readily understood by large segments of the general public. General-circulation newspapers, aware that a large percentage of their readers have not been to college, strive to write news stories at the fourth- to sixth-grade level. A writer's word choice is further limited by the statistic that an estimated 30 million adults in the United States lack basic reading skills and often cannot comprehend messages written beyond the second-grade level.

If your target audience is the general public, remember that a short word—one with fewer syllables—is more easily understood than a longer one. *Communication Briefings* gives the following list of "stately," multisyllable words and some shorter, more reader-friendly options:

"Stately" Word	Reader-Friendly Word
frequently	often
majority	most
regulation	rule
subsequent	future
reiterate	repeat
approximately	about
additional	more
fundamental	basic
individual	person
requirement	need
accomplish	achieve

"Stately" Word	Reader-Friendly Word
characteristic	trait
initial	first
additional	more
residence	home

More complex words, of course, can be used if the target audience is well educated. Most readers of *The Wall Street Journal*, for example, are college graduates, so the writing is more complex than that found in a small-town daily.

Also, if the target audience is professionals in a field such as law, education, science, or engineering, the standard for word choice is different. Educators, for example, seem to like elaborate expressions such as "multiethnic individualized learning" or "continuum."

Scientific writing, too, is loaded with esoteric words. Newspaper editors often complain that they receive news releases from high-technology companies that are so full of jargon that neither they nor their readers can understand them.

Of course if your audience is engineers, you can use specialized words and phrases. Good writing, however, requires that you simplify the message as much as possible. Eric Hatch, writing in *Communication World*, gives an example of the "engineering style" of writing:

A plan will be implemented to incorporate performance database already available from previous NASA 8 2 6 and BTWT tests on the various UDF® models with the code currently under development to yield more accurate spanwise Cd (drag coefficients) distributions and velocity diagrams between blade-rows for our acoustics prediction use.

In this example, notes Hatch, "the author has jammed everything into one polysyllabic elephant of a sentence." He suggests the following rewrite; although still complex, it is more readable to an educated audience:

A database compiled during earlier wind tunnel tests on the various UDF® blade models will be incorporated into the new code. This should give us more accurate drag coefficients and velocity diagrams between the blade rows, resulting in better predictions of the engine's acoustical behavior.

Active Verbs and Present Tense

Verbs vitalize your writing. Don't sacrifice verbs by burying the action in nouns or adjectives. You will boost clarity and add vigor to your writing by stripping away excess words around a verb. A sentence using active voice is also more direct and usually shorter than a passive sentence. Here are some examples:

original statement: The annual report produced a disappointed reaction among the board of directors.

revised statement: The annual report disappointed the board of directors.

original statement: Our consultants can assist you in answering questions about floor treatments.

revised statement: Our consultants can answer your floor treatment questions.

Use of present tense also improves writing. It is better to write "The copier *delivers* 100 copies per minute" than to write "The copier *will deliver* 100 copies per minute." In most public relations writing, particularly news releases, use present and active tense as much as possible. In quotations, for example, it is better to write "The copier is being shipped next month," *says* Rowena Jones, sales manager. Doesn't this sound better than "The copier *will be* shipped next month," *said* Rowena Jones, sales manager? Other tips on how to improve your writing are given in the Tips for Success.

☑ tips FOR SUCCESS

How to Improve Your Writing

Writing is hard work. It takes a good understanding of basic English composition, plenty of practice, and a lot of rewriting and editing to produce interesting and readable copy. The following are some good tips adapted from an article by Katie Badeusz that appeared in Ragan.com.

Be Clear

Don't use technical terms and convoluted sentence structures. If it's not written clearly, nothing else will matter because people won't understand it.

Use Action Verbs

Verbs are the basis of good writing. Instead of using weak verbs such as *utilize* or *optimize*, use visual verbs such as *plunge, hover, reveal,* and *rebound.*

Apply Active Voice

Avoid writing in passive voice. Sentences in active voice are more concise and direct because fewer words are needed to express action. Noun–verb construction is best. Say "He made a mistake," not "Mistakes were made."

Avoid Jargon

Don't exclude readers by using words that are not familiar to them. If you must use jargon, limit the number of terms you use, and don't forget to define them.

Focus on People

Writing about processes, programs, and policies is boring because they often lack the human element. For better understanding and readership, explain programs by focusing on the people affected.

Imagery

Strong visual descriptions are better than generalized statements. Writing that Coca-Cola is sold in many nations or marketed internationally does not have much impact on the reader. A stronger image is created if you write that Coca-Cola is now sold on all continents and is readily available to two-thirds of the earth's population. Or, as Coca-Cola stated in a recent annual report to stockholders: "If all the system's customers lined up along the equator, a thirsty consumer could purchase a Coca-Cola every 16 feet."

Visual descriptions can even be used to portray the wealth of Bill Gates, one of the world's richest people. One writer came up with the following imagery: "If Mr. Gates' fortune were converted to dollar bills, it would take 296 747s to fly the pile from Microsoft's Redmond, Wash., headquarters to New York. And once there, the loot would cover every square inch of Manhattan, not just once, but six times."

Don't Neglect the First Paragraph

An enticing first sentence or paragraph attracts readers. The writing should be short, punchy, and to the point. A good question to ask yourself when writing a lead is "What is this story about?" Answer that question in a creative inviting way.

Include Quotes

Too many quotes, particularly from executive and officials, are too long-winded and full of jargon. Avoid losing readers by incorporating quotes that sound authentic and reflect what a person might say in a normal conversation.

Write with Your Ear

You can improve your writing by reading it out loud to hear what actually works in terms of rhythm and pacing. If you find yourself gasping for air as you read through a long, convoluted sentence, break it into several sentences or use more punctuation.

Allow Yourself to Write Crap

Don't write perfect sentences in your head. Let your thoughts go and then fix them. Good writing involves rewriting. Take a break and come back to your manuscript to reorganize your thoughts, move things around, and do it again.

Take Chances

Writing is a creative process. Think outside the box and ask yourself questions such as "Why should I care about this?" "So what?" and "Why should my readers care about this?" also are good questions. And don't forget to have fun. If you enjoy writing the story, it's likely that you're audience will enjoy reading it. ■

Source: Ragan.com, March 26, 2008.

Another enterprising writer, commenting on Bill Gates' expensive home, notes, "he still has enough money left to buy every house in Alaska, Wyoming, and the two Dakotas."

Errors to Avoid

Errors in your writing will brand you as careless, unprofessional, and inconsiderate of your audience. Errors also call into question the credibility of the entire message. Professional writing requires attention to detail and repeated review of your draft to catch all potential errors.

Spelling

Credibility is sacrificed when spelling errors appear in public relations materials. For example, one news release for a company that offered a spell-checking program included the nonwords "tradmark" and "publishere." Naturally, the company was embarrassed about the typos—especially after *The Wall Street Journal* poked fun at the company on page 1. We can only guess at how much these typos cost the company in sales and consumer confidence.

Time magazine does know the actual cost of a spelling error. Some years ago, *Time* ran a cover headline reading "New Plan for Arms Contol." More than 200,000 covers were printed without the "r" in the word "control" before the error was discovered. The presses were stopped and the error was corrected; putting the "r" back in "control" cost the magazine $100,000. Of course, there are always chuckles when someone writes about "pubic relations" instead of "public relations."

Gobbledygook and Jargon

Every occupation and industry has its own vocabulary. Telephone executives talk about "LATAs" and "attenuation rates." Cable people talk about "pay-to-basic ratios," and even public relations professionals talk about "mug shots," "ANRs," "VNRs," "boilerplate," and "evergreens." All too often, business people slip into a pattern of gobbledygook. Things don't get "finished"; they get "finalized." An event didn't happen "yesterday"; it occurred "at that point in time." In education, we don't have a child "failing"; he's just "motivationally deprived."

All these terms and acronyms may be fine if professionals are talking to each other or sending material to a trade publication, but using such terms in news releases and other messages to the public is a major roadblock to effective communication. Public relations consultant Joan Lowery, writing in *Communication World*, says, "Knowingly or unknowingly, jargon has become the lazy man's way to avoid wrestling with how to communicate clearly, concisely, and with passion to others who may not understand the concepts that some of us live and breathe each day."

The solution, says broadcast news veteran David Snell, is for public relations people to "de-geekify" their superiors. In an article for *The Strategist*, he writes, "To function with maximum efficiency, the public relations person needs to be the 'Outsider's Insider'; the person who understands the jargon, but maintains an active memory of the level of ignorance brought with them to the job." In other words, the public relations writer must always ask the question "Will someone unfamiliar with this profession or industry be able to easily understand the message?"

Lowery takes another approach. She encourages public relations writers to always ask "so what?" This forces executives, as well as engineers, to understand that the news release to the daily newspaper should skip all the technical details and concentrate on how the new product benefits the consumer. Or, if you like jargon, you can always say "the end-user."

The public relations writer is a wordsmith, not a scribe. He or she has the obligation to educate executives and engineers of the need to provide message context and easy-to-understand analogies to explain technical concepts. Often, the use of jargon comes across almost as a foreign language. Your job is to translate the material into basic English.

Poor Sentence Structure

The subject and the words that modify it often become separated in a sentence, causing some confusion about what exactly is being discussed. Here are some examples from news stories:

> Police will be looking for people driving under the influence of alcohol and distributing pamphlets that spell out the dangers of drunken driving.

> The proposed budget provides salary increases for faculty and staff performing at a satisfactory level of 2 percent.

> The student was charged with possession and consumption of an opened beer can, which is against university rules.

Poor sentence structure can also lead to embarrassment. A company newsletter, detailing an employee's illness, once reported: "Jeff was taken to the hospital with what was thought to be thrombus phlebitis. After spending a restless night with a nurse at the hospital, the results were negative."

Wrong Words

A good writer not only checks spelling, but also verifies the meaning of words. An Associated Press (AP) story once told about a man who had inherited a small scenic railroad from his "descendants," who had started it in the nineteenth century. The writer meant "ancestors" but used the wrong word. Another publication also used the wrong word when it reported "The iPhone: a High-Tech Coupe for Consumers." The actual word is "coup."

More mistakes involve the usage of "it's" and "its," "effect" and "affect," "there" and "their," and "presume" and "assume." A common error is using the pronoun "their" when referring to an impersonal object such as a company. The proper term is "its" as in "Starbucks announced *its* (not *their*) new blend of coffee."

Other frequently confused words are listed in the next section. When in doubt, take the time to use the dictionary. It will save you embarrassment later.

"Sound-alike" Words

Many words sound alike and are similar in spelling but have very different meanings. Although it might be somewhat humorous to read that a survey is "chalk full" of information (instead of "chock-full"), a company's management team is doing some "sole" searching (instead of "soul searching"), or an employee was in a "comma" (instead of a "coma") after a car accident, such mistakes are the mark of a careless writer.

> **Use spell-check as a starting point, but never use it as a substitute for a thorough proofreading.**

A spell-checking program is extremely efficient at catching misspelled words, but it often does not catch "wrong" words because they are spelled correctly. Therefore, it is essential to proofread your copy, even after it has been corrected by a spell-checker program.

Here is a list of words that are frequently confused. Do a self-test and write a sentence correctly using the right word.

adapt, adept, adopt	implicit, explicit
callow, callous	lose, loose
canvas, canvass	negligent, negligible
compliment, complement	peak, peek, pique
dominant, dominate	pore, pour
desert, dessert	principle, principal
ensure, insure, assure	stationary, stationery
imply, infer	there, their
foreword, forward	precedent, precedence
who's, whose	adverse, averse
less, fewer	antidote, anecdote

Redundancies

Another major error in writing is redundancy. It is not necessary to use the word "totally" to modify a word such as "destroyed," or "completely" to modify "demolished." Many writers also say that something is "somewhat" or "very" unique. "Unique," by definition, means one of a kind; either something is unique or it isn't. The following redundancy appeared in a news release: "In addition, the company lists $50 million in receivables that it hopes to collect. These are unpaid bills, largely from customers, that have yet to be paid." See the Tips for Success on page 29 for some more additional tips on achieving a clear writing style.

Too Many Numbers

People can digest a few figures but not a mass of statistics. Use numbers sparingly in your writing, and don't put too many in a single sentence. Avoid such constructions as "During 2009, the corporation acquired 73 companies in 14 nations on five continents to achieve revenue of $14.65 billion, up $3 billion from the $11.65 billion in 2008." Consider the following tips for using numbers:

- Write "$92 million" instead of "92,000,000 dollars."
- Provide a readily understood comparison instead of an abstract number. Few people will readily grasp the size of a new warehouse that is 583 feet long, but they will immediately form an image if you say that it's about the length of two football fields.
- Check your math. The price of something can go up more than 100 percent, but it can never go down more than 100 percent.

Hype

You can ruin the credibility and believability of your message by using exaggerated words and phrases. When Sharp Electronics Corporation introduced a new handheld computer, the news release called it "the next true revolution in man's conquest of information." Other companies often describe their products as "first of its kind," "unique," "a major breakthrough," and even "revolutionary," which tends to raise suspicion among journalists.

High-tech companies were once singled out by *The Wall Street Journal* for overusing adjectives. After analyzing 201 news releases, reporter Michael Miller issued a "hype hit parade." In descending order of overuse were the following words: *leading, enhanced, unique, significant, solution, integrated, powerful, innovative, advanced, high performance,* and *sophisticated.* According to a content analysis by Factiva, overused words in business include *robust, next generation, groundbreaking, world class,* and *cutting edge.*

Bias and Stereotypes

Stereotypes often creep in as a writer struggles to describe a situation, group, or person. How often have you seen a writer describe a woman with such adjectives as "pert," "petite," "fragile," "feminine," "stunning," "gorgeous," "statuesque," or "full-figured"? How about "blond and blue-eyed"? Would you describe a man as a "muscular, well-built 6-footer with sandy hair and blue eyes"?

In general, avoid descriptive terms of beauty or physical attributes and mannerisms whenever possible. In most cases, such descriptions have no bearing on the story and can be considered sexist. For example, here's how one Chicago company described its president in a news release: "A tall, attractive blonde who could easily turn heads on Main Street is instead turning heads on Wall Street." Or consider the news release from a Los Angeles firm about the appointment of a woman to a management position: "Demure, naturally pretty and conservative in her dress and manner, Miho Suda could easily pass as a college student."

You should also avoid any suggestion that all members of any group have the same personal characteristic, be it ambition, laziness, shrewdness, guile, or intelligence. Don't suggest that some characteristic sets an individual apart from a stereotyped norm either. For example, it is inappropriate to write, "John Williams, who is black, was promoted to senior vice president." Nor would you write, "Linda Gonzales, a U.S. citizen, will serve as assistant treasurer." In both cases, you are implying that these individuals are exceptions to some norm for their ethnic group.

Avoid gender bias by using non-gender-related words. Awareness of the irrelevance of an employee's gender is why airlines now have "flight attendants" instead of "stewardesses" and why the U.S. Postal Service hires "mail carriers" instead of "mailmen." It also is unnecessary to write that something is "manmade" when a neutral word such as "synthetic" or "artificial" is just as good. "Employees" is better than "manpower," and "chairperson" is more acceptable than "chairman." Some terms may seem difficult to neutralize—"congressperson," "businessperson," and "waitperson" don't exactly trip off the tongue. However, with a little thought, you can come up with appropriate titles, such as "legislator," "executive," and "server."

The problem of avoiding gender bias is particularly difficult because much of our language is geared to the use of the word "man" as a generic term for both males and females. Attempts to avoid this lead to messy constructions such as "he/she" or "his/her" often make for difficult reading. However, another word can be used in most cases. If you make the noun in question plural, the pronoun "their" or "them" will serve nicely. For example, you can write "When a customer requests a brochure, tell them. . . ." In other cases, you can use words such as *personnel*, *staff*, *employee*, *worker*, *person*, or *practitioner* to describe both men and women in the workplace.

Politically Incorrect Language

Beyond avoidance of stereotypes, there is an ongoing controversy about what constitutes **politically correct** (commonly called "PC") language. In today's world of diversity at all levels of national life, there is increased sensitivity about what words and images are used to describe minorities and other groups of people.

For example, the Alliance for the Mentally Ill of New York State picketed a Daffy's discount clothing store because of a billboard showing an empty straitjacket with the headline, "If you're paying over $100 for a dress shirt, may we suggest a jacket to go with it?"

Such concern has merit, and writers should be sensitive to words and images that may offend individuals or groups. However, critics charge that a flood of euphemisms can cause a loss of clarity and may result in a kind of nonsensical bureaucratic language that impedes effective communication.

For example, some groups think the word "civilization" is politically incorrect because it infers that some people are not civilized. Still others object to the word "disabled" and want to substitute "physically challenged" or "differently abled." In this situation, we no longer have short people, but "vertically challenged" people. Although the terms "handicapped" and "crippled" are considered insensitive, it is acceptable to use the term, "mobility disabled" or "physically disabled."

You must also be sensitive to words describing ethnic groups. Today's writers use "Asian American" instead of the now pejorative "Oriental." And the term "Hispanic" is now more acceptable than the politically charged "Spanish-speaking." The term "Latino," however, raises some controversy; some women say it is sexist because the "o" in Spanish is male. The term "Afro-American" is a generally accepted term, and the term "black" is also widely accepted by African Americans and the media.

Language, and its connotations, is constantly changing. The professional public relations writer must be aware of the changes and make decisions based on such factors as sensitivity to the audience, accuracy, and clarity of communication.

■ Summary

- Public relations writing and media placements are accomplished within the framework of the complete public relations process—research, planning, communication, and evaluation.

- Public relations personnel who write news releases and other materials fulfill a valuable role as technicians because they implement and execute the tactics of a public relations program.

- Public relations writing is similar to journalism in that both strive to provide accurate, credible information. They differ with respect to objectives, audience selection, and the variety of media channels that are used.

- A computer, either a desktop or a laptop, is essential for public relations work.

- A reference library is a must for any writer. In addition to books, a person can also do research through search engines, such as Google, and library databases.

- The most widely used stylebook for journalistic writing is the *Associated Press Stylebook and Briefing on Media Law*.

- Media directories are available in print and CD formats, but online databases are now the norm because they can be updated on a daily basis.

- Public relations writers should keep current in the field by reading publications such as *PRWeek* and *Jack O'Dwyer's PR Report*. They should also read daily newspapers and weekly newsmagazines.

- Blogs about public relations and marketing communications are another way to keep up with developments in the public relations field.

- Search engines such as Google, Yahoo!, and MSN help public relations writers find information on the Internet. Electronic databases are good for gathering in-depth information and full-text articles.

- All public relations writing starts with the basic steps of determining the purpose and content of the message.

- Word choice, sentence structure, grammar, and spelling are important. Sloppiness loses credibility.

- Public relations writers should work as "translators" of organizational jargon so messages can be understood by the public.

- Hype and exaggerated claims ruin a message's credibility.

- Writers should be sensitive to words and terms that can be considered sexist or racist.

Skill Building Activities

1. Select a topic, such as public relations, and look it up on Wikipedia. Compare the information with that from another online encyclopedia, such as *Encarta* or *Britannica*. How are the entries similar? How are they different? Which entry, in your view, is the most complete and credible?

2. Go to the library and review several media directories that are provided in the reference section. Or, if possible, make arrangements with a public relations firm to show you the online media databases it uses. Compare and contrast the various directories (databases).

3. Read an issue of a trade publication in the public relations field. You may choose such publications as *PRWeek*, *PR Tactics*, *O'Dwyer's PR Report*, or the *Ragan Report*. You can also go online, using the URLs listed on page 14; however, note that full access to the articles on some of these sites is only available with a paid subscription.

4. Several public relations blogs were mentioned on page 15. Visit at least two of them. What aspects of each blog did you like? What did you dislike?

5. Visit the websites of several public relations organizations, such as PRSA, IABC, IPRA, and so on. Explore their various links and pages. Write a short report on what you found. The URLs are in the Tips for Success on page 14.

6. Select a topic that interests you and "Google it." In addition, use at least two electronic databases available in your library (see box on page 20) to find information on the same topic. What are the pros and cons of using a search engine versus using a library database?

7. Review the list of "sound-alike" words on page 28. Can you write a sentence correctly using each of these words?

Suggested Readings

Badeusz, Katie. "Twelve Tips to Improve Corporate Writing." www.ragan.com, March 26, 2008.

Beaubien, Greg. "An End to Verbiage: Fewer Words Make Stronger Writing." *PR Tactics*, February 2008, p. 21.

Bowerman, Peter. "Writing Better Today: Eight Tips for Instantly Improving Your Marketing Copy." *PR Tactics*, February 2005, p. 20.

Cohen, Noam. "Start Writing the Eulogies for Print Encyclopedias." *The New York Times*, March 16, 2008, p. D2.

Dugan, Kevin. "Lasting Impact: Storytelling Makes Messages Memorable." *PR Tactics*, February 2008, p. 26.

Goldstein, Norm, Editor. *Associated Press Stylebook and Briefing on Media Law*. New York: Basic Books, 2007.

Hacker, Diana. *A Pocket Style Manual*, 5th ed. Boston: Bedford/St. Martin's, 2008.

Jacobs, Ken. "Checkpoints: A Dozen Tips to Power Your PR Writing." *PR Tactics*, February 2008, p. 22.

Klipstine, Thomas. "Time to Take Our Own Advice: Five Simple Principles for Effective Web Writing." *PR Tactics*, February 2008, p. 25.

Marsh, Charles, Guth, David W., and Short, Bonnie. *Strategic Writing: Multimedia Writing for Public Relations, Advertising, and More*, 2nd ed. Boston: Allyn & Bacon, 2009.

Mossberg, Walter S. "Consider Your Needs, Then Use This Guide to Buying a Laptop." *The Wall Street Journal Online*, April 10, 2008.

Mossberg, Walter S. "Three Machines with Three Functions: All-in-One Devices Print, Scan, Copy for Around $100." *The Wall Street Journal*, April 2, 2008, p. D7.

Priest, Joseph. "Word(s) to the Wise for 2008: Brushing Up on New Phrases and Those Oldies but Goodies." *PR Tactics*, January 2008, p. 18.

Schellhardt, Timothy. "Operation Precisely: Top 10 Grammar Reminders." *PR Tactics*, February 2005, p. 21.

Schulz, John J. *Please Don't Do That: The Pocket Guide to Good Writing.* Spokane, WA: Marquette Books, 2008.

Warneke, Kevin. "It's Grammar Time: Paying More Attention to Strunk & White." *PR Tactics*, October 2004, p. 16.

Wylie, Ann. "Start Making Sense: How to Remove Jargon and Other Gibberish from Your Copy." *PR Tactics*, October 2004, p. 17.

Becoming a Persuasive Writer

2

TOPICS covered in this chapter include:

Persuasion: As Old as Civilization   34

The Basics of Communication   35

Theories of Communication   37

Factors in Persuasive Writing   42

Persuasive Speaking   54

Persuasion and Propaganda   55

The Ethics of Persuasion   56

Persuasion: As Old as Civilization

Persuasion has been around since the dawn of human history. It was formalized as a concept more than 2,000 years ago by the Greeks, who made *rhetoric*, the art of using language effectively and persuasively, part of their educational system. Aristotle was the first to set down the ideas of *ethos*, *logos*, and *pathos*, which translate roughly as "source credibility," "logical argument," and "emotional appeal," respectively.

A more recent scholar, Richard Perloff, author of *The Dynamics of Persuasion*, says, "Persuasion is an activity or process in which a communicator attempts to induce a change in the belief, attitude, or behavior of another person or group of persons through the transmission of a message in a context in which the persuadee has some degree of free choice." Such a definition is consistent with the role of public relations personnel in today's society. Indeed, Professor Robert Heath of the University of Houston says:

> . . . public relations professionals are influential rhetors. They design, place, and repeat messages on behalf of sponsors on an array of topics that shape views of government, charitable organizations, institutions of public education, products and consumerism, capitalism, labor, health, and leisure. These professionals speak, write, and use visual images to discuss topics and take stances on public policies at the local, state, and federal levels.

Public relations writers, in particular, spend most of their working day crafting and disseminating information that will persuade and motivate people. The International Public Relations Association (IPRA) succinctly makes the point:

> Public relations is the cultivated landscape drawing our attention to concepts, opinions and conclusions. Through sight, sound, and action, professional communica-

tors do much more than deliver messages and impressions. They motivate audiences to participate and to act—both locally and globally. Persuasive communication is an art form with a direct impact upon our willingness to change the way we live, to change the way we work, to change the way we think.

Indeed, messages are designed to change attitudes and opinions, reinforce existing predispositions, and influence people to buy a product, use a service, or support a worthy cause. To be an effective writer, you need to understand the basic elements of communication and the complex process of how individuals respond to different messages. In an age of information overload, writers must constantly analyze public attitudes and shape persuasive, credible messages that cut through the clutter.

You need to keep asking questions. How do you appeal to self-interests? Which spokesperson has the most credibility? What information is most salient to the target audience? What is the most effective communication channel? What are my ethical responsibilities as a writer?

This chapter gives a thumbnail sketch of some communication theories that are applicable to public relations writing and what social science research tell us about the way people receive, interpret, and act on information. It also provides guidelines about how to make your writing—whether it's on behalf of the Sierra Club or General Electric—more persuasive. Later in the chapter you'll learn about the ethical guidelines and professional standards that should guide the content of your writing.

The Basics of Communication

To communicate is to make known—to project ideas into the minds of others. This process depends on four elements: a *sender*, a *message*, a *channel*, and a *receiver*. If all these elements are present, there will be communication. If any component is missing or not operating, there will be no communication. Because your purpose is to persuade, you want to communicate your ideas to a particular group of people—those who can help or hinder your organization in attaining its objectives. The following sections review the basic communication process from a public relations perspective.

Sender

The sender is the organization from which the message comes. Every organization has different publics, divergent interests, dissimilar objectives, unique problems, distinctive beliefs and peculiarities. As a writer, you must know the organization's objectives so that the messages you prepare will advance these objectives.

Message

Planning the message starts with a determination of exactly what key messages you want your receivers to receive and what you want them to think, believe, or do. Then you must acquire a solid knowledge of what your audience currently knows and believes. If you want to affect attitudes and opinions, you must find out about those that already exist. This often calls for research, which was discussed in Chapter 1.

Your message must be applicable, believable, realistic, and convincing. It must be expressed clearly and understandably in familiar words and phrases. Above all, you must convince the receivers that the idea you are presenting is beneficial to them.

Channel

The media are the physical channels that carry the message to the receiver. They may include newspapers, magazines, radio, television, letters, speeches, audiovisuals, pictures, newsletters, leaflets, brochures, and the Web. Every medium has advantages and disadvantages, as explored in future chapters.

Your job is to determine which medium or combination of media will be most effective in reaching a selected public. If you are trying to reach female college students, it is important to know that there is a vast difference between the readers of *Cosmo*, *Redbook*, and *Glamour* in terms of readership. This will be discussed further in Chapter 10.

It is also important to know the message format that each media requires. Television, for example, requires highly visual material and short **soundbites**. Websites on the World Wide Web require strong graphics and interactive mechanisms. A social media site such as YouTube requires short videos done with a great deal of creativity. A newspaper story requires a strong lead paragraph that attracts the reader.

Receiver

The receivers are the people you must reach. In public relations, potential or actual audiences are commonly referred to as **publics**. A public can be defined in many ways. For marketing purposes, a public is often defined as a market segment—a group of people who have comparable demographic (income, age, education, etc.) characteristics that will cause them to respond to messages in a similar way. A public also can be defined as natural groupings of elected officials, customers, stockholders, or employees. At times, geography defines a particular public—citizens of a town or registered voters in a district.

You will also hear the word **stakeholder** mentioned in relation to publics. Stakeholders, by definition, are groups of people who can be affected by the actions of an organization. The obvious example is the organization's employees, but the list can become quite long when you consider the fact that many "publics" can be affected—consumers, neighbors, suppliers, environmental groups, investors, just to name a few.

Thus, it is extremely important to always think of publics in the plural sense instead of as a collective entity called "the general public." By defining publics by income, age, gender, geography, and even psychographic characteristics, you are much better prepared to design message strategies that are more targeted and relevant to each public or audience. In sum, the more you can segment your publics and understand their characteristics, the better you can communicate with them.

As business becomes more global, there is also a growing need to understand the attitudes, customs, and cultures of people in other nations. Poor conceptualization of messages can cause a number of gaffs when one does not understand the language and culture of a nation. A baby formula manufacturer discovered that in its product introductions in one Spanish-speaking country the term used for "nipple" was a vulgar expression.

Theories of Communication

A message may move from the sender through the media to the receiver without necessarily conveying ideas and getting them accepted. Yet ideas do get accepted, and there are several theories about how this is accomplished. Space does not allow a full discussion of each theory, but this section provides a brief summary of the theories that are most applicable to public relations writers.

Media Uses and Gratification

Recipients of communication are not passive couch potatoes. The basic premise of uses and gratification theory is that the communication process is interactive. The communicator wants to inform and, ultimately, motivate people to act on the information. Recipients want to be entertained, informed, or alerted to opportunities that can fulfill their needs.

Thus, people make highly intelligent choices about what messages require their attention and meet their needs. This is why people are very selective about what articles they will read in the local daily. The role of the public relations writer, then, is to tailor messages that are meaningful to the audience.

A good example is how Burson-Marsteller tailored messages on behalf of the National Turkey Federation to generate year-round sales. The public relations firm used a psychographics model developed by SRI International, a research organization. The model, known as VALS, has several lifestyle typologies:

- *Survivors and sustainers* are at the bottom of the hierarchy. Generally, members of this group have low incomes, are poorly educated, and are often elderly. These people eat at erratic hours, consume inexpensive foods, and seldom patronize restaurants.
- *Belongers* are family oriented and traditional and tend to be lower- or middle-income people.
- *Achievers*, the uppermost level of the VALS scale, are often college-educated professionals with high incomes. They are also more experimental and open to new ideas.

By segmenting the consumer public into these lifestyles, Burson-Marsteller selected appropriate media for specific story ideas. An article placed in *True Experience*, a publication reaching the "survivors and sustainers" group, was headlined "A Terrific Budget-Stretching Meal" and emphasized bargain cuts of turkey. *Better Homes & Gardens* was used to reach the "belongers," with articles that emphasized tradition, such as barbecued turkey as a "summer classic" on the Fourth of July. The "achievers" were reached through *Food and Wine* and *Gourmet* magazines, with recipes for turkey salad and turkey tetrazzini.

By identifying the magazines that catered to these three lifestyle groups and tailoring the information to fit each magazine's demographics, Burson-Marsteller was able to send an appropriate message to each audience. The result was increased turkey sales on a year-round basis. See the Tips for Success box below for some of the various findings of research on persuasion.

Cognitive Dissonance

People will not believe a message, or act on it, if it is contrary to their predispositions. This is the crux of Leon Festinger's theory of cognitive dissonance. In essence, it says that people will not believe a message contrary to their predispositions unless the communicator can introduce information that causes them to question their beliefs.

Dissonance can be created in at least three ways. First, the writer needs to make the public aware that circumstances have changed. Oil companies, for example, say

---

☑ tips FOR SUCCESS

A Persuasion Sampler

A number of research studies have contributed to our understanding of the persuasion process. Ronald Rice and Charles Atkins, in their book *Public Communication Campaigns*, published by Sage Publications, have summarized these findings:

- Positive appeals are generally more effective than negative appeals, in terms of both retention of the message and actual compliance with it.

- Messages presented on radio and television tend to be more persuasive than those seen in print. If the message is complex, however, better comprehension is achieved through print media.

- The print media are more appropriate for conveying detailed, lengthy information; broadcast channels are best for presenting brief, simple ideas. Television and radio messages tend to be consumed passively, whereas the print media allow for review and contemplation.

- Strong emotional appeals and the arousal of fear are most effective when the audience has some minimal concern about or interest in the topic.

- Highly fear-arousing appeals are effective only when some immediate action can be taken to eliminate the threat.

- With highly educated, sophisticated audiences, logical appeals, using facts and figures, work better than strong emotional appeals.

- Like self-interest, altruism can be a strong motivator. Men are more willing to get physical checkups for the sake of their families rather than for themselves.

- A celebrity or an attractive model is most effective when the audience has low involvement, the theme is simple, and broadcast channels are used. An exciting spokesperson attracts attention to a message that would otherwise be ignored. ■

---

that the era of cheap gasoline is over because a rising middle class in such nations as India and China also have cars and are now competing with U.S. drivers for the available supply. Second, the writer needs to provide information about new developments. Public perceptions about China making unsafe toys changed somewhat when Mattel finally admitted that it recalled 18 million toys because of design flaws, not manufacturing problems. Third, the writer should use a quote from a respected person that the public trusts. Chevron, for example, attempts to overcome unfavorable public attitudes about its "green" initiatives by getting endorsements from respected leaders in the conservation and environmental movement.

In many cases, public attitudes can be changed by presenting facts that counter the public's perceptions. A good example is what happened to the lowly potato when the diet industry demonized the vegetable as a fattening, high-carbohydrate food. One survey, for example, showed that almost 25 percent of female heads of households believed that potatoes were fattening. The U.S. Potato Board and its public relations firm, Fleishman-Hillard, countered this perception by pointing out that potatoes—although a carbohydrate—have positive nutritional benefits because they are a good source of vitamin C and potassium, are low in calories, and are sodium free. As a result of the campaign, a positive shift occurred in public perceptions about the potato as a nutritious vegetable, increasing potato consumption.

Framing

Historically, the term *framing* was used to describe how journalists and editors select certain facts, themes, treatments, and even words to "frame" a story in order to generate maximum interest and understanding among readers and viewers. For example, how media frame the debate over health care and the policies of health maintenance organizations (HMOs) plays a major role in public perceptions of the problem. Many people, because they lack specific knowledge and experience about an issue, usually accept the media's version of reality.

Framing theory also applies to public relations because, according to more than one study, about half of the content found in the mass media today is supplied by public relations sources. Indeed, Kirk Hallahan of Colorado State University says that public relations personnel are essentially *frame strategists*, because they construct messages that "focus selectively on key attributes and characteristics of a cause, candidate, product, or service." This framing, in turn, is echoed in the context and content of stories that the mass media disseminate.

The issue of bottled water is a good case study in framing. The $12 billion bottling industry, of course, "frames" bottled water as being better than tap water, a healthy alternative to sodas, and a part of an active lifestyle. Activist groups, such as the National Resource Defense Council (NRDC), frame the consumption of bottled water as environmentally irresponsible because the transport of bottled water from exotic places such as Fiji generates greenhouse gasses, a primary cause of global warming. In addition, plastic bottles not only require oil to make, but an estimated 2 billion pounds of plastic bottles are now clogging landfills. Public relations on both sides, including the tap water filter manufacturers, influence how the media frames the issue in its news coverage.

Another example of framing is how competing interests portrayed the Beijing Olympics. Activists concerned about human rights in China, religious freedom in Tibet, and China's involvement in Darfur (Sudan) worked hard to frame the event in the media as the "Genocide Olympics." In contrast, the International Olympic Committee (IOC) and the Chinese government sought to frame the event as integral to the Olympic goal of promoting international harmony, peace, and cross-cultural understanding.

Political candidates, of course, constantly work to frame their image through the media. Hillary Clinton, for example, used the theme of experience in Washington, whereas Barack Obama sought to frame himself as the candidate of change.

Diffusion and Adoption

The diffusion theory was developed in the 1930s and expanded on by Professor Everett Rogers of Stanford University. It holds that the process of acquiring new ideas has five steps:

1. **Awareness.** The person discovers the idea or product.
2. **Interest.** The person tries to get more information.
3. **Trial.** The person tries the idea on others or samples the product.
4. **Evaluation.** The person decides whether the idea works for his or her own self-interest.
5. **Adoption.** The person incorporates the idea into his or her opinion or begins to use the product.

In this model, the public relations writer is most influential at the *awareness* and *interest* stages of the process. People often become aware of a product, service, or idea through traditional mass media outlets such as newspapers, magazines, radio, and television. Indeed, the primary purpose of advertising in the mass media is to create awareness, the first step in moving people toward the purchase of a product or support of an idea.

At the interest stage, people seek more detailed information from such sources as pamphlets, brochures, direct mail, videotape presentations, meetings, and websites. This is why initial publicity to create awareness often includes an 800 number or a website where people can get more information.

Family members, peers, and associates become influential in the trial and evaluation stages of the adoption model. Mass media, at this point, serves primarily to reinforce messages and predispositions.

Note that a person does not necessarily go through all five stages of adoption with any particular idea or product. A number of factors affect the adoption process. Rogers lists at least five:

- **Relative advantage.** Is the idea better than the one it replaces?
- **Compatibility.** Is the idea consistent with the person's existing values and needs?

- **Complexity.** Is the innovation difficult to understand and use?
- **Trialability.** Can the innovation be used on a trial basis?
- **Observability.** Are the results of the innovation visible to others?

You should be aware of these factors and try to formulate messages that address them. Repeating a message in various ways, reducing its complexity, taking competing messages into account, and structuring the message to the needs of the audience are ways to do this. Another aspect of adoption theory is that some people are predisposed to be *innovators* and early adopters, whereas others, known as *laggards*, won't adopt an idea or product until it is well established. Public relations campaigns often are directed toward the early adopters, also known as *influentials* or *catalysts*, to launch a new product. This is discussed further in future chapters.

Hierarchy of Needs

The hierarchy of needs theory has been applied in a number of disciplines, including communication. It is based on the work of Abraham H. Maslow, who listed basic human needs on a scale from basic survival to more complex needs:

- **Physiological needs.** These involve self-preservation. They include air, water, food, clothing, shelter, rest, and health—the minimum necessities of life.
- **Safety needs.** These comprise protection against danger, loss of life or property, restriction of activity, and loss of freedom.
- **Social needs.** These include acceptance by others, belonging to groups, and enjoying both friendship and love.
- **Ego needs.** These include self-esteem, self-confidence, accomplishment, status, recognition, appreciation, and the respect of others.
- **Self-actualization needs.** These represent the need to grow to one's full stature after all other needs are met. Individuals may learn a new language for the fun of it, volunteer for a cause, or travel.

The campaign for the National Turkey Federation, mentioned earlier, is a good example of the application of Maslow's concepts. Low-income people got an economical recipe that satisfied basic physiological needs. However, the fancy recipes in upscale magazines were designed to meet the ego and status needs of people not worried about food costs.

At times, a public relations or advertising writer can appeal to several needs at once. An ad for a new car, for example, often emphasizes economic, safety, social, and ego needs. For the Baby Boomer who just turned 60, a red sports car may even satisfy self-actualization needs.

The main point is to understand that your audience is looking for messages that satisfy needs. If you can identify and articulate those needs, you are well on your way to being a persuasive writer.

■ Factors in Persuasive Writing

Your purpose is to persuade your target audience. Your message may be delivered in one way, a few ways, or many ways. Techniques for getting your messages into the mass media are detailed in later chapters. As you work on message content, however, keep in mind the concepts of audience analysis; source credibility; appeal to self-interest; clarity of the message; timing and context; symbols, slogans, and acronyms; semantics; suggestions for action; and content and structure. See the Tips for Success below for additional guidelines.

Audience Analysis

A message, as already stated, must be compatible with group values and beliefs. People who commute by car, for example, become more interested in carpooling and mass transit when the message points out the increasing cost of fuel and how gridlock increases every year.

> **" Communicators must have a thorough understanding of their audiences, and they must stay very current with the media being used by these audiences. "**
>
> ■ Jerry Swerling, director of the USC Annenberg Strategic Public Relations Center

Tapping a group's attitudes and values in order to structure a meaningful message is called **channeling**. It is the technique of recognizing a general audience's beliefs and suggesting a specific course of action related to audience members' self-

---

✓ tips FOR SUCCESS

How to Write Persuasive Messages

Philip Lesly, a pioneer in the public relations field, offered these tips for effective, persuasive communication at the Vern C. Schranz Distinguished Lectureship series at Ball State University.

1. Approach everything from the viewpoint of the audience's interest. What is on its mind? What is in it for each person?

2. Make the subject matter part of the atmosphere in which audience members live—what they talk about, what they hear from others. That means tailoring the message to their communication channels.

3. Communicate *with* people, not *at* them. Communication that approaches the audience as a target makes people put up defenses against it.

4. Localize—get the message conveyed as close to the individual's own setting as possible.

5. Use a number of communication channels, not just one or two. The impact is far greater when a message reaches people in a number of different forms.

6. Maintain consistency so that the basic content is the same regardless of audience or context. Then tailor that content to the specific audience as much as possible.

7. Don't propagandize, but be sure you make your point. Drawing conclusions in the information itself is more effective than letting the audience draw its own conclusions.

8. Maintain credibility—which is essential for all these points to be effective. ■

---

interests. In this example, the incentive to participate in carpooling or mass transit offers more motivation than the more abstract concept of saving the environment.

Professor emeritus James Grunig of the University of Maryland says audiences can be defined as either passive or active. *Passive audiences* have to be lured into accepting your message. Consequently, messages directed to them need to be highly visual, use catchy themes and slogans, and contain short messages. A number of communication tools provide this format: dramatic pictures and graphics, billboards, radio and television announcements, posters, bumper stickers, buttons, and special events that emphasize entertainment.

A variation of the passive audience is what Kirk Hallahan of Colorado State University calls the *inactive public*. This public typically has low knowledge and low involvement in the subject—whether a political campaign or a new product or service on the market. This presents a massive challenge to the communicator who must devise strategies for effective communication with such publics in order even to engage them at the basic level of generating awareness. Indeed, most public relations campaigns for new products and services tend to focus on passive or inactive publics.

Active audiences, by contrast, are usually aware of the product, service, or idea. They have reached the second stage of the diffusion process—*interest*—and are seeking more detailed information. Appropriate communication tools for them include brochures, in-depth newspaper and magazine stories, detailed websites, videotapes, seminars, speeches, and display booths at trade shows. Indeed, research shows that visits to websites often are driven by stories in the traditional mainstream media.

In most cases, the competent communicator acknowledges the existence of both passive and active audiences by preparing a number of messages that vary in content and structure. A daily newspaper may receive an attractive publicity photo with a short caption, whereas a specialized trade publication might get an in-depth news release detailing the product's features. On another level, a customer assessing the corporate website may review multiple details about the product or service by clicking on multiple links. The strategy of developing multiple messages for a variety of channels is emphasized throughout this book.

Source Credibility

A message is more believable to an audience if the source has credibility, which is why writers try to attribute information and quotes to people who are perceived as experts. Indeed, expertise is a key element in credibility. The other two elements are sincerity and charisma. Ideally, a source will have all three attributes.

Steve Jobs, president of Apple, is a good example. His success in revitalizing the company in 1999 made him highly credible as an expert on Apple products and a high-tech visionary. In countless news articles and speeches, he also comes across as a personable, laid-back "geek" who really believes that the MacBook, iMac, and the iPhone are the best products on the market. Jobs also has that elusive element of charisma—he is self-assured, confident, and articulate. As *Time* magazine notes, he also has his fan club: "adoring legions at MacWorld."

Not every company has a Steve Jobs for its president, nor is that necessary. Studies, such as the annual Edelman Trust Barometer, show that certain occupational groups have more credibility with the public than others. In its 2008 report, Edelman found that financial or industry analysts, academics, doctors or health care specialists, and nonprofit/NGO representatives are highly credible and trusted by the public. CEOs of companies and government officials are somewhat less trusted, but still ranked higher than bloggers and entertainers/athletes, who are trusted the least. Also ranking quite high in terms of credibility and trust is the category "people like me." In other words, using an average mom as a spokesperson can be very persuasive if you are persuading people about the benefits of using a particular household product.

The Edelman survey gives some insight to what kinds of individuals are credible and trusted, but you need to evaluate the message and the audience to determine the most appropriate spokesperson. For example, if you are writing a news release about a new product for a trade magazine, perhaps the most credible source to quote would be the company's director of research and development. This person is credible because of his or her personal knowledge and expertise. If the news release is about a company's fourth-quarter earnings, however, the most credible person to quote in the news release would be either the CEO, the vice president for finance, or a financial or industry analyst.

Source credibility also can be hired. The California Strawberry Advisory Board, for example, quotes a home economist in its news releases, and this individual appears on television talk shows to discuss nutrition and demonstrate easy-to-follow strawberry recipes. The audience for these programs, primarily homemakers, not only identifies with the representative but also perceives the spokesperson to be an expert. Additional credibility is gained if the spokesperson comes across as being sincere about the message.

Here's a sampling of hired experts who have been quoted and have provided media interviews for various public relations campaigns:

- A veterinarian for a campaign by Novartis Animal Health to launch a new arthritis drug for dogs
- Two professors of nutrition for a campaign by Frito-Lay to tell the public that its potato chips are now made with sunflower oil, a "good" fat
- A celebrity interior designer for a campaign by Olympic Paints and Stains to position itself as a home decorating brand
- A well-known food expert in the African American community for a campaign by Lawry Seasoned Salt to show how its product line enhances this ethnic group's favorite recipes

Celebrities often are used to call attention to a product, service, or cause. Celebrities, as already noted, attract passive audiences to a message. The sponsor's intent is to associate the person's popularity with the product and provide more "glamour" to the product. This is called *transfer*. This is why Kodak chose the Academy Awards to highlight its new dual-lens digital camera. The company's objective was to position itself as a lifestyle brand among women who take their cues from the world of celebrity. In addition to giving cameras with a diamond monogram to the five best actress nominees, Kodak also preselected celebrities, such as Keira Knightley, to take photos of other celebrities attending an Oscar-viewing party at a swank restaurant in New York. The resulting photos were distributed to the media and generated almost 40 million media impressions.

Not all celebrities need to be Hollywood stars or even famous athletes. Again, it depends on finding the appropriate, credible spokesperson for the situation. The Kansas City Health Department had a much less glamorous assignment—educating the gay community and sex workers about the risk of syphilis and the availability of free testing. Flo, a local celebrity drag queen, was chosen as a spokesperson because she was widely accepted in the gay and straight communities. According to Fleishman-Hillard, the public relations firm handling the campaign, "She possessed the ability to take sensitive topics, such as syphilis, and motivate people at risk to take action. Her personality and credibility gave far more exposure to the issue than a straight public health message would have received."

Appeal to Self-Interest

Self-interest was mentioned in connection with both Maslow's hierarchy of needs and audience analysis. A public relations writer must at all times be aware of what the audience wants to know.

Writing publicity for a new food product can serve as an example. A news release to the trade press serving the food industry (grocery stores, suppliers, wholesalers, and distributors) might focus on how the product was developed, distributed, and made available to the public, the manufacturer's pricing policies, or the results of marketing studies that show consumers want the product. This audience is interested in the technical aspects of distribution, pricing, and market niche.

You would prepare quite a different news release or feature article for the food section of a daily newspaper. The consumer wants information about the food product's nutritional value, convenience, and cost and wants to know why the item is superior to similar products. The reader is also looking for menu ideas and recipes that use the product. The Tips for Success below provides a list of common message themes that appeal to an audience's self-interests.

☑ tips FOR SUCCESS

Appeals That Move People to Act

Persuasive messages often include information that appeals to an audience's self-interest. Here is a list of persuasive message themes that author Charles Marsh compiled for an article in IABC's *Communication World*:

Make money	Satisfy curiosity	Save money	Protect family
Save time	Be stylish	Avoid effort	Have beautiful things
More comfort	Satisfy appetite	Better health	Be like others
Cleaner	Avoid trouble	Escape pain	Avoid criticism
Gain praise	Be individual	Be popular	Protect reputation
Be loved/accepted	Be safe	Keep possessions	Make work easier
More enjoyment	Be secure ■		

Clarity of the Message

Communication, as already stated, does not occur if the audience does not understand your message. It is important to produce messages that match the characteristics of your target audience in content and structure.

A bar association once thought it was a great idea to produce a brochure to help motorists understand liability in an accident. However, by the time the committee of lawyers added all the legalese, the brochure became useless as an aid to the general public.

One solution to this problem is to copy test all public relations materials on the target audience. Another solution is to apply readability and comprehension formulas to materials before they are produced and disseminated. Most formulas are based on the number of words per sentence and the number of one-syllable words per 100 words.

In general, standard writing should average about 140 to 150 syllables per 100 words, and the average sentence length should be about 17 words. This is the level of newspapers and weekly newsmagazines such as *Time*.

Timing and Context

Professional communicators often say that timing is everything. In the earlier example about car commuters, it was pointed out that the best time to talk about carpooling and mass transit to owners of sport utility vehicles is when there is a major increase in gas prices. Another good context is when the state highway department releases a study showing that the average commute on a congested highway from point A to point B now takes 20 minutes longer than it did last year. Both of these situations are good examples of keying messages around events and related news stories that provide a context for your message.

Your message also must arrive at a time when it is most relevant to the audience. If it is too early, your audience might not be ready to think about it. April is not the time to talk about new facilities at a ski resort, but October might be just right. Cruise ships also distribute news releases and travel features about tropical destinations as the temperature drops in the Midwest and East Coast. Information about a new software program for doing taxes is relevant in the weeks before the April 15 deadline, but the news value drops after this date. News about a new club would get attention from single, young professionals almost any time.

Symbols, Slogans, and Acronyms

The Red Cross (known as the Red Crescent in the Middle East) is well known throughout the world. The name is totally unenlightening, but the symbol is recognized and associated with the care and help given by the organization. Flags are symbols. Smokey the Bear is a symbol. Even the Nike Swoosh is a familiar symbol on a global scale. You are not likely to produce a symbol that will become world famous, but, if at all possible, you should try to find something graphic that symbolizes a given organization. This is called **branding**, and corp'rations often spend millions to establish a symbol that immediately means reliability and quality to a consumer.

Slogans can be highly persuasive. They state a key concept in a few memorable and easily pronounceable words. The American Revolution had the rallying cry of "No taxation without representation," and today's corporations are just as slogan conscious.

Nike tells us to "Just Do It" and McDonald's assures us that "You Deserve a Break Today." Coca-Cola wants us to have "The Pause That Refreshes," and MasterCard talks about things that are "Priceless." Perhaps one of the most successful slogans of all time is DeBeers assurance that "A diamond is forever." If you can come up with a slogan that expresses the essence of what you are trying to promote, it will help you attain your objective.

Acronyms range from the effective to the ridiculous. Coined from the initial letters of the name of some organization or cause, an acronym can be highly useful in some cases. A good acronym is NOW, for the National Organization for Women. It is pronounceable and memorable, and it makes a succinct political point. These women are striving for equality, and they want it "NOW." Another good reason for using acronyms is to shorten a lengthy name. AIDS is much easier to comprehend and write about than "acquired immune deficiency syndrome."

Semantics

The dictionary definition of words may be clear and concise, but there is another dimension to words—the connotative meaning to various individuals and groups of people. The study of meaning given to words and the changes that occur in these meanings as time goes on is the branch of linguistics called **semantics**.

For example, consider the evolution of the word "gay" in American society. The word was traditionally defined as merry, joyous, and lively. Thus, in the nineteenth century, we had the "Gay Nineties" and people often referred to bright colors or sprightly music as "gay." By the 1920s and 1930s, however, "gay" started being applied as a code word for prostitutes who were said to be in the "gay life." Today, "gay" is only used in the context of the homosexual community.

By the same token, the terms "pro-life" and "pro-choice" have very definite connotations to certain groups of people. "Affirmative action" means opportunity to some and exclusion to others. The controversy over politically correct language was cited in Chapter 1. Even the expression "politically correct" has different connotations to different groups of people. To some, it is derogatory, an attempt by radical groups to censor freedom of expression. To others, the concept stands for equality and an effort to eliminate sexism and racism.

To write persuasively and to influence target audiences, you must be sensitive to semantics. The protracted argument between the Republicans and the Democrats over Medicare funding is a good example. The Republicans say they want to "preserve, protect, and strengthen" the program, whereas the Democrats say such rhetoric is just code words to disguise legislation that will lead to major "cuts" in funding. The issue is again a matter of framing.

Suggestions for Action

Persuasive writing must give people information on how to take action, and the suggestions must be feasible. A campaign by a utility provides a good example. If the company really wants people to conserve energy, it must provide them with information about how to do so. The suggestions may be as simple as turning the thermostat down to 68 degrees, wearing sweaters in the house during the winter months, or purchasing a roll of weather stripping to place around the windows and doors. All these suggestions are within the capability of the utility's customers.

However, if the suggestion is to insulate your house thoroughly, this might not be feasible for consumers with limited incomes. In this case, the utility might accompany the suggestion with a special program of interest-free loans or a discount coupon to make it easier for customers to take the recommended action. In this way, the suggestion becomes feasible to thousands of homeowners.

Environmental organizations, to use another example, make a point of providing information on how to write to your legislator. They provide not only the legislator's address and e-mail, but also a sample letter that you can copy. Greenpeace simply mails its members postcards with preprinted messages. All people have to do is sign the postcard and affix a stamp.

Content and Structure

People are motivated by theatrics and a good story. They are moved by bold action and human drama. Your message should go beyond cold facts or even eloquent phrases. If you can vividly describe what you are talking about—if you can paint word pictures—your message will be more persuasive.

> **" PR is based on presenting compelling stories about products, corporations, and points of view. "**
> ■ Helen Ostrowski, CEO of Porter Novelli

A number of techniques can make a message more persuasive; many of these have already been discussed. The following is a summary of some additional writing devices.

Drama ■ Everyone likes a good story. This is often accomplished by graphically illustrating an event or a situation. Newspapers often dramatize a story to boost reader interest. Thus, we read about the daily life of someone with AIDS, the family on welfare who is suffering because of state cuts in spending, or the frustrations of a middle-class family who is facing eviction from their home because they couldn't pay the balloon mortgage payments. In the newsroom, this is called *humanizing the issue.*

Drama, or human interest, is also used in public relations. A good example is how Harden & Partners used the human interest element when Covenant House opened in Oakland, California. The basic news was that the nonprofit organization was opening a new multipurpose shelter to serve homeless and at-risk youth in the San Francisco Bay area. Such an announcement lacks drama, but the story became more interesting when a human interest element was added. Journalists were given the names of some of Covenant House residents who had agreed to be interviewed. Consequently, a front page story in the *Oakland Tribune* started this way: "For

Marcus, the bed and the hot food he found at Covenant House gave him a chance to rejuvenate and get his life organized. 'You can't think when you are hungry,' said the 22-year-old Missouri native, one of the dozen or so homeless young people who began staying at the new youth shelter in Jack London Square last week."

Relief organizations, in particular, attempt to humanize problems to galvanize public concern to attract donations. Saying that nearly 2 million people in Sudan's Darfur region have become homeless doesn't have the same emotional impact as describing a young mother in a refugee camp sobbing over the lifeless form of her 11-year-old daughter who was raped and then murdered by a Janjaweed militia that also burned down her village and murdered many of her neighbors. Readers and viewers can identify with the mother's loss, which graphically illustrates the need for aid. Large numbers alone are cold and impersonal and generate little or no emotional involvement.

A more mundane use of dramatizing is the application story that is sent to the trade press. With this technique, sometimes called the *case study technique*, a manufacturer prepares an article on how an individual or a company is using its product. Honeywell Corporation, for example, provides a number of application stories about how offices and businesses have saved money by installing Honeywell's temperature-control systems. More examples of the application story are found in Chapter 7.

Statistics ▪ Although numbers can be cold and impersonal, they also can convey objectivity, largeness, and importance in a credible way. For some reason, people are awed by statistics. For example, Toyota, seeking to portray itself as an important contributor to the American economy, once placed ads in major metropolitan dailies that used impressive numbers. One ad stated, "Over the last 5 years Toyota in America has purchased $20 billion in parts and materials from 510 U.S. suppliers. Today, more than half the Toyota vehicles sold in America are built at our plants in Kentucky and California."

Such numbers can be effective, but a writer should use them sparingly. A news release crammed with statistics tends to overwhelm the reader. Consequently, efforts are often made to dramatize statistic in a way that paints a more vivid picture for readers and viewers. Gun control advocates, for example, say that 13 children are killed daily by guns in the United States—the equivalent of 365 Columbine High School killings each year. Antismoking advocates compare the number of deaths each day attributed to smoking as the equivalent of two loaded 747s crashing every day. On a less horrific note, Kimberly-Clark, the market leader in the sales of toilet paper, said it sold 4.5 billion rolls one year—enough to stretch from the earth to the sun. One can also dramatize statistical percentages by putting them in terms that people can readily understand. For example, one MIT professor was quoted as saying, "You can take a flight every day for 21,000 years before you would be statistically likely to be in a fatal accident."

Surveys and Polls ▪ The public and the media express a great deal of interest in what might be called popularity ratings. During a presidential election campaign, various polls and surveys about who is ahead and why seem to dominate coverage. People are also interested in what product ranks number one in cost or satisfaction or what airline is first in service or leg room.

Polls and surveys are related to the persuasion technique called the *bandwagon*. The idea is to show overwhelming support for a particular idea or product by saying that "four out of five doctors recommend . . ." or that "65 percent of the voters support. . . ." Consequently, everyone should get on the "bandwagon."

Various organizations use polls and surveys as a way of getting media publicity and brand recognition. A mattress company once did a poll on how many people slept in the nude. Gillette launched a campaign urging young men to shave more often by citing an online survey that only 3 percent of women liked scruffy men. The possibilities are endless, and the use of surveys as publicity opportunities is elaborated upon in Chapter 4.

☑ tips FOR SUCCESS

Why Writing Fails to Persuade

Many product news releases and marketing brochures don't persuade because key components are missing. Dianna Huff, a business-to-business marketing writing specialist, gives 10 reasons why marketing materials often remain unread:

Emphasis on the company instead of the customer. It's all right to tell customers about your company and its great manufacturing facility, but it's important to tell customers how it benefits them. Do they get a better product or service? Lower prices? Faster turnaround?

All features, no benefits. Don't let engineers write your copy. Focus instead on how your product or service will benefit your customers.

Copy that fails to say, "What's in it for me?" Stay away from generalities. Be specific about how the product or service will help the consumer save money, do things easier, or enhance his or her quality of life.

Too much jargon. Make sure phrases and sentences are not corporate or engineering lingo. Translate concepts into basic English.

Redundancies. Are you using the same words or phrases in several places? Edit them out or use other words.

No call to action. The number one rule in promotional writing is to tell potential customers what you want them to do. Pick up the phone? Visit the website? Visit a store? Buy the product?

Copy not addressed to target audience. Try to picture a person that represents your audience and write directly to him or her.

Failure to nail down messaging. Don't use vague, meaningless phrases about the product or service. Keep asking management about specific benefits, how the product differs from the competition, etc.

Poor grammar. Yes, people do notice.

Failure to edit or proofread. Ask others to also proofread copy. They will no doubt find typos you have missed. ■

Examples ▪ A general statement becomes more persuasive when a specific example can clarify and reinforce the core information. A utility company, when announcing a 5 percent rate increase, often clarifies what this means by giving the example that the average consumer will pay about $5 more per month for electricity. The railroad industry, competing with the trucking industry, gives the example that moving freight by train is three times more fuel efficient than using trucks. A school district, fighting for more funds, could bolster its case by giving examples of overcrowded classrooms, high teacher/student ratios, and poor student achievement compared to wealthier school districts.

As you read this text, you will notice that "for example" is a frequently used phrase. The purpose of these examples, of course, is to help you better understand the basic concept and how it is applied to actual situations.

Testimonials ▪ A testimonial is usually a form of source credibility that comes from individuals who have directly benefitted from using a product, program, or service. Thus, a happy consumer is quoted in a news release or an advertisement about how much he or she likes a particular product or service. A university might use favorable quotes from outstanding alumni about the value of their education. A celebrity on a television talk show might say that a particular drug helped her cope with severe migraine headaches.

Some testimonials are indirect, but powerful. The American Cancer Society may have a woman in her 50s who is dying of lung cancer do a testimonial about the dangers of smoking. Mothers Against Drunk Driving (MADD) might feature a medical doctor talking about the effects of three drinks on a driver's perceptions. Or, it might feature a young woman who is the victim of a drunk driver talking about the many months of hospitalization and plastic surgery that she had to endure.

Endorsements ▪ The endorsement is a variant of the testimonial. Advocacy on behalf of a product, service, or event is often called **third-party endorsement** because often there is no personal connection, as in a testimonial, to what is being endorsed. One form of endorsement is the proclamation by a mayor, governor, or even the president endorsing the celebration of a particular day or week. Thus, we have officials proclaiming "Red Cross Day" or "National Library Week." The U.S. president even proclaims "National Heart Health Month" to help raise public awareness about heart disease. In almost all of these cases, some organization has requested the proclamation as part of its public relations strategy.

A second kind of endorsement is generated by media. These endorsements can come through editorials, product reviews, surveys, news stories, and even blogs. A daily newspaper may endorse a political candidate or a community cause, review restaurants and movies, or even compile a reader survey ranking the best pizza joints. Popular bloggers can make or break a new product by posting favorable or unfavorable reviews. Magazines endorse products by giving "seals of approval" that can be touted by the winning companies. *Allure* magazine, for example, has a "Best of Beauty" awards in

> **❝ Popularization happens when you get credible third parties to speak for your brand, and that is something PR can do extremely well. ❞**
> ▪ Scott Keogh, chief marketing officer of Audi

two categories: beauty products chosen by readers and those chosen by the magazine's editors with the help of beauty experts. *Allure*'s "endorsement" pays dividends for many companies. Becca, a maker of a high-end crème blush, saw its sales triple after winning an award.

The third kind of endorsement is statements by experts, credible organizations, and celebrities; these usually involve payment or some other kind of financial arrangement. Thus, a well-known medical specialist may publicly state that a particular brand of exercise equipment is best for general conditioning. Organizations such as the American Dental Association, the National Safety Council, and even a group called Cosmetic Executive Women also endorse a variety of products and services.

Celebrities, of course, endorse all kinds of products and services for a fee. Indeed, they often make more money in endorsements than what they actually do for a living. The primary purpose of using celebrity endorsements, as already noted, is to add glamour and attract passive audiences that ordinarily would not pay attention to information about a particular product or service. But the cost isn't cheap. Nicole Kidman got $5 million for 2-minutes of air time endorsing Chanel No. 5, and Madonna charged designer Donatella Versace $12 million to endorse a spring collection. However, Toyota got considerable publicity for its Prius hybrid at a very reasonable cost by chauffeuring environmentally conscious Hollywood celebrities to the Academy Awards ceremony. Celebrities who opted for the free ride in a Prius instead of a stretch limo included Orlando Bloom, Selma Hayek, Kirsten Dunst, and Kate Bosworth.

By all accounts, Tiger Woods is the world's most marketable athlete. He endorses a variety of products from Buick to Asahi beer, and his multiyear deals makes him the wealthiest of all celebrity endorsers. He has a 5-year deal with Nike for $105 million, and Gillette is paying up to $20 million in another deal. In 2008, Tiger signed a 5-year agreement with Gatorade to bring out "Gatorade Tiger," which will pay him about $100 million (Figure 2.1). Many experts say Tiger is getting overexposed and that some of his endorsements aren't very credible. As one media columnist noted, "No one believes Tiger drives a Buick."

Emotional Appeals ■ Persuasive messages often play on our emotions. Fundraising letters from nonprofit groups often use this writing device, as demonstrated in the letter from the American Society for the Prevention of Cruelty to Animals (ASPCA)

▶ **FIGURE 2.1** Tiger Woods is literally out of this world when it comes to endorsements. Here the famous golfer poses in a space suit for a Gatorade commercial that launches Gatorade Tiger. His endorsement deal with Gatorade is worth about $100 million over a 5-year period.

in the PR Casebook below. Another fundraising letter, one from the Marine Mammal Center in California, began as follows:

> She was just 5 months old, a feisty sea lion pup practicing what sea lions do best—fishing. But this time the fish she swallowed had a hook in it. She was

PR casebook

Emotional Appeals Humanize an Issue

A basic approach to many fundraising letters is to humanize the problem with a strong emotional component.

The American Society for the Prevention of Cruelty to Animals used a letter in 2008 that starts with a story about an abused dog named Marcus. It follows up with his rescue by ASPCA and gives facts and information about the organization's efforts to rescue hundreds of animals from abuse.

The four-page letter ends, of course, with a note about Brutus being back to "his happy handsome self" and requests the reader's help in saving dogs like him. The following is the first page of the fundraising letter. It starts with an introductory note in large type that states:

The 5 pound chain was so tight it had turned into a deadly noose. The wound was so deep it was nearly to the bone. No food. No water. Locked in a yard, alone and covered with feces. Brutus had only a few days to live.

The letter continued:

"You wouldn't treat a dog that way."

No, you and I wouldn't. But too many people would—and do. Brutus's story is sadly not unique or unlike the multitudes of others the ASPCA Humane Law Enforcement Team witnesses day in and day out.

By the time a neighbor called us about Brutus, the dog was nearly dead. Empowered by law to investigate cases of cruelty and seize abused animals, our ASPCA Humane Law Enforcement Agents entered the backyard. Brutus was too weak to bark or even stand up. In the place of a collar was a 5 pound chain that was so tight it was embedded into his neck. He was so emaciated that you could count every single rib on his weak, dehydrated body.

The Agents knelt down, speaking gently to Brutus. They didn't want to frighten him so they moved very slowly—and at first, they didn't pet him.

Then they saw it. Brutus was wagging his tail. He was barely moving, but yes—the poor, sick dog was saying, "Welcome, friends!"

Brutus was rushed to the ASPCA Bergh Memorial Animal Hospital where he was examined by expert veterinarians who immediately discovered the severity of his abuse and the gaping wound where his collar should have been. Several major surgeries were required to close the wound and repair the tissue around Brutus's neck. While he went through rehabilitation for his injuries, our certified behaviorists spent time showering Brutus with the love, affection and socialization skills he had lived without for so many years.

Brutus's abuser was charged with animal cruelty, and now Brutus is eagerly waiting for a new loving home.

yanked violently from the sea and left dangling from the end of a fishing rod. Then someone aimed a high-powered crossbow and fired a metal arrow point-blank, directly into her neck.

Such "stories" can elicit strong emotions and galvanize public opinion, but they can also backfire. If the appeal is too strong or shocking, it tends to raise people's ego defenses, and they tune out the unpleasant message. The key is to relieve the stressful situation by providing a happy ending. In the case of the ASPCA and Marine Mammal letters, the animals were successfully rescued.

Fear arousal is another form of emotional appeal. Many public service information campaigns use this approach. First, a question is raised. An example is "What would happen if your child were thrown through the windshield in an accident?" or "What would happen to your wife and children if you died of a heart attack?" Second, a relatively simple solution is given to relieve the emotional anxiety. A young mother is told that her baby should always be placed in a secured infant seat. Or, the husband might be encouraged to regularly exercise or even buy more life insurance. Moderate fear arousal, accompanied by a relatively simple suggestion for avoiding the situation, is considered an effective persuasive technique.

Psychologists say the most effective emotional appeal is one coupled with facts and figures. The emotional appeal attracts interest, but logical arguments also are needed. For more practical tips on formulating persuasive appeals, see the Tips for Success on page 50.

■ Persuasive Speaking

Psychologists have found that successful speakers (and salespeople) use several persuasion techniques:

- **Yes–yes.**   Start with points with which the audience agrees to develop a pattern of "yes" answers. Getting agreement to a basic premise often means that the receiver will agree to the logically developed conclusion.

- **Offer structured choice.**   Give choices that force the audience to choose between A and B. College officials may ask audiences, "Do you want to raise taxes or raise tuition?" Political candidates ask, "Do you want more free enterprise or government telling you what to do?"

- **Seek partial commitment.**   Get a commitment for some action on the part of the receiver. This leaves the door open for commitment to other parts of the proposal at a later date. "You don't need to decide on the new insurance plan now, but please attend the employee orientation program on Thursday."

- **Ask for more, settle for less.**   Submit a complete public relations program to management, but be prepared to compromise by dropping certain parts of the program. It has become almost a cliché that a department asks for a larger budget than it expects to receive.

A persuasive speech can be one sided or offer several sides of an issue, depending on the audience. A series of studies by Carl Hovland and his associates at Yale conducted in the 1950s determined that one-sided speeches were most effective with persons favorable to the message, whereas two-sided speeches were most effective with audiences that might be opposed to the message.

■ Persuasion and Propaganda

No discussion of persuasion would be complete without mentioning propaganda and the techniques associated with it. According to Garth S. Jowett and Victoria O'Donnell, in their book *Propaganda and Persuasion*, "Propaganda is the deliberate and systematic attempt to shape perceptions, manipulate cognitions, and direct behavior to achieve a response that furthers the desired intent of the propagandist." Its roots go back to the seventeenth century, when the Roman Catholic Church set up the *congregatio de propaganda* ("congregation for propagating the faith"). The word took on extremely negative connotations in the early twentieth century as a result of World Wars I and II, when competing sides accused each other of using "propaganda" to further their military objectives.

Some critics have even argued that propaganda, in the broadest sense of the word, also includes the advertising and public relations activity of such diverse entities as Exxon and the Sierra Club. Social scientists, however, say that the word *propaganda* should be used only to denote activity that sells a belief system or constitutes political or ideological dogma. Advertising and public relations messages for commercial purposes, however, do use several techniques commonly associated with propaganda. The following are the most common:

- **Plain folks.** An approach often used by individuals to show humble beginnings and empathy with the average citizen. Political candidates, in particular, are quite fond of telling about their "humble" beginnings.

- **Testimonial.** A frequently used device to achieve credibility, as discussed earlier. A well-known expert, popular celebrity, or average citizen gives testimony about the value of a product or the wisdom of a decision.

- **Bandwagon.** The implication or direct statement that everyone wants the product or that the idea has overwhelming support; for example, "Millions of Americans support a ban on assault rifles" or "Every leading expert believes global warming is a significant problem."

- **Card stacking.** The selection of facts and data to build an overwhelming case on one side of the issue while concealing the other side. Critics of the Beijing Olympics, for example, emphasized China's record on human rights, but didn't mention that the quality of life for most Chinese has risen dramatically in the past 20 years.

- **Transfer.** The technique of associating the person, product, or organization with something that has high status, visibility, or credibility. Many corporations, for example, paid millions to be official sponsors of the 2008 Olympic Games, hoping that the public would associate their products with excellence.

- **Glittering generalities.** The technique of associating a cause, product, or idea with favorable abstractions such as freedom, justice, democracy, and the American way. The White House named its military action in Afghanistan "Enduring Freedom" and the Iraqi campaign "Operation Iraqi Freedom." American oil companies lobby for drilling in the Arctic wilderness area to keep "America energy independent."

A student of public relations should be aware of these techniques to make certain that he or she doesn't intentionally use them to deceive and mislead the public. Ethical responsibilities exist in every form of persuasive communication; guidelines are discussed next.

The Ethics of Persuasion

Robert Heath, coauthor of *Rhetorical and Critical Approaches of Public Relations*, writes, "A theme that runs throughout the practice and criticism of public relations is its ability to influence what people think and how they act." He continues:

> Even when practitioners' efforts fail to establish their point of view or to foster the interests of their sponsors and influence stakeholders, their comments become part of the fabric of thought and over time add to societal beliefs and actions. Practitioners create opinions, reinforce them, or draw on them to advocate new opinions and actions.

To many observers, persuasion is a somewhat unsavory activity that distorts the truth and manipulates people. The public distrusts professional "persuaders," and the media often refer to public relations people and political consultants as **spin doctors**. Yet persuasion is an integral part of society. Everyone uses words and visual symbols to share and evaluate information, shape beliefs, and convince others to do or think things. The ancient Greeks recognized rhetoric, the "science of persuasion," as worthy of study and an essential part of public discourse.

In sum, persuasion is not a nasty concept. It does not have to be manipulative, propagandistic, or full of half-truths. Thomas Collins, manager of public affairs for Mobil Oil Company, sounded this theme when he addressed the annual meeting of the Public Relations Association of Indonesia. He said:

> PR counselors must ensure the messages we create, package, and target are efficient and cost-effective, but they must also be believable. This requires that the images we engineer reflect the reality of our clients' existence. We reject deliberate fabrication because bogus images pollute the public mind and do not serve the public interest, and ultimately undermine the trust we seek. . . . The essential ingredient underlying any successful relationship is trust.

A large measure of public trust, which Collins just described, comes from telling the truth and distributing accurate information. A core value of the Arthur W. Page Society, a group of senior communication executives, is to tell the truth by providing an accurate picture of the company's character, ideals and practice.

The IPRA has a core tenet in its charter that states, "Each member shall refrain from subordinating the truth to other requirements." And the PRSA states, in part, "We adhere to the highest standards of accuracy and truth in advancing the interests of those we represent and in communicating with the public."

On a more practical note, *PRWeek* writer Anita Chabria simply says, "Do make sure your statements are accurate. The press will pick up on even innocent mistakes as potential lies." See the Tips for Success below for a model regarding personal ethics.

Thus, it can be seen that public relations writers are, by definition, advocates in the marketplace of public opinion. It is their professional and personal responsibility, however, to be persuasive, using techniques that are forthright, truthful, and socially acceptable. Professor Richard L. Johannesen of Northern Illinois University lists the following persuasive techniques that should be avoided in persuasive writing:

- Do not use false, fabricated, misrepresented, distorted, or irrelevant evidence to support arguments or claims.
- Do not intentionally use specious, unsupported, or illogical reasoning.

☑ tips FOR SUCCESS

An Ethics Test for Public Relations Writers

Persuasive efforts require an ethical framework for decision making. Professors Sherry Baker of Brigham Young University and David Martinson of Florida International University have developed a model they call the TARES test. Public relations writers should test their persuasive communication against five basic moral principles:

1. *Truthfulness.* Are you just telling the literal truth and not the whole story? "Truthfulness (material and substantial completeness) is essential to ethical persuasion."

2. *Authenticity.* Are you intentionally deceiving or manipulating others for the practitioner's or client's self-interest? "A good test for authenticity is whether the practitioner is willing to openly, publicly, and personally be identified as the persuader in a particular circumstance."

3. *Respect.* Are you giving respect to your audience as persons of dignity and intelligence? "Respect for others includes facilitating their ability to be informed and to make good choices."

4. *Equity:* Are you taking advantage of the public's lack of knowledge or information about a topic, a product, or an idea? "The equity/fairness principle requires, for example, that practitioners avoid fashioning persuasive messages in such a manner as to play upon the vulnerabilities of a particular audience."

5. *Social responsibility:* Are your persuasive efforts serving the broader public interest? "Ethically proactive practitioners find ways to make positive contributions to the common good as an integral part of achieving their basic professional objectives." ∎

- Do not represent yourself as informed or as an "expert" on a subject when you are not.
- Do not use irrelevant appeals to divert attention or scrutiny from the issue at hand. Among the appeals that commonly serve such a purpose are "smear" attacks on an opponent's character, appeals to hatred and bigotry, innuendo, and "God" or "devil" terms that cause intense but unreflective positive or negative reactions.
- Do not ask your audience to link your idea or proposal to emotion-laden values, motives, or goals to which it is not actually related.
- Do not deceive your audience by concealing your real purpose, your self-interest, the group you represent, or your position as an advocate of a viewpoint.
- Do not distort, hide, or misrepresent the number, scope, intensity, or undesirable features of consequences.
- Do not use emotional appeals that lack a supporting basis of evidence or reasoning and would therefore not be accepted if the audience had time and opportunity to examine the subject itself.
- Do not oversimplify complex situations into simplistic, two-valued, either/or, polar views or choices.
- Do not pretend certainty when tentativeness and degrees of probability would be more accurate.
- Do not advocate something in which you do not believe yourself.

It is also clear that as a writer of persuasive messages the public relations writer is more than a technician or a "hired gun." Responsibility to a client or an employer should never override responsibility to the profession and the public interest. This is discussed further in Chapter 3.

However, writers often lack the technical and legal expertise to know whether information provided to them is accurate. Robert Heath explains, "In this regard, they are uneasy partners in the public relations process. They are often given information regarding managerial or operating decisions or practices that they are expected to report as though it were true and just."

This does not excuse writers from ethical responsibility. Heath continues:

> The problem of reporting information that they cannot personally verify does not excuse them from being responsible communicators. Their responsibility is to demand that the most accurate information be provided and the evaluation be the best available.

■ Summary

- Persuasion is part of the human fabric and has been around since the beginning of civilization.
- Public relations writers spend most of their day crafting and disseminating messages that will persuade and motivate people.
- The basic communication model has four elements: sender, message, channel (medium), and receiver.
- Several useful theories provide insight as to how people are persuaded and motivated. Public re-

lations writers should be familiar with such theories as (1) media uses and gratification, (2) cognitive dissonance, (3) framing, (4) diffusion and adoption, and (5) hierarchy of needs.

- Public relations writers, as part of message design, use the technique of framing—selecting certain facts, situations, and context—that are then disseminated by the media.

- A number of factors are involved in preparing persuasive messages. They include (1) audience analysis, (2) source credibility, (3) appeal to self-interest, (4) clarity of message, (5) timing and context, (6) use of symbols and slogans, (7) semantics, and (8) suggestions for action.

- A communicator recognizes that there are two kinds of audiences—passive and active (information seeking)—and plans messages and communication channels accordingly.

- Mass and directed media messages are most influential in the awareness and interest stages of the adoption process. Opinion leaders and peers are influential in the later stages.

- Some persuasive writing devices are the use of (1) drama and human interest, (2) statistics, (3) surveys and polls, (4) examples, (5) testimonials, (6) endorsements, and (7) emotional appeals.

- Endorsements are part of establishing credibility for a message. There are several kinds of endorsements: (1) proclamations by civic officials, (2) editorials and product reviews by the media, (3) statements by trade or professional organizations, and (4) celebrity spokespersons.

- Emotional appeals and fear arousal are most effective when accompanied by suggestions and solutions for solving the situation.

- Persuasive speaking techniques include (1) yes–yes, (2) structured choice, (3) seek partial commitment, and (4) ask for more, settle for less.

- Some common techniques of propaganda include (1) plain folks, (2) testimonial, (3) bandwagon, (4) card stacking, (5) transfer, and (6) glittering generalities. All, to some degree, are also used in public relations writing.

- Persuasion should not be manipulative and misleading. It should be based on truthful information and the presentation of ideas in the marketplace of public discussion.

■ Skill Building Activities

1. A state university, facing major cuts in its public funding, wants to persuade the state legislature and the taxpaying public to not make any budget cuts. Use drama, statistics, surveys and polls, examples, testimonials, endorsements, and emotional appeals to make a persuasive argument.

2. The concept of channeling is discussed in terms of tailoring messages to audience self-interests. A city zoo wants to increase memberships and donations. Identify the message theme you would use for the following audiences: (a) business and industry, (b) teachers, (c) parents, (d) senior citizens, and (e) conservation groups.

3. Public relations and advertising practitioners often use experts and celebrities to build credibility and acceptance for the product. Select (1) an expert endorser and (2) a celebrity that you would use for each of the following situations: (a) lightweight luggage, (b) suntan lotion, (c) a laptop computer, (d) hiking boots, and (e) a high-end outdoor gas grill.

4. The text points out that passive audiences and active (information-seeking) audiences require different kinds of messages and media channels. Given this situation, what kinds of messages and media would you use to reach passive audiences about National Breast Cancer Awareness Month? By the same token, what information and media channels would you use to satisfy active audiences?

5. The TARES model on page 57 suggests that public relations practitioners should test their persuasive messages against five basic moral principles. Here's a practical situation: A student accuses a popular football coach at a university of forcing her to have sex with him. The coach

claims the encounter was consensual, but the student is threatening to file a rape charge unless he resigns. The administration, in order to avoid scandal, convinces the coach to resign by giving him a $100,000 separation agreement. The director of university relations tells you to write a news release that the coach has voluntarily resigned to "explore new challenges." No other details are mentioned. Would the news release meet the principles outlined in the TARES test?

■ Suggested Readings

Andsager, Julie L., and White, H. Allen. *Self Versus Others: Media, Messages, and the Third-Person Effect.* Mahwah, NJ: Lawrence Erlbaum Associates, 2007.

Baker, Sherry, and Martinson, David L. "Out of the Red-Light District: Five Principles for Ethically Proactive Public Relations." *Public Relations Quarterly*, Fall 2002, pp. 15–18.

Blumenstein, Rebecca, and Rose, Matthew. "Name That Op: How U.S. Coins Phrases of War." *The Wall Street Journal*, March 24, 2003, pp. B1, B3.

Edgett, Ruth. "Toward an Ethical Framework for Advocacy in Public Relations." *Journal of Public Relations Research*, Vol. 14, No. 1, 2002, pp. 1–26.

Fitzpatrick, Kathy, and Bronstein, Carolyn. *Ethics in Public Relations: Responsible Advocacy.* Thousand Oaks, CA: Sage Publications, 2006.

Gass, Robert H., and Seiter, John S. *Persuasion, Social Influence, and Compliance Gaining*, 3rd ed. Boston: Allyn & Bacon, 2007.

Huff, Dianna. "Ten Reasons Marketing Materials Remain Unread." *PR Tactics*, April 2002, p. 13.

Jowett, Garth S., and O'Donnell, Victoria. *Propaganda and Persuasion*, 4th ed. Thousand Oaks, CA: Sage Publications, 2006.

Larson, Charles U. *Persuasion: Reception and Responsibility*, 11th ed. Belmont, CA: Thomson/ Wadsworth, 2006.

Perloff, Richard M. *The Dynamics of Persuasion: Communication and Attitudes in the Twenty-First Century.* London: Routledge, 2007.

Walsh, Bryan. "Back to the Tap: Bottled Water May Be a Commercial Success Story, but the Environment Pays a Very Heavy Price." *Time*, August 20, 2007, p. 56.

Avoiding Legal Hassles

3

TOPICS covered in this chapter include:

A Sampling of Legal Problems   61

Libel and Defamation   62

Invasion of Privacy   65

Copyright Law   69

Trademark Law   76

Regulatory Agencies   82

Other Federal Regulatory Agencies   86

Working with Lawyers   88

A Sampling of Legal Problems

Public relations writers, once they have mastered the basics of persuasive writing, also have the responsibility to work within the law. You must understand basic legal concepts that provide a framework for all your writing. A false product claim in a news release or the unauthorized use of a celebrity's photograph can lead to costly lawsuits for you and your employer or client.

Here's a sampling of recent government regulatory agency cases and lawsuits that involved public relations materials and the work of practitioners:

- A public relations counselor was quizzed in a California courtroom regarding his role in writing a misleading news release stating that all of the Oakland Raiders's games were sold out for the season. The lawsuit was between the football team and the Oakland Coliseum.

- Tyson Foods was ordered by a federal court to stop promoting and publicizing the claim that its chickens didn't contain antibiotics believed to cause drug resistance in humans. The judge agreed with competitors that said the claim was misleading.

- Bonner & Associates and its client, the Pharmaceutical Research and Manufacturers of America, were charged with violating Maryland's lobbying disclosure laws. A citizens group claimed that the firm used "deceptive tactics" by distributing materials under the name of a fictitious consumer-based organization set up by the pharmaceutical industry.

- The Securities and Exchange Commission (SEC) fined a former employee of Ogilvy PR Worldwide $34,000 for passing "material, nonpublic information" to his father, who then used the information to purchase stock. The employee violated "insider trading" rules.

- The Federal Trade Commission (FTC) fined four manufacturers of weight loss pills, including Xenadrine EFX and One A Day Weight Smart, for making false advertising claims.
- A Chicago man sued for invasion of privacy after he appeared in a video news release for a cholesterol-lowering drug because the company and video producer didn't tell him the actual purpose of the taping.
- An 81-year-old man sued the United Way of America for using his picture on campaign posters and brochures without his permission.
- Enron Corporation and its major executives, including the director of investor relations, were fined and imprisoned for inflating company earnings through various news channels, including news releases.

These examples provide some idea of the legal pitfalls that a public relations practitioner may encounter. Many of the charges were eventually dismissed or settled out of court, but the organizations paid dearly for the adverse publicity and the expense of defending themselves.

Public relations personnel must be aware that they can be held legally liable if they provide advice or tacitly support a client or employer's illegal activity. This area of liability is called *conspiracy*. You can be named as a coconspirator with other organizational officials if you:

- Participate in an illegal action such as bribing a government official or covering up information of vital interest to the public health and safety
- Counsel and guide the policy behind an illegal action
- Take a major personal part in the illegal action
- Help establish a "front group" whereby the connection to the public relations firm or its clients is kept hidden
- Cooperate in any other way to further an illegal action

These five concepts also apply to public relations firms that create, produce, and distribute materials on behalf of clients. The courts have ruled on more than one occasion that public relations firms cannot hide behind the defense of "the client told me to do it." Public relations firms have a legal responsibility to practice "due diligence" in the type of information and documentation supplied by a client. Regulatory agencies such as the FTC (discussed shortly) have the power under the Lanham Act to file charges against public relations firms that distribute false and misleading information.

Libel and Defamation

According to the *AP Stylebook*, "Libel is injury to reputation. Words, pictures or cartoons that expose a person to public hatred, shame, disgrace or ridicule, or induce an ill opinion of a person are libelous." Traditionally, the term *libel* was a printed falsehood and *slander* involved an oral communication, such as a speech or a broadcast mention. Today, however, the courts often use the term *defamation* as a collective term.

Juries award defamation damages to the extent that the following four points can be proved by the injured party: (1) the statement was published to others by print or broadcast; (2) the plaintiff was identified or is identifiable; (3) there was actual injury in the form of monetary losses, impairment of reputation, humiliation, or mental anguish and suffering; and (4) the publisher of the statement was malicious or negligent.

With public figures—people in government, politics, and entertainment—the test is whether the publisher of the statement knew that it was false or had a reckless disregard for its truth. The question of who is a public figure cannot be answered arbitrarily, and the courts are inconsistent on this. It often depends on the context. With private figures—such as corporate executives and even average citizens—the test is whether the publisher of the statement was negligent in checking the truth of the statement. In quoting someone, for instance, be sure you state exactly what was said.

Corporations also are considered "public figures" by the courts for several reasons: (1) they engage in advertising and promotion, voluntarily offering products to the public for purchase and even criticism; (2) they are often involved in matters of public controversy and public policy; and (3) they have the resources for regular access to the media that enables them to respond and rebut criticism. Consequently, corporations have little recourse when an activist group, rightly or wrongly, includes a company on its annual "dirty dozen" of polluters or a consumer affairs reporter flatly calls a product a "rip-off." Such statements are in the realm of fair comment, which will be discussed shortly.

At times, however, corporations do have a legitimate concern about defamation and have good reason to pursue legal action or demand an apology. A good example is General Motors (GM), which filed a multimillion-dollar defamation suit against NBC after the network's *Dateline* news program carried a story about gas tanks on GM pickup trucks exploding in side-impact collisions.

In a news conference, GM's general counsel meticulously provided evidence that NBC had inserted toy rocket "igniters" in the gas tanks, understated the vehicle speed at the moment of impact, and wrongly claimed that the fuel tanks could be ruptured easily. Within 24 hours after the suit was filed, NBC caved in. It agreed to air a 9-minute apology on the news program and pay GM $2 million to cover the cost of its investigation.

In thinking about defamation, you should not confine your precautions to what is printed or broadcast in the mass media. An item on a company blog or a widely distributed e-mail saying that "Jack was feeling no pain" at the office party could be construed as defamation. An unflattering picture of a disheveled employee walking out the door after the annual Christmas party could also lead to a defamation lawsuit if it is published in the company newsletter.

It's also worth noting that a defamation suit can also be filed even if you don't name a specific individual or organization. A recognizable description serves the same purpose if the subject remains unnamed, but the public readily recognizes who or what is being discussed. In one case, a hospital was sued by another hospital for implying in a news release that the number of patient deaths in "another local hospital" was the highest in the region. Because there were only two hospitals in town, the public easily identified the name of the competing medical facility.

In recent years, a number of defamation suits have been filed because of what was included in a news release. One example is a $20 million defamation lawsuit that a former employee of J. Walter Thompson advertising agency filed after an agency news release said she was "let go" because of financial irregularities in the department she headed. The lawsuit was dismissed because she couldn't prove that the agency acted in a "grossly irresponsible manner."

The Fair Comment Defense

Lawsuits, such as those just described, provide a warning of what can happen, but this does not mean that an organization has to avoid statements of fact or opinion in public relations materials. Truth is the traditional defense against libel charges, but opinions also have a degree of legal protection under the First Amendment to the U.S. Constitution, which protects the freedom of speech. This legal concept is known as *fair comment privilege*.

This defense, for example, explains why theater and music reviewers can skewer a play or concert with impunity. It also means that mainstream journalists and even bloggers are protected when they write or post comments blasting a company's policy or products even if they have some of the facts wrong. As already stated, when individuals and companies voluntarily display their wares to the public for sale or consumption, they have no real recourse against criticism done with honest intention and lack of malicious intent.

A utility company in Indiana, for example, once tried to sue a citizen who wrote a letter to a newspaper criticizing it for seeking a rate hike. The judge threw the suit out of court, noting that the rate increase was a "matter of public interest and concern" even if the letter writer didn't have all the facts straight.

Fair comment also protects the critical comments of organizational executives, which may be included in a news release or as the result of a media interview. In one case, the owner of the New York Yankees was sued for libel by an umpire when a news release from the team called him a "scab" who "had it in" for the Yankees and "misjudged" plays. A lower court awarded the umpire libel damages, but a higher court overturned the judgment by ruling that the comments in the news release constituted protected statements of opinion. In another case, a judge found the Genesis One Computer Corporation innocent of libel when it characterized another firm's breach of contract as a "device" to avoid payment of commissions due to Genesis.

If you ever have occasion to write a news release that makes critical comments about another individual or organization, you can use the fair comment defense. However, take several precautionary measures. Experts suggest (1) that opinion statements be accompanied by the facts on which the opinions are based; (2) that opinion statements be clearly identified with quote marks and attribution to a particular individual; and (3) that the context of the language surrounding the expressions of opinion be reviewed for possible defamation.

Avoiding Defamation Suits

The key phrase for avoiding defamation suits is to "watch your language." Words, as explained in Chapter 1, have denotive and connotative meanings. In either case, an executive can invite a lawsuit by simply calling the leaders of a labor union a "bunch of crooks using Nazi tactics" during a labor dispute. Or an executive might call a news reporter "a pimp for all environmental groups." Such language, although highly quotable and colorful, can provoke legal retaliation.

ABC found out the hard way about the fallout from poor word choice. In a news story about Philip Morris, the commentator said the company "spiked" cigarettes with nicotine. The unfortunate use of that term resulted in ABC making a public apology and agreeing to pay $15 million to Philip Morris for its legal expenses after it filed a defamation suit.

In situations involving personnel, organizations often avoid potential lawsuits by saying that an employee left "for personal reasons" or to "pursue other interests," even if the real reason was incompetence or a record of sexual harassment. There are two reasons for using fairly innocuous language. First, the organization is liable for defamation if the individual has not been formally charged and convicted of an illegal action in a court of law. Second, news releases and product publicity should be written in accordance with FTC and SEC regulations, which will be discussed shortly.

It's also a good idea to avoid unflattering comments or accusations about the competition's products or services. Although comparative advertising is the norm in the United States, a company must walk a narrow line between comparison and "trade libel" or "product disparagement." Statements should be truthful, with factual evidence and scientific demonstration available to substantiate them. Companies often charge competitors with overstepping the boundary between legitimate, factual comparison and defamation.

Subway, for example, sued Quiznos because it sponsored a contest for the best homemade video showing why Quiznos sandwiches are superior to Subway's. The winning video showed a race between two wagons. The Quiznos wagon, in the form of a meaty sandwich, blasted smoke at the plain-looking Subway car, causing it to crash in defeat. The ad's creator got $10,000, and the video was shown on the Internet as well as on a giant screen in Time Square. Subway claimed that the video, and others entered in the contest, made "false statements" and depicted Subway in a "disparaging manner." Quiznos, of course, claimed that it was not legally liable for the content of a contest entry.

An organization, however, can offer the opinion that a particular product or service is the "best" or "a revolutionary development" if the context clearly shows that the communication is a statement of opinion attributed to someone. Then it is classified as "puffery" and doesn't require factual evidence, according to Federal Trade Commission (FTC) guidelines.

Invasion of Privacy

One area of possible liability and potential lawsuits is an organization's treatment of its employees with regards to privacy. Public relations writers and staff are vulnerable to litigation with regard to invasion of employees' privacy in at least five areas:

- Employee newsletters
- Photo releases
- Product publicity and advertising
- Media inquiries about employees
- Employee blogs and virtual communities

Employee Newsletters

It is no longer true, if it ever was, that an organization has an unlimited right to publicize the activities of its employees. In fact, Morton J. Simon, a Philadelphia lawyer and author of *Public Relations Law*, once wrote, "It should not be assumed that a person's status as an employee waives his right to privacy." Today, Simon's comment is still correct. A company newsletter or magazine does not enjoy the same First Amendment protection that the news media enjoy when they claim "newsworthiness" and "public interest." A number of court cases have shown that company newsletters are considered commercial tools of trade.

This distinction does not impede the effectiveness of newsletters, but it does indicate that editors should try to keep employee stories organization oriented. Indeed, most lawsuits and complaints are generated by "personals columns" that may invade the privacy of employees. Although a mention that Joe Smith collects baseball caps or that Mary Worth is now a great-grandmother may sound completely innocent, the individuals involved—for any number of reasons—might consider the information a violation of their privacy. The situation could be further compounded into possible defamation by "cutesy" editorial asides in poor taste.

In sum, one should avoid anything that might embarrass or subject an employee to ridicule by fellow employees. Here are some guidelines to remember when writing about employee activities:

- Keep the focus on organization-related activities.
- Have employees submit "personals" in writing.
- Double-check all information for accuracy.
- Ask: "Will this embarrass anyone or cause someone to be the butt of jokes?"
- Don't rely on secondhand information; confirm the facts with the person involved.
- Don't include racial or ethnic designations of employees in any articles.

Photo Releases

Ordinarily, a public relations practitioner doesn't need a signed release if a person gives "implied consent" by posing for a picture and is told how it will be used. This is particularly true for "news" photographs published in internal newsletters or posted on the organization's intranet.

Public relations departments, however, should take the precaution of (1) filing all photographs, (2) dating them, and (3) giving the context of the situation. This precludes the use of old photos that could embarrass employees or subject them to ridicule. In other cases, it precludes using photographs of persons who are no longer employed or have died. This method also helps to ensure that a photo taken for the employee newsletter isn't used in an advertisement. If a photo of an employee or customer is used in product publicity, sales brochures, or advertisements, the standard practice is to obtain a signed release.

Product Publicity and Advertising

As already noted, an organization must have a signed release on file if it wants to use the photographs or comments of employees and other individuals in product publicity, sales brochures, and advertising. An added precaution is to give some financial compensation to make a more binding contract.

Chemical Bank of New York unfortunately learned this lesson the hard way. The bank used pictures of 39 employees in various advertisements designed to "humanize" the bank's image, but the employees maintained that no one had requested permission to use their photos in advertisements. Another problem was that the pictures had been taken up to 5 years before they began appearing in the series of advertisements.

An attorney for the employees, who sued for $600,000 in damages, said, "The bank took the individuality of these employees and used that individuality to make a profit." The judge agreed and ruled that the bank had violated New York's privacy law. The action is called *misappropriation of personality*, which is discussed later in this chapter.

Written permission also should be obtained if the employee's photograph is to appear in sales brochures or even in the corporate annual report. This rule also applies to other situations. A graduate of Lafayette College sued the college for using a photo of his mother and him at graduation ceremonies, without their permission, in a financial aid brochure.

> **❝ If I used my mother in an ad, I'd get her permission—and I almost trust her 100 percent. ❞**
> ■ Jerry Della Femina, advertising executive

Media Inquiries About Employees

Because press inquiries have the potential of invading an employee's right of privacy, public relations personnel should follow basic guidelines as to what information will be provided on the employee's behalf.

In general, employers should give a news reporter only basic information:

Do Provide
- Confirmation that the person is an employee,
- The person's title and job description,
- The date of beginning employment, or, if applicable, date of termination.

Do Not Provide Employee's

- Salary,
- Home address,
- Marital status,
- Number of children,
- Organizational memberships, or
- Job performance.

If a reporter does seek any of this information, because of the nature of the story, several methods can be followed. First, you can volunteer to contact the employee and have the person speak directly with the reporter. What the employee chooses to tell the reporter is not the company's responsibility. Second, many organizations do provide additional information to a reporter if it is included on an optional biographical sheet that the employee has filled out. In most cases, the form clearly states that the organization may use any of the information in answering press inquiries or writing its own news releases. A typical biographical form may have sections in which the employee can list such things as memberships in community organizations, professional affiliations, educational background, past titles and positions, and even special achievements. This sheet should not be confused with the person's official employment application, which must remain confidential.

If an organization uses biographical sheets, it is important that they be dated and kept current. A sheet compiled by an employee 5 years previously may be hopelessly out of date. This is also true of file photographs taken at the time of a person's employment.

Employee Blogs

Many organizations now encourage employees to have a blog as a way of fostering discussion on the Internet and obtaining informal feedback from the public. In some large companies, even top executives have a blog, even if public relations professionals do most of the actual writing. In most cases, the blog is clearly identified with the creator and gives information (and images) about the employer. As John Elasser, editor of *PR Tactics*, says, "Some of that content may be innocuous; other types may be embarrassing or come back to haunt the company in litigation."

Consequently, many organization have policies that provide guidelines for what rank-and-file employees, as well public relations writers, can and cannot say on their blogs. In general, organizations prohibit employee bloggers from talking about fellow colleagues or making comments about supervisors and executives. Such postings can invade the privacy of other employees and even lead to lawsuits if someone feels that he or she has been ridiculed or defamed in some way.

On another level, companies are concerned about the distribution of confidential information. Sun Microsystems, for example, prohibits discussion of a wealth of nonpublic information, including financial data, personal information about individuals, and work-related legal proceedings or controversies.

Cisco extends this concept by stating that employees must reveal their affiliation with the company on their blogs if they are talking about the company. The policy states, "If you comment on any aspect of the company's business or any policy issue the company is involved in . . . you must clearly identify yourself in your postings or blog site and include a disclaimer that the views are your own and not those of Cisco." Additional rules regarding online communication are provided in Chapter 12. In addition, the Electronic Frontier Foundation has a "Legal Guide for Bloggers" at its website (www.eff.org/bloggers/lg).

Virtual Online Communities

A newer innovation is virtual online communities, such as Second Life, Entropia, Universe, and There.Com. Although these communities are sometimes used for gambling and adult entertainment, increasingly they are home to multinational companies advertising their brands and promoting communication among employees and with customers.

IBM, realizing the potential for hosting meetings with clients and partners, has published guidelines for more than 5,000 of its employees who inhabit Second Life and other virtual worlds. Some of its basic rules are (1) don't discuss intellectual property with unauthorized people, (2) don't discriminate or harass, and (3) be a good Netizen. IBM, whose employees are often parodied as cogs in matching navy suits, doesn't have a dress code for its employee avatars, but it does suggest being "sensitive to the appropriateness of your avatar or persona's appearance when you are meeting with IBM clients or conducting IBM business."

> **If someone is a fisherman and they want to talk about fly fishing outside of work, that's not our business. But if someone is going to talk about notebooks, they have to say they are from Dell.**
>
> ■ Bob Pearson, vice president of Dell computers

Copyright Law

Should a news release be copyrighted? What about a corporate annual report? Can a Dilbert comic strip be featured in the company magazine without obtaining permission from the strip's creator? What about reprinting an article from *Fortune* magazine and distributing it to the company's sales staff? Are government reports copyrighted? What about posting a video clip from Comedy Central on the Internet? What constitutes copyright infringement?

These are just some of the bothersome questions that a public relations writers should be able to answer. Knowledge of copyright law is important from two perspectives: (1) what organizational materials should be copyrighted and (2) how to correctly utilize the copyrighted materials of others.

In very simple terms, *copyright* means protection of a creative work from unauthorized use. A section of the U.S. copyright law of 1978 states: "Copyright protection subsists . . . in the original works of authorship fixed in any tangible medium of expression now known or later developed." The word *authorship* is defined in seven categories: (1) literary works; (2) musical works; (3) dramatic works; (4) pantomimes and choreographic works; (5) pictorial, graphic, or sculptural works; (6) motion pictures; and (7) sound recordings. The word *fixed* means that the work is sufficiently permanent or stable to permit it to be perceived, reproduced, or otherwise communicated.

Thus, a copyright does not protect ideas, but only the specific ways in which those ideas are expressed. An idea for promoting a product, for example, cannot be copyrighted—but brochures, drawings, news features, animated cartoons, display booths, photographs, recordings, videotapes, corporate symbols, slogans, and the like that express a particular idea can be copyrighted. It should be noted, however, that the Supreme Court did rule in 1991 that directories, computer databases, and other compilations of facts may be copied and republished unless they display "some minimum degree of creativity."

Under current law, a work is automatically copyrighted the moment it is "fixed" in tangible form. Although such a "work" doesn't have to carry a notice of copyright, many organizations take the extra precaution of using the letter "c" in a circle (©), followed by the word *copyright* and citing the year of copyright to discourage unauthorized use. A more formal step is official registration of the copyrighted work within 3 months after creation. This is done by depositing two copies of the manuscript (it is not necessary that it has been published), recording, or artwork with the Copyright Office of the Library of Congress. Registration isn't necessary for copyright protection, but it is often helpful in a court case against unauthorized use by others.

A copyright, under current U.S. law, protects original material for the life of the creator plus 70 years for individual works and 95 years from publication for copyrights held by corporations. This is often called the "Mickey Mouse" law because in 1998 Congress extended copyright projection to its current level after extensive lobbying from Walt Disney Company. Its copyright on its Mickey Mouse character would have expired in 2003 under the previous guidelines. The main point that you must remember is that any works created since 1978 are automatically copyrighted for the term of the author's life plus 70 years.

Not all materials, however, have copyright protection. Some material is considered to be in the **public domain** because of its age. Shakespeare's works are in the public domain, as are many literary classics. The music of many great composers, such as Chopin and Mozart, can also be used without violating copyright. On a more basic level, most works published in the United States prior to 1923 are in the public domain. Works created between 1923 and 1963 are in the public domain if the copyright was not renewed. Materials produced by the federal government can also be used freely, but there are some guidelines regarding their use that are discussed further in the next section about fair use.

Fair Use versus Infringement

Public relations writers are in the business of gathering information from a variety of sources, so it is important to know where fair use ends and infringement begins. This also applies to plagiarism, which is explained in the Tips for Success on page 71.

Don't Plagiarize: It's Unethical

Copyright infringement and plagiarism differ. You may be guilty of copyright infringement even if you attribute the materials and give the source but don't get permission from the author or publisher to reproduce the materials.

In the case of plagiarism, the author makes no attempt to attribute the information at all. As the guide for Hamilton College says, "Plagiarism is a form of fraud. You plagiarize if you present other writer's words or ideas as your own." Maurice Isserman, writing in the *Chronicle of Higher Education*, explains, "Plagiarism substitutes someone else's prowess at explanation for your own efforts." At its most basic level, plagiarism is using sentences and paragraphs from someone else's work without attribution or quote marks.

The World Wide Web has increased the problems of plagiarism because it is quite easy for anyone, from students to college presidents, to cut and paste entire paragraphs (or even pages) into a term paper or speech and claim it as their own creation. Of course, getting away with it has become more difficult because of sophisticated tools such as Turnitin (www.turnitin.com), which can scan the Internet and find the exact sentence or paragraph that the student copied and pasted into a paper.

John Barrie, founder of Turnitin, told *The Wall Street Journal* that ". . . 85 percent of the cases of plagiarism that we see are straight copies from the Internet—a student uses the Internet like a 1.5 billion-page cut-and-paste encyclopedia." Most universities have very strong rules about plagiarism, and it is not uncommon for students to receive an "F" in a course for plagiarism. In the business world, stealing someone else's words and expression of thought is called theft of intellectual property and employees, including CEOs, are fired. In sum, don't use "cut-and-paste" as a substitute for producing your own work. If someone's sentence or paragraph is really great, at least put it in quotes and give proper attribution. ■

Fair use means that part of a copyrighted article can be quoted directly, but the quoted material must be brief in relation to the length of the original work. It may be, for example, only one paragraph in a 750-word article and up to 300 words in a long article or book chapter. Complete attribution of the source must be given regardless of the length of the quotation. If the passage is quoted verbatim, quote marks must be used.

It is important to note, however, that the concept of fair use has distinct limitations if part of the copyrighted material is to be used in advertisements and promotional brochures. In this case, permission is required. It also is important for the original source to approve the context in which the quote is used. A quote out of context often runs into legal trouble if it implies endorsement of a product or service.

The copyright law does allow limited copying of a work for fair use such as criticism, comment, or research. However, in recent years the courts have considerably narrowed the concept of fair use when multiple copies of a copyrighted work are involved. In 2003, for example, a federal court awarded almost $20 million in damages to a financial newsletter after it filed a copyright infringement suit against Legg Mason, a large securities firm. The company had purchased a single subscription to the newsletter but then proceeded to redistribute the newsletter internally by photocopying it and posting it on its intranet.

Such lawsuits can be avoided if an organization orders quantity reprints from the publisher and pays a licensing fee that permits it to make paper or electronic copies. Dow Jones, publisher of *The Wall Street Journal*, has a whole department (see www.djreprints.com) that arranges reprints that can be used in print, e-mail, PDF, or URL formats. In the case of using entire articles or book chapters from a variety of sources, individuals and organizations can get permission and pay a royalty fee to the Copyright Clearance Center, which has been established to represent a large number of publishers. Easy selection and payment of royalties can be accomplished through its website (www.copyright.com).

Government documents, as already noted, are in the public domain. Public relations personnel, under the fair use doctrine, can freely use quotations and statistics from a government document. Care must be exercised, however, to ensure that the material is in context and not misleading. The most common problem occurs when an organization uses a government report as a form of endorsement for its services or products. An airline, for example, might cite a government study showing that its on-time arrivals are the best in the industry, but neglect to state the basis of comparison or other meditating factors.

Photography and Artwork

Copyright law makes it clear that freelance and commercial photographers retain ownership of their work. In other words, a customer who buys a copyrighted photo owns the item itself, but not the right to make additional copies. That right remains with the photographer unless transferred in writing to the individual or organization that has bought the photographs.

In a further extension of this right, the duplication of copyrighted photos is also illegal. This was established in a 1990 U.S. Federal District Court case in which the Professional Photographers of America (PP of A) sued a nationwide photofinishing firm for ignoring copyright notices on pictures sent for additional copies.

Freelance photographers generally charge for a picture on the basis of its use. If it is used only once, perhaps for an employee newsletter, the fee is low. If, however, the company wants to use the picture in the corporate annual report or on the company calendar, the fee may be considerably higher. Consequently it is important for a public relations person to tell the photographer exactly how the picture will be used. Arrangements and fees then can be determined for (1) one-time use, (2) unlimited use, or (3) the payment of royalties every time the picture is used.

Computer manipulation of an original artwork can also violate copyright. One photographer's picture of a racing yacht was used on a poster after the art director electronically changed the numbers on the sail and made the water a deeper blue. In another case, a photo distribution agency successfully sued *Newsday* for unauthorized use of a color image after the newspaper reconstructed the agency's picture using a computer scanner, then failed to credit the photographer. FPG International was awarded $20,000 in damages, 10 times the initial licensing fee of $2,000. In sum, slightly changing a copyrighted photo or a piece of artwork can be considered a violation of copyright if the intent is to capitalize on widespread recognition of the original artwork.

This was the case when the estate of the late children's author, Dr. Seuss, won a $1.5 million judgment against a Los Angeles T-shirt maker for copyright infringement. The manufacturer had portrayed a parody of Dr. Seuss's Cat in the Hat character smoking marijuana and giving the peace sign. In another situation, the Rock and Roll Hall of Fame filed a copyright suit against a freelance photographer who snapped a picture of the unique building at sunset and sold posters of his work without paying a licensing fee.

Similarly, sports logos are registered trademarks, and a licensing fee must be paid before anyone can use logos for commercial products and promotions. This will be discussed in the section on trademarks.

Work for Hire

Copyright automatically belongs to the creator of the work, but the "work for hire" concept provides a notable exception. If you create a work as an employee of an organization, the copyright belongs to the organization. In other words, all those wonderful news releases and brochures that you write and produce on the job belong to your employer.

It gets a bit more complicated, however, when an organization outsources work to a freelancer to write a brochure or a feature story. In the now famous *Reid* case (*Community for Creative Nonviolence v. Reid*), the U.S. Supreme Court in 1989 ruled that freelance writers retain ownership of their work and that purchasers of it simply gain a "license" to reproduce the copyrighted work.

Prior to this ruling, the common practice was to assume that commissioned articles were work for hire and that the purchaser owned the copyright. In other words, a publication or an organization could use the material in a number of ways, even selling it to another publication, without the writer's permission. Under the new interpretation, ownership of a writer's work is subject to negotiation and contractual agreement. Writers may agree to assign all copyright rights to the work they have been hired to do or they may give permission only for a specific one-time use.

In a related matter, freelance writers are pressing for additional compensation if an organization puts their work on CD-ROM, in online databases, or on the World Wide Web. They won a major victory in 2001 when the Supreme Court (*New York Times v. Tasini*) ruled that publishers, by making articles accessible through electronic databases, infringed the copyrights of freelance contributors.

Public relations firms and corporate public relations departments are responsible for ensuring compliance with copyright law. This means that all agreements with a freelance writer must be in writing and the use of the material must be clearly stated. Ideally, a public relations department should negotiate multiple rights and even complete ownership of the copyright.

The importance of copyright ownership is highlighted by a case involving Wal-Mart. The retail giant hired a video-production company to document the activities of top executives over a 30-year period. The video company was given unlimited access and recorded a number of activities, such as a former executive vice president challenging store mangers to continue his work opposing unionization. Other videos showed male store managers in drag leading thousands of coworkers in the corporate cheer. Not exactly the kind of material appropriate for public consumption.

However, in 2008 the video-production company announced that almost 15,000 of its Wal-Mart tapes were available for sale, much to the delight of union activists and lawyers pursuing various legal suits against Wal-Mart. Wal-Mart claimed that the videos were owned by the company and that the video-production company was violating copyright. The only problem was that the video-production company had never signed an agreement assigning copyright ownership to Wal-Mart. A checklist of copyright guidelines is provided in the following Tips for Success.

☑ tips FOR SUCCESS

Guidelines for Using Copyrighted Material

Keep the following guidelines in mind when reproducing materials:

- Ideas cannot be copyrighted, but the expression of those ideas are protected.
- An entire article that is e-mailed to a large number of people or posted on a website or a blog requires the permission of the publication or creator of the work.
- Using news clips to track coverage is acceptable, but distribution of clips to a large audience is a violation of copyright.
- Major public relations materials (brochures, annual reports, videotapes, motion pictures, position papers, and the like) should be copyrighted, if only to prevent unauthorized use by competitors.
- Although there is a concept of fair use, any copyrighted material intended directly to advance the sales and profits of an organization should not be used unless permission is given.
- Copyrighted material should not be taken out of context, particularly if it implies endorsement of the organization's services or products.
- Quantity reprints of an article should be ordered from the publisher.
- Permission is required to use segments of television programs or motion pictures.
- Permission must be obtained to use segments of popular songs (written verses or sound recordings) from a recording company.
- Photographers and freelance writers retain the rights to their works. Permission and fees must be negotiated to use works for other purposes than originally agreed upon.
- Photographs of current celebrities or those who are now deceased cannot be used for promotion and publicity purposes without permission.
- Permission is required to reprint cartoon characters, such as Snoopy or Garfield. In addition, cartoons and other artwork or illustrations in a publication are copyrighted.
- Government documents are not copyrighted, but caution is necessary if the material is used in a way that implies endorsement of products or services.
- Private letters, or excerpts from them, cannot be published or used in sales and publicity materials without the permission of the letter writer.
- Original material posted on the Internet and the World Wide Web has copyright protection.
- The copyrighted material of others should not be posted on the Internet unless specific permission is granted. ■

Copyright Issues on the Internet

The Internet and World Wide Web raise new issues about the protection of intellectual property. Two issues regarding copyright are (1) the downloading of copyrighted material and (2) the unauthorized uploading of such material.

The Downloading of Material ■ In general, the same rules apply to cyberspace as to more earthbound methods of expressing and disseminating ideas. Original materials in digital form are still protected by copyright. The fair-use limits for materials found on the Internet are essentially the same those for materials disseminated by any other means.

Related to this is the use of news articles and features that are sent via e-mail or the Web to the clients of clipping services. An organization may use such clips to track its publicity efforts, but it can't distribute the article on its own website or intranet without permission and a royalty payment to the publication where the article appeared.

The Uploading of Material ■ In many cases, owners of copyrighted material have uploaded various kinds of information with the intention of making it freely available. Some examples are software, games, and even the entire text of *The Hitchhiker's Guide to the Galaxy*. The problem comes, however, when third parties upload copyrighted material without permission. Consequently, copyright holders are increasingly patrolling the Internet and World Wide Web to stop the unauthorized use of material.

Viacom constantly monitors sites such as YouTube for unauthorized postings of video clips from its various television programs on MTV or CBS. Under the 1998 Digital Millennium Copyright Act, Internet businesses such as YouTube are immune from liability for material posted by its users, but are required to take down any infringing material after it is notified by the copyright owner. In a single year, YouTube removed 230,000 clips at Viacom's request, which is one reason why a video might be available on YouTube one day and gone the next. The posting of illegal video clips continues to dog the entertainment industry, causing a great deal of lobbying for more protective legislation and even major lawsuits. In 2007, for example, Viacom filed a $1 billion copyright infringement suit against Google, which owns YouTube.

Consider some additional examples of controversies regarding online materials:

- Dutton Children's Books threatened a lawsuit against a New Mexico State University student for using Winnie the Pooh illustrations on his home page.
- Paramount Pictures sent warning notes to Star Trek fans against using the Internet to disseminate photos from the TV series.
- Corbis Corporation, which has millions of photos for licensing or purchase, threatened legal action against a retirement community for using a photo of an elderly couple on its website without paying the licensing fee.

Trademark Law

What do the names Big Gulp, iTunes, Dockers, eBay, Academy Awards, Xbox, American Idol, Bubble Wrap, Frappucino, and even Ziploc have in common? Or what about "A diamond is forever," "Priceless," or "Just do it." They are all registered trademarks protected by law.

A trademark is a word, symbol, or slogan, used singly or in combination, that identifies a product's origin. According to Susan L. Cohen, writing in *Editor & Publisher's* annual trademark supplement, "It also serves as an indicator of quality, a kind of shorthand for consumers to use in recognizing goods in a complex marketplace." Research indicates, for example, that 53 percent of Americans say brand quality takes precedence over price considerations.

The concept of a trademark is nothing new. The ancient Egyptians carved marks into the stones of the pyramids, and the craftsmen of the Middle Ages used guild marks to identify the source and quality of products. What is new, however, is the proliferation of trademarks and service marks in modern society. Coca-Cola, Google, and Microsoft are some of the world's most recognized brands, but they are only some of almost 1 million active trademarks registered with the U.S. Patent and Trademark Office. According to the International Trademark Association, the number of trademarks is increasing at a rapid rate.

The Protection of Trademarks

The three basic guidelines for using trademarks are as follows:

- Trademarks are proper adjectives and should be capitalized and followed by a generic noun or phrase. For example, Kleenex tissues or Rollerblade skates.
- Trademarks should not be pluralized or used in the possessive form. Saying "American Express's credit card" is improper.
- Trademarks are never verbs. Saying "The client FedExed the package" violates the rule.

In addition, organizations take the step of designating brand names and slogans with various marks. The registered trademark symbol is a superscript, small capital "R" in a circle—®. "Registered in U.S. Patent and Trademark Office" and "Reg. U.S. Pat. Off." may also be used. A superscript "TM" in small capital letters indicates a trademark that isn't registered. It represents a company's common-law claim to a right of trademark or a trademark for which registration is pending. For example, 3M™ Post-it® Notes (see Figure 3.1).

A service mark is like a trademark, but it designates a service rather than a product, or is a logo. An "SM" in small capitals in a circle℠ is the symbol for a registered service mark. If registration is pending, the "SM" should be used without the circle.

© 1996, 3M. "Post-it" is a registered trademark of 3M.

Remember,

There's only one Post-it® Note and it's from 3M. Please help us protect our trademark by including the ® when you write about Post-it® Notes or our other Post-it® products. And since a trademark is an adjective, follow it up with an appropriate noun: Post-it® Software Notes, for example. The Post-it® trademark is a name you can trust — please help us keep it that way.

Post-it® Notes

3M Innovation

FIGURE 3.1 Brand names are important assets. As shown in this ad, the "R" with a circle around it indicates that the name Post-it is a registered trademark.

These symbols are used in advertising, product labeling, news releases, company brochures, and so on to let the public and competitors know that a name, slogan, or symbol is protected by law. Many news releases, for example, include a statement at the end that gives a brief description of the company and its trademarks. Here is one example: "Deckers Outdoor Corporation builds niche products into global lifestyle brands by designing and marketing innovative, functional, and fashion-conscious footwear developed for both high performance outdoor activities and everyday casual styles. Teva®, Simple®, and UGG® are registered trademarks of Deckers Outdoor Corporation." This kind of statement is often referred to as "boilerplate" and will be further explained in Chapter 5.

Public relations writers play an important role in protecting the trademarks of their employers. They safeguard trademarks and respect other organizational trademarks in the following ways:

- Ensuring that company trademarks are capitalized and used properly in all organizational literature and graphics. Lax supervision can cause loss of trademark protection.
- Distributing trademark brochures to editors and reporters and placing advertisements in trade publications, designating names to be capitalized. An example is the FedEx ad in Figure 3.2.
- Educating employees as to what the organization's trademarks are and how to use them correctly.
- Monitoring the mass media to make certain that trademarks are used correctly. If they are not, send a gentle reminder.
- Checking publications to ensure that other organizations are not infringing on a registered trademark. If they are, the company's legal department should protest with letters and threats of possible lawsuits.

FIGURE 3.2 Protection of trademarks requires corporate diligence. FedEx® places ads in journalism

- Making sure the trademark is actually being used. A 1988 revision of the Trademark Act no longer permits an organization to hold a name in reserve.

- Ensuring that the trademarks of other organizations are correctly used and properly noted. A good source is the International Trademark Association (www.inta.org); it has a directory of more than 3,000 trademarks and service marks with their generic terms.

- Avoiding the use of trademarked symbols or cartoon figures in promotional materials without the explicit permission of the owner. In some cases, to be discussed, a licensing fee is required.

Organizations adamantly insist on the proper use of trademarks in order to avoid the problem of having a name or slogan become generic. Or, to put it another way, a brand name becomes a common noun through general public use. Some trade names that have become generic include *aspirin, thermos, cornflakes, nylon, cellophane,* and *yo-yo.* This means that any company can use these names to describe a product. An additional list of trademarked brands is provided in the following Tips for Success.

The Problem of Trademark Infringement

There are thousands of businesses and organizations, so finding a trademark that is not already in use is extremely difficult. The task is even more frustrating if a company wants to use a trademark on an international level.

A good example is what happened to Nike at the Olympic Games in Barcelona. The athletic shoe manufacturer paid millions to be an official sponsor of the games, and it planned to introduce a new line of clothes at the event. There was a snag, however. A Spanish high court ruled that the firm's trademark infringed on the trademark of a Barcelona sock company that had registered "Nike" more than

---

✔ tips FOR SUCCESS

Trademarks Require a Capital Letter

Trademarked names are like proper nouns: They are capitalized and should be followed by a generic noun or phrase. The International Trademark Association (INTA) also recommends that trademarks should never be pluralized, used in possessive form, or used as verbs. Currently, more than 700,000 trademarks are registered with the U.S. government. Here is a sampling of trademarks that are often assumed to be generic words:

Jaws of Life	Band-Aid	Chap Stick	Day-Timer	DeskJet
Frisbee	Gatorade	Hula Hoop	Handi Wipes	Muzak
Realtor	NutraSweet	Spandex	Express Mail	Rolodex
StairMaster	Teflon	MapQuest	WebCrawler	Scotch tape ■

Source: International Trademark Association, *www.inta.org.*

60 years earlier. The court barred Nike from selling or advertising its sports apparel in Spain, an action that cost the company about $20 million in marketing potential.

More recently, eco-friendly brands have become a hot commodity. *Advertising Age* reported in 2008 that there was a "green gridlock" at the U.S. Patent and Trademark office as companies rushed to embrace Earth Day and environmentalism. In 2007, *green* was the most popular word, with 2,400 trademark filings. Companies also sought to trademark names with the words *energy*, *clean*, and *eco* in them. Glen Gunderson, chair of Dechert's trademark practice, told *Advertising Age*, "Clearly, it's not easy being green, since a trademark by definition is a distinctive term . . . . Many of these me-too filings will either not merit legal protection or will be very weak trademarks."

The complexity of finding a new name, coupled with the attempts of many to capitalize on an already known trade name, has spawned a number of lawsuits and complaints claiming trademark infringement. Here are some examples:

- *Entrepreneur* magazine was awarded $337,000 in court damages after filing a trademark infringement lawsuit against a public relations firm that changed its name to "EntrepreneurPR."
- Fox News filed a suit against satirist and author Al Franken because the title of his new book was *Lies and Lying Liars Who Tell Them: A Fair and Balanced Look at the Right*. Fox claimed that the phrase "fair and balanced" was trademarked.
- Martha Stewart's attempt to trademark the name "Katonah" for a new line of home furnishings raised the ire and organized protest of a suburban New York town of the same name and the Ramapough Lenape Indian Nation, which honors the original Chief Katonah.
- StoryCorps, a national oral-history project that uses "Sound Portraits," asked JetBlue airlines to cease using the term "Story Booth" in a promotional program to record passengers' anecdotes. StoryCorps believed the similar sounding name was a misappropriation of its trademark and the credibility that it had generated over the years.
- Anheuser-Busch filed a trademark infringements suit against a North Carolina college student for producing and selling T-shirts that said "Nags Head, NC— King of Beaches" and "This Beach is for You."
- Cisco Systems, claiming that it had already trademarked the term "iPhone," filed an infringement suit against Apple after Steve Job's announcement of a new product by the same name at MacWorld in early 2007. Cisco lost, and the rest is history.

In all of these cases, organizations claimed that their registered trademarks were being improperly exploited by others for commercial or organizational purposes. Sports franchises are particularly protective of their trademarks. Teams in the National Football League and the National Basketball Association earn more than $3 billion annually just selling licensed merchandise. Major college teams also rake

FIGURE 3.3 The Olympic rings logo is one of the world's most recognized brands. It is trademarked by the International Olympic Committee (IOC) and cannot be used without the hefty payment of licensing fees. The logo for the 2012 London Olympics is also trademarked and can only be used by official sponsors, who pay up to $100 million in licensing fees.

in millions of dollars annually by licensing their logos to be placed on everything from beer mugs to T-shirts.

Perhaps the most zealously guarded and expensive sports trademark is the Olympic rings. For the Beijing Olympics, companies paid up to $20 million just to sponsor the Olympic Torch relay, which also gave them to right to use the Olympic symbol in their marketing and public relations efforts. See the logo for the London 2012 games in Figure 3.3.

The following are the major guidelines that the courts use when considering cases of trademark infringement:

- Has the defendant used a name as a way of capitalizing on the reputation of another organization's trademark—and does the defendant benefit from the original organization's investment in popularizing its trademark?

- Is there an intent (real or otherwise) to create confusion in the public mind? Is there an intent to imply a connection between the defendant's product and the item identified by trademark?

- How similar are the two organizations? Are they providing the same kinds of products or services?

- Has the original organization actively protected the trademark by publicizing it and by actually continuing to use it in connection with its products or services?

- Is the trademark unique? A company with a trademark that merely describes a common product might be in trouble.

Misappropriation of Personality

Another form of trademark infringement can result from the unauthorized use of well-known entertainers, professional athletes, and other public figures in an organization's publicity and advertising materials. A photo of a rock star or movie star might make a company's brochure or newsletter more interesting, but the courts call it *misappropriation of personality* if permission and licensing fees have not been negotiated.

Deceased celebrities also are protected. To use a likeness or actual photo of a personality such as Elvis Presley, Marilyn Monroe, or even Princess Diana, the user must pay a licensing fee to an agent representing the family, studio, or estate of the deceased. The Presley estate, more than 30 years after his death, is still the "King," generating about $50 million annually from music royalties, DVDs, licensing deals, and tourism at Graceland. The estate of John Lennon generates about $45 million annually, and the estate of Peanuts comic strip creator Charles Schulz collects about $35 million annually. Even Albert Einstein's estate receives about $20 million annually.

The legal doctrine is the right of publicity, which gives entertainers, athletes, and other celebrities the sole ability to cash in on their fame. The legal right is loosely akin to a trademark or copyright, and many states have made it a commercial asset that can be inherited by a celebrity's descendents. One California artist, for example, was sued by the heirs of the Three Stooges because he made a charcoal portrait of the famous acting team and reproduced it on T-shirts and lithographs.

In sum, you need to be familiar with what might be considered trademark infringement. Don't use stock photos of living or dead personalities or a Dilbert or Peanuts comic strip unless you have permission. Also, be cautious about using a known slogan as the basis for coming up with a similar slogan. One nonprofit was sued by the International Olympic Committee for having a "Reading Olympics."

Regulatory Agencies

The promotion of products and services, whether through advertising, product publicity, or other techniques, is not protected by the First Amendment. Instead, the courts have traditionally ruled that such activities fall under the doctrine of commercial speech. This means that messages can be regulated by the state in the interest of public health, safety, and consumer protection. In other words, public relations writers involved in product publicity and the distribution of financial information should be aware of guidelines established by two major government agencies: the Federal Trade Commission and the Securities and Exchange Commission.

The Federal Trade Commission

The Federal Trade Commission (FTC) ensures that advertisements are not deceptive or misleading. The agency also has jurisdiction over product news releases and other forms of product publicity, such as videos and brochures.

In the eyes of the FTC, both advertisements and product publicity materials are vehicles of commercial trade—and therefore subject to regulation. In fact, Section 43(a) of the Lanham Act makes it clear that anyone, including public relations personnel, are subject to liability if that person participates in the making or dissemination of a false and misleading representation in any advertising or promotional material. This includes advertising and public relations firms, which also can be held liable for writing, producing, and distributing product publicity materials on behalf of clients.

For example, an FTC complaint was filed against Campbell Soup Company for claiming that its soups were low in fat and cholesterol and thus helpful in fighting heart disease. The FTC charged that the claim was deceptive because publicity and advertisements didn't disclose that the soups also were high in sodium, a condition that increases the risk of heart disease.

The Campbell Soup case raises an important aspect of FTC guidelines. Although a publicized fact might be accurate in itself, the FTC also considers the context, or "net impression received by the consumers." In Campbell's case, advertising copywriters and publicists ignored the information about high sodium, which placed an entirely new perspective on the health benefits of the soup.

Hollywood's abuse of endorsements and testimonials to publicize its films also has attracted the scrutiny of the FTC. The FTC investigated Sony Pictures when it found that Sony had concocted quotes from a fictitious movie critic to publicize four of its films. In a similar vein, Twentieth Century Fox admitted that it had hired actors to appear in "man in the street" commercials to portray unpaid moviegoers.

More recently, the FTC has been focusing on the marketing of food and beverages to children. In 2007, the agency subpoenaed 44 food marketers for detailed reports on how much they spend promoting their products to children and adolescents to determine if more federal regulations might be required.

FTC investigators are always on the lookout for unsubstantiated claims and various forms of misleading or deceptive information. Some of the words in promotional materials that trigger FTC interest include *authentic*, *certified*, *cure*, *custom-made*, *germ-free*, *natural*, *unbreakable*, *perfect*, *first-class*, *exclusive*, and *reliable*.

> ❝ **There is a trend toward potential claims, including PR firms, for their role in disseminating a message that is misleading or . . . has omitted material facts.** ❞

In recent years, the FTC also has established guidelines for "green" marketing and the use of "low-carb" in advertisements and publicity materials for food products. The following general guidelines, adapted from FTC regulations, should be taken into account when writing product publicity materials:

- Make sure the information is accurate and can be substantiated.
- Stick to the facts. Don't "hype" the product or service by using flowery, non-specific adjectives and ambiguous claims.
- Make sure celebrities or others who endorse the product actually use it. They should not say anything about the product's properties that cannot be substantiated.
- Watch the language. Don't say "independent research study" when the research was done by the organization's staff.
- Provide proper context for statements and statistics attributed to government agencies. They don't endorse products.

- Describe tests and surveys in sufficient detail so the consumer understands what was tested under what conditions.
- Remember that a product is not "new" if only the packaging has been changed or the product is more than six months old.
- When comparing products or services with a competitor's, make certain you can substantiate your claims.
- Avoid misleading and deceptive product demonstrations.

Companies found in violation of FTC guidelines are usually given the opportunity to sign a consent decree. This means that the company admits no wrongdoing but agrees to change its advertising and publicity claims. Companies may also be fined by the FTC or ordered to engage in corrective advertising and publicity.

The Securities and Exchange Commission

Company megamergers, stock offerings in new companies, and major financial scandals have made the Securities and Exchange Commission (SEC) practically a household name. This federal agency closely monitors the financial affairs of publicly traded companies and protects the interests of stockholders.

SEC guidelines on public disclosure and insider trading are particularly relevant to corporate public relations staff members who must meet the requirements. The distribution of misleading information or failure to make a timely disclosure of material information may be the basis of liability under the SEC code. A company may even be liable if it satisfies regulations by getting information out but conveys crucial information in a vague way or buries it deep in the news release.

A good example is Enron, the Houston–based energy company that became a household word overnight when it became the largest corporate failure in U.S. history. The company management was charged with a number of SEC violations, including the distribution of misleading news releases about its finances. According to Congressional testimony, the company issued a quarterly earnings news release that falsely led investors to believe that the company was "on track" to meet strong earnings growth in 2002. Three months later, the company was bankrupt. Later, in criminal trials, Enron's CEO, Jeffrey Skilling, was sentenced to 24 years in prison. The head of investor relations, Mark Koenig, received 18 months for aiding and abetting securities fraud.

The SEC has volumes of regulations, but there are three basic concepts that you should remember:

- Full information must be given on anything that might materially affect the company's stock. This includes such things as (1) dividends or their deletion, (2) annual and quarterly earnings, (3) stock splits, (4) mergers or takeovers, (5) major management changes, (6) major product developments, (7) expansion plans, (8) change of business purpose, (9) defaults, (10) proxy materials, (11) disposition of major assets, (12) purchase of own stock, and (13) announcements of major contracts or orders.

- Timely disclosure is essential. A company must act promptly (within minutes or a few hours) to dispel or confirm rumors that result in unusual market activity or market variations. The most common ways of dispensing such financial information are through use of electronic news release services, contact with the major international news services (Dow Jones Wire), and bulk faxing.

- Insider trading is illegal. Company officials, including public relations staffs and outside counsel, cannot use inside information to buy and sell company stock. The landmark case on insider trading occurred in 1965, when Texas Gulf Sulphur executives used inside information about an ore strike in Canada to buy stock while at the same time issuing a news release downplaying rumors that a rich find had been made.

The courts are increasingly applying the mosaic doctrine to financial information. Maureen Rubin, an attorney and professor at California State University, Northridge, explains that a court may examine all information released by a company, including news releases, to determine whether, taken as a whole, they create an "overall misleading" impression. One such case was *Cytryn v. Cook* (1990), in which a U.S. District Court ruled that the proper test of a company's adequate financial disclosure was not the literal truth of each positive statement, but the overall misleading impression that it combined to create in the eyes of potential investors.

As a result of such cases, writers of financial news releases must also avoid such practices as:

- Unrealistic sales and earnings reports
- Glowing descriptions of products in the experimental stage
- Announcements of possible mergers or takeovers that are only in the speculation stage
- Free trips for business reporters and offers of stock to financial analysts and editors of financial newsletters
- Omission of unfavorable news and developments
- Leaks of information to selected outsiders and financial columnists
- Dissemination of false rumors about a competitor's financial health

The SEC also has regulations supporting the use of "plain English" in prospectuses and other financial documents. Companies and financial firms are supposed to make information understandable to the average investor by removing sentences littered with lawyerisms such as *aforementioned*, *hereby*, *therewith*, *whereas*, and *hereinafter*. The cover page, summary, and risk factor sections of prospectuses must be clear, concise, and understandable. A SEC booklet gives helpful writing hints such as (1) make sentences short; (2) use *we* and *our*, *you* and *your*; and (3) use active verbs. More information about SEC guidelines can be accessed at its website (www.sec.gov).

A very important SEC regulation is the Fair Disclosure regulation (known as Reg FD). Although SEC regulations already mandated "material disclosure" of information that could affect the price of stock, the new regulation expands the concept by requiring publicly traded companies to broadly disseminate "material" information via news releases, webcasts, or SEC filings.

According to the SEC, Reg FD ensures that all investors, not just brokerage firms and analysts, will receive financial information from a company at the same time. Schering-Plough, a drug maker, was fined $1 million by the SEC because the company disclosed "material nonpublic information" to analysts and portfolio managers without making the same information available to the public.

Other Federal Regulatory Agencies

Although the FTC and the SEC are the major federal agencies concerned with the content of advertising and publicity materials, you should also be familiar with the general guidelines of the Federal Communications Commission (FCC), the Food and Drug Administration (FDA), and even the Bureau of Alcohol, Tobacco, and Firearms (BATF).

The Federal Communications Commission

The Federal Communications Commission (FCC) provides licenses to radio and television stations, allocates frequencies, and ensures that the public airwaves are used in the public interest. On occasion, the commission's policies and procedures directly impact the work of public relations personnel and writers who produce and distribute video news releases (VNRs) on behalf of employers and clients.

The FCC ruled in 2005 that broadcasters must disclose to viewers the origin of video news releases produced by the government or corporations when the material runs on the public airways. The agency didn't specify what form such disclosure should take, but broadcasters argued that the FCC was curtailing their First Amendment rights. FCC Commissioner Jonathan Edelstein disagreed, saying the issue was not free speech, but rather identifying who is actually speaking. He told the *Washington Post*, "We have a responsibility to tell broadcasters they have to let people know where the material is coming from. Viewers are hoodwinked into thinking it's really a news story when it might be from the government or a big corporation trying to influence the way they think."

The issue of source attribution came about as a result of critics complaining that VNRs produced by the Bush administration and aired as part of local television reports was "government propaganda." In addition, public relations firms came under fire from citizen watchdog groups who say the actual client for a VNR is often obscured. For example, television stations used a VNR that featured two prominent "debunkers" of global warming under the rubric of the "TCS Daily Science Roundtable," which was actually owned by a Republican public relations firm that included ExxonMobil as a client.

Both the broadcast and public relations industry have joined together to call for voluntary controls and disclosure instead of "government intrusion" into the news process. Both industries have adopted codes of practice regarding disclosure.

The Food and Drug Administration

The FDA oversees the advertising and promotion of prescription drugs, over-the-counter medicines, and cosmetics. Under the Food, Drug, and Cosmetic Act, any "person" (which includes advertising and public relations firms) who "causes the misbranding" of products through the dissemination of false and misleading information may be liable.

The FDA has specific guidelines for video, audio, and print news releases on health care topics. First, the release must provide "fair balance" by telling consumers about the risks as well as the benefits of the drug or treatment. Second, the writer must be clear about the limitations of a particular drug or treatment, for example, that it might not help people with certain conditions. Third, a news release or media kit should be accompanied by supplementary product sheets or brochures that give full prescribing information.

Because prescription drugs have major FDA curbs on advertising and promotion, the drug companies try to sidestep the regulations by publicizing diseases. Eli Lilly & Co., the maker of Prozac, provides a good example. The company sponsors ads and distributes publicity about depression. The Glaxo Institute for Digestive Health conducts information campaigns about the fact that stomach pains can be an indication of major problems. Of course, Glaxo also makes the ulcer drug Zantac.

Another public relations approach that has come under increased FDA scrutiny is the placement of celebrities on television talk shows who are being paid by the drug companies to mention the name of a particular drug while they talk about their recovery from cancer, a heart attack, or depression. Some programs, such as the *Today* show, have now banned such guests.

Bureau of Alcohol, Tobacco, and Firearms

If you are writing publicity or advertising copy for an alcoholic beverage, you should be aware of the laws and regulations under the Federal Alcohol Administration Act, which is enforced by the Bureau of Alcohol, Tobacco, and Firearms (BATF). One section prohibits "any statement that is false or untrue in any particular or that, irrespective of falsity, directly or by ambiguity, omission, or inference, or by addition of irrelevant, scientific, or technical matter tends to create a misleading impression." In other words, don't make any product claims about the health benefits of a particular alcoholic beverage.

Wineries have run into problems by implying that there are health benefits associated with drinking wine. For example, the BATF prohibited Geyser Peak winery from using the slogan, "As age enhances wine, wine enhances age." However, after intense lobbying efforts on the part of the California wine industry, the BATF did allow wineries to use the following statement: "The proud people who made this wine encourage you to consult your family doctor about the health benefits of wine consumption."

Working with Lawyers

You now have an overview of how various laws and government regulations affect your work as a public relations writer and specialist. A basic knowledge of the law should help you do your work in a responsible and appropriate manner, but you also should realize that a smattering of knowledge can be dangerous.

Laws and regulations can be complex. You are not a trained attorney, so you should consult lawyers who are qualified to answer specialized questions regarding libel, copyright, trademarks, government regulation, and invasion of privacy. Your organization's staff attorneys or outside legal counselors are your first source of information.

At the same time, remember that lawyers can tell you about the law; they should not tell you what to say or how to say it. They are legal experts, but not experts on effective writing and communication. They don't understand that the media want information now or that "no comment" is perceived as a guilty plea in the court of public opinion.

Indeed, a major area of friction can be the clash between the legal and public relations departments. Lawyers generally prefer to say little or nothing in most situations, whereas the public relations staff perceives its role as providing a steady flow of information and news about the organization to multiple publics. The result is often a never-ending tug-of-war. At the same time, it is essential that the legal and public relations staffs cooperate in the best interests of the organization.

Great care must be taken in releasing information about litigation, labor negotiations, complex financial transactions, product recalls, and plant accidents. Numerous laws and regulations, to say nothing of liability considerations, affect what should or should not be said. Out-of-court settlements, for example, often stipulate that the amount of the settlement will not be publicly disclosed. This is why it is often important to submit a draft news release to legal counsel as a first step.

Your relations with legal counsel will be more pleasant and more productive if you keep abreast of new developments. To do this, you should maintain a file of newspaper and magazine articles that report on legal developments and decisions relating to public relations. This might include new regulatory guidelines, consent decrees, libel awards, trademark infringement suits, product recalls, and court decisions on employee privacy.

The following guidelines can go a long way in ensuring cooperation and mutual respect between the legal and public relations functions:

- Each department should have a written definition of its responsibilities.
- The heads of both departments should be equal in rank and should report to the organization's chief executive officer or executive vice president.
- Both departments should be represented on key committees.
- The legal counsel should keep the public relations staff up-to-date on legal problems involving the organization.
- The public relations staff should keep the legal staff up-to-date on public issues and media concerns that will require an organizational response.
- The departments should regard each other as allies, not opponents.

Summary

- A public relations practitioner can get caught up in a lawsuit or a case with a government regulatory agency in a number of different ways. Practitioners may be held legally liable if they provide advice or support the illegal activity of a client.

- The concept of defamation involves a false and malicious (or at least negligent) communication with an identifiable subject who is injured either financially or by loss of reputation or mental suffering. Libel suits can be avoided through the careful use of language.

- Companies cannot assume when publishing newsletters that a person waives his or her right to privacy due to status as an employee. It is important to get written permission to publish photos or use employees in advertising materials and to be cautious in releasing personal information about employees to the media.

- Employees are limited in expressing opinions. Online communication can be monitored by the employer. Employees can be fired for revealing trade secrets or harassing fellow employees through e-mail or websites.

- Companies also have guidelines for employee blogs and participating in virtual online communities, such as Second Life. Employees, as well as public relations writers, should identify their affiliation if they are writing a blog or posting messages in an Internet chat group.

- Copyright is the protection of creative work from unauthorized use. It is assumed that published works are copyrighted, and permission must be obtained to reprint such material.

- The "fair use" doctrine allows limited use of copyrighted material if it is properly attributed and quotation marks are used.

- Unless a company has a specific contract with a freelance writer, photographer, or artist to produce work that will be exclusively owned by that company (a situation called "work for hire"), the freelancer owns his or her work.

- New copyright issues have been raised by the popularity of the Internet and the ease of downloading, uploading, and disseminating images and information.

- A trademark is a word, symbol, or slogan that identifies a product's origin. Trademarks are always capitalized and used as adjectives rather than nouns or verbs. Companies vigorously protect trademarks to prevent their becoming common nouns.

- Misappropriation of personality is a form of trademark infringement. It's the use of a celebrity's name or image for advertising purposes without permission.

- Commercial speech is regulated by the government in the interest of public health, safety, and consumer protection. Among the agencies involved in this regulation are the Federal Trade Commission (FTC), the Securities and Exchange Commission (SEC), and the Food and Drug Administration (FDA).

- A cooperative relationship must exist between public relations personnel and legal counsel. It helps if both groups report to the same top executive and both are represented on key committees.

Skill Building Activities

1. Rosanna's, a chain of coffee shops, wants to launch a marketing and public relations program to promote its brand. Some ideas include the following: (1) establish a website that would include photos of celebrities drinking a cup of coffee; (2) develop a series of ads showing customers in store locations enjoying a cup of coffee; (3) hire a freelance writer to develop some feature stories about the origin of various coffee beans that also provides some guidelines for selecting various blends sold by the chain; (4) distribute a news release giving the results of a

survey that showed coffee drinkers preferred Rosanna's coffee over Starbucks; and (5) post reprints of articles that have been written about the company on its website. What are the legal concerns surrounding each of these activities?

2. You work for a company that is experiencing a downturn in its stock price. The company president suggests the stock could go up if you write a news release about a new, highly advanced product. The R&D department, however, says the product is only in the prototype stage and may not available for another year. Does writing

and distribution of such a news release violate any SEC rules?

3. You work in media relations for a company. A local reporter calls you to tell you that one of the company's employees has just been named "Citizen of the Year" by the chamber of commerce. She's on deadline and wants you to give her as much information as possible about the employee's position, home address, marital status, number of children, hobbies, and so on to make a write a good profile of this outstanding citizen. What should you do?

Suggested Readings

Bunker, Matthew D., and Bolger, Bethany. "Protecting a Delicate Balance: Facts, Ideas, and Expression in Compilation Copyright Cases." *Journalism & Mass Communications Quarterly*, Vol. 80, No. 1, 2003, pp. 183–197.

Goldsborough, Reid. "Blogging and the Law: Letting Loose is Not Without its Risks." *PR Tactics*, August 2005, p. 11.

Gower, Karla K. *Legal and Ethical Restraints on Public Relations*. Long Grove, IL: Waveland Press, 2003.

Hazley, Greg. "PR, Legal Need to Play on Same Team." *O'Dwyer's PR Services Report*, December 2005, pp. 1, 12–13.

Karnitschnig, Matthew. "Media Titans Pressure YouTube Over Copyrights." *The Wall Street Journal*, October 10, 2006, p. B1.

Koppel, Nathan. "A Battle Erupts Over the Right to Market Marilyn." *The Wall Street Journal*, April 10, 2006, pp. A1, A11.

Kupferschmid, Keith. "Copyright Compliance is Easy Choice." *PRWeek*, October 7, 2007, p. 2.

Langston, R. Carter. "Public Relations and the Law: Six Keys to Winning in the Court of Law—and Public Opinion." *PR Tactics*, March 2006, p. 14.

McWilliams, Gary. "Candid Camera: Trove of Videos Vexes Wal-Mart." *The Wall Street Journal*, April 9, 2008, pp. A1; A12.

Parkinson, Michael G., and Parkinson, L. Marie. *Law for Advertising, Broadcasting, Journalism, and Public Relations*. Mahwah, NJ: Lawrence Erlbaum Associates, 2002.

Reber, Bryan, Gower, Karla, and Robinson, Jennifer. "The Internet and Litigation Public Relations." *Journal of Public Relations Research*, Vol. 18, No. 1, 2006, pp. 23–44.

Rundle, Rhonda. "Critical Case: How an Email Rant Jolted a Big HMO." *The Wall Street Journal*, April 24, 2007, pp. 1, 16.

Silver, David. "Managing the Litigation PR Process in the Court of Public Opinion." *The Strategist*, Summer 2006, pp. 42–43.

Story, Louise. "Can a Sandwich Be Slandered?" *The New York Times*, January 29, 2008, pp. C1, C4.

Finding and Making News

4

TOPICS covered in this chapter include:

The Challenge of Making News   91

What Makes News   92

How to Find News   101

How to Create News   103

The Challenge of Making News

A major purpose of many public relations programs is to provide information to the media in the hope that it will be published or broadcast. The resulting coverage is called *publicity*. The public relations writer who writes and places stories in the media is commonly referred to as a *publicist*.

Effective publicists need to know three things. First, they must be thoroughly familiar with traditional journalistic news values. Second, they must know where to find news and how to select the angle that will be most interesting to journalists and the public. Third, they must be problem solvers and come up with creative publicity tactics that effectively break through a forest of competing messages. These topics are the subject of this chapter.

Indeed, the publicist must navigate at least four obstacles on the way to generating coverage in the news media. The first obstacle is media gatekeepers. Reporters and editors decide what information qualifies as news and is worthy of being published or broadcast. Only one sentence or paragraph of the news release that you spent hours on may be used or, more often than not, the entire release might be thrown away.

The second obstacle is the incredibly shrinking news hole. The increasing migration of advertising to the Internet, for example, has caused most daily newspapers and many magazines to reduce the number of pages in each issue, which has also affected the amount of space available for news and features. This, in turn, has increased the competition for getting material published, because publications literally receive hundreds of news releases and story ideas every day.

The third obstacle is the reality that the traditional mass media is now fragmented, and it is no longer possible to reach the larger public through a single medium. That means that today's public relations writer must be adept at preparing and packaging publicity materials in a variety of formats—for print, broadcast, video, direct mail, e-mail, and the World Wide Web. Increasingly, interactive social media websites are being used (see Chapter 12).

Information overload is the fourth obstacle. In today's world of 24/7 news, everything from suburban weeklies to cable channels, online networks, and websites compete for an individual's attention. As a consequence, your organization's news may never even get the audience's attention.

Overcoming these obstacles can be a daunting task for any publicist responsible for informing, persuading, and motivating various audiences on behalf of an employer or client. You can take several steps, however, to make your efforts more effective. These include (1) understanding news values, (2) targeting the right media with your information, (3) thinking continuously about the interests of the readers or listeners, (4) keeping in mind the objectives of the client or employer, and (5) exercising creativity in thinking about how to present information that will meet the requirements of media gatekeepers.

What Makes News

Students in news writing classes are taught the basic components of what constitutes "news." Publicists must also be familiar with these elements if they are to generate the kind of information that appeals to **media gatekeepers**. The following is a brief overview of traditional news values from a public relations perspective.

Timeliness

Timeliness may be the most important characteristic of news. By definition, news must be current. A publicist can make a story angle timely in four ways.

One way to make news timely is to announce something when it happens. An organization usually contacts the press as soon as an event occurs. This might be the announcement of a new CEO, the merger of two companies, the launch of a new product or service, or even the settlement of a labor dispute. Such items are fairly routine and don't require much creativity, because the emphasis is on providing the basic facts. A delay in conveying this kind of information, however, could result in a news item being rejected as "old news."

A second approach to timeliness is providing information or story ideas that relate to an event or situation that is already being extensively covered by the news media. A good example is how a tax and financial planning firm, Gilman Ciocia, used the U.S. government's announcement of a tax stimulus package to issue a news release reminding people that they had to complete their tax returns in order to get a rebate check. Another example is the Homeownership Preservation Foundation. After President Bush gave a speech on the rising rate of foreclosures, the Foundation's executive director issued a news release that included the statement, "Today's developments underscore the importance of using trained mortgage counselors to understand how President Bush's announcement impacts individual homeowners."

Even scandal can provide a publicist with a timely opportunity. While the media was having a field day covering the revelations that Governor Eliot Spitzer of

New York was a client of a high-end prostitution service, publicist Michael Darden successfully arranged to have his client, couples expert Rich Hammons, appear on the *Oprah & Friends* XM satellite radio show.

At other times, a topic or issue generates media and public interest over a period of weeks and months. For example, health care issues continue to hold media interest, so pharmaceutical firms tailor their news releases around the idea that new "wonder drugs" are a cost-effective way to reduce hospital stays. Global warming and environmentalism also get frequent media coverage. First Act, one of the world's leading makers of musical instruments, successfully placed a story with the *Los Angeles Times* about its "green guitars" during the annual convention of the International Music Products Association in that city. As another example, travel publicists successfully placed articles in travel magazines about how to save money on a European vacation after the dollar sank to new lows against the euro.

> **" In the public relations business, the name of the game is finding a hook that links your press release to the news. "** ■ Joshua Harris, reporter for *The Wall Street Journal*

A third approach to timely distribution of publicity materials is to relate the organization's products or services to another event that has national recognition and interest. Kimberly-Clark and its public relations firm, Ketchum, used this approach to publicize its toilet tissue by capitalizing on the effects of America's potty break during the halftime of the Super Bowl. The company used former player and coach, Mike Ditka, to be a spokesperson and sponsored an essay contest, "Share Your Cloggiest Moment." The efforts generated considerable media coverage, and 98 percent of the media placements mentioned that Scott Bath Tissue dissolves four times faster than the leading brand—something to consider for Super Bowl fans racing to the bathroom during the long commercial breaks.

A popular movie also provided a timely opportunity. *The Lord of the Rings* trilogy was filmed in New Zealand and, after the film won an Oscar for cinematography, the New Zealand government launched an international public relations and advertising campaign billing the nation as "best supporting country."

A fourth aspect of timeliness is offering information linked to events and holidays that are already on the public agenda. Auto clubs and insurance companies, for example, have excellent placement success with articles about safe driving just before the Labor Day and July Fourth holiday weekends, when millions of Americans take to the road. Even April Fool's Day can be used as a hook. Mr. Handyman International, for example, used the day to send a news release not to be "fooled" by handyman scam artists when hiring professionals to do home improvements. It cautioned homeowners not to fall for such pitches as "I have a special offer that's good for you today, only."

Halloween is another timely holiday. The American Academy of Ophthalmology issued a news release warning that "some ghoulish things can happen to your eyes" unless you take some precautions. The same theme was sounded by the American Optometric Association, which said that masks can be very scary if they limit your peripheral vision. Of course, the American Association of Orthodontists, which knows about candy and teeth, sent out a news release about the "tricks treats can play" and offered orthodontic tips.

At Thanksgiving, Butterball Turkey achieves a publicity bonanza by operating a Turkey Talk-Line and website (www.butterball.com), which is used by about 200,000 novice cooks each year. Information about Butterball's hotline, plus articles about how to cook a turkey, receive considerable print and broadcast coverage. One story that usually gets media pickup is a summary of what questions callers ask. One common question is "What is the best way to thaw a turkey?" And almost 20,000 people asked that question in a recent year.

Christmas is the major season for purchasing children's toys, so the media are receptive to news releases from toy manufacturers about new products on the market. Duracell capitalizes on the holiday gift-giving season with its annual "Duracell Kids' Choice Toy Survey." It publicizes a "Top 10" toy list based on a survey of children in YMCA afternoon programs. Ameritech used the holiday season to release publicity material about its home security systems, which will protect all of those packages under the tree. The American College of Gastroenterologists reminded people to see a doctor if all the holiday food and drink causes stomach problems.

Timing is everything, but sometimes events cause havoc with even the best-laid plans. The Hong Kong Tourist Board had just launched a campaign to attract more tourists when the SARS epidemic hit and more than 100 people in China and Hong Kong died from the mutant strain of pneumonia. Unfortunately, it was too late to change or recall advertisements in international magazines promising that "Hong Kong Will Take Your Breath Away."

A fifth area of building publicity is gearing activities around a self-designated day, week, or even month. See the Tips for Success on page 95.

Prominence

The news media rarely cover the grand opening of a store or anything else unless there is a prominent person with star power involved. For example, a bank might use a music or film celebrity from the 1960s to open a new branch to attract senior citizens as customers. Home Depot got publicity mileage by having Brad Pitt appear at a news conference to talk about the company's partnership with Pitt and Global Green to rebuild New Orleans.

Beauty queens still attract attention too, even in New York City. When the city inaugurated its 311 number to answer citizen questions about such mundane things as how to recycle trash, Miss Universe was enlisted to make a call and ask a question about a swimming pool's hours of operation. *The New York Times* carried a photo of the 18-year-old beauty queen from the Dominican Republic talking on the phone and devoted 16 column inches to the new service. The headline: "Miss Universe Dials 311 (Don't Ask For Her Number)."

The presence of movie stars, rock stars, and professional athletes at special events invariably draws crowds and the media, but an organization can attract media coverage by using other kinds of prominent people as well. An immunization clinic for low-income

> **" If a celebrity doesn't show up to an event or party, what will the media write about? "**
>
> ■ Lori Levine, founder of Flying Television, a talent booking and brokering firm

☑ tips FOR SUCCESS

If It's May, It's National Asparagus Month

National organizations and trade groups often designate a day, a week, or even a month to focus on a cause, an industry, or even a product. May is a popular month, with such designations as National Barbecue Month, National Paint Month, National Physical Fitness and Sports Month, and even National Arthritis Month.

The National Asparagus Association selected May as National Asparagus Month because it marks the peak of asparagus production. By promoting the month, the trade group hopes to encourage consumption of its product at home and in restaurants. Surveys show that more meals are eaten out on Mother's Day than on any other day, and the asparagus association makes a special effort to encourage restaurants to put its product on the menu.

The warm weather in May also prompts the National Paint and Coating Association to sponsor National Paint Month. As a spokesperson says, "It's the time of the year when people are thinking about home improvements, and hence it is the perfect month to alert the public to the power of paint."

If a special day, week, or month is well organized and promoted, it can provide a focus point for media coverage on an annual basis. Breast Cancer Awareness Week, for example, was started almost 20 years ago by ICI Pharmaceuticals with the assistance of its public relations firm, Burson-Marsteller. The week is still going strong with a coalition of 17 organizations supporting a variety of educational efforts and events during the designated week. As a result of continued media coverage, the majority of American women now recognize the phrase "early detection."

However, experts say Breast Cancer Awareness Week is an exception in a very crowded field. "Clients often think these national days are a fantastic way to get publicity when in fact it is one of the least interesting kinds of news you can present to the media," says Audrey Knoth, vice president at Pennsylvania–based Goldman & Associates.

Echoing Knoth's thoughts is Reg Henry, a columnist at the *Pittsburgh Post-Gazette*. He notes, "The Awareness Month industry has proliferated to such an extent that observances often overlap and the result is almost nobody is aware of anything." Making his point is a partial list of designated weeks from Chase's Calendar of Events (www.chases.com) for just the first week of May. The list includes: (1) Be Kind to Animals Week, (2) National Family Week, (3) Reading is Fun Week, (4) Teacher Appreciation Week, (5) Astronomy Week, (6) National Wildflower Week, and (7) National Nurses Week. After all that, it's no wonder that May 7 is designated as the "Great American Grump Out."

If you insist on creating a special day, week, or month for your client, *PRWeek* suggests the following tips:

- Do have an educational component or call to action.
- Do make sure the campaign has a human element.
- Do find credible experts and partners for the media to interview. ■

children usually gets first-page coverage if a governor, or even a mayor, pays a visit. A former astronaut or a retired Olympic medalist visiting a local high school also generates media interest.

Giving an issue celebrity status is one way of cutting through the clutter of competing causes and less-than-exciting news. Take the issue of obesity and good health. Former U.S. Surgeon General C. Everett Koop was tapped by a consortium of food

FIGURE 4.1 Giving awards generates publicity, especially if a celebrity receives it. Here, seven-time NBA All-Star Alonzo Mourning receives an award from the American Association of Kidney Patients for his commitment to raising awareness of chronic kidney disease. The award ceremony was at the halftime of an NBA game, which also guaranteed a large audience.

manufacturers to talk about the importance of exercise and a healthy diet—and was immediately overwhelmed by requests for talks and media interviews.

Many events, of course, don't have the high-priced glamour of Brad Pitt or the high public visibility of a governor, but you can still gain from the use of officials and other well-known individuals in quotes and pictures. One common tactic is the award photograph. Organizations often honor prominent individuals, which attracts media coverage. For example, Figure 4.1 shows NBA star Alonzo Mourning receiving an award. On a more routine level, even photographs of an organization's national president giving an award can generate publicity in local media.

Note that prominence is not restricted to people; it also extends to organizations. Large multinational corporations such as IBM and ExxonMobil automatically get more media attention, because they control so many resources and affect so many lives. If you work for a smaller, less prominent company, you will have to try much harder to get media coverage.

Proximity

Surveys have shown that the news releases most acceptable to media gatekeepers are those with a local angle. These stories, often called **hometowners**, are custom tailored for an individual's local newspaper or broadcast station by emphasizing the local angle in the first paragraph of the news release.

Professor emeritus Linda Morton of the University of Oklahoma, for example, once conducted a survey of hometown releases from a major university and found a 36 percent acceptance rate by newspapers. In contrast, generalized news releases had only a 3 to 8 percent acceptance rate. She concluded: "Because a primary goal is to bring the writer's work before the general public through the media, hometowners are clearly an effective tool to bring this about."

PR Data Systems, a distribution service, did a content analysis of seven dailies in Illinois and Wisconsin and came to the same conclusion. Almost 70 percent of all news coverage in the business and financial sections of these newspapers, according to a report in *O'Dwyer's PR Newsletter*, was devoted to local companies. Ed Harrington of PR Data Systems noted, "One business editor reported he used only three of 150 releases received during the study period because all of the others lacked a local angle."

Obviously, the local angle—proximity—has strong news value. Whenever possible, it is important to "localize" information. Publicists should take the time and effort to include the names of local dealers, retailers, and other area representatives for the news media serving a particular city.

Today it is easy to localize news releases and to tailor them to specific kinds of media by using software applications that can automatically merge the names of local people into a news release. An insurance company, for example, may announce that 150 of its agents nationwide qualified for induction into the "Million Dollar Roundtable" in sales. The publicist would localize this event by using software to insert the names of individual agents into the lead paragraph of the news release. Thus, a newspaper editor in Lexington, Kentucky, would receive a news release that begins, "Denise Smith of Lexington, an agent for Northwestern Mutual Insurance Company, has been inducted into the company's 'Million Dollar Roundtable.' " The names of the other 149 agents, who live elsewhere, would not be mentioned. Hometown news releases are discussed further in Chapter 5.

Another form of localizing is highlighting various aspects of a person's background in different publications. In the case of Denise Smith of Northwestern Mutual Insurance Company, various audiences would be interested in her achievement. For example, the weekly newspaper in the small town where Denise graduated from high school needs a news release that mentions Denise's parents, her graduation year, and the fact that she was president of the senior class. In contrast, the suburban weekly in Lexington would appreciate a paragraph giving her business address and noting the fact that she is the past chair of the local planning commission. A trade newspaper covering the insurance industry would be more interested in a news release that details her professional career.

In sum, always keep the local angle in mind when you write a news release. This often requires additional research and writing, but the resulting media coverage is worth the effort. As news correspondent Mort Rosenblum once wrote, "A dogfight in Brooklyn is bigger than a revolution in China."

Significance

Any situation or event that can affect a substantial number of people is significant. Global warming continues to be a hot topic, so to speak, but the concept and the scientific debate about the problem is somewhat abstract to the public. Publicists for environmental groups have worked to make the topic more significant to the average person by focusing on a popular consumer items. The Natural Resources Defense Council (NRDC), for example, points out that consuming bottled water is not environmentally friendly because it takes oil to make all of those plastic bottles and only a quarter of them are ever recycled. The result is about a billion pounds of plastic bottles clogging landfills every year. In addition, the transport of bottled water contributes to greenhouse gasses, a major source of global warming. The transport of a case of bottled water from Fiji to Los Angeles, for example, produces about 7 pounds of greenhouse gasses on its 5,500 mile journey.

The major media coverage of the NDRC's "Think Outside the Bottle" campaign has, of course, become a significant issue for the $11 billion American bottled water industry. Bottlers such as Coca-Cola are publicizing their efforts to make thinner, more ecologically correct plastic bottles, but publicists from manufacturers of tap water filters also are finding renewed media interest in their products.

In judging significance, you must know not only *how many* people will be affected but also *who* will be affected. A major task, of course, is to convince media gatekeepers that the issue, product, or service is significant to their readers, listeners, or viewers. In sum, be prepared when the journalist says, "So what?"

Unusualness

Anything out of the ordinary attracts press interest and public attention. The presence of a giant inflated King Kong hugging an office building in Portland to promote the Oregon lottery is certainly unusual. So is a 75-foot birthday cake in the shape of a snake that the San Diego Zoo made to celebrate its 75th year of operation. Even the National Education Association (NEA) got media coverage for its Read Across America campaign by staging events with a costumed Dr. Seuss character (see Figure 4.2).

FIGURE 4.2 Special events need interesting photo opportunities. The National Education Association (NEA) held an event at the New York Public Library to launch its Read Across America program by having a Dr. Seuss theme. Actresses Constance Marie and Kyla Pratt and Miss Universe 2008, Zuleyka Rivera, were enlisted to pose with a Dr. Seuss character for this publicity photo.

A lot of products are pretty ordinary, so it's always a challenge for a publicist to think of something "unusual" that will attract media interest. Duct tape, a common staple for home handymen, is a good example of a dull product. So what to do? Heckel Consumer Adhesives, the parent company of the Duck brand of duct tape, decided on a series of unusual events featuring the tape. One such effort was inviting students to design prom dresses made of duct tape. That led to a duct tape fashion show in New York where all the designer dresses were fashioned out of duct tape. The company also exhibited a giant American flag made entirely of multicolored duct tape in New York on Flag Day.

Melanie Amato, director of advertising and research for the Heckel Company told *PRWeek* that all Duck brand public relations efforts have to involve four elements the company wants the brand to convey: They have to be fun, they have to project friendliness, they must display resourcefulness, and they have to be imaginative. Such efforts have made the Duck brand the number-one brand in the United States.

The opening of a new bank branch also falls into the category of less than exciting news. The typical ribbon cutting won't cut it, so to speak, so publicists need to be more creative in thinking up something more unusual. Colorado–based Peter Webb Public Relations came up with a winner for Safeway Select Bank in Phoenix with a campaign called "Cold Hard Cash." The firm capitalized on Phoenix's high summer heat by creating 10 ice sculptures fashioned into various shapes, such as computer terminals, grocery bags, and dollar signs. Frozen inside each sculpture was a cash prize; $10,000 was divided among the sculptures. More than 400 people registered, and 10 got the chance to melt their ice blocks and take home whatever cash they could get their hands on by rubbing away the ice. The *Arizona Republic* ran a front-page business story and photo of the event, and the three network affiliates also covered the event.

Human Interest

People like to read about other people. That is why the news media often focus on the lives of the rich and famous and why *People*, *US Weekly*, and *OK!* magazines are such a success. The love lives of movie stars and the antics of rock singers provide constant grist for the tabloids and the mainstream media.

Interest in people, however, is not restricted to celebrities. A journalist may focus on the plight of one family on welfare to illustrate the problems of the entire social services system. Television news, which tries to explain complex issues in a minute or two, often uses the vehicle of personalizing an issue by letting one individual or family speak. Indeed, people would rather listen to the problems of a welfare mother in her own words than view a series of bar charts showing the decline in state and federal funding for social services.

Public relations writers also have opportunities to humanize stories. Here are some examples:

- A university graduates 10,000 students every spring, but the news release focuses on an 80-year-old grandmother who is graduating with her daughter and her granddaughter.

- A company that manufactures a voice-activated cellular phone for disabled people prepares a feature article about how the phone helps one disabled Iraq war veteran.
- A brilliant research engineer for a computer company is the subject of a company feature story that is sent to the trade press.
- A food bank, after getting permission, gives the names of clients to a reporter who wants to interview some of them for a story on how the agency has helped them.
- *The Wall Street Journal* is approached about doing an in-depth profile on the first woman CEO in the company's history.
- The background and expertise of a restaurant chef is the subject of a feature article in the living section of the local daily or weekly.

Conflict

When two or more groups advocate different views on a topic of current interest, this creates news. Indeed, reporters often fuel the controversy by quoting one side and then asking the other side for a comment.

Organizations get coverage when they state a position or viewpoint regarding a local or even international controversy. Labor disputes between management and employees, for example, are often accompanied by competing media interviews, news releases, and picket lines, as shown in Figure 4.3.

Organizations, groups, and individuals also receive media coverage for stating various opinions about such ongoing controversies as global warming, illegal immigrants, universal health care, the price of gasoline, and increased automobile fuel efficiency. Managed health care and patient rights, for example, was supported by such groups as the American Medical Association and the Trial Lawyers of America, but strongly opposed by insurance companies and the United States Chamber of Commerce.

In sum, publicists should be aware of on-going public issues and conflicts to determine if their clients or employers should publicize a particular viewpoint or perspective on the issue. A publicist, however, must first assess whether the particular issue is relevant to the orga-

FIGURE 4.3 Conflict generates media interest and coverage. During labor disputes, labor unions often use a picket line and signs to provide a highly visible statement about their grievances. The availability of photos and video clips generates more media coverage than just a news story.

nization. Rising gasoline prices may not be particularly relevant to a chain of restaurants, but highly relevant to delivery services such as UPS, FedEx, or even local pizza parlors that deliver.

Newness

Advertising and marketing people say that the two words they find most useful are "new" and "free." You will seldom use "free," but you should constantly search for something "new." Any news release announcing a new product or service has a good chance of being published if you can convince a journalist that it is truly "new." Apple's iPod and iPhone, for example, generated thousands of articles and blog posts when they were introduced. New, updated models of these products, however, receive considerably less media coverage.

New uses for old products are the basis of most food publicity. There is nothing new about potatoes, walnuts, yams, or avocados; yet food editors steadily publish new recipes for these and scores of other foods. A growing trend is relating food to health. James Cury, executive editor of Epicurious (www.epicurious.com), told *O'Dwyer's PR Newsletter* that he likes food publicists who can relate their products to such buzzwords as "organic," "clean," and "sustainable."

Publicists for new products often work to have reviews of the product published in leading publications. A favorable product review by Walt Mossberg in *The Wall Street Journal* is the Holy Grail for the high-tech consumer goods industry. By the same token, a review or product mention on Epicurious or in *Food & Wine* is highly sought by the food and restaurant industry.

One note of caution: The news media are getting somewhat distrustful of claims that a product or service is "new." In many cases, the only thing "new" about a product is the packaging; from an editor's point of view, that is not "new" enough. High-technology companies have also raised reporter suspicions about new products that often turn out to be what cynical reporters call "vaporware."

How to Find News

Now that you understand what constitutes traditional news values, you should have a good framework as you approach the process of finding news.

Internal News Sources

The first step in finding news is to become totally familiar with the organization you represent. One way to learn about an organization is to do research. According to Professor Robert Kendall in his text, *Public Relations Campaign Strategies*, this involves looking at a variety of sources, including the following:

- **Important papers.** Policy statements, annual reports, organizational charts, position papers, research reports, market share, sales projections, and biographies of top managers.

- **Periodicals.** Current and past issues of employee newsletters and magazines.
- **Clipping files.** Published articles and online postings about the organization and the industry. Review the local press as well as the national and international press.
- **Other published materials.** Copies of the organization's brochures, speeches, slide presentations, videotapes, and sales material.

In addition to reviewing all of these sources, which are available primarily in published form, you must also play the role of roving reporter. Talk to a variety of people, ask a lot of questions, and constantly be on the lookout for something new or different. Most news stories don't come to you; you have to seek out stories. Most people have no clue whether an event or a situation is newsworthy, so you must be alert to clues and hints as well as hard facts.

A new process or technique may be just business as usual to a production manager, but it might lead you to several possible stories. For example, AlliedSignal received news coverage for a new fiber by pointing out that it could be used in automobile seat belts to slow the movement of a passenger's upper body in a collision. The company publicist did two things to make this story newsworthy. First, she related the new fiber to a use that the public could readily understand. Second, she arranged and distributed an interesting photo that showed the manufacturing process.

A change in work schedules may affect traffic and thus be important to the community. Personnel changes and promotions may be of interest to editors of business and trade papers. A new contract, which means hiring new employees, might be important to the regional economy. By the same token, the loss of a major contract—and its implications for the employees and community—also qualifies as significant news.

External News Sources

Ideas on how to get your organization into the news can come from almost any source. For example, you might attend a Rotary Club meeting and hear a speaker talk about the national need to train more engineers in the computer sciences. That might spur you to investigate how the problem affects your employer or client. This, in turn, might lead to the idea that you could generate some media coverage by telling the media what your company is doing about the problem in terms of providing college scholarships or even recruiting engineers from other nations. Or perhaps you might offer the media an interview with the company president, who can articulate some solutions to the problem. Another approach might be to have the CEO write an **op-ed** piece for the local daily or even *The Wall Street Journal*. Op-eds are discussed in Chapter 7.

As discussed earlier, you should always think about how you can use news events to create publicity. In order to do this, you need to read, listen to, and watch the news for events and situations that may affect your organization. As Michael Klepper, a New York publicist, says, "This requires becoming a media junkie, which is an absolute necessity for anyone wanting to be successful in the media relations part of the business."

Reacting to a news event is exactly what the Child and Family Services of New Hampshire did when the media reported that a newborn baby had been abandoned. The day the story hit, Renee Robertie, communications director of the agency, faxed all state dailies, radio stations, and television stations the options a mother experiencing a crisis pregnancy would have if she were to call Child and Family Services. This got an immediate media response, and there were many stories of the "What a mother can do" type, which prominently featured the agency's services. Robertie adds, "The key to success is being prepared so when something like this happens, you are able to step in as the voice of authority and provide reporters with good data and soundbites at a moment's notice."

All news events can be used to create news, but you must think of applications to your particular organization and industry on a moment's notice to take advantage of timeliness, which is a core news value. That's the hard part. To help you do this, we will discuss creativity and brainstorming later in this chapter.

Other external sources that you can tap for ideas are polls and surveys, census reports, trade media, financial analyst reports, findings of governmental commissions, sales figures for entire industries, and updates on competitors.

Professional periodicals and newsletters serving the public relations industry should not be overlooked. They often include results of surveys indicating what the "hot" topics are in the media. A national survey of newspaper editors by News USA, a news release and feature article distribution firm, illustrates the point. The survey found that the topic of health care generated the most interest on the part of editors. Other topics of media interest included retirement strategies, medicine, environment, food, education, consumer issues, recreation, and finance. A survey of food editors by another firm indicated that low-fat and fat-free recipes were "hot" topics. In addition, the interests of individual editors and publications are part of media databases such as Cision, which was mentioned in Chapter 1.

How to Create News

There is no hard-and-fast definition of what is news. A Hearst editor once declared, probably with more truth than he realized, "News is what I say it is." It's also true that most "news" is created by individuals and organizations that plan activities and events for the purpose of creating public awareness to inform, persuade, and motivate.

Historian Daniel Boorstin even coined the term **pseudoevent** to describe events and situations that are created primarily for the sake of generating press coverage. Some classic examples of the pseudoevent are the Miss America pageant, the Academy Awards, and the Super Bowl.

The Miss America contest was a creative solution by a publicist hired by the Atlantic City Chamber of Commerce, which wanted to extend the summer tourist season past Labor Day. The contest was not only good for business in Atlantic City, but it also provided the American public with a form of entertainment.

The Academy Awards, another American institution, also had its beginnings as a publicity stunt. It was begun in 1929 by the movie industry to garner media attention and also increase movie attendance during the Depression. Today, the

Academy Awards has grown into a $100 million industry that not only continues to increase box office revenue for winning films, but also serves as a showcase for celebrities, jewelers, designers, and even caterers.

The Super Bowl is essentially a pseudoevent invented by the National Football League (NFL) in 1961. As in the case of the Miss America pageant, it was originally designed to extend the professional football season and increase revenues. The event generates considerable hype and media coverage. It is the most watched television event of the year; in 2008 about 100 million people watched the XLII game (Roman numerals is part of the hype) as two American teams vied for the "world" championship.

Although the term *pseudoevent* has a somewhat negative connotation, the main point is that such events are considered legitimate news if they also meet the standards of traditional news values. A news conference by Apple's Steve Jobs announcing a new product, for example, may be carefully planned and staged, but it also provides useful information to the media and consumers. A product launch of a new cleaning product from Clorox, in contrast, requires considerable creativity to generate media attention.

Indeed, such creativity and vision are essential attributes for work in public relations, but such things are difficult to teach and even more difficult to learn. Hal Lancaster, author of the "Managing Your Career" column in *The Wall Street Journal*, says creative people share some common traits: "keen powers of observation, a restless curiosity, the ability to identify issues others miss, a talent for generating a large number of ideas, persistent questioning of the norm, and a knack for seeing established structures in new ways."

Judith Rich, now a Chicago-based creativity consultant and former vice president of Ketchum, gives some tips for developing your creative instincts. Writing in PRSA's *The Strategist*, she offers the following:

- Look at things with new eyes.
- Hear with new ears. Listen to the world outside of yourself for a change.
- Ask questions and start learning from people you might not usually consider as resources.
- Stop saying or thinking "No." Be more open to possibilities.
- Keep things in perspective and, at the same time, try to expand your horizons.
- Don't be put off by rules that may not even exist. Don't limit your thinking.
- Get excited about ideas that may change the way you do business.
- Inspiration comes easiest to a rested mind. Escape, on occasion, from the daily grind.
- Record ideas whenever they occur.
- Don't just look for information and ideas in the "normal" places.
- Draw heavily on personal resources—remember the content of your dreams. Your unconscious may sometimes solve your conscious concerns.

Brainstorming

Public relations firms such as Ketchum generate creative ideas by conducting **brainstorming** sessions. The point of such a session is to encourage everyone to express any idea that comes to mind. An idea may be totally impractical and off the wall, but no one is allowed to say "it won't work" or "that's a stupid idea." This inhibits creative thinking and people's willingness to participate.

All ideas, regardless of their merit, can be placed on a flip chart or whiteboard. As the team looks at all the ideas, new ideas that combine and refine the original list are usually generated. Another approach is to give everyone three colored dots and ask them to place the dots next to the three ideas they believe are best, based on feasibility, cost-effectiveness, and timeliness. Those ideas receiving the most dots are emphasized and shaped.

If a large team of people is trying to come up with creative ideas, a similar approach is to give each participant 25 to 50 note cards and ask them to jot down one idea per card. Through a system of sorting, five or six common ideas will emerge that warrant further discussion.

A good example of how brainstorming can lead to a creative program is PETCO. The objective of the brainstorming session was to create an event that would attract customers but also raise PETCO's brand on a national level. A brainstorming session by the public relations staff finally came up with the idea of hosting a Chihuahua race—not exactly a breed associated with racing. The team publicized the races at various stores and also put race footage on YouTube and on PETCO's website. In addition, the original idea was expanded to taking dogs on the road, holding races in TV studios and parking lots in partnership with dog-rescue groups and local humane societies.

You, too, can create news in a variety of ways. See the Tips for Success on page 106 for a list of 32 ways to generate news. The next several pages highlight various tactics for making news: (1) special events, (2) contests, (3) polls and surveys, (4) top 10 lists, (5) stunts, (6) product demonstrations, (7) rallies and protests, (8) personal appearances, and (9) awards.

Special Events

Any number of events are created or staged to attract media attention and make the public aware of a new product, service, or idea. This goes back to the concept of the "triggering event" that becomes the catalyst for individuals to adopt new ideas or modify their behavior.

It is less certain, however, what exactly constitutes a "special event." Some say that any event that is out of the ordinary is "special," whereas others say that any event can be "special" if the organizers are particularly creative at organizing it. At times, things that occur on a routine basis can become the focus of media coverage if some creativity is exercised. A new store may quietly open its doors for business, or it can have a "grand opening" with a celebrity cutting the ribbon and a circus in the parking lot.

32 Ways to Create News for Your Organization

1. Tie in with news events of the day.
2. Cooperate with another organization on a joint project.
3. Tie in with a newspaper or broadcast station on a mutual project.
4. Conduct a poll or survey.
5. Issue a report.
6. Arrange an interview with a celebrity.
7. Take part in a controversy.
8. Arrange for a testimonial.
9. Arrange for a speech.
10. Make an analysis or prediction.
11. Form and announce names for committees.
12. Hold an election.
13. Announce an appointment.
14. Celebrate an anniversary.
15. Issue a summary of facts.
16. Tie in with a holiday.
17. Make a trip.
18. Make an award.
19. Hold a contest.
20. Pass a resolution.
21. Appear before a public body.
22. Stage a special event.
23. Write a letter.
24. Release a letter you received (with permission).
25. Adapt national reports and surveys for local use.
26. Stage a debate.
27. Tie in to a well-known week or day.
28. Honor an institution.
29. Organize a tour.
30. Inspect a project.
31. Issue a commendation.
32. Issue a protest. ■

New product launches are often accompanied by special events or activities. When J. K. Rowling's *Harry Potter and the Deathly Hallows* was released, bookstores around the world hosted midnight parties the night of the release complete with games, costumed customers, and music. Borders, for example, reported that 800,000 people attended the parties at its locations around the world.

Another example is Visa, an Olympic sponsor for more than two decades. It organized a Visa Olympic Media Summit in New York City to introduce its team of athletes for the Beijing Olympics and to unveil its integrated marketing plan in support of the 2008 games. Other corporations sponsor rock concerts as part of a product launch.

Even nonprofits, such as the World Wildlife Fund, do special events that are global in scope. The organization sponsored an Earth Hour in March 2008 in which millions of people and many landmarks around the world, including San Francisco's Golden Gate Bridge, turned their lights off for an hour to raise awareness about global climate change.

A major special event category is anniversaries. Major milestones in the age of a product, an institution, or a service are often the "triggering event" that provides the "news hook" for extensive media coverage. Detroit, for example, held a year-long celebration of its 300th birthday, and a resort hotel in Florida celebrated its 75th anniversary by inviting all the couples married there back for a 3-day celebration. The Museum of Art in Dallas celebrated its 100th anniversary by keeping the museum open 100 hours straight for a series of events occurring at all hours of the day. Hershey's celebrated its centennial by unveiling the world's largest Hershey's Kiss during a gala event at the company's headquarters (Figure 4.4).

Planters rolled out a number of special events to celebrate its 100th anniversary and its famous icon, Mr. Peanut. One event was a national vote to decide whether Mr. Peanut should get a new fashion accessory, such as a pocket watch, cuff links, or a bow tie. In addition, a NutMobile traveled the country, visiting state fairs and festivals to distribute product samples and to allow visitors to take a virtual tour of milestones in Planters' history. The company's creative media kit for the celebration is highlighted in Chapter 6.

Creating a compelling special event is more art than science. However, reporter Anita Chabria of *PRWeek* says an event or a publicity stunt should do more than grab media coverage. She writes, "While their wacky or weird imagery may draw camera crews quicker than an interstate pile-up, the end result is that consumers receive a message about the brand identity."

Chabria offers three tips to public relations staffs:

1. Think about how the event will reflect on the brand identity and the message it will send to the consumers.

2. Create fun and engaging visuals for the media that will look good on camera.

3. Make sure you give the media a very clear idea of what those visuals will be in advance of the event.

Additional details about organizing and managing events are presented in Chapter 17.

FIGURE 4.4 Special events can also include publicity stunts. Hershey's celebrated the 100th anniversary of its Kisses Chocolate brand at a gala event in which it unveiled the world's largest piece of chocolate. The 12-foot-high structure weighing 30,540 pounds was certified by *Guinness Book of Records* representative Jane Boatfield (left) who attended the unveiling.

Contests

The contest is a common device for creating news. In fact, it is often advised that "if all else fails, sponsor a contest." There are contests of every kind. At the local level, the American Legion sponsors high-school essay contests on citizenship, and Ford Dealers enthusiastically sponsor safe-driving contests for teenagers. There are also numerous Elvis look-alike contests, tractor pulls, beauty pageants, and eating contests.

> " *The hardest thing is to convince the media that your contest or sweepstakes is going to deliver real informational interest as opposed to pure commercialism.* "
>
> ■ Julie Hall, Vice President of Schneider & Associates

Here are some examples of creative contests:

- Kimberly-Clark, as a way of promoting its toilet tissue as a tie-in with the Super Bowl (described earlier), sponsored an essay contest on the topic of "Share Your Cloggiest Moment," in which the winner received $25,000 to "Flush Your Worries Away."
- Procter & Gamble, to generate interest in its antiperspirant as being a "hot" product, enlisted Jennifer Lopez to launch "Secret's Show Us Your Moves" in a nationwide casting call to find a female dancer to appear in her upcoming video.
- Tommy Hilfiger sponsored a contest with By Kids for Kids for the "Signature Style Challenge," giving a $10,000 prize to the young person with the best sketch and explanation of a fashion idea.
- Martinique, an island in the Caribbean, sponsored a travel essay contest among bloggers, with the winner receiving a complete expense-paid vacation to the French island.
- Google announced a $20 million prize for the first team that builds a privately funded spacecraft and lands it on the moon by 2012.
- Since 1998, Intel has sponsored the annual Intel Science Talent Search competition that encourages high school students in the sciences. Forty high school seniors are named as finalists, and the top winner receives a $100,000 scholarship.

Publicists and organizations, however, are warned that sponsoring a contest takes a great deal of planning and legal considerations. David Ward, a reporter for *PRWeek*, gives these tips:

DO

- Get your planning done early. There are a lot of regulations and details.
- Get some well-known celebrities involved to establish credibility and interest with the media.
- Think local, especially when you get down to finalists. Most outlets love stories on locals who do well.

DON'T

- Go it alone. Hire experts to help you run the contest or sweepstakes.

- Worry about the size of the prize. Even million-dollar prizes don't attract media attention.
- Go to media too often unless they are cosponsors. The same outlet won't cover the launch, the finalists, and the winner. Spread various angles around to various media.

Polls and Surveys

The media seem to be fascinated by polls and surveys of all kinds. Public opinion is highly valued, and much attention is given to what the public thinks about issues, lifestyles, political candidates, product quality, and so on.

Author Peter Godwin, writing in *The New York Times Magazine*, says the public's fascination with polls and surveys is "a uniquely American trait—a weakness for personal comparative analysis." He continues, "It's the reason we devour surveys about success, weight, love, family and happiness. And why not? Political polls tell us only how one candidate is faring against another. Polls about other people's personal lives let us gauge how we're faring relative to our friends and neighbors."

Given this media and public interest, many organizations are willing to oblige by conducting polls and surveys on a range of topics. Larry Chiagouris and Ann Middleman, in a *Public Relations Quarterly* article, say that "publicity-driven research" is one of the most effective ways for an organization to get media coverage and position itself as a market leader. In addition, surveys have high credibility because quantitative data is perceived as accurate.

Some journalists, however, are more cynical about the use of surveys to get media attention. John Kay, a columnist for the *Financial Times*, writes "This is the age of the bogus survey. . . . Public relations professionals understand these triggers, to such an extent that commissioning a bogus survey is now a standard element in the pitch they present to prospective clients."

Here are some examples of polls or surveys that have generated media coverage:

- Cheapflights.com (www.cheapflights.com) conducted a survey on its blog site about airplane etiquette. It found that 2,000 respondents thought the incessant talker was the most offensive behavior. Ranking a close second was the person who immediately reclines his or her seat—into your lap. Third was the arm rest hog, which tied with the carry-on luggage champ who tries to stuff suitcases in the overhead rack.
- Rand-McNally, celebrating its 150th anniversary, commissioned a survey that found, among other things, that respondents would like most to share a family road trip with Chevy Chase. The survey also found that the top road disagreement was personal space and seating arrangements.
- Securian Dental conducted the "Tooth Fairy Poll" among its clients and found that the U.S. children received an average of $2.09 per tooth from the Tooth Fairy, which was a 22 percent increase from the previous year's average of $1.71. The results were also localized; a release for Minnesota showed that children received an average of $2.10 per tooth, a 44 percent increase from $1.46 the previous year.

- Blue Rhino, a supplier of propane gas to outdoor grills, conducted a survey of 2,000 men and women to name their favorite grilling song. The number one song was "Cheeseburger in Paradise" by Jimmy Buffet, but "Ring of Fire" by Johnny Cash also was popular.

Many surveys, including some of those just mentioned, aren't very scientific. *Food & Wine* magazine once conducted an online survey and announced to the world that the supermarket checkout line is the most popular choice for where to meet a mate. It also found, in its admittedly unscientific poll, that whipped cream is the sexiest food but that chocolate mousse is better than sex.

Even the prestigious American Medical Association (AMA) has publicized the results of dubious surveys. The AMA reported, for example, that 92 percent of college-aged women participating in an online survey said it was easy to get alcohol on a spring-break trip, and that 20 percent of them regretted the sexual activity they engaged in during spring break. An AMA spokesperson admitted to *The Wall Street Journal* that the organization used the online poll, in which women self-selected themselves to participate, to merely call attention to the dangers of excessive alcohol consumption and high-risk sexual behavior on spring breaks. And it worked. Since the survey had an element of sex in it, the media found it newsworthy.

Nancy Hicks, a senior vice president of Hill & Knowlton, says surveys and polls can be marvelous publicity opportunities if a few guidelines are followed. In an article for *PR Tactics*, she suggests:

- **The topic.** It should be timely, have news value, and fit the needs of the organization.
- **The research firm.** It should be one that has credibility with journalists. That's why many commissioned surveys are done by the Gallup Organization or similar nationally known firms.
- **The survey questions.** They should be framed to elicit newsworthy findings.

Hicks also suggests paying attention to how the material is packaged for the press. "The lead in the news release should feature the most newsworthy findings, not what is of most interest to the sponsoring organization," says Hicks.

Media kits, discussed in Chapter 6, should include background information on the organization and on the research firm, a summary of the major research findings, and simple charts and graphs that can be easily reproduced as part of a news story. See the Tips for Success on page 111 for more information on how to conduct and report the results of a survey or poll.

Top 10 Lists

A good alternative to polls and surveys is to simply compile a "Top 10 List." Fashion trade groups announce the "Top 10 Best Dressed Women," and environmental groups compile lists of the "Top 10 Polluters." Newspapers and magazines also get into the act by compiling a list of the "Top 10 College Basketball Players" or the "Top 10 Newsmakers" of the year.

How to Conduct a Credible Survey

A survey of topical interest can generate considerable publicity for an organization. Mark A. Schulman, president of a market research and opinion polling firm in New York, offers these tips in an article for *O'Dwyer's PR Report*:

- Choose a topic that captures the interest of key targets and the media.
- Results must not appear to be self-serving. Journalists look for balance. Don't shy away from some negative findings.
- Find the story hook in advance by doing some preliminary research, often focus groups.
- Choose a sample size that will be credible. Don't skimp on sample size and undercut the project's appeal to media outlets. Sample the appropriate target groups.
- Put a human face on the percentages. Sprinkle some respondent quotes into the report.
- Plan your media strategy at the beginning of the process, not as an afterthought. Build excitement in the survey by including in the press kit some additional background material and sources to help the press build the story. Provide a list of outside experts who can be interviewed.
- Provide key press contacts with an advance peek in exchange for premium coverage.
- Don't sit on your data. Release it quickly. News events can make even the best study stale.
- Release all the results, not just the ones that are favorable to your client.
- Guidelines for release of survey results are issued by the American Association for Public Opinion Research (www.aapor.org) and the Council of American Survey Research Organizations (www.casro.org). You should always include information on the method of interview, the number of people interviewed, dates, and the exact question wording. Journalists may not use this information in their stories, but it gives them confidence that the survey findings are credible. ■

Briggs & Stratton, a leading manufacturer of lawnmowers and other outdoor power equipment, builds its brand identity with an annual list of the "Top 10 Lawns in America." And the American Kennel Club gets publicity for announcing the 10 top dog breeds in the United States based on AKA registrations of purebred dogs. The Labrador retriever has been the most popular dog in the United States for a number of years, but the Yorkshire terrier is now in the number two spot, beating out the golden retriever and the German shepherd.

There are endless possibilities for top 10 lists. The California Association of Winegrowers issued a news release on Earth Day, for example, giving the "Top 10 Reasons California Wines Are an Eco-Friendly Choice." A San Francisco public relations firm even got 8 inches in *The Wall Street Journal* for its "Top 10 Most Humiliating Public Relations Gaffes of the Year." First place went to the District of Columbia Housing Authority, which issued a news release about a drug bust the night before the raid was planned. The dealers heard about it on the radio and failed to make an appearance.

Product Demonstrations

The objective of a product demonstration is to have consumers or media representatives actually see how a product performs. Auto manufacturers do "product demonstrations" by inviting journalists to test-drive a new model. Hotels and resorts invite travel writers to spend a weekend at the facility. Food companies do demonstrations by getting representatives on cooking and home shows. Weber Grills, for example, hired a well-known chef to give tips on talk shows about the proper way to barbecue.

A cosmetic company, Styli-Style, introduced its newly designed flat makeup pencil at a New York champagne bar. It hired a celebrity makeup artist to demonstrate the various colors and to also apply makeup to the various journalists and guests attending the event.

Another kind of makeup was done by PetSmart, a pet-supply chain. PetSmart publicized a grand opening of a store by offering its pet grooming services to some of the local Humane Society's grubbiest guests and then putting them on display for adoption. It was a win-win situation. The idea clearly demonstrated the value of its grooming services and also placed the new store in a favorable light because of its community outreach. Even a television news reporter covering the event took a dog home after his wife saw a made-over mutt on television.

On occasion, a product demonstration is built around a press junket. Procter & Gamble introduced its new Head & Shoulders HydraZinc shampoo by taking editors to Arizona where they could experience the benefits of the zinc-rich desert landscape. Briefings included a celebrity stylist and a P&G research scientist to highlight the benefits of the HydraZinc formula. According to *PRWeek*, "Zinc-rich foods were also served during dinner and a customized spa treatment allowed editors to discover the healing powers of zinc." The results were articles about the new shampoo in such publications as *Elle*, *Shape*, and *Redbook*.

Blendtec, a manufacturer of blenders, took a viral video approach to a product demonstration. The company's marketing director made several 1-minute videos showing its blender pulverizing such items as a 12-pack of Coke, a white lab coat, and even a golf club; he then posted the videos on the company's website and on YouTube. He also posted the videos on Digg (www.digg.com), a bookmarking site where readers rank content. The "Will it blend?" videos were a big hit and, according to Ragan.com (www.ragan.com), an online public relations newsletter, the videos have been viewed by more than 100 million people. The popularity of the videos on YouTube and Digg prompted the *Today* show to invite the company president to demonstrate the Blendtec by using it to create a "Cochiken" (Coca-Cola and half a chicken, bones and all).

Stunts

Journalists often disparage publicity stunts, but, if they are highly visual, they often get extensive media coverage. One popular theme is doing something that qualifies for the *Guinness World Records*. Thus, newspapers print photos and television stations use video clips of "the world's largest quiche Lorraine," "the world's largest apple pie," "the world's largest ice cream cake," or even "the world's longest salad bar."

Baskin-Robbins made the world's largest ice cream cake (5.5 tons) in one of the hottest spots on earth, Dubai, to celebrate International Ice Cream Month. Hidden Valley Ranch salad dressings sponsored the world's longest salad bar in New York's Central Park. It took 17,000 pounds of vegetables to make the salad, which, of course, was topped with Hidden Valley's Original Ranch dressing.

" You need something that is fun and irresistible to get people's attention. "

■ Kathy Carliner, Senior Vice President of Golin Harris

Hershey's, mentioned earlier, received a certificate from the *Guinness Book of Records* for constructing the world's largest Chocolate Kiss to celebrate its 100th anniversary. The 12-foot tall chocolate, shown on page 107, weighed 30,540 pounds. In contrast, Israeli manufacturer Modu made the *Guinness Book of Records* by making the world's lightest mobile phone. It weighs 1.4 ounces.

Other kinds of stunts can be staged with a bit of creative thinking. A German software firm, for example, celebrated its listing on the New York Stock Exchange by converting a block of New York's financial district into a "beach party." It took 60 tons of sand, 5,000 beach balls, and several volleyball nets to accomplish the transition. Because of the visual element, the company received more extensive coverage than just a short paragraph on the business page. Another creative stunt was an ice golf tournament sponsored the Canadian Tourist Commission (see Figure 4.5).

▶ **FIGURE 4.5** Ice golf anyone? The Canadian Tourism Commission turned the frozen pond at Bryant Park in New York City into a golf course as part of a publicity stunt to promote Canada. While two Canadian Mounties watch, a contestant tees off in an effort to win a two-carat Polar Bear Canadian Diamond worth about $40,000.

A stunt done by upscale stores, such as Neiman Marcus, is listing over-the-top gifts in the annual Christmas catalogue. One year, Neiman Marcus offered a $7,000, 44-inch high "crystal case" dog house with a mini armchair of Italian leather. It didn't sell, but the item generated media coverage worth millions for the store. Victoria's Secret advertises a jewel-encrusted bra every Christmas for about $3 million, but only one has ever been sold.

Rallies and Protests

A rally or protest generates news because one of the traditional news values, discussed earlier, is conflict. Some rallies involve thousands of protestors, such as a series of rallies throughout the United States to protest proposed legislation restricting the legal status of Hispanic immigrants. On a more modest scale, even a group of local high school students holding a rally protesting the firing of a favorite coach generates media interest.

Other groups use demonstrations as a tactic to publicize their cause. The Save Darfur Coalition, for example, organizes small groups of protestors to "picket" the offices of financial institutions and corporations that have investments in Sudan. They carry signs about companies condoning genocide and show graphic photos of victims (see Figure 4.6).

Few television stations or newspapers can resist covering such rallies or protest demonstrations, each of which has high news value from the standpoint of human interest and conflict. Moreover, a rally or protest is highly visual, which is ideal for television coverage and newspaper photographs.

Although television often gives the impression that demonstrations are somewhat spontaneous events, the reality is that they are usually well planned and organized. The manuals of activist groups, for example, give guidelines on everything from contacting potential participants via an e-mail network to appointing "marshals" who will assure that the protestors won't destroy property or unnecessarily provoke police confrontations. The idea is to make a statement, not create a riot that will damage the organization's cause.

When planning a protest or demonstration, the media should be contacted in advance to ensure coverage. More than one rally has been rescheduled to

FIGURE 4.6 Protests and demonstrations are highly visible and involve conflict, a traditional news value. The Save Darfur Coalition, as part of its tactics to promote its cause, holds protests at the offices of financial institutions and corporations doing business in Sudan.

accommodate the media. Prominent people and celebrities, if possible, should be asked to join the march or give a talk at a rally. Prominence, as activists know, is another important news value.

On a humorous note, Gillette capitalized on the media's tendency to cover protests. It organized a fake protest movement called the "National Organization of Social Crusaders Repulsed by Unshaven Faces (NoScruf)" to counter the trend of the unshaven look among young men. A group of young women were hired to do a mock demonstration in New York, complete with banners, bull horns, and fake underarm hair to give the message, "We won't shave until you do." The effect was so real that a CNN producer on his way to work called in a news crew to cover it.

Personal Appearances

Two kinds of personal appearances generate news. The first is the kind where the publicity is incidental to something else. The second is the appearance where the publicity is the only objective. Most typical of the first type is the situation where someone makes a speech to an organization. If the president of the XYZ Company addresses the local chamber of commerce, he will be heard by all who attend the meeting.

The audience for the speech, however, may be greatly increased if the media are supplied with copies of the speech, a news release, or several **soundbites**. As a general rule, every public appearance should be considered an opportunity for news both before and after the event. And, of course, there should always be an effort to get reporters to attend the meeting and get the story themselves.

Appearances where publicity is the sole objective take several forms. One is an appearance on a local radio or television talk show. There are numerous opportunities for appearing on such shows. For example, more than 1,000 radio stations (out of 10,000) in the nation now emphasize talk instead of music.

Talk shows with a national audience include *Meet the Press*, *Oprah Winfrey*, *Larry King Live*, and the *Today* show. The American Fly Fishing Trade Association (AFFTA), for example, scored a coup by getting on three major television shows in a 3-day period. First was the *Late Show with David Letterman*, where Sister Carol Anne Corley ("The Tying Nun") enlightened the host about some of the finer points of the sport. The next morning, two AFFTA representatives—clad in boots, waders, and vests—garnered prime time in front of the *Today* show window in New York's Rockefeller Plaza. Two days later, on the opening day of the trout fishing season, Estee Lauder model and fly-fishing instructor Karen Graham bellowed "Good morning, America" for the ABC cameras and gave a clinic for members of the media. Chapter 9 discusses how to get on such shows.

Another approach is the media tour. Increasingly, this is done via satellite and the Internet to save travel time and costs. The **satellite media tour (SMT)**, explained further in Chapter 9, is essentially the process of placing a spokesperson in a television studio and arranging for news anchors around the country to do a short interview via satellite. It is the same process that news programs use to get reports from their correspondents in the field.

Awards

Last, but not least, you can create news for your organization by giving and receiving awards. The California Pharmacists Association (CPhA), for example, inducts several outstanding pharmacists into its Hall of Fame every year at its state convention. By honoring these individuals, the organization also generates the opportunity to send a news release to the inductees' local newspapers, generating even more media coverage.

At the local level, there are awards given by any number of organizations. The YMCA honors the "Outstanding Woman of the Year," the chamber of commerce names the town's "Outstanding Business Owner of the Year," and even the local college honors the "Graduate of the Year" and the "Alumnus of the Year."

If an organization receives an award, that also can generate news. Intel, for example, sent out a news release announcing that it was ranked number one in the "100 Best Corporate Citizens" list by *CRO*, a magazine for corporate responsibility practitioners. The news release also noted that Intel has received more than 50 corporate social responsibility recognitions worldwide, including the "Most Responsible Multinational Corporation in China" from Beijing University.

At times, however, an award can be more hype than substance. The Hollywood Walk of Fame, sponsored by the Hollywood Chamber of Commerce, is somewhat suspect. The impression is that a celebrity gets a "star" embedded in cement because he or she has achieved something. The reality is that no "star" gets considered unless a film studio agrees to pay $15,000. In other words, the "award" often boils down to being part of a publicity campaign to bolster a star or promote an upcoming movie. One Hollywood publicist told *The Wall Street Journal*, "I've been in meetings where they say, 'We're going to have this poster, this outdoor campaign, and a Hollywood Boulevard star.'"

■ Summary

- A major objective of many public relations programs is to generate publicity for the employer or client.

- Publicity is not an end in itself. It is a means to help achieve organizational goals and objectives.

- Publicists should thoroughly understand the basic news values of (1) timeliness, (2) prominence, (3) proximity, (4) significance, (5) unusualness, (6) human interest, (7) conflict, and (8) newness.

- The first step in preparing publicity is to become thoroughly familiar with the company or organization through use of internal documents and interviews. Use of external sources, such as media coverage, also is recommended.

- A public relations writer should constantly monitor current events and situations that may affect the organization and provide opportunities for publicity.

- Problem-solving skills and creativity are required to generate publicity. One way to get creative ideas is through brainstorming with colleagues.

- Some tactics for generating news include (1) special events, (2) contests, (3) polls and surveys, (4) top 10 lists, (5) stunts, (6) product demonstrations, (7) rallies and protests, (8) personal appearances, and (9) awards.

- The satellite media tour and the cyber media tour are now used by organizations to book a spokesperson on a television or radio news program.

Skill Building Activities

1. A Japanese restaurant chain is celebrating its 25th anniversary next year. What activities and special events would you recommend to attract more customers and generate media coverage?

2. Surveys indicate that the topic of health generates a lot of media interest. How would a manufacturer of vacuum cleaners use this "hook" to generate some publicity for the company and its products?

3. A beer company is interested in doing some sort of poll or survey that would generate media coverage. What would you recommend?

4. An architectural firm likes the idea of creating a "Top 10 List." What ideas do you have for such a list?

5. A company is introducing a new, lightweight laptop computer that is "full" size but 2 pounds lighter than its competitors. How would you generate media interest and publicity for this new product?

6. Organize an in-class brainstorming session to generate ideas about how the women's soccer team at the university can get more media coverage. Alternatively, conduct a brainstorming session on how you would organize a campus campaign to make students more aware about the dangers of binge drinking.

Suggested Readings

Austin, Cathy. "Embracing Your Firm's Right Brain: Wake Up Your Creativity." *PR Tactics*, August 2007, p. 16.

Chabria, Anita. "Pulling a Stunt That Will Whip Up the Media." *PRWeek*, September 23, 2002, p. 22.

Chabria, Anita. "The Right Way to Seize the Day." *PRWeek*, December 3, 2001, p. 18.

Frank, John N. "Duck Tape Reaps Rewards of Sticking to Innovative PR Plan." *PRWeek*, August 5, 2002, p. 10.

Kay, John. "Research that Aids Publicists but not the Public." *Financial Times*, October 31, 2007, p. 6.

LaMotta, Lisa. "Launches Must be Products of Creativity." *PRWeek*, May 22, 2006, p. 30.

McKay, Betsy, and Vranica, Suzanne. "Firms Use Earth Day to Show Their Green Side." *The Wall Street Journal*, April 22, 2008, p. B7.

Newman, Andrew. "How Dictionaries Define Publicity: The Word of the Year." *The New York Times*, December 10, 2007, p. C5.

O'Connell, Vanessa. "It's the Publicity That Counts: Even Unsold, Over-the-Top Gifts Offer a Bonus for Retailers from Neiman Marcus to Sam's." *The Wall Street Journal*, November 17, 2006, pp. B1, B4.

Rich, Judith. "Waiting for Inspiration: Why You Need to Be Prepared to Be Inspired." *Strategist*, Spring 2007, pp. 12–13.

Schmelzer, Randi. "The Most Effective Use of Star Power." *PRWeek*, September 17, 2007, p. 22.

Schulman, Mark A. "PR Surveys Break Through the Clutter." *O'Dwyer's PR Services Report*, May 2002, p. 33.

Trickett, Eleanor. "Brainstorming Ideas for a New Campaign." *PRWeek*, November 18, 2002, p. 20.

Ward, David. "Tax Stories Can be Relevant Year-Round." *PRWeek*, March 24, 2008, p. 11.

Ward, David. "Designing a Contest to Win Media Attention." *PRWeek*, June 6, 2005, p. 20.

Werner, Bret. "Consumers Connect With Credible Celebrity Endorsements." *O'Dwyer's PR Services Report*, December 2007, p. 11.

Writing the News Release

5

TOPICS covered in this chapter include:

The Backbone of Publicity Programs   118

The Value of News Releases   119

Planning a News Release   119

Types of News Releases   122

Parts of a Traditional News Release   124

Writing the E-mail News Release   134

Preparing the Multimedia News
   Release   136

The Backbone of Publicity Programs

The basic news release, also called a **press release,** is the backbone of almost every publicity plan. There are, however, two sobering facts. First, various studies have found that between 55 and 97 percent of all news releases sent to media outlets are never used. Second, there is massive competition for the attention of reporters and editors.

Feature Photo Services, for example, estimates that daily newspaper editors receive about 2,000 news releases a day. Many come via snail mail, but the majority is now sent via e-mail and electronic distribution services such as Business Wire and PR Newswire. Each of these services distributes about 20,000 news releases a month to media outlets all over the world.

Given the odds, this means you must do three things if your release is to stand a chance of being published. First, you must follow a standardized format. Second, you must provide information that will interest the audience. And third, your material must be timely.

This chapter outlines how to prepare news releases that will meet these criteria. The focus is on writing the traditional news release, but many of the basic elements also apply to the formatting of news releases for electronic distribution via the Internet and the World Wide Web. It is pointed out, for example, that an e-mailed news release should be much shorter than a standard news release. In addition, this chapter will include information about the development of "smart" news releases that include everything from photos to videos and Internet links to various search engines and bookmarking sites. Chapter 9 will discuss how to prepare material for radio and television stations.

The Value of News Releases

So why write a **news release**? The primary reason, of course, is to help achieve organizational objectives. News releases, when they form the basis of stories in the news columns of newspapers and magazines or are part of a TV news hour, create awareness about ideas, situations, services, and products. A new product on the market, or an appeal for Red Cross blood donations, is brought to the attention of the public. A manufacturer of a potato-chip maker, for example, sold out its entire stock after *The New York Times* included parts of a news release in an article about new kitchen gadgets.

> ❝ *A recent survey of journalists by Atlanta PR firm Arketi Group found news releases are used by 90 percent of business journalists as sources for story ideas.* ❞ ■ Craig McGuire, *PRWeek*

News releases are also cost-effective. Almost any organization, from a garden club to IBM, can create and distribute news releases at nominal cost compared to the cost of buying advertising. There is also the factor of credibility. News releases appear in the news columns of newspapers, and studies consistently show that people consider information in a news story to be much more believable than an advertisement.

In one such study, the Wirthlin Group surveyed a sample of 1,023 adults. Almost 30 percent of the respondents said that a news article would affect their buying decisions, whereas only 8 percent indicated that an advertisement would. In another study reported by eMarketer, it was found that consumers buying electronic products and automobiles were most influenced by "reading articles on product" compared to a variety of other media, including direct mail, in-store promotions, and other traditional advertising channels.

Planning a News Release

Writing a news release requires the tools and equipment described in Chapter 1. The following sections discuss the selection of paper, some fundamentals about word processing a release, and the style you should follow. But before writing anything, the public relations writer should complete a planning worksheet.

The Basic Questions

Your planning worksheet should answer the following questions:

- What is the subject of the message? What is the specific focus of this release?
- Who is this message designed to reach? For example, is it aimed at local citizens, or is it mainly for executives in other companies who read the business page and might order the product?
- What is in it for this particular audience? What are the potential benefits and rewards?

- What goal is the organization pursuing? What is the organization's purpose? Is it to increase sales of a product? Position the company as a leader in the field? Show company concern for the environment?

- What do you want to achieve with the news release? Is the objective to inform, to change attitudes and behavior, or to increase attendance at a local event?

- What key messages should this news release highlight? How can they be tailored to the format of a specific publication and its readers?

These questions enable you to select and structure the content of a news release from a public relations perspective. The release can still meet the journalistic goal of presenting information objectively and in correct newspaper or broadcast style, but it must also be carefully crafted to include key messages. This kind of planning is the major difference between writing as a journalist and writing as a public relations professional.

At the same time, however, you must think like a journalist. In terms of format and content, a news release should be the same thing as a news story. Many of the same rules apply, including the news values discussed in Chapter 4. Like a journalist, a public relations writer needs to include the five Ws and H: *who*, *what*, *when*, *where*, *why*, and *how*. If you have the answers to these questions at your fingertips, you are ready to begin.

Selection of Paper

The traditional news release in the United States, for the past century, has been written on letter-sized white paper measuring 8.5 by 11 inches. The paper should be 20- or 24-pound weight and designed for multiple purposes—inkjet printers, laser printers, plain-paper fax machines, and high-speed photocopy machines. In Europe and most of Asia, the standard letter size paper is A4—about 1 inch longer and a bit narrower than the U.S. letter size.

The use of colored paper for a news release does not get much support from experienced publicists, despite the logic that a colored release will stand out from the hundreds of releases that pile up in a newsroom. Most editors say that news value is the major factor—not the color of the paper. If color does strike your fancy, use pastel colors such as ivory, light blue, light green, or pale yellow. Don't use dark colors; they make words hard to read. The same goes for brilliant colors such as shocking pink, Day-Glo green, or bright yellow. The editor wants facts, not a rainbow.

At the same time, however, you should be alert to opportunities for some creativity. Amann & Associates, a Virginia-based public relations firm, sent news releases on light blue paper with a bottom border of colorful tropical fish because the client was Tetra Systems, a manufacturer of fish food. The approach was effective because the paper gave the effect of looking into an aquarium.

Spacing and Margins

Double-spacing is the standard for printed news releases distributed via fax or regular mail. Double-spaced copy is easier to read at the draft stage, and editors have traditionally found that the extra space allows them to do editing and rewrites.

FIGURE 5.1 This is the first page of a traditional news release prepared by Ketchum on behalf of its client, Aetna. The release is double-spaced, has a summary headline, and has the contact information of the Ketchum staffer working on the account.

Contact: Noelle Perillo
(202) 835-7289
noelle.perillo@ketchum.com

Parents: Are Your Grads Ready for the Real World?
National Survey Finds College Grads Likely to Fall through Gaps in Health Insurance Coverage

Aetna and the Financial Planning Association Help Parents of Upcoming College Grads

HARTFORD, Conn. — A new national survey finds as parents celebrate their child's graduation, they and their children may not be prepared for all the "real world" costs. When asked if their child had a medical emergency or needed health care while uninsured, only 44 percent of parents say they would pay for their child's health expenses, while 39 percent would offer to share the cost or teach their child how to take out a loan.

More than 1.4 million students will graduate from college this year – many of whom will no longer be eligible as dependents under their parents' health insurance plan, and may no longer qualify for the student plan provided by their alma mater. While parents want to be supportive, 40 percent admit that they do not have the tools and resources to help their children plan for their health benefits.

Aetna (NYSE: AET) and the Financial Planning Association® (FPA®) are helping parents do their homework to make smart health benefits and financial decisions – for themselves and for their children – through the *Plan for Your Health* public education program (www.PlanforYourHealth.com). *Plan for Your Health* is a free web resource for parents who are helping new grads with the transition between health plans, without becoming uninsured.

To find out what parents think about health benefits during this important transition, Aetna and FPA conducted a survey of parents of upcoming and recent college graduates to gauge their knowledge and concerns regarding their child's health benefits after graduation.

1

However, if you are distributing news releases via e-mail and the Internet, single-spacing is the standard format. You may electronically send a double-spaced news release to an electronic distributor such as Business Wire or PR Newswire, but it will be reformatted to single-spacing for distribution directly to a newspaper's computer. Editors, by calling up the news release or fact sheet on their computers, can change the format to anything they want.

In sum, if your news releases are mailed or faxed to a variety of publications, double-space them. If you are distributing them via e-mail and the Internet, single-space them. More details about e-mail news releases will be given later in the chapter.

Standard margins for a printed news release are 2 inches from the top of the page and about 1.5 inches from each side and the bottom of the page. If you have a letterhead, start writing copy about 2 inches below it. See Figure 5.1 for an example of a standard news release distributed by Ketchum on behalf of its client, Aetna.

Some other formatting rules for a printed news release are as follows:

- Use 10- or 12-point standard type. Courier and Times Roman are popular fonts because they are easy to read. Avoid "squeezing" copy to fit on one page by reducing the size of type: this is self-defeating.
- Don't split sentences or paragraphs between pages.
- Never hyphenate a word at the end of a line. Unjustified right margins are acceptable.
- Number the pages of a news release.
- Place a *slug line* (a short description) at the top of each page after the first one. This identifies the story in case the pages get separated.
- Write "more" at the end of each page if the news release continues.
- Write one of the old journalistic terms "-30-," "end," or "###" at the end of your news release.

Use AP Style

The *Associated Press Stylebook* is the standard reference for writing news releases because most American newspapers use "AP style" or some variation of it. If a news release conforms to AP style, it makes the work of reporters and editors much easier.

Lorry Lokey, founder of Business Wire, says that thorough knowledge of AP style helps tailor your news release to the person who ultimately decides if it is published. He says, "Editors are your customers, to put it bluntly; you are trying to sell them on your 'story.' Put roadblocks in their way via faulty style and they are likely to take their business to someone else's release."

Lokey also complains that public relations writers don't seem to notice that most newspapers keep paragraphs limited to fewer than six typeset column lines. Instead, far too many news releases have paragraphs that are 6 to 10 typed lines, the equivalent of 9 to 18 newspaper column lines. More aspects of style are discussed later in this chapter.

Types of News Releases

A news release can be prepared on virtually any subject that would affect or interest a general or specialized audience. Indeed, in the course of a year, an organization prepares and distributes news releases on a variety of subjects. There are five basic types of news releases, although the lines between them often blur. They are (1) announcements, (2) spot announcements, (3) reaction stories, (4) bad news, and (5) local news.

Announcements

Announcements herald such occurrences as personnel appointments, promotions, and changes; new products or services (if they are really new and interesting); reports of sales, earnings, acquisitions, mergers, events, awards, contests, policy changes, employment opportunities, anniversaries, price changes, new employees, layoffs, construction, openings and closings of facilities, contracts received (or canceled), and legal actions.

In general, it is a good idea for the highest-ranking person in the organization to make the announcement. As pointed out in Chapter 4, prominence is a news value. The president of a company making an announcement garners more news interest than a vice president or a department manager. However, when it comes to localizing news, the local plant manager is more prominent to the local press than the company president whose office is in a distant city.

Spot Announcements

When things due to some outside action or influence happen to an organization, a spot news release may be in order. When a storm disrupts the services of a public utility, a fire or an accident stops work, a flood closes roads, a strike closes a factory, or any other type of incident occurs, the organization can issue a release that tells what has happened and what effect it is having.

If the affected organization does not give the news to the media, reporters will write their own stories and may do a poor job because they don't have all the facts. In many cases, follow-up stories must be released later. These may carry additional detailed information and report on progress toward solving the problem.

Reaction Releases

Reaction releases are used when an event or situation has an impact on the organization. When the price of oil rose to record highs in 2008, a number of airlines, trucking firms, and delivery services issued news releases about how the price of gasoline was forcing them to charge higher prices for their services. In another situation, banks and mortgage companies issued news releases commenting on proposed federal legislation to stem the tide of foreclosures in the housing market.

Another use of the reaction release is to hitch on to a news event or public issue that, although not directly involving the organization, has some bearing on it. For instance, national restaurant chains issued news releases speculating on how a U.S. economic recession would affect future earnings if potential customers reduced their visits to restaurants.

Bad News

Some organizations suppress news that might reflect badly on them. This is a sure way to make things worse. People will talk, rumors will spread, and investigative reporters will take a major interest in exposing the "cover-up."

The only way to make the best of such a situation is to confront the issue. A release giving facts and the organization's point of view should be drafted immediately. If reporters ask for more information, it should be given to them.

Another approach is to bury bad news within a story. One corporation started a news release about its year-end results by reporting "progress in our strategic program by divesting companies outside our core consumer business." In the second paragraph, the company said it had declared dividends on preferred stock. The news that the company had a loss of $109 million didn't come until the second page, and it wasn't until the fourth page that the company said it was omitting its dividend on common stock.

This approach to reporting bad news may slip by some journalists, but most alert reporters will detect the clumsy attempt and make a mental note that all future company news releases should be taken with a grain of salt. As discussed in Chapter 3, a professional public relations writer should convince the company that such a news release is not only unethical, but also can violate state and federal regulatory agency guidelines.

Local News

The most common reason that news releases get used is the presence of a local angle, which was one of the strong news value mentioned in Chapter 4. Although many publications and broadcast outlets serve a national audience, the reality is that most media outlets serve local audiences.

A case in point is the *Grosse Pointe* (MI) *News*, a weekly newspaper serving an affluent suburb of Detroit. John Minnis, news editor of the paper, and Cornelius Pratt, a professor of public relations at Michigan State University, found that the newspaper received 189 news releases in a single week. Of that number, 65 (34 percent) were selected for publication. Overall, 57 percent of the releases printed were chosen for their local angle. The two researchers, who reported their findings in *Public Relations Quarterly*, concluded, "Location, location, location is the axiom of real estate agents. In public relations, it should be localization, localization, localization."

There are two ways to localize. One is to use the names of local people; the other is to use information that is of local significance. The computer makes it possible to easily alter a basic news release by inserting information that emphasizes the local angle. An example of this was how to "localize" the insurance award news release in Chapter 4.

The technique of "hometown" releases is used by many organizations. Colleges and universities, for example, often prepare individualized releases about entering freshmen for newspapers in their hometowns. The Defense Department sends releases about the positive accomplishments of enlisted men and women to their hometown media. In one recent year, the U.S. Navy prepared and distributed 1.13 million "hometown" releases.

Localizing information is another way to get releases published. An airline, for example, usually issues a quarterly summary giving the total number of passengers, the number of flights, and other statistical details. This information, by itself, does not have much local interest except in the city where the airline is headquartered. You can, however, gain more publicity by extracting local statistics from the general report. For example, the media outlets in Boise, Idaho, would get a "localized" release from the airline that would give the number of passengers boarding the plane in Boise and the most frequent destinations. The release might also give the number of flights per month out of Boise. The last part of the news release would give the airline's overall statistics.

Any number of state and national organizations also "localize" information. The National Association of Realtors, for example, may break down national statistics by city. Editors in Tucson get a release about the real estate market in their area, whereas media outlets in Dayton get another "localized" version.

Parts of a Traditional News Release

A news release has six basic components: (1) letterhead, (2) contacts, (3) headline, (4) dateline, (5) lead paragraph, and (6) body of text. A seventh element, often included at the end of a news release, is a short summary of the organization.

Letterhead

The first page of a news release is usually printed on an organization's letterhead. The letterhead gives the name of the organization, its complete address, and its telephone numbers, fax numbers, e-mail addresses, and even websites. If the organization does not have a letterhead, you should create an attractive template using Microsoft Office or similar software.

Many organizations tailor a letterhead specifically for news releases. The news release from Shedd Aquarium in Figure 5.2 is an example. In addition to giving the organizational information, the term "News Release" or something similar appears as part of the letterhead. The term "For Immediate Release" also appears near the letterhead of many releases, but many publicists say that this is just a tradition and not really necessary. New York public relations counselor Alan Hirsch told *Jack O'Dwyer's Newsletter*, "Using 'for immediate release' on any news announcement is extreme ignorance because the term is obsolete and has no meaning. Media don't hold up the news any more...."

That may be true in the age of instant global communication, but there are times that a writer will request a specific release time. For example, you may write: "For Release after 9 P.M. January 16." This often occurs when the release concerns a speech by someone or an award that is announced at a certain time.

The primary reason is that unplanned things happen. The speaker or award recipient, because of a plane delay or another emergency, may not show up. In such a case, the media would look foolish reporting a speech or an award that was never given.

At times, you may also wish to indicate that an advance news announcement is "embargoed" until the organization makes a formal announcement at a news conference. The idea behind this is that a particular news outlet won't "scoop" the opposition by broadcasting or publishing the announcement ahead of time. This approach, however, is risky unless you get an ironclad agreement by a news organization to honor your request. This is usually done *before*

News Release

For Immediate Release

Media Contacts:
Melissa Holland
Shedd Aquarium
312-692-3330
mholland@sheddaquarium.org

Emily Mason
Public Communications, Inc.
312-558-1770, ext. 136
emason@pcipr.com

THE KOMODO DRAGON, THE WORLD'S LARGEST LIZARD, MAKES FIRST-EVER APPEARANCE IN CHICAGO AT NEW MUST-SEE EXHIBIT

"Lizards and the Komodo King" Opens April 8 for a Limited Time at Shedd Aquarium

CHICAGO – From snakelike glass lizards to stocky Gila monsters, geckos that can curl up on a quarter to monitor lizards as long as a canoe, lizards come in a wild variety of shapes and sizes. And from the tiny day gecko to the world's largest lizard, the Komodo dragon, they'll all be at Shedd as part of a new must-see special exhibit, *Lizards and the Komodo King*, opening April 8.

There are more than 3,000 species of lizards in the world, each with unique and remarkable adaptations. Visit *Lizards and the Komodo King* and you'll learn why some lizards bark, eject their tails to evade predators, have "beards" and even use their tails to hang from treetops while they sleep. The basilisk can even walk on water! Enter this kingdom of lizards, where your hosts are spectacular creatures—some beautiful, some ferocious, but every one of them fascinating.

"All the animals in the exhibit will engage Shedd guests," said Mark Schick, collection manager at Shedd Aquarium. "They will learn the important role that lizards play in the environment, as well as how they are threatened in the wild by invasive species, unmanaged human development and the pet trade."

In *Lizards and the Komodo King*, guests can explore the world of lizards and learn through several interactive features, including a texture-rubbing station. They can even listen to recordings of geckos barking. This visual exhibit will connect you to more than 25 lizard species, including the crocodile monitor – the world's longest lizard – the bearded dragon, green tree monitor, caiman lizards, shield-tail agamas and much more.

"Lizards have so many bizarre characteristics and behaviors that our guests are constantly asking questions and crowding around the lizard habitats that we currently have on display, like the blue iguanas," said Schick. "We decided to feature *Lizards and the Komodo King* so guests could indulge their curiosity and learn about more about the textures, colors, forms and behaviors of these fascinating animals."

But the highlight of *Lizards and the Komodo King* is certainly Faust, the Komodo dragon. Shedd guests will come face to face with all 8 feet and 120 pounds of him. With his forked tongue, unbelievable size, and ability to take down water buffalo, Faust will show guests why the Komodo is a ferocious predator. Visitors will learn about Faust's razor-sharp teeth and toxic saliva, which harbors a dangerous mix of bacteria that cause deadly infections.

-more-

FIGURE 5.2 Many organizations use "news release" letterheads. This is the first page of a release from Shedd Aquarium about a lizard exhibit. This news release, single-spaced, was also included in an electronic media kit, which is discussed in Chapter 6.

you send them the advance news release or press kit. If they decline to honor your embargo, you then have the option of not sending them any advance information. In general, publicists use the embargo sparingly—usually in the case of announcing a major new product, a merger between two major companies, or a change in executive leadership.

Contacts

The contact person is listed directly after the letterhead. The contact person is often the writer of the news release, but it could also be the organization's director of public relations. Ideally, you should include the contact person's full name, title, telephone number, fax number, and e-mail address. In many cases, however, only a name, a telephone number, and an e-mail address are given.

An example is a news release sent by the St. Louis Convention & Visitors Commission. The top of the news release included the following:

For More Information:

Donna Andrews or Rebecca Rodgers

St. Louis Convention & Visitors Commission

314-421-1023 or pr@explorestlouis.com

If a public relations firm has prepared the release, the contact may be an account executive assigned to the account. If the news release is distributed nationally, or even internationally, it often is a good idea to also provide an after-hours number to accommodate time zone differences.

When a contact is given on a news release, it is assumed that he or she is qualified to answer any reporter inquiries about the subject of the news release. It is also important that the person be readily available to take phone calls and respond immediately to e-mail inquiries. Reporters often complain that the contact is impossible to reach, or doesn't seem to know anything more than what is already stated in the news release. So, if you are listed as a contact, make sure you are thoroughly prepared and can respond almost immediately. Many stories never see the light of day simply because a reporter couldn't reach a contact before the publication's deadline.

As a contact, however, you will often be busy with other projects and unable to just sit by the phone waiting for a call that may never come. If you are away from your phone, it is common practice to leave a voice-mail message that gives reporters on deadline your pager or cell phone number. Another approach is to give the caller the name and telephone number of another person who can be contacted in your absence.

Headline

Most news releases, particularly product-related ones, carry a brief headline. This usually appears in boldface and in a slightly larger type than that used in the body of the news release. Thus, if the body is in 12-point type, the headline often is in 14- or 16-point type.

The purpose of the headline is to give an editor or journalist a quick indication of what the news release is about. Headlines are supposed to give the "bottom line," the most newsworthy aspect of the story. Headlines should be factual, devoid of hype, and to the point.

Here are some examples:

Merck Develops New Drug for Asthma Sufferers

UFCW Members Reach Agreement with Grocers

Northwest Airlines Names Richard B. Hirst Senior Vice President

Increasingly, news releases include a second headline, known as a **subhead**. This provides additional key information to journalists and editors, because they scan virtually hundreds of news releases in a short amount of time. Here are some examples of using a subhead:

Intel Science Talent Search Finalists Announced

40 Young Scientists to Compete for $1.25 Million in Scholarships

The World Turns Out for World Wildlife Fund's Earth Hour

Over 400 Cities Participate in Historic Global Event to "Turn Off Lights"

Parents: Are Your Grads Ready for the Real World?

National Survey Finds College Grads Likely to Fall Through Gaps in Health Insurance Coverage

Note that these headlines are written in the active present tense. Avoid past tense; it gives the impression that the news item is not timely. If you do use a headline, place it two or three lines above the first line of the news release.

You should also notice that all of these examples have a single subject or focus. Media trainer Jerry Brown says, "One message is better than two. Two are usually better than three. If you have more than three messages for a story, you're not focused enough." This idea of a single message is explored further when we discuss lead paragraphs in a news release.

Dateline

The dateline, in all capital letters, appears at the start of the lead paragraph, which is discussed in the next section. The dateline is simply the city where the release originated, plus the date. You don't have to mention the state if the city is a major one, but smaller, more unfamiliar cities and towns usually include the state. For example, a news release might be datelined RICHMOND, VA, or MANCHESTER, NH, whereas one from CHICAGO or SAN FRANCISCO doesn't need a state because everyone knows the state in which they are located.

After the name of the city, the date of the release is often given. For example, a complete dateline would be as follows: ST. LOUIS—February 11, 2008. Global companies often use the day first, followed by the month and the year (28 April 2004). This sequence is used by almost every nation in the world except the United States, which has a tradition of using month, day, and year (April 28, 2004). By spelling out the month, the date is clear whether you use the U.S. style or the international method. If you simply write, "4/12/99," there can be confusion. Are you saying "April 12" (U.S.) or "December 4" (international sequence)?

Another approach to the dateline is simply to put the date on the release above the contact's name. If the release is being sent via one of the electronic newswires, such as Business Wire, the date and time of the distribution is automatically added to the release. Those who favor this approach say a date should not clutter up the lead paragraph.

The Lead

The most important part of any release is the lead paragraph. In one to three sentences, you must give the reader the basic details of the story or entice the reader to read the second paragraph. Marvin Arth, author of *The Newsletter Editor's Desk Book*, says the trick to good lead writing is to focus immediately on the most newsworthy or interesting point and to reserve other details until later in the story. In other words, keep a lead paragraph to no more than three to five lines.

Unfortunately, a common "sin" among organizations and public relations firms is to write leads crammed with too much information. The result is an elongated lead paragraph of 9 or 10 lines that tends to turn off journalists and readers because such a mass of words in one paragraph is visually unattractive to the average person.

> ❝ *Aside from the news item itself, the most important parts of a news release are the headline and the first paragraph.* ❞
> ■ Ron Consolino, columnist for the *Houston Chronicle*

There are two other common "sins." One is too much hype and the use of flowery adjectives. This is particularly true in the tourism and entertainment industry. One news release for a Caribbean resort had a lead paragraph that used such terms as "a hidden gem in paradise" with rooms featuring "breathtaking ocean views," "fabulous outdoor pools," and the "world's most incredible cave diving."

The second "sin" is a lead paragraph of 9 or 10 lines filled with techno babble. Here is an example:

> Applied Micro Circuits Corporation, a global leader in embedded Power Architecture processing, optical transport, and storage solutions, announced its two new versions of its successful family of Rubicon products that enable low cost Carrier Grade Ethernet services over Metro and Core SONET/SDH and OTN networks.

And that was only the first four lines of the eight-line lead paragraph.

Inexperienced writers, even those not writing a high-tech release, often clutter up a lead paragraph with unnecessary words and a tangle of information that is difficult to digest in. Here is an example:

> Medical Careers College is pleased to announce a Medical Career Education Expo to be held this Saturday, March 29, 2008, from 10 A.M. until 4 P.M. Both Richmond

campuses, South Side at 800 Moorehead Park Drive and West End at 2809 Emery-wood Parkway, will be participating in this exciting event.

This lead is cluttered in several ways. First, it's not necessary to give the year; this is assumed. Second, there are unnecessary "hype" words such as "pleased to announce" and "this exciting event." Third, two locations and addresses are given that would be better placed in a subsequent paragraph. See the following Tips for Success for a list of classic news release mistakes.

Clutter also occurs when a writer tries to put too many of the five Ws and H in the lead paragraph. The solution is to put only the most important element of the story in the lead paragraph. The other Ws, or the H, can be woven into the succeeding paragraphs. Here are examples of leads that emphasize only one element:

- **Who:** Recording artist Lisa Atkinson will lead a sing-along and entertain preschool children.

- **What:** "Fire, Earth, and Water," a major exhibit of pre–Columbian sculpture from the Land Collection, opens Friday.

✓ tips FOR SUCCESS

10 Classic News Release Mistakes

Alan Caruba, a public relations consultant and publicist for three decades, has prepared this list of 10 "Classic News Release Mistakes":

1. **Failure to provide a headline.** "It's a news story and headlines articulate the theme. Subheadlines, too, are useful."

2. **Boiler-plate.** "A first paragraph that jams in the client's name, their title, the company, its location, etc., while ignoring the primary theme of the release, kills it."

3. **Spelling and grammatical errors.** "Very harmful to any release because it suggests its writer is either uneducated or the release was not proofread."

4. **Punctuation errors.** "Because editors and reporters, as well as broadcast news personnel, make their living writing, these mistakes are 'red flags,' raising doubts about the source of the release."

5. **Hyperbole.** "The word from which we get the term 'hype' in which ordinary things are given extraordinary qualities. It's instantaneously recognizable, creating barriers to credibility."

6. **Documentation.** "Failure to attribute data to verifiable, independent sources diminishes credibility."

7. **Contacts.** "Failure to provide the names, phone and/or fax numbers of informed, articulate spokesperson(s) renders a release useless."

8. **Too long.** "The best releases are the briefest. Too much initial data can be a turn-off. If more is wanted, it will be requested."

9. **Localize.** "Whenever possible, 'localize' the release."

10. **Be accessible at all times.** "The best news release makes the media come to you. Opportunity ceases after the third ring of your phone." ■

- **When:** November 15 is the last date for filing claims for flood damage caused by . . . .
- **Where:** A golden retriever has won Best of Show honors at the 90th Golden Gate Kennel Club Dog Show.
- **Why:** Farnell of Britain will merge with Premier Industrial of Cleveland. The deal, valued at $2.8 billion, is an effort to consolidate the worldwide distribution of electronics equipment.
- **How:** Flextime, the system that permits employees to set their own starting and stopping times, has reduced labor turnover at Kellogg Enterprises by . . . .

Several types of leads are possible. They are the (1) straight summary lead, (2) the informal lead, and (3) the feature lead. The type of lead used often depends on the subject matter. If you are making an announcement, a straight summary lead is preferred. Here are some examples:

- Northwest Airlines today announced that Richard B. Hirst has been named senior vice president of corporate affairs and general counsel.
- More than 25,000 grocery workers in the Baltimore-Washington area represented by the United Food and Commercial Workers Union (UFCW) have reached a tentative agreement with Giant Foods and Safeway.
- The American Red Cross and the Greater Cleveland Business Planning Association (BEPA) will host a series of extreme crisis communications seminars, led by communications expert Bruce Hennes.
- Forty high school seniors today were named finalists for the Intel Science Talent Search. The competition, called the "junior Nobel prize," is America's oldest and most prestigious high school science competition.

The second type of lead is the informal lead, which often provides factual information but in a more informal way. Such leads are often used for publicizing community events or reporting the results of surveys, which are timely but not exactly "hard" news. Here are some examples:

- The sky will be ablaze with the crackle of scale-model machine-gun fire this weekend at the Hill Country Air Museum in Morgan Hill.
- A new national survey finds as parents celebrate their child's graduation, they and their children may not be prepared for all the "real world" costs. When asked if their child had a medical emergency or needed health care while uninsured, only 44 percent of parents say they would pay for their child's expenses, while 39 percent would offer to share the cost or teach the child how to take out a loan. (A news release from Aetna, an insurance company.)
- The results are in!!! The Tooth Fairy Poll from Securian Dental Plans reports an increase in the current average "gift" U.S. children receive from the Tooth Fairy. Children receive an average of $2.09 per tooth, which is up from last year's gift of $1.71—a 22 percent increase. Tooth Fairy gift amounts range from a low of five cents to a high of $50 per tooth.

The third type of lead is the feature lead, which raises the reader's interest. Essentially, the lead is a "hook" that encourages the reader to read the second paragraph for more information. Feature leads are often used for news releases that are sent to specialized sections of a daily newspaper, such as travel, auto, lifestyle, and food. These news releases, which are also discussed in Chapter 7, are topical but are not as time sensitive as announcement releases. Here are some examples:

- One hundred years ago, Italian immigrant Amedeo Obici "cracked the nut" on how to deliver fresh-tasting peanuts when he established Planters, known today as America's grandest nut company. This year, Planters marks 100 years of history, heritage, and delivering consistently fresh-tasting nuts with a year-long anniversary celebration.

- A trans–Atlantic trip to Naples, Italy, is no longer necessary to dine on the best lasagna, but instead can be found in Naples, Florida, at the namesake Italian restaurant, Naples Tomato.

- Things are getting green in St. Louis—and we're not talking about the foliage. St. Patrick's Day is practically upon us and the Gateway City is gearing up to celebrate its Irish heritage in grand style. In addition to "family ties" with sister cities Donegal and Galway, Ireland, St. Louis has a rich history and strong connection to the Emerald Isle—and we're not afraid to show it.

- What makes maps so hypnotic? Is it their endless detail that magically draws us in? The worlds of possibilities they offer as they take us on vicarious journeys? The connection to a moment in history? Their sometimes dazzling beauty? (News release from the Field Museum in Chicago on an exhibition of maps.)

The mechanics of a lead paragraph are relatively simple. Use strong declarative sentences, keep the number of dependent clauses to a minimum, keep it to five lines or less on your computer screen, and rewrite if any sentence comes out more than three lines long. All of this helps readers to grasp the key information quickly, even if they don't read the rest of the story. In addition, you should avoid the following pitfalls that lead to weak leads:

- **Prepositional phrases.** "At a meeting held in the . . ." or "For the first time in history . . ." These phrases, used at the beginning of a lead paragraph, tend to weaken the force of the sentence.

- **Participial phrases.** "Meeting in an atmosphere of confidence . . ."

- **Dependent clauses.** "That all high school students are required to . . ."

- **Clutter.** "Joe Gonzales, a veteran retailer and former mayor, at a meeting of the Chamber of Commerce to . . ." or "The XYZ Corporation is pleased to announce . . ."

Body of the Text

The lead paragraph is an integral and important part of the text. As such, it forms the apex of the journalistic "inverted pyramid" approach to writing. This means that the first paragraph succinctly summarizes the most important part of the story and succeeding paragraphs fill in the details.

There are three reasons for using the inverted pyramid structure. First, if the editor or reporter doesn't find something interesting in the first few lines, he or she won't use the story.

Second, editors often cut the length of an item, and they start at the bottom. In fact, Business Wire estimates that more than 90 percent of news releases published are edited to be much shorter than the original text. If the main details of the story are at the beginning, the release will still be understandable and informative even if most of it ends up in the trash basket.

A third reason for using this structure is that the public does not always read the entire story. Statistics show, for example, the average reader spends fewer than 30 minutes reading a metropolitan daily newspaper. This means that most readers read a lot of headlines, some beginning paragraphs, and a few stories in their entirety. If they read only the headline and the first paragraph, readers should get the main facts.

Once the lead is written, you must add information until the story is complete. Michael Ryan, professor of communication at the University of Houston, says a news release should have four basic paragraphs. His model is as follows:

Paragraph 1

a. Most important facts of release

b. Attribution, less essential information

Paragraph 2

a. Essential background material, names of key characters or sources, a second important element

b. Names of secondary characters or sources

Paragraph 3

a. Elaboration on material in paragraph 1

b. Background material, attribution

Paragraph 4

a. Most important material in sentence

b. Background material, attribution

This model does not mean that all news releases should be four paragraphs long. Ryan points out that there could be several paragraphs of the same kind in a news release. For example, your particular news release may require more background or include several important and interesting supporting quotations. Thus, in order to tell the story fully, you may use several "3" paragraphs.

The basic idea, however, is to use a structure that enables you to write a succinct news release that includes all the important and interesting information. There is no rule that news releases should be a specific length, but most writers strive to tell their stories in one or two pages, or fewer than 400 words. Space and time are always a premium in the news business, so reporters appreciate news releases that are short and to the point.

The body of the news release should also include your employer or client's stock symbol and stock exchange if it is a publicly traded company. For example, the lead sentence from an airline started as follows: "Northwest Airlines (NYSE:NWA) today announced . . ."

Lorry Lokey of Business Wire says that this is a good idea if you are distributing news releases electronically, because the full text is sent to more than 300 databases and Internet news systems. These databases often use the stock symbol as a way of indexing information about companies and industries. It is also a good idea to include an organization's website and major e-mail address somewhere in the news release so reporters, and even customers, can easily access important background information.

Description of the Organization

Many news releases will include a standard paragraph at the end to give some basic information about the company so reporters get some idea about the organization's size and purpose. This standard paragraph is often called **boiler-plate** in the jargon of the field.

Other supplemental information at the end of a news release might include a listing of trademarked names used in the release. This alerts the reporter to what products and services must be capitalized. Thus, there will be a notation such as "Windows is a U.S. registered trademark of Microsoft Corp."; this notation was discussed in Chapter 3. Here are some examples of boiler-plate:

About Visa

Visa operates the world's largest retail electronic payments network providing processing services and payment product platforms. This includes consumer credit, debit, prepaid and commercial payments, which are defined under Visa, Visa Electron, Interlink, and PLUS brands. Visa enjoys unsurpassed acceptance around the world and Visa/PLUS is one of the world's largest global ATM networks, offering cash access in local currency in more than 170 countries. For more information, visit www.corporate.visa.com.

About Google, Inc.

Google's innovative search technologies connect millions of people around the world with information every day. Founded in 1998 by Stanford Ph.D. students Larry Page and Sergey Brin, Google today is a top web property in all major global markets. Google's targeted advertising program provides businesses of all sizes with measurable results, while enhancing the overall web experience for users. Google is headquartered in Silicon Valley with offices throughout the Americas, Europe, and Asia. For more Information, please visit www.google.com. Google, Google Apps. Google Docs, Google Calendar, and Google Talk are registered trademarks of Google, Inc.

About Intel

Intel, the world leader in silicon innovation, develops technologies, products, and initiatives to continually advance how people work and live. Additional information about Intel is available at www.intel.com/pressroom and blogs.intel.com. Intel and the Intel logo are trademarks of Intel Corporation in the United States and other countries.

See the Tips for Success on page 135 for a list of tips on how to write an effective news release.

■ Writing the E-mail News Release

The traditional news release, double-spaced on an 8.5- by 11-inch page, is still used by many publicists despite pronouncements that "The traditional news release is dead." One only needs to review the stacks of news releases that still arrive by snail mail at newspaper offices around the country, or even the media kits (discussed in Chapter 6) that are still being produced in paper form. As one publicist explains, "Our job is to offer the information in any format that the journalist or media outlet desires." For example, if you visit a corporate newsrooms on the Web you will find any number of traditional news releases posted on the site that can be downloaded by journalists and the public.

It's now widely recognized, however, that the news release format has changed somewhat to better fit distribution via e-mail or an electronic distribution service. The basic components of the traditional news release are still present, but one no longer needs to double-space the copy. A second major change is length. The traditional standard is fewer than 400 words, but the new standard for an e-mail release is fewer than 200 words and only four or five paragraphs. The goal is brevity so that journalists can see most of the news release on one screen and don't have to scroll. If a journalist has hundreds of e-mails in his or her inbox, scrolling becomes a real chore. The Intel news release in Figure 5.3 shows the standard format of an e-mail release.

February 20, 2008 08:00 AM Pacific Time

Intel Tops Corporate Citizen List

SANTA CLARA, Calif.–(BUSINESS WIRE)–Intel Corporation took the No. 1 spot in this year's "100 Best Corporate Citizens" list. Released today by CRO Magazine (stands for corporate responsibility officer), the list has gained national recognition as an indicator of best practices in the area of corporate responsibility.

The list identifies companies that best combine business objectives with responsible practices across eight categories: environment, climate change, human rights, employee relations, corporate governance, lobbying, philanthropy and financial performance. Rankings are based on research and analysis by IW Financial, and the companies are drawn predominantly from the Russell 1000 Index. Intel has been in the top 20 on the list since its inception 9 years ago.

"At Intel, we define success not only by our business performance, but how we transform the world in which we live and work," said William A. Swope, corporate vice president and general manager of Intel's Corporate Affairs Group. "We invest a great deal of effort and resources toward corporate responsibility and have high expectations for ethical conduct in all parts of our business. This recognition is a testament to the ongoing work and commitment of our employees worldwide."

Intel's approach to global citizenship includes an annual $100 million commitment to improving education around the world and a long-term commitment to sustainability in its operations and in its products. In fact, in the past year Intel produced 45-nanometer chips that deliver industry-leading energy-efficient performance and come from the most advanced manufacturing process incorporating environment-conscious lead- and halogen-free design. Additionally, the company recently topped EPA's Green Power Partner List by becoming the largest purchaser of renewable energy credits in the United States.

In 2007, Intel received more than 50 corporate social responsibility recognitions world-wide including the U.S. EPA 2007 Water Efficiency Leader award for reducing, reusing and recycling water; the Most Responsible Multinational Corporation in China from Beijing University; the Supersector Leader for Technology by the Dow Jones Sustainability Index and the Corporate Knights/Innovest's list of the "100 Most Sustainable Corporations in the World." More information about Intel's efforts can be found at intel.com/go/responsibility.

CRO is the only membership media platform for corporate responsibility practitioners. CRO publishes 'CRO' Magazine, TheCRO.com, bi-weekly e-newsletters, webinars and produces the four-time-annual CRO Conferences. More details regarding the 100 Best Corporate Citizens list are available at www.TheCRO.com.

About Intel

Intel, the world leader in silicon innovation, develops technologies, products and initiatives to continually advance how people work and live. Additional information about Intel is available at www.intel.com/pressroom and blogs.intel.com.

Intel and the Intel logo are trademarks of Intel Corporation in the United States and other countries.

Contacts

Intel Corporation
Christine Dotts, 480-554-7959
christine.dotts@intel.com

▶ **FIGURE 5.3** This release from Intel Corporation is the standard format for an e-mail release sent to editors and posted on the corporation's Web newsroom. It is one page, single-spaced, and includes a short description of the organization at the end. Note that the contact information is at the end of the release instead of the beginning, as in the traditional news release.

Rules for Writing a News Release

All news releases should be "news centered" according to Schubert Communications, a Pennsylvania public relations firm. Lisa Barbadora, director of public relations and marketing content for Schubert, gives these rules for writing news releases:

- Use short, succinct headlines and subheads to highlight main points and pique interest. They should not simply be a repeat of the information in the lead-in paragraph.

- Do not use generic words and phrases such as "the leading provider" or "world-class" to position your company. Be specific, use phrases such as "with annual revenues of."

- Do not describe products using phrases such as "unique" or "total solution." Use specific terms or examples to demonstrate the product's distinctness.

- Use descriptive and creative words to grab an editor's attention, but make sure they are accurate and not exaggerated.

- Do not highlight the name of your company or product in the headline of a news release if it is not highly recognized. If you are not a household name, focus on the news instead.

- Tell the news. Focus on how your announcement affects your industry and lead with that rather than overtly promoting your product or company.

- Critique your writing by asking yourself, "who cares?" Why should readers be interested in this information?

- Do not throw the whole kitchen sink into a release. Better to break your news into several releases if material is lengthy.

- Do not use lame quotes. Write like someone is actually talking—eliminate the "corporatese" that editors love to ignore. Speak with pizzazz to increase your chances of being published.

- Target your writing. Create two different tailored releases that will go out to different types of media rather than a general release that isn't of great interest to either group.

- Look for creative ways to tie your announcement in to current news or trends.

- Write simply. Use contractions, write in active voice, be direct, avoid paired words like "clear and simple," and incorporate common action-oriented phrases to generate excitement. Sentences should be no longer than 34 words.

- Follow the *Associated Press Stylebook* and specific publications' editorial standards for dates, technical terms, abbreviations, punctuation, spellings, capitalization, etc.

- Do not use metaphors unless they are used to paint a clearer picture for the reader.

- Do not overdo it. It's important to write colorfully, to focus on small specific details, to include descriptions of people, places, and events, but do not write poetry when you want press.

- Do not be formulaic in your news release writing. Not every release must start with the name of the company or product. Break out of the mold to attract media attention.

- Do not expect editors to print your entire release. Important information should be in the first two paragraphs.

- Make it clear how your announcement is relevant for the editors' readers. ■

The traditional news release has a headline, which has been discussed, but an e-mail news release must also have a subject line that identifies exactly what the news release is about. If the subject line is vague or dull, there's no incentive for the recipient to open it. B. L. Ochman, writing in *The Strategist*, suggests that you should "Think of the electronic news release as a teaser to get a reporter or editor to your website for additional information." He makes the following additional suggestions:

- Use bullets to convey key points.
- Write only two or three short sentences in each of the five paragraphs.
- Above the headline, or at the bottom of the release, be sure to provide a contact name, phone number, e-mail address, and URL for additional information.
- Never send a release as an attachment. Journalists, because of possible virus infections, rarely open attachments unless they know and trust the source.

Ochman concludes, "Write like you have 10 seconds to make a point. Because online, you do."

Preparing the Multimedia News Release

The major change in the evolution of the humble news release is the advent of the multimedia release, which has also been dubbed the "smart media release" (SMR). These releases, pioneered by the major electronic distribution services, such as Business Wire, PR Newswire, and Marketwire, now make it possible to embed a news release with high-resolution photos/graphics, video, and audio components. In addition, these services have teamed up with search engines such as Google, Yahoo!, and MSN to promote maximum exposure of the news release through search engine optimization. An example of a "smart" release is shown in Figure 5.4.

May 26, 2008 10:15 AM Pacific Daylight Time

Creator of Beloved Military Mascots Presents Nation With Original Painting by Famed Artist Stewart Moskowitz

SAN DIEGO--(BUSINESS WIRE)--Diann Wall-Wilson, creator of the official mascot of the U.S. Marine Corps and the beloved mascots of the U.S. Army, Navy, Air Force and Coast Guard, accompanied by Paul Shiffman, her associate, presented the nation with an original painting by world renowned artist Stewart Moskowtiz at a Memorial Day ceremony held in the White House Gift Shop in Washington, D.C.

The painting, entitled "United Stars of America," depicts a large American flag on which are emblazoned the five mascots of the five branches of the U.S. military. Commissioned by Wall-Wilson, the painting is a tribute to the men and women who across two centuries have bravely and honorably served the country.

According to Wall-Wilson, "This painting is my way of paying tribute to the country and the men and women who have sacrificed so much for it. I hope that this token of my appreciation will give pleasure to all who see it and remind them of the courage and dedication of our armed forces and the role they play in protecting and preserving our rights as a free people."

Wall-Wilson went on to say, "I asked Stewart Moskowitz to execute this painting because I know of no one better equipped or who has a greater love for his country."

Moskowitz is a well-known American poster artist whose works are enjoyed around the world. Plans call for his latest work to be released to the public in the form of a limited edition print (www.militarycreationsllc.com).

Contacts

for Military Mascots, Inc.
Paul Shiffman
818-223-8969
pshiffman@gbcglobal.net

Smart Multimedia Gallery

Graphic
A loving tribute to the U.S. Armed Forces, the limited edition print was unveiled at a special Memorial Day Ceremony held at the White House Gift Shop by Diann Wall-Wilson, creator of the official mascot of the U.S. Marine Corp and the beloved mascots of the Army, Navy, Air Force and Coast Guard. (Graphic: Business Wire)

FIGURE 5.4 This "smart" news release was distributed by Business Wire, an electronic news distribution firm. The release includes a high-resolution graphic that can be downloaded by editors to accompany the story. Other "smart" releases may include videos, audio, and hyperlinks to other websites.

Michael Lissauer, executive vice president of Business Wire, told *PRWeek*, "The most important thing to our clients is seeing their news release on these search engines. They know consumers go there. If they write a news release effectively, they can bypass the gatekeepers, the journalists, who always had the opportunity of interpreting the release how they wanted." In other words, the SMR has expanded the audience beyond just the traditional media outlet.

The popularity of social media has also been incorporated into the SMR. An SMR will include social media tags so the content can be circulated through Digg, Technorati, del.icio.us and other social bookmarking sites to increase search engine rankings of the release and to drive targeted traffic to the organization's website. Other links will be to blogs, an organization's on-line newsroom, and even a space where readers can post comments about the news release.

> 66 *No matter how much technology you employ to help make your message stand out from the crowd, if the message doesn't resonate, the photos, links, and videos won't help it.* 99 ■ Michael Pranikoff, PR Newswire

Marketwire, in particular, has added services to address social media. According to Craig McGuire writing in *PRWeek*, "The service includes social bookmarks and tags, Second Life, news channel distribution, audio headline summaries, search-engine-friendly permalinks, social video hosting on Photobucket, photo hosting on YouTube, and more." According to Paolina Milana, vice president for Marketwire, "Social media releases are generally formatted so information is easy to scan, utilizing bullets and lists of ready-made quotes instead of dense text." See the components of Marketwire's social media release in Figure 5.5.

McGuire gives some techniques for incorporating social media into SMRs:

DO

- Include links to pages where multiple instances of your key words/phrases reinforce your message.
- Place terms in key positions like headlines and first paragraphs.
- Distribute a release through a service that carries hyperlinks to downstream sites such as Yahoo! Finance, AOL News, and Netscape.

DON'T

- Go link crazy. Too many links will confuse journalists and draw focus away from key messaging.
- Use low-resolution images. Opt for high-resolution multimedia that can be easily used by layout pros.
- Use all tools, all the time. Focus first on the message. Use the bells and whistles to complement the campaign.

The SMR fulfills the prediction of Manny Ruiz, president of Hispanic PR Wire, that "The press release of the last century is dead." He enthusiastically adds, "In its place is a dynamic service that is more of an interactive marketing tool, more relevant and compelling for journalists; the difference is it's not only for journalists." This may be true, but it's still worth remembering that the vast majority of news

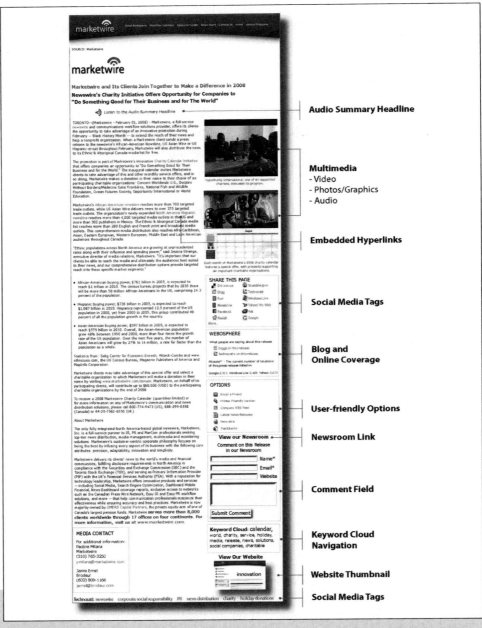

FIGURE 5.5 This ad for Marketwire highlights the components of the smart media news release. The annotations on the side of the sample news release shows the placement of such tools as multimedia, embedded hyperlinks, social media tags, blogs, and newsroom links. These news releases are designed to directly reach consumers through search engine optimization and make the information readily accessible on any number of Internet sites.

releases, even those carried by the electronic distribution services, are still basic releases about mundane activities that don't require photos, videos, or audio components. However, the number and variety of channels receiving news releases has expanded considerably beyond traditional media outlets. More discussion of placement and distribution is provided in Chapter 10, "Distributing News to the Media."

Summary

- The media are flooded with hundreds of news releases. To beat the odds and get space or time, your release must be newsworthy, timely, and well written.

- News releases are a basic element of almost every publicity plan. When published or broadcast, they can raise public awareness and influence decision making.

- Planning worksheets and answering the five Ws and H are the basic first steps in writing a news release.

- News releases should be produced on letter-size white paper and conform to Associated Press (AP) style.

- There are several types of news releases: announcements, spot announcements, reaction stories, bad news, and hometown releases.

- One key to successful news release writing is to emphasize the local angle.

- The news release has six components: organization name, contacts, headline, dateline, lead paragraph, and body of text. A seventh component can be a standard paragraph, often called boilerplate, at the end of the news release that provides basic information about the organization.

- Contacts listed on a news release should be knowledgeable about the topic and highly accessible to reporters who call for more information.

- Lead paragraphs summarize the basic story in five lines or less. Feature leads should arouse interest and encourage people to keep reading or listening.

- Don't try to get all five Ws and H (who, what, when, where, why, and how) in the lead paragraph. Choose the most important one or two elements.

- Write news releases that will appeal to editors and their audiences. Too many releases please the client or employer, but violate journalistic standards.

- News releases are highly structured pieces of writing. Use inverted pyramid style, with the most important facts first.

- Keep news releases factual. Avoid puffery and hype.

- News releases distributed via e-mail or the Internet should be restructured to be about five paragraphs, single-spaced. The subject line should be specific and arouse enough interest for the journalist to open it. A link to the organization's website should also be included if reporters want additional information.

- The multimedia media release is often used for major event and product launches. Also called the *smart media release* (SMR), it includes photos, video, and audio. Hyperlinks are embedded into the text, and links are made to social media networking sites.

Skill Building Activities

1. There is a list of six questions on pages 119–120 that a writer should answer before writing a news release. Answer these questions as if you were pre-paring a news release for the following situations:

   a. A new play is opening at the city's professional repertory theater.

   b. A food company is introducing a completely fat-free potato chip.

c. The local Red Cross chapter is kicking off its annual drive for blood donations.

2. Study the lead paragraphs of stories in the daily newspaper. Find three examples of each of the following: (a) a straight summary lead, (b) an informal lead, and (c) a feature lead. Note in what sections of the newspaper that you found the various kinds of leads, such as local news, lifestyle, business, travel, etc.

3. The websites for Visa, Google, and Intel are given on pages 133–134 as part of examples showing standardized company descriptions that often appear at the end of a news release. Go to these websites and visit each company's "pressroom" to review the various news releases. Write a short memo about the content, subject matter, and format of the news releases you find.

4. Write a news release for your college newspaper about the upcoming meeting of a student organization that has invited a guest speaker. Follow the guidelines in the chapter regarding the six basic elements of a news release. At the end of the release, include a brief description of the organization.

Suggested Readings

Aronson, Mary, Spetner, Don, and Ames, Carol. *The Public Relations Writer's Handbook in the Digital Age.* New York: John Wiley & Sons, 2007.

Bivens, Thomas H. *Public Relations Writing: The Essentials of Style and Format*, 6th edition. Boston: McGraw-Hill, 2007.

Consolino, Ron. "How to Write an Effective News Release." *Houston Chronicle*, www.chron.com, April 12, 2008.

Dyer, Paul. "Addressing Common Concerns: The Social Media Release Defined." *PR Tactics*, November 2007, p. 22.

Friedman, Mitchell. "25 Ways to Perfect Your Press Release." *PR Tactics*, July 2002, p. 15.

Garcia, Tonya. "Hot Off the Wire: Newswires Keep up with Changing Media and Financial Climate." *PRWeek*, September 17, 2007, p. 22.

LaMotta, Lisa. "Press Releases Go the DTC Route: Many Releases Now Written with the Consumer In Mind." *PRWeek*, July 17, 2006, p. 18.

McGuire, Craig. "Keeping Your Press Releases Relevant." *PRWeek*, February 2, 2008, p. 14.

Newsom, Doug, and Haynes, Jim. *Public Relations Writing: Form and Style*, 8th edition. Belmont, CA: Thomson/Wadsworth, 2007.

O'Brien, Laurel. "The Value of the Common News Release." *The Strategist*, Winter 2001, pp. 28–31.

Ochman, B. L. "The 'Death' of the Traditional Press Release." *The Strategist*, Summer 2000, pp. 16–18.

Smith, Ronald D. *Becoming a Public Relations Writer: A Writing Process Workbook for the Profession.* New York: Routledge, 2007.

Sweetland, Bill. "Don't Waste Readers' Time by Burying the Lead." Ragan.com, www.ragan.com, April 8, 2008.

Walker, Jerry. "18 Simple Rules for Writing a Press Release." *O'Dwyer's PR Services Report*, November 2002, pp. 32–33.

Woyk, Elizabeth. "Teaching the Press Release a New Trick." *BusinessWeek*, July 3, 2006, p. 16.

Wylie, Ann. "Anatomy of a Press Release: What to Include—and What to Avoid—in a Successful Media Relations Piece." *PR Tactics*, September 2003, p. 9.

Preparing Fact Sheets, Advisories, Media Kits, and Pitches

6

TOPICS covered in this chapter include:

Expanding the Publicity Tool Kit   141

Fact Sheets   141

Media Advisories   144

Media Kits   146

Pitching a Story   152

Expanding the Publicity Tool Kit

As discussed in the previous chapter, the news release is the backbone of most publicity programs. This chapter explores several other basic publicity tools that are regularly prepared and distributed to encourage and facilitate media coverage: fact sheets, media kits, and media advisories.

Fact sheets are one-page background sheets about an event, a product, or even the organization. Such fact sheets may be distributed with a news release or even be part of a media kit. A **media kit**, frequently called a **press kit**, contains a variety of materials, such as news releases, fact sheets, and photos. They are often assembled for the introduction of new products/services and major events.

Public relations professionals also need to know how to create a **media advisory**, also called a **media alert**, which is used to let assignment editors know about a newsworthy event or an interview of opportunity that could lend itself to photo or video coverage.

This chapter also details how to write effective memos and e-mails that will persuade reporters and editors to cover your product, service, or event. In the trade, this is called making a **pitch**.

Fact Sheets

A fact sheet often accompanies a news release or a media kit. It is essentially what the name implies—a list of facts in outline or bullet form that a reporter can use as a quick reference when writing a story. A fact sheet may form the basis of a whole story for a reporter, or the reporter might use just one or two of the facts provided to supplement the information in the news release.

There are several kinds of fact sheets. You can write one for an upcoming event, for example, that uses boldface headings to give such basic information as (1) the name of the event, (2) its sponsor, (3) the location, (4) the date and time, (5) the purpose of the event, (6) the expected attendance, (7) a list of any prominent people attending, and (8) any unusual aspects of the event that make it newsworthy.

The "event" may be a community-wide activity, such as a Jazz Festival, but it could also be the grand opening of a facility for homeless youth. In another situation, the Field Museum of Chicago prepared a basic fact sheet about the opening of a new exhibit on maps. The fact sheet gave (1) the dates of the exhibit, (2) the number of maps on display, (3) a short description of some rare maps on exhibit, (4) hours of the exhibit, (5) admission fees, (6) the museum's address and telephone numbers, and (7) the corporate sponsors.

Another Chicago institution, the Shedd Aquarium, used several "fact sheets" to provide background information on an exhibit featuring 30 species of lizards. One fact sheet gave some "pop culture" facts about lizards. One bulleted item, for example, noted "In ancient Egyptian and Greek symbolism, the lizard represented divine wisdom and good fortune." Another fact sheet, shown in Figure 6.1, was titled "Fun Facts on Lizards and the Ko-

Fact Sheet

For Immediate Release

MEDIA CONTACTS:
Melissa Holland
Shedd Aquarium
312-692-3330
mholland@sheddaquarium.org

Emily Mason
Public Communications Inc.
312-558-1770, ext. 136
emason@pcipr.com

FUN FACTS ON *LIZARDS AND THE KOMODO KING*

Did you know? Lizards will change their skin color to camouflage themselves, "bark" to attract a mate and even twist out of their scales or squirt blood from their eyeballs to escape predators! Check out the true colors of lizards at Shedd's *Lizards and the Komodo King* opening Saturday, April 8. Find out why some lizards have "beards," how some sleep in the treetops by their tails and much more!

Here are more fun facts about some of the lizards in Shedd Aquarium's new special exhibit *Lizards and the Komodo King*, opening April 8:

Komodo Dragon

- The largest lizard in the world, the Komodo dragon, makes its first ever appearance in Chicago at Shedd.

- The actual saliva of a Komodo dragon harbors a fatal mix of bacteria that causes deadly infections and is just as lethal as the Komodo's vicious bite.

- Although the toxic saliva of a Komodo dragon is lethal enough to kill it s prey, Komodos are immune to other Komodo bites.

- Komodo dragons will devour its entire meal, even the hooves, horns, bones and hide. However, it will not eat anything inside the digestive tract of its prey and can go several weeks between meals.

- The real name for the Komodo dragon is Komodo Island monitor. A 1927 *National Geographic* article described the Komodo as a "dragon" and the word stuck.

- With hawk-like vision and unbelievable sense of smell, the Komodo dragon can see up to 1,000 feet away and can sniff out rotting flesh from miles away!

- Komodos have ancestors that date back more than 100 million years.

- The Komodo at Shedd gets his name, Faust, from the German-based legend of a man who sold his soul to the devil, but ultimately fell in love, thus discovering the full meaning of life. This broke his pact with the devil; consequently, Faust was believed to hold the power to control the devil.

-more-

FIGURE 6.1 Fact sheets can be compiled on almost any subject. This one, distributed by Shedd Aquarium in Chicago for its lizard exhibit, gives some basic background about the star attraction, a Komodo dragon. Note that bullets are used to give factoids that journalists may select to include in their stories.

modo King." See also the PR Casebook on page 150 about the media kit that promoted the exhibit.

A second kind of fact sheet is a one-page sheet giving key facts about an organization. This is also referred to as a **corporate profile**. Typical headings may include (1) the organization's name, (2) the products or services produced, (3) the organization's annual revenues, (4) the total number of employees, (5) the names of top executives, (6) the markets served, (7) its position in the industry, and (8) any other pertinent details.

A fact sheet on Medtronic, a medical technology firm, is a good example. It gives a one paragraph description of the company's services and products followed by bulleted items giving the organization's (1) address; (2) main telephone number; (3) website address; (4) stock symbol; (5) key executives; (6) name, phone, and e-mail of the director of investor relations; (7) name, phone, and e-mail of the director of public relations; (8) number of employees; and (9) annual revenues. Another example of an organizational profile is shown in Figure 6.2.

The third kind of fact sheet is simply a summary of a new product's characteristics. A fact sheet for a company's new snack product, for example, might give such details as (1) nutrition information, (2) the production process, (3) pricing, (4) availability, (5) convenience, and (6) how it serves a consumer need. A good example of such a fact sheet is one by Philips Norelco about a new razor, which is shown in Figure 6.3.

A variation on the traditional fact sheet is information presented in a question-and-answer

FIGURE 6.2 Another kind of fact sheet is the corporate or organizational profile. This one outlines gives a brief overview of the Cruise Lines International Association and its activities. Such fact sheets are useful to journalists who may be unfamiliar with an organization and the scope of its activities.

FACT SHEET

CRUISE LINES INTERNATIONAL ASSOCIATION, INC.

OVERVIEW: The nonprofit Cruise Lines International Association (CLIA) is North America's largest cruise industry organization. CLIA represents the interests of 24 member lines and participates in the regulatory and policy development process while supporting measures that foster a safe, secure and healthy cruise ship environment. CLIA is also engaged in travel agent training, research and marketing communications to promote the value and desirability of cruise vacations and counts as members nearly 16,000 travel agencies across the United States and Canada.

MEMBERSHIP:
- Twenty-four cruise lines with approximately 175 ships representing 97 percent of North American cruise capacity
- Nearly 16,000 member travel agencies that display the CLIA seal, identifying them as cruise vacation experts
- Almost 100 of the most innovative suppliers of goods and services to the cruise industry make up CLIA's Executive Partner program.

TRAVEL AGENT EDUCATIONAL PROGRAMS: Through live training programs in 185 cities, agent seminars at industry conferences and online courses, CLIA offers agents more than 65,000 training events annually. Only agents at CLIA member retailers are eligible to enroll in CLIA's four exclusive levels of certification: Accredited Cruise Counsellor (ACC), Master Cruise Counsellor (MCC), Elite Cruise Counsellor (ECC) and Elite Cruise Counsellor Scholar (ECCS), and CLIA also offers a Luxury Cruise Specialist designation. Credits are earned through a combination of training seminars, cruise experience; attendance at CLIA co-sponsored and endorsed conferences, ship visits and cruise experience, and more. CLIA agents report that certification program completion has led to an average 261 percent increase in sales productivity.

KEY PERSONNEL:
- Terry L. Dale, President and Chief Executive Officer
- Michael Crye, Executive Vice President, Technical and Regulatory Affairs
- Robert Sharak, Executive Vice President, Marketing and Distribution
- Eric Ruff, Executive Vice President, Public Policy and Communications
- Capt. Ted Thompson, Senior Vice President, Technical and Regulatory Affairs

CLIA OFFICES:

FLORIDA	WASHINGTON, D.C.
910 SE 17th Street, Suite 400	2111 Wilson Blvd., 8th Floor
Fort Lauderdale, FL 33316	Arlington, VA 22201
Telephone: (754) 224-2200	Telephone: (703) 522-8463
Fax: (754) 224-2250	

Web site: www.cruising.org

PHILIPS NORELCO

PHILIPS NORELCO BODYGROOM

Norelco gets up close and personal with its latest grooming gadget that removes unwanted hair below the chin... even below the belt!

Norelco BODYGROOM BG2020

Recommended Retail Price: $39.99

Availability: Target and Amazon.com in April 2006

For Additional Information Visit: www.norelco.com

Features:	Benefits:
Take it ALL Off	Specifically designed for all body parts below the chin – it grooms unwanted hair from legs, chest, back, groin area and more!
Feelin' Good	Chromium Steel trimmer blades combined with a hypoallergenic shaving foil leave even the most sensitive skin smooth with less irritation.
Make it Your Own	Three interchangeable attachment combs trim hair different lengths because sometimes we don't want to take it all off!
Rechargeable and cordless	Can be charged for 50 minutes of cordless trimming time.
We got your back	Full Two Year Warranty

FIGURE 6.3 Publicists usually prepare a fact sheet for a new product. This one, for Philips Norelco, provides the basic information about a new shaving product. The format is easy to read, and it gives a website for more information. In addition, journalists can also call or e-mail public relations representatives at a public relations firm who are familiar with the product.

format. This format, often used on websites and the Internet, is called an **FAQ**. This is cyberspace jargon for "Frequently Asked Questions." Hewlett-Packard, for example, supplemented its Internet news release on a new ScanJet printer with a FAQ that answered typical consumer questions about the new product. When you write an FAQ, try to place yourself in the shoes of the consumer who is hearing about the product for the first time. What questions would you ask? FAQs on websites also give consumers, as well as editors, the opportunity to click various links (video, audio, photos, product specifications) to get even more information about a product.

Media Advisories

Advisories are also called *media alerts* because they tell assignment editors about upcoming events that they might be interested in covering from a story, photo, and video perspective.

The most common format uses short, bulleted items rather than long paragraphs. A typical one-page advisory might contain the following elements: a one-line headline, a brief paragraph outlining the story idea, some of journalism's five Ws and H, and a short paragraph telling the reporter who to contact for more information or make arrangements.

A typical media advisory is the one from Greyhound Friends, Inc., shown in Figure 6.4. The advisory was about an upcoming fashion show to benefit retired

> **FIGURE 6.4** A media advisory, or media alert, is sent several weeks in advance to let editors and reporters know about an upcoming event. An advisory is usually organized around the journalistic five Ws and H to give editors a quick overview of the event details. An advisory also gives some suggestions for photo or video opportunities that help assignment editors plan coverage.

Home   FPSnewswire   Feature Photo Service   Corporate   RSS

Commontales

Central Park Fashion Show to Benefit Retired Greyhounds and Spanish Galgos

Boston, MA/April 25, 2007/FPSnewswire/--

WHAT:
Commontales.com and Greyhound Friends, Inc., are partnering to produce an Egyptian-inspired fashion show featuring twelve canine models. Retired greyhounds and Spanish galgos will be escorted around the Central Park landmark, Cleopatra's Needle, by twelve models in Egyptian garb. The event is the launch debut for Commontales.com's Greyhound/Galgos section.

WHERE:
"The Obelisk," Cleopatra's Needle, is located directly behind the Metropolitan Museum of Art on the East Side of Central Park at 81st Street. The entrance is located at Fifth Avenue and 79th street.

WHEN:
Thursday, April 26, 2007 from 2:00 p.m.-5:00 p.m.

PHOTO OP:
The fashion show will begin at 2:00 p.m. with press availability until 5:00 p.m. Please call Tom Kane at (646) 519-1556 or Louise Coleman at (617) 817-6706 for more details.

WHO:
Commontales.com, a site developed for members to trade stories, photos, and video about their hounds, has partnered for this event with Greyhound Friends Inc., a non-profit organization located in Hopkinton, Massachusetts, dedicated to placing retired racing greyhounds and Spanish galgos in loving homes.

WHY:
Once the favored dog of the ancient Egyptians and the medieval nobility greyhounds began being breed in the United States in the 1920's for the racing industry. The greyhounds' cousins, the galgos, are bred in Spain for hunting and coursing where they often face brutal deaths and serious injury. It was normal practice to kill racing greyhounds after their careers or if they did not make the grade until adoption organizations like Greyhound Friends were established to find suitable homes. Currently other countries involved with greyhounds and galgos are seeing a rise in awareness about the treatment of these dogs.

http://www.featurephoto.com/release.asp?id=932   3/7/2008

Greyhounds. The advisory used such heads as What, Where, When, Who, and Why. In addition, it suggested the best time for a photo opportunity and who to contact for making arrangements.

Another example of a media alert for an event is the "World's Longest Salad Bar," a publicity stunt in New York's Central Park sponsored by Hidden Valley Ranch dressings. It was written in such a way that local reporters knew the details of "when" and "where," and television stations in other cities knew how to get video footage and soundbites via satellite.

Media alerts are also used to announce the time and location of a scheduled news conference. Increasingly, news conferences are broadcast over the Web so reporters in other cities can "attend" without having to actually travel to the location. In such cases, the media advisory lets reporters know how and when they can sign on to the Webcast or teleconference. Advisories also are sent regarding satellite media tours by experts and celebrities (see Chapter 9 for more on satellite media tours).

A third kind of media advisory is one that lets reporters and editors know about an interview opportunity. Korbel Champagne Cellars, for example, let journalists know that its "marriage proposal" expert was available for interviews during a 2-week period in July. The "interview opportunity" even suggested five other timely topics that he could discuss.

The fourth kind of advisory alerts the press to a local angle as part of a national story. Korbel Cellars also sent print media and broadcast stations in the Dallas area an announcement that a Dallas couple was one of the three finalists in its "perfect proposal contest." Also made available to the press was a photo of the actual marriage proposal on the stage of the Palace Theatre in New York where "Aida" was playing. And finally, the advisory let the editors know that the couple was available for interviews.

■ Media Kits

A media kit, also called a **press kit**, is usually prepared for major events and new product launches. Its purpose is to give editors and reporters a variety of information and resources that will make it easier for the reporter to write about the topic.

A basic media kit may include (1) a main news release; (2) a news feature; (3) fact sheets on the product, organization, or event; (4) background information; (5) photos and drawings with captions; (6) biographical material on the spokesperson or senior executive; and (7) some basic brochures. All materials should be clearly identified; it's also important to prominently display contact information, such as e-mail addresses, phone numbers, and website addresses.

Such a list is a good starting point, but remember that each press kit you produce will no doubt have variations depending on the specific event or product. A media kit for the Boston Beer Company, brewers of Samuel Adams, contained the following materials:

- A news release announcing that Irish Red Ale received the most votes among 42,000 beer enthusiasts at over 1,000 tasting events across the country.
- A backgrounder giving a short description of its 21-member "family of beers."
- A two-page history of the Boston Beer Company (corporate profile).
- A two-page profile of Jim Koch, brewer and founder of the company.
- A packet of Bavarian hop seeds, which is used in the brewing process.

Another example of a basic media kit is the one distributed by the Field Museum in Chicago when it opened its "Maps: Finding Our Place in the World" exhibit. A print version of the media kit was sent to major media. The kit also included a CD that contained all of the basic print material plus 30 high-resolution photos that could be downloaded as jpeg files. The kit and the CD contained the following material:

- About 30 photographs of rare maps and globes on display, with captions
- The main news release about the exhibit
- A media advisory announcing a media preview 2 days before the public opening

- A description of the exhibits in each of the seven galleries, dubbed a "walk-through"
- A feature on the technologies used for mapping today
- Short background stories about the rare maps and globes being exhibited
- A schedule of public lectures and gallery programs
- Texts of radio public service announcements (PSAs) about the exhibits

Adventures by Disney took a more visual approach with its media kit. It distributed a primarily photo-based media kit that showed scenes from various travel itineraries around the world that the company was offering in 2008. The media kit contained:

- A two-page news release announcing new exotic locations for the entire family and returning trips that had been offered in previous years
- A seven-page overview of each trip, highlighting key sightseeing opportunities
- Several pages of color photos illustrating each itinerary and the URL of a specific Disney Web site that journalists could access to download high-resolution files of the images
- A CD containing extensive captions for each photo and high-resolution photos that could be downloaded

Compiling a Media Kit

The various informational materials, many of which have just been described, are traditionally placed in a folder with the organization's name on it. The typical media kit folder is 9 by 12 inches and has four sides—a cover, two inside pages (often with pockets to hold news releases, etc., in place), and a back cover that has the organization's name, address, and website address. Another common feature is to include a business-card slot on one of the inside pockets. Folders can also include slots for CDs.

A company can also invest in custom-designed folders to package the contents of a media kit more creatively. Crayola, for example, created a colorful media folder to publicize its 25-city bus tour celebrating the 100th anniversary of the company. The package was a self-mailer that unfolded into a large round sheet 2 feet in diameter that featured artwork in a rainbow of crayon colors. The packet also included a colorful news release (localized for each city) and two backgrounders. It also included an interesting piece of trivia: "Since 1903, more than 120 billion crayons have been sold throughout the world. End to end they would circle the earth 200 times." Media kits should reflect the company's image and products; the colorful Crayola media kit is a classic example.

Another classic example is the media kit that Planters peanuts designed to generate publicity for its 100th birthday. The

> **Fact sheets, background materials, and other supporting documents should be made available in a format that is easy for the journalist to recognize and access.** ■ Gary Glenn, eNR/NewsWire One

"folder" was actually a large can that was a replica of its famous blue and yellow container for its peanuts. Inside the can was a news release about various events and activities that were planned to celebrate the anniversary. There was also a spiral-bound circular brochure giving the history of Planters, the evolution of the Mr. Peanut logo, and other historical notes about the development of various products. And, of course, the "kit" contained a can of peanuts. See Figure 6.5 for photos of the Planters kit.

The Crayola and Planters media kits, however, are the exception. The vast majority of kits are in the traditional folder, but these, too, can be expensive to supply if they are custom-designed, use glossy paper, and feature full-color printing. The Adventures by Disney folder (shown in Figure 6.6), for example, was highly visual with multiple full-color photos (complementing the theme of the content) on three of its four pages. Such appealing packaging, designed to attract the interest of reporters and editors, can raise the cost of each media kit to $10 or $15 by the time all the materials are produced and the folder cover is designed. Consequently, printed press kits are distributed somewhat selectively to major media and key editors.

Media kits represent a valuable opportunity to get publicity placements, but several surveys of editors indicate that such kits often miss the mark. They are too large, contain too many sales brochures, include poor-quality photos, and have poorly written news and feature stories. Consequently, you should keep press kits

▶ **FIGURE 6.5** A media kit is usually in an attractive folder. Planters, however, celebrated its 100th birthday by preparing a media kit that reflected the company's business. The media kit was a large can that replicated its well-recognized product tins. Inside, the theme was continued by a spiral-bound anniversary booklet in the round shape of an open can of peanuts. The kit also contained a tin of peanuts. The kit generated more than 1,000 placements, including coverage on the "Today" show and *The New York Times*. Radio stations in 46 states mentioned the anniversary, and 178 television stories were produced throughout the year. Planters and its public relations firm, Weber Shandwick, received a bronze anvil from the Public Relations Society of America (PRSA) in the category of press/media kits.

FIGURE 6.6 This is the cover of a media kit distributed by Adventures by Disney to travel editors at major media outlets throughout the country. Media kit covers are attractively designed to attract attention and to reinforce a theme. This kit, about tours around the world designed for families, featured a number of photos from travel locations that editors could download from an enclosed CD or a website.

slim and cost-effective; they should not be repositories for all the company's product brochures. Provide reporters and editors with information that is simple, factual, and relevant to their audiences. Give them story ideas, local angles, photos, and interesting graphics.

Electronic Media Kits

The traditional printed media kit is still used, as illustrated by the various examples just described, but their numbers are rapidly declining as organizations find it more cost-efficient to distribute the same information via CDs, e-mail, and online newsrooms. Electronic press kits, also known as **EPKs**, or **e-kits**, are also more versatile than traditional printed media kits, because they can include multiple pieces of information in a variety of formats (text, video, photo, audio, animation, etc.). All this gives the journalist much more flexibility and choice than the traditional printed kit.

Another advantage of the EPK is that it expands the potential audience. Traditional media kits were sent only to media outlets. Today's EPK, if well designed, has the potential of reaching a wider audience of consumers, bloggers, online forums, and other websites via social media tags and RSS feeds.

The cost savings, in particular, is a very convincing argument for organizations. For one trade show, Hewlett-Packard (HP) issued all of its press materials online rather than spend the money to print and send hundreds of press kits to editors covering the event. The cost savings was about $17,000, according to Michael Spataro, vice president of Weber Shandwick Worldwide. In another example, a company developed an Internet press kit that included eight documents, five photos,

> **" The days of a thousand press kits are gone. Instead, well-designed online press kits can have an ongoing shelf life with constantly updated content. "** ■ Tom Bucktold of Business Wire

and a PR Newswire distribution to hundreds of media outlets for a total cost of $4,000. The same material, printed and mailed to 500 reporters, would have cost about $15,000.

Journalists also seem to prefer EPKs over printed kits. In 2004, Weber Shand-wick polled 1,500 media outlets and found that 70 percent preferred to receive information via electronic communications such as e-mail or the Web. The major reasons were (1) storage and filing simplicity, (2) ease in forwarding materials to others, (3) faster access to company or public relations contacts, and (4) elimination of newsroom clutter. Kelly Brooks, marketing communications manager for Coca-Cola offers another reason why reporters covering events, such as the Olympics, prefer EPKs. She says, "Reporters would rather use a Web-based tool when it's convenient for them than lug around a bulky kit."

Not every journalist, however, likes the digital approach. Daniel Cantelmo, writing in *Public Relations Quarterly*, quotes one senior editor for a high-technology magazine who said, "In 5 or 10 minutes, I can go through 25 printed

■ **PR** casebook

Leapin' Lizards!!! CD Media Kit Makes Giant Lizard a Star

How do you stir up public interest in lizards? That was the challenge of the public relations staff at Chicago's Shedd Aquarium when the institution planned a special exhibit on lizards. The highlight of the show would be the first-ever public display of the world's largest lizard, a Komodo Dragon, in the city.

The solution was the development of an interactive media kit on CD because of its ability to supply large amounts of information in an approachable, engaging format. Roger Germann, director of public relations for Shedd, and his team concentrated on packaging the CD to be eye-catching and inviting to the media. The cover of the CD, for example, conveyed a jungle-like scene in which the Komodo king dominates the world of lizards. The jungle theme was then carried throughout the elements and pages of the kit. The intro, for example, featured an up-tempo drumbeat that introduced four short videos featuring lizards in their natural habitat to convey a sense of what the public would see at the exhibit.

FIGURE 6.7 The new lightweight media kit is the CD. The Shedd Aquarium designed an attractive cover for its CD that publicized its lizard exhibit. Digital formats are now the norm. Providing an electronic media kit on CD or posting a media kit online is economical and enables multimedia content.

press kits . . . and pick out exactly what I need. If I had to go through 25 CDs or on-line press kits, it would take hours. I don't have the time." Because of editors like him, e-kits probably will never totally replace the traditional media kit. In many cases, public relations firms and organizations continue to produce and distribute both a printed kit and a CD, often in the same package. The idea, again, is to provide whatever format the particular editor or journalist wants. As already mentioned, both Adventures by Disney and the Field Museum sent a traditional media kit, but included a CD and directed journalists to website. In contrast, the Shedd Aquarium put all of its resources into a CD media kit about a new lizard exhibit. See the PR Casebook below for a description.

Echoing the argument for both print and electronic versions is Glen Stone, public affairs manager at the Toronto Board of Trade. He told *PRWeek*, "I give electronic information to journalists via email and in kits, but my kits always include paper versions of the essentials so that reporters, particularly radio reporters who have 24 deadlines a day, have something they can use immediately."

The kit also included news releases and fact sheets about the exhibit and the subject of lizards. One of these fact sheets, "Fun Facts on Lizards and the Komodo King," is shown in Figure 6.7. Another fact sheet was titled, "Lizards Leap into Pop Culture." Other materials gave a thumbnail description of the more than 30 lizard species on exhibit and even a tip sheet on "Responsible Lizard Ownership." A dozen high-resolution photos of various lizards that could be printed or downloaded was also provided (Figure 6.8). According to Germann, "Most importantly, the inherently interactive nature of a CD-ROM, with its ability to deliver sound and animation, helps convey the exciting nature of the exhibit and build enthusiasm for it among the media."

The media kit was a hit. It generated almost 250 print and broadcast placements, reaching an audience of about 30 million. In addition, outreach to online media resulted in 80 placements, reaching an estimated than 60 million people. The publicity helped the aquarium generate 2.1 million visitors to the exhibit, making it one of the top two attended aquariums in the country. The successful program received a bronze anvil from the Public Relations Society of America (PRSA) in the category of electronic media kits. The total budget of the campaign was less than $75,000. ■

FIGURE 6.8 The Shedd Aquarium media kit included more than 30 high-resolution photos of lizards in their natural habitat that editors could download to illustrate stories about the exhibit. Several photos of the Komodo dragon, the star of the exhibit, were included. The kit also included a fact sheet on the Komodo dragon. It can, for example, devour a whole pig in 20 minutes.

The main point to remember is that an EPK, much like the traditional news release, should have the same components of the traditional print version. Craig McGuire of *PRWeek* explains, "There should be a well-written, fact-filled description of the subject, as well as product/event sheets, press releases regarding newsworthy items, bios, and backgrounders on key subjects, testimonials, articles from archives, perhaps a calendar or itinerary, and always a contact sheet."

McGuire, however, adds that the major change is how all these materials are presented. E-kits have the technical capacity to enrich content by offering a gallery of outstanding photos, embedding hyperlinks to websites, or even providing video demonstrations of how a product works. Electronic Arts (EA), for example, effectively uses a CD format to show entertainment reporters and editors simulations from its various video games. Movie studios use websites and CDs to promote new films by providing film clips, interviews with the stars, and production facts.

Shel Holtz, author of *Public Relations on the Net*, says organizations often fail to understand the medium. Instead of taking full advantage of the technology, some organizations merely post news releases with some stock photos. The EPKs for NASA's space shuttles, he laments, "are nothing more than long, linear paper documents—good text-based information with no photos of the astronauts or vehicles involved." Holtz concludes, "The access to information offered by online press kits is a good first step, but the techniques will provide real value over old models only when we begin tapping into the differences between the Web and print, and using them to create something more than an online version of our old brick-and-mortar kits." The use of Web pages and their use in media kits is discussed more thoroughly in Chapter 12.

Pitching a Story

Publicists spend a lot of time and energy preparing materials such as news releases, fact sheets, and even media kits. These efforts, however, don't amount to much unless they can convince an editor or reporter that a particular story is newsworthy and relevant to their readers or viewers.

A common approach, of course, is to simply distribute the publicity materials and let nature, so to speak, take its course. Editors, as already noted, review hundreds of news releases and media kits every day and select the few that interest them. Another approach, however, is for publicists to make a pitch directly to the media gatekeeper if a particular situation or story angle is more "special" than just a routine news release.

Media kits, in particular, often include a short, personalized letter to the editor that is considered a pitch for using the material. One publicist for an author of a kosher cookbook, for example, included a short letter in a media kit that let editors know that high-resolution photos of recipes and publicity photos of the author were available on a particular website. In addition, the letter ended with an offer to set up a personal interview with the book author.

Another standard pitch letter was included in a media kit distributed by Sunkist Growers about its "Take a Stand" campaign to provide lemonade stands to youth who wanted to raise money for a worthy cause. Here is the template for the letter:

Dear (name),

With schools letting out and summer approaching fast, parents are presented with the challenge of finding fun and meaningful ways for their kids to pass the time. This summer, instead of watching tv and playing video games, why not get your kids started on the path of becoming an entrepreneur? What better way for kids to spend the dog days of summer than to learn how to run a business and raise money for charity through an old-fashioned lemonade sale!

In its third year, the Sunkist "Take a Stand" Program encourages kids, ages 7–12, across the country to get involved in their communities and raise money for a charitable cause that's near and dear to their hearts.

In 2005, Sunkist gave away more than 2,000 free lemonade stands to kids who wanted to give back to their communities through the "Take a Stand" Program. From those 2,000 stands alone, participants reported raising an estimated $400,000 for hundreds of charities nationwide.

The "Take a Stand" Program is back by popular demand and Sunkist is giving away an unprecedented 5,000 lemonade stands in 2006. So far this year, Sunkist has received pledges from kids in every state who will be coming soon to a neighborhood corner near you.

And getting involved is as easy as logging on to www.sunkist.com/takeastand and submitting a "Take a Stand" pledge. Sunkist will then send a free, limited edition Sunkist Summer Fun Lemonade Stand and Juicer Kit complete with tools kids need to be successful, while supplies last.

With summer vacation on the horizon, now is the perfect time to report on how kids in your area are getting involved in your local community. Enclosed is a press kit with additional information on the "Take a Stand" Program, including lemonade recipes and some fun facts on lemons.

I'll be following up with you soon to discuss your interest in a story on the "Take a Stand" Program. In the meantime, if you have any questions or are interested in finding out if kids in our area are setting up a lemonade stand, please contact me directly at (phone), or at (email).

Thanks for your time and consideration.

Kind regards,

(name)

On behalf of Sunkist Growers, Inc.

As you might guess, there is considerable competition to get the attention of an editor or broadcast producer. According to *Ragan's Media Relations Report*, a typical example is *Barron's*. Richard Rescigno, managing editor of this influential business weekly, gets about 30 to 35 phone calls from public relations people each week.

In addition, he receives more than 200 "pitches" by mail and e-mail every week. Rescigno estimates that only 1 or 2 percent of all the ideas that are pitched actually result in stories. Another 5 percent serve as supporting material for larger stories. "PR people have to have a high tolerance for rejection," he told *Ragan's* reporter.

That's the bad news. The good news is that many other journalists get most of their story ideas from pitches by publicists. *The New York Times* leading tech columnist, David Pogue, told Ragan.com (www.ragan.com) that about 60 to 70 percent of his columns come from pitches. However, the rate of rejection still remains quite high. Pogue receives about 150 e-mail pitches daily.

Given these statistical odds, it is important that you understand the components of an effective pitch that will substantially increase your odds for getting a story published or broadcast. A good pitch has three phases: (1) researching the publication or broadcast show, (2) writing the e-mail or letter and making the call, and (3) following-up.

Researching the Publication

Perhaps the most important component is the first phase—doing your homework. Pitches must be customized to a particular editor and publication. There is no such thing as a "one size fits all" pitch that is appropriate for all media. Visa or Master-Card, for example, would pitch a bride's magazine to do a story about the challenges of a young couple combining their finances. In contrast, a story might be pitched to the AARP monthly magazine about how senior citizens can reduce credit card transaction fees while traveling abroad.

❝ Media relations specialists should not send out a pitch without knowing the reporters and publications in advance. ❞ ■ David B. Oates, ContentOne Communications

Lynn Lipinski, a senior media specialist for GCI public relations in Los Angeles, writes in *PR Tactics*, "You must . . . familiarize yourself with the publication's style, format, readership, deadlines, and regular features. Media guides can provide the basic information about a publication, but the only way to truly know if it is right for your client is to read it."

In addition to media databases, which were mentioned in Chapter 1 and are explained further in Chapter 10, public relations writers rely on "media profile" reports that are published by such publications as *PRWeek*, *Ragan's Media Relations Report*, *Bulldog Reporter*, and *O'Dwyer's Newsletter*. These articles give the background of the publication, the key editors, the kinds of stories they want, and how to make a "pitch."

PRWeek, for example, regularly has a "media profile" about a particular publication. One article was about *Parade* magazine, which is distributed in Sunday newspapers, reaching about 75 million people each week. *PRWeek* advised its readers, "Editors prefer e-mail pitches that are short, sweet, and to the point. Don't send attachments or samples until they are asked for. Don't send mass e-mails, and know what is appropriate for the magazine. You have to prove that you've read *Parade*."

Even publications that appear to focus on the same subject matter often don't have the same audience characteristics. Tripp Whetsell, a New York public relations counselor, writes in *PR Tactics*, "Even if you're pitching the same story about prostate cancer to *Esquire*, *Men's Journal*, and *GQ*, doesn't automatically assume that the content is the same just because all three are men's magazines." The same goes for broadcasting; Fox News targets 30- to 40-year-olds, whereas CNN draws viewers with an average age of 60. Blogs also have different audiences; the following Tips for Success offers some advice about pitching them.

Lipinski adds, "Read articles written by the reporter you are pitching. Familiarize yourself with the reporter's style, interests, background, and regular beat." At the same time, she urges would-be writers of pitch letters to be aware of current

---

☑ tips FOR SUCCESS

How to Successfully Pitch Bloggers

The "blogosphere" is now part of the media landscape; media databases (discussed in Chapter 1) now track the contact information and coverage areas of bloggers who have gained a national audience. Therefore, in addition to pitching stories to traditional media, a savvy publicist also needs to include bloggers in order to reach the widest possible audience.

Pitching a blogger, however, has its perils. Unlike traditional media, which just ignore an off-base pitch, bloggers will gleefully post critical comments about the quality of your pitch and even make snide remarks about your intelligence. Consequently, it's critical to do your homework before you pitch a blogger. Kevin Dugan, cowriter of the Bad Pitch Blog (www.badpitch.blogspot.com), suggests six questions that public relations professionals should ask themselves before aiming a pitch at key bloggers:

1. **Have you read more than the blog's most recent posts?** A blogger's most recent posts might not be representative of his or her overall interest in topics and issues.

2. **Have you searched the blog for relevant product/service/industry terms to see if they have already been mentioned?** You should be aware of what the blogger has already said about you or your organization. "If they are already covering you, you have a conversation opener for your pitch," says Dugan.

3. **Have you subscribed to the blog's RSS feed or e-mail delivery system?** This makes it easier for you to follow a blog and tailor a pitch around something that is already being discussed.

4. **Have you left a comment on the blog that continues a discussion and is unrelated to your pitch?** Blogs are designed to start conversations about a subject. Become a participant in the discussions so that you will have a relationship with the blogger before you make the pitch.

5. **Have you looked at posts and links from the blogger's home page to find out how they want to be pitched?** Knowing their preferences and guidelines goes a long way in delivering a pitch that will be considered.

6. **Have you sent the blogger an e-mail unrelated to your pitch?** If you leave a public comment, Dugan says, "You should come up with another reason to introduce yourself to the blogger."

Dugan, interviewed by Ragan.com, says building relationships with bloggers comes first and pitching comes second. He even suggests that you develop media contacts on social networking sites such as LinkedIn and Facebook. These sites, Dugan warns, are for building relationships—not making a pitch. ■

---

issues, business trends, and societal issues, so you can angle your pitch within the framework of a larger picture. If the company is expanding by purchasing smaller companies, perhaps the story can be pitched from the angle that it is an example of consolidation in a particular industry.

In sum, knowledge of the publication and the demographics of its audience are crucial to a successful pitch. David Pogue of *The New York Times* expresses the frustration of many journalists. He told Ragan.com, "I get the idea that a lot of PR people inherit some database and they just blast everything to the whole list and I cannot tell you what a waste of time that is. It just turns the busy journalists against the person, that firm, and that client."

Preparing the Pitch

Once you've done your research and have ascertained what kind of pitch would be most appropriate for a particular publication, broadcast show, or even a blogger, the next step is to write a succinct, attention-grabbing memo or e-mail. As Richard Rescigno of *Barron's* notes, you have about 60 seconds (either in an e-mail or a telephone call) to grab an editor's interest.

David Pogue of *The New York Times*, for example, prefers short e-mail pitches. One of his favorites, which resulted in a story, was "David, my client sells a laptop that can be dropped from 6 feet, get dunked in water, and survive 300-degree heat. Let me know if you're interested." Another attention-getting pitch that resulted in a story was, "David, I see you've been covering digital cameras a lot. Wondering if you'd be interested in one that shoots underwater and costs less than $100? Press release below. Contact me if you have any questions."

Therefore, the first rule of a pitch is brevity—less than a page or a screen. Second, Whetsell's advice regarding good writing should be followed: "Your sentences should be clean, sharp, and to the point. Your syntax, as well as your spelling, should be flawless. Don't give journalists a reason not to take you and your clients seriously by being sloppy."

Third, a pitch should have an enticing lead. That means that you should avoid beginning a pitch with something trite such as "I'm writing to inquire if you would be interested in a story about . . ." That's a good way to turn off an editor. See the Tips for Success on page 157 for more tips on writing pitches.

Ragan's Media Relations Report has published several articles on how to write pitches and create great opening lines. Here are some examples of opening lines that generated media interest:

- "How many students does it take to change a light bulb?" (Story about a residence hall maintenance program operated by students who receive financial aid.)
- "Would you like to replace your ex-husband with a plant?" (Story about a photographer who is an expert at removing "ex's" and other individuals from old photos.)
- "Our CEO ran 16 Boston Marathons . . . And now he thinks we can walk a mile around the river." (Story about a CEO leading employees on a daily walk instead of paying for expensive gym memberships or trainers.)

- "You are cordially invited to the Dirtiest Event in Boulder." (A story about staging a coal-dumping event to show people how much fossil fuel it takes to heat an average house. The slightly "smutty" approach worked; major dailies and television stations covered the coal dumping.)
- "For almost 25 years, Jack Osman has been drinking shots of oil. He also sings songs about such foot-tapping topics as breakfast and grease. And sometimes, just for fun, he cooks down ground beef to find out its fat percentage." (Pitch about the availability of a nutrition professor to give media interviews on diet and health.)

As these examples show, a pitch should immediately raise curiosity or get to the point as soon as possible. Here is a letter written by Michael Klepper, owner of a New York public relations firm, that netted 8 minutes on NBC's *Today* show.

> Plastics!
>
> How can we get rid of them? Some environmentalists say we can't. Ralph Harding says we can. He is executive vice president of the Society of Plastics Industry. He has just returned from Europe where they easily dispose of plastics in modern incinerators.
>
> I'll call you in a week to see if the *Today* show would be interested in talking to him.

Klepper, who has written hundreds of pitch letters in his career, adds, "The pitch letter should be newsy, not groveling. It shouldn't read 'respectfully submitted' or 'I need this one' or 'my client is breathing heavy.' You are never asking for a favor; you are submitting good, topical, newsworthy material that is directed to a decision maker."

A good example of a succinct pitch is one written by Samantha Schoengold of Fineberg Publicity in New York on behalf of her client, Danskin Plus clothes. It was sent to the producer of the 5 P.M. news program on WCBS-TV in New York. The pitch, which resulted in a segment titled "The Forgotten Woman," was summarized by *O'Dwyer's Newsletter* as follows:

> Did you know that most women in the United States are a size 14 or larger? These women are not necessarily overweight; they can be tall or just big boned, and they have long been forgotten and overlooked by most fashion manufacturers.

Danskin caters to women of all ages and sizes by addressing and dressing their fitness and fashion needs. . . .

Let our Danskin Plus expert, Phyllis Moroney, offer her advice on fashion, fitness and health for the larger size woman. We can create a fashion segment incorporating Danskin Plus styles to show the different ways it can be worn from the office to the gym or just to hang out in. . . .

E-Mail Subject Lines ■ The vast majority of pitches today are sent to editors, reporters, television producers, and bloggers via e-mail. Consequently, probably the most important aspect of the pitch is the subject line. If it doesn't generate interest and curiosity on the part of the receiver as they quickly scan hundreds of e-mails, it's deleted without a second thought. Such a challenge requires a lot of creativity on the part of the publicist to come up with a good subject line. Ragan.com compiled a list of creative subject lines that generated media stories. Here are some examples:

- "Call it a display of Howly Muttrimony sealed with a sniff." (Story about a dog wedding at a shopping center staged as a benefit for an animal rescue group.)
- "The Man Who Will End iPod Whiplash." (Story about an engineer who created a new technique for searching music online.)
- "Wearing Prada Can Be the Devil for Your Spine." (Story from a hospital involved in spinal therapy about women injuring their spines by lugging around ever-larger designer handbags.)
- "Weather to Pack Sunscreen or an Umbrella." (Story about a new online weather service and its trip planner services.)
- "Veggies for Dessert? Blue Cheese Gelato!!" (Story about new fruit and vegetable flavors for an ice cream store chain.)
- "New Book Says Hormones May be Making You Fat." (Story about a weight loss program authored by a chiropractor.)

Not all subject lines, however, need to be creative and clever. An informative subject line, such as "Free Public Hurricane Seminar Tomorrow Night at Nauticus," satisfies the key word requirement and tells the receiver exactly what the story is about. As Margo Mateas, president of the Public Relations Training Company writes in *PR Tactics*, "Writing a powerful media pitch doesn't take a lot of words. It takes a lot of thought and planning. Put your effort into being succinct and concise, and it will pay off." See the Tips for Success on page 159 for more guidelines for writing an e-mail pitch.

The Telephone Pitch ■ Despite the popularity of e-mail, it still remains somewhat impersonal and easy to ignore. Consequently, a case can be made for actually picking up the phone and having a real-time conversation with an editor or journalist. As Susan Balcom Walton and Nick Kalm explain in *PR Tactics*, "Pitching a story face-to-face, or at least voice-to-voice, can help develop stronger journalist relation-

Guidelines for Pitching Stories by E-Mail

Publicists frequently pitch story ideas by e-mail. In fact, many editors prefer this method over letters, faxes, or even phone calls. However, it's important to remember some guidelines:

- Use a concise subject line using key words that tells the editor what you have to offer.

- Keep the message brief, one screen at the most.

- Get to the point in the first or second sentence. Don't engage in trite "How are you" comments.

- Don't include attachments unless the reporter is expecting you to do so. Most reporters, due to possible virus attacks, never open attachments unless they personally know the source.

- Don't send "blast" e-mails to large numbers of editors. E-mail systems are set up to filter messages with multiple recipients in the "To" and "BCC" fields—a sure sign of spam. If you do send an e-mail to multiple editors, break the list into small groups.

- Send tailored e-mail pitches to specific reporters and editors; the pitch should be relevant to their beats and publications.

- Personally check the names in your e-mail database to remove redundant recipients.

- Give editors the option of getting off your e-mail list; it will make your list more targeted to those who are interested. By the same token, give editors the opportunity to sign up for regular updates from your organization's website. If they cover your industry, they will appreciate it.

- Establish an e-mail relationship. As one reporter said "The best e-mails come from people I know; I delete e-mails from PR people or agencies I don't recognize." ■

ships, greater preparation and knowledge of your subject, and greater flexibility during the pitch."

Calling a reporter or editor requires the same preparation that goes into preparing a written pitch. You need to thoroughly research the publication, broadcast outlet, or blog so you are totally familiar with the content and demographics of its audience. You also need to use media databases, which often give short profiles of editors and reporters so you have some familiarity with their interests and even pet peeves. It's even wise to figure out when to call so it doesn't interfere with deadline pressures. If you call on a deadline, you most likely will receive a quick brush-off.

Before making the call, prepare a brief outline or script of what you will say in the first 30 seconds. You should give your name and organization/client before starting and, in one or two sentences, tell them what you are calling about. Get to the point; don't try to exchange mundane openers such as "How are you today?" or "I was wondering if you would be interested in a story about XYZ's new widget." It's much better to give the story angle up front and why it would be of interest to readers or viewers.

Walton and Kalm add that you need to say why the story is significant and how it fits into other stories/trends already being covered by the publication, broadcast outlet, or website. As freelance writer Amy Gunderson observes, "Good pitchers think about the larger implications. They are always thinking 'What's the angle?' They are always thinking like journalists." At the same time, listen to what the journalist is telling you. Don't be an insistent telemarketer and ignore the message that he or she is not interested.

Melvin Helitzer, author of *The Dream Job: Sports Publicity*, says a pitch should have the following six elements:

- Enough facts to support a full story
- An angle of interest to the readers of that specific publication
- The possibility of alternative angles
- An offer to supply or help secure all needed statistics, quotes, interviews with credible resources, arrangements for photos, and so on
- An indication of authority or credibility
- An offer to call the editor soon to get a decision

Follow Up on Your Pitch

The advantage of a telephone call, of course, is that you get instant feedback. If you have e-mailed, faxed, or even mailed a pitch to an editor or broadcast producer, it is important to follow up. It is not good enough to end a pitch by asking a reporter to call you if they have questions. A better approach is what Julie Schweigert of Edelman Worldwide wrote at the end of her pitch letter for Korbel's "perfect proposal contest." She takes the initiative in a nice way by writing "I will contact you next week to follow-up, but in the meantime you can reach me at 312/233-1380 with any questions." Remember, in public relations, keep the ball and the responsibility for follow-up in your court.

In your follow-up, the reporter may ask you to send more information. If that is the case, make sure you provide all the information within 24 hours. You should also ask how the reporter would like to receive the information—by e-mail, fax, U.S. mail, or special messenger. Reporters all have their own preferences.

Reporters and editors can also be quite blunt and tell you in no uncertain terms that they aren't interested. Or they may be more polite and say they have already done a similar story recently, so they are not interested at the moment. But you can impress them, and even change their minds, if you have done your homework and can say accurately why your story is different from the last three articles about similar subjects.

Follow-up, however, often means that you graciously accept "No" for an answer. Don't keep pitching the idea or arguing with the editor over the merits of the story; it is better to cut your losses and keep the door open for future pitches to the same editor. You must continually develop good, productive relationships with the reporters you typically pitch; you won't win all the time, but you will improve your batting average by remaining cordial and gaining trust as a good resource person.

Summary

- Fact sheets are a brief outline of an event, an organization, or a new product. The purpose is to place basic and supplemental information at the editor or journalist's fingertips.

- Media advisories, also called *media alerts*, tell assignment editors about an upcoming event. They often suggest photo, video, and interview opportunities. Media alerts about upcoming events typically include the five Ws and H in outline form.

- Media kits are packets of material that may include news releases, photographs, feature stories, fact sheets, position papers, backgrounders, and brief biographical sketches.

- Electronic press kits (EPKs) are prepared in CD format or are available online from organizational Web sites. They can include all the information in a printed media kit, but also include audio sound bites, high-resolution photos, video clips, and product demonstrations.

- The purpose of a pitch letter is to convince editors and reporters to cover an event or do a story. Pitches to editors must be brief, raise interest, and come immediately to the point. Pitch letters are customized to each editor based on the publication's content, demographics, and circulation. E-mail pitches must have succinct, creative subject lines. A telephone pitch requires the same preparation as writing a memo or sending an e-mail pitch.

Skill Building Activities

1. Select a local nonprofit organization or a company and write a basic fact sheet about it.

2. The Minnesota Zoo is opening a major exhibit about insects on May 1. A variety of "bugs" from around the world will be included in the exhibit, but the major attraction will be a walk-through butterfly garden where a thousand butterflies will be feeding, resting, and emerging as adult butterflies. Write a media advisory (alert) inviting the media to the opening and make some suggestions about interview, photo, and video opportunities.

3. The Minnesota Zoo exhibit on insects will have thousands of live bugs on display. Write an e-mail pitch to the lifestyle editor at the *Minneapolis Tribune* to do a story on the exhibit. Also, write another e-mail pitch to the assignment editor at the leading television station in the Twin Cities.

4. The Hard Rock Hotel and Casino in Las Vegas has completed an $800 million renovation project and wants to attract new business from men and women aged 21 to 49. A media kit needs to written and produced to start generating coverage and "buzz" about the renovated facilities. Write a memo outlining what materials would be included in a digital media kit (either a CD or website).

Suggested Readings

Brown, Lorra M. "Faulty Pitches: How to Avoid Sending Irrelevant, Infuriating Material to Editors." *PR Tactics*, December 2007, p. 12.

"Great Opening Lines: Boost Your Chances at Coverage by Writing Pitch Leads that Get Reporter's Attention." *Ragan's Media Relations Report*, February 3, 2003, pp. 1, 6.

Kent, Christine. "Brilliant Media Pitches: How to Craft E-Mail Subject Lines." Ragan.com, www.ragan.com, April 2, 2008.

Kent, Christine. "Eight Pitches that Caught Reporters' Attention." Ragan.com, www.ragan.com, January 30, 2008.

Lewis, Benjamin. *Perfecting the Perfect Pitch: Creating Publicity Through Media Support.* Potomac, MD: Larstan Publishing, Inc., 2007.

McGuire, Craig. "The New, Lightweight Press Kit." *PRWeek*, May 15, 2006, p. 18.

Oates, David B. "A Pitch Must Keep the Editor in Mind." *PR Tactics*, December 2003, p. 13.

Sebastian, Michael. "How to Pitch the *Times*' David Pogue." Ragan.com, www.ragan.com, April 23, 2008.

Seitel, Fraser. "The Art of Pitch Emails." *O'Dwyer's PR Report*, May 2007, pp. 48–49.

Walton, Susan Balcom, and Kalm, Nick. "Conversation Starter: Why You Should Resuscitate the Verbal Media Pitch." *PR Tactics*, May 2007, p. 17.

Creating News Features and Op-Ed 7

TOPICS covered in this chapter include:

The Value of Features   163

Planning a News Feature   164

Types of Features   168

Parts of a Feature   175

Placement Opportunities   180

Writing an Op-Ed   181

The Value of Features

Perhaps the best way to show the value of news feature stories is to contrast them with basic news releases. The news release emphasizes the timely disclosure of basic information about situations and events. The **feature story**, in contrast, can provide additional background information, generate human interest, and create understanding in a more imaginative way.

In other words, news release writing requires left-brain skills emphasizing the logical, analytical, and sequential development of ideas. Feature writing, in contrast, requires right-brain skills, such as intuition, image-making, and creativity. Facts form the basis of feature writing in public relations, just as they do in news release writing, but the approach is different.

Consider, for example, the appointment of a new company president. The news release will give the basic information in one or two paragraphs. It will give the new president's name and perhaps a brief summary of her professional career—all pretty dry, routine stuff. A feature article, however, could give the new president a human dimension. It would focus on her philosophy of management, college experiences, hobbies and interests, and vision of the future. Such an article might run 1,500 words instead of two paragraphs.

Features are considered "soft news" rather than "hard news." In journalistic terms, this means that features are not as time-sensitive as the "hard" news of quarterly earnings, mergers and acquisitions, contracts, expansions, and lay-offs. They entertain, provide background, and give consumer tips. They often show up in the specialty sections of the daily newspaper—entertainment, food, business, real estate, automotive, technology—and most of them originate from public relations sources.

Feature stories come in all sizes and shapes, but all of them have the potential to (1) provide more information to the consumer, (2) give background and context about organizations, (3) provide behind-the-scenes perspective, (4) give a

> ❝ *Feature news has an indefinite shelf life, and can be used by the media when it's needed, not just when it's distributed.* ❞ ■ Business Wire

human dimension to situations and events, and (5) generate publicity for standard products and services.

Regarding the last point, many products are not particularly newsworthy and would never get coverage if a feature writer didn't exercise some creativity. Think of the lowly potato. It would seem that no self-respecting editor would be interested in a news release from the National Association of Potato Growers. However, a feature directed to the food editor can generate coverage and also increase sales of potatoes. Some possible features might discuss (1) potatoes as a source of vitamins, (2) potatoes as a low-cost addition to daily nutritional needs, and (3) creative recipes using potatoes as an ingredient. Another possibility is a short history of the potato, its origins, and its economic impact.

Indeed, evidence suggests that feature materials are becoming increasingly popular with newspapers and magazines. A survey of trade editors conducted by Rhode Island–based Thomas Rankin Associates, for example, found that more than half of the editors wanted more case histories and technical "how to" features from public relations sources. Mike Yamomoto, managing editor of CNET, says, "The future of media is a greater concentration on the feature story as a branding vehicle. The challenge for the media is to capture audiences with a unique presentation of information."

The new interest in feature articles, particularly by print media, no doubt is related to where people get their news. Radio, TV, and the Internet now provide the instant "hard" news, so many newspapers are shifting their focus to publishing more in-depth stories on news events and features that provide consumer tips. A readership study by the Newspaper Association of America and the American Society of Newspapers, for example, found that feature-style writing increased reader satisfaction, was easier to read than the traditional inverted-pyramid news approach, and even made it more "fun" to read the newspaper.

The concept of publishing consumer tips and "news you can use" is referred to as **service journalism**. According to *News Reporting and Writing* by Brooks, Kennedy, Moen, and Ranly, a key component of service journalism is to demonstrate how the reader can use the information to do such things as (1) save time, (2) make more money, (3) save money, or (4) get something free. In other words, the idea is WIIFM—what's in it for me?

If public relations professionals keep this axiom in mind, the print media will be more than happy to use their material.

■ Planning a News Feature

Coming up with a feature idea takes some creative thinking. There are three things to keep in mind. First, you have to conceptualize how something lends itself to feature treatment. Second, you have to determine if the information would be interesting to and useful for a particular audience. Third, you must be sure that the feature helps achieve organizational objectives. Does it position the organization in a favorable light? Does it encourage the use of a particular product or service?

Good feature writers ask a lot of questions. They need a natural curiosity about how things work and how things are related to each other. If the company has just produced a new video game, for example, you would find out exactly how the game was developed. By asking questions, you might find out that a 19-year-old computer "nerd" invented the game, or that a new technology was used to create "real-life" animated effects. In each case, you have a potential feature. A story about the inventor would make interesting reading, but so would a story about how the new computer technology could be applied in other fields.

News events and issues can also trigger ideas for feature stories. If Congress passes a law, how does that affect your organization or industry? If media attention is being given to global warming and greenhouse gasses, perhaps you can develop a feature on how your company is using new technologies to reduce its carbon footprint. The possibilities are limited only by your own imagination and creativity.

Ways to Proceed

Once you have a feature idea, there are four ways you can proceed. The most common approach is to write a general feature and distribute it to a variety of publications in much the same way as news releases are sent or posted on the organization's website. A similar method is to have a feature service distribute it for you in various formats, ranging from straight text to more elaborate layouts that include headlines, photos, and stories already prepared for newspaper columns and pages. Such layouts are called **camera-ready** in the trade, and a good example is shown in Figure 7.1. Distribution by feature service firms is discussed further in Chapter 10.

In most cases, such features are topic-specific and are sent to the editor in charge of a particular section. A feature on the lowly potato is sent to the food editor, but a feature on a new "smart" phone goes to the business or technology editor. A feature on how to have a

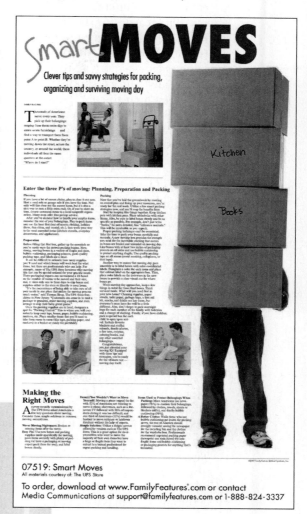

07519: Smart Moves
All materials courtesy of: The UPS Store

To order, download at www.FamilyFeatures.com or contact Media Communications at support@familyfeatures.com or 1-888-824-3337

FIGURE 7.1 Feature releases are often distributed in camera-ready format, which means that they are already set up in regular newspaper columns, complete with a headline and even photos. All an editor has to do is insert the article into the page. This service feature, prepared and distributed by Family Features, was for The UPS Store.

beautiful green lawn, of course, goes to the garden editor. In a more sophisticated version of this approach, newspapers in the same circulation area will receive different features and photos about the same subject. This way, editors know the material is somewhat exclusive to them and won't show up in a competing publication.

The second approach is to write an exclusive feature for a specific publication. In this case, you need to target a publication that reaches your selected audience, be they engineers, architects, educators, or purchasing agents. You also need to review several issues of the publication to determine the topics it has covered and the style used in similar articles.

Once you are familiar with the publication, phone the editor, outline the subject in about 60 seconds, and ask if he or she would be interested. You can also send a brief letter. Carol Haddix, food editor of the *Chicago Tribune*, says the ideal public relations professional "just sends a note explaining his or her idea in a way that is phrased to interest me."

The reason for the short phone call or a note (called a *query*) is to determine if there is enough interest to justify writing an exclusive feature. Perhaps the editor has recently run several features much like the one you have in mind. Or the editor might suggest another story angle that would appeal to more readers.

Many editors, simply on the basis of a phone call or a brief note, will give you the green light to submit an article for consideration. This does not mean that they are obligated to use it.

Other editors, particularly those for popular magazines, will ask you to submit a *proposal* that outlines the entire article and explains why the magazine should publish it. A proposal should include the following points:

- Tentative title of the article.
- Subject and theme.
- Significance. Why is the topic important? Why should readers know about it?
- Major points.
- Description of photos and graphics available.

The third approach is not to write the feature at all. Instead, you give a journalist a story idea that he or she might want develop on his or her own. In other words, you phone or e-mail the person and make a pitch, which was discussed in Chapter 6. If the journalist is interested, you can offer to help by sending background information, providing photos and other artwork, and even setting up interviews with potential sources for the story.

The advantage of this approach is that the publication's staff actually writes the story. Thus, the publication has invested time and money in the story and is more likely to publish it. The disadvantage is that you can't always control how the story will be developed and whether it will advance organizational objectives.

The fourth approach is simply to post the feature on your organization's website for possible downloading by journalists and consumers. Hewlett-Packard (HP), for example, has a link on its online newsroom (www.hp.com) simply titled "feature stories." Figure 7.2 shows a feature story about how to use HP software and equipment to make customized wedding invitations. Other placement opportunities for features are discussed later in this chapter.

» HP Home   » Products & Services   » Support & Drivers   » Solutions   » How to Buy

» Contact HP

Search: [   ] »

⦿ HP Newsroom ○ All of HP U.S.

Newsroom > Feature stories

Get a warm reception

Wedding guests will love receiving these HP Activity Center projects

■ Share/tag this page

Readers have rated this story
3.69 out of 5

» Company information

» Newsroom home

News
» News releases
» **Feature stories**
» HP Videos
» Blogs
» Podcasts
» RSS Feeds
» Awards

Journalist resources
» Media relations contacts
» Fast facts
» Press kits
» Executive team
» Financial information
» Global citizenship
» History & Milestones
» News archives

Related links
» HP Ads
» HP Images
» Recalls and replacement programs
» Student Inquiries
» Trademark and Product names

by Susan Twombly, April 2008

There's nothing more personal than your wedding day. And there's no better way to make the day more personal than with beautifully colored and customized wedding invitations, programs and more.

At the HP Activity Center, you'll find FREE projects to do with your honey – and for not much money. In fact, HP printers, paper and inks are designed to work better together – so there's no need to waste precious wedding dollars on multiple reprints. With easy instructions, each professional-looking project is a piece of cake.

So, after he pops the question, pop on over to the HP Activity Center. And, don't forget to tell friends and family about the Bridal Shower Kit!

Say "I do" to these projects

Bella Flora Wedding Collection
» View enlarged image
» View project page

Find your perfect match with the **Bella Flora Wedding Collection** to create a colorful, consistent look before, during and after your day. When you think of flowers, think beyond your bouquet with the botanically inspired **Bella Flora Wedding Invitation Kit.**

The kit includes matching invitations, RSVP, reception cards and envelopes. Choose from four themes in chartreuse, chocolate, plum or grey. Then, add text, colored overlays and up to six photos to create a couple-customized look. Add an artistic touch to the return address label with **Bella Flora Envelope Label Wraps.**

The **Bella Flora Wedding Kit Assembly and Tips** gives you helpful hints on how to write, put together and mail your wedding invitations and thank you notes – from composing casual or more formal greetings to printing and postage guidelines. Get help choosing the right paper for a traditional or contemporary look or – for brides that want to wear white but think green – recycled paper.

Engage your guests with a **Bella Flora Wedding Program,** a pretty and practical way to

Choose your project!
» HP Activity Center
» Bella flora wedding collection
» Bella flora wedding invitation kit
» Bella flora envelope label wrap
» Bella flora wedding program
» Wedding wrap sets
» Bella flora wedding CD/DVD sleeve
» Bella flora wedding CD/DVD tattoos
» Bella flora thank-you note and envelope
» Bridal shower kit
» Wedding wrap sets
» Fortune gift box kit
» Vintage nouveau wine gift set
» Basil & twill 5 x 7 photo frames

Choose your printer!
» HP A626 Compact Photo Printer
» HP Photosmart C7280 All-in-One Printer

» Your feedback is important to us, tell us more

Give the gift that keeps on giving

HP A626 Compact Photo Printer
» View enlarged image

▶ **FIGURE 7.2**   Feature stories are often found in the online newsrooms of major corporations, which are accessible to both journalists and the public. One feature posted by HP offered tips to couples on how to do their own wedding invitations and thank you notes using applications in the HP Activity Center. The feature included photos that could be enlarged for better viewing, as well as links to other "how to" sites for bridal showers, wedding programs, and creating customized CD covers and wine labels.

■ Types of Features

There is no formal classification of feature stories and no practical limit to the variety of stories that can be written. Whenever you find something that can be made interesting to some segment of the public, it may be the beginning of a feature. Some ideas are obvious, but many more can be developed if you hunt for them. Among the most frequently seen features are (1) case studies, (2) application stories, (3) research studies, (4) backgrounders, (5) personality profiles, and (6) historical pieces. These categories are not mutually exclusive, and the lines between them often blur, but some familiarity with them will help you understand the range of possibilities.

Case Study

The **case study** is frequently used in product publicity. Case studies often tell how individual customers have benefited from a company's product or service or how another organization has used the product or service to improve efficiency or profits. In other words, case studies are a form of third-party endorsement or testimonial that helps illustrate the acceptance or popularity of a particular service or product in the marketplace.

Organizations providing various services often use the case study feature. One company, Great Date, distributed a feature release that related the stories of two men (a lawyer and a stock broker) who found love and happiness after signing up with the matchmaking service. The founder of the service is quoted later in the feature saying, "Jim is typical of many male clients who want a professional matchmaker to help them. In just the last month, we have worked with a 40-year-old never-married surgeon, a 38-year-old real estate lawyer, and a 48-year-old stockbroker whose wife had died of cancer several years ago." The idea, of course, is to encourage readers to relate the service to their own needs by showing "typical" clients who are benefiting from its services.

In October, at the beginning of the skiing season, Great Date issued another feature titled "Skiers Turn to Professional Matchmakers." The angle was timely, and again the feature gave several case histories of men and women finding love on the slopes thanks to the efforts of the matchmaking firm. In sum, the skiing angle was yet another way to package the same message with a seasonal focus.

❝ *Case studies are an essential aspect of many PR programs, providing rich information on the value and strength of a company's offering.* ❞
■ Catherine M. Wolfe, director of marketing services, Toshiba America Medical Systems

Technology may not be as interesting as finding love, but HP develops a number of features to demonstrate the versatility and durability of its many products. In one case study, for example, the company explains how Nissan uses HP computer equipment to monitor prototype electronic engine-control systems in its racing cars. The story quotes a Nissan executive saying, "Our jobs are simplified knowing that the engine computer will perform up to specifications under severe race conditions. With HP's help, we can get down to the business of winning races."

Another HP feature described how a Mt. Everest expedition used its portable Deskjet printer to print weather reports and other data at its base camp, which was located in the bitter cold at 17,000 feet. The expedition leader is quoted as saying, "For a portable, its speed and resolution are remarkable." Consumers may not be climbing Mr. Everest anytime soon, but they get the impression that this is an extremely durable and reliable product.

A word of caution about case studies. Although most customers and organizations are flattered that you want to use them in a case study about your products and services, you should always ensure that they have given permission and have approved the feature story—in writing. See the following Tips for Success for more tips on how to write a case study.

Application Story

The **application story** is similar to the case study. The major distinction is that the application story focuses primarily on how consumers can use a product or a service in new and innovative ways. The advantage to the organization is that it can show multiple, practical applications of a product or service over a period of time, which generates increased consumer awareness and usage.

Much food publicity consists of application stories—new recipes or new variations on familiar ones. The food pages of newspapers carry many such features. There's nothing new about apples, walnuts, beef, or even artichokes, but the producers and distributors of such commodities regularly send the media new recipes and ways of preparing such foods. Most of these features are accompanied by mouth-watering, high-resolution color photos that entice consumers to try the

☑ tips FOR SUCCESS

Writing a Case Study

A satisfied customer is the key to writing a case history that shows how a company's product or service was used successfully. G. A. "Andy" Marken, president of Marken Communications, offers a list of questions that a public relations writer should keep in mind:

- What can be told about the company, its place in the industry, its size, and other details?
- Why did the company first need the products or services in question?
- Who was involved in the application?
- What did the products or services do for those people? What can they do now, as a result of the products or services, that they couldn't do before?
- How does the solution save time and money and add quality?
- Could the company get the same results with a competitive solution? If not, how does this solution provide savings that couldn't otherwise be achieved?
- What is the customer contact protocol? Who should clear and approve the article? ■

FIGURE 7.3 Food features are made more attractive with mouth-watering photos of prepared dishes. This photo from Boggiato Produce, Inc., features its romaine lettuce as part of a shrimp tempura recipe that was made available to food editors. A CD media kit contained numerous recipes and corresponding high-resolution photos.

recipes that, in turn, generate sales for the ingredients. See Figure 7.3 for a typical food publicity photo.

Another approach is to give consumers tips and advice that relate to an organization's products and services. Homewood Suites, for example, issued a feature story titled "Taking Your Kids—and Visiting Colleges." It was distributed in March by Business Wire just as the "season" started for parents and high school seniors to visit various prospective colleges. The application story was a list of 10 tips by a travel expert for "visiting colleges with your kids." One tip: "Whenever possible, leave the younger siblings behind. They'll be bored." Another useful tip: "Move on if you arrive on campus and your child refuses to get out of the car." The complete news feature is provided in Figure 7.4.

> ❝ *A succession of application stories about customers utilizing the same product in different ways can show varied uses for a product or service.* ❞
>
> ■ Donna St. Jean Conti, owner of St. Conti Communications

Smead Corporation, a manufacturer of office supplies, also used a feature approach to give consumers advice on how to get organized. The story was titled, "The Three Big Myths of Getting Organized." The first myth was "All I have to do is buy organizing products to get organized." The refutation of the myth was "Don't stop here. You have to use organizing materials."

Gold's Gym generates publicity and name recognition by sending reporters features on fitness topics ranging from how to get in shape for bikini season or reducing the tire found on many middle-aged men. The opportunities for offering consumer tips are boundless and are limited only by the writer's imagination. An orchid farm issued a feature story by offering the tip that men could really impress their significant others by skipping the roses on Valentine's Day and giving a potted orchid instead. According to the feature, an orchid is really a "babe magnet for the clueless guy."

Research Study

Surveys and polls, as well as scientific studies, can provide opportunities for features. This is particularly true if the **research study** is about some aspect of contemporary lifestyles or a common situation in the workplace. One study, sponsored by a Korbel Champagne Cellars, was about how Americans propose marriage. It found, among other things, that 25 percent of men still propose marriage on bended knee.

Residence Inn, a chain owned by the Marriott Corporation, got extensive coverage with a research study about the effects of long business trips on female man-

FIGURE 7.4 A hallmark of a good feature story is providing information and tips that help consumers in their daily lives. This release from Homewood Suites gives 10 tips for parents taking their children on a tour of prospective colleges. Such trips, of course, include staying in hotels, and such a feature positioned Homewood well for generating business during the spring "tours."

March 11, 2008 01:35 AM Pacific Daylight Time

Taking Your Kids—And Visiting Colleges

Travel & Leisure I

MEMPHIS, Tenn.–(BUSINESS WIRE)–In the next few months, college campuses across the country will begin to see the ubiquitous cluster of parents and high school seniors and juniors narrowing down their top picks. Campus touring as a family can be valuable bonding time as well as an extra reason to get away. Spring and summer are the busiest as families visit more campuses than ever.

Syndicated Family Travel Columnist, Eileen Ogintz, author of Taking the Kids (www.takingthekids.com) has toured campuses from Maine to Illinois to California with her kids and others and interviewed plenty of parents and admissions experts along the way. Below are her top ten tips for visiting colleges with your kids:

1. Whenever possible, leave the younger siblings behind. They'll be bored. Use the opportunity to focus on your college-bound child.

2. Build some fun into the trip—include some pool time, or visit some area attractions. Think of this as a special time with your child that you won't have again.

3. Take a virtual tour of the campus first - you might cross it off the list before you visit. One site, www.campustours.com offers tours of hundreds of colleges and universities.

4. Plan on no more than two campuses a day, if that, and don't schedule more than three days in a row or all of the schools will start to look alike. Allow time for a tour, information session and coffee or lunch in the student center–so your son or daughter can get a feel for the place.

5. Refrain from asking too many questions or offering comments. That will only embarrass your child.

6. If you know a child at the school you're visiting, invite them to lunch or dinner so your child can get another perspective.

7. If you are touring near a city or suburban campus, consider staying at a "suite - hotel" like Homewood Suites where you and your family with have lots of room to spread out. They even offer great perks like free internet, free breakfast and a complimentary grocery shopping service. Visit homewoodsuites.com for more information and additional locations.

8. If the process is entirely too stressful, consider sending your teen on organized college tours like those run by former Johns Hopkins University admissions official Bob Rummerfield. (www.college-visits.com)

9. Bring along a laptop and suggest your child write some initial impressions after each visit.

10. Move on if you arrive on campus and your child refuses to get out of the car.

Even if your kids are too young to think about college, introduce them to your alma mater or even plan your next vacation near a college campus. With these tips in mind, a little patience, and smart planning, college touring can be a great time for bonding with your children before they leave the nest.

Contacts

for Homewood Suites
Brad Carmony, 901-374-6518
brad.carmony@hilton.com
http://www.hiltonworldwide.com

agers and executives. The feature concentrated on the research finding that women feel more productive and stimulated by extended business trips than men, who report feeling lonely and bored. The feature went on to quote psychologists, female executives, and Residence Inn managers about the findings of the study. According to Marriott, women now comprise 31 percent of all business travel "roomnights."

Philips Norelco distributed feature stories relating to the introduction of its new Bodygroom all-purpose shaver for men. A commissioned survey by Opinion Dynamic Corporation found that more than half of the male respondents prefer a hairless back to any other body part. Among the other earthshaking findings was that "More than 72 percent of the men surveyed indicated that they use a razor blade to remove hair in even the most sensitive areas—ouch!"

Research studies can also have seasonal themes. The Abundant Forests Alliance, for example, distributed a research study during the pre–Christmas season by reporting that nearly 6 out of 10 Americans purchase artificial trees rather than real ones. The second sentence in the lead paragraph, however, went on to say that "about the same number mistakenly believe buying an artificial Christmas tree is better for the environment than a real Christmas tree." The story went on to expand on the themes of the forest industry—that real Christmas trees are biodegradable and recyclable.

Backgrounder

There are several kinds of **backgrounders**. One focuses on a problem and how it was solved by an organization or a product. Often there is some historical material and an opportunity for injecting human interest into the story. One example is a story on the reclamation of strip-mined land and how a coal company restored an area to productive use for farming.

Another kind of backgrounder explains how a technology or product has evolved over the years. A good example is a feature about the evolution of the Global Positioning Systems (GPS), which is based on a network of satellites circling the earth. The company that supplies road data to in-car navigation systems is NAVTEQ, which is not exactly a household name. It was a major sponsor of a map exhibition at Chicago's Field Museum, and a feature was distributed about how the company generates the data used by MapQuest, Google, and almost all GPS systems. It's a fascinating story of two-person teams literally driving millions of miles a year recording "navigation attributes." See Figure 7.5 to see the entire news feature.

Cisco Systems, which had developed a new technology for enhancing global teleconferencing, issued a backgrounder on the problems and challenges of creating a global "virtual team" that could meet as if all the team members were in the same

 The Field Museum

 THE NEWBERRY LIBRARY CHICAGO

State-of-the-Art Navigation Looks to the Future…and the Past

"Take a left by the McDonald's, go past the old Burma Shave signs, look for the big oak tree and take a right. You can't miss it."

If you've ever gotten turn-by-turn directions from someone, you know they work perfectly…until they don't. Maybe you've turned at the wrong McDonald's (there are so many!), or maybe the oak tree was uprooted in last week's storm. You miss one stoplight, go a bit too far before you realize it, and pretty soon you're completely lost, with no way to get back to a familiar landmark.

That's where the in-car navigation system takes us a big step forward. Global Positioning Systems (GPS) are based on a network of satellites circling the earth that can pinpoint exactly where you are at any moment. In combination with digitized maps, the navigation system can tell you exactly how to get there from here, wherever "there" and "here" may be. They're also used in day-to-day business – for example, making sure your package gets to its exact address. And they can be a life-saving feature of your local emergency response team, helping them locate a crisis quickly and accurately. These are feats that would have seemed like science fiction a generation ago; to many of us, they *still* feel futuristic.

But a little-known secret of high-tech digital mapping is revealed here: it depends on old-fashioned legwork – make that wheelwork – by a couple of people in a car, collecting data as they drive the roads.

On the Road Again…and Again…and Again…

The company that supplies road data to your in-car navigation system, to the Internet mapping sites of MapQuest, Google, and Yahoo, to truck fleets and the U.S. Army, is Chicago-based NAVTEQ. To create their database they begin with existing maps, charts, and satellite images obtained from the Census Bureau, local governments, and other sources. They digitalize this data, bring it all together…and then the fun begins.

Based in field offices around the world are more than 600 NAVTEQ geographic analysts. All together they drive millions of miles a year, in two-person teams, collecting information known as "navigation attributes." What's the speed limit on this stretch of road? Can you make a left turn at that intersection? Is this still a one-way street? Where is the entrance to this public building? What do the road signs say? There are more than 200 of these attributes that teams collect – in addition to verifying the data they have, looking for new roads, and noting changes to old ones. While one team member drives (slowly!), the other feeds the data into a laptop computer connected to a GPS that is concurrently tracking their route.

Geographic analysts are on the road virtually every day. Back in the office they compile the new data and update the database. NAVTEQ provides its clients with the data, updated regularly, and companies like Google and OnStar put it to use in Internet map directions and navigation systems. Companies use their own algorithms – sophisticated mathematical formulas – to map the route you request. In many cases, it's not the shortest route but the quickest, so the algorithms figure in a number of the navigational attributes NAVTEQ collects, such as road speeds, stoplights, and toll plaza.

Currently, most in-car systems are getting this information from data stored in the program of the in-car system, not from real-time data feeds. So they can't include up-to-the-minute information on road repairs, accidents, and rush-hour traffic jams. But state-of-the-art navigation systems – in cars, mobile phones, and other devices – are beginning to provide real-time information, offering more routing alternatives and views much closer to what you see through your windshield. Get a sneak preview of what lies ahead in The Field Museum's *Maps: Finding Our Place in the World*.

# # #

FIGURE 7.5 The Field Museum, as part of its media kit on an exhibition entitled "Maps: Finding Our Place in the World," included a feature about the exhibit's major sponsor, NAVTEQ. The Chicago–based company provides information for road maps and GPS systems around the world. This well-written feature provides a "behind the scenes" insight into how the company compiles its data.

room. As the feature states, "Advances in communication technologies have not only created new opportunities to reach new markets and suppliers, but also a workplace that is becoming virtual, with team members located around the world." The feature, which was posted on its website and distributed to technology trade journals, cited the findings of two experts in the field who had written a book on effectively communicating in a global company.

Personality Profile

People like to read about people, particularly if they are celebrities. A review of any magazine newsstand is a graphic confirmation that the "cult of personality" is alive and well. Such profiles are highly readable because they "humanize" the celebrity by giving a glimpse of what's behind the curtain, so to speak.

Personality profiles of "movers and shakers" also are popular in the business press. Cover articles in *Fortune* magazine often profile the lives and management philosophies of successful CEOs. Other profiles of prominent executives can also be found in such publications as *BusinessWeek*, *Forbes*, *The New Yorker*, *Financial Times*, and *The Wall Street Journal*.

In most cases, these profiles are written by journalists with, quite often, a strong assist from public relations personnel who (1) "sell" the idea of a profile, (2) make the executive available, (3) provide background information, and (4) even arrange photo shoots.

Another approach is writing a profile of the CEO that can be used in media kits and posted on the organization's website. A media kit for Boston Beer Company, producers of the Samuel Adams brand, includes a two-page, single-spaced profile of its founder, Jim Koch. In it, readers get a sense of Koch's values and philosophy about making beer. We also learn that he has three degrees from Harvard, taught adventure skills for Outward Bound, and told his dad that he wanted to start a brewery. To which his dad responded, "You've done some dumb things in your life, but this is just about the dumbest."

A person doesn't have to be a CEO, however, in order to qualify for a personality profile. There is any number of employees in any organization who would make an interesting profile because they have an unusual job, an interesting hobby, or have distinguished themselves in some way. A San Francisco company, for example, once distributed a feature on the new manager of the company's Vietnamese Service Center because the woman had a compelling story about her escape from war-torn Vietnam. Bowling Green State University once got a major feature in the *Chronicle of Higher Education* by profiling the director of the university's research center on fruit flies, which the publication dubbed "Fruit-Fly Capital of the World." The Tips for Success on page 174 offers additional tips for writing a personality profile.

Historical Piece

Anniversaries, major changes, centennials, and many other events lend themselves to historical features. Significant milestones may present an opportunity to report on the history of the organization, its facilities, or some of its people. Stressing the

Writing a Personality Profile

A writer attempts to capture the essence of an individual in a personality profile by creating a full-color picture in words. Ragan Communications, Inc., publisher of various newsletters about communication, gives the following tips on how to enhance the writing of your profile features:

- **Give the "essence."** Tell the reader who the profile subject is and why he or she is interesting.

- **Take some chances.** A profile is an interpretation, not an official biography. Give the reader a picture of your subject as you see him or her.

- **Get a different view.** Try to see the world through the subject's eyes. A profile works when you understand a person's motivations.

- **Don't write in chronological order.** Most people are more interesting at 40 than they are at 4. Don't begin at the beginning. Write about what makes your subject interesting now.

- **Make your subject reflect.** Ask profile subjects to evaluate themselves, describing good points and bad, high and low points.

- **Don't focus on work alone.** Don't limit your profile to a piece about somebody's job. Try to see the whole person who goes home after work and has an interesting hobby.

- **Describe, describe, describe.** Paint a picture of your subject. Is he or she serious, jovial, upbeat? What kind of personality does the person exhibit under stress, or at play? ■

---

history of an organization lends it an air of stability and permanence. The public can logically deduce that if an organization has lasted "that long," it must have merit.

Planters, discussed in Chapter 6, used its 100th anniversary to distribute features about the founder of the company, Italian immigrant Amedeo Obici, who started the company in 1906 after observing a person eating peanuts and dropping the shells behind him. That led to Obici's idea to sell fresh, roasted peanuts without the shells. The rest is history, so to speak. The Hershey company celebrated the 100th anniversary of Kisses Chocolates by issuing a feature about the evolution and unique packaging of the product.

One doesn't have to wait for century, however, before writing a historical feature. Logitech, Inc.—the world's largest manufacturer of the computer mouse—was able to generate a large number of feature stories by highlighting its 30th birthday. According to *Ragan's Media Relations Report*, the inventor of the mouse was invited to come see the 200 millionth mouse come off the assembly line. Of course, the press also was invited to the celebration and to interview the man who made "click" part of the world's vocabulary.

Another example of a **historical piece** is a 200-word feature distributed by Fisher Nuts titled "The Humble Peanut Has History as Essential Food." The release begins, "Having nurtured the dawn of civilization in the Amazon River basin, the peanut moved on to support European explorers as early as the 15th century." Historical features are also a staple of tourism publicity. The Alaska Division of

Tourism distributes features about the history of the state to encourage visitors. One article was titled, "Following 19th-Century Russians Across Alaska." The lead paragraph was: "Visitors to Alaska who have forgotten their American history are quickly reminded that the 49th state was once a Russian colony. One reminder is the large number of Russian names sprinkled across the map."

Chicago's Field Museum took a somewhat different approach for its exhibition on maps. It compiled four 200-word stories about the role of maps through history. Cortez described the Aztec capital of Tenochitlan by sending a map to Charles V, King of Spain. Maps also helped American and British negotiators determine the boundaries of the United States after the Revolutionary War, and a doctor in the 1850s "mapped" the spread of cholera in London by neighborhoods, thus limiting its spread.

Parts of a Feature

The formatting of a feature is similar to that of a news release. You should use the organization's letterhead and give the standard information such as contacts, headlines, and datelines. The test can be double-spaced or single-spaced, depending on its distribution, and sentences or paragraphs should not break between pages or computer screens. The following sections detail the components of a feature news release, and additional tips are given in the Tips for Success on page 176.

The Headline

"Newspaper and broadcast editors pick daily from over 10,000 releases online and on paper," says Ron Levy, the founder of North American Precis Syndicate, but you can get hundreds of placements if you use headlines that "editors find delightful and charming."

"Headlines are vital," says Steven Gossett, editorial manager of PR Newswire's feature news unit. He suggests headlines of 20 words or less and to use the name of the organization or product if it is well known. If your client or employer isn't a household name, then the next best approach, says Gossett, is to tell what's new, unusual, different, or important about your product, service, or organization.

There are two kinds of headlines that you can use. The first is the informational headline, which gives the crux of the story. Some informational headlines are "Travel Tips: Travel Insurance Offers Peace of Mind on Family Vacations" and "Expert Advice for Buying Power Tools as Gifts." Another informational headline is "Good News for Caffeine Lovers: Study Shows Caffeinated Beverages Hydrate Like Water."

The informational headline works well for the results of research studies or when the organization is offering advice and tips (10 tips seem to be the standard) on how to purchase a product, book a cruise, or even improve your wardrobe. Essentially, these headlines make the promise of a "reward" for the consumer by helping them save money, buy a good product, achieve better health, or prevent illness. Verizon, for example, got extensive media placements by sending out a news feature offering tips on how to help a child succeed in the classroom.

Writing a Great Feature Story

An organization may get more media exposure by doing a feature story instead of a straight news release. Fred Ferguson, head of PR Newswire's Feature News Service (www.prnewswire.com), offers the following advice on how to write a feature news release:

- Grab the editor's attention with a creative headline that tells the story.
- Tell the same story in the first paragraph, which should never be cute, soft, or a question.
- Support the lead with a second paragraph that backs it up and provides attribution. Place the product and service name at the end of the second paragraph so it becomes less advertorial.
- Try to keep all paragraphs under 30 words and to three lines. This makes it easier for editors to cut to fit available space, holds the reader's attention, and is attractive in most page layouts.
- Do not excessively repeat the name of the product or service. It dilutes the value of the story.
- Forget superlatives, techno-babble, and buzzwords. Instead, tell consumers why they should care.
- Never say anything is the first or the best, express an opinion, or make claims unless you directly attribute it to someone else.
- Avoid using a self-serving laundry list of products or services.
- Discard a telephone number acronym in favor of numerals. It makes it easier for consumers to make a telephone call for more information.
- Don't put the corporate name in all capital letters. It violates AP style.
- Don't give a standard paragraph about the organization at the end of the article. ■

The second kind of headline is one that uses a play on words, alliteration, or a rhyme to raise the curiosity of the editor or the consumer. Levy, mentioned earlier, offers the following examples of word play:

"School Day Stress Busters That Get High Marks" (Procter & Gamble)

"Work and Money Problems Are One Big Headache" (Tylenol)

"Knight of the Road Spend Nights on the Road" (American Trucking Association)

"The Good the Bad and the Bubbly—Celebrating Safely" (American Academy of Ophthalmology)

Other examples of creativity are found in the following sampling of headlines from the feature news website of PR Newswire:

"New Parents Need the Scoop on Cat Litter" (a new cat litter product)

"Help Your Teen Put His Best Face Forward" (a new acne medicine)

"See Your Way Through the Next Power Outage" (a new flashlight)

"New National Water Gardening Group to Dive into Deep End on Important Issues" (organization of a new water conservation group)

Whatever your choice of headline, whether it is an informational one or one that generates curiosity, make sure it grabs the interest of editors and readers. Philips Norelco's Bodygroom feature, for example, merely stated, "Look Better Naked."

The Lead

News releases usually have a summary lead that tells the basic facts in a nutshell. The name of the organization is in the lead, and readers will get the key information even if the summary is all they read.

In contrast, the purpose of the lead in a news feature story is to attract attention and get the reader interested enough to read the entire article. A good lead requires creativity on the writer's part because it must intrigue people and appeal to their curiosity. A lead is a promise; it tells people that they will learn something that will be beneficial to them.

The problem-solving angle often makes a good lead. Here is the lead that Plast World used on a feature news release for its product:

> Mom alert! The solution to summer "blahs" and Father's Day gift giving can be found on the shelves of the nearest gift or toy store. GEOMAG, the world's strongest magnetic building system from Italy, is both the perfect gift for dads and the answer to the most irritating summer question. "I'm bored . . . what can I do?"

Here are some other creative leads that generate interest, give information, or promise a benefit:

- "Many home improvement enthusiasts will tell you that new tools are at the top of their wish lists. But for those with little knowledge of power tools, shopping for them can be an intimidating and confusing experience." (A feature release by Dremel, a manufacturer of power tools, that gives five tips on shopping for power tools.)
- "The joy of the perennial bloom, children's carefree laughter, and a relaxed drive in an old convertible bring to mind the wonderful, cheerful months of summer. The essence of this anticipated season is captured when Filoli, one of America's greatest treasures, hosts its new event, 'Summer at Filoli: A Family Celebration,' on June 28 from 10 A.M. to 3:30 P.M." (A feature release by Filoli Estate, Woodside, California.)
- "More and more men and women, who are regular skiers, are turning to professional matchmakers to find affluent companions who are also skiers." (A feature release by Great Date Now, a matchmaking service.)
- "Tired of staying up all night assembling your kids' holiday gifts? Does the thought of deciphering lengthy, complicated instructions make your skin crawl?

If so, you're not alone." (A feature release by Huffy Sports Company about a "no tools" portable basketball hoop stand.)

Notice that these leads are brief and concise. Most experts recommend a lead paragraph of no more than 30 words. A good lead also focuses on the most unusual part of the story. A lead introducing a machine that builds curbs without forms could start with these words: "The formless curber lays concrete curbs without the use of expensive forms." This statement is factual and true, but the feature would be much more interesting if it started like this: "It's just like squeezing toothpaste out of a tube. In fact, it works on the same principle. By squeezing the concrete through a die shaped like the final curbing, it is possible to lay concrete curbs without the labor and materials needed for forms." This lead should appeal to the contractor who is a prospective buyer of the machine. It is unusual, interesting, and promises the reward of savings.

The Body

Chapter 5 pointed out that news releases use the inverted pyramid, presenting the most important facts first and elaborating on them in the succeeding paragraphs. It also pointed out that news releases should be relatively short.

The feature story, in contrast, has none of these constraints. It doesn't need to follow Ryan's four basic paragraphs, and it can even be longer than one single-spaced page. The practical guide to length is to use enough words to tell the story thoroughly, but to stop writing when it is told. Because most features are planned for specific publications, you should look at the average length of features in the chosen medium. Food sections in the newspaper, for example, tend to want features that are 200 to 750 words long. Business Wire, which distributes features on behalf of clients, recommends a six-paragraph story of 400 words or less. In other words, less is better. In addition, tips should be in bullet form, not numbered.

Feature stories usually include the following:

- Direct quotes from people
- Concrete examples and illustrations
- Basic statistics or research findings
- Descriptive words that paint mental pictures
- Information presented in an entertaining way

Keep in mind the use of parallels. A strange subject will be more understandable if it is explained in familiar terms—as in the curbs-as-toothpaste example. In the amplification of that story, the writer would undoubtedly explain how the concrete is squeezed out of the die using a screw like that in a meat grinder, which extrudes the concrete mix and at the same time pushes the machine away from the newly cast curb.

If a feature does run longer than 200 to 400 words, insert subheads. The subheads, which often are boldfaced or underlined, indicate the major sections of the story. Subheads, however, should also provide information. Instead of saying something vague such as "Adaptability," it is better to write "Adaptability at Local Offices."

The body of the story essentially delivers the reward promised in the lead.

The Summary

In many cases, the summary is the most important part of the feature. It is often quite brief, but it must be complete and clear. Essentially, it is the core message that the writer wants to leave with the reader. Abundant Forests Alliance, for example, ended its feature on Christmas trees by stating the two key points: Recycle your "real" Christmas tree and make Christmas presents out of this year's tree by making holiday potpourri or sachets out of the dried needles.

It's also important to provide sources of more information and product information. Abundant Forests added, "For more Green Tips for the holiday, visit www. abundantforests.org." In the case of Norelco, the final sentence stated, "Bodygroom is available at Target and Amazon.com and retails for $39.99." A feature news article that gave tips to travelers on the benefits of travel insurance ended with the following information:

> HTH Worldwide provides travel insurance services and global health and security information for travelers. For more information or for a free quote, visit www. travelhealthinsurance.com or call HTH Worldwide at (866) 501-3254.

Photos and Graphics

A feature story is often accompanied by photos and graphics to give it more appeal. Food producers typically send mouth-watering color photos of prepared food. See Figure 7.3 to see how a lettuce and vegetable producer used such a product photo.

Media outlets also like **infographics**, computer-generated artwork that attractively displays simple tables and charts. *USA Today* pioneered the use of infographics, and newspapers around the nation now use them with great frequency. A key finding of MCI's "Meetings in America" survey, for example, was chosen by *USA Today* for its front-page "USA Snapshot" series. It was a simple bar chart giving the primary reasons why people get stressed about business travel. Leading the list was "time away from family" with 75 percent. Only 20 percent reported stress filling out expense reports. Chapter 8 gives more information about photos and graphics.

Features have also become multimedia in scope. Stories can be illustrated with photos, audio, video, or podcasts, which broaden their visibility and online life. Distribution services such as Business Wire, PR Newswire, and MarketWire can facilitate these add-ons, but they can also be offered on an organization's website. HP's feature story (Figure 7.2) on using its applications and products to create wedding invitations and programs, for example, included six photos and even had a space where readers could post comments about the article. Feature stories, like news releases, can also be embedded with a URL and Technorati tags to better reach blogs and other online sites such as Facebook. This is discussed further in Chapter 12.

Placement Opportunities

The possibilities for feature story placement are endless. *Bacon's* has more than 100,000 media outlets and 900,000 editors, broadcasters, freelance writers, syndicated columnists, and bloggers in its database.

Your challenge is to figure out what kind of publication would be most interested in your feature story. It may be only one particular trade publication, or it may be all weekly newspapers in the country. See Chapter 10 for a discussion of databases that can help you make that decision.

In general, placement opportunities for the print media include newspapers, general-circulation magazines, specialty/trade magazines, and internal publications. Placement opportunities for broadcast media are discussed in Chapter 9; opportunities for online media are discussed in Chapter 12.

Newspapers

The primary use of features generated by public relations personnel is in the special sections of daily newspapers. The food section is a popular place for manufacturers and producers of food products, and the automotive section gets its fair share of features from Ford, General Motors, and Chrysler.

Weekly newspapers are not as specialized, but editors are always on the lookout for features that affect the average citizen. The Internal Revenue Service, the Social Security Administration, and even producers of grass seed often get space because they give tips to the public about how to save on taxes, file for Social Security, or grow a great lawn.

General Magazines

Although it can be argued that there is no longer any such thing as a "general" magazine, we use the term to mean "popular" magazines such as *Glamour*, *Cosmopolitan*, *Travel & Leisure*, and *People*.

These magazines usually have their own staffs and regular freelancers who write features, but they do rely on public relations sources for ideas and information. Thus, *Seventeen* magazine might carry an article about the difference between suntan lotions and sunscreens. Most of the information would probably have originated with a sunscreen manufacturer that hired a public relations firm to create publicity and increase sales to female teenagers.

Specialty/Trade Magazines

There are two kinds of magazines in this category. The first is magazines that serve particular interest and hobby groups. There are magazines for golfers, surfers, car buffs, stamp collectors, scuba divers, joggers, gardeners, and even soap opera fans. The list of hobbies and interests is endless.

Whenever your organization has something bearing on a special field of interest, there may be a theme for a feature—and it is possible to write more than one feature on the same subject. With a new line of golf clubs, one story might tell how the line was developed under the guidance of a well-known player; another might deal with unusual materials and manufacturing techniques; and a third could describe the experiences of several golfers with the new clubs. Each of these stories might be placed with a different golf magazine.

The second category is publications that serve a particular industry. For example, about 2,600 publications cover the computer industry. The Internet has spawned a whole new set of publications.

Another thing to remember in preparing features for business or trade publications is that a given subject might be of interest in several fields. The remodeling of a hotel could lead to features for a number of unrelated publications. Engineering magazines might be interested in structural problems and solutions, architectural magazines might use stories about design and decoration, travel publications might use stories about the renaissance of a former favorite destination, and hotel supply magazines might use stories about new carpeting, furniture, kitchen facilities, and so on.

Internal Publications

Many internal publications use material from outside sources. The most likely prospects are those where there is a built-in interest. A feature telling how something produced by your organization is helping another organization has innate interest. For example, you might have a feature describing exactly how your company makes the special insulating material that the XYZ Company is using to produce cold-weather footwear. The XYZ Company newsletter or magazine might welcome such a piece.

▉ Writing an Op-Ed

The term *op-ed* literally means "opposite the editorial page." The concept originated at *The New York Times* in 1970 and has now spread to many major newspapers and magazines across the country. The purpose of op-ed articles is to present a variety of views on current news events, governmental policies, pending legislation, and social issues.

From a public relations standpoint, op-ed pieces provide an excellent opportunity for individuals and organizations to reach an audience of readers who also tend to be opinion leaders or, in the jargon of the industry, "influentials." Indeed, if an organizational executive wants to become a spokesperson (the new jargon is "thought leader") for a particular industry or cause, public relations counsel often recommends writing one or more op-ed pieces.

This was the case in Minneapolis when a former mayor was asked by a development company and its public relations firm to write an op-ed piece supporting the immediate opening of a $134 million

> **❝ The whole point of an Op-Ed is to illuminate the issue in a new way. It isn't just opinion; it's an opinion grounded in facts, data, and research. ❞**
>
> ▪ Henry Miller, chief operating officer, Goodman Media

entertainment complex in the downtown area. About the time the complex was ready to open and tenants were preparing to move in, a political controversy about the wisdom of the building the complex in a tight economy started to surface. Even the City Planning Commission was threatening to call public hearings and delay issuing occupancy permits.

McCafferty Interests, the developer of the complex, sought the services of Carmichael Lynch Spong to devise a strategy to get the project back on schedule and to dampen the "political bickering." The firm's recommendation was to place an op-ed in the *Minneapolis Star Tribune* under the by-line of the former mayor who was a strong supporter of the project.

Carmichael Lynch Spong researched past media coverage of the complex, compiled historical data, and consulted with the former mayor to develop a persuasive op-ed piece under her name. It was published in the *Star Tribune* with two photos, one showing the former derelict neighborhood and a current photo showing the new complex.

The op-ed reached an estimated audience of 2.3 million residents in the Twin Cities, and it turned the tide in terms of public support for the project. The *Star Tribune* also wrote an editorial supporting the project after the op-ed piece was published, and even the City Planning Commission changed its mind. Due to these efforts, the complex opened on schedule.

Nintendo also used an op-ed by its president, Satoru Iwata, to position him as a visionary in the industry. The context was the opening of Electronic Entertainment Expo (E3), the major trade show for the electronic entertainment industry, in Los Angeles. Nintendo was introducing its new game console, the Wii, which supported its strategy of expanding into the video game market.

Golin Harris, the public relations firm, commissioned to craft, pitch, and place the op-ed, which was written to accomplish the following:

- Build support for Nintendo's strategy to broaden the appeal of video games.
- Demonstrate how the video game industry had paralleled Hollywood to localize Nintendo's vision beyond the E3 audience to the greater Los Angeles community.
- Position Nintendo president Satoru Iwata as a spokesperson for the video game industry.
- Secure placement in a high-profile outlet, specifically the *Los Angeles Times*.
- Build buzz for Nintendo leading into E3.

The op-ed was written in Iwata's voice and pitched to the *Los Angeles Times*, which published it on the opening day of the E3 conference. According to Golin Harris, "The op-ed . . . helped Nintendo communicate its key messages effectively in a nationally recognized forum and created tremendous buzz for Nintendo going into the event."

Universities and think tanks such as the Brookings Institution and the Hoover Institution also make considerable use of op-ed pieces. The objective is to gain visibility for an institution and establish its experts as "thought leaders" in a particular field. The public relations department of Washington University in St. Louis, for example, got 426 placements in one year by sending op-ed articles written by 62 faculty members.

The op-ed pages of *The New York Times*, *The Wall Street Journal*, *Financial Times*, and the *Washington Post* are the best known and the most prestigious in terms of placement. They regularly carry op-eds written by ambassadors, former presidents, CEOs of major corporations, senators, and a host of other prominent or influential people. The competition is steep; *The Wall Street Journal* receives about 500 to 700 op-ed articles a month and has space for only a few of them.

Your employer or client may not be a former ambassador or a CEO of a global company, but that should not discourage you from submitting op-ed pieces to these newspapers and to other U.S. dailies. Editorial page directors are always looking for fresh insights from anyone who has expertise or a new perspective on a particular topic of current public concern. David Shipley, op-ed editor of *The New York Times*, says it best: "We look for timeliness, ingenuity, strength of argument, freshness of opinion, clear writing, and newsworthiness." Indeed, op-eds must have a current news angle to fulfill the journalistic requirement of timeliness. The following Tips for Success offers more tips on writing an op-ed.

✓ tips FOR SUCCESS

Writing the "Perfect" Op-Ed

- Daily newspapers prefer articles of about 400 to 750 words, which are about three double-spaced pages.

- Concentrate on presenting one main idea or a single theme.

- Have a clear editorial viewpoint. Get to your point in the first paragraph and then proceed to back up your opinion.

- Use facts and statistics to add credibility to what you say. Double-check your facts before using them. John Budd, chairman of The Omega Group, says, "Ratio of opinion to fact should be about 20 percent to 80 percent."

- Don't ramble or deviate from your principal points. An op-ed is not an essay that slowly builds to its point.

- Use short, declarative sentences. Long, complex sentences and paragraphs cause readers to tune out.

- Be timely. The article should be about a current social issue, situation, or news event.

- Avoid the use of "I" in stating your opinion. Write in journalistic third person.

- Use active verbs; avoid passive tense.

- Describe the background of the writer in the cover letter to the publication. This helps editors determine the person's qualifications.

- Don't do a mass mailing of an op-ed piece. Standard practice is to offer the piece to one publication at a time.

- Query editors before sending an op-ed; it will save you time and energy. ■

In addition, you should not overlook the trade press. Publications that serve a particular industry or profession also use commentaries and short opinion articles. A company's head of research or the vice president of human resources might have something to say that would be interesting to the readers of these publications.

Public relations writers often do the initial work of drafting an op-ed for a client or employer. Another way to approach it is to ask a person for notes from a recent speech. Speeches to organizations are often recycled as op-eds to newspapers.

Op-eds, by definition, are short and to the point. The most effective in terms of placement are 400 to 750 words, which are about three to four word-processed pages, double-spaced. Various publications establish their own guidelines for length. The *Atlanta Journal and Constitution* prefers 200 to 600 words, whereas the *Washington Post* wants submissions of 600 to 700 words. *The New York Times* suggests 650 words.

Such restrictions in length mean that you must write well in terms of organization and conciseness. Jennie Phipps, in an article on how to write an op-ed for *PRWeek*, gives the basic format:

> Start with a catchy lead paragraph that is about 30 words. Use the second 35- or 40-word paragraph to explain further what you said in the first graph. The third graph is the nut graph—that's the place where you make your point, preferably in a sentence or two. Use the next half-dozen or so paragraphs to support your point— logically and with verifiable statistical information and quotes from experts. Banish the phrase "I think" altogether. Throw in humor whenever possible. Wrap it all up with a concluding graph that clearly ties back to the nut graph.

This is good advice, but there are some other guidelines to keep in mind. As in pitch letters, you need to do some homework on the audience and geographic reach of the targeted publication. It is also wise to read the editorial pages of the publication and find out, either from the newspaper or a media directory, how op-ed submissions are handled. Some editorial page directors prefer an e-mail or fax query outlining the subject of the proposed op-ed piece and the author's credentials. Others simply want a brief phone call and a pitch in 60 seconds or less.

If the editor is interested, he or she will most likely ask you to submit the op-ed for consideration. This gives you the "green light" to proceed with this particular publication, because you at least have an editor's commitment to review the piece. This is important, because an op-ed should be submitted to only one publication at a time; it is not like a news release that is distributed to numerous publications.

You can always retool the basic op-ed for submission to other publications, but each publication expects exclusive rights to the piece you send them. In fact, publications "lock up" these exclusive rights by paying op-ed authors, even if they are CEOs or millionaires in their own right. *The New York Times*, for example, pays $450+, and *USA Today* pays $300+. Smaller dailies often pay less.

Letters to the Editor

The next best thing to an op-ed article is a published letter. Letters are generally shorter than op-ed pieces. They focus primarily on rebutting an editorial, clarifying information mentioned in a news story or column, or adding information that might not have been included in the original story.

Burton St. John III, writing in *PR Tactics*, calls a letter to the editor an **LTE**. He says:

> LTEs often react to negative editorials, unbalanced news stories or unfavorable letters from other readers. But, increasingly, newspapers are running letters when an organization has positive news to share—perhaps recognizing important civic contributions by their employees or stating public support for an important community movement like downtown development.

An example of a good LTE, reprinted in *PR Tactics*, is the following:

Advertising Mail Has Value

I note with considerable consternation the repeated use of the term "junk mail" in your recent article concerning expanded recycling services in St. Paul. The truth is that most Americans, most of the time, use advertising mail.

According to the *Guide to Mail Order Sales*, $200 billion a year is generated by advertising mail for business and charities. According to the American Newspaper Association, the typical Sunday newspaper is 67 percent advertising. How would you react if a third party referred to the *Star Tribune* as a "junk newspaper"? Just doesn't seem right, does it?

Peggy Larson
Postmaster, St. Paul

There is limited space for letters, so you should follow closely any guidelines that the publication has established. Most newspapers and magazines publish these guidelines as part of an LTE page. The *San Jose* (CA) *Mercury News*, for example, has the following policy: "Letters of up to 125 words will be considered for publication. All letters must include a full name, address, and daytime phone number, plus any affiliations that would place your opinion in context."

Many of the op-ed guidelines apply, but here are some that relate directly to letters:

- Keep it short. A letter of 200 words or less has a much better chance of being published than one with 500 words.
- Be temperate and factual. Don't call the editor or the author of an article names or question their integrity.
- Identify the subject in the opening paragraph. If your letter is in response to a specific article, refer briefly to the article and the date it appeared.
- State the theme of your letter in the second paragraph. Do you agree, disagree, or want to clarify something?
- The next several paragraphs should give your viewpoint, supported by convincing facts, examples, or statistics.
- Close. At the end of your letter, give your name, title, organization, and telephone number. Publications often call to confirm that you wrote the letter.

Another aspect of the editorial page, working with the publisher and editor to have the publication write an editorial supporting your idea or project, will be discussed in Chapter 11.

■ Summary

- News feature writing requires right-brain thinking—intuition, image-making, and conceptualization.

- A feature story can generate publicity for "ho-hum" products and services. It also can give background, context, and the human dimension to events and situations.

- Features and background stories are part of a trend in the print media to do what is called *service journalism*—"news you can use."

- Feature writing uses the "soft sell" approach. The name of the organization, the product, or the service should appear only once or twice. Stay away from hype and provide editors with information that is factual and informative.

- A good feature writer is curious and asks a lot of questions. He or she can conceptualize and see possibilities for the development of a feature article.

- There are four approaches to feature writing: (1) distribute a general feature to a variety of publications; (2) write an exclusive article for a publication; (3) interest a freelancer or reporter in writing a story; and (4) post feature articles on the organization's website.

- There are several types of features: (1) case study, (2) application story, (3) research study,

(4) backgrounder, (5) personality profile, and (6) historical feature. Features can also be a blend of several types.

- Feature stories are formatted much like news releases in terms of using letterheads, contacts, headlines, and datelines.

- A feature should use extensive quotes, concrete examples, highly descriptive words, and information presented in an entertaining way.

- Photos and graphics are an integral part of a feature story package.

- There are numerous placement opportunities for feature articles in specialty newspaper sections (food, real estate, etc.), general-circulation magazines, special-interest magazines, business and trade magazines, and internal publications.

- Op-ed pieces are an opportunity to portray the organization and its executives as "thought leaders" on a particular subject or issue of current public interest. Op-eds must feature strong writing, use facts, and be concise, only about 400 to 700 words.

- Letters to the editor usually are written to comment on, add information, or rebut an article or editorial that has already been published. Most letters should be 200 words or less to better ensure publication.

■ Skill Building Activities

1. Review the contents of your local daily for a week and compile a scrapbook of feature articles you find in the categories of (a) case study, (b) application story, (c) research story, (d) backgrounder, (e) personality profile, and (f) historical piece. In addition, identify the company or association that probably sent the release to the newspaper as part of its publicity efforts. A good

place to look for such features will be the specialty sections of the newspaper, such as food, lifestyle, auto, business, real estate, and so on.

2. A feature article can be written on almost any subject. Write a 200- to 400-word feature for one of the following organizations:

   a. A paint manufacturer

b. The Florida orange industry

c. A national chain of fitness centers

d. A national hotel chain

e. A national restaurant chain

Remember that the information should be useful to prospective customers and appeal to editors.

3. Select a business executive or the head of a charitable organization in your community and write a personality profile about him or her. An alternative is to write a personality profile on a university professor or administrator who has just received a major honor or award.

4. The state legislature is considering a 10-percent increase in tuition at public universities. Draft an op-ed for the president of your university's student government opposing the tuition hike. The audience is readers of the town's daily newspaper.

5. The local business daily has profiled the owner of a successful public relations firm. In the interview, she is quoted as saying, "You don't need a degree in journalism or public relations to work in the field. I have a B.A. in English and worked my way up from a secretary's job." You're majoring in journalism or public relations. Write a letter to the editor (200 words or less) disagreeing with her assessment.

Suggested Readings

Aamidor, Abraham. *Real Feature Writing*. Mahwah, NJ: Lawrence Erlbaum Associates, 2006.

Chang, Irene. "Making Sure That Your Opinion Is Noted." *PRWeek*, April 2, 2007, p. 14.

Conti, Donna St. Jean. "Marketing a Company by Telling Customer Stories: Real Solutions for Real Problems." *PR Tactics*, February 2006, p. 22.

Friedlander, Edward Jay, and Lee, John. *Feature Writing for Newspapers and Magazines*. Boston: Allyn & Bacon, 5th edition, 2004.

Ward, David. "Producing Feature Packages: Giving Reporters the Perfect Package." *PRWeek*, November 14, 2005, p. 18,

Wolfe, Catherine M. "Letting Customers Speak for Your Value: Case Studies Provide Media Coverage Cachet." *PR Tactics*, December 2007, p. 19.

Wylie, Ann. "Increase Readership with a Feature-Style Story: Inverted-Pyramid Stories Take a Beating in Studies and Trends." *PR Tactics*, July 2006, p. 17.

Selecting Publicity Photos and Graphics 8

TOPICS covered in this chapter include:

The Importance of Publicity Photos   188

Components of a Good Photo   188

Working with Photographers   196

Writing Photo Captions   200

Creating Other Graphics   202

Maintaining Photo and Art Files   205

Distributing Photos and Artwork   205

The Importance of Publicity Photos

Photographs and graphics are important components of news releases and feature stories. They add interest and variety, and they often explain things better than words alone.

Helen Dowler, director of photo services at PR Newswire, told *O'Dwyer's PR Services Report*, "Images should be an integral part of every PR plan. Photos alone, or with a press release, will increase interest in a story. In fact, if your picture illustrates a story well, it can be the deciding factor for an editor on whether to report on a story or someone else's."

Today, the digital revolution has made it relatively easy to provide photos and graphics to the media almost instantly via the Internet and the World Wide Web. Thom Weidlich, a reporter for *PRWeek*, explains: "These days, seemingly nothing could be simpler than supplying a newspaper, magazine, or other publication with a needed photo; just attach a JPEG to an e-mail and whisk it through cyberspace."

This chapter explores the elements that make a good publicity photo or graphic and explains how to prepare the material for media consideration. Its purpose is not to make you a professional photographer, but to give you a better working knowledge of what constitutes a good photo and how to work with photographers to achieve maximum media placement results.

Components of a Good Photo

The adage says that a picture is worth a thousand words. A picture in a newspaper or magazine often takes the same space as a thousand words, but it has much more impact. Studies have shown that more people "read" photographs than read articles. The Advertising Research Foundation found that three to four times as many people notice the average one-column photograph as read the average news story. In another study, Professor Wayne Wanta of the University of Missouri found that articles accompanied by photographs are perceived as significantly more important than those without photographs. This also applies to graphics, which will be discussed later in the chapter.

Publicity photos, however, are not published if they are not high resolution and if they do not appeal to media gatekeepers. Although professional photographers should be hired to take the photos, the public relations writer often supervises their work and selects the photos that are best suited for media use. Therefore, you need to know what makes a good publicity photo. Product photos are particularly challenging. See the following Tips for Success for some guidelines on taking product photos.

> **Motion and still images are valuable. Somebody might not read the story, but they'll recall the images.** ● Amanda Watlington, owner of a marketing consulting

Technical Quality

The technical quality of a photo is very important. Indeed, a common complaint of editors is the poor content and technical quality of publicity photos. They look for

---

✓ tips FOR SUCCESS

How to Take Product Photos that Get Published

- Show the product in a scene where it would logically be used. If it is used in an office, show it in an office.
- Clean up the area where the picture is to be taken. Remove any litter or extraneous items. Repaint if necessary.
- If people are in the picture, be sure that they are dressed for the situation. They should wear the kind of clothing that they would wear while using the product.
- Put perspective into the photo so viewers will know how big the item is. For example, show a hand, a person, or a pencil.
- Use a top-of-the-line digital camera to ensure maximum quality and resolution.
- Don't accept anything but the best in photographs. They have a potential shelf life of 5 years; many may be used by others to illustrate books or brochures. Give them quality.
- Take at least two photos—vertical and horizontal—of each new product. This makes them adaptable to a variety of situations. When possible, show the product in use. Application stories need illustrations.
- If there are other products in the picture, be sure that the new one is in the dominant position.
- The setting should be realistic, with everything hooked up and ready to go.
- Every picture must have an identifying caption.
- Be sure that the background contrasts with the product. Make the product stand out. ■

---

the key elements of good contrast and sharp detail so the photo reproduces well on everything from glossy magazine pages to cheap newsprint. You must also consider that photos are often reduced in size or, on occasion, enlarged when they are published. If they have good resolution to begin with, they will hold their quality.

Back in the days before the digital revolution, the traditional approach was to submit photos printed on glossy paper in an 8- by 10-inch or 5- by 7-inch format. Today, professionals use digital cameras, and the traditional process of taking photos on film, developing the film, and making prints has practically disappeared. In fact, 2003 marked the year that digital cameras began to outsell film cameras.

Although the process of taking photos has changed radically, the key elements of a good photo remain the same. Photos must have high resolution and sharp detail to be used. Online media, for example, are willing to sacrifice quality for the speed of download, so they typically use images at 72 dpi (dots per inch). Print publications, however, require much higher resolution, and 300 dpi is the norm. Distribution services such as NewsCom and Feature Photo Service distribute publicity photos in a 300-dpi JPEG or GIF format to accommodate the needs of almost any publication—from monthly glossy magazines to small weekly newspapers.

Subject Matter

There is a wide variety of subjects for a publicity photo. On one level, there are somewhat static photos of a new product or a newly promoted executive. On another level, photos are used to document events such as a groundbreaking or a ribbon-cutting ceremony.

Trade magazines, weekly newspapers, and organizational newsletters often use the standard "grip and grin" photo of a person receiving an award, a company president turning the first shovel of dirt on the site of a new building, or the traditional "ribbon-cutting" ceremony to open a new store. These shots have been a traditional staple of publicity photos for years, and there is no evidence that they are going out of fashion even in the digital age. At the same time, you should be aware that such photos can be quite boring, and editors want more unusual or artistic material.

Group pictures nearly always present a problem; it is relatively easy to violate the concepts of newsworthiness, action, and central focus. There is often the danger of showing too many people, so a good rule is to have no more than three or four people in any one photo. Such a rule provides for more action, keeps the picture simple, and makes every face easily identifiable.

A common mistake is to please everyone by having people pose for a group photo. This might mean the entire board of directors, 60 real estate salespeople, 125 college graduates, or even all 250 members of a club. A group photo may be legitimate when you want to give a souvenir of a particular meeting or conference or provide documentation for a specialized publication, such as a fraternal or alumni magazine. However, pictures of this kind should not be sent to general-circulation newspapers and magazines.

One way to handle large groups is to take a series of small group pictures of individuals from the same town or company. These then let you multiply the coverage by localizing the event for hometown newspapers or employee publications.

In general, you should show activity in the picture: people talking to each other, looking at a display, or shaking hands with a notable person in an informal pose. The people should not be lined up looking at the camera. A common composition is to show three people all talking or listening to a fourth person who is at the left of the picture. This fourth person may be a keynote speaker, the president of an organization, or someone who has just received an award. Such a composition can provide a focus and add some interest, but even these pictures are somewhat of a tired cliché.

In a group situation, it is extremely important to take down the names and titles of people as they are photographed. This will make your job much easier later on, when you have to write the caption, which will be discussed in another section. Don't rely on memory—yours or anyone else's.

Composition

We have already discussed ways to compose photographs of groups. Inherent in all this is the concept of keeping the photo simple and uncluttered. A look at the family album will illustrate the point. We have Aunt Minnie and Uncle Oswald looking like pygmies because the family photographer also wanted to include the entire skyline of New York City. Consequently, Aunt Minnie and Uncle Oswald are about 35 feet from the camera.

In most cases, the photographer should move into, not away from, the central focus of the picture. If the purpose is to show a busy executive at his or her desk, the picture should be taken close up so that the subject fills most of it. Sufficient background should be included to provide context, but it is really not necessary to show the entire surface of the desk—including the disarray of papers, picture of spouse and kids, and paperweight from a recent convention. All of this conflicts with what the viewer is supposed to focus on in the picture.

Another reason for moving in on the subject and minimizing the background or foreground is to achieve good composition. That picture of Aunt Minnie and Uncle Oswald also shows the Empire State Building growing out of Uncle Oswald's head.

Experts have made the following suggestions about composition and clutter:

- Take tight shots with minimal background. Concentrate on what you want the reader to get from the picture. A good example of a tight shot is Figure 8.1.

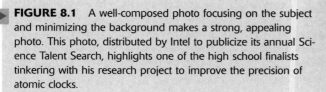

FIGURE 8.1   A well-composed photo focusing on the subject and minimizing the background makes a strong, appealing photo. This photo, distributed by Intel to publicize its annual Science Talent Search, highlights one of the high school finalists tinkering with his research project to improve the precision of atomic clocks.

- Emphasize detail, not whole scenes.
- Don't use a cluttered background. Pick up stray things that intrude on the picture.
- Try to frame the picture.
- Avoid wasted space. There should not be a large gap between an object, such as an award, and the person's face. In the case of a group picture, people should stand close to each other.
- Ask subjects wearing sunglasses to remove them.

All this advice is logical, but there may be times when the background plays an important role. If the purpose of the photo is to show someone in his or her work setting, it is important to capture a sense of the person's environment. A photo of a manager in management information systems, for example, might show him or her surrounded by three or four computers and a stack of printouts. Phil Douglis, a widely known photographic consultant, calls it the "environmental portrait." He continues, "Such portraits blend posed subjects with their supporting context to symbolize jobs, capture personalities, and ultimately communicate something about them to readers."

Action

Action is important because it projects movement and the idea that something is happening right before the reader's eyes. A picture of someone doing something— talking, gesturing, laughing, running, operating a machine—is more interesting than a picture of a person standing still and looking at the camera. Douglis says, "Interactive exchanges are the most productive form of communication. Photojournalism is an ideal medium for visually expressing how people communicate interactively with each other."

America's amateur photographers have filled the nation's family albums with pictures of Aunt Minnie and Uncle Oswald in rigid, formal poses, staring blankly, but a quick look through your daily newspaper will not turn up this kind of shot. Prize-winning news photographs bear out that action and interaction among people are the key elements in successful photography. In other words, take pictures of people doing something or interacting with others—not just staring at the camera. A good example is the photo on page 98 in Chapter 4 showing celebrities at a National Education Association (NEA) gathering to kick off the "Reading Across America" campaign.

With some thinking, an action photo can be taken of almost any situation. Professional photographers recommend, however, that the best "action" photos are those taken when the subjects are being spontaneous and are not conscious of the camera. Consequently, photographers will often take multiple shots over a period of several minutes to get the best facial expressions and portrayal of more natural interaction.

However, sometimes a straight head-and-shoulders portrait is exactly what is needed. For example, a press release announcing a promotion or the new president of a club or organization is often accompanied by what is referred to as a **mug shot**. See Figure 8.2 for a typical example.

FIGURE 8.2 Organizations usually distribute a short news release and a photo to announce the promotion of an executive. These head-and-shoulder photos, also known as "mug shots," are commonly used in business publications. The caption is simply the name of the individual and perhaps his or her new title.

You should not conclude, however, that all good pictures must suggest overt action. Some of the greatest photos have been character studies of people whose faces reflected their happiness at having won an award, their intense concentration on a critical issue, or their sorrow at having lost an election.

Scale

With inanimate objects, it is important to consider the scale. The picture should contain some element of known size so that the viewer can understand how big or small the object is. With large machines, it is common and effective to place a person in the picture. This helps the viewer estimate the approximate size of the picture's subject. A good example is the person standing beside Panasonic's new 155-inch HD plasma screen in Figure 8.3.

When smaller things are photographed, the scale guide is even more important. This also offers an opportunity to provide drama and adds the news value of novelty. For example, a new computer chip from Intel was photographed beside a penny—and the chip was even a bit smaller. The product publicity photo in Figure 8.4 (on page 194) demonstrates another approach to scale.

Camera Angle

Interest can also be achieved through the use of unusual camera angles. Starbucks illustrated its decision to carry Naked Juice (100 percent juices and smoothies) in its 7,000 outlets using the perspective of the camera inside the refrigeration unit looking out,

FIGURE 8.3 Showing scale and size are important in many product publicity photos. The size of Panasonic's new 150-inch HD plasma screen is better understood by having a person standing beside it. The large image of the panda, which fills the entire screen, is also attention getting and illustrates a key feature of the product—picture clarity.

FIGURE 8.4 A small square-shaped, black memory card isn't very compelling from a visual stand-point. It attracts much more interest if it is compared to something in our everyday lives. The memory card, for example, can hold the equivalent of a briefcase full of photos, documents, videos, CDs, slide presentations, and more. This photo graphically displays this by showing a Panasonic executive holding the memory card while surrounded by the contents of his briefcase. The caption for the photo is "Your Briefcase the Size of a Postage Stamp."

capturing an employee framed at the door reaching in to get a bottle of the product. See Figure 8.5.

Another approach is the extreme close-up that emphasizes shapes and patterns. A photo of a new mainframe computer isn't very interesting, so it's important to look at the situation and come up with an interesting angle that makes a better photo. IBM, for example, chose to show to use the unusual angle of a technician assembling part of a module that was part of the new "super" computer. See Figure 8.6 on page 196 for the publicity photo that was made available to the media.

Some other camera angles commonly used are (1) shooting upward at a tall structure to make it look even taller, (2) an aerial shot giving the viewer a chance to see something that might otherwise be unnoticeable, and (3) using a fish-eye lens to capture a 180-degree image.

Lighting and Timing

Indoor pictures often require more than a flash on a camera. Depending on the subject, a photographer may have to use supplemental lighting to remove or en-

FIGURE 8.5 An unusual angle can make even a bottle of fruit juice more interesting. This publicity photo, distributed by the Naked Juice Company, shows the perspective of looking out of the refrigeration unit and focuses on a person reaching in to get a container. This element of "action" in the photo elevates a ho-hum product picture into something much more interesting.

hance shadows to highlight a key element—a person's face, a product, or some aspect of the background. Even simple product photos, where the background is plain white or black to ensure that the product stands out, requires considerable lighting expertise.

Outdoor photos also have their challenges. If you want a picture of the company's executives in front of the new headquarters and the photo has to be taken in a westward direction, you should schedule the shooting in the morning; otherwise the glare of the afternoon sun may have a detrimental effect. In general, outdoor pictures taken in the morning or late afternoon are better for contrast than pictures taken at midday. Of course, the photographer can use a flash to lighten dark areas.

Selecting the location or setting of a picture is important if you want good, sharp results. For example, if you know that the people involved will be wearing light colors, you should not use a white background. Conversely, don't select a dark background if your photo subjects will be wearing dark clothing. In both cases, the result will be "floating heads," because the clothing will blend into the background. In all situations, you want to strive for high contrast between the background and the individuals being photographed.

FIGURE 8.6 Mainframe computers are big square boxes that are really dull to look at, let alone photograph for publicity purposes. IBM solved the problem by focusing on the assembly of the computer using an unusual camera angle that emphasized shapes and the human element.

Color

Before the digital age, most publicity photographs were produced in black and white because they were economical, versatile, and acceptable to most publications. However, color photographs are now the industry standard and used by all kinds of publications as printing technology has become more sophisticated and less expensive. If a publication plans to use black-and-white photos, color photos can easily be converted. Most of the photos in this book, for example, were originally in color.

Everything that has been said about composition and quality should be underlined in relation to color pictures. To be used, they must be outstanding in both interest and technical quality.

The preferences of various publications vary; many consumer and trade publications still prefer color slides or a CD, whereas newspapers have a strong preference for digital files that can be downloaded from the website of an organization or a distributor such as NewsCom. Some publications may even prefer glossy photos that can be scanned, but this is a rarity in the instant world of the Internet. Distribution methods will be discussed shortly.

Working with Photographers

It is important to use a skilled photographer with professional experience. Too many organizations try to cut corners by asking an employee with a point-and-click digital camera to take pictures. Often, the public relations writer is also asked to take the photos. This may be all right for the company newsletter, but publicity photos sent to the media must be extremely high quality if they are going to be competitive with the thousands of other photos that are readily available.

It will cost more money to hire a professional photographer, but at least you won't end up with pictures that are dull, poorly composed, and generally unusable. Another reason is that it's better business practice to use a professional who has formal training in visual communications. They are experienced and use high-quality equipment, which usually produces much better results. Your job, as the public relations professional, is to figure out the purpose of the photograph and its objective. It's the photographer's job to figure how to accomplish the objective from a visual perspective.

Finding Photographers

You should have a file of photographers, noting their fees and particular expertise. If you have no such file built up, you might consult colleagues to find out if they can make any recommendations. If you are unfamiliar with a photographer's work, ask to see his or her portfolio. This is important, because photographers are skilled at different things.

A good portrait photographer, for example, may not be good at photographing special events. A news photographer, by contrast, may be an expert at special events but unable to take good product photographs. In sum, you should find the best photographer for each kind of job.

Three experts at a workshop sponsored by MediaLink/WirePix (see the following Tips for Success) say that public relations professionals should always ask three questions of a prospective photographer before hiring him or her: (1) Do you shoot digital? (2) Can you show me examples of other similar photos you have taken? and (3) What contacts do you have with the media and how will you help me distribute the photo once it has been shot?

☑ tips FOR SUCCESS

Photo Advice from the Experts

The following 10 tips were given by three photo experts at a workshop sponsored by MediaLink/WirePix at the National Press Club in Washington, D.C. The list was originally compiled by Jerry Walker for *O'Dwyer's PR Report*.

1. Remember that photographs, even for publicity, are not advertising. Make sure you identify the news value of the story you want to illustrate.

2. Wire services like AP get a thousand or more photos a day. Your photo needs to tell a story quickly and creatively and have real news value to make the cut.

3. Capture images that tell your story at a glance. If your story is you're donating money to build homes for the homeless, get a photo of people building homes, not a "grip and grin" check presentation.

4. Write a complete and proper caption. Don't be misleading.

5. Identify the audience you are trying to reach. Photos for newspapers and trade publications are different than those for annual reports or brochures.

6. Get stories out in a timely fashion. Day-of-event photos are important. Use a respected distributor who is experienced with newsroom operations.

7. Try to create photos that have a shelf life and can be used for other projects down the road.

8. If you are organizing a press event, make sure you provide the media, both print and broadcast, with a visual opportunity. Talking heads at the podium are not visual.

9. Don't try to overbrand the photo. It should look spur-of-the-moment, even if it isn't.

10. PhotoShop is a wonderful tool. Don't abuse it by altering reality in your photos. ■

Contracts

Any agreement with a photographer, as pointed out in Chapter 3, should be in writing. A written document helps you to avoid misunderstandings about fees, cost of materials, and copyright ownership of the images.

A letter of agreement with a photographer should cover the following matters:

- What is the photographer's professional fee for taking pictures? Is it on a project basis or based on an hourly fee?
- How are out-of-pocket expenses, such as meals, mileage, lodging, etc., handled while on assignment? Does the photographer get a daily per diem or submit receipts?
- What will be delivered upon completion of the assignment? Will it be photos on a CD, website downloads, or even actual prints?
- Who will supervise the photographer? Will you or someone else in the organization help the photographer set up shots?
- Who will retain the images? Under copyright law, photographers retain ownership unless the signed agreement gives full ownership and control to the organization commissioning the work.
- Nature of use. Does the organization have unrestricted use of the photograph, or does it have to get permission from the photographer each time it wants to use the shot?
- Photographer's use of negatives or digital images. Can the photographer sell images to outside parties, or does the organization want exclusive use?

Ideally, you want to sign agreements with photographers that give unrestricted, exclusive use of all images. But be prepared to pay more for the photographer's services if that is the case.

The Photo Session

You will save time and money with regard to the photo session if you plan ahead.

- Make a list of the pictures you want. For pictures of people, arrange for a variety of poses.
- Know who you need, where and when you need them, and what props will be required.
- Notify people whose pictures are to be taken. Get releases, if needed (see Chapter 3).
- Be sure that the location for the photo session is available, clean, and orderly.
- Consider lighting. Will the photographer have everything needed, or should you make preparations?
- Have everyone and everything at the right place at the right time.
- Tell the photographer what you need, not how to do the job.

Cropping and Retouching

In most cases, the quality and composition of the photos can be improved through editing. The two primary techniques for editing photos are cropping and retouching. **Cropping** is editing the photo by cutting off parts of the picture that you don't want. Eliminating parts of the photo provides a tighter focus on the key elements. A photo of the CEO talking to a major stockholder, for example, may also include the waiter clearing a table at one side. It is relatively easy to "crop out" the waiter and any other surrounding background.

The second technique, **retouching**, is usually done to alter the actual content of the photo. Let's assume that the photo just mentioned was taken in such a way that a basket of flowers on the stage behind the CEO looks like it is planted on top of his head. In such a situation, cropping may not be the answer, because it also would scalp the top of the CEO's head. The solution, of course, is to simply eliminate the flowers through "airbrushing," or digital manipulation.

Today, even amateurs can use software such as Adobe Photoshop to crop and retouch photographic images at will. Too much "red eye" in the subject's eyes? No problem. Is the background a bit dark or the sky not blue enough? With a few keystrokes, the problem is solved. Indeed, amateur photographers armed with digital cameras and software programs can manipulate and improve the quality of their photos with relative ease. Even expert photographers rely on Photoshop to "electronically" create the perfect picture.

Ethical Considerations

Cropping and retouching are common practices in photography, but there are increasing ethical and legal concerns about the boundaries of altering photographic images. An original photograph, for example, can be scanned or downloaded. An editor can then use photo editing software to make any number of alterations. For example, a person's dark suit can be changed to a light tan, and a shadow on a person's face can be removed. The editor can also change the background from a plain wall to an oak bookcase or even a desert by merging the photo with another one stored in the computer's memory. An output device generates the new image on a printed page.

Advertising and public relations people often use photo editing tools to enhance the quality of publicity photos. Thus, a company's board of directors is shown in front of the production line, even though the original photo was taken in a studio. Or, a new product is enhanced by blacking out the background and putting more light on the actual product.

The examples presented thus far are relatively harmless, but news editors continue to express deep concern about additional liberties that may be taken. A Chinese photographer, for example, received considerable international criticism for taking a photo of China's new high-speed train to Tibet crossing a trestle, and then doctoring it by adding a herd of rare antelope peacefully grazing

66 In PR advocacy, you can choose whether to use photographs. If a photo doesn't meet your needs, don't use it. But once you decide to use it, don't alter it. 99 ○■ Carri Jenkins, director of communications, Brigham Young Uni-

nearby. The idea, of course, was to visually show how the train had not disturbed the wildlife habitat. One media critic said, "It's the perfect propaganda photo."

As a public relations professional, you should be concerned about the digital manipulation of photos. You have a professional responsibility to honor the original photographer's work and not make alterations that would violate the integrity of the original photo.

When does a cosmetic correction become a violation of the photographer's copyright—or even an outright deception? Would you, for example, use a composite photo to show gender and racial diversity in your organization? If an altered photo misleads and deceives the public in a significant way, do not use it.

Susan Balcom Walton, a professor of public relations at Brigham Young University, suggests that public relations firms and departments should have a photo manipulation policy. Such a policy can be formed, she says, by first asking three questions:

1. Does the image alter reality?
2. Does the image intend to deceive in any way?
3. Has anything in the image been manipulated to imply endorsement of, or agreement with, your organization's views when that might not have been the photographer's or subject's intent?

Writing Photo Captions

All photos sent to the media need a **caption**. This is the brief text under the photo that tells the reader about the picture and its source. However, a caption is not a description of the photo. Some novice caption writers make the mistake of writing, "Pictured above . . ." or "This is a picture of . . ." or "Jane Doe is shown talking to . . ." Don't write the obvious; write to provide context and additional information that are not readily apparent by looking at the picture.

Most captions, when they accompany a news release, are two to four lines long. In fact, one study by Gallup Applied Science showed that two-line captions are the most effective. This guideline, however, does not apply to **photo news releases**. PNRs, as they are called, are simply photos with longer captions that are distributed to the media without any accompanying news release—the caption tells the entire story.

According to Deborah S. Hauss, writing in *PRWeek*, "Photo news releases enable PR pros to get pictures out more quickly and stand out amidst a sea of written press releases. . . . Sometimes all it takes to capture the media's attention is a visually compelling image and a short caption." See the PR Casebook on page 201 for a photo news release distributed by Adventures by Disney.

Regular captions and PNRs are written in the active, present tense. Don't write "The park gates were opened by Mayor Jones"; say instead, "Mayor Jones opens the park gates." Here are the first sentences of several photos used in this chapter that illustrate the use of active, present tense:

- "Nathaniel Hipsman, 17, of Marietta, GA, a finalist at the 2008 Intel Science Talent Search (STS) displays his research . . ." (Figure 8.1)

The Photo News Release

Photos sent to the media with a long caption can serve as a stand-alone, visual news release. Adventures by Disney vacations used photos and extensive captions to publicize its family vacations. A photo and a caption for each vacation were included in its CD media kit sent to travel editors.

Here is the photo and caption that described one excursion to Italy:

On Adventures by Disney vacations, kids become "Junior Adventurers," with programs, experiences, guide books and other resources designed especially for them. In addition to visiting historic places like Saint Mark's Square in Venice, Adventures by Disney vacation to Italy offer Junior Adventurers the chance to learn to make Carnivàle masks, cook tasty Italian dishes, and play bocce ball from local experts. Launched in 2005, Adventures by Disney provide immersive, hassle-free and exhilarating guided family vacation experiences to destinations in Europe, the Americas, Asia, and Australia. In 2008, families traveling with Adventures by Disney can take part in extraordinary experiences from Prague to Paris, Yellowstone to Costa Rica, the ruins of Pompeii to the ruins of Machu Picchu, the Great Barrier Reef to the Great Wall of China, and more. ■

- "Panasonic displays its 150-inch HD plasma, which it says is the world's largest, at the 2008 Consumer Electronics Show (CES) in Las Vegas, Nevada." (Figure 8.3)
- "IBM technician Len Centonze, Highland, NY, assembles a 'multi-chip' module at the company's Poughkeepsie, NY, plant." (Figure 8.6)

A caption for a head-and-shoulders picture of a person (a mug shot) can be even shorter. The caption may be just the person's name. For full identification, you can also add the person's title and company; for example, "Douglas M. Schosser, director of finance, Associated Banc-Corp."

Captions for publicity photos of new products should include a key selling point. For example, the caption for the Dell product photo on page 8 in Chapter 1 carried the following caption:

> An employee of Dell Japan displays its new laptop computer "Vostro 1000" during a press conference in Tokyo. The computer maker put two desktops and three laptops of "Vostro" series for medium and small-sized businesses on the market today.

There is some argument about stating "from left to right" in a photo caption. To many people, this seems redundant, because people read copy—and probably scan photographs—from left to right anyway. If there are two or three people in the picture, it is assumed that you are identifying them from left to right. You can also indicate identity by the action taking place in the picture—for example, "John Baroni presents Nancy Southwick with a $5,000 scholarship at the annual awards banquet."

In general, the most important person in the photograph should be the first person at the left side of the picture. This ensures that this person is mentioned first in the photo caption. The most important person may alternatively be in the center of the picture, surrounded by admirers. In this case, you can write, "Sharon Lewis, the singer, is surrounded by adoring fans after her concert in Denver." Any reader should be able to figure out which person in the picture is Sharon Lewis.

However, the use of "left," "right," and "center" is perfectly acceptable if clarity is achieved. Here is the caption used under a photo of the top three winners of its Science Talent Search competition:

> Washington, DC/March 11, 2008—First place winner Shivani Sud, 17, of Durham, NC, (Center); second place winner Graham Van Schaik, 17, of Columbia, SC (Right); and third place Brian McCarthy, 18, of Hillsboro, Oregon, (Left) celebrate winning the 2008 Intel Science Talent Search. Intel Chairman Craig Barnett presented the top winners with college scholarships of $100,000, $75,000, and $50,000, respectively. These top award recipients were chosen from an applicant pool of more than 1,600 American high school seniors.

Creating Other Graphics

Photographs are not the only art form that you can use for publicity purposes. Charts, diagrams, renderings and models, maps, line drawings, and clip art are widely used. Many of these visuals can be formatted on your own computer using Microsoft Office, PowerPoint, or other software applications, but you should also consider using graphic artists and commercial illustrators. This is particularly true if you are preparing material for distribution to the media, which requires simple and well-designed, colorful graphics.

Charts

The primary reason for using charts is to make figures understandable. There are three basic charts for this purpose, and each seems to work best for certain kinds of information.

- **Pie chart.** Ideal for showing what part of a total is used for each of several purposes. An organization may use such a chart to show how a budget or revenues are divided.
- **Bar chart.** Ideal for showing comparisons between years in such things as income, population, sales, and prices.
- **Graph.** Somewhat like a bar chart, but better suited for showing changes over a long period of time. A simple graph may track sales and profits in relationship to each other.

Today, charts are being dressed up with graphics so that they are more appealing and easier to understand. Reading a copy of *USA Today* makes the point. Instead of showing a simple bar chart or graph, an attempt is made to incorporate representations of the subject into the chart.

A media kit prepared by Rand McNally, for example, made effective use of pie and bar charts to report the findings of a survey about families taking vacations by car. The charts, in vibrant colors, give readers an instant view of key findings. One fun question: What celebrity would you most want as a fellow passenger on a family driving vacation? Chevy Chase won by a landslide. See Figure 8.8 to see the mapmaker's charts.

Infographics can be prepared using Microsoft Office applications

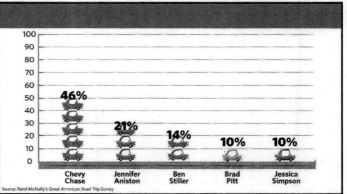

FIGURE 8.8 Charts and graphs can be interesting if some creativity is exercised. Rand McNally made the results of a survey very visual by using colorful charts. The pie chart, in a suitcase, gives the destinations of families that were planning to take a driving vacation. The bar chart graphically gives the results of a poll asking people what celebrity they would like as a fellow passenger on a driving vacation.

or more sophisticated software from Adobe, such as InDesign or Illustrator. Large dailies usually have their own graphics departments and make their own infographics. However, many smaller dailies and thousands of weeklies lack such capabilities and often are interested in receiving simple, colorful charts in addition to high-resolution photos.

Diagrams

Diagrams are most valuable in showing how something works. How an engine works, how an accessory should be attached, or how a product can be used can all be made more clear with a diagram.

In planning diagrams, you should not only check with the engineers, but you should also pretest the final diagram on potential readers for comprehension and understanding. The key to effective artwork, particularly diagrams, is simplicity.

Renderings and Scale Models

A rendering is an architect's drawing that shows how a finished structure will look. Increasingly, such artwork is being produced by computer drawing programs or the photo editing software.

Photos of scale models are also used to give readers a thorough understanding of what is being built or renovated. Both renderings and scale models are widely used in news and feature stories about construction projects. Simple maps showing the location of a construction site or a new freeway ramp, etc. often accompany architectural drawings and photos. The availability of such artwork often makes the difference between a major news story and a brief mention.

Line Drawings and Clip Art

Cartoons are a form of line art, but most people think of line art as drawings of symbols, designs, and objects. These drawings are still made by artists using paper and ink, but the process is now available to almost anybody with a personal computer.

Barnaby Feder, a *New York Times* reporter, summarizes the state of the art as follows:

> Today's PC graphics programs typically come with hundreds or even thousands of stored images, called clip art, which users can put into their graphics as building blocks. Photographs, shots from video clips and animation can be pasted in as well. Users can also choose from virtually infinite varieties of color and quickly change perspectives, shading, overlapping images and other features.

Adobe's InDesign and Illustrator include clip art and the tools needed to create line drawings. **Clip art** can be ordered on floppy disk, CD, or even downloaded from the Internet. Microsoft Office and Word Works also feature clip art. Another source of design templates and stock photos is Google Images (images.google.com).

Line drawings and clip art are used primarily for organizational advertisements, leaflets, brochures, and newsletters. They can also be used to illustrate press kits, position papers, and camera-ready features sent to the media.

Maintaining Photo and Art Files

A properly indexed photo and illustration file is a necessity. Without this, negatives, digital images, or artwork can be lost for future use. The long-term employee who knows where everything is located and can remember the situation will eventually retire or take another job. In other words, don't rely on the collective memory of individuals to keep track of photos and artwork.

Digital photos should be stored on the organization's file server with readily identifiable tags. In addition, back-up CDs or DVDs should be made. Corporate files may be identified by names such as "J. Jones, Chairman," or topical areas such as "Employee Recognition Banquet," "Grand Opening of Lansing Store," or "Scale Model of Springfield Office Bldg."

It is important to place all pertinent data in the file. This may include (1) the date of the event; (2) when the photo was taken; (3) the location; (4) releases from people portrayed; (5) complete names and titles of people shown; and (6) the name and address of the photographer, including any restrictions on the use of the picture.

Distributing Photos and Artwork

Digital technology makes it relatively easy to distribute photos and other artwork. However, there are several approaches that are used. The first approach is to simply e-mail a news release or an advisory to a specific journalist or editor and let them know that you have photos and artwork if they are interested. You can offer four different formats: (1) a thumbnail, (2) a slightly bigger preview image, (3) a low-resolution version, and (4) a high-resolution (300 dpi) one. An editor, for example, may just want to preview thumbnails and then order a specific photo. The main point to remember is to never send an attachment (photos or anything else) to an editor unless you are specifically asked to do so. The proliferation of viruses means that no editor will open an attachment unless they personally know and trust you.

A variation of this approach is to simply give a website in the news release where editors can download the photos and artwork. In many cases, journalists are given a special URL or link that allows them to access high-resolution photos that are not readily available to the general public. HP, for example, requires media to register for access to its "library." Ryan Donovan, HP's director of corporate media relations, told *PRWeek*, "You want to protect the brand so you have to know how those images that represent the brand are being used."

The second approach is a shotgun tactic. You mail a media kit that includes a CD that contains at least two files. One file contains high-resolution photos and artwork, the other file contains the captions keyed to the photographs. In many cases, the kit will also provide a printed page of thumbnail (2 × 2 inches) photos, as well as a print version of the captions. This allows the editor to quickly review the contents of the CD without actually having to open it. Adventures by Disney, mentioned earlier, used this approach.

The third approach is to use an electronic distribution service such as Business Wire, PRNewswire, MarketWire, or Feature Photo Service. Editors receive daily feeds from these services that let them know what's being distributed and, with a few clicks, access any story or related photo for downloading into their computers. In many cases, photos and graphics are embedded into the news release so editors can preview a thumbnail of the photo. If they like it, they can download a high-resolution copy with a few clicks. The concept of the "smart" news release was discussed in Chapter 5.

These distribution services also archive past stories and photos. This makes it easy for an editor to review all of the news releases and photos that Intel, for example, has distributed over a period of several years. Newscom is a particularly valuable resource; it maintains a searchable database of over 20 million images, graphics, and text from more than 100 photo agencies, wire services, and freelance photographers. Access to Newscom, however, is restricted to registered users.

Distribution, of course, also occurs online via social networking sites. It is important to tag photos (as well as news releases) with key words so search engines can index them.

■ Summary

- Photographs and graphics add appeal and increase media usage of news releases or features.

- Digital cameras are now used for publicity photos; such photos can be taken and distributed almost instantly.

- A public relations writer should be familiar with the elements of a good publicity photo: quality, subject matter, composition, action, scale, camera angle, lighting, and color.

- Publicity photos should be sharp, clear, and high contrast.

- Photos should be creative. Traditional pictures of "ribbon cuttings" no longer work.

- A publicity photo should have no more than three or four people in it. Save the large-group shot for the photo album.

- Photos with action and informality are more interesting than rigid, posed shots.

- Use professional photographers if you plan to send materials to news organizations.

- Crop photographs to remove clutter and get a tighter focus on the main subject.

- Photo captions are short, use present tense to describe the action, and provide context.

- Charts, diagrams, maps, etc., should be simple, colorful, and uncluttered.

- Through computer technology, charts can be made more visually attractive. They are often called "infographics."

- It is important to keep a well-organized photo and graphics file for reference purposes.

- Photos and graphics can be distributed by e-mail, CDs, websites, and electronic news wires.

- Never send an attachment (photo or otherwise) to a reporter or editor unless specifically requested to do so.

■ Skill Building Activities

1. News releases and features are more attractive to editors if photos are enclosed. Describe the type of photo(s) you would use to illustrate the following situations.

   a. The appointment of a new company president

   b. An announcement that a 22-story hotel will be built

   c. A story about the opening of a new microbrewery

   d. A "how to" feature on how to get organized

e. A feature on the growth and success of a local pizza chain

f. A feature about the ethnic diversity of a college campus

g. A production of "Mamma Mia" by the local repertory theater

2. Product publicity photos pose a major challenge because it takes creativity to make a product look interesting. What kinds of publicity photos would you recommend for the following products:

a. An electric frying pan

b. A new portable GPS navigation system for cars

c. A laptop computer

d. A golf cart

e. Nonfat potato chips

f. An improved solar panel

g. A new MP3 player

3. A local food bank is having a grand opening of its new facilities, including the traditional ribbon cutting by city officials and an open house for the community. Describe the types of publicity photos that could be taken of this event to ensure media interest and acceptability. After you decide on the type and content of some photos, write a caption for each one.

4. A civic organization is honoring five outstanding citizens at its annual banquet. Describe how you would organize and compose publicity photos of this event that would be acceptable to the local newspaper.

5. Charts and graphs are more attractive if some creativity is used. A bottled water company wants to show how much water a person needs per day based on the person's weight and activity level. Create a rough draft, either freehand or on a computer, of an "infographic" that would show this data in an attractive way.

Suggested Readings

Burns, Heather. "Photography 101: An Editor's Crash Course." Ragan.com (www.ragan.com), February 25, 2008.

Kobre, Kenneth. *Photojournalism: The Professional Approach.* St. Louis: Focal Press, 6th edition, 2008.

Lewis, Tanya. "A Picture Can Be Worth a Thousand Hits." *PRWeek*, January 14, 2008, p. 22.

Lipp, Danielle. "Crafting the Picture-Perfect Pitch." *PRWeek*, April 30, 2007, p. 14.

McGuire, Craig. "A Picture Tells a Thousand Words." *PRWeek*, April 24, 2006, p. 18.

Murray, David. "The Secrets of Good Corporate Photography." Ragan.com (www.ragan.com), June 3, 2008.

Spencer, Jane, and Ye, Juliet. "China Eats Crow over Faked Photo of Rare Antelope." *The Wall Street Journal*, February 22, 2008, pp. A1, A13.

Sweatland, Bill. "Captions That Say Exactly Nothing." Ragan.com (www.ragan.com), January 15, 2008.

Walker, Jerry. "Photo Editors Give Tips for Shooting PR Photos." *O'Dwyer's PR Services Report*, August 2001, pp. 41–42.

Walton, Susan Balcom. "The Truth of a Single Instant: Focusing on the Issue of Photo Manipulation." *PR Tactics*, November 2007, p. 25.

Weidlich, Thom. "Providing Quality Photos Puts Your Story in Sharper Focus." *PRWeek*, August 18, 2003, p. 18.

Whittle, Scott. "Digital Photography Can Improve Your Chances for Media Placement." *O'Dwyer's PR Services Report*, May 2003, p. 29.

Writing for Radio and Television

9

TOPICS covered in this chapter include:

The Wide Reach of Broadcasting   208

Radio   208

Television   223

Personal Appearances and
    Product Placements   239

The Wide Reach of Broadcasting

Radio and television offer many opportunities for the public relations writer who wants to reach both mass and specialized audiences effectively.

Radio reaches about 94 percent of adults over the age of 18 on a daily basis, with a total estimated audience of about 225 million. A 2008 study by Edison Media Research found that college graduates aged 25 to 54 listen to the radio almost 16 hours a week. Noncollege graduates listen more than 21 hours a week. Radio is particularly strong among Hispanics, the largest and fastest growing minority in the United States; families tune in an average of 24 hours a week. Teenagers also are big listeners of radio, primarily through online sites. According to Arbitron and Edison Media Research, 33 million Americans aged 12 and over listen to a radio station over the Internet during an average week.

Television, despite the advent of the Internet and social networking sites, also continues to have large audiences. The National Association of Broadcasters (NAB) says that local television news still attracts about 150 million viewers on a daily basis, and that the average American family still spends about 7 hours daily watching television.

Writing and preparing materials for broadcast outlets requires a special perspective. This chapter explains how to write for the ear, integrate audio and visual elements into a script, and harness the power of satellite and digital communications to conduct media tours that can reach a global audience. It also tells you how to get your spokesperson on broadcast talk and magazine shows.

Radio

Radio lacks the glamour of television and the popularity of the Internet, so it is not always the first medium that public relations people think of when planning an information campaign.

On a local level, however, radio is a cost-effective way to reach large numbers of people in various age, ethnic, and income groups. Radio can be heard almost anywhere. It is the only mass medium that can reach millions of Americans as they commute to and from work in their cars. In addition, the miracle of the transistor brings radio to mail carriers on their routes, carpenters on construction sites, homeowners pulling weeds in their gardens, and exercise enthusiasts working out at a gym or jogging.

Approximately 13,500 radio stations are on the air in the United States, ranging from low-powered outlets operated by volunteers to large metropolitan stations audible for hundreds of miles. In addition, radio stations are increasing their audience reach through the Internet. An estimated 2,000 stations now have an Internet presence, and many are concurrently broadcasting and Webcasting their programming. The station's format often determines the nature of the audience. There are "top 40" stations for teenagers, all-news stations for commuters, classical stations that appeal to an older and better-educated group, and stations that play "adult contemporary" for aging baby boomers. One popular format is "country," which reaches a variety of age and occupational groups.

A public relations practitioner should study each station's format and submit material suitable to it. There is little sense in sending information about senior citizen recreation programs to the news director of a hard rock FM station with an audience made up primarily of

> **" It (radio) is the medium the demographics of age, gender, economic standing, and ideology. "**
> ■ Michele Wallace, MediaLink

teenagers. You can determine the demographics of a station by consulting radio and television directories or by contacting the station's advertising and marketing department. One common source of advertising rates and demographic data is published by Standard Rate and Data Services. Another source is the *Radio Marketing Guide and Fact Book for Advertisers*. See Figure 9.1 for an example of a typical broadcast listing from *Bacon's Media Directories*, which is published by Cision.

Radio News Releases

Although radio station staffs often find themselves rewriting print releases to conform to broadcast style, the most effective approach is to send news releases that are formatted for the medium. Radio is based on sound, and every radio release must be written so that it can be easily read by an announcer and clearly understood by a listener.

Format ■ There are several major differences between a radio release and a news release prepared for print media. Although the basic identifying information is the same (letterhead, contact, subject), the standard practice is to write a radio release using all uppercase letters in a double-spaced format. You also need to give the length of the radio release. For example, "RADIO ANNOUNCEMENT: 30" or "RADIO ANNOUNCEMENT: 60." This indicates that the announcement will take 30 or 60 seconds to read.

The timing is vital, because broadcasters must fit their messages into a rigid time frame that is measured down to the second. Most announcers read at a speed

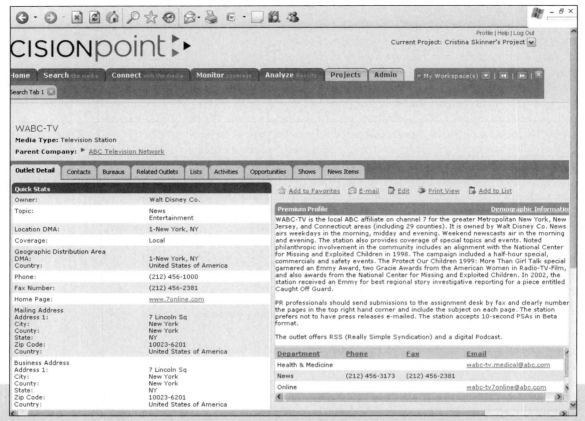

FIGURE 9.1 A publicist has more success placing materials on the radio or television if he or she knows the format and demographics of the station. Armed with such information, the publicist can tailor the material and also find out who should be contacted. This is an excerpt of a television station listing from a Cision database, which was formerly *Bacon's*. Such databases also let publicists know how the station prefers to receive information. In this case, the preferred method is a fax to the assignment desk. See also page 251 for a radio station listing.

of 150 to 160 words per minute. Because word lengths vary, it is not feasible to set exact word counts for any length of message. Instead, the general practice is to use an approximate line count. With a word processor set for 60 spaces per line, you will get the following lengths:

2 lines = 10 seconds (about 25 words)

5 lines = 20 seconds (about 50 words)

8 lines = 30 seconds (about 75 words)

16 lines = 60 seconds (about 150 words)

There are also differences in writing style. A news release for a newspaper uses standard English grammar and punctuation. Sentences often contain dependent and independent clauses. In a radio release, a more conversational style is used, and the emphasis is on strong, short sentences. In fact, you can even write radio copy using incomplete or partial sentences, as you would do in a normal conversation. This allows the announcer to draw a breath between thoughts and the listener to follow what is being said. An average sentence length of 10 words is a good goal. More tips on writing a radio news release are provided in the Tips for Success on page 212.

Here is a an example of a 60-second news feature distributed by North American Precis Syndicate (NAPS) for Champion, a sports clothing manufacturer:

BUILDING A BETTER SPORTS BRA

THE LAST FEW DECADES HAVE SEEN GREAT STRIDES IN FEMALE

ATHLETICS—FROM THE PASSAGE OF TITLE NINE LEGISLATION, WHICH

REQUIRED EQUALITY IN MEN'S AND WOMEN'S SCHOOL SPORTS FUNDING,

TO THE INTRODUCTION OF THE SPORTS BRA. TODAY, CUTTING-EDGE

TECHNOLOGY HELPS DESIGN SPORTS BRAS FOR COMFORT AND CONTROL,

AND SCIENCE-BASED RESEARCH PROGRAMS TEST AND EVALUATE BRAS

FOR EFFECTIVE USE DURING DIFFERENT ACTIVITIES. COMPANIES SUCH AS

CHAMPION USE EXCLUSIVE BIOMECHANICAL RESEARCH TO ESTABLISH A

MOTION CONTROL REQUIREMENT SYSTEM. THIS MEANS EACH SPORTS

BRA CAN BE RATED BASED ON HOW EFFECTIVELY IT CONTROLS MOTION

AND BOUNCE. EACH OF THE SPORTS BRAS INDICATES A RATING BY CUP

SIZE WITH CORRESPONDING FITNESS ACTIVITIES, USING A COLOR-CODED

SYSTEM TO ENSURE SUPPORT, FIT, AND COMFORT. FOR EXAMPLE, IF A

BRA IS RATED AS LIGHT SUPPORT, IT MIGHT BE APPROPRIATE FOR

ACTIVITIES SUCH AS YOGA, PILATES, AND WEIGHT TRAINING. MAXIMUM

SUPPORT WOULD BE MORE GEARED TO HIGH-IMPACT SPORTS SUCH AS

RUNNING, BASKETBALL, AND HORSEBACK RIDING. EXPERTS RECOMMEND

REPLACING ALL SPORTS BRAS AFTER ONE HUNDRED WEARINGS. FOR

MORE INFORMATION, VISIT CHAMPION-U-S-A—DOT—COM.

Notice the spacing in the website address. This alerts the news announcer to read the URL slowly so people can remember it. The same rule is applied to telephone numbers. Oftentimes, a number or URL is repeated a second time for listeners who are in the process of grabbing a pencil and pad.

Audio News Releases

Although news releases or features in broadcast style can be mailed or faxed to radio stations for announcers to read, the most common and effective approach is to send the radio station a recording of the news announcement.

An **audio news release**, commonly called an **ANR**, can take two forms. One simple approach is for someone with a good radio voice to read the entire announcement; he or she may or may not be identified by name. This, in the trade, is called an **actuality**. The second approach is a bit more complex, but relatively easy to do. In this instance, you use an announcer but also include a **soundbite** from a satisfied customer, a celebrity, or a company spokesperson. This approach is better than a straight announcement because the message comes from a "real person" rather than a nameless announcer. These combination announcements are also more acceptable to stations because local staff can elect to use the whole recorded announcement or take the role of announcer and use just the soundbite.

Format ■ The preferred length for an ANR is 60 seconds, including a soundbite of 20 seconds or less. It is advisable to accompany any sound tape with a complete script of the tape. This enables the news director to judge the value of the tape without listening to it.

☑ tips FOR SUCCESS

How to Write a Radio News Release

- Time is money in radio. Stories should be no longer than 60 seconds. Stories without actualities (soundbites) should be 30 seconds or less.
- The only way to time your story is to read it out loud, slowly.
- A long or overly commercial story is death. Rather than editing it, a busy radio newsperson will discard it.
- Convey your message with the smallest possible number of words and facts.
- A radio news release is not an advertisement; it is not a sales promotion piece. A radio news release is journalism—spoken.
- Announcers punctuate with their voices; not all sentences need verbs or subjects.
- Releases should be conversational. Use simple words and avoid legal-speak.
- After writing a radio news release, try to shorten every sentence.
- Listeners have short attention spans. Have something to say and say it right away.
- Never start a story with a name. While listeners are trying to figure out who the person is, they forget to listen to the sentences that follow. ■

Source: News Broadcast Network, New York.

Here is the script of an ANR that includes a soundbite from a spokesperson. TVN Productions in New York produced it on behalf of its client, Hidden Valley Ranch:

WORLD'S LONGEST SALAD BAR: 60 SECONDS

THIS IS A TVN REPORT. WHAT IS 160 YARDS LONG, BOASTS MORE THAN

17,000 POUNDS OF PRODUCE, AND IS FREE TO ANYONE WHO HAS AN

APPETITE FOR HEALTHY LIVING? WHY, IT'S THE WORLD'S LONGEST SALAD

BAR, OF COURSE, AND IT'S HAPPENING THURSAY, MAY 27TH IN NEW YORK

CITY'S CENTRAL PARK TO KICK OFF MEMORIAL DAY WEEKEND. JOSIE

WELLING OF HIDDEN VALLEY RANCH EXPLAINS:

"RANCH DRESSING IS AS MUCH AN AMERICAN ORIGINAL AS CENTRAL

PARK AND MEMORIAL DAY WEEKEND, WHICH IS WHY WE DECIDED TO

BRING THEM TOGETHER FOR A GOOD OLD-FASHIONED MEMORIAL DAY

PICNIC. IT'S ALSO A GREAT WAY TO CELEBRATE OUR 25TH ANNIVERSARY."

THE SALAD BAR FEATURES COUNTLESS VARIETIES OF FRUITS,

VEGETABLES, GREENS AND GARNISHES, AS WELL AS 20 DIFFERENT

SPECIALTY SALADS ALL FEATURING HIDDEN VALLEY ORIGINAL RANCH

DRESSING—A PRODUCT WHICH TURNS 25 THIS YEAR. THE EVENT IS

EXPECTED TO BE RECOGNIZED BY THE GUINNESS BOOK OF RECORDS AS—

YOU GUESSED IT—THE WORLD'S LONGEST SALAD BAR.

Notice that the above script is written in a somewhat breezy manner, reflecting the nature of the event. The World's Longest Salad Bar is a fun and oddball event.

Organizations announcing new products, however, tend to be more low-key and play it straight. The American Psychological Association (APA), for example, used ANRs to highlight the various topics of research papers at its annual convention. About 25 researchers were selected to give soundbites on topics that would be of interest to the general public. Topics included stopping brain cell loss, violence in video games, differences between men and women, high school hazing, substance abuse, and childhood mental health.

Each ANR began by announcing that the annual APA convention was examining a wide range of issues affecting society and ended with giving the website address to those wanting more information. The ANRs were targeted to news talk and adult consumer stations, and they reached an audience of more than 20 million listeners on a budget of only $10,000.

Production ▪ Every ANR starts with a carefully written and accurately timed script. The next step is to record the words. In doing this, it is imperative to control the quality of the sound. A few large organizations have complete facilities for this; some get help from moonlighting station employees; but most organizations use a professional recording service.

The recording services have first-class equipment and skilled personnel. They can write and format a script and even edit a spokesperson's comment to the desired length. They also provide the announcer best suited to the kind of message to be delivered.

Delivery ▪ Once the ANR has been produced, the public relations professional must notify the news department that an ANR is available. You need to give the subject of the release and tell editors how to retrieve it. VNR-1 Communications, in a survey of 305 news-talk stations, found that almost 75 percent of respondents preferred to receive e-mail notification about ANRs. Another 20 percent preferred notification via news network feeds, and 10 percent preferred fax notification.

Radio stations, like newspapers, have preferences about how they like to receive news releases. One survey by DWJ Television indicated that almost 75 percent of the radio news directors preferred to receive actualities by phone. An organization can set up a dedicated phone line that has recordings of various news releases or it can contract with an organization such as Strauss Radio Strategies, which will set up and maintain an actuality line for its clients.

Another method of delivery is via satellite or the World Wide Web. Strauss Radio Strategies, for example, also has the ability to deliver an ANR to more than 3,000 ABC-affiliated radio stations throughout the United States via a satellite network. A compact disk (CD) can also be mailed to stations, along with a script, but this only works if the "news" is not particularly time-sensitive. MP3 formats also are popular, and the use of ANRs can be extended by making them available as podcasts.

Use ▪ Producing ANRs is somewhat of a bargain compared to producing materials for television. When Sears distributed a radio news release responding to charges of overcharging customers at auto repair centers in California, the cost of preparing and distributing a national release was $3,900. Ford spent $3,500 for a news release on battery recycling as part of Earth Day festivities. It got 624 broadcasts and reached more than 5 million people with the message.

Despite the cost-effectiveness, you should still be selective about distribution to stations that have an interest in using such material. Radio releases, like news releases, should not be shot-gunned to every radio station.

You also need to monitor usage. Many organizations send a return postcard on which the station can report use. However, News Broadcast Network estimates that usage cards generate only a 5 to 7 percent response rate. Other organizations simply call the station and ask how many times a particular story or announcement has aired. By using Arbitron ratings, which give estimated audience figures, public relations professionals can then calculate how many listeners were exposed to the message. In addition, monitoring services now scan radio and television talk and news programs in major markets across the nation and can offer a report within 24 hours of something being aired. Evaluation procedures are discussed in Chapter 19.

The use of audio news releases is increasingly popular with radio stations. Thom Moon, director of operations at *Duncan's American Radio*, told *PRWeek* that he thinks the major reason for this is the consolidation of ownership in radio broadcasting (Clear Channel owned 1,200 stations when it was sold to a private equity firm), which has resulted in cost-cutting and fewer news personnel.

Jack Trammell, president of VNR-1 Communications, told *PR Reporter*, "They're telling us they're being forced to do more with less. As long as radio releases are well produced and stories don't appear to be blatant commercials, newsrooms are inclined to use them." Trammell conducted a survey of radio stations and found that 83 percent of the newsrooms use radio news releases (RNRs). Thirty-four percent say RNRs give them ideas for local stories. The editors look for regional interest (34%), health information (23%), and financial news (11%). They also like tech stories, business trends, children's issues, politics, seasonal stories, agriculture, and local interest issues.

A good example of "localizing" a story is the ANR that Moultrie News Generation produced about the need for air bags and seat belts that was distributed around Memorial Day weekend. To localize the story for individual markets, the release included statistics for each area.

Some Tips ■ Trammell, in an article for *PR Tactics*, gives some additional "rules" for successful radio and television story placement:

- **Topicality.** Stories may fail every other judgment criteria and still get airtime simply because they offer information on a hot topic. *Newsroom Maxim*: News is about issues that matter to the majority of our listeners or viewers.

- **Timeliness.** Stories should be timed to correspond with annual seasons, governmental rulings, new laws, social trends, etc. *Newsroom Maxim*: The favorite word in broadcasting is "now" followed by "today" and then "tomorrow." The least favorite word is "yesterday."

- **Localization.** Newsrooms emphasize local news. A national release should be relevant to a local audience. Reporters are always looking for the "local angle." *Newsroom Maxim*: If it's not local, it's probably not news.

- **Humanization.** Show how real people are involved or affected. Impressive graphics and statistics mean nothing to audiences without a human angle. *Newsroom Maxim*: People relate to people—and animals.

- **Visual appeal.** Successful stories must provide vibrant, compelling soundbites or video footage that subtly promotes, but also illustrates and explains. *Newsroom Maxim*: Say dog, see dog.

Public Service Announcements

Public service announcements are another category of material that public relations writers prepare for radio stations. A **public service announcement (PSA)** is defined by the Federal Communications Commission (FCC) as an unpaid announcement that promotes the programs of government or nonprofit agencies or that serves the public interest. In general, as part of their responsibility to serve the public interest, radio and TV stations provide airtime to charitable and civic organizations, although there is no legal requirement that they do so. Thus, a PSA may be a message from the American Heart Association about the necessity of regular exercise or an appeal from a civic club for teacher volunteers in a literacy project.

According to DWJ Television, a video producer, PSAs give various governmental and nonprofit organizations an opportunity to use the same channels of communication as major business advertisers, but at only a fraction of the cost. DWJ further states, "It is not unusual for a television campaign, produced and distributed on a budget of $25,000 to $40,000, to get airtime that would have cost $1 to $5 million or more for paid advertising."

Profit-making organizations do not qualify for "free" PSAs despite the "public service" nature of their messages, but an informational campaign by a trade group or foundation can qualify. For example, the Homeownership Preservation Foundation used radio PSAs in late 2007 and early 2008 to reach homeowners worried about possible foreclosures. The following 30-second and 60-second PSAs were used, which received a Bronze Anvil award from the PRSA:

30 SECONDS

HOW ANNOYING IS DEBT? IMAGINE THE MOST ANNOYING PERSON YOU KNOW, ONLY LIKE DEBT, IT'S WITH YOU EVERY DAY. YOU KNOW THE GUM-SMACKING, LOUD-CHEWING, INCESSANT-THROAT-CLEARING, NO-TURN-SIGNAL-USING, TOO-MUCH-COLOGNE-WEARING, OPEN-MOUTH-BREATHING, HAIRY-KNUCKLES-HAND-SHAKING, 7 A.M.-LEAF-BLOWING, DUCK-TAIL-HAVING, CARELESS-CIGARETTE-FLICKING, DOUBLE-PARKING PERSON WHO COULD COST YOU YOUR HOME.

IF YOU'RE WORRIED ABOUT MISSING MORTGAGE PAYMENTS, CALL 888-995-HOPE. THERE YOU'LL GET ADVICE FROM FINANCIAL EXPERTS, FREE OF JUDGMENT, AND FREE OF COST. 888-995 HOPE. OR VISIT 995HOPE.COM.

60 SECONDS

HOW ANNOYING IS DEBT? THINK OF THE WORST DAY OF YOUR LIFE, ONLY IT'S EVERY DAY BECAUSE DEBT IS ALWAYS THERE. IT'S AS IF EVERY DAY YOU'VE OVERSLEPT TO FIND YOUR DOG HAD RUN AWAY, AND YOUR CAR WON'T START, SO YOU HAVE TO SEARCH THE NEIGHBORHOOD ON YOUR

DAUGHTER'S BIKE, WHICH HAS TWO FLAT TIRES, AND WHEN YOU

FINALLY MAKE IT TO WORK, YOU FIND OUT YOU'VE BEEN LAID OFF

BECAUSE THE RAISE YOU GOT LAST MONTH MADE IT CHEAPER FOR YOUR

COMPANY TO MANUFACTURE ITS PRODUCTS IN INDONESIA, AND THAT

YOU'RE LOSING YOUR PENSION SO THAT THE OVERPAID CEO CAN ADD A

NEW CABANA TO HIS COMPOUND IN TAHITI, AND WHEN YOU GET HOME

YOU LEARN THAT YOUR MOTHER-IN-LAW HAS TO MOVE IN WHILE SHE

RECOVERS FROM HER GALL BLADDER SURGERY, AND SINCE YOU'RE OUT

OF WORK YOU'LL BE THE ONE GIVING HER THE REQUIRED DAILY SPONGE

BATH WHILE BEING TOLD HOW HER BABY SHOULD HAVE MARRIED SO

AND SO, THE ASTRONAUT BRAIN SURGEON PHILANTHROPIST WHO

RESCUES PUPPIES WITH ARMLESS ORPHANS IN HIS SPARE TIME.

KEEP YOUR HOME YOURS. IF YOU'RE WORRIED ABOUT MISSING

MORTGAGE PAYMENTS, CALL 888-995-HOPE. THERE YOU'LL GET ADVICE

FROM FINANCIAL EXPERTS, FREE OF JUDGMENT, AND FREE OF COST. 888-

995 HOPE. OR VISIT 995HOPE.COM.

This example shows the potential effectiveness of PSAs. To get the attention of public service directors at radio stations, the PSA package mimicked the stamped "past due" and "foreclosed" notices on late bills. As a result, the PSAs aired 42,000 times on stations nationwide, reaching an audience of 59 million. The foundation received more than 28,400 phone calls and more than 36,700 website hits. Remember, however, that such successes are the exception, not the rule. Only those PSAs that are timely, creative, and of high recording quality stand a chance of being used.

Here are a few more points to remember about PSAs:

- Only nonprofit, civic, and voluntary organizations are eligible to use PSAs. Announcements by profit-making organizations are considered advertisements, and stations charge regular advertising rates for carrying them.
- Stations are no longer required by the FCC to provide evidence of public service as a condition of license renewal. In other words, there is no legal requirement that stations must air PSAs, but most of them do so to a limited degree. A survey by the Pew Research Center in 2008 found that less than 1 percent of air time (0.5%) is dedicated to PSAs. As a result, some nonprofits negotiate with stations to actually buy time for PSAs to ensure they are aired.

- Few PSAs are aired during periods of peak listening, when a station can run revenue-producing advertisements. The Pew Research Center survey also found that almost 50 percent of all PSAs air after midnight. WestGlen Communications, a producer of PSAs, claims that only about 35 percent of all PSAs run after midnight and that most (about 60 percent) are aired between 6 A.M. and midnight.

Format ■ PSAs, like radio news releases, are usually written in uppercase and double-spaced. They can be 60, 30, 20, 15, or 10 seconds long. The most popular length, according to a survey of stations conducted by Atlanta-based News Generation, are PSAs between 15 and 30 seconds in length. Sixty percent of the respondents use this length; less than 20 percent use 60-second PSAs.

Unlike ANRs, the standard practice is to submit multiple PSAs on the same subject in various lengths. The idea is to give the station announcer flexibility in using a particular length to fill a particular time slot throughout the day. DWJ Television, a producer of PSAs, further explains: "Some stations air PSAs in a way that relates length to time of play, for example placing one length in their early news shows and another in the late news show. Supplying both lengths allows a campaign to be seen by people who only watch one of these shows."

Here are some examples of varying lengths that were distributed by the National Foundation for Infectious Diseases:

10 SECONDS

PROTECT YOURSELF AND YOUR LOVED ONES THIS FLU SEASON. MORE

INFLUENZA VACCINE IS AVAILABLE THAN EVER BEFORE. TALK WITH

YOUR DOCTOR NOW ABOUT IMMUNIZATION. A MESSAGE FROM THE

NATIONAL FOUNDATION FOR INFECTIOUS DISEASES.

15 SECONDS

PROTECT YOURSELF AND YOUR LOVED ONES THIS FLU SEASON. MORE

INFLUENZA VACCINE IS AVAILABLE THAN EVER BEFORE. THE NATION'S

LEADING HEALTH EXPERTS ENCOURAGE VACCINATION FOR EVERYONE

WHO WANTS TO REDUCE THEIR RISK FOR INFLUENZA INFECTION THIS

SEASON. A MESSAGE FROM (STATION) AND THE NATIONAL FOUNDATION

FOR INFECTIOUS DISEASES.

20 SECONDS

THE NATION'S LEADING HEALTH EXPERTS ENCOURAGE EVERYONE WHO

WANTS TO REDUCE THEIR RISK FOR INFLUENZA INFECTION TO GET

VACCINATED THIS SEASON AS SOON AS POSSIBLE. MORE INFLUENZA

VACCINE IS AVAILABLE THAN EVER BEFORE. TALK WITH YOUR DOCTOR

ABOUT IMMUNIZATION FOR YOURSELF AND YOUR LOVED ONES. A

MESSAGE FROM (STATION) AND THE NATIONAL FOUNDATION FOR

INFECTIOUS DISEASES.

30 SECONDS

THE NATION'S LEADING HEALTH EXPERTS ENCOURAGE EVERYONE WHO

WANTS TO REDUCE THEIR RISK FOR INFLUENZA INFECTION TO GET

VACCINATED THIS SEASON, EVEN IF INFLUENZA HAS ALREADY BEEN

REPORTED IN THE AREA. MORE INFLUENZA VACCINE IS AVAILABLE THIS

SEASON THAN EVER BEFORE. CONTACT YOUR DOCTOR OR HEALTH

DEPARTMENT AS SOON AS POSSIBLE TO GET YOURSELF AND YOUR LOVED

ONES VACCINATED. A PUBLIC SERVICE MESSAGE FROM (STATION) AND

THE NATIONAL FOUNDATION FOR INFECTIOUS DISEASES.

Adding Sound ■ An announcer reading a script is OK, but adding sound effects can make a radio PSA more interesting. Many PSAs have background music. Larry Saperstein, vice president of production at WestGlen Communications, told *PRWeek*, "Music can be dramatic. It can change, uplift, and give a message of hope. It can be used very effectively, but should never dominate." A second approach is to include sound effects that reinforce the theme and subject matter. Here are two PSAs of varying length from the National Heart Lung and Blood Institute, part of the U.S. Department of Health and Human Services, that included sound effects:

30 SECONDS

(The dramatic sound of a stock car)

Announcer: BLOCK THE FLOW OF AIR IN A STOCK CAR ENGINE, AND

YOU'VE GOT A PROBLEM ON YOUR HANDS.

(Engine starts to shut down)

IF YOU HAVE EMPHYSEMA, WHEEZING, CHRONIC BRONCHITIS OR

SMOKER'S COUGH, YOU KNOW THE FEELING. WHAT YOU DON'T KNOW IS

IT COULD BE COPD, THE NUMBER 4 CAUSE OF DEATH. BUT IT CAN BE

TREATED. SO TALK TO YOUR DOCTOR ABOUT COPD AND GET A SIMPLE

BREATHING TEST. LEARN MORE. BREATHE BETTER. GO TO

WWW.LEARNABOUTCOPD.ORG.

A MESSAGE FROM THE NATIONAL HEART, LUNG, AND BLOOD INSTITUTE

OF THE U.S. DEPARTMENT OF HEALTH AND HUMAN SERVICES.

60 SECONDS

(The dramatic sound of a stock car)

Announcer: WHAT'S ONE OF THE MOST IMPORTANT ELEMENTS OF A HIGH-

PERFORMANCE STOCK CAR ENGINE?

(Engine revs higher)

AIR. FLOWING THROUGH THE SYSTEM. MIXING WITH FUEL. COMBUSTING.

BRINGING THE SPEED AND THRILLS OF STOCK CAR RACING TO LIFE.

BLOCK THE EXHAUST? THE FLOW OF AIR? YOU'VE GOT A PROBLEM ON

YOUR HANDS.

(Engine starts to shut down)

IF YOU HAVE EMPHYSEMA, WHEEZING, CHRONIC BRONCHITIS OR

SMOKER'S COUGH, THEN YOU KNOW WHAT IT'S LIKE WHEN THE AIR CAN'T

GET THROUGH. WHAT YOU PROBABLY DON'T KNOW IS THAT IT COULD BE

COPD, THE NUMBER 4 CAUSE OF DEATH IN AMERICA.

BUT COPD CAN BE TREATED. SO TALK TO YOUR DOCTOR ABOUT COPD

AND GET A SIMPLE BREATHING TEST. THEN GET BACK ON TRACK FOR

TREATMENT.

LEARN MORE. BREATHE BETTER. GO TO WWW.LEARNABOUTCOPD.ORG

A MESSAGE FROM THE NATIONAL HEART, LUNG, AND BLOOD INSTITUTE

OF THE U.S. DEPARTMENT OF HEALTH AND HUMAN SERVICES

Production Most PSA scripts are mailed or e-mailed (no attachments, please) to the station's director of public or community affairs. The scripts allow station announcers to make selections and to read them on the air. Many stations also have a website that includes a PSA template that allows local organizations to just fill in the blanks with the standard questions of who, what, when, where, and why. This is particularly helpful when local organizations are announcing community events, such as festivals, 5K runs, and so on.

A more sophisticated approach is to record your PSAs, particularly those with music and sound effects, and use a good production house to make CD copies. Figure 9.2 shows an example of a PSA distributed on a CD. Another way is to make the recorded PSAs available via a dedicated phone line. The National Foundation for Infectious Diseases and the National Heart Lung and Blood Institute mailed CDs of recorded announcements in both English and Spanish to stations. They also included a basic fact sheet giving more detail about the topics presented in the PSAs. In many cases, scripts are also included for the convenience of station personnel.

Use ■ Almost any topic or issue can be the subject of a PSA. However, stations seem to be more receptive to particular topics. A survey of radio station public affairs directors by WestGlen Communications, a producer of PSAs, found that local community issues and events were most likely to receive airtime, followed by children's issues. The respondents also expressed a preference for PSAs involving health and safety, service organizations,

> **66 In PSAs, speak to the common man. . . . Make it as simple as possible. 99**
>
> ■ Christiane Arbesu, vice president of production, MultiVu

breast cancer, and other cancers. A 2008 study by Pew Research confirms this. It found that the most common topic of PSAs was health (26%), followed by fundraising (23%), family and social concerns (12%), community organizations or events (8%), and volunteerism (6%).

The majority of respondents also prefer PSAs that include a local phone number rather than a national toll-free number. Because of this preference, many national groups, including the American Cancer Society and the American Red Cross, have a policy of distributing scripts to chapters that can be localized.

Other studies have shown that an organization needs to provide helpful information in a PSA and not make a direct pitch for money. Radio stations tend to shun PSAs that ask people for money directly. A more

FIGURE 9.2 A popular method for distributing radio PSAs is by CD. This CD, produced by the American Veterinary Medical Association, uses graphics to give the CD more visibility on the desk of the public affairs director at a station. The subject of the PSAs is well marked, and the varying lengths are given.

subtle approach is to tell people about the organization and give them a phone number or a website to get more information.

Some Tips ■ Phil Rabin, writing in *PRWeek*, gives some tips for successful PSAs—whether they are for radio or television. You should:

- Do your research so your PSA reaches the appropriate station and its primary audience.
- Keep it simple. The short length of PSAs means that you must minimize the points you want to make.
- Always send PSAs to the director of public or community affairs, not the news department.
- Send broadcast PSAs in different lengths.
- Establish an effective tracking system.
- Try to localize your PSAs; a local number is often more effective than a national toll-free number.

An additional tip is to send your PSAs to the station 5 or 6 weeks before you want them to air. This gives time for mailing and for the station to put the PSAs in its rotation schedule. Radio stations literally receive stacks of CDs containing PSAs, and it often takes time for the station's public affairs director to sort through all of them.

Experts also recommend that the best time to submit PSAs is in January when stations have a lull in paid advertising. In contrast, the 4 months leading up to Christmas are very advertising intensive, so stations use fewer PSAs.

Radio Media Tours

Another approach in radio is the **radio media tour (RMT)**. Essentially, this can be described as a spokesperson conducting a series of round-the-country, one-on-one interviews from one central location. The publicist prebooks telephone interviews with DJs, news directors, or talk show hosts around the country, and the personality simply gives interviews on the phone, which is then recorded for later use or broadcast live.

A major selling point for RMTs is their relatively low cost and the convenience of giving numerous interviews from one central location. David Thalberg, vice president of Ruder/Finn, told *Ragan's Media Relations Report*, "You don't have to go to a TV station, and you don't have to put on a suit. Your client can do the interview over the phone, seated in his or her office, with all the supplementary material he or she needs to come across as authoritative and informed."

A good example of an effective RMT is one organized by Strauss Radio Strategies for the Children's Defense Fund (CDF) to discuss child health care issues. The president of CDF and four family spokespersons conducted 14 radio interviews over a period of several hours and reached an estimated audience of 6 million listeners. According to Strauss, this represented 150 airtime minutes; comparable advertising costs would have been more than $300,000. Television media tours, known as satellite media tours (SMTs), will be discussed in the next section.

Television

The fundamental factor that separates television from the other traditional media and gives it such pervasive impact is the visual element. The combination of color, movement, sound, and sight on a screen in your own living room is hard to resist. No wonder the medium is the primary source of news, information, and entertainment for most people. In fact, the National Association of Broadcasters (NAB) says that local TV news attracts 150 million viewers. Network news reaches 30 million; prime-time national cable, 3 million; and regional cable, 31 million.

There are almost as many television stations (1,500) in the United States as there are daily newspapers (1,532), and there are numerous opportunities for the placement of public relations materials at the local level. However, you need to know how a television station is organized and who is in charge of various programs. The titles may vary somewhat, but the following positions are common at both radio and television stations:

- **General manager.** This person, comparable to the publisher of a newspaper, determines general policy and manages all the departments.
- **Program director.** This person decides which programs to produce and broadcast—including news, public affairs, and entertainment programs.
- **Directors and producers.** These people moderate the various interview and talk shows that are the staple of many stations. They are comparable to the section editors of daily newspapers.
- **News director.** This person, comparable to the managing editor of a newspaper, manages the entire operation of gathering and producing newscasts.
- **Assignment editor.** This person, comparable to the city editor of a newspaper, assigns reporters and camera crews to cover news stories.
- **Reporters.** These are the people who write and report the news, as well as the sound and camera technicians who accompany them on assignments.
- **Public affairs or public service director.** This person is the station's public relations representative. Duties may include working with community organizations to broadcast public service announcements and organizing public affairs programming.
- **Promotion director.** This person promotes the station by sponsoring contests and events, often in partnership with other community groups.

You may have reason to contact all of these people at one time or another. Specific placement opportunities for talk shows, call-in programs, product placement, community calendars, and other messages are discussed later in the chapter. Here, we focus on working with television news directors, assignment editors, and reporters to generate news coverage of your organization or client.

There are four approaches to getting your news story on local television. First, you can send the television station the same news release that you send to the local print media. If the news editor thinks the topic is newsworthy and lends itself to visual representation, he or she might tell the assignment editor to have a reporter and camera crew follow up on the news release.

A second approach is to prepare a media alert or advisory advising the news department about the particular aspect of an event or occasion that would lend itself to video coverage. These media alerts can be sent via e-mail, fax, or by a newswire. Figure 9.3 shows an example of a media advisory.

A third approach is to phone or e-mail the assignment editor and make a "pitch" to have the station do a particular story. The art of writing pitch letters was discussed in Chapter 6.

The fourth approach is to write and produce a **video news release** (VNR) that, like an audio news release, is formatted for immediate use with a minimum of effort by station personnel. The VNR also has the advantage of being used by numerous stations on a regional, national, or even global basis.

Serena Williams, Rafael Nadal 'Walk On Water' in World's First Tennis Match on Liquid Terrain

Footage to Be Available for Downlink Tuesday, March 25 20:00 to 20:15 GMT

—(BUSINESS WIRE)—

WHERE: Domestic United States and Canada
Satellite Galaxy XI/15K Slot 1 @ 91W Ku Band
Downlink 11985 Horizontal
FEC 3/4
Symbol Rate 4.42 Msps

Latin America-Europe and Caribbean
Satellite IS-9/24C Slot 6 @ 58W C Band
Downlink 4175 Horizontal
FEC 3/4
Symbol Rate 4.42 Msps

Australia-Asia
Satellite IS-2/12C Slot 4 @ 169E C Band
Downlink 4035.5 Horizontal
FEC 3/4
Symbol Rate 4.42 Msps

WHAT: Two of the world's leading tennis players, Serena Williams and Rafael Nadal, took to a custom-made court to try their luck on a more challenging surface in the first ever game of tennis on water. The event took place Monday, March 24, 2008, atop Miami's new Gansevoort South Hotel overlooking South Beach on its first day of business.

HOW: The water-covered court was constructed in the 110-foot swimming pool set in the Gansevoort's exclusive 22,000-square-foot rooftop retreat. A specialist underwater team took five days to construct two invisible platforms at either end of the pool using a combination of bespoke acrylic sheets and supporting acrylic tubes.

WHY: Sony Ericsson hosted the revolutionary event to celebrate the start of this year's Sony Ericsson Open March 26 to April 6. The Sony Ericsson Open is the World's fifth largest tournament. It is the only 12-day tennis event on both the ATP and Sony Ericsson WTA Tour calendars. The Sony Ericsson Open features all of the world's top-ranked men and women players.

(NOTE TO EDITORS: FOR SHOT DESCRIPTIONS EMAIL WILL@SPICERANDMOORE.COM)

Contacts

For Spicer and Moore, London

Gigi Otero Public Relations
Gigi Otero, +1 818 752 2151
go@gopr.biz

FIGURE 9.3 Television stations receive news advisories like this one to inform them of news feeds and how to downlink the material if they are interested. This advisory, distributed by Business Wire, gives the satellite coordinates, the subject matter, and contacts for more information.

Video News Releases

It's estimated that more than 5,000 VNRs are produced annually in the United States. Large organizations seeking enhanced recognition for their names, products, services, and causes are the primary clients for VNRs. The production of VNRs can more easily be justified if there is potential for national distribution and multiple pickups by television stations and cable systems. It's now common for VNRs to also be posted on company websites; social media sites, such as YouTube; and as video podcasts.

So what exactly constitutes a VNR package? MultiVu, a video production firm, gives these four components:

- 90-second news report with voiceover narration on an audio channel separate from that containing soundbites and natural sound.
- Extra soundbites and B-roll.
- Clear identification of the video source.
- Script, spokespeople information, media contacts, and story background information provided electronically.

VNRs are not cheap. A typical VNR, says one producer, costs a minimum of $20,000 to $50,000 for production and distribution. Costs vary, however, depending on the number of location shots, special effects, and staff required to produce a high-quality tape that meets broadcast standards.

One producer, WestGlen Communications, advertises a basic VNR package for about $20,000 that includes (1) consultation on story concept and news positioning; (2) production; (3) script, 1-day shoot, edit, and voiceover; (4) distribution; and (5) distribution to newsrooms, satellite feed, and 2 days of pitching assignment editors to use it. Other producers, such as MultiVu, TVN Productions, DWJ Television, and DS Simon Productions offer similar packages.

Because of the cost, you must carefully analyze the newsworthiness of your information and consider whether the topic lends itself to a fast-paced, action-oriented visual presentation. If you have nothing to show except talking heads or graphs and charts, you should think twice about producing a VNR.

66 *Today's VNRs are much more than just broadcast placement tools. They are being targeted to a variety of audiences through Web syndication, strategic placements in broadcast cable, and site-based media in retail outlets and hospitals.* 99

■ Tim Bahr, managing director, MultiVu

You should also consider whether the information will be current and newsworthy by the time a VNR is produced. On the average, it takes 4 to 6 weeks to script, produce, and distribute a high-quality VNR. In a crisis situation or for a fast-breaking news event, however, VNRs can be produced in a matter of hours or days.

A good example of rapid response is Pepsi's response to news reports that syringes and other sharp objects had been found in cans of Diet Pepsi. Within a week, the soft-drink company produced and distributed a VNR showing that it was virtually impossible for someone to insert foreign objects into cans as they moved down the high-speed bottling lines. This VNR reached an estimated 186 million television viewers and helped avoid a massive sales decline of Pepsi. Subsequently, Pepsi commissioned three more VNRs, which included a message to consumers from Pepsi's president, a surveillance camera catching an alleged tamperer, and a "thank you" to consumers for their support. According to MediaLink, the producer and distributor of the VNRs, the VNRs were seen by an aggregate of 500 million viewers on 3,170 news programs.

Format ■ Essentially, a VNR is a television release converted to a finished tape that can be broadcast. The standard length is 90 seconds, the length preferred by the overwhelming majority of TV news directors.

Writing a script for a VNR is a bit more complicated than writing one for an ANR, because you also have to visualize the scene, much like a playwright or a film writer. Adam Shell, former editor of *PR Tactics*, describes the required skills:

> Producing a VNR requires expert interviewing skills, speedy video editing, a creative eye for visuals, and political savvy. The job of the VNR producer is not unlike that of a broadcast journalist. The instincts are the same. Engaging sound bites are a result of clever questioning. Good pictures come from creative camera work. A concise, newsworthy VNR comes from good writing and editing. Deadlines have to be met, too. And then there are all the tiny details and decisions that have to be made on the spot. Not to mention figuring out subtle ways to make sure the client's signage appears on the video without turning off the news directors.

Perhaps the best way to illustrate Shell's comments is to show a typical VNR storyboard and a more detailed script. Figure 9.4 shows a thumbnail storyboard for a VNR that was produced by DS Simon Productions on behalf of the March of Dimes about Hurricane Katrina victims. Figure 9.5 shows the script of a VNR about cervical cancer that was produced by the College of American Pathologists.

Production ■ Although public relations writers can easily handle the job of writing radio news releases and doing basic announcements for local TV stations, the production of a video news release is another matter. The entire process is highly technical, requiring trained professionals and sophisticated equipment. Consequently, the public relations writer serves primarily as an idea creator and a facilitator.

The public relations professional may come up with the idea, write a rough script (storyboard) outlining the visual and audio elements, and make arrangements for a video production and distribution service to produce the video. Such firms are listed in the Yellow Pages under "Video" and "Television." The advertisements in the public relations trade press such as *PRWeek* and *O'Dwyer's PR Report* are also good sources.

It is important to keep in mind that the video producer follows the basic **storyboard** (outline of who and what should be included) to achieve the organizational objective, but will usually videotape many minutes of footage and use the editing room to make the finished 90-second product.

DS Simon Productions
Storyboard for March of Dimes B-Roll During Hurricane Aftermath
Help the Babies of Katrina

More than 100 premature newborns were evacuated to Baton Rouge during Katrina, and the March of Dimes helped reunite them with their families.

The shelter in Baton Rouge housed more than 6,000 in one large room on cots. Everyone slept side by side, some on cots, others -- including pregnant women -- slept on the floor.

Eight-months pregnant, Crystal Sulliven walked from New Orleans with her one-year-old son to a Baton Rouge shelter. There she received help from the March of Dimes.

Ingrid Olivas fled New Orleans while eight-months pregnant with her first child. She told her story in English and Spanish of receiving pre-natal vitamins, clothes and help relocating from the March of Dimes.

March of Dimes volunteers distributed clothes to pregnant women and children at crowded shelters. They also provided pre-natal vitamins, diapers and other supplies for families with young children.

March of Dimes volunteers like Liza Cooper worked to help move pregnant women and families with newborn babies into smaller shelters. Stress is one known cause of premature birth, and they wanted to alleviate some of the stress on pregnant women during Katrina's aftermath.

FIGURE 9.4 This is the storyboard created by DS Simon Productions for a video news release on behalf of the March of Dimes. The March of Dimes mounted a major effort after Hurricane Katrina to provide aid and care for mothers and children who were left homeless. The VNR not only raised public awareness of the problem, but also raised money to continue the assistance. The VNR was seen by an estimated 4.5 million viewers and generated about $50,000 in donations.

FIGURE 9.5 Video news releases must be scripted to show both the video and audio components and how they work together. This VNR, from the College of American Pathologists, shows the typical format of a script. The video description is on the left side, and the audio is in the right column. These scripts are often provided along with a Beta tape or a satellite download so news editors can quickly assess the subject and content of the VNR.

Consequently, it is not necessary to write a prepared script for everyone who appears on video. It is better, and more natural, to have them talk informally in front of the camera and then use the best soundbite. The Tips for Success on page 229 offers additional information on writing for video.

MediaLink, a major producer and distributor of VNRs, offers the following tips for producing VNRs that best meet the needs of TV news directors:

- Give TV news directors maximum flexibility in editing the tape so that they can use their own anchors or announcers. This can be done by producing the VNR on split audio (the announcer track on one audio channel and the natural sound of the VNR on another). This way, producers have the option of "stripping" the announcer's voice.

- Produce the VNR with news footage in mind. Keep soundbites short and to the point. Avoid commercial-like shots with sophisticated effects.

- Never superimpose your own written information on the actual videotape. TV news departments usually generate their own written notes in their own typeface and style.

- Never use a stand-up reporter. Stations do not want a reporter who is not on their staff appearing in their newscast.

- Provide TV stations with a local angle. This can be done by sending supplemental facts and figures that reflect the local situation. These can be added to the VNR when it is edited for broadcast.

- Good graphics, including animation, are a plus. Stations are attracted to artwork that shows things in a clear, concise manner.

Pintak Communications, a public relations firm in Washington, D.C., offers the following suggestions for preventing a VNR disaster:

- **Use outside experts to give credibility.** A VNR with only corporate spokespeople is not a good idea. In addition, don't clutter up the VNR with an excessive number of corporate logos.

- **Avoid commercialism and hype.** The VNR is a news story, not a corporate advertisement.

- **Avoid overproduction.** Slick dissolves and flashy effects are great for music videos, but news producers equate it with advertising.

Delivery ■ Your VNR package should include 2 or 3 minutes of **B-roll,** or background pictures and soundbites, for use by the TV news producer in repackaging the story. Typical B-roll includes additional interviews, soundbites, and file footage. A Nielsen Media Research survey of 130 TV news directors, for example, found that almost 70 percent wanted a VNR with a B-roll attached.

In fact, many stations now prefer to use a B-roll because of controversy about stations using VNRs without attribution. Watchdog groups have complained to the Federal Communications Commission (FCC) that stations using VNR content without telling viewers the original source are presenting "fake news." The Center for

Media and Democracy, for example, conducted a 6-month probe and found that 46 stations in 22 states aired unsourced video material supplied by VNR production firms on behalf of their clients.

The controversy also put the spotlight on the public relations industry. The issue was whether public relations firms and VNR producers were adequately labeling VNR packages that identified the sponsor and the client. As a consequence, the National Association of Broadcast Communicators (NABC) was formed and established new standards calling for the complete identification and disclosure of indi-

---

■ PR casebook

Television B-Roll Is an Explosive Hit

Television stations often prefer B-roll footage of an event instead of a packaged VNR. A B-roll allows the station to supply its own reporting based on the video segments provided. The Hoffman Agency, which is based in San Jose, California, scored an impressive hit for its clients, Sony and A4S Security, by providing a B-roll of how a new surveillance product could withstand extreme conditions, providing video coverage even after the detonation of a bomb in a bus or a building.

Sony and A4S Security planned to demonstrate the video surveillance system by setting off an explosion in a retired bus from the Denver transit system. For verification purposes, the companies would document the testing process and the methodology. Hoffman Agency was in charge of planning media coverage of the demonstration and producing a video segment that would be attractive to television stations.

Sheri Baer, broadcast director of Hoffman and a former television reporter, worked with the demolition crew to organize a detailed shot list and suggested interview questions for Sony and AS4 Security executives. These interviews were integrated into the final footage. Baer also suggested getting soundbites from law enforcement and Homeland Security officials so they could be included in soundbites as part of the total package.

The big day arrived. At a testing facility in the Colorado desert, Sony and A4S blew up the bus with 10 pounds of explosives, tearing off the roof and stripping the bus down to bare metal. The Shiftwatch product withstood the blast and provided data and video to within seconds of the explosion. The video footage provided enough images that Hoffman was able to craft a media-friendly and highly compelling B-roll that that could be offered to selected media.

Billed as the "Simulated London Bus Blast, the Latest in Anti-Terror Tech," Baer and her colleagues began pitching television stations in key markets. Baer pitched the Sony and A4S video surveillance product by sending a personal e-mail to television reporters. The most important targets were the Fox News Network and Kurt, "The Cyber Guy," Knutsson of KTLA in Los Angeles, which was also syndicated to other major television stations. Here is the text of her note to reporters at KPIX in Los Angeles:

Hi Sue, Tony & the KPIX Assignment Desk:

I wanted to alert you to an extraordinary B-roll tape I'll be distributing next week on behalf of A4S Security and Sony. The two companies have created a new video surveillance product for terrorism detection and prevention geared toward public transportation systems (busses, subways, etc.) A4S recently tested the product by stimulating the London bus bombing at a testing facility in Colorado. A4S blew up a retired city bus with 10 pounds of explosives, literally tearing off the roof and stripping the bus down to bare metal. The product withstood the blast and provided data and video of the event up to within seconds of the explosion.

viduals or organizations paying for and sponsoring a VNR. This disclosure is to be made part of the VNR, rather than just a supplementary note to the TV station. Unfortunately, even if public relations firms apply these standards, they cannot stop television stations from stripping the sources out and using the VNR or the B-roll as a product of their own reporting.

A good example of effective placement for a B-roll is one produced by the Hoffman Agency for its clients, A4S Security and Sony, about a new video surveillance product for terrorism detection. See the PR Casebook starting on the facing page.

As you can imagine, the footage is quite chilling but it also dramatically shows the effectiveness of the new high-tech tools law enforcement officials can rely on in their efforts to detect, deter, and prevent terrorist activities. The footage is well shot with long unedited sequences and natural sound. The tape also has sound bites from A4S, Sony, the Larimer County Sheriff's Department, a Homeland Security expert, and the Colorado Bureau of Investigation.

We have a limited number of hard copy Beta tapes and want to confirm interest before shipping a dub. The tape (including story background materials) is scheduled for delivery next Wednesday, February 1. If you're interested in localizing the story, we could arrange an interview with a Sony spokesperson in San Jose.

Please let me know as soon as possible if you would like to receive a tape.

Best Regards,
Sheri

The result was excellent. The B-roll was used on the Fox News Network and *Fox and Friends*, reaching an audience of 2 million. The initial coverage through Fox generated coverage by Fox affiliates. In Los Angeles alone, KCBS, KABC, KTLA, and KTTV all carried stories crafted from the B-roll tape. Says Baer, "By personally guiding the production and distribution of high-quality B-roll tape, Hoffman effectively reduced the story's exploitive potential—and delivered quality coverage that consistently integrated Sony

FIGURE 9.6 B-roll footage often provides the video element of a television news report. This scene of a bus exploding was shown on WGN in Chicago as part of the news report about a new surveillance technology developed by A4S Security and Sony to deter terrorism.

Notification ■ Television newsrooms are usually notified in advance that a VNR and B-roll are available. E-mail is the most popular and efficient notification method. Another technique—e-advisories—is also used on a national and global basis. E-advisories provide story information as well as links to streaming media previews of VNRs, scripts, and related story information. E-advisories, according to MultiVu, "also allow reporters to download broadcast-quality MPEG-3 versions over the Internet." Such advisories are also posted on newswire sites such as Business Wire.

Some experts prefer faxing a notification to television newsrooms, using the logic that a paper version tends to be passed around a newsroom so a number of staffers see it. Faxes also avoid the problem of competing with hundreds of e-mails that assignment editors get every day. Ideally, MultiVu recommends that stations be notified about a VNR 48 to 72 hours before the initial satellite feed. When a story breaks with little advance notice, of course, the notification process can be shortened.

VNRs that are not time-sensitive can be mailed to selected stations. These are known as **evergreens**, because they are always in season. A VNR on general research into AIDS could be held by a producer for use in an eventual series, or a VNR from the U.S. Forest Service on how to prevent fires could be held in reserve until summer, when the danger is highest.

Mail distribution, as well as Web downloads, can also used for what is known as **stock footage**—standard video shots of a company's production line, headquarters, or activities that the station can store until the company is in the news. Then, as the anchor gives the news, the viewer sees the stock footage on the screen. A news story about an electric power plant, for example, may use stock footage from the utility company showing interior scenes of the facility.

Use ■ VNRs are widely used by television stations and cable systems, particularly in smaller markets. A survey by WestGlen Communications, for example, found that 90 percent of TV stations regularly use outside-produced video for newscasts. This optimistic statistic, however, is tempered by the reality that TV stations today receive so many VNRs that they are drowning in them.

A survey by KEF Media Associates in Atlanta, for example, found that almost 90 percent of the local TV newscasts in the top 100 markets devoted less than 5 percent of their airtime to VNR material. In a 44-minute news hour (allowing for advertising), that represents only 2 or 3 minutes. At the same time, some stations in top markets receive more than 100 VNR pitches a week, which graphically illustrates the stiff competition any VNR has for being used at all.

In other words, VNRs go through the same gatekeeping process as news releases and features submitted to newspapers and magazines. Emil Gallina, a senior vice president of Hill & Knowlton's Electronic Media Services, once made the comparison in a *Communication World* article:

> Video releases look like TV news in the same way that press releases read like newspaper articles. And the moving pictures we distribute for television are the equivalent of the 8 by 10 photos we send to newspapers and magazines. Their purpose is the same: to encourage coverage and to provide materials the reporter might not

otherwise obtain . . . They are merely one source of raw material from which news reports can be created.

The comparison is appropriate, but many public relations practitioners worry about the expense and whether the potential audience reached is worth the investment. And even if it is used, the typical VNR rarely reaches millions of people. A well-done VNR, according to surveys, usually gets 40 to 50 station airings with an audience of 2 to 3 million people. This is a far cry from the blockbusters by the Insurance Institute for Highway Safety, which garnered 213 million viewers with a VNR about the ability of pickup trucks to survive crashes.

Consequently, it is important that you understand the value, purpose, and limitations of VNRs. Before you commit the money to have a quality VNR produced and distributed, you should first assess (1) the news value of the topic, (2) whether the topic lends itself to a visual treatment, (3) whether it can be recycled for use in social networking sites and blogs, and (4) whether this is a cost-effective method of reaching your target audience.

There are other, more cost-effective ways to achieve broadcast coverage. One is the satellite media tour, which will be discussed shortly.

Public Service Announcements

Television stations, like radio stations, use public service announcements on behalf of governmental agencies, community organizations, and charitable groups. In fact, a survey by News Broadcast Network found that the typical TV station runs an average of 137 PSAs per week as part of its commitment to public service. DWJ Television, another video producer, says that 70 percent of televisions PSAs are used between the hours of 7 A.M. and 1:30 A.M., with about 40 percent of this number used between 6 P.M. and 12:30 A.M.

Many of the guidelines for radio PSAs, which were discussed previously, apply to television PSAs. They must be short, to the point, and professionally produced. Television is different, however, in that both audio and visual elements must be present. Thus, the soundbites or actualities must have someone with not only a good voice, but also an attractive appearance. As a result, many, television PSAs use a well-recognized celebrity or spokesperson. Ronald McDonald House Charities, for example, distributed a 60-second television PSA using Sarah, the Duchess of York, who is its official "global ambassador." The video showed scenes of children around the world in less than ideal circumstances. In a voiceover (V/O), Sarah gave the following message:

HELLO, I'M SARAH, THE DUCHESS OF YORK. GLOBAL AMBASSADOR FOR

RONALD MCDONALD HOUSE CHARITIES. WE ALL FEEL THE PAIN OF

CHILDREN WHEN WE SEE THEM SUFFERING, AND WE ALL WISH THAT WE

COULD DO SOMETHING ABOUT IT. IN MY TRAVELS, I'VE BEEN TOUCHED

BY SO MANY CHILDREN WHO NEED OUR HELP. THEY AREN'T GETTING THE

PROPER CARE THAT THEY NEED. SOME CHILDREN DON'T HAVE ACCESS TO
MEDICINE OR DOCTORS. SOME DON'T EVEN HAVE ANY OF THE THINGS WE
TAKE SO MUCH FOR GRANTED . . . LIKE CLEAN DRINKING WATER OR
FOOD. SOME NEVER GET TO BE HELD BY THEIR OWN PARENTS.
NOVEMBER 20TH IS WORLD CHILDREN'S DAY. AND IT'S A GREAT DAY TO
DO SOMETHING ABOUT IT. JOIN US IN HELPING THE CHILDREN WHO
REALLY NEED US MOST. TO FIND OUT HOW YOU CAN GET INVOLVED AND
FOR MORE INFORMATION VISIT WWW.DOT.RMHC.DOT.ORG. ALL OF US
TOGETHER, CAN REALLY MAKE A DIFFERENCE. THIS HAS BEEN A PUBLIC
SERVICE MESSAGE FROM RONALD MCDONALD HOUSE CHARITIES.

When there are a number of elements, the script begins to look more like a page from the manuscript of a play. In film and video production, it is often called a **storyboard**. Its purpose is to provide dialog, but it also describes the scenes and visual aspects so a camera crew knows the general outline. The storyboard by Rotary International, shown in Figure 9.7, is a good example of a storyboard.

Some PSAs get considerable airtime. A 30- and 60-second PSA on behalf of the German National Tourist Office promoted the 2006 World Cup in that nation. The spots, called "A Time to Make Friends," invited reviewers to visit the "land of ideas, rich in artistic and cultural activities." They were seen by an estimated 50 million people. A series of PSAs on anxiety disorders got more than 100,000 air plays. A Salvation Army PSA series reached more than 43 million Americans. The National Organization on Fetal Alcohol Syndrome (NOFAS) reported a 400 percent increase in calls to its hotline in the 2 to 3 days following a PSA featuring TV star Laura San Giacomo. Many PSAs also seem to stick in people's minds. "McGruff, the Crime Dog," is recognized by 98 percent of children between the ages of 6 and 12.

> ❝ The traditional media is always going to be on the menu. The trick is trying to maximize impact with new media tools. ❞

The Internet, of course, has opened up new opportunities for video PSAs. The Ad Council, which produces many PSAs on behalf of national and international charitable organizations, also posts them on more than a dozen new media streams. By the end of 2007, for example, Ad Council PSAs had generated a half million YouTube views. Another PSA, featuring Mark Zupan, a member of the U.S. Paralympic rugby team, received 700 television airings, as well as 6,500 YouTube views.

Satellite Media Tours

The television equivalent to the radio media tour (RMT) is the satellite media tour (SMT). This is essentially a series of prebooked, one-on-one interviews from

Lending a hand :30 psa

Alone our reach is limited. No matter how great our intentions, on our own, we can only stretch so far. But at Rotary, we believe the right group of people working together can make our communities, our world, a better place. Learn more at rotary.org. Rotary. Humanity in motion.

You Can :30 psa

You can eradicate polio. You can promote peace. You can feed the hungry. You can help children do better in school. Because you can get involved with Rotary. Learn more at rotary.org.

When You Start With Rotary :30 psa

When you start with Rotary, good things happen. Rotary is ordinary people working together to clean the environment, stop disease and accomplish other extraordinary things. Learn more at rotary.org.

FIGURE 9.7 Television PSAs must have video. This is the storyboard of three 30-second announcements that Rotary International made available on an international basis.

a fixed location via satellite with a series of television journalists and, sometimes, talk show hosts.

The SMT concept started in the mid-1980s when companies began to put their CEOs in front of a television camera. The public relations staff would line up reporters in advance to interview the spokesperson via satellite feed during allotted timeframes and, in this way, television journalists across the country could interview them personally. For busy CEOs, the satellite was a time-efficient way of giving interviews. All they had to do was visit a corporate or commercial television studio near their office. See Figure 9.8 for an illustration of how a satellite media tour works.

Today, the SMT is a staple of public relations and the television industry. One-on-one interviews, as well as news conferences via satellite, are widely used. In fact, a survey by WestGlen Communications found that nearly 85 percent of the nation's television stations participate in satellite tours, including stations in the top 10 markets. Reporters like SMTs because they can ask their own questions and get an exclusive interview with a source anywhere in the world. This is in contrast to the VNR, which is a set piece, much like an ordinary news release. See the Tips for Success on page 237 for more on SMTs.

The easiest way to do an SMT is simply to make a spokesperson available for an interview. Celebrities are always popular, but an organization can also use articulate experts in its subject area. Essentially, the spokesperson sits in a chair or at a desk in front of a television camera. Viewers usually see the local news anchor asking questions and the spokesperson on a newsroom monitor, via satellite, answering them in much the same way that anchors talk with reporters at the scene of an event.

Basically, the format is two talking heads—the news anchor and the spokesperson. An example of such an SMT is one done by Best Buy on "Black Friday," the day after Thanksgiving when stores are jammed with shoppers. Best Buy enlisted pop commentator Mo Rocca to add some lighthearted rumor to the frantic day and partnered him with a personable Best Buy employee who was knowledgeable about electronic products and what was "hot" that season. In the space of 3 hours, the pair gave 23 media interviews to television stations across the country. According to

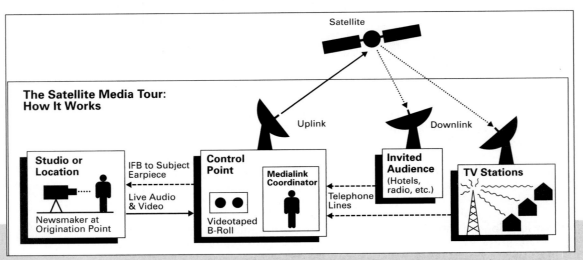

FIGURE 9.8 Satellite media tours are efficient and save travel time. This illustration shows the mechanics of an SMT. The process is interactive because the spokesperson and the interviewer can talk as if they are in the same room.

(Copyright by MediaLink, New York)

Guidelines for a Successful SMT

Anecdotal evidence indicates that four out of five pitched satellite media tours don't get aired. You can increase the odds if you follow these "do's" and "don'ts" compiled by *PRWeek*:

Do

- Include a relevant angle for the stations in every market you pitch.

- Use an interesting, visually appealing background or set. It often makes the difference between your SMT getting on the air or not.

- Get stations involved by sending items that will help them perform and promote the interview.

- Respect producer's wishes when they tell you they will get back to you. Incessant follow-up will only annoy those who you are trying to convince.

- Localize your SMT. If local audiences aren't going to be interested, neither are the producers airing the story.

- Be clear in your pitch. Provide producers with the who, what, when, and why right away.

- Use credible, knowledgeable spokespersons that project confidence and are personable.

Don't

- Don't let the SMT become a commercial. If producers think there is the possibility of too many product mentions, they won't book it.

- Don't be dishonest with producers about the contents of your SMT.

- Don't pitch your SMT to more than one producer at a station.

- Don't be conservative with the amount of talent. A boring medical SMT will pack more punch if you present a patient along with the doctor.

- Don't surprise the producer. Newscasts are planned to the minute and unexpected events (spokesperson cancels) will not be appreciated. ■

public relations firm Manning, Selvage & Lee, which handled the SMT, "Together, they brought a unique element of irreverence to the campaign, connected emotionally with consumers, and distinguished Best Buy from other retailers on one of the busiest shopping days of the year . . ."

Although **talking heads**, as they are known in the industry, are often used for SMTs, today's most successful SMTs are more interactive and dynamic. As Sally Jewett, president of On-The-Scene Productions, told *PRWeek*, "It's important to offer reporters something beyond the talking head, especially since competition is increasing as more firms realize the benefits of SMTs."

One approach is to integrate additional video into the SMT. As discussed in the section about VNRs, this is called B-roll material. Essentially, video footage of an event or activity is run while the spokesperson talks off-screen. For example, Abbott Labs hired Simon Productions to do an SMT on a new product for diabetics. While the spokesperson was talking about the new product, Simon showed people using it, being checked out by a doctor, and eating the "wrong" foods.

WestGlen Communications, in a survey of television news directors, found that almost 95 percent of the stations prefer B-roll footage to accompany the interview.

"Stations like to put together a background piece to air prior to the interview," says Annette Minkalis, senior vice president of WestGlen's broadcast department. She adds, "Many stations prefer B-roll and a hard copy summary 3 to 4 days in advance of the tour. Having footage in advance, as opposed to having it fed during the interview, gives stations time to prepare the story, especially in a live interview." At times, an SMT is also coordinated with the release of a VNR about the same topic.

Another popular approach to SMTs is to get out of the television studio and do them on location. When the National Pork Producers Council wanted to promote outdoor winter grilling, its public relations staff hired a team from Broadcast News Network to fire up an outdoor grill in Aspen, Colorado, and put a chef in a parka to give interviews, via satellite, while he cooked. In another example, the Hawaii Tourism Board targeted television stations in New England on a cold winter day with an SMT originating from Hawaii's sunny and attractive beaches.

Log Cabin Syrup, a division of Aurora Foods, opted for an even more remote locale to do an SMT. WestGlen Communications organized an SMT from the north rim of the Grand Canyon to show Log Cabin's sponsorship of a project called "Restoration of America's Log Cabins." The SMT, and a VNR, featured interviews with a restoration team that was restoring a 1930s log cabin. Of course, the grandeur of the Grand Canyon also made the site attractive, despite the considerable logistical details of providing satellite links to the remote location. However, Michael Hill of News Broadcast Network told *O'Dwyer's PR Services Report*, "A remote location adds value to the story itself, and increases the likelihood—and quality—that the SMT will be picked up by the media."

Organizing an SMT from a remote location, however, does involve more planning. Here are some tips from various production companies:

- Do a site survey. Figure out the logistics for sound, lighting, telephones, and satellites.
- Make contingency arrangements in case of bad weather.
- Make sure your spokesperson is adaptable and prepared to answer all sorts of questions.
- Arrange for necessary permits and permissions if using public or private property.
- Make sure the location has some tie-in with your subject.
- Make certain that the location is free from general public access to avoid background distractions.
- Be conscious of other complications, such as noise from honking horns and even air traffic.

Another aspect to consider is whether the SMT has enough news value to justify its cost. In general, a basic SMT costs $10,000 to $25,000. The Best Buy SMT cost $40,000, but it also included the cost of celebrity talent. If it is done outside a television studio, costs can rise substantially, depending on the location and logistics involved. Given the cost, many organizations try to get maximum benefit by combining an SMT with ANRs and VNRs. Interviews can also be reformatted for the organization's website and made into audio podcasts. Bev Yehuda, vice president of

MultiVu, adds, "With your spokesperson already in a TV studio, it's easy to initiate an Internet connection and produce a video webcast."

News Feeds ■ A variation on the SMT is a news feed that provides video and soundbites of an event to TV stations across the country via satellite. The news feed may be live from the actual event as it is taking place (real time), or it could be video shot at an event, edited, and then made available as a package.

In either case, the sponsoring organization hires a production firm to record the event. DWJ Television, for example, was hired by Christie's to cover the auction of 56 outfits worn by women at Academy Award ceremonies. DWJ engineers managed everything from setting up cameras and lighting to troubleshooting problems for crews during the auction.

The event, which benefited the American Foundation for AIDS Research, was made available in real time to television stations around the country and the world via satellite. Stations could air the whole auction, or simply make a video clip for use in later newscasts. Stations in 9 of the top 10 markets used the news feed, which reached almost 12 million viewers.

An example of a packaged news feed is one done for Korbel Champagne Cellars to announce the three winners of its "perfect marriage proposal" contest. Edelman Worldwide, the public relations firm, worked with distributor WestGlen Communications to offer TV stations video clips and soundbites showing the three winning proposals—which ranged from a proposal at a Broadway production to tuxedo-clad men skiing down a Colorado slope armed with roses and, of course, champagne.

Personal Appearances and Product Placements

So far in this chapter we have concentrated on how to prepare and generate timely material for newscasts. Here we will present an overview of other placement opportunities in broadcasting, from getting people booked on talk shows to having a popular sitcom use your employer's or client's product on the show.

In these cases, your contact is no longer the news department, but rather the directors and producers of various specialty features and shows. Your most valuable communication tools are the telephone and the persuasive pitch letter (see Chapter 6).

Before using either tool, however, it is necessary to do your homework. You must be familiar with a show's format and content, as well as the type of audience that it reaches. You can obtain this information in several ways.

One method is to study the station and descriptions of its shows in a broadcast database. Directory listings can tell you program format, types of material used, and the name of the director or producer. Directories are discussed in the next chapter, but see Figure 9.1 on page 210 for an example of a television station listing.

A second approach is to watch the program or feature and study the format. In the case of a talk or interview show, what is the style of the moderator or host? What kinds of topics are discussed? How important is the personality or prominence of the guest? How long is the show or a segment? Does the show lend itself to demonstrations and visual aids? The answers to such questions will help you tailor your phone calls and pitch letters to achieve maximum results.

Talk Shows

Radio and television talk shows have been a staple of broadcasting for many years. KABC in Los Angeles started the trend in 1960, when it became the first radio station in the country to convert to an all-news-and-talk format. Today, more than 1,110 radio stations have adopted the format. Other stations, of course, also include talk shows as part of their programming. In fact, it is estimated that there are now more than 5,000 radio talk shows in the United States.

The same growth rate applies to television. Seven years after KABC started the talk show format, Phil Donahue began his TV show. Today, there are more than 20 nationally syndicated talk shows and a countless number of locally produced shows. For the past decade, the number one syndicated daytime talk show has been the *Oprah Winfrey Show*, attracting about 8 million viewers on a daily basis. On the network level, three shows are the Holy Grail for publicists: NBC's *Today*, ABC's *Good Morning America*, and CBS's *Early Show*. Collectively, these three shows draw about 14 million viewers between 7 and 9 A.M. every weekday. As *PRWeek* says, "there's simply no better way to hit millions of consumers in one shot."

The advantage of talk shows is the opportunity to tell your views directly to the American public without the filter of journalists and editors interpreting and deciding what is newsworthy. Another advantage is the opportunity to be on the air for longer than the traditional 30-second soundbite in a news program.

You may never have the opportunity to book a guest on the *Today* show, but you should be aware of such shows and their ability to reach large audiences. Talk shows and public affairs programs on local radio and television stations, as well as a proliferation of cable channels, provide excellent placement opportunities for organizational spokespersons talking on any number of topics.

Here are some questions to consider when thinking about placement on a talk show:

- Is the topic newsworthy? Do you have a new angle on something in the news?
- Is the topic timely? Can you tie the idea to some lifestyle or cultural trend?
- Is the information useful to the viewers? How-to ideas may be welcomed.
- Does your spokesperson have viewer appeal? A celebrity may be acceptable, but there must be a logical tie-in to your organization and to the topic to be discussed. A professional athlete might be plausible talking about running shoes but out of place in a discussion about the economy.
- Can the spokesperson stay on track? It is easy for celebrities to get involved in discussions of their professional activities and personal lives.
- Can you keep the speaker from stressing the commercial angle? Most talk show hosts will allow a brief mention of a brand name or sponsor identification. If your speaker gets too commercial, the entire interview may be deleted—and your organization may land on the list of those who will not be invited back.

When you know the answers to these questions, you will be ready to look for a booking—or several. Here are some tips that should help:

- Be sure that your speaker fits the program. If he or she isn't a fast thinker, avoid shows full of rapid exchanges and loaded questions.

- Be sure that you know the requirements of the program and the abilities of your spokesperson.

66 *We expect our hosts (spokespersons) to be able to put the products in a newsworthy context and answer unexpected questions.* 99

■ Michael Friedman, executive vice president of DWJ Television

- Plan to use visuals if possible. Charts, diagrams, samples, and videotapes may help the producer decide.

- Deal with only one person on the program. But you may certainly approach producers of other programs on the same station.

- Be careful about exclusivity. Some stations will refuse to book a guest who appears on a competing station. Find out before you commit. By committing to one station, you may miss an opportunity to get on others.

- Plan variations so that you can offer the same person to different shows or different stations without giving the same thing to each.

- Prepare your speaker.

After you have done your homework on the format of a radio or television talk show, contact the show's producer or associate producer. If it is a network or nationally syndicated show, the contact person may have the title of talent coordinator or talent executive. Whatever the title, these people are known in the broadcasting industry as **bookers** because they are responsible for booking a constant supply of timely guests for a show.

You can place a phone call briefly outlining the qualifications of your proposed speaker and why the person would be a timely guest, or you can write a one-page pitch letter or send an e-mail (see Chapter 6) to convince the producer to book the guest. In many cases, the booker will ask for video clips of the spokesperson on previous TV shows, and even newspaper clips relating to past interviews. As mentioned previously, the more you know about the format and the audience of the show, the better you can tailor a persuasive pitch.

It is also important to be honest about your client's expertise and personality. According to Marsha Friedman of Event Management Services in Clearwater, Florida, which specializes in booking guests, talk show producers often complain that guests often bear little resemblance to their publicist's pitch. Barbara Hoffman, producer of *Doctor to Doctor*, told *O'Dwyer's PR Newsletter* that the best pitches come from publicists whose "clients are always exactly what they say they are, always prepared, interesting, on time, and always have something unusual or cutting edge to offer my program."

In general, talk shows book guests 3 to 4 weeks ahead of time. Unless a topic or a person is extremely timely or controversial, it is rare for a person to be booked on 1 or 2 days' notice. Keep this in mind as you plan talk show appearances as part

The Ideal Talk Show Guest

What constitutes a killer TV guest? Senior producer for *Your World with Cavuto*, Gresham Strigel, shared his thoughts with *Bulldog Reporter*, a public relations newsletter:

■ The spokesperson is personable and approachable when producers conduct pre-interviews on the phone. They are forthright in a nonaggressive way. "If you're wishy-washy, noncommittal, or stilted, you're not going much further."

■ Guests should have strong opinions. "We don't call certain people back because they've been trained not to say anything. The stronger your position is, and the higher up it is, the more media attention you're going to get. Nobody likes guests who play it safe."

■ Guests should be passionate about the subject. "We don't want people who are robotic—who just spit out facts. If you convey passion about what you're talking about, you jump off the screen."

■ Debate without getting personal or mean-spirited. "Smile. . . . Audiences like to see someone who is comfortable on-screen—someone who is happy to be there."

■ Have an engaging, outgoing personality. "Talking heads and ivory tower types don't do well on television. They're better suited to print, where their personality—or lack of one—can't turn audiences off." ■

of an overall public relations plan. See the accompanying Tips for Success for more on what makes a good talk show guest.

On occasion, it's possible that a local television station will let you create your own talk show. Rex Healthcare did just that in Raleigh, North Carolina, by creating a monthly medical call-in TV show titled *Rex on Call*. The show, which featured doctors and medical researchers as guests, had a mix of health advice and took "house calls" from interested viewers. Additional viewers were reached through archived Web episodes available on the company's website.

Magazine Shows

Magazine shows, like talk shows, are excellent outlets for topical feature stories. Depending on the program, they can be human-interest features or in-depth investigative stories on some contemporary issue such as the high cost of medical care or the plight of the homeless in major cities.

On the local level, there are many human-interest magazine shows. A sampling of magazine shows in one large city featured such subjects as a 1-pound baby who survived, a treatment for anorexia nervosa, a couple who started a successful cookie company, remedies for back pain, tips on dog training, a black-belt karate expert, blue-collar job stress, and the work habits of a successful author.

Most, if not all, of these features came about as the result of someone making a pitch to the show's producers. The objective of the segment, at least from the perspective of the people featured, is exposure and the generation of new business. The tips on dog training, for example, featured a local breeder who also operated a dog obedience school. The karate expert ran a martial arts academy.

Product Placement

Television's dramatic and comedy shows, as well as the film industry, are good vehicles for promoting a company's products and services. It is not a coincidence that the hero of a detective series drives a Dodge Viper or that a United Airlines plane is shown taking off or landing. Such product placements, often called **plugs**, are often negotiated by product publicists and talent agencies. This is really nothing new. *IPRA Frontline* reports, "In the early 1900s, Henry Ford had an affinity for Hollywood and perhaps it is no coincidence that his Model T's were the predominant vehicle appearing in pictures of that era."

Product placements, however, came of age in the movie *ET* back in the early 1980s. The story goes that M&M Candies made a classic marketing mistake by not allowing the film to use M&Ms as the prominently displayed trail of candy that the young hero used to lure his big-eyed friend home. Instead, Hershey's *Reese's Pieces* jumped at the chance, and the rest is history. Sales of Reese's Pieces skyrocketed, and even today, more than 20 years after the film's debut, *Reese's Pieces* and *ET* remain linked in popular culture and in the minds of a whole new generation of *ET* fans.

The placement of Reese's Pieces in *ET*, according to marketing experts, was one of the most famous product-placement scenes of all time. And it spawned a whole new industry of product placements in television shows and movies. Clothing manufacturers and retailers are particularly active in product placements, because studies show that today's young people get most of their fashion ideas from watching television shows. This is why upscale retailers were eager, and paid large fees, for the main characters in *Sex in the City* to be seen using their clothes, handbags, jewelry, and shoes.

Indeed, product placements have become a major part of the television and film industry, and many of them are full-fledged marketing communications campaigns. Coca-Cola, for example is prominently featured on *American Idol*. In another popular series, the *Sopranos*, Carmela drove a new Porsche Cayenne, and Tony used a cell phone from Cingular (now AT&T). Even Horatio Caine arrives in a Hummer on *CSI: Miami*. Indeed, *O'Dwyer's Newsletter* quotes Frank Zazza of iTVX productions saying that a 20-second product placement on *Desperate Housewives* would be worth about $400,000, about the same as a 30-second commercial on the show.

Another opportunity, of course, is on game shows. *The Price Is Right*, for example, uses a variety of products as prizes to contestants. In one episode, the prize was a tent, a camp table and chairs, and lanterns. It was a great low-cost product placement for Coleman for less than $200. At the minimum level, a product appears in a TV series or a film and that's it. A hotel or resort, for example, may be only a location shot, but it no doubt has been selected because the hotel was willing to provide rooms and food for the show's personnel. This is called a "trade-out."

Although product placements and tie-ins on a high-profile television series or a major film can cost millions of dollars, you should remember that not all product placements are in that league. A low-profile item such as a can of soda or a bag of chips in a scene may cost virtually nothing. However, be prepared to provide samples of the product to the crew for daily use or special events, such as the "wrap party" for the crew at the end of filming.

You should always be alert to opportunities for publicity on television programs and upcoming movies. If the company's product or service lends itself to a particular program, contact the show's producer directly or through an agent who specializes in matching company products with the show's needs. If you are dealing with a national television show or a film studio, you particularly need the services of a product placement firm located in Hollywood or New York. At last count, there were about 50 agencies engaged in this booming specialty area.

Issue Placement ■ A logical extension of product placements is convincing popular television programs to write an issue or cause into their scripts. Writers for issue-oriented shows such as *Grey's Anatomy*, *ER*, and *Law & Order* are constantly bombarded with requests from a variety of nonprofit and special interest groups.

The National Campaign to Prevent Teen Pregnancy, for example, worked very hard to get the issue of teen pregnancy on *Dawson's Creek* because it reached so many young people. The result was a scene where Dawson's mom talked to her son's girlfriend, Joey, about ways to prevent pregnancy. Many social and health organizations also lobby the producers of daytime soap operas to write scripts where major characters deal with cancer, diabetes, drug abuse, alcoholism, and an assortment of other problems.

The idea is to educate the public about a social issue or a health problem in a popular television show or a movie. Someone once said, "It's like hiding the aspirin in the ice cream." Even the federal government works with popular television programs to write scripts that deal with the dangers and prevention of drug abuse. Remember, however, that you can only suggest themes and ideas to show producers and script writers. They retain the creative independence to determine how they will write a scene.

The flip-side of asking script writers to include material is asking them to give a more balanced portrayal of an issue. The health-care industry, for example, is concerned about balance in such programs as *ER*. The popular program deals with a variety of health issues and, in many cases, health maintenance organizations (HMOs) get portrayed in an unfavorable light. Consequently, these organizations often meet with the program's script writers to educate them about the facts so the program is more balanced.

Radio Promotions

Public relations representatives for nonprofit organizations, record companies, concert promoters, and community events committees often generate publicity and exposure through radio promotions.

Promotions are beneficial to both the station and the outside organization. For example, a concert promoter may arrange with a radio station's disc jockey to award tickets to every 10th listener who calls the station and correctly answers a trivia question on the air. Prize giveaways tend to increase the number of listeners, and the concert promoter gets publicity.

A nonprofit group sponsoring a fund-raising festival may make arrangements for a radio station (or a television station) to cosponsor the event as part of the station's own promotional activities. This means that the station will actively promote the festival on the air through public service announcements and disc jockey chatter between songs.

The arrangements may also call for a popular disc jockey to broadcast live from the festival and give away T-shirts with the station's logo on them. This, too, is good promotion for the station and often attracts people to the fund-raising event because the disc jockey is a well-known personality. It is a win-win situation for both the station and the nonprofit group.

Organizations that have a creative idea can often get publicity by providing newscasters and disc jockeys with something unusual to talk about. A public relations firm for Burger King, for example, came up with the idea of introducing the fast-food chain's new Breakfast Buddy sandwich by delivering the sandwiches to morning radio DJs live on the air. The announcers were asked to sample them and ask listeners to call in and win a free phone call to their "best buddy" anywhere in the United States. One delivery resulted in a 10-minute interview on one major New York show; in all, the promotion secured time on 150 stations and more than 391 minutes of announcer endorsements.

If you are handling an event or a cause that is suitable for this type of promotion, contact the director of promotions for the radio or television station. If the station is interested, negotiate the terms of the sponsorship. For example, the station may promise to air a specified number of announcements for the event in return for being listed in the organization's news releases, programs, and print advertising as a sponsor of the event. Such terms are spelled out in a standard contract, often supplied by the radio or television station.

Stations will not necessarily promote or cosponsor your event just because it is worthy. They must be convinced that their involvement will benefit the station in terms of greater public exposure, increased audience, and improved market position.

Community Calendars

Civic clubs and other community groups can publicize upcoming events by sending short announcements to local broadcast outlets. Radio stations, in particular, operate community calendars as a service to their listeners.

To be used, however, the event must be open to the public and of general interest. A meeting of the local automobile dealers' association doesn't qualify, but a forum on the global economy sponsored by the local chapter of the World Affairs Council would be acceptable. Radio stations serving specialized audiences have variations on the community calendar. For example, a classical radio station might have an "arts calendar" that would list upcoming plays, musicals, and art shows. By the same token, a rock music station might have a "concert calendar" that lists upcoming rock concerts.

You write a calendar announcement in much the same way as you write a PSA. The announcement should be to the point. It should give the name of the event, the sponsoring organization, the date and time, location, cost, and a telephone number that listeners can call for more information.

Here is an example of a community calendar announcement for the Field Museum's map exhibition, which has been mentioned in previous chapters:

- **10 seconds:** Maps can tell us both *where* and *who* we are. The Field Museum's exhibition, **Maps: Finding Our Place in the World**, allows visitors to take a look at some of the most historically valuable maps ever created. For more information, visit www.fieldmuseum.org.

- **15 seconds:** Maps not only tell us where we are, but more importantly, who we are. The Field Museum's exhibition, **Maps: Finding Our Place in the World**, allows visitors to take a look at some of the most historically valuable maps ever created. For more information, visit www.fieldmuseum.org.

- **30 seconds:** Maps can tell us both *where* and *who* we are. The Field Museum's exhibition, **Maps: Finding Our Place in the World**, allows visitors to take a look at some of the most historically valuable maps ever created. Besides direction, maps can also give us clues on how a people, nation, government or organization viewed their worlds. Through contemporary, historical, flat or three-dimensional maps, this exhibition will explore a variety of themes, ranging from the history of maps to the map makers political, cultural, or spiritual worldview. For more information, call (312) 922-9410 or visit www.fieldmuseum.org.

Community calendar items should be sent to the station via e-mail or fax at least 3 weeks in advance.

Documentary Videos

Television stations and especially cable systems require a vast amount of programming to fill their schedules. Short features of 2 or 3 minutes and productions that run 20 minutes or more are often used to fill gaps in the programming day.

This is another public relations opportunity to increase awareness and visibility of an organization. A good example is the Fireman's Fund Insurance Company's documentary *Into the Fire*, which supported a multimillion-dollar corporate philanthropy program to provide grants to fire departments and fire-service organizations.

Ketchum was commissioned to produce the documentary with the goal of raising awareness of the need for fire departments to have more resources. The target audience was affluent 34- to 65-year-old men and firefighters. The History Channel was chosen as a partner in this documentary effort because it reached the target audience. *Into the Fire*, which was produced by a high-profile director who had won Emmy awards, shared firefighters' stories in their own voices. The result was an airing on the History Channel that reached more than 2.7 million viewers. In addition, private screenings were held for Fireman's Fund agents in 29 cities, where they were encouraged to get other agents to sign up to participate in the grant program.

The campaign received the Entertainment and Media Campaign of the Year in 2008 from *PRWeek*. One judge noted, "The very definition of entertainment today requires that the audience become invested in the concept and part of the experience. This film provided them in a big way."

Such documentaries are produced and distributed by businesses, nonprofit organizations, trade associations, and professional groups. For maximum acceptability, they must be relatively free of commercial hype and must concentrate on informing or educating the viewing audience. The following are a few examples of documentaries that have been made available to television stations and cable systems:

- *Waltzing Matilda*, a 32-minute travelogue on Australia, sponsored by the Australian Tourist Commission
- *Rethinking Tomorrow*, a 28-minute report on energy conservation, sponsored by the U.S. Department of Energy

- *Oil over the Andes*, a 27-minute account of the building of an oil pipeline, sponsored by the Occidental Petroleum Company
- *Noah Was an Amateur*, a 27-minute history of boat building, sponsored by the National Association of Engine and Boat Manufacturers

Getting such videos distributed requires some method of informing the broadcast stations of their availability. You can handle this yourself by contacting media outlets and letting them know about the subject of the video. National distribution services also market such videos. These organizations can distribute your materials by mail or satellite, depending on the preferences of the TV stations or cable systems that order them. In addition, these distribution services have an established program that can place your films and videos with schools, clubs, special-interest groups, and civic groups.

Increasingly, organizations also are making longer documentaries available 24 hours a day through video podcasts that can even be viewed on mobile phones.

Summary

- The broadcast media are important channels of communication, but using them requires thinking in terms of sound and visual elements.
- Radio releases are similar to press releases, but they require more concise writing and a conversational tone.
- Audio news releases (ANRs) are more interesting because they include soundbites, music, and sound effects.
- Public service announcements (PSAs) are short broadcast announcements used by nonprofit groups and public agencies.
- Radio media tours (RMTs) are a cost-effective way to reach many stations with an exclusive interview over a wide geographic area.
- Television is an excellent medium of communication because it combines the elements of sight, sound, motion, and color.
- Television news releases must contain both sound and visual elements such as graphics, slides, or videotape.

- Video news releases (VNRs) are widely used by TV stations and cable systems. They are also posted on organizational websites and social media sites such as YouTube.
- VNRs require professional preparation and high technical quality. To be used, they must be newsworthy and timely. Satellite distribution is the most cost-effective method.
- Satellite media tours (SMTs) are widely used in the broadcast industry. A popular format is setting up interviews from a location that reinforces the story.
- A good, persuasive query or pitch letter is used to get placements on news programs and talk shows.
- Talk shows offer numerous opportunities for reaching mass and specialized audiences.
- Organizations and groups can get exposure by making use of community calendars, radio promotions, creative publicity ideas, and documentaries.

Skill-Building Activities

1. The U.S. Forest Service wants to warn campers that lack of rain has made forests and campgrounds more vulnerable to forest fires this summer. Write 10-, 20-, 30-, and 60-second radio PSAs on this subject.

2. The international programs office on campus wants to encourage students to study abroad for a summer or a semester. Write a 60-second audio news release (ANR) that includes a soundbite.

3. The city is sponsoring its annual jazz festival in September. Write 10-, 20-, and 30-second announcements for the community calendars of local radio stations.

4. The National Coalition of Student Health is very concerned about binge drinking on college campuses. The coalition wants to raise public awareness about the issue nationwide. Write a memo giving your suggestions on how a satellite media tour (SMT) could be organized around this subject. For example, who would you use as a spokesperson?

5. The Bally Company wants to promote exercise among busy young professionals and, of course, get visibility for its national chain of fitness centers. Write a newsworthy video news release (VNR) script showing both video and audio components.

6. Red Bull, the energy drink, is a client of your public relations firm. What TV entertainment programs might be good outlets for product placements? Name some popular shows and suggest how Red Bull could be used in the script.

■ Suggested Readings

Chang, Irene. "Bringing a Broadcast's Message Home: Giving SMTs a New Look." *PRWeek*, October 8, 2007, p. 14.

Garcia, Tonya. "The Right Balance: Even With Explosion of Web Video, There Are Some Campaigns Where Traditional Media Play a Part." *PRWeek*, December 24, 2007, p. 19.

Hazley, Greg. "VNRs, Oversight Rank Among Top PA Issues." *O'Dwyer's PR Report*, February 2007, pp. 1, 19.

Hill, Bob. "A Guided Tour: Tips for SMT Spokespeople." *PR Tactics*, July 2003, pp. 15, 17.

Iacono, Erica. "PR Can Take Lead in Product Placement." *PRWeek*, June 5, 2006, p. 14.

Iacono, Erica. "Broadcast Tools Find Second Home: Putting VNRS, B-roll, and SMTs on the Web are Quickly Becoming Corporate Necessity." *PRWeek*, May 1, 2006, p. 18.

Lewis, Tanya. "Going Beyond the Traditional Avenues: There Are Far More Options for Distributing Your PSA." *PRWeek*, December 17, 2007, p. 22.

Lewis, Tanya. "The Language of Motivation: With PSAs, You Have Just a Short Time to Get People to Act." *PRWeek*, December 11, 2006, p. 26.

Longpre, Marc. "Satellite Radio Boosts Niche Audience for Healthcare." *PRWeek*, May 21, 2007, p. 11.

Purushothaman, Shoba. "Resuscitate Your VNR Using B-roll." *PR Tactics*, June 2003, p. 26.

Trammell, Jack. "Five Rules for Television and Radio Placements." *PR Tactics*, June 2003, p. 21.

Walker, Jerry. "Ten Tips for Making a Good Impression in a TV Interview." *O'Dwyer's PR Services Report*, July 2003, p. 32.

Ward, David. "The Mid-Morning Treasure Trove." *PRWeek*, July 10, 2006, p. 18.

Distributing News to the Media

10

TOPICS covered in this chapter include:

Reaching the Media   249

Distribution of Materials   254

Reaching the Media

Previous chapters emphasized that an essential part of public relations writing is making sure that the right media—and the right audience—receive your material. This chapter is about selecting the appropriate channels of distribution that will ensure that your materials will reach the correct media and intended audience.

A number of distribution methods can be used. This chapter details such methods as e-mail, online newsrooms, electronic wire services, feature placement firms, mail, and faxing. Each method has its advantages and disadvantages, which will be discussed in the following pages.

Indeed, a common complaint of editors is that they receive hundreds of news releases that are not relevant to their publication or their audience. A second major complaint is that news releases are often sent to the wrong person. Compounding this problem is the estimate that nearly one-third of all journalists change their job or beat every 90 days.

So how do you find the right medium and the correct, current contact person? How do you reach the business editor on every daily newspaper in the nation? How do you contact every Spanish-speaking radio station in Texas? How do you know what specialized trade publications would be interested in your company's new product?

Finding media, their addresses, and the names of editors would be nearly impossible if not for the existence of media databases in print and electronic form. Thus, the basis of all distribution channels is an up-to-date media database.

Media Databases

Media databases vary in format and scope. However, a common denominator is that they usually provide such essential information as (1) names of publications and broadcast stations, (2) mailing addresses, (3) telephone and fax numbers, (4) e-mail addresses, and (5) names of key editors and reporters. Many directories also give a profile of the media outlet in terms of audience, deadlines, and placement opportunities.

Cision (www.us.cision.com), for example, publishes *Bacon's* media directories, which are available in print format or online. There are three main databases: (1) newspapers and magazines, (2) radio/TV/cable, and (3) Internet media. In addition, Cision also publishes two regional directories: *Bacon's Metro California Media* and *Bacon's New York Publicity Outlets*. Another specialized database is a listing of editorial calendars for print media, which outlines special supplements that a publication may offer throughout the year. Editorial calendars will be discussed shortly.

Cision says that its *Bacon* directories and media databases have contact information on more than 900,000 editors, analysts, freelancers, syndicated columnists, broadcast journalists, and bloggers. Embedded in this information are preferred contact methods, beats covered, pitching tips, biographical information, audio interviews, and even photos of journalists. Sample listings from Cision's online media database and print edition are shown in Figure 10.1.

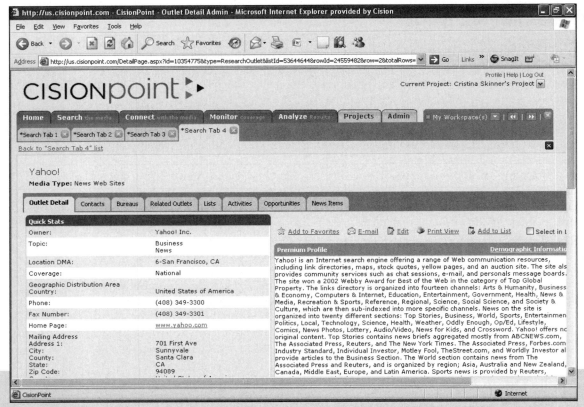

▶ **FIGURE 10.1A** A comprehensive media directory does more than just provide the name and address of a publication or a broadcast service. It also provides a thumbnail description of the media company, what topics are of interest to it, and how to contact various personnel. Shown here is an example from Cision's (A) online database and (B) a listing from its print directory.

Another major directory is Burrelles/Luce (www.burrellesluce.com). It offers an online database that includes contacts at daily newspapers, magazines, radio, non-daily newspapers, and television and cable. It claims to have detailed listings for about 76,000 media outlets in North America, including 380,000 staff listings and their contact preferences. Electronic news-wires such as Business Wire and PR Newswire also maintain databases of media contacts. Business Wire's PressCenter, for example, contains regular media contacts, as well as the details of influential writers at thousands of blogs.

Although print and CD directories are still used, online databases have the advantage of always being up-to-date with the latest information because they often are updated on a daily basis. A promotional letter from Cision, for example, claims that its staff makes about 10,000 updates on a daily basis. In one year alone, the company advertises that it made more than 1 million updates to its database, which is one reason that print directories are practically an artifact of the past.

These online databases enable you to rapidly compile a tailored media list for your messages, print out mailing labels, or even e-mail or fax your news release directly to a journalist. For example, if you need a list of business editors in four markets at dailies with a circulation above 50,000, you can compile it with a few keystrokes on your computer. With a few more keystrokes, you can print out the entire list on mailing labels or e-mail the news release to the selected media.

The computer has made it relatively easy to launch a thousand news releases with the click of the mouse, but publicists should avoid this approach to distribution

▶ **FIGURE 10.1B**

WOL-AM, 1450   A
5900 Princess Garden Pkwy 8th Fl   **(301) 306-1111**
Lanham, MD 20706-2925   Fax: (301) 306-9510
    Home Page: wolam.com

Network: ABC Radio Network, Wall Street Journal Radio, Bloomberg Radio, American Urban Radio Network
Owner: Radio One Inc   **Wattage:** 1,000
Profile: Talk, News; Target Audience: 18 thru 64; News: 8 B'casts, 100% Staff Prod.; Talk: 90% Staff. Prod.; Guests: Live, Phone, Taped; Releases/Scripts; Avg. Arbitron: 0.53; PSAs: Written.
Ethnicity: African-American.
Lead Times: Advertising - 3 days prior.
Management/News Executives:
Vice President & GM . . . . Michele Williams   (301) 429-2601
          mwilliams@radio-one.com
Operations Manager . . . . Kathy Brown   (301) 429-2680
          kb@radio-one.com
Program Director . . . . Ron Thompson   (301) 429-2673
          rthompson@radio-one.com
News Director . . . . Sheila Stewart   (301) 429-2639
          sstewart@radio-one.com
Public Service Director . . . . Vaughn Holmes   (301) 429-2677
          vholmes@radio-one.com

Programs:
Dean's Talk Room
Air Time: Mon-Fri, 1:00 - 4:00 PM
Profile: General Interest; **Format:** Talk, Interviews.
Interviews: Live, Phone, Taped; **Can Use:** Guests, Press Releases, Books.
Focus: Program features discussion of current events and hot topics. Guests of the show include individuals knowledgeable about the topic at hand.
Show Personnel:
Host . . . . Bernie McCain
Producer . . . . Dana Carl
          dcarl@radio-one.com

Madison the Black Eagle

       Home Page: www.joemadison.com
Air Time: Mon-Fri, 6:00 - 10:00 AM
Profile: General Interest, News/Weather/Sports; **Format:** Talk, Interviews, Listener Phone-In.
Interviews: Live, Phone; **Can Use:** Guests, New Products, Press Releases, Books, Calendar.
Focus: General interest morning program offers a mix of entertaining talk, issues-driven discussion and top news headlines of the day.
Show Personnel:
Host . . . . Joe Madison
          Phone: (301) 429-2631
          beagle980@aol.com
          www.joemadison.com
Producer . . . . Darryl Greene
          Phone: (301) 429-2624
          dgreene@radio-one.com

because it creates a blizzard of unwanted, irrelevant news releases at every media outlet in the country. Indeed, as already mentioned, the indiscriminate distribution of news releases is the major complaint that journalists have about publicists.

Ruth McFarland, senior vice president of Cision, points out that media databases such as Bacon's should only be the starting point for thinking more strategically about what particular media outlet should be contacted. She told *O'Dwyer's PR Report*, "The paradox of PR media research is that less is more; the fewer entries you have in your database of regular contacts, the better your results will be." She continues, "Making only 10 calls to the right editors with just the right story idea will get you 10 times better coverage than sending out 100 releases and following up with 100 perfunctory phone calls or e-mails."

> 66 *Don't fall for the 'spray and pray' method by using a media database to blast e-mails to anyone remotely connected with your client. You will only damage your company's reputation as well as your own.* 99 ■ Eric Hall, executive vice president of MyEdcals

However, every news release doesn't require extensive media research. Some organizations have several standard mailing lists that accommodate most of their releases. One list might include only local media in the organization's headquarters city. A second list might include local media in cities where the organization has manufacturing plants. A third list might be statewide media, and a fourth list might include regional and national media. Yet another list might include trade and business media covering the industry. In each case, the news release should be tailored to the particular mailing list.

Many professional publicists, in order to ensure total accuracy, also take the time to call the media outlet and double-check an editor's name before sending out an important news release. Bill Clapper, a public relations practitioner, posted a note on PRFORUM that sums up the problem. He writes, "I think we buy fancy software that can sort, slice, and dice all the media in the galaxy. But it doesn't guarantee that my press release will get to the right person in a timely manner. Only way to do that is to call and find out who the business editor is today."

If you have compiled your own media list, you must update it regularly. Whenever, and however, you learn of a change, correct your mailing list immediately. Nothing annoys an editor or reporter more than a useless news release, but a close second is a release sent to someone who hasn't been around for months—or years.

Some public relations people try to solve this problem by addressing envelopes to titles instead of people. For example, a news release will be sent to the "news editor" or the "features editor" of a publication. Although this seems a logical approach, recipients react much as they do to junk mail addressed to "occupant." Releases sent to a generic e-mail address at a media outlet have the same fate; no one bothers to open it.

Editorial Calendars

Not only do media databases help you find the names and addresses of media gatekeepers, several of them also tell you when to approach publications with specific kinds of stories.

Trade publications and business periodicals, in particular, tend to operate on what is known as an **editorial calendar**. That means that certain issues have a special editorial focus. Special issues are used to attract advertising, but news stories and features on the subject are also needed.

For example, a high-technology magazine may have a special issue on laptop computers planned for April. Companies that manufacture laptop computers will no doubt want to advertise in that issue. If you're in the public relations or marketing communications department of the company, this special issue should also alert you that the publication is also open to news and feature stories about laptop computers.

Indeed, one of your major duties for a client or an employer is to review the editorial calendars of various publications to determine stories and features that might be submitted to coincide with the editorial focus of a particular issue. It also pays to check your local daily to get a list of special supplements planned for the year. Doing this sort of homework will dramatically increase your story placements.

Periodicals often set their editorial calendars a year in advance, and many keep the same special-issue calendars from one year to the next. MyEdcals (www .myedcals.com) has a Google-like database that tracks the editorial calendars of about 7,000 publications in the United States and Canada. According to Eric Hall, executive vice president of MyEdcals, this equates to more than 400,000 story opportunities for publicists. He points out, however, that publicists should always double-check a publication's editorial calendar, since about 50 percent of publications make changes during the year. Several media directories also provide the editorial calendars of publications, including *Bacon's* and Burrelles/Luce.

Tip Sheets

Another good way to find media personnel who might have an interest in your material is **tip sheets**. These are weekly newsletters that report on recent changes in news personnel and their new assignments, how to contact them, and what kinds of material they are looking for. Some even tell you how to pronounce people's names.

Public relations newsletters such as *Bulldog Reporter*, *Jack O'Dwyer's Newsletter*, *Ragan's Media Relations Report*, *PRWeek*, and *PartyLine* provide regular tips as part of their content. Here are two sample items from the weekly edition of *PartyLine* (www.partylinepublishing.com), a newsletter exclusively devoted to listing media placement opportunities:

> The Hollywood Reporter's deputy editor Andrew Wallenstein is interested in information in stories about the impact of digital media on the entertainment industry. He is reached at The Reporter, 5055 Wilshire Blvd., Los Angeles, CA 90036. The editorial fax is: (323) 525-2377.

> Garage Style Magazine is the first magazine devoted to garages. Launched by publisher–editor Don Weberg, an automotive journalist, the magazine, a quarterly, will showcase spectacular garages, especially those of car collectors. The magazine is designed to be a resource for amazing garages, with technical how-to articles,

product reviews and buyer's guides. Information for inclusion should go to *Garage Style Magazine*, PO Box 812, LaHabra, CA 90633, (562) 833-8085; www .garagestylemagazine.com

Armed with this kind of information, a public relations professional considerably increases the odds of getting a media placement. Tip sheets allow you to use the rifle approach, instead of shot-gunning material all over the country in the hope that some editor, somewhere, is interested in it.

■ Distribution of Materials

The vast majority of publicity materials are now distributed in digital and electronic formats. E-mail is now universal and so pervasive in our society that it's difficult to conceive of a time in the not so distant past when snail mail was the primary distribution method. Snail mail has not disappeared from the publicist's tool kit, and will be discussed later, but today's primary distribution channels are (1) e-mail, (2) online newsrooms, (3) electronic newswires, (4) mat distribution companies, and (5) photo placement firms.

66 *With so many avenues for communications these days, PR and marketing professionals must use a mix of distribution channels to ensure their message is heard.* 99 ■ Vocus white paper, Five Key Ways to Distribute Your News

This section also discusses the continued use of mail and overnight package delivery, as well as the faxing of materials. Each distribution channel, of course, has its advantages and disadvantages, and a summary of the various methods is provided in the Tips for Success on page 255. The focus in the chapter is reaching traditional media; Chapter 12 further explores additional distribution and placement opportunities in the new media, often called *social media*.

E-Mail

Electronic mail, or **e-mail**, is the oldest feature of the Internet. It was invented in 1971, but wasn't widely adopted by business until the late 1980s. Today, having an e-mail address (or even several) is practically universal. In fact, e-mail is so pervasive in today's society that IDC, a research firm, estimated that 10 trillion e-mails were sent worldwide in 2006, compared to less than a trillion in 1997. People put their e-mail addresses on their business cards, organizations publicize their e-mail addresses, and media personnel use e-mail as their primary source for news releases, media advisories, and other communications.

Indeed, more than one survey has confirmed that e-mail is the major form of communication among public relations writers, clients, and journalists. One survey conducted by the Center for Media Research, for example, found that journalists prefer communicating via e-mail over any other medium. In fact, 98 percent of the journalists surveyed said they prefer to receive news releases via e-mail. Another survey of journalists by Vocus public relations found similar results. According to *PR Reporter*, "While spam is a problem, 83 percent still choose e-mail as their preferred way of receiving news releases over fax and mail."

Selecting a Distribution Channel

This chapter describes a number of media distribution channels. That still leaves the question, "Which channel should I use for my material?" The answer is not simple. It depends on the purpose and objectives of your message—and who you want to reach with it. In many cases, you should use a mix of distribution channels. The following are some general tips:

- **E-mail.** Good for suggesting story ideas to journalists and editors, answering media questions and queries, and sending news releases.

- **Online newsrooms.** This is a comprehensive library of information for the journalist. Good for distributing news releases, media kits, features, corporate background information, and high-resolution photos and graphics. Distribution is enhanced by sending e-alerts and having journalists sign up for RSS feeds from the online newsroom.

- **Electronic wire services.** Best for distribution of financial news to large newspapers and major broadcast outlets on a national or international basis where immediate disclosure is needed. Ideal for multimedia news releases that incorporate photos, graphics, and video. Distribution also includes Internet search engines, bloggers, and other social networking media.

- **Feature placement firms.** Good for reaching suburban newspapers and small weeklies. Best for feature-type material that remains relevant over a period of time and can be used in various sections of the newspaper. Distribution can be done in multiple formats.

- **Photo placement firms.** Best for distributing high-resolution publicity photos on an international basis. Makes it possible to index images for access by search engines.

- **Mail.** A common method for distribution of routine materials to local and regional media. Mailing houses are effective for mailing news releases, media kits, and CDs on a local, regional, or national basis.

- **Fax.** Good for sending media advisories and alerts and late-breaking important news. Not recommended for mass distribution of news releases.

- **CD-ROMs.** Best used for background material, such as corporate profiles, executive bios, and product information sheets. Increasingly used in place of printed media kits. ■

The Vocus survey also found that most respondents prefer news releases to have links to websites so that they can easily click the links to get supplemental information. If you provide links in your news releases, Vocus notes that it is better to link journalists to a customized website that pertains to the news release. All too often, the only link on the news release is the organization's home page, and reporters have to do more clicking to find the actual material. One common solution is online newsrooms, which will be discussed in the next section.

If you do send an e-mail news release, here are some general rules that supplement the guidelines given in Chapter 5:

- Write a subject line that contains keywords and concisely tells the subject of the news release.

- Put useful information—not contact numbers—at the beginning of a news release.

- Don't send attachments unless requested. File attachments often carry viruses.
- Don't send HTML e-mail messages.
- Provide links to a website that contain additional information and graphics.
- Use an extended headline at the top of the news release to give the key message or point.
- Try to use bullets for key points.
- Keep it short; reporters hate to scroll through multiple screens.
- Don't mass distribute releases; it's called spam.
- Don't rely entirely on use of e-mail for distribution of news. Support it with fax or hard copy distribution.
- Use blind copy distribution, and don't reveal your entire mailing list. No reporter wants to know they are part of a mass mailing.
- Remember to provide contact e-mail addresses and phone numbers.
- Continually update your e-mail addresses.
- Make sure your news release is factually correct and free of any spelling, grammar, or punctuation errors.

E-mail offers several advantages. Ron Solberg, one of the pioneers in using new technologies for public relations purposes, wrote in *PR Tactics* some years ago:

> Reporters receiving news releases by e-mail don't have to re-key your words. They can easily save or discard the document. And if a reporter wants to keep the release for future reference, it's more convenient to store it on their computer's hard drive than in an overstuffed file drawer. In addition, any copy you key in and send directly to a reporter by e-mail will appear on his or her computer screen exactly as you sent it. There is less opportunity for re-keying error if the reporter uses a quote from your electronic news release in a story.

Advocates of e-mail also say that it is less intrusive than a phone call. If a reporter or editor receives the message at deadline, they can read it at a more convenient time. Others say e-mail is much more efficient and less annoying to editors than faxes. E-mail also eliminates telephone tag. Reporters and public relations personnel can easily engage in an e-mail dialogue, posting messages on each other's computer, instead of trying to reach each other by telephone and leaving messages on voicemail.

The downside, of course, is the problem of getting noticed in a deluge of 200 or 300 e-mails that typically flood an editor's inbox on a daily basis. The Vocus study, for example, found that 17 percent of the respondents received over 200 e-mail releases a week and another 33 percent received 100 to 200 releases a week. In another survey, research firm Radicati Group estimated the average corporate e-mail user sent and received about 171 messages a day in 2006, and the number is expected to double by 2010.

Spamming has become a common complaint among journalists and practically everyone else. *Spam*, broadly defined, is unsolicited e-mail, and many journalists say there is little difference between mass e-mails from public relations firms and those from organizations that want to enhance your physical attributes with various potions. Consequently, public relations professionals increasingly are finding that their news releases are blocked by highly sophisticated antispamming software.

Jennifer Martin, corporate communications manager for CipherTrust, has one solution: "Try to go through and personalize each e-mail, and don't blind copy a press release." What she means is that you should not copy (even if it's hidden) multiple reporters at the same time.

Online Newsrooms

Sending e-mail news releases on a regular basis is called a "push" approach to distribution. A "pull" strategy, in contrast, is to make information readily available that attracts or "pulls" journalists to your information. A good example is a fully operational newsroom on an organization's website. HP has an extensive newsroom, which is shown Figure 10.2.

Indeed, an online newsroom is a vital necessity because it's often the first place journalists turn to for basic information about the organization, its products, and its services. An online newsroom link should be highly visible on an organization's home page, and it should be easy to navigate with a minimum number of clicks.

Vocus, a supplier of public relations software and owner of PRWeb, says that an online newsroom has five key components:

1. **Contact information.** The names, e-mail addresses, and phone numbers of the primary public relations contacts for the organization should be listed and easy to find. The Center for Media Research surveyed journalists on the usefulness of company newsrooms, and 97 percent said contact information was very important. At the same time, the most frequent complaint of journalists is that such information is not included or difficult to find.

2. **Corporate background.** The site should include a comprehensive company history, a basic fact sheet, executive profiles, and product descriptions. You can also highlight the awards of the organization, major executive presentations, and position papers. This was important to almost 90 percent of the journalists.

3. **News releases and media kits.** News releases should be traditionally formatted and listed in reverse chronological order. Media kits should be posted in a similar way. This was important to 92 percent of the surveyed journalists. In addition, it's important to have "printer friendly" capability availability for visitors.

4. **Multimedia gallery.** You should provide executive photos, product photos, charts, graphs, and other artwork in both low (72 dpi) and high (300 dpi) resolutions to meet the needs of visitors to the site. Materials should be downloadable in JPEG or PDF format. This was important to about 70 percent of the journalists.

5. **Search capability.** Include a search component in your newsroom to allow journalists, consumers, investors, and other visitors to easily find information by topic or date. This component was important to 95 percent of the surveyed journalists in the Center for Media Research survey.

HP Newsroom

Share/tag this page

» Company information

» Newsroom home

News
» News releases
» Feature stories
» HP Videos
» Blogs
» Podcasts
» RSS Feeds
» Awards

Journalist resources
» Media relations contacts
» Fast facts
» Press kits
» Executive team
» Financial information
» Global citizenship
» History & Milestones
» News archives

Related links
» HP Ads
» HP Images
» Recalls and replacement programs
» Student Inquiries
» Trademark and Product names

» HP Graphic Arts: Progressive, Profitable Printing

» HP Labs Advances Sustainable IT with New Research Projects

HP announced new research initiatives from HP Labs, the company's central research arm, aimed at developing new technologies and business models that leave a lighter carbon footprint.

» **News releases** RSS

» HP Labs Advances Sustainable IT with New Research Projects

» HP Licenses Technology to Xtreme Energetics for Creation of Super-efficient Solar Energy System

» HP Board Declares Regular Dividend

» HP Names Don Grantham Chief Sales Officer

» HP Announces Multimillion Dollar Sale of HP Indigo Digital Press Technologies to Consolidated Graphics

» More news releases

» **Feature stories** RSS

» Defending the Desktop: What can your company do to help protect business data?

» Green up: Save energy while you help reduce your impact on the environment

» Moving to greener pastures: Better ways to increase energy efficiency across your business

» Activity Center: Great Wedding & Bridal Shower projects for you & your guests

» HP helps reduce costs and improve business processes

» More feature stories

»View HP's FY07 Global Citizenship Report

Executive corner

» Executive viewpoints
» Biographies
» Speeches
» Articles

Most popular:

News releases
» HP Introduces Full-function Mini-notebook PC for Education Market

» HP to Acquire EDS for $13.9 Billion

» HP Names Don Grantham Chief Sales Officer

» HP Offers Customers World's Broadest Portfolio of Digital Color Printing Products to Capture Digital Page Growth

» HP Announces Multimillion Dollar Sale of HP Indigo Digital Press Technologies to Consolidated Graphics

Feature stories
» HP Graphic Arts: Progressive, Profitable Printing

» Defending the Desktop: What can your company do to help protect business data?

» DreamWorks Animation artists go over the top with HP technology

» HP Compaq dc7800 Business Desktop PC

» New HP Thin Client solutions — easy, secure & affordable computing

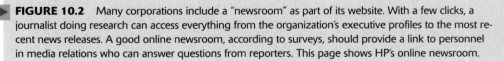

FIGURE 10.2 Many corporations include a "newsroom" as part of its website. With a few clicks, a journalist doing research can access everything from the organization's executive profiles to the most recent news releases. A good online newsroom, according to surveys, should provide a link to personnel in media relations who can answer questions from reporters. This page shows HP's online newsroom.

TEKgroup International (www.tekgroup.com), which designs online newsrooms, also conducts an annual survey of journalists that asks what functions they prefer in an online newsroom. In the 2008 annual survey of more than 400 journalists, it was found that 70 percent of journalists often visited online newsrooms. Their reasons for visiting were mixed: to access breaking news (97%), to access news releases (98%), to access photos (92%), to access executive biographies

(89%), to access company background information (97%), to search archives (100%), and to access public relations contacts (99%).

The journalists in the TEKgroup survey also indicated that almost all of journalists (97%) preferred receiving information via a newsroom e-mail alert or an RSS feed. Another large percentage (92%) preferred receiving pitched stories via a newsroom e-mail alert. Basically, an e-mail alert contains the company logo, a subject head, a one-paragraph summary, and a link to the full release in the organization's online newsroom.

Journalists and bloggers that cover specific industries or companies often sign up for e-mail alerts and RSS feeds because information is then automatically forwarded to them for their review. It saves them the trouble of taking the time to do their own searches and access multiple websites.

> **❝ I find sites that are organized both by release date and by topical information are the easiest to navigate. The quicker I can find the information I need, the quicker I'll be able to turn the story around. It's always helpful to have a point person's contact information available for brief follow-up questions. ❞** ■ A journalist quoted in the TEKgroup survey

Online newsrooms are particularly important when there's a crisis and there's a need to rapidly disseminate information to the media and other important publics, such as employees, investors, and members of the community. The TEKgroup survey indicated that more than 90 percent of the journalists thought it was important to be able to access an online newsroom during a crisis. There's the expectation, however, that the organization will provide up-to-date and relevant information throughout a crisis. Indeed, one complaint of online newsrooms is that the information is not frequently updated. A website that never changes, quips John Gerstner of IntranetInsider.com, is a "cobweb."

There's some debate whether online newsrooms should be password protected, which would require journalists to register before entering the newsroom. In the TEKgroup survey, only 34 percent of journalists said they would be willing to register, and another 47 percent said they might register. Many corporations, including Cisco and IBM, allow anyone to visit their newsrooms and to download materials. Thomson Financial advises "Do not password-protect your site. You do not want to exclude anyone from spreading the words about your company." Other organizations, such as HP, believe that some areas of the pressroom should be password-protected, such as those areas offering access to high-resolution photos and graphics. The argument is that the brand must be protected, so it's necessary to determine who is downloading material and for what purpose.

Electronic Wire Services

Many organizations regularly distribute their news releases and other publicity materials, such as photos, through electronic wire services. This is particularly true for corporate and financial news that requires immediate, timely disclosure to media over a wide geographic area to meet Securities and Exchange Commission (SEC) regulations.

The three major newswires are Business Wire (www.businesswire.com), PR Newswire (www.prnewswire.com), and Marketwire (www.marketwire.com). It's estimated that each one distributes more than 200,000 news releases annually to daily newspapers, broadcast stations, trade publications, and online news services. Other major distributors are PrimeZone Media Network, PRWeb, Black PRWire, Hispanic PRWire, and USAsianWire.

To submit a news release, you send the release online via a form on a service's website. There is no e-mail involved. The wire services make lists of news releases available to editors and reporters. Editors and reporters can access the lists from their computers and click the news releases that interest them. A reporter can edit the news release on the screen, write a headline for it, and then push another key to have it printed in the right typeface and column width. Of course, the editor or reporter can also push the delete key and send the whole release to the electronic trash can.

The advantage of electronic distribution services is the timely and immediate delivery of a large amount of material via a website that can be easily accessed by everyone in the news department. E-mailed news releases, by contrast, must be processed one at a time and are usually sent to specific reporters or editors. Electronic wire services can customize the distribution of material to specific media. They can send your news release to every daily newspaper in Ohio, or you can send it to a select list of financial publications in North America, Europe, and Asia. They can also distribute full-text news releases and color photos to African American and Hispanic publications or a select list of high-tech trade magazines.

Electronic news wires also offer clients the additional opportunity of distributing their news releases to online search engines such as Google, Yahoo!, and MSN, which also enables consumers and the general public to access the full text of news releases and other publicity materials. In recent years, as social media networks have proliferated and become part of the landscape, wire services have kept up by including bloggers and social network sites, such as Facebook and YouTube, in the distribution mix.

Indeed, news releases can be transmitted with an increasing number of bells and whistles. Although the vast majority of news releases distributed by the public relations wire services are still in the "text only" category, multimedia news releases—which can include video and audio—often are used to launch new products, promote major events, and make major organizational announcements. According to Janet Lynn, a vice president at Business Wire: "Included within the release are high-resolution photos, streaming audio, streaming video, and spreadsheets. All a person visiting our website has to do is click on any of these options and be hyperlinked to their choice." See Chapter 5 for a discussion of "smart" news releases.

A good example of the use of electronic wire services is Domino's launch of its Cheesy Garlic Bread Pizza. Its multimedia news release, distributed by PR Newswire, incorporated text, video, several screen shots, and links to del.Icio.us, Digg, Technorati, Reddit, Newsvine, Google, and Yahoo! Another multimedia news release distributed by Marketwire on behalf of Zero Gravity, a company marketing suborbital flights, featured a video clip of well-known scientist Stephen Hawking in zero-gravity flight, which was downloaded 110,000 times on YouTube. For an example of a multimedia news release, see Figure 10.3 or refer back to a Marketwire illustration on page 138.

In other words, the news release isn't just for the press anymore. The public can also access various wire services online to read news releases and other materials that have been distributed to the media. As *PRWeek* reporter Craig McGuire notes, "Business Wire converts the traditional news release into a search engine optimized page of Web content that includes photos, graphics, video, and multimedia, logo branding, keyword links, formatting, and social media tags." PR Newswire has a program titled "Web Widget," that enables online users to integrate news and video into their own homepage, blog, or website. Tips for maximizing distribution of your online news release in terms of keywords and social tags is provided in the following Tips for Success.

> 66 *Our EON delivery platform provides our client's news releases with the long tail which allows the release to be found and highly ranked on search engines, expanding their life cycle.* 99
>
> ■ Laura Sturaitis, vice president of new media development at Business Wire, as quoted in *PRWeek*

✔ tips FOR SUCCESS

Maximizing Distribution of Online News Releases

Online news releases must include several key components to achieve maximum distribution via the traditional media, online media, and social media networks. The following is adapted from a white paper by Vocus, owner of the distribution service PRWeb.

■ **Keywords.** Headlines should be no longer than 80 characters and contain keywords related to the major theme of your news. It's important for search engine optimization (SEO), but it's also the first opportunity to engage your viewer. Additional keywords should be placed in the release to create content that is easily retrievable. In general, a maximum of four to six keywords should be used.

■ **Enhanced URL.** Search engines look at the keywords used in a hyperlink to a website to determine its ranking. If a hyperlink has keywords included and points to your website, then a person searching for these words is more likely to find you among the results.

■ **Anchor text/embedded keywords.** Embedding hyperlinks into your release can also increase your ranking and drive traffic to your website. Make sure, however, that the hyperlink goes to a specific page directly connected to the idea or concept highlighted in the news release.

■ **Multimedia content.** Adding a photograph, a video, or an audio to your release will not only make your news release more consumable and graphically pleasing, but it will also ensure your news is indexed in image search engines and create more visibility for your message.

■ **Social media tags.** Allowing your content to be circulated through Digg, Technorati, del.Icio.us and other social bookmarking sites will not only increase the search engine rankings of your release, but also drive traffic to your website. ■

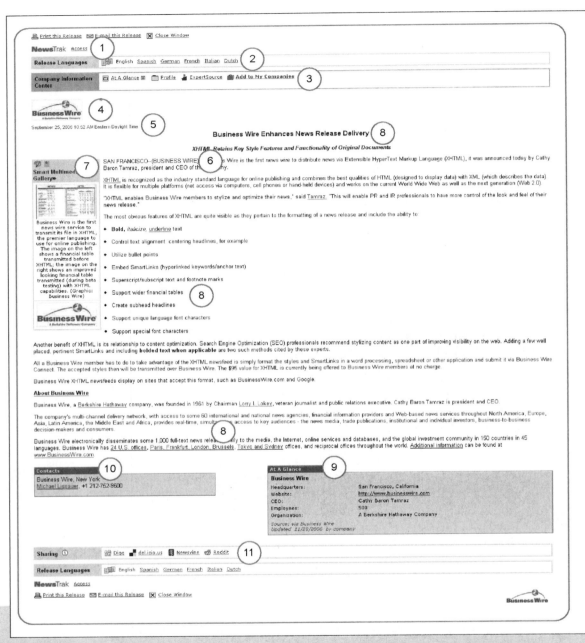

FIGURE 10.3 Several services distribute electronic news releases directly to a publication's servers via phone lines or satellite. This illustration identifies the various elements of a Business Wire "smart" news release that embeds such elements as photos, graphics, video, spreadsheets, and slideshows into the basic news release. In addition, news releases also include social media tags and keywords for maximum search engine optimization (SEO). Journalists and bloggers can access these elements with a simple click of the mouse.

1. Tracking reports provide valuable audience and visibility information for sender

2. Multilingual delivery options for audiences worldwide

3. Quick links to key company information

4. Downloadable logo for brand visibility

5. Time and date stamp

6. Dateline and source wire slug guarantee news from a credible, trusted source

7. Multimedia gallery includes hi-resolution photos and graphics, streaming audio and video, and other web- and print-ready elements

8. XHTML formatting and transmission allows for centered and stylized headlines, bold, italic and underlined text, bulleted lists, embedded hyperlinks and other features that increase attractiveness and optimize for search engines

9. At-A-Glance Information displays key company statistics

10. Contact information including live email link

11. Social media tags allow for easy bookmarking and sharing by internet users including consumers, journalists and bloggers

The *Holmes Report* notes that "by appearing on wires such as Business Wire, press releases are being read by potential investors, by potential customers, and even employees." Michael Lissauer, senior vice president of marketing for Business Wire, sums it up, telling *PRWeek*:

The press release is reaching an additional audience today. Press releases were always aimed at the media, which would interpret those releases, write what they wanted to write based on those releases, that was what consumers ultimately saw. But with the advent of the Internet, the target audience can see press releases in their original form.

Cost ▪ National distribution of a basic news release transmitted to major media in all 50 states is about $600. A regional news release is about $250 to $400, and a statewide release is between $125 and $225. Distribution to media in a single city, such as Cleveland, is about $125.

Business Wire, among others, also has worldwide distribution packages. If you want the whole planet to get your news release, it can be arranged for about $6,000. Individual nations are much cheaper; a news release to media in Australia is about $500. Ethnic media can also be reached. The Black PR Wire is $475 per release, and the national Hispanic PR Wire is about $400 for a basic release.

Multimedia news releases, of course, cost much more. PR Newswire, for example, charges an additional $1,325 for including a photo in a standard news release.

Embedding audio and video, plus additional distribution to social media networks, adds more costs.

In sum, however, distributing news releases via an electronic wire service is extremely cost-effective in terms of reaching multiple media outlets and the vast majority of the U.S. population that is now online. A 2007 study, for example, estimated that 70 percent of adult Internet users in the United States go online on an average day. As a result, electronic distribution has been touted as the wave of the future: It is fast, cost-effective, global in scope, and highly compatible with the extensive use of the computer in processing today's news.

Feature Placement Firms

A number of distribution services specialize in preparing columns and features that are distributed as entire layouts, complete with headlines, photos, and graphics. Such materials are called **mat releases** or **camera-ready art**. Editors simply cut the article out from a glossy sheet of paper (called a **repro proof**) and paste it into the newspaper layout.

Cutting and pasting, however, has become less common. News USA and others, for example, now package camera-ready stories for their clients on CD-ROMs that editors can pop into their PCs. Editors receive a new disk every month. E-mail and direct mail also are used to send material.

Perhaps the most popular and efficient way of delivering camera-ready materials is to post them on the website of a feature placement firm. Editors sign up for a stream of continuing content and then download the articles and high-resolution graphics that interest them. Brian Agnes, vice president of marketing for Family Features Editorial Syndicate, explains:

> Due to the wide variety of publishing platforms for columns and mat releases (as opposed to our formatted full pages), we release our syndicated column material in unformatted fashion as Word docs, JPEGs, and PDFs. We find it encourages greater publishing frequency by allowing editors to reformat the content to suit their space needs—as releases and columns are typically used as filler material rather than occupying a fixed position in every publication.

Camera-ready stories often are used by weekly and daily newspapers to fill news space inside the newspaper. According to the distribution services, the demand for camera-ready stories is booming as a result of rising costs and fewer staff writers. Thousands of newspapers, which receive the stories free, find that using such materials keeps staffing costs to a minimum and fills their inside pages. Such features are often found in the specialty sections of a newspaper, such as the auto, food, real estate, travel, and computing sections.

Feature placement firms distribute features and other information that is relevant over a period of several months. In the business, these stories are often called **evergreens**. They may include camera-ready features are about food, travel, health, education, special events, and consumerism. Here are some headlines of typical feature stories, with the client in parentheses:

- "What to Do About Childhood Cancer" (National Childhood Cancer Foundation)
- "Transform Your Green Space into Livable Space" (Ace Hardware)
- "How to Protect Your House When You Go on Vacation" (Schlage Lock Company)
- "Furry Valentines With Wet Kisses" (Nestle Purina PetCare Company)

Trade groups, national charitable organizations, national membership organizations, state tourism departments, and any number of corporations use camera-ready releases to create awareness and visibility. The most successful ones emphasize consumer tips and keep commercialism to a minimum. In fact, most camera-ready features only mention the organization once or twice in the entire article. For more tips on how to write a mat feature, see the following Tips for Success.

Camera-ready features are relatively short. A one-column feature is about 225 words, and a two-column story is about 350 to 500 words. Family Features specializes in full-page features. Figure 10.4 shows an example of a full-page

☑ tips FOR SUCCESS

The Components of a Successful Food Feature

Mat feature releases must be informative and appealing to consumers. In addition, they must be about somewhat "evergreen" subject matter so that they are relevant over a period of months. The following is adapted from tips provided by Family Features about how to write a food feature, but many of the suggestions are relevant to other "camera-ready" features.

Copy

- Think like an editor.
- Use AP style.
- Use short, snappy headlines.
- Use subheads to augment the headline.
- Provide short, reader-friendly copy.
- Use sidebars to break out copy.
- Use subtle branding (in ingredients, Web addresses, spokesperson's tips or quotes, booklet offers, and contests).

Photos

- Provide more than one photo, if possible.

- Keep lighting consistent and even for all photos.
- Provide good contrast.
- Avoid backlighting.
- Keep product, graphic in sharp focus.

Recipes

- Instructions should be clear, logical, and reader-friendly.
- Use ingredients easily found in most supermarkets.
- List ingredients in order of use.
- Keep measurements consistent. ■

07527: Stars & Stripes Sizzle!
All materials courtesy of: The Beef Checkoff through National Cattlemen's Beef Association / Northwest Cherry Growers / Wilton Industries, Inc.

To order, download at www.FamilyFeatures®.com or contact
Media Communications at support@familyfeatures.com or 1-888-824-3337

▶ **FIGURE 10.4** Distributors of camera-ready features are adept at writing materials that focus on consumer tips instead of a commercial pitch. In general, the name of the sponsoring organization should be buried in the middle of the story or at the end of it. The idea is to create brand awareness and credibility, but to do so in a subtle way. This full-page, camera-ready feature on recipes for grilling was distributed by Family Features for the National Cattlemen's Beef Association and the Northwest Cherry Growers.

feature offered by Family Features that was prepared for the National Cattlemen's Beef Association and Northwest Cherry Growers. To attract editor and reader interest, camera-ready features usually also include a photo or a graphic of some kind. Radio stations receive short spots professionally voiced on CD, and TV stations often receive video features.

Cost ■ Several companies write, produce, and distribute camera-ready features. North American Precis Syndicate (www.napsinfo.com) is one of the oldest and largest in the business; other national firms include Metro Editorial Services (www.metrocreativegraphics.com), NewsUSA (www.newsusa.com), and Family Features (www.familyfeatures.com).

NAPS, for example, distributes its client features to 10,000 daily and weekly newspapers across the country and says that an organization typically will get 100 to 400+ placements. The cost for a two-column feature, which includes writing, formatting, and distribution, is about $5,550; a one-column feature is about $4,000. A camera-ready release to a television station (four slides, plus a script) costs about $6,500 for distribution to 1,000 TV stations. According to NAPS, the client typically receives 100 to 150+ placements. NAPS also prepares and distributes radio releases to about 6,500 stations and claims clients receive about 400 to 500+ placements. The cost of a radio release is about $5,000.

NewsUSA specializes in packages of multiple releases. For example, it will send 26 different camera-ready features over the course of a year to 10,500 newspapers for about $80,000. The same number of radio features will cost a similar amount. Of course, there is always the success story. NewsUSA prepared and distributed 23 camera-ready features for American Century Investments and received a total of 4,304 placements, representing 242 million potential readers. You should note, however, that audience size is based on the total circulation of the newspaper, not how many people actually read the feature.

In addition to regular mailings, distribution services prepare camera-ready stories on a central theme. Metro Publicity Services, for example, has mailings on everything from Mother's Day to Fall Home Improvement. Many of these articles show up in advertising supplements of daily newspapers. For example, the home improvement supplement might use a camera-ready story from a paint manufacturer that offers tips on what kind of paint would be best for a bathroom or kitchen.

Photo Placement Firms

Several firms specialize in the distribution of publicity photos and captions. Newscom (www.newscom.com) is a major source of high-resolution photos and graphics for registered journalists and editors on any number of subjects. In fact, its website houses more than 20 million images, graphics, and text from more than 100 different photo agencies, wire services, and 100 freelance photographers.

An editor, for example, may receive an e-alert or a news release that includes a link to Newscom to retrieve a particular photo or graphic that illustrates the story. Or perhaps an editor may be looking for a particular photo that shows celebrities at a corporation's sponsored event. In most cases, Newscom will have a variety of photos available from the event, and the editor can select one that fits the publication's needs. Publicity photos provided by clients can usually be downloaded at no cost, but there are royalty and licensing fees that must be paid for other photos in its inventory.

A second major photo distribution firm is Feature Photo Service (www .featurephoto.com). It distributes publicity photos, captions, and graphics for clients. The company offers worldwide news release and photo distribution via more than 25 news agencies worldwide. In addition, it distributes photos to 1,200 U.S. news media via Associated Press (AP) and Newscom. According to its website, for about $450 you can distribute a 400-word news release "to more than 100,000 desktops at 2,300 newsrooms . . . as well as to more than 8,000 editors at over 2,300 worldwide publications via Newscom." In addition, Feature Photo Service distributes photos to various search engines, including Google, MSN, and Yahoo! An example of a Feature Photo Service media advisory is shown in Figure 10.5.

Mail

A widely used distribution method, even in the Internet age, is still regular mail. It is often referred to as **snail mail** by dedicated users of the Internet, but newsrooms still receive thousands of news releases, CDs, and media kits via this method every day. For many weeklies in small towns across America with limited computer servers and Internet accessibility, daily mail delivery is just fine. Mail is delivered by the U.S. Postal Service or by private companies such as FedEx, Airborne Express, and DHL Worldwide.

As mentioned earlier in the chapter, surveys have shown that journalists prefer e-mail by a large margin, but e-mail is not without problems. As one journalist notes, "E-mail isn't as good as it was. Haven't you heard? SPAM is driving us crazy just like you." Another journalist says, "After 9/11, all I wanted was e-mail. Now, I want only fax. I get hundreds of e-mails weekly and I seldom read any but those from people I know."

FPS feature photo service | FPS newswire

Home   FPSnewswire   Feature Photo Service   Corporate   RSS

Read Across America

Attention Photo Editors:

Phoenix, Ariz./February 4, 2008/FPSnewswire/-- Maxine O. Bush Elementary School Kindergarteners, Jair Perez, left and Nayeli Carrasco read Seuss classic "Green Eggs and Ham" as part of NEA's Read Across America celebrations in Phoenix, Ariz. More than 45 million people are expected to participate in this year's Read Across America celebrations. (Feature Photo Service)

Contact:
Staci Maiers
(202) 822-7150
smaiers@nea.org

Photo Available Associated Press & NewsCom

Source: NEA
Web Site: http://www.nea.org
Image Available: http://www.newscom.com/cgi-bin/pub/s?f=FPS%2ffpspub

Providers of press releases are responsible for content and accuracy not FPSnewswire, Feature Photo Service, Inc., or related entities.

Feature Photo Service - FPSnewswire © 2004-2007   Disclaimer | Contact Us

FIGURE 10.5 Placement firms such as Feature Photo Service (FPS) distribute a variety of publicity photos on behalf of clients. This media advisory, sent to newspaper photo editors, gives a thumbnail of the photo and the caption. Interested editors can then download the photo from a website.

Many organizations and public relations firms continue to mail hard copies of news releases and media kits even when they have companion electronic versions. Daniel Cantelmo, writing in *Public Relations Quarterly*, says there are some good reasons for this. He quotes, for example, one senior editor for a high-technology magazine who said, "In 5 or 10 minutes I can go through 25 printed press kits . . . and pick out exactly what I need. If I had to go through 25 CDs or online press kits, it would take hours. I don't have the time."

In sum, the U.S. Postal Service continues to be a cost-effective method for distributing news releases, media kits, fact sheets, position papers, and other background materials. As indicated in Chapter 9, many PSAs are produced on CDs and then mailed to radio and television stations. All materials, however, must be sent first class mail or by overnight express. It is never acceptable to send materials by second- or third-class mail.

Many organizations also use services such as FedEx on a routine basis to mail everything from letters to packages. Overnight delivery is usually guaranteed, and these services are quite adequate for sending materials on a regional, national, or even international level. Another advantage is that they offer sophisticated tracking so you know exactly when a package has been delivered.

Some publicists think that delivery by overnight service increases an editor's perception of the material's importance and newsworthiness, but the widespread use of these services has pretty much eliminated any feeling that the material is special or urgent. In fact, most editors say they treat such envelopes just like any other mail that is delivered to their desks from the mail room.

Mailing can be done by the organization. All you need is a good address list, properly prepared labels, and a postage meter. If you mail in the morning, chances are good that media in the area will receive the material the next working day. Letters sent nationally are received in 2 or 3 days. However, if you are mailing materials to international media, you will be better off using another distribution channel, such as fax, electronic wire services, or e-mail.

Another approach to mailing is to use a distribution firm, also called a **mailing house**. A number of firms serve the public relations industry, including Media Distribution Services (MDS) and Cision, which were discussed earlier. MDS (www .mdsconnect.com) has centers in 10 U.S. cities and offers full-service printing, production, and mailing of everything from news releases to media kits, newsletters, and brochures.

Fax

Many news releases are still sent by facsimile transmission, despite the perception that a fax is an artifact of the past. A **fax** is as quick as a telephone call and has the advantage of providing information in written and graphic form. The other advantage is that a fax often receives more attention and readership than an e-mail that can be easily deleted without ever opening it.

Ideally, the fax is used only if there is a late-breaking news development or you are sending a media advisory about an upcoming event or alerting editors of an upcoming satellite feed. The reality is that modern technology has made it possible to send faxes to every media outlet in the country within minutes. One fax distribution service, for example, claims that it can transmit information over as many as 1,000 phone lines simultaneously. This is called **broadcast fax**, or **bulk fax**. Political candidates, for example, use bulk fax extensively to let media editors know their latest statements on the economy, health care, and a host of other public issues. They also used bulk fax to provide media alerts about upcoming speeches, rallies, and public appearances.

Sending bulk faxes, however, is not popular with editors. In fact, many newspapers actively discourage faxes of routine news releases and even change their fax numbers on a regular basis to avoid reams of "junk" faxes—which are like "junk" mail. Another approach tried by more than one daily is to have 900 numbers so that the publicists are charged for sending unsolicited faxes.

But the problem still remains. George Condon, Washington bureau chief for Copley News Service, told *Jack O'Dwyer's PR Services Report* that "Junk faxes are one of our biggest problems. There is nothing more annoying to me than having those faxes clog up our machines."

The opposite of sending bulk faxes is **fax on demand** (FOD). In this situation, a reporter can call an 800 number and, through a series of custom-designed prompts, ask for various organizational materials to be sent by fax. This service helps reporters on deadline if they can't reach an organizational spokesperson.

In sum, fax material only if the medium specifically requests it or gives permission in advance. Check with your regular media contacts to ascertain whether they want material sent by this method and under what circumstances.

Summary

- Media directories, whether print, CD-ROM, or online, are essential tools for compiling media lists and distributing information.

- Media lists and e-mail addresses must be updated and revised on a regular basis; journalists frequently change jobs.

- Publicists use editorial calendars to find out what special editions or sections various publications are planning for the year.

- Tip sheets let publicists know what kind of material a publication or broadcast station is seeking for a particular purpose.

- Mailing labels must be accurate; they should be addressed to a specific editor by name and include such details as the floor or suite in an office building.

- The vast majority of news releases and other press materials are now distributed via e-mail and through electronic news wires.

- E-mail is now a popular way of communicating with reporters and editors about possible story ideas. It works best, however, when the publicist and the reporter have already established a working relationship.

- Online newsrooms, which are part of an organization's website, have become the primary source for journalists seeking late-breaking news and other information about an organization.

- Electronic newswires now distribute multimedia news releases that include photos, graphics, and video clips embedded into the basic news release.

- Electronic newswires, such as Business Wire, distribute news releases to Internet search engines and social networking sites, which allows the public to access the information in addition to the traditional media.

- Keywords are important for search engine optimization (SEO). Publicists must use keywords that consumers will likely use to search for information.

- Camera-ready features are widely used by newspapers and other media outlets because they reduce staff costs and fill space. Feature service firms distribute camera-ready articles on paper, CDs, or online.

- Mail, often called snail mail, is still widely used to distribute publicity materials. Organizations often mail news releases and media kits in addi-

tion to providing the same materials online or on a CD format.

- The fax machine is a good way to send media advisories and late-breaking news releases. However, it is not wise to mass distribute routine news releases by fax.

Skill Building Activities

1. A manufacturer of sunscreen has developed a feature article about the need for protection to avoid the dangers of skin cancer. The target audience is women ages 18 to 35. Using media databases and directories available in the library or online, compile a list of magazines that reach this particular audience.

2. News releases sent by e-mail should have a concise subject line using keywords. What subject line would you use for the sunscreen news release?

3. Check out the online newsrooms of two or three corporations or organizations. What are the contents? Is the site user-friendly? Why or why not?

4. Log on to Business Wire, PR Newswire, or MarketWire. Explore these websites and access

some of the news releases filed by various organizations. Write a brief analysis of what you found.

5. Camera-ready or mat news features usually contain about 400 to 500 words. Select a product or service and write a release that would appeal to consumers. What photos, line art, or graphics would you use to illustrate the article? See the Tips for Success on page 265 for some guidelines.

6. Review the contents of several weekly or daily publications in your area. Try to identify articles/features that probably were distributed by a feature placement firm. Write a critique of the article(s) in terms of appeal, information, relevance, and readability.

Suggested Readings

Garcia, Tonya. "Hot Off the Wire: A Number of Issues Are on the Radar for Newswires." *PRWeek*, September 17, 2007, p. 21.

Lacono, Erica. "The News Business: Newswires Have Evolved from Conduits to Partners." *PRWeek*, September 12, 2005, pp. 20–21.

LaMotta, Lisa. "Straight from the Horse's Mouth: Online Pressrooms Can Ensure that Journalists Get the News from the Right Source." *PRWeek*, April 17, 2006, p. 14.

Lewis, Tanya. "Newswires Search for the Right Words: SEO Tools Help." *PRWeek*, November 20, 2006, p. 18.

McQuire, Craig. "Newswires Strive to Bolster Releases: Tags That Can Be Picked Up by Social Networks are Now a Must." *PRWeek*, July 23, 2007, p. 18.

Momorella, Steve, and Woodall, Ibrey. "Tips for an Effective Online Newsroom." *PR Tactics*, November 2005, pp. 22–23.

Wylie, Ann. "What Do World-Class Web Sites Do That Yours Doesn't Do." *PR Tactics*, May 2006, p. 13.

Wylie, Ann. "Write Web Headlines That Reach Readers Online." *PR Tactics*, February 2006, p. 27.

Getting Along with Journalists

TOPICS covered in this chapter include:

The Importance of Media Relations   272

The Media's Dependence on Public Relations   273

Public Relations' Dependence on the Media   274

Areas of Friction   275

Working with Journalists   282

A Media Relations Checklist   297

Crisis Communication   300

The Importance of Media Relations

Media relations is the core activity in many public relations jobs. In fact, one survey of 539 large companies by the Public Affairs Group (PAG) found that media relations was the number one job responsibility of their public relations staffs. A survey by *PRWeek* found that media relations was the number one activity performed by corporate public relations departments. Similar surveys have indicated that media relations is the primary activity of public relations firms. In other words, public relations personnel are the primary contact between the organization and the media. Consequently, it is important to discuss the concepts of effective media relations and how to establish a good working relationship with journalists.

> **Media relations is the crux of all PR. It is about getting your clients in—and keeping your clients out of—the press.**
>
> ■ Ray Kerin, executive director of media relations for Merck, as quoted in *PRWeek*

Public relations professionals and journalists have long had a love–hate relationship. There are flashpoints of friction and distrust, but there is also the realization that they are mutually dependent on each other. A national survey of journalists by a New York public relations firm is indicative. Two-thirds of journalists don't trust public relations people, but 81 percent say they need them anyway.

This chapter explores the symbiotic relationship between publicists and journalists from several perspectives. First we explore how publicists and journalists depend on each other. Then we examine some friction areas, such as excessive hype, advertising influences, sloppy reporting, and tabloid journalism. The chapter concludes with guidelines for giving effective media interviews, organizing news conferences, conducting media tours, and handling crisis situations. By keeping these guidelines in mind, you will be able to build trusting and productive relationships with journalists.

▪ The Media's Dependence on Public Relations

The reality of mass communications today is that reporters and editors spend most of their time processing information, not gathering it. And, although many reporters deny it, most of the information that appears in the mass media comes from public relations sources, which provide a constant stream of news releases, features, planned events, and tips to the media. Even Gary Putka, the Boston bureau chief of *The Wall Street Journal*, admits that "a good 50 percent" of the stories in the news-paper come from news releases.

A number of surveys and analyses of media content over the years have documented the media's reliance on public relations. One such study goes back to 1973, when L. V. Sigal wrote *Reporters and Officials: The Organization and Politics of Newsmaking*. He studied 1,200 *New York Times* and *Washington Post* front pages and found that 58.2 percent of the stories came through routine bureaucratic channels, official proceedings, news releases and conferences, and other planned events. Just 25.2 percent were the products of investigative journalism, and most of these were produced by interviews, the result of routine access to spokespersons. Sigal explained, "The reporter cannot depend on legwork alone to satisfy his paper's insatiable demand for news. He looks to official channels to provide him with newsworthy material day after day."

More recent studies have confirmed Sigal's work. Jericho Promotions (New York) sent questionnaires to 5,500 journalists worldwide and got 2,432 to respond. Almost 40 percent of respondents said they got at least half of their story ideas from public relations people. The percentage was even higher among editors of lifestyle, entertainment, and health sections of newspapers.

PRWeek conducted a national survey of journalists and found that almost 60 percent used news releases "all the time" or "often." Thirty percent acknowledged that they relied more on public relations sources than they did

> ❝ In a lot of ways, PR people do the legwork of journalists—feeding them stories and sources, and doing research. ❞
>
> ▪ Sheldon Rampton, research director of PRWatch, as quoted in *The New York Times*

5 years earlier. A 2007 survey by Arketi Group explored what sources journalists used to write their stories. Industry sources and news releases were cited by 90 percent of the journalists, and 89 percent cited public relations contacts. Organizational websites, often maintained by public relations departments, was cited by 74 percent of the respondents.

Perhaps another indication of the media's reliance on public relations sources is the extensive use of "spokespeople" as primary sources in news stories. Journalists often use "spokesman" or "spokeswoman" as a code word for public relations personnel who provide information. Bob Williams, an ethics fellow at the Poynter Institute for Journalism, conducted a computer search of articles in the top 50 U.S.

newspapers for references to "spokesperson" or similar terms. He found that the term appeared 501,101 times in 2000, up 81 percent from the 292,308 times in 1995.

All this amounts to what O. H. Gandy calls "information subsidies" to the press. In his book, *Beyond Agenda Setting: Information Subsidies and Public Policy*, he explains that material such as news releases constitutes a "subsidy," because the source "causes it to be made available at something less than the cost a user would face in the absence of a subsidy."

In other words, public relations materials save media the time, money, and effort of gathering their own news. Indeed, no medium—including *The New York Times*—has enough reporters to cover all the available news. As one editor of the *San Jose* (CA) *Mercury News* once said, publicists are the newspaper's "unpaid reporters."

Despite such statements, most journalists are loath to admit any reliance on public relations sources because they think it reflects negatively on their abilities as reporters. Denise E. DeLorme and Fred Fedler comment on this in a *Public Relations Review* article that offers a historical analysis of journalist hostility to public relations. They write:

> In one contradiction, journalists wanted information to be easily available, yet resented the men and women who made it available. By the mid-twentieth century, journalists were dependent upon PR practitioners for a large percentage of the stories appearing in newspapers. But admitting their dependence would shatter cherished ideals. Journalists were proud of their ability to uncover stories, verify details, and expose sham. Thus, they were unlikely to admit their dependence, lack of skepticism, failure to verify, and failure to expose every sham.

■ Public Relations' Dependence on the Media

The purpose of public relations, as mentioned throughout this book, is to inform, to shape opinions and attitudes, and to motivate. This can be accomplished only if people receive messages constantly and consistently.

The traditional media, in all their variety, are still cost-effective channels of communication, even in the Internet age. They are the multipliers that enable millions of people to receive a message at the same time. Thousands of newspapers and magazines, plus hundreds of radio, television, and cable outlets, enable the public relations communicator to reach very specific target audiences with tailored messages designed just for them. For example, Cision's *Internet Media Directory* contains nearly 6,000 online news outlets, all but 400 of which are tied to traditional print or broadcast outlets. Demographic segmentation and psychographics are now a way of life in advertising, marketing, and public relations.

The media's power and influence in a democratic society reside in their independence from government control. Reporters and editors make independent judgments about what is newsworthy and what will be disseminated. They serve as filters of information, and even though not everyone is happy with what they decide, the fact remains that media gatekeepers are generally perceived as more objective than public relations people, who represent a particular client or organization.

This is important to you, because the media, by inference, serve as third-party endorsers of your information. Media gatekeepers give your information credibility and importance by deciding that it is newsworthy. The information is no longer from your organization, but from *The New York Times*, *The Wall Street Journal*, or CNN.

The Internet, of course, has considerably changed the media landscape in the past decade. Today, public relations professionals are less dependent on the traditional mass media to reach large audiences, because, for the first time in history, an organization, or even an individual, can literally reach billions of people, bypassing traditional mass media gatekeepers. Some have called this the "democratization of information," in which anyone now has the ability to communicate with large numbers of people on a global scale. One manifestation of this is the more than 100 million blogs in existence as of 2008. See the Tips for Success on page 276 for tips on how to work with bloggers. Chapter 12 further discusses blogs and other social networking media.

Areas of Friction

The relationship between public relations and the media is based on mutual cooperation, trust, and respect. Unfortunately, certain actions compromise the relationship. On the public relations side, these actions often involve the use of excessive hype, not doing the necessary homework, and making a nuisance of themselves. Perhaps Peter Himler, executive vice president of Burson-Marsteller in New York City, said it best: "Overt commercialism, hyperbole, artificiality and manipulation are the best ways to turn off a reporter and, in so doing, damage the fragile, but vital relationship between our two professions."

On the journalistic side, these actions include name calling, sloppy/biased reporting, and tabloid sensationalism. Both groups face the issue of improper advertising influence, which tends to undermine the credibility of the news coverage.

Hype and News Release Spam

As noted in Chapter 5, journalists receive hundreds of news releases every month. Far too many of them contain hype words such as "unique," "revolutionary," "state-of-the-art," and "sophisticated." Journalists, dulled by the constant flow of news releases that sound like commercials, generally conclude that the majority of publicists are incompetent. In fact, the *PRWeek* survey mentioned previously found that slightly more than 50 percent of the responding journalists thought "poorly written materials" was a major problem with public relations.

Although this complaint was near the top of the list, almost 60 percent of the journalists thought the biggest problem was public relations people who were "unfamiliar with our editorial requirements and format." Other major complaints, in descending order, were (1) too many unsolicited e-mails, faxes, and phone calls; (2) don't know the product or service; (3) repeated calls and follow-up; (4) spokespersons not available; and (5) don't meet publication deadlines.

Working with Bloggers

The blogosphere has had a significant impact on traditional media relations. The influence of the blogosphere now means that public relations professionals now include bloggers—or citizen journalists—in their media relations outreach efforts.

According to Aaron Heinrich and Adam Brown of Ketchum, writing in PRSA's *The Strategist*, "Creating an outcome favorable to our companies or clients will mean creating a relationship with a blogger or podcaster in the same way we have relationships with members of traditional media."

Indeed, key bloggers are finding themselves being courted with the same intensity as regular journalists. The American Petroleum Institute (API), for example, organized teleconference briefing sessions for bloggers on gasoline prices and other oil industry issues. CBS included "mommy bloggers" when it wanted to publicize its new show, *The New Adventures of Old Christine*. Key bloggers were invited to spend the day on the set, and *The Wall Street Journal* reported, "The bloggers got free swag, watched a rehearsal, and made videos with actors that they could post on their sites."

A number of organizations now invite bloggers to news conferences and special events. An example is IMG, the organizer of New York Fashion Week. It now issues 10 percent of its press credentials to fashion bloggers.

Building relationships with bloggers, however, takes time, because they are more independent and wary of using public relations materials. Here are some tips for working with bloggers:

- Do your homework. Use research tools, such as Technorati and Google Blog Search, to identify major blogs in your subject or industry area that have a following.

- Read posts and comments on the blog to gauge readership and the blogger's personality.

- Begin posting comments on the blog about topics being discussed. As *The Wall Street Journal* notes, "Some bloggers may need to see that you are a regular reader in order to take your pitch seriously."

- Tailor your approach in subject matter and tone. Some blogs are extremely casual, whereas others are more formal in tone.

- Don't blanket bloggers with untargeted, irrelevant pitches and releases. They will consider it spam and many will criticize you online.

- Regularly monitor blogs for mentions of your client or organization. A number of sites, such as Google Reader and Bloglines, can do this. A mention is an opportunity for you to post a comment.

It's wise to keep in mind that blogs often have a major influence on coverage by the mainstream press. In a study conducted by Brodeur and Marketwire, 62 percent of the journalists surveyed said blogs had a significant impact on the "tone of discussion" in news reporting. The same study found that almost 30 percent of the journalists had their own blogs, either a personal one or as part of their job. Another study by the Arketi Group found that almost 60 percent of journalists say they sometimes get story ideas from blogs. ■

Indeed, a major sore spot for many editors and journalists is the large number of news releases they receive that reflect a total ignorance of a publication's format and content. Many reporters label such news releases as nothing but spam, and some get so irritated that they "blacklist" the senders to block any further messages from them. Chris Anderson, executive editor of *Wired*, went even further. He posted on his blog the sources and addresses of 329 unsolicited e-mails, many from leading public relations firms, and told the senders that he had permanently blocked them.

Many journalists applauded his action, and some public relations professionals also agreed. Peter Shankman, author of *Can We Do That?! Outrageous Stunts That Work*, posted a reply that rather than spraying buckshot, public relations people should research beats and specify a single reporter. "Don't want to do that?" he asked, "Get the hell out of my industry."

Other practitioners were more sanguine about the whole *Wired* flap, which resulted in a 15-inch *New York Times* story. Sheldon Rampton, director of research for PRWatch (an organization that reports on dubious PR practices), told the newspaper that editor complaints about the volume of unsolicited e-mail news releases was more of an etiquette transgression and nuisance than a big ethical concern.

Journalists also resent the gimmicks that often accompany news releases and media kits. T-shirts, coasters, caps, paperweights, pens, and mugs have historically been the most popular items, but *PRWeek* columnist Benedict Carver says these items are dull and overdone: "Everyone has 50 mugs and T-shirts."

Consequently, public relations people and their marketing counterparts try to come up with more creative gimmicks that, in theory, will make their media kit stand out from all the others that arrive daily in the newsroom. Mindbridge Software, for example, wanted to raise the profile of the company's efficiency-improving products, so it sent custom-printed rolls of toilet paper to reporters. The catchphrase printed on the toilet paper, next to the company logo, was "Helps you with the bottom line."

Other creative, and sometimes bizarre, methods of catching an editor's eye have included the following:

- A new light bulb along with a lamp to test its use
- A miniature Harry Potter broomstick wrapped in a scroll announcing a press luncheon and movie screening
- Two volleyballs emblazoned with details of a press event to announce the creation of a new professional women's volleyball league
- Four popcorn balls to announce the opening of a new roller coaster

Journalists often refer to such items as "trash and trinkets." Most items are innocuous, but some are downright tasteless or show poor judgment. A movie studio, for example, once sent editors a box of sirloin steaks to announce its cannibal-themed movie, *Ravenous*. And publicists for the book publisher Harlequin decided to announce a new book, *Fish Bowl*, by sending journalists fish bowls containing *Betta splendens*, also known as "Siamese fighting fish." The gimmick made the press all right; PETA, the animal rights organization, fired off a public letter demanding that the book publisher and its public relations firm desist from using live animals in promotions.

Although many publicists think sending such gimmicks helps separate their media kits and releases from the pack, most journalists say they are a waste of time. In a national survey by Bennett & Company, an Orlando public relations firm, only 16 percent of the responding journalists ranked gimmicks as a good way of gaining attention.

June Kronholz, education reporter at *The Wall Street Journal*, told *PRWeek*, "Trinkets won't sell a story." As for the idea that promotional items will influence journalists to use a story, Kronholz says, "No one's going to buy anyone with a coffee mug. What PR people know and what they're counting on is that we'll open the boxes first. But they think that if we open the package first, we'll give it more consideration, and that's not true." Matt Lake, a senior editor at CNET, an online publication, was even more blunt, telling *The Wall Street Journal*, "These things are really stupid."

However, if you do decide to include a promotional item with your news release or media kit, *PRWeek* recommends the following guidelines.

- Make sure there is a "news hook" and a clear connection between the promotional item and the news you are announcing.
- Try to send items that reporters can use. Otherwise, they may be viewed only as an annoyance that takes up space.
- Consider creative packaging instead of a promotional item. A brightly colored envelope is likely to be opened before a white one.
- Think simply. Rather than sending a basketful of items, consider sending one item that represents the message you are trying to convey.

As a general rule, the value of such gimmicks and giveaways should not exceed $15 to $20. This helps avoid conflicts with a media outlet's ethics guidelines, which often limit the value of items that can be accepted. Some newspapers even have a policy that forbids staff to accept any promotional item. See the section on Gift Giving later in the chapter.

Name Calling

The excesses of hype and promotion have caused many journalists to openly disdain public relations as nothing but covert advertising, deception, and manipulation. Or, as one columnist wrote, public relations people make their living by "sticking Happy Faces over unpleasant realities." Frank Rich, a columnist for *The New York Times*, has used a number of adjectives over the years to describe public relations, including "propaganda," "sloganeering," and "lacking in principles and substance."

As a consequence, many old-time journalists tend to call public relations people "flacks," a derogatory term for press agents. It is somewhat like calling all lawyers "ambulance chasers" or all reporters "hacks." "I grew up in this business 30 years ago learning that flacks were your enemies, with an asterisk," says Roy Peter Clark, vice president of the Poynter Institute for Media Studies. He told *New York Times* reporter Andrew Newman, "The asterisk was unless you really needed them, when you were on a tough deadline, and couldn't get around them or through them."

Some reporters still use the term "flack," or "flak," but most mainstream publications and broadcast outlets now refrain from using the "F" word in print. *The Wall Street Journal*, as a matter of policy, simply uses the official title of the public relations person in a story. Unfortunately, many reporters and bloggers haven't gotten the word. Instead of the word "flack," however, they often use the term "spin doctor" to describe anyone working in public relations. Such name calling by reporters impedes mutual respect and cooperation.

Sloppy/Biased Reporting

The quality of reporting does not seem to inspire much confidence among public relations people and organizational executives. One survey, for example, found that 82 percent of executives think news coverage today reflects the reporter's personal opinions and biases. Another survey of *Fortune* 500 communications executives found that 43 percent of them would give reporters a "B" grade on covering their companies, and another 38 percent would give reporters a "C" grade.

The biggest complaint of the *Fortune* 500 communication executives is that journalists are perceived as having no background in the subject they cover or are considered to be biased. These findings echo a survey some years ago by the American Management Association. It found that the majority of the public relations directors who participated thought that sloppiness on the part of reporters was the major reason for inaccurate stories. Reporters were also faulted for not doing their homework before writing a story, having a tendency to sensationalize, and making simplistic generalizations. See the Tips for Success on page 280 about how to correct errors in the media.

However, business executives often don't have a clear idea of how the media operate and what they need to write a fair, objective story. Many times, for example, executives give vague answers and stonewall reporters—and then complain that the story is not totally accurate. Executives also don't seem to realize that news stories go through various levels—writing, editing, headline writing, and placement—that are done by several people. This, of course, increases the chance of distortion.

You can reduce the chances for sloppy reporting by doing four things:

- Educate executives about how the media operate and how reporters strive for objectivity. That means other viewpoints, sometimes unfavorable, will be in a story.
- Train executives to give 30-second answers to questions. This reduces the possibility of answers being garbled and distorted.
- Provide extensive briefing and background material to reporters who are not familiar with the topic or the organization.
- Familiarize executives with basic news values. Even *The Wall Street Journal*, says senior editor Dennis Kneale, looks for stories with "conflict, drama, and obstacles. . . . Our readers love to read about people, and about how egos and ambitions are shaping companies."

Tabloid Journalism

Newspapers and broadcast shows are not all alike, and the level of commitment to journalistic standards ranges from wholehearted to nonexistent. For example, *The Wall Street Journal* is highly praised for its high standards and fair reporting,

☑ tips FOR SUCCESS

Correcting Errors in News Stories

News coverage isn't always objective, factual, or accurate. Mistakes happen, and it is likely that you or your employer will have complaints on occasion about inaccurate and unfair news coverage. The following are some approaches you can take:

- **Ascertain the facts.** Analyze the offending article or broadcast news segment. What exactly is inaccurate, incomplete, or unfair about it? If it's simply a matter of not liking the tone of the story, there probably isn't much you can do about it. Oftentimes, organizational executives think any article that doesn't praise the organization is unfair and biased. At other times, the damaging effect of the inaccuracy or distorted headline is somewhat minor. As public relations counselor Fraser Seitel says, "Don't sweat the small stuff."

- **Talk to the reporter.** If the error is significant, contact the reporter to discuss the incorrect facts or references. You should politely provide the correct facts with documentation. Avoid confrontation; the reporter no doubt will be writing future stories about your organization, so it's wise to maintain a good relationship. In many cases, the reporter will voluntarily correct the information in subsequent articles or broadcast. Many newspapers also print corrections under the rubric of a clarification.

- **Talk to the editor.** If you don't get satisfaction from the reporter and the complaint is a major one, you may wish to contact the editor and make a formal request for a correction. If the answer is no, be prepared to negotiate a remedy such as letter to the editor or even an op-ed piece where you can pre-sent the accurate facts. If you believe that the reporter consistently writes unfavorable stories about your organization or client, it's a good idea to request a meeting with the reporter and the editor.

- **Go public.** An old adage holds that you should never pick a fight with anyone who buys ink by the barrel; nevertheless, many companies take the offensive and make every effort to inform key publics about their side of the story. Letters can be sent to community opinion leaders, employees, or even stockholders, depending on the story. Another approach is to purchase advertising to rebut the allegations.

- **File a lawsuit.** The last resort is to file a lawsuit if legal counsel believes that the newspaper or broadcast outlet has intentionally distorted the truth. A threatened libel suit often encourages the media outlet to print a correction or an apology. A lawsuit also gets media coverage, which gives the organization a platform to inform the public about inaccuracies in the original story. ■

whereas the *National Enquirer*, the *Star*, the *Globe*, and the *Sun* are famous for sensational headlines, manipulated photos, and often less than accurate stories about the private lives of celebrities.

The same situation exists in television. Shows such as *Hard Copy, Inside Edition*, and *A Current Affair* are known as "tabloid television" and "trash TV" because they concentrate on the sensational and have used the facade of traditional journalism on what is pure entertainment. This has been called "journaltainment."

Organizations are even becoming more wary of traditional shows such as *60 Minutes*, *20/20*, and *Dateline NBC*. In the race for ratings, these shows have started to offer more sensationalism and to manipulate events for greater effect. As mentioned earlier, NBC was sued by General Motors and had to make an on-air apology for rigging a sequence that showed gas tanks on GM trucks exploding. The people responsible were all fired.

Such lapses of journalistic standards are a major concern for the media because the antics of an isolated few affect the credibility of all journalists. Your challenge is to make sure you don't paint all media with the same brush. You should continue to give service to responsible journalists and provide information. However, if a reporter has a reputation for sensationalism and doing hatchet jobs, you are probably better off politely declining to participate in an interview.

Advertising Influence

It is a fact of economic life that most media are dependent on advertising revenues for survival. Increased competition, coupled with a recession in the magazine industry, has made competition for ad dollars stiffer than ever. "As a result," writes *Wall Street Journal* reporter Fen Montaigne, "some publications are feeling more pressure to please advertisers, either by running positive spreads on them, plugging them into captions, or including them in roundups of the best new products to buy."

Although mainstream news periodicals and daily newspapers generally keep a high wall between the news and advertising department, this is not always the case in the trade press and among specialized magazines. Beauty, fashion, auto, and home decorating magazines, for example, are well known for running fashion layouts and other features that prominently promote their advertisers. *Architectural Digest*, for example, actually has a policy of mentioning only advertisers in the magazine's captions for photo layouts. Linda Wells, editor of *Allure*, told *The Wall Street Journal*, "We write about people who advertise in the magazine. That's what magazines do."

All of this, of course, raises troubling questions about journalistic ethics and integrity. The editors and reporters on specialty publications loudly proclaim that advertising and consulting assignments don't affect their editorial judgment, but their protestations seem a bit hollow and hypocritical.

The situation also affects public relations personnel. If the public increasingly takes a skeptical view of what they read and hear, the value of the media as an objective, independent source of information is compromised. Thus, messages from organizations won't have the same impact and believability that the media now bestow on such messages.

Advertising influence also presents practical problems for the public relations practitioner. How do you sort out the publications that are "for sale" and those that maintain high ethical standards? Should you build an advertising budget into your plans to pave the way for product reviews in some specialty publications?

If a publication insists that you buy an ad to get news coverage, should you go along with it? The PRSA Code of Ethics (Chapter 3) states that you should not engage in any activities that would "compromise the integrity of communication channels. Is buying a full-page ad in a publication or paying an editor a consulting fee a violation of professional ethics? Or is it just good business?

Working with Journalists

There will always be areas of friction and disagreement between public relations people and journalists, but that doesn't mean there can't be a solid working relationship based on mutual respect for each other's work. Indeed, one definition of public relations is that it is the building of relationships between the organization and its various publics, including journalists.

Press interviews, news conferences, media tours, and other kinds of gatherings provide excellent opportunities to build these working relationships. They are more personal than just sending written materials and helping reporters get direct answers from news sources.

Company executives who are prone to stage fright may view such contact with the media as a nightmare. They fear that they will say something stupid, be misquoted, or be "ambushed" by an aggressive reporter who will slant the interview to imply that the organization is guilty of some wrongdoing.

Nevertheless, regular one-on-one contact with journalists helps the organization accomplish the objectives of increasing visibility, consumer awareness, and sales of services or products. They key is preparation. As book author Dick Martin points out, "In dealing with the press, as in any other business dealing, preparation is compulsory." The following discussion will provide tips and techniques to make sure that you and your organization's executives are prepared to meet the press.

Media Interviews

An old public relations joke goes, "You know you're going to have a bad day when your secretary tells you *60 Minutes* or *A Current Affair* is in the lobby." A local newspaper or television reporter can cause the same sort of discomfort, particularly if he or she shows up unannounced. However, most press interviews are set up in advance. You can pitch a possible interview, or one can be requested by a reporter who is looking for credible experts to fill out a story.

There are many tip lists on how to conduct media interviews, but some points are worth noting here. First, if a reporter calls to request an interview, you should interview the reporter first. Some common questions are:

- Who are you?
- What is the story about?
- Why did you call me?
- What are you looking for from me?
- Who else are you speaking with?
- Are you going to use my comments in your story?
- When is the story going to run?

By asking such questions, you can decide if you are qualified to answer the reporter's questions or whether someone else in the organization would be a better source. You may also decide that the context of the story is not appropriate for your organization and decline to be interviewed. For example, the reporter may ask you to comment on some topic that has nothing to do with your organization.

One danger in a telephone interview is that you may be caught off guard and will not have time to formulate your thoughts. Before you know it, you and the reporter are chatting away like old friends about a number of topics. This is fine, but do remember that your name and a quote will probably appear in the article or as a soundbite on a newscast. It may be used accurately, or it may be completely out of context.

A better approach for a major interview, whether initiated by you or the reporter, is to schedule it in advance. If you know the purpose of the story, you can better prepare yourself or other spokespersons for the session.

Here are some tips, compiled from a number of sources, on how to handle interviews with print or broadcast personnel:

- Determine, in advance, what key point or message you want to convey on behalf of the organization or client.

- Answer questions, but link them to your key message whenever possible.

- Anticipate questions and plan answers. Be totally familiar with facts, figures, details that will help you sound credible.

- Prepare for the worst. Think of every question that might possibly be asked, reasonable or unreasonable. Then prepare answers for each.

- Use examples and anecdotes. Don't tell half-truths. Don't exaggerate. Don't brag about your organization or its products or services.

- Be quotable. Say it briefly, clearly, and directly in 30 seconds or less.

- Speak conversationally and use personal anecdotes when appropriate.

- Don't let reporters put words in your mouth. Rephrase their words, avoiding negative ones.

- Don't lie. If you know information that's not appropriate to give out at that moment, say so.

- Never say "no comment." It conveys the impression that you are hiding information or are guilty of something. Try to give the reporter a reason you can't comment, and offer alternative information if appropriate. See the accompanying Tips For Success for more on how to say "no comment."

- There is no such thing as "off the record." Assume anything you say will appear in print or broadcast.

✓ tips FOR SUCCESS

Alternatives to Saying "No Comment"

Most media guidelines emphasize that public relations personnel should always be helpful to and cooperative with the media. However, there are times when the best course of action is to not answer a reporter's question. Instead of saying "no comment," however, you should explain why you can't respond to the question.

Betsy Goldberg of Waggener Edstrom Worldwide offers some tips in an article written for *PR Tactics*. She says that no practitioner should feel compelled to answer a question, particularly if (1) it's not your area of expertise, (2) your organization is not prepared to reveal details at the present time, (3) the issue is before the courts, and (4) government and financial regulations prohibit you from talking about the subject.

Ron Levy, former president of North American Precis Syndicate, adds two more reasons: (1) the question deals with proprietary information that would benefit competitors and (2) the question violates the privacy of employees.

In general, Goldberg believes journalists will understand if you follow three steps: (1) I can't discuss that, (2) here's why I can't discuss that, and (3) this is what I can discuss. ■

- Don't answer hypothetical questions.
- Don't speak ill about the competition or other individuals.
- Dress and act appropriately. Don't distract your listeners with defensive non-verbal language, such as crossing your arms.
- Watch for loaded questions. Take time to think. Don't repeat a derogatory remark; shift to another subject.
- Always answer positively. It's the answer that counts, not the question.
- Watch your attitude. Don't be arrogant, evasive, or uncooperative. Don't argue. Don't use jargon. Don't lose your temper.
- Avoid memorizing your statements, but do use notes for reference. Speak from the public viewpoint; it is the public's interest that is important. Look at the interviewer when he or she is asking a question, but face the camera when you are answering a question being recorded by a television crew.
- Be cooperative, but don't surrender. Watch for presumptive questions: "Why are you resisting the efforts to control pollution?" "Why do you charge such outrageous prices?" Deny the statement and shift to another topic.
- If a question is unfair or too personal, say so and refuse to answer. You are not required to answer every question.
- Don't challenge figures unless you know for certain they are wrong. Remember that there are too many ways to cite statistics.
- Discuss only activities and policies that lie within your area of responsibility.
- Admit that you don't know the answer if that is the case. If you promise to provide more information later, make sure you do.
- Smile. Be as relaxed and informal as possible. A humorous remark may be used if it is appropriate, but don't be facetious; you might be misunderstood.

Other media training experts have added to and elaborated on this list. One common suggestion is to provide reporters with company background materials in advance. This will help them get facts and names correct. Body language is important. Be confident and relaxed, always look a reporter in the eye, keep your hands open, smile and lean forward when you're talking. The idea, says Stephen Rafe of Rapport Communications, is to be assertive and avoid being defensive, passive, submissive, or aggressive.

There are additional tips that apply to interviews on broadcast talk shows. Ketchum gives the following advice:

- Say it in 60 seconds.
- Deliver your message with sincerity.
- Know your facts.
- Rehearse your message.
- Stay alert.
- Participate in discussion.

- Get your message across.
- Don't get mad.
- Don't look at the camera.

Grooming and dress are also important in a television program. Men should wear conservative suits. A sports jacket might be permissible in some cases, but it must not be loud. Wild plaids or violent colors won't do. Suits should be dark; if there is a pattern it should be so subdued as to be almost invisible. Men should avoid white shirts. Pale blue, gray or tan with no noticeable pattern is best. Flashy rings, large cuff links, and big belt buckles are unacceptable. If a man has a dark beard, a shave just before the appearance is a good idea. For any television appearance, the producer may suggest some makeup. This should not be resisted; even the nation's presidents have used it. Women should dress conservatively in dresses or suits. Makeup should be the kind that is normally worn for business. Any jewelry that dangles, jingles, or flashes is taboo.

Another important point is that the speaker is "on stage" at all times. A surreptitious scratch or adjustment of clothing may be seen by some members of the audience or picked up by a TV camera. A speaker should assume that an inelegant gesture will be seen.

News Conferences

A news conference is a setting where many reporters ask questions. It is called by an organization when there is important and significant news to announce, news that will attract major media and public interest.

Bulldog Reporter, a media relations newsletter, gives the following list of instances that are appropriate for news conferences:

- An announcement of considerable importance to a large number of people in the community is to be made.
- A matter of public concern needs to be explained.
- Reporters have requested access to a key individual, and it is important to give all media equal access to the person.
- A new product or an invention in the public interest is to be unveiled, demonstrated, and explained to the media.
- A person of importance is coming to town, and there are many media requests for interviews.
- A complex issue or situation is to be announced, and the media need access to someone who can answer their questions.

The two major reasons for having a news conference are to give all media an opportunity to hear the announcement at the same time and to provide a setting where reporters can ask follow-up questions. Many announcements, particularly those involving research breakthroughs, major corporate decisions, or crises, raise numerous questions, as reporters seek information on all aspects of an issue or event.

Your role as a public relations professional is to determine when and if a news conference is needed. All too often, executives in an organization want to call a news conference to stir up publicity and make routine announcements that can just as easily be handled with a news release. Not only is this an expensive proposition, it also alienates the media, who have better things to do than attend news conferences when there is no news.

Scheduling a News Conference ■ The news conference should be scheduled at a time that is convenient for the reporters—that is, with an eye on the deadlines of the media represented. In general, Tuesday, Wednesday, or Thursday mornings are best for dailies and broadcast media. This allows sufficient time for reporters to get stories in the next morning's daily or on the 6 P.M. news. If the primary audience is the trade press—reporters representing publications in a particular industry—late afternoon news conferences may be more convenient.

Avoid Saturdays and Sundays, as well as major holidays. Most media operate with skeleton staffs on these days and hence don't have the personnel to cover news conferences. Also, avoid news conferences after 5 P.M. Major newspapers and broadcast outlets are unionized, and they prefer not to pay reporters overtime.

Another consideration, which often can't be planned for, is to schedule the news conference on a day when there are not other major announcements or news events. In many major cities, for example, local bureaus of the Associated Press (AP) keep a "day book" of upcoming events, including news conferences that have already been scheduled by various organizations.

Selecting a Location ■ A location for a news conference must meet several criteria. First, it must be convenient for the media invited and be relatively close to their places of work. Second, the room selected must have the necessary facilities to accommodate both print and broadcast media.

Organizations often use hotels and conference centers for news conferences, as well as the corporate headquarters. It is important for the room to have plenty of electrical outlets, particularly for radio and television crews. Television people may prefer a room on a ground floor near an entrance so that they can park a mobile communications center outside the room. In some cases, they will want to run cables from the truck to the room for live broadcast.

Live radio can involve microwave, cellular phone, or land-line transmission. Radio reporters will want a room with phone jacks or a bank of phones nearby.

You should make the room available 1 or 2 hours in advance so that radio and television crews can set up. You should have a general seating plan to make sure that the equipment doesn't obstruct the view or hinder the work of print reporters. An elevated platform for TV cameras in the back of the room is helpful. See Figure 11.1, which shows a news conference in session.

If you think journalists from out of town would be interested in the news conference, it is now standard procedure to hire your own video and audio crew to provide a transmission via closed-circuit television or the Internet. When the music

FIGURE 11.1 Tennis star Anna Koumikova gives a news conference in Washington, D.C., before a match with the Washington Kastles. A good way to reach many reporters at the same time is to have a news conference. A brief statement or presentation is given, and the majority of the time is spent answering reporters' questions. In general, a news conference by a celebrity is always well attended, even if there isn't much news.

industry announced a new copyright protection plan to allow music to be distributed on the Internet, 2,500 journalists and industry experts received press materials and heard the announcement online through their personal computers. Only 25 reporters actually attended the event, which was held in New York City. Another consideration is to have several smaller rooms reserved nearby for exclusive interviews with a company representative after the general news conference.

Invitations ■ The invitation list should include all reporters, and even influential bloggers, who might be interested in the announcement. It is better to invite too many than to omit some who may feel slighted.

Invitations take various forms, depending on the event and the creativity of the public relations person. The standard approach is an invitation that can be delivered by first class mail, e-mail, fax, or even messenger. A second approach is a more formal invitation that incorporates some graphical elements. This approach is often used for events and new product announcements. A third approach is the stunt. When Swatch invited reporters to a news conference announcing a new line of divers' watches, it had people in SCUBA gear deliver aquariums containing invitations.

If the news conference will also be broadcast live via satellite to reporters in various cities, a satellite distribution firm will send a media advisory. SGI, for example, held such a news conference when it announced a joint business venture with movie producer Steven Spielberg. Apple regularly uses live satellite feeds whenever Steve Jobs gives a news conference about a new product. Use the telephone or e-mail if the conference is being scheduled on short notice. In any case, the invitation should state the time and place, the subject to be discussed, and the names of the principal spokespeople who will attend.

Print or fax invitations should be sent 10 to 14 days in advance and should be marked "RSVP" so that you can make appropriate decisions regarding the size of the meeting room, the number of media kits needed, and what special equipment will be required. Reporters are notorious for not responding to RSVPs, so it is standard procedure to phone or e-mail them several days before the event and encourage their attendance.

Handling the Conference ■ It is important that a news conference be well organized, short, and punctual. It is not a symposium or a seminar. A news conference should run no more than an hour, and statements by spokespeople should be relatively brief, allowing reporters time to ask questions.

You should brief your employer or clients on what they are going to say, how they are going to say it, and what visual aids will be used to illustrate their announcement. Reporters should receive copies of the text for each speech and other key materials such as slides, PowerPoint presentations, charts, executive bios, and background materials. These are often given to reporters in the form of a media kit, which was discussed in Chapter 6.

It's also important to establish ground rules for the conduct of the news conference. Usually, brief opening statements are made followed by a Q&A session. If there are many attendees, it might be wise to consider the format of one question and follow-up per person. This ensures that more people can ask a question rather than having one or two reporters dominate the session. The other consideration is to keep on track. Reporters often take the opportunity to ask oddball questions that distract from the stated purpose and objectives of the new conference.

Coffee, fruit juice, and rolls can be served prior to the opening of a morning news conference. Avoid trying to serve a luncheon or cocktails to reporters attending a news conference. They have deadlines and other assignments and don't have time to socialize.

After the Conference ■ At the conclusion of the news conference, the spokespeople should remain in the room and be available for any reporters who need one-on-one interviews. This can be done in a quiet corner or in a room adjacent to the site.

As the public relations person, you should be readily accessible during the remainder of the day in case reporters or bloggers need more information or think of other questions as they prepare their stories. You should know where the spokespeople are during the day and how they can be reached, just in case a reporter needs to check a quote or get another.

Another duty is to contact reporters who expressed interest but were ultimately unable to attend. You can offer to e-mail them the materials from the news conference and, if you have recorded the news conference, offer excerpts of videotape or soundbites. Another possibility is to arrange a one-on-one interview with one of the spokespeople. In media relations, as stated previously, service is the name of the game.

Teleconferences and Webcasts

A news conference can also be a teleconference (phone) or Webcast (video). The technology is simple: a speakerphone hookup or a video streamed via the Internet or a satellite dish. According to a survey by the National Investors Relations Institute (NIRI), almost 75 percent of *Fortune* 500 companies use large-scale conference calls to announce and disseminate quarterly financial results. In addition, NIRI estimates that one in three U.S. businesses use teleconferences at least once a month.

A teleconference or Webcast can be effective for several reasons. First, it is a cost-effective way to interact with reporters on a somewhat one-to-one basis. Second, it is convenient for the media. Rather than taking time to travel to and from a news conference, reporters can participate from their desks. Third, conference calls and Webcasts can generate more "attendance" by journalists in other cities.

Here are some guidelines for holding a teleconference or Webcast:

- Invite reporters and key bloggers to participate in advance.
- The teleconference or Webcast should last no more than 45 to 60 minutes.
- Remember time zones when scheduling such an event.

Media Tours

An alternative to the news conference, which is held in one location, is the media tour. Unlike the satellite media tour (SMT), which was described in Chapter 9, a media tour involves personal visits to multiple cities and a number of media throughout the region or the nation. Although the ultimate purpose of any media tour is to generate news coverage for the client or employer, there are two kinds of media tours. The first has the immediate objective of generating media coverage. The second is focused on providing background and establishing a working relationship.

Generating Coverage ■ If the goal is to generate coverage, a spokesperson goes on a media tour and is booked on locally produced broadcast shows in various cities. The publicist also will arrange local print media interviews. This concept, already mentioned in Chapter 4, capitalizes on the idea that a "local" angle often gets more media attention.

A good example of how this works is a marketing communications program conducted on behalf of Step Reebok, an adjustable device for step training. The objective was to promote the product and physical fitness in general.

Rich Boggs, founder of Sports Step and creator of the adjustable step, was an ideal spokesperson. He was once an overweight, three-pack-a-day smoker who completely changed his lifestyle and now has a strong commitment to health and fitness.

Boggs went on a 14-city media tour to promote step training and his product. Because physical fitness was topical and trendy, he was able to get on 24 different TV news and talk shows, 4 of which were national. He also gave 21 radio interviews and was the subject of more than 20 newspaper feature articles.

The media tour, a key element in an overall marketing communications program, led to a 45 percent increase in sales of Step Reebok. A comparable advertising campaign would have cost almost $750,000.

Relationship Building ■ The second purpose of a media tour is of longer range in terms of results. An organization's officials visit key editors for the purpose of acquainting them with the organization and what products or services it provides. This, in today's jargon, is called a **desktop tour**, because it takes place at the editor's or reporter's desk. In reality, it usually takes place in a conference room or at a local Starbucks. Unlike the first kind of tour, which focuses on the general media, these tours primarily involve publications that cover specific industries. At times, a desktop tour is also used to reach financial analysts who track a specific industry and make stock recommendations.

It would be difficult to get representatives from national business and trade publications to visit the offices of a small company. Yet by taking the president, the director of public relations, and perhaps the chief financial officer to the publication, it is possible to arrange for a one-on-one meeting with the editors. Your presentation may not result in a story immediately, but you will have laid the groundwork for future coverage. See the following PR Casebook for a case study of a media tour.

The Role of a PR Firm ■ Public relations firms often are hired to arrange media tours. Their job is to (1) schedule appointments with key editors; (2) conduct media training for the organization's spokespeople; (3) prepare an outline of key talking points; (4) make airline, hotel, and local transportation arrangements for each city; and (5) prepare a briefing book about the background of the editor and the publication that will be visited. Of course, an account executive from the public relations firm goes on the media tour and coordinates all the logistics. Figure 11.2 shows a page from a briefing book.

PR casebook

A Media Tour Pays Off

Handspring, Inc. faced a challenge. Although the company was already established in the media as a leading innovator of handheld computing products, it needed a strategy to launch its new Treo product line. With such respected giants as Nokia and Ericsson commanding this market, how could a small handheld computer manufacturer compete?

Handspring and its public relations firm, Switzer Communications, decided that an aggressive media tour—including product demonstrations—conducted with a wide range of media and financial analysts, would be vital to the launch of the Treo product line and subsequent product reviews. The objectives were (1) position Handspring as a leading innovator of new products and technologies, (2) launch and establish credibility for a new communicator product line, and (3) educate consumers about the extension of product lines, not a replacement for current products.

Switzer Communications organized a media tour that included a broad range of publications, including technology, business, and consumer-focused media, through an extensive series of briefings. The tour, which took place several weeks before the product was actually available for purchase, consisted of a 10-day sweep of the West and East coasts, including Boston, New York, Washington D.C., Los Angeles/San Diego, and the San Francisco/Bay Area. In addition, Switzer organized briefings with top wire syndicates, online news and trade sites, and daily newspapers on the Thursday and Friday before the Monday launch to secure announcement-day coverage.

The media tour gave journalists an early preview and demonstration of the Treo product line. According to Switzer, publications with a combined circulation of 43 million covered the launch of the new product line. Ellen Sheng of *The Wall Street Journal*, for example, reported, "Shares of Handspring, Inc. sprang up as much as 53 percent Monday following announcements that its highly anticipated integrated wireless device would be on the market." ■

Thursday, April 22

Breakfast is on your own. Please check-out on Thursday by 8:45 a.m. Car service will pick you up at the upper ramp mezzanine level entrance of the hotel at 9:00 a.m.

Car Service
Music Express
1-800/255-4444
Confirmation #772388
Pick up from the Grand Hyatt is at 9:00 a.m.

- ***Fortune Magazine*** **10:00 a.m.**

Directions from the Grand Hyatt New York to *Fortune Magazine*: Approx. 5 minutes

Go Southeast on E 44TH ST towards 2ND AVE. Turn RIGHT onto 2ND AVE. Turn RIGHT onto E 42ND ST. Turn RIGHT onto 6TH AVE.

1271 Avenue of the Americas
New York, NY
212/502-1212

- ***Computer Shopper*** **11:30 a.m.**

Directions from *Fortune Magazine* to *Computer Shopper*: Approx. 5 minutes

Go Northeast on 6TH AVE towards W 51ST ST. Turn LEFT onto W 51ST ST. Turn LEFT onto BROADWAY -BROADWAY becomes JACK DEMPSEY COR. Turn LEFT onto W 48TH ST. Turn RIGHT onto 7TH AVE. 7TH AVE becomes ACTOR SQ. Stay straight to go onto 7TH AVE. 7TH AVE becomes BROADWAY. BROADWAY becomes GREELEY SQ. Turn LEFT onto W 32ND ST. Turn LEFT onto PARK AVE.

One Park Avenue
11th Floor
New York, NY
212/503-3900

FIGURE 11.2 A briefing book, often prepared by a public relations firm, gives organizational spokespersons a schedule of appointments and directions to a publication.

Previews and Parties

Three basic situations warrant a press preview or party: (1) the opening of a new facility, (2) the launch of a new product, and (3) announcement of a new promotion for an already established product.

Journalists are often invited to tour a new facility before it is open to the general public. This allows them to prepare stories that will appear one or two days before the grand opening. From a public relations standpoint, this kind of coverage helps generate public awareness of the new facility and often increases opening-day crowds. See Figure 11.3 for a press invitation to an amusement park. Press previews

are routine for a new corporate headquarters, hospital wings, shopping malls, department stores, restaurants, even a new toxic waste dump. In most cases, the press gets a background briefing, a media kit, and a tour.

Demonstrations of new products also lend themselves to press previews. This is particularly true in high technology, where sophisticated products can be put through their paces by the engineers who developed them. Many companies have a press preview of their products just before a major trade show. The advantage is that reporters from all over the country are already gathered in one place.

New campaigns for old products also generate their share of press previews and parties. The Champagne Wine Information Bureau, for example, invited food and wine journalists to a tasting at the Bubble Lounge in New York to kick off Champagnes Week, a nationwide promotion.

Planning a press preview is like planning any other event (see Chapter 17). Great attention must be paid to detail and logistics to ensure that the guests have a positive experience.

Of course, even the best plans sometimes go awry. The staff of Daniel Edelman Public Relations was red-faced when a USAir 757 flight crew did not show up to fly a plane for a demonstration of In-Flight Phone's new air-to-ground communication system. On board waiting for the demonstration were more than 100 newspeople who had been brought to Washington, D.C., to cover it.

Previews may also include a cocktail party or a dinner. One national company combined a press preview of its new headquarters building with a party that included cocktails and dinner. This kind of event falls into the category of relationship building and networking. It allows company executives to mingle and socialize with reporters in a casual atmosphere. Ultimately, this helps executives feel more relaxed when a reporter they already know wants to interview them for a story. Unlike news conferences, press previews are often held after "working hours," when reporters are not on deadline.

Press Junkets

A variation on the press preview is the press tour. In the trade, such events are also called **junkets**. Within the travel and tourism industry, they are called **fam trips**, which is shorthand for *familiarization tour*. By whatever name, they usually involve invitations to key reporters, bloggers, and experienced freelance writers for an expense-paid trip to witness an event, view a new product, tour a facility, or visit a resort complex. See Figure 11.4 for a fam trip invitation to Lake Tahoe.

Here are some examples of press tours:

- Joe Boxer Corporation took 150 fashion and lifestyle reporters on an all-expense-paid weekend trip to Reykjavik, Iceland, to unveil its new line of underwear and pajamas.

WINTER MEDIA *FAM* ITINERARY

Wednesday, March 5, 2008
All Day ~ Journalist Arrivals,
Equipment Fitting & Hotel Check in, Opening Night Dinner

Thursday, March 6, 2008
Breakfast
Lake Tahoe Skiing & Non-Skiing Activities
Lunch
Dinner in Lake Tahoe
Return to Hotel

Friday, March 7, 2008
Breakfast
Snowmobiling
Lake Tahoe Skiing & Non-Skiing Activities
Dinner & Entertainment

Saturday, March 8, 2008
All Day ~ Departures

This Itinerary is subject to change

FIGURE 11.4 An important tool in travel promotion is the familiarization trip, often called a "fam" trip. Travel writers are taken as guests to inspect a travel destination such as a resort complex. This invitation invited writers to enjoy a weekend in Lake Tahoe, all expenses paid.

- Weber-Stephens Products took 25 journalists on a four-day trip to the Bahamas to launch its new line of charcoal and gas grills.
- Ford Motor Co. took 14 auto editors and journalists on a 5-day trip to France, where it was unveiling a new model at the Paris auto show.
- The Australian Tourist Commission regularly invites groups of travel writers "down under" to acquaint them with the country's natural wonders.

Although all-expense-paid junkets are a well-established practice, journalists remain somewhat divided about the ethics of participating in them. Some feel the acceptance of free trips is a corrupting influence on journalistic freedom. Some large media organizations, such as *The New York Times*, *Conde Nast Traveler*, and *USA Today* even have policies against free trips. They see no reason why a reporter has to travel all the way to Iceland for the unveiling of a new underwear line. Other organizations, such as *The Chicago Tribune* and CNN, will not accept expense-paid trips but will pay a discount "press rate" on airfares and hotel rooms if they think the tour is sufficiently newsworthy. Still other media outlets, smaller and less wealthy, have no qualms whatsoever about accepting free trips.

As a consequence, public relations people must consider carefully all aspects of sponsoring a junket and determine whether the cost is justified in terms of potential benefits. One of the most important things to remember, says Andrea Graham in *O'Dwyer's PR Services Report*, "is that a sponsored trip is not accepted in exchange for a rave review. It's simply a means of facilitating a writer's research." In other words, there is no guarantee that a story will be written or that it will be positive.

To be effective and generate good media relations, a press tour must be well planned and organized. There must be a legitimate news angle, and it should not be just a vacation with plenty of free food and booze. Lavish entertainment and the giving of expensive gifts are frowned upon in the ethics code of the Society of Professional Journalists (SPJ) and the Public Relations Society of America (PRSA). Journalists, although they may attend, generally "bad-mouth" the affair if they think there has been an overt attempt to "buy" favorable coverage.

Public relations firms often are hired to organize media tours. Their job is to take care of virtually everything—airline tickets, press kits, itineraries, hotel rooms, local transportation, event tickets, menus, and even special requests from somewhat jaded journalists who expect first-class treatment. According to Teri Grove, owner of a Denver firm specializing in travel tourism, "Hosting a press trip is extremely labor intensive, since no detail can be overlooked during the trip, from the moment guests are greeted at the airport to their departure."

Editorial Board Meetings

The key editors of a newspaper or a magazine meet on a regular basis to determine editorial policy. Your client or employer, on occasion, may wish to meet with them as part of an overall strategy of developing long-term relationships. Editors usually are long-term employees of a publication.

Joan Stewart, writing in *PR Tactics*, says there are five reasons for meeting with an editorial board:

1. You want the newspaper's support for a cause or issue.
2. You're about to announce a sensitive and possibly controversial news story and want to meet with the board before the story appears to provide background and context so that the publication can do a better job of reporting the story.
3. The newspaper has been printing unfavorable editorials about you, and you want to present your side in hopes they change their perspective.
4. You feel the newspaper has been treating you unfairly in its news stories, and you've gotten nowhere with the reporter or junior editors.
5. You want to introduce your new CEO to the board for a "getting-to-know you" session.

In general, you phone or write the editorial page director and request a meeting with the publication's editorial board. Most editors want a tightly written, one-page letter outlining who you represent, what issues you would like to cover, and why your representatives are the best qualified to discuss the issue. Don't weigh down your first letter or e-mail with a media kit or other background information.

Once you have an appointment, you should develop a message that focuses on three or four key points. You should also decide in advance what you want to accomplish in the meeting. Do you simply want the editors to know about your viewpoint so it can perhaps be incorporated into future news stories and editorials, or do you want them to write an editorial supporting you? The best approach is to have a well-informed senior person from your organization give the presentation. This may be the company president, but it can also be an expert in a particular field, such as law, accounting, environmental standards, technology, etc., depending on the issue. In general, your role as the public relations person is not to give the presentation, but to make arrangements for the meeting, prepare the background materials, and help your spokesperson prepare for it.

Here's a list of tips from the experts for meeting with editorial boards:

- Conduct a practice session before the meeting, responding to difficult questions; it helps to know something about previous editorial positions.
- Take no more than three or four people. Well-known experts with credentials are great as long as they can explain their views simply.
- Don't expect more than a half-hour. Make your presentation brief and to the point, so there is sufficient time for Q&A.
- Bring the same materials you would have sent had there been no meeting.
- Leave videos at your office (they won't watch them).
- Offer to submit an op-ed piece if the editors do not adopt your position.
- Write a follow-up note offering further information and the names of third-party experts who can be contacted.

Ann Higbee, managing partner at Eric Mower and Associates, sums up the value of editorial boards. She writes, in *PR Tactics*, "Building good working relationships with the editorial board can help your organization get credit for the positive things it does and lays the groundwork for public understanding in tough times." See Figure 11.5 for an example of an editorial about Rotary International.

THE WALL STREET JOURNAL.

TUESDAY, APRIL 12, 2005   © *2005 Dow Jones & Company, Inc. All Rights Reserved.*

REVIEW & OUTLOOK

Polio and Rotary

Today marks the 50th anniversary of the Salk polio vaccine. Poliomyelitis, also know as infantile paralysis, used to be one of childhood's most feared diseases. A few years after Dr. Jonas Salk announced his vaccine on April 12, 1955, nearly every child in the U.S. was protected. Today polio has disappeared from the Americas, Europe and the Western Pacific and is nearly gone from the rest of the world.

A too-little known part of this feat is the role played by Rotary, the international businessman's club, which 20 years ago adopted the goal of wiping out the disease. Rotary understood that medical breakthroughs are worthless unless people aren't afraid to immunize their children and efficient delivery systems exist to get the vaccine to them. And so it mobilized its members in 30,100 clubs in 166 countries to make it happen.

In 1985, when Rotary launched its eradication program, there were an estimated 350,000 new cases of polio in 125 countries. Last year,

1,263 cases were reported. More than one million Rotary members have volunteered their time or donated money to immunize two billion children in 122 countries. In 1988, Rotary money and its example were the catalyst for a global eradication drive joined by the World Health Organization, Unicef and the U.S. Centers for Disease Control. In 2000 Rotary teamed up with the United Nations Foundation to raise $100 million in private money for the program. By the time the world is certified as polio-free—probably in 2008—Rotary will have contributed $600 million to its eradication effort.

An economist of our acquaintance calls Rotary's effort the most successful private health-care initiative ever. A vaccine-company CEO recently volunteered to us that the work of Rotary and the Gates Foundation, both private groups, has been more effective than any government in promoting vaccines to save lives. It's become fashionable in some quarters to deride civic volunteerism, but Rotary's unsung polio effort deserves the Nobel Peace Prize.

FIGURE 11.5 One reason for meeting with editorial boards of newspapers is to request an editorial supporting your cause. This editorial, published in *The Wall Street Journal,* supported and saluted the activities of Rotary International to eradicate polio around the world.

A Media Relations Checklist

Many checklists and guidelines for dealing effectively with the media have been compiled. Most of them are well tested and proven, but you must always remember that there are no ironclad rules. Media people are also individuals to whom a particular approach may or may not be applicable. Here's a list of common sense guidelines, many of which will be familiar to you from earlier chapters:

- **Know your media.** Be familiar with the publications and broadcast media that are used regularly. Know their deadlines, news format, audiences, and needs. Do your homework on other publications and broadcast shows before sending a pitch letter or news material.

- **Limit your mailings.** Multiple news releases are inefficient and costly, and they alienate media gatekeepers. Send releases only to publications and broadcast outlets that would have an interest in the information. You are not running a mass-mailing house.

- **Localize.** Countless surveys show that the most effective materials have a local angle. Take the time to develop that angle before sending materials to specific publications.

- **Send newsworthy information.** Don't bother sending materials that are not newsworthy. Avoid excessive hype and promotion.

- **Practice good writing.** News materials should be well written and concise. Avoid technical jargon and hype.

- **Avoid gimmicks.** Don't send T-shirts, teddy bears, balloon bouquets, or other frivolous items to get the attention of media gatekeepers.

- **Be environmentally correct.** Avoid giant media kits and reams of background materials. Save trees.

- **Be available.** You are the spokesperson for an organization. It is your responsibility to be accessible at all times, even in the middle of the night. Key reporters should have your office and cell phone numbers.

- **Get back to reporters.** Make it a priority to make a quick response to any media inquiries. One survey of journalists found that this was the number one rule to establishing a good working relationship with reporters. Quick response is even more necessary when you are working with an online publication, because they work within a very tight time frame.

- **Answer your own phone.** Use voicemail systems as a tool of service, not as a screening device. Reporters (like other people) hate getting bogged down in the electronic swamp of endless button pushing.

- **Be truthful.** Give accurate and complete information even if it is not flattering to your organization. Your facts and figures must be clear and dependable.

- **Answer questions.** There are only three acceptable answers: "Here it is," "I don't know but I'll get back to you within the hour," and "I know but I can't tell you now because . . ." "No comment" is *not* one of the three alternatives.

- **Avoid "off-the-cuff" remarks.** Don't say anything to a reporter that you would not wish to see in print or on the air.

- **Protect exclusives.** If a reporter has found a story, don't give it to anyone else.

- **Be fair.** Competing media deserve equal opportunity to receive information in a timely manner.

- **Help photographers.** Facilitate their work by getting people together in a central location, providing necessary props, and supplying subjects' full names and titles.

- **Explain.** Give reporters background briefings and materials so that they understand your organization. Tell them how decisions were reached and why.

- **Remember deadlines.** The reporter must have enough time to write a story. One good rule is to provide information as far in advance as possible. In addition, don't call a reporter at deadline time.

- **Praise good work.** If a reporter has written or produced a good story, send a complimentary note. A copy to the editor is also appreciated.

- **Correct errors politely.** Ignore minor errors such as misspellings, inaccurate ages, and wrong titles. If there is a major factual error that skews the accuracy of the entire story, talk to the reporter who wrote the story. If that doesn't work, talk to the editor or news director.

Media Etiquette

The points above constitute the core of effective media relations, but here are some additional tips about basic media etiquette that should be observed. Failure to do so often leads to poor media relations.

Irritating Phone Calls ■ Don't call a reporter or an editor and say, "Did you get my news release?" You should assume that it was received if you used a regular channel of distribution, such as first-class mail, a courier service, fax, or e-mail.

Unfortunately, the practice of phoning reporters with such an inane question is widely used as a pretext for calling attention to the news release and making a pitch for its use. Although the approach seems logical, and some publicists strongly defend callbacks as an obligation to their employer or client, surveys continue to show that such calls are a major irritant to journalists. The *PRWeek* survey mentioned earlier in this chapter found that "repeated calls and follow-up" was one of the top five complaints journalists had about public relations people.

However, if your boss still insists on doing callbacks, it's better to call a reporter to offer some new piece of information or a story angle that may not be explicit in the news release. The telephone call then becomes an information call instead of a desperate plea to read the release and use it.

If you do call a journalist, the best time is usually in the morning. Never call when a publication or a broadcast news show is close to deadline unless you have late-breaking news.

Inappropriate Requests ■ Don't call reporters to ask them when a story will be used. Most reporters don't know when the story will be used, or even *if* it will be used. Editors make that decision based on the space and time available.

In addition, don't ask the publication or broadcast station to send you a news clipping or broadcast segment. If you want such materials, make arrangements with a clipping service or broadcast monitoring firm.

Finally, don't ask to see a story before it is published or broadcast. The media, citing policy and the First Amendment, usually refuse. It is permissible, however, to ask a reporter if you can check any quotes attributed to you. In many cases, you will still get a frosty no.

Lunch Dates ■ Don't take a reporter to lunch unless the purpose is to discuss a possible story or to give a background briefing on some upcoming event. In other words, a lunch should have a business reason. You need to be well informed about the product or idea and be organized. Reporters don't like to waste time in idle chitchat, nor are they impressed by dining at an expensive restaurant.

If you do have lunch, give the reporter the opportunity to select the restaurant and pay for his or her portion of the meal. Many publications have strict rules forbidding reporters to accept free lunches. Others, of course, have no such restrictions. In your case, it is always acceptable to ask and then do whatever feels comfortable for the reporter.

Gift Giving ■ Many organizations like to give reporters a souvenir for attending a preview or party. Gifts can be appropriate if they have nominal value, such as a coffee mug, a T-shirt, calendar, or even a letter opener. However, it is not wise to give expensive gifts (more than $25), because it raises questions of "influence buying." In any case, the gift should be available at the door, and reporters should be given the option of taking the gift or bypassing it.

Some organizations also send Christmas gifts or even birthday presents to reporters, but this is becoming a rarity. The days of giving big bottles of booze and season tickets are long gone, says Larry McQuillian, director of communications at American Institutes in Washington, D.C., in a Ragan.com article. Indeed, most major media outlets have policies that discourage gift giving. *The New York Times*, for example, has a policy that states, "New York Times staff members may not accept gifts, tickets, discounts, reimbursements, or other inducements from any individuals or organizations covered by the Times or likely to be covered by the Times." Other major media, including the *Washington Post*, the *Chicago Tribune*, and the *Los Angeles Times*, have similar policies.

Although the mainstream press discourages gifts, the trade press is often more receptive. Moderately priced gift baskets of food items are popular, and many public relations professionals also send such gifts to freelance writers that regularly cover their organization or industry. Another suggested gift, under the $25 limit, are books about journalism or related to the field that the reporter regularly covers.

Janelle Brown, an Internet news service reporter, posted a story on Salon.com about all the gifts that landed on her desk during the Christmas season. She notes:

> More often than not, the thought of all that marketing money being blown on undeserved presents leaves me slightly nauseated. If a company really wanted to stand out this holiday season, it could put all those funds toward a better cause: a hefty donation toward a deserving charity. It may not make headlines, but then neither do all the baubles they send us.

In other words, gifts to reporters are rarely appreciated, nor are they necessary to generate a good working relationship. At the same time, many public relations professionals say a personal note or card at holiday time thanking the reporter for his or her work during the year goes a long way in cementing a continuing, positive relationship with reporters.

■ Crisis Communication

A good working relationship with the media is severely tested in times of crisis. All the rules and guidelines stated previously about working effectively with the press are magnified and intensified when something out of the ordinary occurs and thus becomes extremely newsworthy. There are many dimensions of what constitutes a crisis for a company or an organization. Kathleen Fearn-Banks, in her book *Crisis Communications: A Casebook Approach*, says, "A crisis is a major occurrence with a potentially negative outcome affecting the organization, company, or industry, as well as its publics, products, services, or good name."

Here is a sampling of major crises that have hit various organizations:

- Wendy's fast-food chain had a major decline in sales after media reported a customer had found a severed finger in her bowl of chile. Sales rebounded when it was found that the incident was a hoax.

- JetBlue received negative publicity and thousands of phone calls from irate passengers when a Valentine's Day snowstorm in the Midwest stranded thousands of passengers. The airline was faulted for not adequately responding to the situation.

- Yahoo!'s reputation was severely damaged after a Congressional committee criticized the company for cooperating with Chinese authorities to reveal the name and e-mail address of a journalist who had posted comments on the Internet. He was sentenced to a prison term.

- The Gap stores implemented a crisis communication plan after media reports surfaced that the company was in business with a vendor that used child labor in India to make clothes for GapKids.

These situations, no matter what the circumstances, constitute major crises because the reputation of the company, industry, or product is in jeopardy. Economic survival is at stake, and a company can lose millions of dollars overnight if the public perceives that a problem exists.

Toymaker Mattel, for example, faced a major loss of market share and consumer confidence in 2007 after it issued a recall of more than 20 million toys made by Chinese companies. Mattel, which makes and sells 800 million toys a year, implemented a crisis strategy of being open and transparent about the situation to regain the trust of parents worldwide.

The CEO of Mattel, Robert Eckert, was an effective and articulate spokesperson for the company and gave countless media interviews about how important toy safety was to the company. He was backed up by an in-house team of public relations professionals who, according to *PRWeek*, "... worked around the clock to manage the logistics of the global recall—including creating materials, translating everything into 20 languages, and establishing call centers."

Mattel, in addition to conducting the massive recall, also conveyed information about what steps it was taking to ensure that similar problems would not occur in the future. One key message, which was used in news releases and full-page newspaper ads was "Our recent voluntary recalls are part of our ongoing promise to ensure the safety of your children. We have strengthened our testing worldwide with a mandatory 3-stage safety check of paint used on our toys."

Mattel's strategy was successful. As a result of its efforts to be open and come across as being concerned about toy safety, consumer confidence was restored and Christmas sales of Mattel toys rebounded.

During a crisis, the media can be adversaries or allies. It all depends on how you and your organization manage the crisis and understand the media's point of view. Keep in mind the following guidelines developed by *PR Newswire*:

- **"No comment" fuels hostility.** Even a simple "Can I get back to you?" can be misconstrued as evasive.
- **Always try to be helpful.** Too many executives are so guarded in conversations with reporters that they miss opportunities to get their own case across.
- **Be familiar with print and broadcast deadlines.** Calling a news conference on or after a deadline may hurt your organization's chance to get fair or full treatment.
- **Get to know the journalists in your area before a crisis hits.** That way, they will already know something about you and your company, and you will have an idea of how they work.

The key to successful dealings with the media during a crisis is to become a credible source of information. The following points are adapted from a PR Newswire brochure:

- Appoint a spokesperson whom the media can trust and who has authority to speak for the company. It also is a good idea to designate one spokesperson, so that the organization speaks with one voice.

- Set up a central media information center where reporters can obtain updated information and work on stories. You should provide telephone lines so reporters can talk with their editors or send e-mail messages. Provide fax machines and computers for their use. Provide food and transportation if necessary.

- Provide a constant flow of information on the organization's website, even if the situation is unchanged or negative. A company builds credibility by addressing bad news quickly; when information is withheld, the cover-up becomes the story.

- Be accessible. Provide after-hours phone numbers and carry a cell phone with you at all times.

- Keep a log of media calls, and return calls as promptly as possible. A log can help you track issues being raised by reporters and give you a record of which media showed the most interest in your story.

- Be honest. Don't exaggerate, and don't obscure facts. If you're not sure of something or don't have the answer to a question, say so. If you are not at liberty to provide information, explain why.

These guidelines reflect plain common sense, but when a crisis hits, it is surprising how many organizations go into a defensive mode and try to stonewall the media. Jack-in-the-Box, for example, violated the tenets of crisis communications in the first days of reported food poisonings. The company initially said "no comment" and then waited 3 days to hold a news conference, at which the company president tried to shift the blame to the meatpacking company.

David Vogel, a business professor at the University of California in Berkeley, says, "There are two principles: accept responsibility and take action." Even if you are not directly at fault, the organization should take responsibility for its product and the public safety.

Mattel's president accepted responsibility for its brand and products from the start, but experts say that Jack-in-the-Box fumbled early on by not showing concern for the poisoned customers. The company would have won more public goodwill and favorable press coverage by more quickly offering to pay all medical bills, which it eventually did.

Summary

- Journalists depend on public relations sources for receiving most of their information; public relations people rely on the media for widespread distribution of information.

- The most common complaints journalists have about public relations people, according to a *PRWeek* survey, are (1) lack of familiarity with editorial requirements and format, (2) poorly written materials, (3) too many unsolicited e-mails and phone calls, (4) lack of knowledge about their product or service, and (5) repeated calls and follow-ups.

- Gimmicks, such as T-shirts and coffee mugs, are not well received by reporters and editors.

- "Flack" or "flak" is a disparaging term for a press agent or publicist.

- The major complaint about journalists is that they are sloppy in their accuracy and often don't take the time to do their homework.

- Publications and broadcast programs that engage in sensational journalism require special handling and precautions. Declining an interview is always an option.

- Media credibility is undercut when publications link advertising contracts with the amount of coverage that an organization receives.

- Spokespersons for an organization should prepare carefully for media interviews. Media training is essential to assure a positive outcome.

- News conferences should be held only if there is significant news that lends itself to elaboration and questions from journalists. News conferences can also be held via teleconferences or Webcasts.

- Media tours involve travel to major cities and setting up appointments with local media outlets. One purpose is to generate coverage; another is to acquaint editors with your product or services.

- Previews and parties are acceptable ways of giving executives and reporters a chance to know each other better. Gifts are not necessary.

- Press tours, often called *junkets*, should be used only if there is a legitimate news story or angle. Avoid junkets that simply wine and dine journalists.

- A meeting with a publication's editorial board is a good way to establish rapport and long-term relationships.

- There are many guidelines for how to conduct effective media relations. The bottom line is to be accurate, truthful and provide outstanding service.

- Don't irritate reporters by asking, "Did you get my news release? Also, don't ask to see an advance copy of the story or when a story will be published.

- If you need to set the record straight, begin with the reporter who wrote the story.

- Crisis communications is a test of excellent media relations. You need to work closely with the media to assure that the public is fully informed.

▮ Skill Building Activities

1. Do a content analysis of your local daily newspaper to determine the number and percentage of news articles that probably originated from news releases, news conferences, interviews with organizational spokespersons, a press preview, or a media tour. Construct a chart and write a summary of what you found.

2. You have been hired to organize a news conference for Target Stores, which is announcing a major expansion into the Florida market. Outline and describe the steps for organizing this news conference. The resulting plan should be a blueprint of the entire event, including selection of the site, use of visual aids, list of invitees, and arrangements for the conference to be Webcast.

3. *BusinessWeek* has decided to write a news feature about your company's innovative approach to conserving energy and reducing greenhouse gasses in its manufacturing plants. A reporter and photographer will be visiting the company headquarters in 10 days. What should you, as director of corporate communications, do to prepare for their visit?

4. The Foster Company operates a chain of clothing stores. Poor earnings and incompetent management have caused the company to declare bankruptcy, but a new CEO has been able to rebuild the brand and make the company profitable again. It's time to let the financial and trade press know about the turnaround. What kind of media tour would you organize for the

CEO? Prepare a memo giving the logistics of a tour, including the media to be contacted.

5. Blogs are now part of the media landscape. Your client makes moderately priced bicycles used for leisure and weekend exercise. The company doesn't have a large advertising budget, but it thinks publicity (and sales) could be generated through blogs devoted to leisure bike riding. Do some research and compile a list of five blogs that would be interested in receiving postings and other information from the manufacturer.

Suggested Readings

Auletta, Ken. "Critical Mass: Everyone Listens to Walt Mossberg." *New Yorker*, May 14, 2007, pp. 104–112.

Bush, Michael. "Worth of Embargoes Subject to Debate." *PRWeek*, December 17, 2007, p. 6.

Bush, Michael. "API Targets Bloggers as Prices at the Pump Rise." *PRWeek*, May 28, 2007, pp. 1, 28.

Bush, Michael. "Playing the Editorial Board Game." *PRWeek*, January 2, 2006, p. 18.

Goldberg, Betsy. "Tackling Tough Topics: Anticipating and Mastering the Media Interview." *PR Tactics*, May 2007, p. 12.

Kent, Christine. "Gifting Sparks PR Ethics Debate." Ragan.com (www.ragan.com), November 20, 2007.

Lewis, Tanya. "Rules of Engagement Change with Blogs." *PRWeek*, September 10, 2007, p. 15.

McKenna, Ted. "CAIR Creates Guide to Improve Media Portrayal of U.S. Muslims." *PRWeek*, November 19, 2007, pp. 1, 28.

Neumeier, Mike. "Journalists Get Web 2.0: Do You?" *PR Tactics*, February 2008, p. 11.

Newman, Andrew Adam. "Things Turn Ugly in the 'Hacks vs. Flacks' War." *The New York Times*, November 5, 2007, p. C9.

Rosenbaum, Carol M. "Friendly Persuasion: How to Excel in Media Interviews." *PR Tactics*, December 2007, pp. 14–15.

Walker, TJ. "When News Breaks, and Reporters Need a Quick Interview, What Do You Do?" *PR Tactics*, May 2007, pp. 13–14.

Ward, David. "Putting Your Products to the Test." *PRWeek*, August 14, 2006, p. 18.

Ylisela, Jimmy. "Five Ways to Improve Reporter Relations." Ragan.com (www.ragan.com), March 7, 2008.

Tapping the Web and New Media

12

TOPICS covered in this chapter include:

The Internet: Pervasive in Our Lives   305

The World Wide Web   306

The Basics of Webcasting   321

The Rise of Social Media   322

The Explosion of Blogs   326

The Continuing Role of Traditional Media   345

The Internet: Pervasive in Our Lives

Today's college students have grown up with the Internet, and it's difficult to imagine life without it. Many of your parents probably do not understand that the Internet is a revolutionary concept that has transformed the media almost as much as the invention of the printing press by Gutenberg in the 1400s.

For centuries, the mass media controlled the flow of information. The media traditionally has had the following characteristics: (1) it is centralized, having a top-down hierarchy; (2) it costs a lot of money to become a publisher; (3) it is staffed by professional gatekeepers known as editors and publishers; and (4) it features mostly one-way communication with limited feedback channels.

Because of the rise of the Internet and the World Wide Web, two spheres of influence have emerged that are constantly interacting with each other. CooperKatz and Company calls them the *mediasphere* and the *blogosphere*. This new media is characterized by (1) widespread broadband; (2) cheap/free, easy-to-use online publishing tools; (3) new distribution channels; (4) mobile devices, such as camera phones; and (5) new advertising paradigms. The Internet, for the first time in history, has caused the democratization of information around the world.

The Internet, which was created as a tool for academic researchers in the 1960s, came into widespread

> ❝ *The blogosphere is terrific from a publicist's point of view. The fact is, the blogosphere is now extending the reach of mainstream media.* ❞
>
> ■ Lloyd Trufelman, CEO of Trylon SMR, as quoted in *O'Dwyer's PR Report*

public use in the 1990s, and the rest is history. Indeed, the worldwide adoption of the Internet has taken less time than that of any other mass medium. Marc Newman, general manager of Medialink Dallas, says, "Whereas it took nearly 40 years before there were 50 million listeners of radio and 13 years until television reached an audience of 50 million, a mere 4 years passed before 50 million users were logging on to the Internet since it became widely available."

The growth of the Internet and the World Wide Web continues at an astounding rate, and any figures given today are out-of-date almost before they are published. Yet some statistics are worth noting as a reference point:

- The number of worldwide Internet users is estimated to be about 1.5 billion people. In North America alone, there are 246 million Internet users, or about 73 percent of the population of the United States, Canada, and Mexico. The use of the Internet grew 127 percent between 2000 and 2008.
- U.S. Internet users spent an average of 15.3 hours a week online in 2007, up from 8.9 hours in 2006.
- More than 113 billion searches were conducted in the United States during 2007, with Google accounting for nearly 64 billion of them.
- The World Wide Web contains 63 billion pages, and there are more than 100 million websites.
- There are an estimated 112 million blogs, and 120,000 blogs are created every day around the world.
- MySpace has more than 100 million accounts worldwide, and an estimated 500,000 people join either MySpace or Facebook every day.
- YouTube hosts about 100 million daily video streams. In January 2008 alone, 79 million users watched over 3 billion videos.
- Podcasts are increasing in popularity. The U.S. audience was 18 million in 2007, and it is projected to be almost 70 million by 2012.
- Globally, there are now 3 billion cell phone subscribers, which is almost half the world's population. In almost 50 nations, there are now more cell phones than people.

The World Wide Web

The exponential growth of the World Wide Web is due, in large part, to its unique characteristics. The Tips for Success on page 307 compares the "traditional media" and the "new media," but here are some major characteristics of the Web that enable public relations people to do a better job of distributing a variety of messages:

- You can update information quickly, without having to reprint brochures and other materials. This is an important element when it comes to major news events and dealing with a crisis
- It allows interactivity; viewers can ask questions about products or services, download information of value to them, and let the organization know what they think.
- Online readers can dig deeper into subjects that interest them by linking to information provided on other sites, other articles, and sources.

Traditional Media versus New Media

The World Wide Web is today's new medium. Many of its characteristics can be better understood by comparing it with traditional mass media. Kevin Kawamoto of the University of Washington compiled the following chart for a Freedom Forum seminar on technology.

Traditional Mass Media

Geographically constrained: Media geared to geographic markets or regional audience share; market specific.

Hierarchical: News and information pass through a vertical hierarchy of gatekeeping and successive editing.

Unidirectional: Dissemination of news and information is generally one-way, with restricted feedback mechanisms.

Space/time constraints: Newspapers are limited by space; radio and TV by time.

Professional communicators: Trained journalists, reporters, and experts tend to qualify as traditional media personnel.

High access costs: Cost of starting a newspaper, radio, or TV station is prohibitive for most people.

General interest: Many mainstream mass media target large audiences and thus offer broad coverage.

Linearity of content: News and information are organized in logical, linear order; news hierarchy.

Feedback: Letters to the editor, phone calls; slow, effort heavy, moderated and edited; time/space limited.

Ad-driven: Need to deliver big audiences to advertisers to generate high ad revenues; mass appeal.

Institution-bound: Much traditional media are produced by large corporations with centralized structure.

Fixed format: Content is produced, disseminated, and somewhat "fixed" in place and time.

News, values, journalistic standards: Content produced and evaluated by conventional norms and ethics.

New Media

Distance insensitive: Media geared toward needs, wants, and interests, regardless of physical location of the user; topic specific.

Flattened: News and information have the potential to spread horizontally, from nonprofessionals to other nonprofessionals.

Interactive: Feedback is immediate and often uncensored or modified; discussions and debate rather than editorials and opinions.

Less space/time constraints: Information is stored digitally; hypertext allows large volumes of info to be "layered" one atop another.

Amateurs/nonprofessionals: Anyone with requisite resources can publish on the Web, even amateur and nontrained communicators.

Low access costs: Cost of electronic publishing/broadcasting on the Internet is much more affordable.

Customized: With fewer space/time restraints and market concerns, new media can "narrowcast" in depth to personal interests.

Nonlinearity of content: News and information linked by hypertext; navigate by interest and intuition, not by logic.

Feedback: E-mail, posting to online discussion groups; comparatively simple and effortless; often unedited, unmoderated.

Diverse funding sources: While advertising is increasing, other sources permit more diverse content; small audiences OK.

Decentralized: Technology allows production and dissemination of news and information to be "grass-roots efforts."

Flexible format: Content is constantly changing, updated, corrected, and revised; in addition, multimedia allows the integration of multiple forms of media in one service.

Formative standards: Norms and values obscure; content produced and evaluated on its own merit and credibility. ■

- A great amount of material can be posted. There is no space or time limitation.
- It is a cost-effective method of disseminating information on a global basis to the public and journalists.
- You can reach niche markets and audiences on a direct basis without messages being filtered through traditional mass media gatekeepers (editors).
- The media and other users can access details about your organization 24 hours a day from anywhere in the world.

A website, from a public relations standpoint, is literally a distribution system in cyberspace. Organizations, for example, use their websites to market products and services and post news releases, corporate backgrounders, product information, position papers, and even photos of key executives or plant locations. The public, as well as media personnel, can access the information and download selected materials into their computers and even print out hard copies. Websites have also become more interactive, giving public relations professionals valuable feedback from consumers and the general public.

Organizations use their websites in different ways. Here's a sampling:

- Federal Express uses its website for investor relations. Stock prices, analyses of company performance, the annual report, and other financial information are available.
- Rutherford Hill Winery in California uses its website to give a video tour of the winery.
- L. L. Bean has a website that gives a history of the company, explains how it hand-sews its shoes, and lists attractions at 900 state and national parks.
- Westchester Medical Center posts a virtual encyclopedia of disease and health care information, freely available to the public. The site also establishes the medical center as the premier medical facility by describing its multiple clinics and medical services (Figure 12.1).
- IBM, a global corporation, has segments of its website devoted to its activities on various continents. One series on Africa, for example, provided PDFs of case studies and short video clips.
- Starbucks, in an effort to revive its brand, launched a website for customers to offer the company suggestions about products and other aspects of its stores. The site was modeled as a social network where users could post comments on each other's ideas.

In many cases, an organization's website is hyperlinked to other Web pages and information sources. A user can visit a related website by clicking a mouse on various icons. Business Wire's website, for example, is linked to the home pages of various organizations that use its distribution services.

Various surveys indicate that journalists use websites extensively to retrieve current news releases and other materials. A survey of journalists by *Bulldog Reporter*

FIGURE 12.1 Westchester Medical Center, located in New York state, has a well-designed website that offers the public a variety of information and services. The site is designed for easy navigation so visitors can find information about the medical center's treatment centers and also basic health care information.

and TEKgroup, for example, found that 49 percent of respondents visited a corporate website or online newsroom more than once a week. Another 24 percent visited about once a week.

According to *NetMarketing*, companies are sending out fewer media kits and getting fewer phone inquiries as a result of putting material on websites. As Rick Rudman, president of Capital Hill Software, told *PR Tactics*, "The days of just posting press releases on your website are gone. Today, journalists, investors, all audiences expect to find media kits, photos, annual reports, and multimedia presentations about your organization at your press center." Online newsrooms were discussed in Chapter 10.

Writing for the Web

Anyone browsing the World Wide Web will testify that the majority of home pages are visually boring and not worth a second look. In order to avoid the pitfalls of having such a home page, experts offer the following advice:

- Define the objective of the site.
- Design the site with the audience in mind.
- Don't just place existing materials on the site; redesign the material with strong graphic components.
- Update the site constantly. This is the real cost of a home page.
- Don't overdo the graphics. Complex graphics take a long time to download.
- Make the site interactive; give the user buttons to click to explore various topics.
- Use feedback (an e-mail address or computer bulletin board) to evolve the site.

Two basic concepts are important when writing for the Web. First, there is a fundamental difference between how people read online and how they read printed documents. According to a study by Sun Microsystems, it takes 50 percent longer for an individual to read material on a computer screen. As a consequence, 79 percent of online readers scan text instead of reading word-by-word.

Second, the public relations writer needs to know the basic difference between linear and nonlinear styles of writing. Printed material usually follows a linear progression; a person reads in a straight line from the beginning of the article to the end of it. Nonlinear means that items can be selected out of order; a person selects a note card out of a stack. Online reading, say the experts, is nonlinear; people seek out particular "note cards" about an organization, a product, or a service. One person clicks the tab for price and availability of a product, whereas another clicks for more information about how to use the product in a specific situation.

This technique is called **branching**. Michael Butzgy, owner of Atomic Rom Productions in Cary, North Carolina, explains in *Communication World*, "Branching allows you to send users in specific directions. The basic idea behind branching is to eliminate the need for viewers to scroll down a long linear document." In another

Communication World article, Jeff Herrington, owner of his own Dallas public relations firm, says:

> Rather than organize information so it runs linearly from the top of the screen to past the bottom, we want to layer the information in sections that sit like index cards in a file box, one screen behind the other. The first card (or screen) of information contains within it all the links to all the cards (or screens) behind it, and so on. That way, the online user rarely, if ever, has to perform the tedious and time-consuming task of scrolling.

Helen L. Mitternight, owner of a communications firm in Annandale, Virginia, explains nonlinear writing in yet another *Communication World* article:

> Think of it as writing in chunks, with each idea or information contained in each "chunk" (or component of your writing) complete unto itself. Identify elements of your writing that contain a single unit of information and recast it into a "chunk" that can both stand alone and work with the rest of your online piece. And, even more than most writing, shorter is better. Documents written for the Web should be 50 percent shorter than their print counterparts, according to the Sun Microsystems study.

How short is "short"? Herrington says sentences should be fewer than 20 words long and that a paragraph should have only two or three sentences. An entire topic should be covered in two or three paragraphs, or about the length of one screen. This approach, he says, recognizes the fact that people scan material and dislike scrolling to view other links to the topic.

Other experts offer additional tips for writing online. *Communication Briefings*, for example, says you should limit line length to fewer than 60 characters. It further states, "Long text lines are hard to read and give your website a claustrophobic 'filled-up' look that discourages visitors from remaining." The newsletter also offers the following tips:

- Use subheads to break long articles into shorter chunks.
- Insert extra space between paragraphs, because it adds visual contrast.
- Avoid distracting backgrounds that make type difficult to read.
- Avoid using "yesterday," "today," or "tomorrow"; use the day of the week or dates.

Shel Holtz, author of *Public Relations on the Net*, offers a number of writing tips:

- **Write the way you talk.** Injecting more personality into the copy will make it easier for people to invest the time in reading it.
- **Limit each page to a single concept.** Provide links to related ideas, allowing the reader to decide which information to pull.

- **Use a lot of bullet-point lists.** Lists are easy to scan, but they also force readers to absorb each item one at a time.

- **Make sure each page provides the context readers need.** You have no way of knowing whether they followed your path to get to this page.

- **Limit the use of italics and boldface.** Italics and bold attract attention, so use them only to highlight your key points.

- **Don't overuse hyperlinks within narrative text.** Each hyperlink forces the reader to make a choice between continuing to read or following the link. Collect your hyperlinks at the bottom of the page, after the narrative.

- **Make sure your hyperlinks are relevant.** Think about your audience and what they are looking for; don't include gratuitous links simply because you can.

- **Provide feedback options for readers.** Feedback can lead you to make revisions and updates that keep the writing current and relevant.

The accompanying Tips for Success expands on what Holtz and others have said about writing for a website.

All too often, however, websites violate many of these guidelines because public relations writers don't understand the medium and simply post printed materials to a Web page without making any changes. This is a big mistake, according to Nick Hernandez, project manager for Frito-Lay. He told *Web Content Report*, "Placing the text from a printed brochure onto a Web page word-for-word doesn't work. It's just static text." He says such a document really needs hyperlinks, graphics, and animation to attract interest and readership.

Ideally, at the very least, a public relations writer should edit articles, brochures, and handbooks into bite-sized chunks so the online reader isn't faced with constant scrolling. One relatively simple approach is to give the reader an executive summary of the material—in one screen or less—and then provide a link to the entire document if it isn't too long.

The ideal way, of course, is to do what Hernandez at Frito-Lay suggests; convert the

☑ tips FOR SUCCESS

Writing for a Website

Diane F. Witmer, in her textbook *Spinning the Web: A Handbook for Public Relations on the Internet*, says writing for the Web is much like any other writing project. You need to follow many of the same basic guidelines, but also be aware that the text will be read on a computer screen. Witmer gives 10 basic tips:

1. As with all effective public relations writing, your text must be mechanically excellent and free of any grammar, punctuation, spelling, or syntax errors.

2. Avoid "puff" words, clichés, and exaggerations.

3. Keep the sentences short, crisp, and to the point.

4. Use active verbs and avoid passive voice.

5. Support main ideas with proper evidence.

6. Keep individual paragraphs focused on one central idea.

7. Make sure each paragraph logically follows the one before it.

8. Set the reading level appropriate to the readership; use short words and sentences for young and inexperienced readers.

9. Avoid a patronizing tone by talking "with" rather than "at" the reader.

10. Avoid jargon, acronyms, and other specialized language that may confuse the reader. ■

entire document to nonlinear style and make it more digestible through graphics and various links. A company's annual report, for example, would get virtually no readership on a Web page if it was a replica of the 36-page printed version. However, news releases and media advisories posted to websites tend to be full-text files because such files are relatively short and reporters often download them and save them for quick referral while they are working on a story.

Building an Effective Website

"You have 10 to 12 seconds to 'hook' an Internet surfer onto your website, or else they'll click onto something else," says consultant Gordon MacDonald in an interview with *O'Dwyer's PR Services Report*. For this reason, considerable attention is given to Web design so a site can compete with the thousands of other Web pages that are readily accessible with the click of a mouse. The idea is to create a website that is attractive and easy to navigate and that offers relevant information. We have previously discussed how a website can be user-friendly, so this section discusses additional aspects of creating a website for your organization.

MacDonald says building a good website requires the following:

- You must have the "vision" of how you want your organization to be perceived by the public.
- You need a copywriter to write the text.
- You need a graphic artist to add the visual element.
- You need a computer programmer to put the ideas together in HTML code for the Internet.

MacDonald mentions having a "vision" for the website. Other experts, such as Ralph F. Wilson of Wilson Internet Services, describes the first step as deciding what you want the website to accomplish. In most cases, an organization wants a website to accomplish multiple objectives—and keeping the press informed is only one of them.

Marketing is a common objective. Indeed, the vast majority of websites in today's world are dedicated to e-commerce. Most businesses, from mom-and-pop enterprises to multinational corporations, have websites to sell products and services directly to the public. Other marketing approaches might be websites where potential customers can learn about the organization and gain a favorable impression or develop a qualified list of prospects for goods or services. Websites with a strong marketing emphasis may have several main sections that feature information about the organization and its reputation for service and reliability, a list of product lines, technical support available to customers, instructions on how to order products or services, and details on the various services available.

Another preliminary step before creating a website is to spend some time thinking about your potential audience and their particular needs. It is one thing to decide what the organization wants to accomplish; it is quite another thing to place yourself in the minds of the audience and figure out how they will use your website.

Are they accessing your site to find a particular product? Are they primarily investors who are looking for financial information? Or are they looking for employment information? Are they likely to download the material and save documents in print form? If that is the case, Diane Witmer, in her book *Spinning the Web: A Handbook for Public Relations on the Internet*, says you need to have light background and dark text to ensure maximum readability.

Focus groups, personal interviews, and surveys often answer these questions and can help you design a user-friendly site. The San Diego Convention Center, for example, redesigned its website by forming a customer advisory board of 28 clients that used the facility. Focus group research was held to find out what they wanted to see in an updated website. According to *PRWeek*, "The Customer Advisory Board feedback enabled SDCC to jettison a great deal of the clutter that plagues many sites and focus on exactly what the target audience wanted. Gone were dense copy and hard-to-navigate pages, replaced by hot links to key portions of the site."

Indeed, paying attention to the needs of the audience helps you decide exactly what links you want to list on the home page. Intel's home page, for example, has a short list of just three categories: Work, Play, and About Intel. Under each category, there are index tabs for specific areas. In the Work area, for example, there are tabs for products, support, downloads, online communities, and technology. Under the About Intel area, there are tabs for such items as the corporate history, executive biographies, the press room, and even how to sign up for RSS feeds and Intel newsletters. Indeed, being able to navigate a website with ease is the key to an effective site. According to *Web Content Report*, "Improved navigation ranks first on nearly every site's priority list. The goal: Fewer required clicks for users to access information because your site loses users at each step in your navigation."

Jakob Nielsen, an Internet consultant, offers a list of additional design elements that enhance usability (www.useit.com):

- Place your organization's name and logo on every page.
- Provide a "search" tab if the site has more than 100 pages.
- Write straightforward and simple headlines and page titles that clearly explain what the page is about and that will make sense when read out of context in a search engine results listing.
- Structure the page to facilitate scanning and help users ignore large chunks of pages in a single glance. For example, use groupings and subheadings to break a long list into several smaller units.
- Don't cram everything about a product or topic into a single page; use hypertext to structure the content space into a starting page that provides an overview and several secondary pages that each focus on a specific topic.
- Use product photos, but avoid pages with lots of photos. Instead, have a small photo on each of the individual product pages and give the viewer the option of enlarging it for more detail.

- Use link titles to provide users with a preview of where each link will take them before they have clicked on it.

- Do the same as everybody else. If most big websites do something in a certain way, then follow along, because users will expect things to work the same way on your site.

- Test your design with real users as a reality check. People do things in odd and unexpected ways, so even the most carefully planned project will learn from usability testing.

Forrester Research says there are four main reasons why visitors return to a particular website. First and foremost is high-quality content. Then, in descending order, are ease of use, quick to download, and frequent updates.

Making the Site Interactive

A unique characteristic of the Internet and the World Wide Web, which traditional mass media does not offer, is interactivity between the sender and the receiver.

One aspect of interactivity is the "pull" concept. The Web represents the "pull" concept because you actively search for sites that can answer your specific questions. At the website itself, you also actively "pull" information from the various links that are provided. In other words, you are constantly interacting with a site and "pulling" the information most relevant to you. You have total control over what information you call up and how deep you want to delve into a subject. In contrast, the concept of "push" is information delivered to you without your active participation. Traditional mass media—radio, TV, newspapers, magazines—are illustrative of the "push" concept, and so are news releases that are automatically sent to media. So are e-mail messages sent to you.

Another dimension of interactivity is the ability of a person to engage in a dialogue with an organization. Many websites, for example, encourage questions and feedback by giving an e-mail address that the user can click and then send a message.

One successful application of this is the website of the Broward County Public Schools in Fort Lauderdale, Florida. The school board was working on two new policies, and it realized that not everyone could attend meetings to discuss the proposals. Therefore, the decision was made to post the policy drafts on the its website and allow the public to e-mail their comments and views to the district. Dozens of e-mail messages were received, and the suggestions were used to revise the policies. The Public Relations Society of America (PRSA) awarded the school district a Bronze Anvil for its website, noting, "For Broward County Public Schools, interactive is much more than a buzzword, it is a working program to make a school district function better."

Unfortunately, the idea of "interactive" and encouraging feedback is more buzz than reality on many websites. According to reporter Thomas E. Weber of *The Wall Street Journal*, "Many big companies invite a dialogue with consumers at their

Internet outposts but are ill-prepared to keep up their end of the conversation." He explains:

> The *Wall Street Journal* zapped e-mail inquiries to two dozen major corporate websites with e-mail capabilities and found many of them decidedly speechless. Nine never responded. Two took 3 weeks to transmit a reply, while others sent stock responses that failed to address the query. Only three companies adequately answered within a day.

A delayed response to an e-mail query, or no response at all, damages an organization's reputation and credibility. Ideally, an e-mail query should be answered by an organization within 24 hours. Although it is good public relations to solicit feedback from the public, you should think twice about providing e-mail response forms on your website if the organization isn't capable of handling the queries.

Book author Diane Witmer sums it up best: "double check that the client's staff is both prepared and able to respond quickly to e-mail messages. If the client fails to meet the expectations of Internet users through slow or inadequate responses, the website is likely to be more harmful than helpful to the client's reputation."

Attracting Visitors to Your Site

Promoters of new sports stadiums often say, "If we build it, they will come." Some "builders" of websites believe the same thing, but that is not necessarily true. Unlike sports stadiums, there are literally thousands of websites, and an organization has to actively promote its presence on the Web.

If you want to attract visitors, you need to do much more than "build" a site. You also have to give a lot of directional signage so people can find your website. The two major "directional" signs are hyperlinks and search engines. Most people find websites by following links, either from other websites or search engines. In fact, one study by the Georgia Institute of Technology found that 85 percent of people begin their online research at a search engine (see Chapter 1).

Hyperlinks ■ According to Joe Dysart, writing in *PR Tactics*, "One of the Web's most powerful promotional tools is also one of its most basic: the hyperlink." In other words, sites that have a lot of links with other sites tend to get more visitors.

You should link your website to organizations or topics that have a direct or indirect interest in your organization or the industry. According to Dysart, "Some businesses, for example, exchange links with a few of their suppliers or trading partners. Others offer links to information directories, free map-making services, and the like." Another approach is to piggyback, so to speak, on already well-established websites that continually come up first in any search by keywords related to your business. If the link is not a direct competitor, you should make an inquiry about exchanging hyperlinks for the benefit of both organizations.

If your site has many links, it also increases your ranking on search engines, says Jan Zimmerman, author of *Marketing on the Internet*. Dysart says, however, that your links should not be posted on your home page. Otherwise, some of your visitors might get distracted even before they get into your site. He suggests "burying" these links within your site. If you are looking for linking partners, he says, "a good source is the Mega Linkage List (www.netmegs.com/linkage), a site that lists more than 1,500 directories, little known search engines, and other clearinghouses where you can post your link."

Search Engines ■ The essential key to the vast, sprawling universe called the World Wide Web is a search engine. There are multiple search engines, many of which were described in earlier chapters, but the major ones are Google, Yahoo!, and MSN. Fredrick Marchini, in a *PR Tactics* article, writes, "According to IMT Strategies, search engines create more awareness about websites than all advertising combined, including banner, newspaper, television, and radio placements."

Search engines play a large role in our daily lives for two reasons. First, most of us begin online research by typing in a few words and seeing the list of sites Google or another engine generates. Second, more than one study has shown that the average Internet user limits his or her search to the first 10 citations. In other words, if your site is mentioned in the top 10 citations—as opposed to being citation number 154 on a 27-page list—you get much greater visibility and traffic.

So how do you get into the top 10? The most common approach is using the technique of Search Engine Optimization (SEO), which has been mentioned in previous chapters, including Chapter 5. The basic idea behind SEO is that an organization uses keywords to describe its business, products, or services; words that might be used by an average consumer. These keywords are embedded as hyperlinks in your website and materials so search engines can identify them. In addition, it's also common to have your keywords and content circulated through social bookmarking sites such as Digg or del.icio.us to drive traffic to your website to increase your ranking in terms of site visitors. Another approach is paying for a higher ranking. Search engines are commercial enterprises, so they earn revenue by charging a fee to get listed on their indexes. As Aleksandra Todorova writes in *PRWeek*, "If you want your client's website to outscore the competition, the choices are to pay, or pay more."

The most expensive option is the concept of "pay-for-position." This is a system of purchasing, more or less in competition with others, the exclusive rights to search words that best describe your organization or products. Say your company, for example, makes ping-pong balls; you would pay Google several cents, or even several dollars, for each click on "ping-pong," and Google would automatically list your organization in the top 10 results. If you are doing a 3-month product publicity campaign, a pay-for-position strategy would be a good approach.

The second method, which is cheaper, is called the "pay for inclusion" strategy. With this strategy you just pay a fee to be listed on search engine indexes. It's something like a lottery, however. You may get listed in the top 10 results on occasion or, then again, you might not. At least it's better than not being listed at all. With this approach, a lot depends on the number of visitors to your site.

A useful resource, says Todorova, for keeping updated on the latest news, tips, and trends on how to get listed on all major search engines is www.searchenginewatch .com.

Advertising ■ Another method of attracting visitors, of course, is a traditional advertising campaign. Victoria's Secret, for example, spent $1.5 million on a Super Bowl TV ad and $4 million on full-page newspaper advertisements to tell the world about its planned lingerie fashion show on its website.

You may not have the budget for sexy models or Super Bowl ads, but you should include your website's URL in print and broadcast advertising. You can also do specialty advertising. If your site has an online "press room," for example, you may wish to advertise this fact in various trade magazines, such as *Editor & Publisher*, that serve the journalism profession. Several studies have shown that advertising in traditional media drives Web traffic. This is discussed further at the end of the chapter.

Another form of advertising is to place your website's URL on the organization's stationery, business cards, brochures, newsletters, news releases, promotional items, and even special event signage. In addition, employees of an organization usually have a standard signature line on their e-mail messages that includes telephone numbers as well as website addresses.

Tracking Site Visitors

An important part of site maintenance is tracking visitors to your site. Management, given its investment, wants to know if the site is actually working. In other words, how well is it fulfilling its objectives? Is it generating sales leads? Is it selling products and services? Is it helping the organization establish brand identity? Are journalists actually using it to write stories?

Fortunately, the digital revolution allows quick and tangible ways to monitor traffic on any website. A number of different measurement terms are used, and it is often confusing as to exactly what each one means.

One term is **hit**. Victoria's Secret, for example, reported that the lingerie fashion show got 5 million hits an hour, which sounds pretty impressive. The term "hit," however, merely describes the number of requests a Web server has received—not the number of actual viewers. In fact, most people trying to log on to the fashion show never got connected, because the servers were only configured to handle 250,000 to 500,000 simultaneous viewers.

Two other often used terms are **page view** or **page impression**. These terms are interchangeable and they refer to the number of times a page is pulled up. Unlike a "hit," one completed visit equals one page view. According to Paul Baudisch, general manager of *Circle.com*, "This term is most often used to describe 'traffic' to a site."

The term **unique visitor** occasionally is used. It basically means first-time visitors to a site. Baudisch says it is a good metric for tracking the number of viewers, whereas page view is better for tracking brand awareness.

Armed with an understanding of these basic terms, a public relations practitioner can track various dimensions of website usage. Each individual page within a website, for example, can be tracked for first-time visitors, return visitors, and the length of time a viewer stays on a particular page. This gives you an indication of what information on your website attracts the most viewers, and it also may indicate what pages should be revised or dropped.

You can even track the number of people who used a search engine or the actual URL to reach your site. If a high percentage of visitors are going directly to your site, it at least indicates that you've done a good job of publicizing the address.

Websites can also track the effectiveness of overall advertising, marketing, and public relations efforts. Was there an increase in site visits after the placement of an advertisement in a major trade publication? What about a major story in a business magazine?

Many organizations also use their sites to gather names and e-mail addresses by having a simple registration form that viewers must fill out before they can open certain pages in the website. As an incentive, organizations run contests and give prizes for those who provide detailed information about themselves. The same kind of information is gathered when viewers request more information or provide comments via links on the site.

Even if you don't "pull" information from a website, you leave something behind. It's called a **cookie**, which is a file that is placed on your hard drive by a website you have visited. According to Shel Holtz, "The next time you visit that particular site, it looks for the cookie, which helps the site remember who you are, what you've done on the site before, and any other information you may have stored."

Tracking Internet and Web users is getting more sophisticated by the month. A number of companies now offer comprehensive services that can easily cut and slice data many ways to find out exactly who is being reached, their demographics, and even their product preferences. To marketers, this is a bonanza. For many individuals, it raises major privacy issues.

Return on Investment

Websites require staffing and budget. One good way to convince management that a website is well worth the investment and contributes to the "bottom line" is to calculate its **return on investment (ROI)**. This means that you compare the cost of the website to how such functions would be done by other means.

Hewlett-Packard, for example, says its saves $8 million a month by allowing customers to download printer drivers instead of the company mailing them out on disks. Cisco Systems says that by distributing news releases via its website—NEWS@Cisco—it saves about $125,000 annually in distribution wire costs, such as for Business Wire.

There can also be substantial savings in the area of brochures and printed materials. Terry Colgan, senior account manager at Oki Business Digital, told *Interactive Public Relations*, "Since I know the cost of printing/warehousing and distributing data sheets, catalogs, and other pre-sales materials, I can calculate ROI based on documents downloaded or ordered via fax. In fact, Oki earned a 285 percent ROI in its very first year on the Web."

Amy Jackson, director of interactive communications at Middleberg Associates, says that calculating the ROI for your website is one of the best ways to evaluate your online success. She told *Interactive Public Relations*, "Companies who invest in developing comprehensive, well-managed online media rooms can save thousands of dollars on printing and faxing costs if the media can readily find what they are looking for on the Web."

Who Controls the Site?

Because websites are becoming ever more important, turf battles often emerge within organizations over who should control the site. One survey of corporate communications and public relations executives by the Institute for Public Relations Research, for example, found that 70 percent of the respondents believed an organization's communications/public relations function should manage and control all content of the website.

Public relations professionals argue that an organization's website is a communications tool and, because they are the communication experts within the organization, they should decide what messages are communicated. This ensures that key messages are disseminated in the proper format and context to accomplish specific objectives.

However, personnel in Information Technology (IT) take a different perspective. IT staffers were the first to develop the capabilities of the Internet and the World Wide Web, before anyone else knew they existed. They argue that the Web is simply an extension of their traditional domain, which is the constant upgrading and maintenance of an organization's computer systems.

The reality, of course, is much more complicated. Neither public relations nor IT, in today's content-rich Web, has sole proprietary rights. An organization's website serves a number of functions, including marketing. Shel Holtz, writing in *Communication World*, says, "As for the Web, electronic commerce falls in the marketing/sales jurisdiction. While communicators can play a role in both these areas, it is highly unusual to expect . . . sales transactions within the communication department."

At the same time, neither public relations nor marketing personnel have the technical expertise to understand all the technical specifications and computer hardware that is needed to actually make a site work. IT people, who are computer programmers and engineers, are the ones best trained to worry about routers, AVI animation files, pixels, Mbone, and so on.

The conclusion, then, is that no one department or function should manage and control an organization's website. Instead, experts such as Shel Holtz and others say the best solution is a team approach, where representatives from various departments are equals. Holtz elaborates, "The team should take ownership of responsibility for the intranet or website, since teams work better than a situation in which one department retains control and others are merely subservient to the demands of the controlling group."

The advantage of cross-functional teams is that various members bring different strengths to the table. IT can provide the technical know-how, the public relations manager can share expertise on the formation of messages, and marketing can provide the perspective of consumer services that can be provided through the site.

Even human resources, as a team member, can contribute ideas on how to facilitate and process employment inquiries.

The Basics of Webcasting

A website is enhanced and supplemented by using Webcasts. Indeed, Webcasting has become more common as bandwidth has increased and better technology has evolved. In fact, one survey found that more than 90 percent of public companies use Webcasts for everything from employee training to briefings for financial analysts and news conferences launching a new product. One big advantage is that they save time and money, eliminating the cost of travel for participants.

Thomson Financial defines a Webcast as "any event, live or archived, which involves the transmission of information from a person or organization to a larger audience over the Internet." The company continues, "Webcasts can be as simple as an audio-only address from a CEO or as elaborate as an audio/video Webcast with a PowerPoint slide show presented from multiple locations with follow-up questions from the audience."

A good example of a media-oriented Webcast was one hosted by the Chocolate Manufacturers Association (CMA) and its public relations firm, Fleishman-Hillard. It sponsored a chocolate-tasting Webcast for food writers around the country who also received a "tasting kit" before the event. They could taste various chocolates as they viewed the Webcast, which featured experts on chocolate. By having a Webcast, the organization doubled attendance from the previous year. Lynn Bragg, CMA president, told *PRWeek*, "It's helped us connect with media and build relationships with them in a way that has increased awareness of CMA." The entire budget for the Webcast was $19,500.

The U.S. Bureau of Engraving and Printing (BEP) also used a Webcast news conference to launch the newly designed $5 bill to 250 reporters from around the world. It featured U.S. Treasury, BEP, Federal Reserve, and U.S. Secret Service officials explaining the bill's new security features to prevent counterfeiting. The Webcast also helped drive traffic to BEP's website; the site experienced a 1,000 percent increase in visitors, and there were about 100,000 downloads of materials explaining the security features and other characteristics. In addition to the Webcast, BEP and its public relations firm, Burson-Marsteller, also conducted a satellite media tour with various media outlets and produced podcasts that were archived on the website. Podcasting will be discussed shortly.

In another application, Clarkson University, located in Potsdam, New York, uses Webcasts to stream campus events in real time to its alumni and other supporters. One event was a lecture by a Nobel Laureate, Dr. Paul Crutzen, who was visiting the campus to talk about global warming. Another event was a "Night at the Opera" featuring a former opera singer.

The audience for such events may not be very large, but Karen St. Hillaire, director of university communications, thinks their promotional value makes the cost and effort worthwhile. She told *Interactive Public Relations*, "It is our belief that eventually this medium can be one of the most effective media to communicate with our alumni. It's a wonderful way to reach people who cannot be physically present for an event."

The value of a Webcast is its delivery system—the computer. You can reach more people via a regular radio or television broadcast, but that requires the involvement of media gatekeepers making a decision to use your information, or you could buy the time at expensive commercial advertising rates. Closed-circuit television is another method, but that requires the audience to gather at a specific location to view the program.

If you do use Webcasting for transmitting audio and video, either in real time or as archived material, you should be aware of two aspects. The first one is quality. People expect the same high-resolution quality from the Internet as they see on television, so top-notch lighting, staging, and production is necessary.

The second aspect is understanding the computer capabilities of the intended audience. Is the website easily accessible? Are there enough servers and broadband width available to handle the traffic? Victoria's Secret's first attempt at streaming a live fashion show of lingerie-clad models, for example, crashed because the IT infrastructure was not able to handle the traffic. You also have to be careful about using too many "cool" technologies and graphics programs that are impressive but that require a lot of broadband that older computers may not be able to handle.

Medialink offers some additional guidelines to ensure successful transfer of images on the Web or an organization's intranet:

- Minimize fast movements and significant screen shifts.
- Emphasize strong foreground images and avoid shadows.
- Tiny details are often lost through digital encoding; provide sharp, clean screens.
- Audio should be clean and without the clutter of distracting background noise.

The Rise of Social Media

The first generation of the Internet, often called Web 1.0, was primarily based on information being transmitted from supplier to receiver. Although websites still serve that function, the second generation of the Internet (Web 2.0) has become an interactive model, and Web users now have multiple tools to talk to each other in real time. Thus, the term *social media* has now entered the mainstream as what Paul Rand of Ketchum calls "one of the most dramatic, if not revolutions, in history."

According to Wikipedia, "Social media describes the online technologies and practices that people use to share opinions, insights, experiences, and perspectives with each other." David Bowen, writing in the *Financial Times*, adds, "Social networks are all about a shift from vertical to horizontal communications on the Web." IDC, a technology consultancy, puts it in more pragmatic terms. By 2010, it estimates that 70 percent of all the digital information in world will be created by consumers.

There are various categories of social media. Blogs are the most dominant manifestation, but social networks such as MySpace, Facebook, and YouTube are also a major presence in today's world, even more social networks are being created almost daily. The rise of podcasts, wikis, and virtual reality sites, such as Second Life, also power conversation between people around the world. A list of social media applications is provided in the following Tips for Success.

This social media conversation is not organized, not controlled, and not on message. Instead, the conversation is vibrant, emergent, fun, compelling, and full of insights. Some experts have even called social networks the world's largest focus group. The *Economist*, for example, noted that "The direct, unfiltered, brutally

☑ tips FOR SUCCESS

Road Signs on the New Media Highway

The Internet keeps evolving. The first generation (Web 1.0) was the extensive development of e-mail and websites that primarily focused on the delivery of information. The second generation, called Web 2.0, was the development of social networking sites that made the Web more interactive as a vehicle of collaboration, sharing, and open conversation. WieckMedia (http://wieck.com) offers a list of important Web 2.0 sites:

Del.icio.us. A social bookmarking Web service for storing, sharing, and discovering Web bookmarks. The site was founded in 2003 and is part of Yahoo! http://del.icio.us.com

MySpace. An interactive social networking website offering a user-submitted network of friends, personal profiles, blogs, groups, photos, music, and videos internationally. It is owned by Fox Interactive Media, which is part of News Corporation. http://myspace.com

Facebook. A social networking site launched in 2004; it has the highest number of users among college-focused sites. http://facebook.com

Twitter. A social networking and micro-blogging service that allows users to send "updates" (text-based posts, up to 140 characters long) via instant messaging or e-mail to the Twitter website. http://twitter.com

Blogger. A blog-publishing system created by Pyra Labs, which was purchased by Google in 2003. www.blogger.com

Technorati. An Internet search engine for searching blogs. http://technorati.com

YouTube. Video-sharing website where users can upload, view, and share video clips. Created in 2005, it is now owned by Google. http://youtube.com

Flickr. A photo-sharing website and Web services suite that features an online community platform. http://flickr.com

Wikipedia. A multimedia, Web-based, free-content encyclopedia project operated by the Wikipedia Foundation. http://en.wikipedia.org

Digg. A community-based popularity website with an emphasis on technology and science articles. It combines social bookmarking, blogging, and syndication with a form of nonhierarchical, democratic editorial content. http://digg.com

Second Life. An Internet-based virtual world that enables users to Interact with each other through avatars. http://secondlife.com ■

honest nature of much online discussion is black gold; Texas tea to companies that want to spot trends or find out what customers really think."

The rise of social networks, which exploded in 2007, has also changed the landscape of public relations. It means that public relations, now more than ever before, needs to be focused on *listening* in order to facilitate conversations between organizations and their constituents. One public relations counselor, in a survey conducted by the Institute for Public Relations (IPR), put it this way: "Social media has provided an opportunity to truly put the public back into public relations by providing a mechanism for organizations to engage in real-time, one-on-one conversations with stakeholders."

Such conversations, however, can't be controlled, so organizations and their public relations staffs must get used to the idea that everything an organization does is more transparent and fair game for comment. David Pogue, technology columnist for *The New York Times*, thinks this is a valuable concept. He writes, "When a company embraces the possibilities of Web 2.0, it makes contact with its public in a more casual, less sanitized way that, as a result, is accepted with much less cynicism. Web 2.0 offers a direct, more trusted line of communications than anything that came before it."

> " Collectively, the social media—including blogs, social networks, RSS feeds, podcasts, wikis, reviews, bulletin boards, and newsgroups—have the power to support or destroy a brand or reputation. Transparency is the key; but it's risky business and requires a new mindset and toolkit. "
>
> ■ Markovsky Company, a public relations and investor relations firm

Tapping into Usenet and Listservs

No one knows for sure, but experts estimate there are more than 10,000 discussion groups (also called "newsgroups" or "bulletin boards") on the Usenet portion of the Internet. **Usenet** dates back to 1974, which makes it the prototype of today's social networking sites. It continues to be an international meeting place where people gather (but not in real time) to discuss events and topics in specialized areas.

Chapter 1 outlined some Usenet groups and blogs that specialize in public relations topics. Other groups may focus on topics such as the environment, television shows, baseball, and Frisbee. There are also numerous discussion groups about specific products and brands. A popular Usenet venue is Yahoo! Groups.

From a public relations standpoint, Usenet is a good way to distribute information to users who are interested in your organization. In fact, many organizations create their own bulletin boards, often within their own websites, for the purpose of posting messages and getting feedback from users. Organizations can also post messages on more generalized bulletin boards. A good example of how this works is Slocan Forest Products, a Canadian company, which was threatened by a hostile takeover bid. In order to drum up support to remain independent, the president of Slocan posted messages on various computer bulletin boards that reached stockholders, the business community, the press, environmental groups, and government regulatory agencies. He also posted his own personal e-mail address so people could comment directly on the takeover bid. The hostile bid was beaten back.

Organizations also use the Usenet to monitor issues and what people are saying, electronically sampling public opinion to determine how people feel about various issues that affect the organization. See Chapter 19 for information on eWatch (http://prnewswire.com/ewatch), a company that monitors Usenet groups for what is said about various products and organizations.

Listserv, started in 1984, is similar to Usenet. Instead of messages being posted to a bulletin board, however, items are sent directly to users via e-mail. The advantage of a listserv is that it eliminates the need for journalists to initiate access to a particular website. Because almost every company now has a website, it is unlikely that a reporter will make this effort unless there is a major news event involving the company.

Listserv, however, automatically sends information via e-mail to anyone who has asked to receive information on a selected topic. Edelman Worldwide (www.edelman.com) has a listserv on its website so a reporter can "subscribe" to information about his or her specialty area, whether it is food, autos, or health care. If a reporter signs up for information regarding the auto industry, for example, Edelman automatically forwards any news releases from its clients in that industry. A more modern version of listserv is RSS.

Using RSS to Distribute and Manage Information

RSS stands for *Real Simple Syndication*, and it's the basic tool for managing the vast amount of information available on the Internet. *PR News* explains, "Simply put, RSS enables the delivery of automatically updated information directly to your desktop based specifically on what you want to read, whether the content comes from a blog, website, social network, or digital news outlet."

Users can subscribe to any number of RSS feeds, which are offered by news organizations, corporations, professional groups, and nonprofits. The Public Relations Society of America (PRSA), for example, has a daily RSS "Trends and Issues" feed to its membership that provides links to news stories and research reports regarding the public relations industry. RSS feeds only include the headline, a short description of the article, and the link to the article.

Many organizations also have RSS feeds that automatically "push" timely information to employees on a regular basis. In fact, RSS feeds often replace mass company e-mails that might not be read or that take up space in employee inboxes. One advantage is that more than one feed can be set up so employees are only subscribed to the feeds that are relevant to their job area. Many organizational websites have a list of RSS feeds that customers can select to receive.

Public relations professionals, in addition to using RSS feeds to distribute information to subscribers, such as journalists, customers, and other publics, also use RSS feeds to monitor blogs, bulletin boards, and websites that mention the employer or client. Instead of having to manually monitor hundreds of possible sites, an RSS feed will give you a daily summary of all mentions in one easy, digestible format.

To do this, however, you need to install an RSS reader on your computer. An RSS reader is a piece of free software that aggregates all the Web content gathered by a user's feeds. Some popular RSS readers are Google Reader, Bloglines, Rojo,

NewsGator, and FeedShow. Once you subscribe to a reader, you can customize your feeds through "browse and search." If you find a feed that you want to receive on a daily basis, just click "subscribe."

■ The Explosion of Blogs

Blogs, which date back to 1998, have now practically become mainstream media in terms of numbers and influence. In the beginning, they were called **Weblogs,** because they were websites maintained by individuals who wanted to post their commentary and opinions on various topics. Today, the abbreviated term "blog" is commonly used.

Although the vast majority of blogs are still the province of individuals who post their diaries and personal opinions, they are now widely recognized by business and public relations personnel as an extremely cost-effective way to reach large numbers of people. The format and mechanics of blogs make them attractive for several reasons:

- Almost anyone can create a blog with open-source software. A blog is ideal for a small business as well as a large company.
- Start-up costs are often minimal.
- The format and writing are informal, which can give an organization a friendly, youthful, human face.
- Links can be made to other blogs and Web pages.
- Readers can post comments directly on the blog.
- Material can be updated and changed instantly.
- Extensive uses of syndication technologies allow aggregation of information from hundreds of blogs at once. An organization can immediately assess what customers and various publics are saying about it.
- Gives an organization an outlet to participate in the online dialogue already being said in other blogs and message boards.
- They allow organizations to post their own points of view unfettered by the editing process of the traditional media.

Ben King, writing in the *Financial Times*, summarizes the advantages of blogs over traditional websites. He writes, "The exchange of links, comments, and trackbacks knits individual blogs into a dense network of mutual reference and endorsement, providing a giant boost in traffic for bloggers who get it right." See the Tips for Success on page 327 for tips on how to write a blog.

Indeed, as already noted, there were about 112 million blogs in 2007, with about 120,000 new ones being created every day. The vast majority do not have much readership, but others have gained a large following because their postings have gained a reputation for credibility and for breaking major stories, which are then picked up by the traditional media. Indeed, surveys have shown that the majority of journalists regularly read blogs for story ideas and blogs heavily influence today's news coverage.

Susan Balcom Walton, writing in *PR Tactics*, says organizations enter the blogosphere for four reasons:

- To achieve real-time communication with key stakeholders
- To enable passionate, knowledgeable people (employees, executives, customers) to talk about the organization, its products, and services
- To foster conversation among audiences with an affinity for or connection with the organization
- To facilitate more interactive communication and encourage audience feedback

Public relations writers are usually involved in three kinds of blogs: corporate or organizational blogs, employee blogs, and third-party blogs.

Corporate Blogs ■ A corporate blog, unlike an employee blog, is usually written by an executive and represents the official voice of the organization. In many cases, someone in the public relations department actually writes the blog for the executive. Some corporate blogs are now even being outsourced to public relations firms, but some critics say this is a guaranteed way to ensure that the blog is artificial and full of "execu-babble."

Larry Genkin, publisher of *Blogger and Podcaster* magazine, gives a good description of what a corporate blog should be. He says:

> In its best incarnation, corporations will use blogs to become more transparent to their customers, partners, and internally. By encouraging employees to speak their minds, companies will be able to demonstrate their heart and character. Not an easy trick for a faceless entity. This will facilitate stronger relationships and act as 'grease in the gears' of a business operation.

An example is how UPS used a corporate blog to connect its employees with its 100th anniversary celebration. It selected 100 outstanding employees from around the world to attend the celebration in Seattle and to also post messages, plus videos of the event, on the corporate blog site for fellow employees. UPS public relations and IT staff helped the employees, many of whom had never blogged, to produce their posts, but the posts came across as authentic and highly personalized about their experience attending the celebration.

In another situation, McDonald's started a blog "Open for Discussion" about its corporate social responsibility (CSR) program. The vice president of CSR, Bob Langert, gave his personal perspective on McDonald's programs, but also invited consumers to engage in dialogue about what the fast-food giant was doing. According to Langert's post, "We want to hear from you because we are always learning and trying to improve. And you can't learn—or improve—without listening."

Although all corporate blogs should provide opportunity for the public to post comments, it's also important to provide useful and informative information that the audience can use. This was the approach Ford & Harrison, a national labor and employment law firm, took when it started a blog to address workplace issues from a legal perspective. The blog, called "That's What She Said," used graphics and humor to explore a workplace issue in terms of how much the behavior of the blog's main character would cost companies to defend in real-life lawsuits. This showcased the firm's legal expertise in a user-friendly way and *PRWeek* noted, "This is pop culture meeting the conservative world of law in a way that sets the blogosphere on fire." See an excerpt from the blog in Figure 12.2.

Another blog worth mention is the GM FastLane Blog, which GM describes as a "forum for GM executives to talk about GM's current and future products and services, although non-executives sometimes appear to discuss the development and design of important products. On occasion, FastLane can be utilized to discuss other important issues facing the company." GM also posted its blogger policy, which provides some good guidelines for all corporate blogs. They are:

1. We will tell the truth. We will acknowledge and correct any mistakes promptly.
2. We will not delete comments unless they are spam, off-topic, or defamatory.
3. We will reply to comments when appropriate as promptly as possible.
4. We will link to online references and original source material directly.
5. We will disagree with other opinions respectfully.

Although GM and many other major organizations have endorsed blogs, it should be noted that a blog may not be a good fit for every organization. As Ben King noted in his *Financial Times* article, "The rapid, spontaneous back and forth discourse of the blogosphere is not an easy fit with the slow, cautious approach favored by most corporate marketing departments." In other words, the organization must realize that a blog is not just another form of online advertising where the message is controlled; it's an open forum where both positive and negative comments may be posted. Michael Wiley, director of new media for GM, told *PRWeek*, "To me, this is what separates blogging from the rest of the Web."

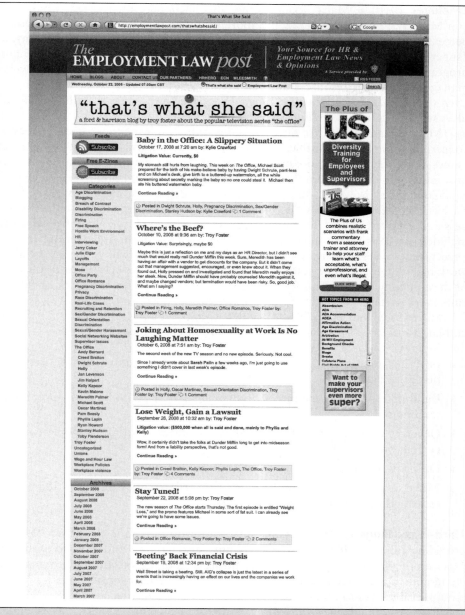

FIGURE 12.2 A corporate blog can often give a human face to the organization and also build brand awareness. Ford & Harrison, a labor and employment law firm, uses a blog written by an employee to give succinct advice about labor law and how to avoid lawsuits. The advice is based on the behavior of the main characters in the popular television series *The Office*. The blog, written in a humorous way, showcases the firm's legal expertise.

Employee Blogs ■ Many organizations also encourage their employees to blog. Sun Microsystems, for example, has more than 4,000 employee blogs, or about 15 percent of its workforce. More than half of them, according to the company, are "super-technical" and "project-oriented," which only appeal to fellow computer programmers and engineers. Others, such as those written by the CEO as well as managers in human resources and marketing, are more general in subject matter. Even the company's legal counsel blogs. He opened a recent post with "I really dislike the word compliance" and went on to explain why.

Many organizations are uncomfortable with employee blogs because they are concerned about liability or that proprietary information will be released. Other companies, those that have a more open system of communication and management, believe employee blogs are great sources of feedback, ideas, and employee engagement.

Companies, however, do establish some guidelines for employee blogs. Cisco, for example, tells employees "If you comment on any aspect of the company's business . . . you must clearly identify yourself as a Cisco employee in your postings and include a disclaimer that the views are your own and not those of Cisco." Dell also expects employees to identify themselves if they do any sort of blogging, social networking, Wikipedia entry-editing, or other online activities related to or on behalf of the company. See the Tips for Success box on page 331 for IBM's list of rules for employees participating in blogs and other social media.

Steve Cody, managing director of Peppercom, a public relations firm, adds several additional important points for employee or client blogs:

- Be transparent about any former, current, or prospective clients being mentioned in the blog.
- Respond in a timely manner to individuals who post comments—pro, con, or indifferent.
- Generate as much original material as possible instead of just commenting on current news events.
- Only link to blog sites that are relevant to your post.
- Make sure that readers know that the blog represents your views and not necessarily those of your employer or client.

Third-Party Blogs ■ Organizations, in addition to operating their own blogs and providing guidelines for employee blogs, must also monitor and respond to the postings on other blog sites. The products and services of organizations are particularly vulnerable to attack and criticism by bloggers, and an unfavorable mention is often multiplied by links to other blogs and search engine indexing.

Roy Vaughn, chair of the PRSA counselor's academy, explains. "Web empowerment has made the consumer king, and it has also made long-standing corporate and individual reputations extremely vulnerable. With Web 2.0, reputations can be made or broken in a nanosecond."

A good example is the 10-day blogstorm that overtook Kryptonite Company, a manufacturer of bike locks. A consumer complaint was posted to bike forums and blogs that a Bic pen could be used to open a Kryptonite lock. Two days later, videos

IBM's Guidelines for Employee Blogs

IBM encourages its employees to participate in blogs and other social media. It has generated a list of 10 guidelines that has evolved over several years.

1. Blogs, wikis, and other forms of online discourse are individual interactions, not corporate communications. Be mindful that what you write will be public for a long time.

2. Identify yourself. Give your name and, when relevant, your role at IBM. When you blog about IBM or IBM-related matters, you must make it clear that you are speaking for yourself and not on behalf of IBM.

3. If you publish a blog or post to a blog outside of IBM, and it has something to do with the work you do or subjects associated with IBM, use a disclaimer such as this: "The postings on this site are my own and don't necessarily represent IBM's positions, strategies, or opinions."

4. Respect copyright, fair use, and financial disclosure laws.

5. Don't provide IBM's or another's confidential or other proprietary information. Ask permission to publish or report on conversations that are meant to be private or internal to IBM.

6. Don't cite or reference clients, partners, or suppliers without their approval.

7. Respect your audience. Don't use ethnic slurs, personal insults, obscenity, etc. and show proper consideration for others' privacy and for topics that may be considered objectionable or inflammatory—such as politics and religion.

8. Find out who else is blogging on the topic and cite them.

9. Don't pick fights. Be the first to correct your own mistakes and don't alter previous posts without indicating that you have done so.

10. Try to add value. Provide worthwhile information and perspective. ■

were posted on blogs showing how to pick the lock. Three days later, *The New York Times* and AP reported the story and it was picked up by the mainstream media. Four days after that, the company was forced to announce a free product exchange that cost $10 million.

Dell has also experienced the wrath of bloggers about its customer service, which caused sales to decline, but it was a good lesson. Today, according to *The New York Times*, "It's nearly impossible to find a story or blog entry about Dell that isn't accompanied by a comment from the company." Comcast, a cable giant, also gets its share of consumer complaints on blogs, but it also has stepped up its Internet monitoring and has customer service representatives follow up with anyone who posts a complaint.

Darren Katz, writing in *O'Dwyer's PR Report*, makes the point that "By engaging in online dialogue, companies are showing their customers that they care about their opinions, value their respect, and plan to rightfully earn their repeat business."

Consequently, it's the responsibility of the public relations department to monitor third-party blogs and even rogue websites, which are discussed in the Tips for

Success below. A list of influential blogs for your industry should be made, and such tools as Technorati, Blogpulse, and Google Search can be helpful.

You should also establish relationships with the most relevant and influential bloggers who are talking about your company. Rick Wion, interactive media director of Golin Harris, told Susan Walton in *PR Tactics*, "Treat them the same as you would any other journalist. In most cases, they will appreciate the recognition. By providing materials directly in a manner that is helpful to bloggers, you can build positive relationships quickly."

☑ tips FOR SUCCESS

Responding to Rogue Websites

Not all websites are established to promote a product, a service, or the image of an organization. The World Wide Web also has sites that attack organizations for a variety of sins: making shoddy products, exploiting Third World labor, selling unhealthy products, polluting the environment, ripping off the consumer, and so on.

Many URLs for these sites, written by disgruntled employees, customers, or social activists, end with "sucks.com," such as www.gapsucks.org, or something similar, like www.ihatestarbucks.com or www.noamazon.com. Others are not so blunt in terms of orientation, such as www.mcspotlight.com or www.walmartsurvivor.com.

In any case, such sites present a public relations challenge to those organizations that are being maligned. Should the organization actively respond to preserve their reputation, or should they ignore such sites? The answer is somewhat mixed.

In general, the rule is to only closely monitor such sites to find out what customers, social activists, and disgruntled employees are saying about you. Such monitoring often detects the "tip of an iceberg" about a problem that the organization should address before the complaint hits the mainstream media, such as *The Wall Street Journal* or *The New York Times*. The issue of Nike using sweatshop labor, for example, was first posted on rogue websites before the mainstream media picked up the story.

Monitoring firms, such as *PRNewswire Ewatch* and *CyberAlert*, can be retained to monitor websites, Usenet groups, listservs, and message boards to give you a sense of what is being said. The general rule, however, is not to respond to the website operator or message board operator unless you want to inform them they are violating trademark rules or engaging in slander that is legally actionable. It is never acceptable to post a response posing as a consumer and not identify yourself as an organizational representative. "Planting information is out of bounds," says Nick Wreden, author of *Fusion Branding: How to Forge Your Brand for the Future*.

PRWeek writer Melanie Shortman says, "It is only appropriate to acknowledge and respond to saboteurs if they break the law or pose an imminent or dangerous threat." She quotes Tony Wright, an account supervisor at Weber Shandwick, who says, "The only times I would ever respond is if the thread of the message is getting out of control. If, all of a sudden there are 50 posts, and everyone is saying something that isn't true, then you can respond."

The main idea is to recognize opinion—for example, "I don't like Starbucks"—as legitimate free speech, but you should respond if the site says something untrue about the brand, such as "Starbucks buys coffee from the Colombian Mafia, who use the plantations as a front for illegal drug operations." ■

A good example is how Weber Shandwick works with about 20 influential food bloggers on behalf of its food industry clients. The public relations firm regularly monitors their posts to find out what they are saying and what the "hot button" issues are being discussed. This, in turn, allows the firm to build relationships with the bloggers and offer information that they can use in their blogs. Janet Helm, director of the food and nutrition practice at Weber Shandwick, told *PRWeek*, "They are an influential source, and we can't leave them out of the marketing mix." See Chapter 11 for additional information on working with bloggers.

To find out more about the content of blogs, or even how to have your very own blog, see the following sites: www.blogger.com (create your own blog); www.weblogs.com (news and links about blogs); and http://blogdex.media (list of blogs and blogging news). Also see the Tips for Success on page 327 for tips on how to write a blog.

Making Friends on MySpace and Facebook

There are multiple online social networking communities, including the business-oriented LinkedIn, but MySpace and Facebook established early leads in popularity and continue to experience astounding growth rates. Mike Spataro, vice president of Visible Technologies, estimated in a 2008 *PRWeek* article that a combined 500,000 people joined these two sites on a daily basis. He went on to say that research shows that 70 percent of Americans ages 15 to 34 were currently actively engaged in some form of social network.

Other research studies have focused on the demographics of social networking sites. One study by Grunwald Associates reported that 96 percent of online teens and "tweens" used social networks. College students are also heavy users of social networks. According to statistics compiled by Youth Trends, visiting social networking sites was the second most popular online activity by college students, after sending and receiving e-mail.

MySpace, founded in 2003, was the first major social networking site and registered its 100 millionth account in 3 three years. Facebook opened registration in 2006 and immediately became popular with college students and young professionals. In fact, a survey by Youth Trends found that Facebook was the students' favorite website in 2007 and 2008. A survey by Student Monitor, a research firm, found that Facebook and beer tied for the most popular "thing" among college students after the iPod.

Although Facebook has fewer registered members than MySpace, it tends to have more unique visitors. In May 2008, for example, the site had 123.9 million unique visitors and was the fifth most visited site on the Web. According to Wikipedia, Facebook is "The world's most popular social networking site." A major part of its growth was the opening of registration to all users in 2007. The site also gained considerable influence by expanding its platform applications to more than 7,000.

The popularity of social networking sites such as MySpace and Facebook has been noted by advertising, marketing, and public relations professionals. They see such sites as an excellent opportunity to make "friends" in several ways. A survey of executives by TNS media intelligence/Cymfony, for example, found that marketing and public relations personnel believed networking sites were vital for (1) gaining consumer insights, (2) building brand awareness, and (3) creating customer loyalty.

Accomplishing these objectives, however, takes a great deal of thought and creativity, because you must shape messages that are relevant and interesting to your "friends." This often requires techniques such as humor, short video clips, music, contests, and audience participation. Paramount, for example, used Facebook to promote *Indiana Jones and the Kingdom of the Crystal Skull* by offering visitors to the website a chance to send friends virtual gifts of the familiar Jones fedora. According to *The New York Times*, "McDonald's is hosting an elaborate game online tied to its sponsorship of the 2008 Summer Olympics."

> ❝ We use tools based on their strengths, and each of the entries in the social media space offers its own strengths and weaknesses, possibilities and limitations. ❞ ■ Shel Holtz, social media guru at an IABC workshop

Coors has also expanded its traditional advertising and product publicity to embrace social networking sites. One initiative on Facebook enabled visitors (aged 21, of course) to send friends a "Code Blue" alert inviting them to meet up for a Coors Light. They could even use Facebook maps to direct their buddies to the nearest bar. Aaron, one of Coor's almost 2,000 fans, gave the site five stars: "This app is epic. I used it to set up my birthday party and it was so easy to invite everyone."

Another Coors campaign, centered on the Super Bowl, sponsored a contest for consumers to create video clips and submit them on various networking sites to win prizes. Tim Sproul, a creative director for a Portland, Oregon, advertising agency, told *The New York Times*, "If you have anything to pitch in a social environment, it makes sense to pitch beer. We feel like we're not intrusive in the online experience, we're relevant, by giving people a chance to connect."

Even companies selling luxury goods have discovered the group and business pages of MySpace and Facebook. Cartier, for example, set up a MySpace profile to promote jewelry in its Love collection. Visitors to the site could do more than look at the jewelry and the high price tags. According to Eric Pfanner, reporting in *The New York Times*, ". . . visitors can also sample music from artists like Lou Reed and Grand National, including several songs with the theme of love that were composed for Cartier. They can watch film clips with a romantic story line. And, of course, they can click on any of those friends' pictures to visit their profiles." Among Cartier's 3,800 friends were Sting, the band Good Charlotte, and Lou Reed.

In general, organizations use social networking sites as part of the overall media mix to execute a campaign. A good example is the Trojan campaign that used advertising, print and broadcast publicity, a dedicated website, and Facebook. The campaign is highlighted in the PR Casebook on page 336.

YouTube: King of Video Clips

An extremely popular medium of communication, thanks to increased high-speed broadband capacity, are video clips. According to data from the comScore Video Matrix service, U.S. Internet users viewed 11.5 billion online videos during March of 2008. In addition, it was found that the average online video was 2.8 minutes in length and the average online viewer watched 235 minutes of online video.

Google's YouTube ranked as the top U.S. video property, with 38 percent of all videos that month, or about 4.3 billion videos. As early as 2007, YouTube was already streaming more than 200 million videos each day. In the same year, it was estimated that YouTube added 831,147 videos to its library. In other words, YouTube is the premier video sharing site for users to upload, view, and share video clips.

Many videos are posted by individuals, but organizations are also creating and posting online videos as part of their marketing and public relations outreach to online communities. These communities, in general, are well-educated and relatively affluent. In addition, research firms such as Nielsen/NetRatings have found that the 35 to 64 age group constitutes about 50 percent of YouTube's audience. Another large audience is college students; research shows that 95 percent of them regularly view videos online.

Such demographics prompted AirTran Airways to use YouTube to publicize its X-Fares, a standby flight program for college students. The airline appealed to students by creating AirTranU, complete with a mascot called Eunice, the AirTran Ewe. The idea was to get students to interact with the brand in a fun way with an online video contest. The airline, according to *PRWeek*, asked students to "Do a little (or big) dance, sing a fight song, chant, or whatever else comes to you." Students could post their videos at www.youtube.com/airtranu to compete for prizes. In addition, AirTran's public relations firm, CKPR, created profiles for Eunice on MySpace, Friendster, and Facebook, attracting more than 600 friends among the target audience. The EweTube contest attracted 24,000 unique visitors, and Eunice even appeared on NBC's *Today*. The campaign received *PRWeek*'s award for "Best Use of the Internet/New Media 2008," with one judge commenting, "This was really a nice approach to engage the jaded college audience in a brave, clever, and irreverent way."

Humor was also used by H&R Block, a nationwide tax preparation company. Taxes and accounting are not exactly a "cool" subject, but the company wanted to reach younger audiences as it introduced such services as do-it-yourself online tax preparation. The campaign started in January, the beginning of tax season, with the arrival of Truman Greene on YouTube. According to *Brandweek*, "In a dozen videos, the fictional oddball raves about the joys of online income tax preparation and spoofs popular YouTube shorts (like the precision treadmill routine dancers)." The YouTube videos received more than 556,000 views, and the MySpace page had about 3,300 friends. In all, *BrandWeek* reported that awareness of H&R Block's digital products increased 61 percent.

A video parody can also be successful on YouTube for increasing awareness of a product and brand. Smirnoff launched a new iced-tea malt beverage on YouTube by creating a 2-minute parody of a rap video titled "Tea Partay." It showed three blond men in polo-shirts rapping lines such as "Straight Outta Cape Cod, we are keepin' it real." It worked because croquet, yachting, and white men aren't typical rap-video imagery. It was viewed more than 500,000 times and created word-of-mouth buzz as people e-mailed it to friends and colleagues.

Kevin Roddy, creative director of BBH, an advertising firm, told *The Wall Street Journal* that the Smirnoff video cost about $200,000 to produce, but it was a good value. A traditional 30-second TV spot costs an average of $350,000 to make plus the cost of air time—which can run into six figures. He also said, "The client bought into it. They understand that advertising is no longer about talking at someone, it's about

Trojan Uses the Web and Social Media to Promote Sexual Health

America is not a sexually healthy country. Each year, for example, 19 million Americans are diagnosed with a sexually transmitted disease (STD). In addition, more than 65 million live with an incurable STD. The Center for Disease Control (CDC) reports, "One in four young women between the ages of 14 and 19 is infected with at least one of the most common sexually transmitted diseases."

Such statistics prompted Trojan, a leading manufacturer of condoms, to launch a multimedia campaign to reframe people's perceptions about using condoms and to start a national dialogue about sexual health in America. A major component of the campaign, titled "Evolve," was extensive use of a well-designed website (www.trojanevolve.com) and establishment of a presence on Facebook (Figures 12.3 and 12.4) and MySpace in order to generate conversations among teenagers and college students.

The website used several components. The centerpiece was a creative video ad that used animated images of pigs in a bar to humorously represent self-centered, immature, and thoughtless behavior. The "hero" evolves from a pig to a man when he demonstrates responsibility and respect for his partner by choosing to use condoms. Another link on the site tells how the video was created. Other videos give short statements from members of the Trojan professional advisory board, including a sexologist, who discuss the importance of responsible sexual behavior and, of course, using a condom.

Another link of interest to college students is a Sexual Health Report Card that "graded" almost 140 colleges and universities on "well-evolved sexually healthy programs." Some of the criteria used were whether the institution had sex education outreach, condom and contraception availability, and student health center walk-in appointments. The five most sexually healthy schools, in descending order, were the University of Minnesota, the University of Wyoming, the University of Washington, Rutgers University, and Purdue University.

The mainstream media, such as newspapers, lifestyle magazines, and consumer publications, were reached through an electronic media kit prepared by Edelman. It featured the background of the Evolve campaign, U.S. sexual health statistics, and the Sexual Health Report Card. Edelman also generated coverage, particularly in the print media, by pointing out that a number of major broadcast stations and networks don't accept ads about sexual health and the use of condoms. According to

evolve. be a man. use a condom every time. nobody likes a pig.
?TROJAN

▶ **FIGURE 12.3** Most public relations campaigns use a mix of traditional and new media.

Edelman, the Evolve campaign generated more than 200 media stories in less than 4 months. The Evolve program received *PRWeek*'s Product Brand Development Campaign of the Year in 2008. ■

FIGURE 12.4 Trojan's Evolve program included print ads and a profile on Facebook.

engaging with the consumer. To do that, you have to play by different rules. It requires you to be more entertaining." Good advice for public relations professionals, too.

Not all YouTube videos, however, have to be humorous and entertaining. The United Steelworkers, during a strike against Goodyear Tire & Rubber Co., posted a 30-second video spot on YouTube that showed a photo montage of auto accidents. As a sport utility vehicle flips over, a question appears on-screen, "What tires do you plan to buy?" The union was making the case against tires made by replacement workers, and the video ranked 24 on YouTube the day it was posted. Even if there aren't many downloads of a video initially, organizations believe it's worth the effort to make one, because the video may be picked up by a blogger who will repost it and give it new life. Ultimately, it may even attract the attention of traditional media outlets.

Flickr: Sharing Photos

If YouTube is the king of videos, Flickr is the queen of photo sharing. The popular site allows individuals to share photos of their vacations, their children's first steps, and even their 21st birthday parties with the rest of the world.

Flickr is primarily for personal use, and organizations are strongly discouraged from trying to sell products or services. Public relations personnel, however, do find creative ways to use the social networking aspect of Flickr to build awareness of an organization or brand. Here are some examples compiled by Christine Kent for *Ragan.com*:

- Peachpit Press publicized a book about working with Adobe Photoshop by setting up a Flickr group for "before" and "after" photos by readers who had used the author's tips to improve their photos. Peachpit also organized a Flickr group on behalf of another photo book that asked people to post photos and give their personal stories about their best photos. Peachpit publicist Laura Pexton notes, "We have found these groups to be great for building enthusiasm for a product, as well as a feeling of involvement."

- Monterey Aquarium has a group on Flickr that encourages the posting of photos taken by visitors at the facility. It even sponsored a photo contest in connection with World Ocean Day. The Aquarium's public relations staff also monitors blogs, and if someone posts a good photo showing the various exhibits, they ask the individual to also post it on Flickr. Ken Peterson, communications director at the aquarium, told *Ragan.com*, "We've let some people know that we're interested in using their photos on the aquarium website or in other vehicles. That creates great word of mouth, since the photographer will likely tell his or her friends to visit the aquarium website—or Flickr group—and see the photo on display."

- *Arizona Highways* set up a Flickr page and encouraged tourists to post their photos that best illustrated the state's natural wonders. Eric Reid, creator of the site, notes, "I don't think Flickr can be used for just anyone—it has to apply to companies that actually have something to show, and something that's interesting to look at on its own."

The programs just mentioned make the strong point that social media sites such as Flickr can be used for public relations purposes only if the focus is on generating participation and involvement on the part of consumers and the general public. In all these programs, the organization was basically a facilitator of people connecting to people.

Getting a Second Life

Social networking can also take place in virtual worlds. Although there were about 30 such sites in 2008, Second Life is the best known Internet-based virtual world video game, with almost 6 million "residents," including people with multiple identities.

Second Life was created by Linden Labs in 2003 but came to international attention in late 2006. Essentially, it allows individuals to interact with each other through animated avatars that they create to represent themselves. Most avatars have human form, but it does allow a short person to be 6 feet tall or an average woman to look like a supermodel. According to Wikipedia, "Residents can explore, meet other residents, socialize, participate in individual and group activities, and create and trade items (virtual property) and services with one another."

Various organizations have established a presence on Second Life. H&R Block, for example, has avatars Hope and Rex giving tax advice. Text100, a public relations firm, has an island where its avatars tell residents and visitors about the values of public relations counsel (Figure 12.5). Other organizations, such as IBM, have used Second Life for employees and customers to interact with each other.

FIGURE 12.5 Text100 created a virtual presence in Second Life where "avatars" could learn how to write a news release or watch a video about the public relations firm's services. Other organizations are using virtual worlds to foster discussion between employees and customers.

Texting, Twitter, and Wikis

Sending text messages via a mobile or cell phone is now pervasive and universal. In fact, *Ragan.com* reports that nearly 75 percent of mobile phone users worldwide send text messages on a daily basis. Text messaging is particularly popular among Americans in the 10 to 25 age group.

Texting ■ Organizations and public relations staffs use texting to reach employees, customers, and key publics. Shel Holtz, a social media expert, told Ragan.com that there are three levels of texting for organizations. One is the broadcast text, which companies often use to send a brief message to all employees at the same time. The message may be as mundane as reminding people to sign up for the company picnic or more serious, such as when updating employees about a crisis situation. A second level of texting is by subscription. Users sign up to receive text messages from groups or organizations in much the same way that they sign up for RSS feeds. A reporter, for example, may sign up to receive text messages from a company that he or she covers on a regular basis. The third method, says Holtz, is the "one-off," where a cell phone user can send a text message to a source to get an answer to a question. They may text Google, for example, to get the address and phone number of a restaurant. An employee may text HR to get a short answer to a health benefits question.

A good example of an organization using texting as a communication tool is the South Dakota Office of Tourism. Skiers visiting the state can sign up to receive daily text message alerts about snowfall and weather conditions. E-mail alerts to subscribers were already being used, but sending messages direct to cell phones seemed to be more logical in terms of accessibility. Wanda Goodman, public relations manager at the tourism office, told *Ragan.com*, "It adds a level of convenience for travelers and builds another level of connectivity with potential visitors to the state."

Randi Schmelzer, writing in *PRWeek*, gives three key points that should be kept in mind about texting:

■ Text messaging is an immediate, cost-effective way for public relations professionals to communicate with a variety of publics.

■ Texting should involve timely and actionable information.

■ Text recipients should have the ability to opt in or out; otherwise, messages are little more than spam.

Twitter ■ Another form of text messaging is Twitter, which gained popularity in 2007. Essentially, it's a free social networking and microblogging service that allows users (known as *twits*) to post messages of up to 140 characters in length on computers and other mobile devices. Messages are displayed on the user's profile page and delivered to other users (called *followers*) who have signed up for them. As of July 2008, more than 2.2 million accounts were registered. The following are some examples of how organizations and their public relations staffs use Twitter:

■ Businesses such as Cisco, Whole Foods, and Comcast use Twitter to provide updates to customers.

- The Los Angeles Fire Department used Twitter to communicate updates about California wildfires.
- CNN and BBC use Twitter to distribute late-breaking news.
- Barack Obama's presidential campaign used Twitter to keep campaign volunteers and supporters up-to-date with motivational messages and late-breaking campaign developments.

Wikis ■ Interaction between individuals working a particular project can be facilitated by wikis. Basically, a *wiki* is a collection of Web pages that enables anyone who accesses it to provide input and even modify the content. Ward Cunningham, coauthor of *The Wiki Way: Quick Collaboration on the Web*, gives the essence of wikis as follows:

- They invite all users to edit any page within the website, using a basic Web browser.
- They promote meaningful topic associations between different pages.
- They involve visitors in an ongoing process of creation and collaboration.

General Motors, for example, created a wiki site for its employees and customers as part of its centennial celebration. It encouraged individuals to contribute first-person experiences relating to the company's history via stories, images, video, and audio. The advantage of the wiki was that individuals could comment on other contributions, correct inaccurate information, and even add supplemental information regarding their experiences and viewpoints.

GM originally considered the standard coffee table book outlining the company's history, but company spokesperson Scot Keller told *MediaPost*, "We felt that a more social, more inclusive approach was appropriate, and the story is best told not by the corporation or media but by men and women who were there." As a spin-off, GM planned to package various stories and materials for distribution to other social networking communities and websites.

Wikis also are used by public relations departments and firms to keep employees and clients up-to-date on schedules and plans for executing campaigns. Joel Postman, executive vice president of Eastwick Communications, told *Ragan.com* that the firm's wiki "allows almost everyone in the agency to set up a well-organized, attractive, customized workspace for any number of tasks. Some of the more popular uses of the wiki are for event management, document version control, and maintenance of standardized documents like client 'boilerplate' and executive bios."

An example is how Eastwick used its wiki to plan a media preview for its client, Fujitsu. Every related document was kept on the wiki, including executive speeches and presentations, FAQs, bios, and the schedule. Staffers at Fujitsu could access the wiki to add their feedback on the site, and Postman said that the wiki reduced e-mail traffic by almost 40 percent. It also reduced paper use by about 15 percent.

Podcasts: The Portable Medium

Podcasting was once described by a public relations expert as "radio on steroids." A more standard definition is provided by Wikipedia: "A podcast is a digital media file, or a series of such files, that is distributed over the Internet using syndication feeds (RSS) for playback on portable media players and personal computers." In other words, a podcast can be delivered to users via computers, MP3 players, iPods, and even smart phones.

So who came up with the word *podcast*, which the *Oxford American Dictionary* designated as the Word of the Year in 2005? According OneUpWeb, a firm specializing in making podcasts for clients, *podcast* comes from "pod" as in Apple's iPod, and "cast" from "broadcast," meaning to transmit for general or public use.

Most podcasts are audio only, but video podcasts are also finding a home on smart phones, websites, YouTube, and other social networking sites. The three major advantages of podcasts for distributing messages are (1) cost-effectiveness, (2) the ability of users to access material on a 24/7 basis, and (3) portability. A person, for example, can listen to an audio podcast while driving to work, walking down a mountain trail, or even while gardening. Simply put, podcasts have many of the same advantages as traditional radio.

Organizations use podcasts for a variety of purposes, including providing news about the company, in-depth interviews with executives and other experts, features giving consumer tips about use of products and services, and training materials for employees. Some examples:

- Whirlpool produces a podcast series titled "American Family." Topics range from advice and discussion about traveling with kids, weight loss, stroke in women, and even snowmobiling safety. Whirlpool, as a policy, never discusses its products within the show, limiting mention of the company to the beginning and end of each transmission. The idea is to build customer loyalty and connect with women, the primary audience of Whirlpool. Dan Cook, director of interactive marketing for Whirlpool, told Ragan.com "We cover topics that are important to the life of the everyday consumer. It's an opportunity for us to connect our brand to her."

- Purina, the pet food manufacturer, has a podcast series offers advice to pet owners. Its introduction of the series on its website gives the essence of content: "Is it unusual for a cat to use the toilet? Is your dog bored out of its skull? Can cats and dogs suffer from heart attacks? Get answers to these questions and more in season two of Animal Advice, where veterinarians field questions from pet lovers like you." Some sample titles in the series were "Animal safety during the summer months" and "Itching dogs and cats." See the Purina podcast illustration in Figure 12.6.

- Disneyland used podcasts as part of its global campaign to generate interest in the park's 50th anniversary celebration. The content included interesting facts about the park's history, current attractions, and in-depth interviews with employees about their work in the park.

FIGURE 12.6 Podcasts should provide relevant and interesting information that consumers can use. The idea is to engage the audience and build brand loyalty in an informal and conversational way. Purina's series of podcasts about pet care is a good example.

- The University of Pennsylvania's Wharton School produces podcasts that primarily feature insights from professors at the business school regarding current trends and issues.

The equipment for producing a podcast is relatively simple. You need (1) a computer; (2) a good microphone; (3) software, such as Audacity, to record, edit, and finish audio files; (4) a Web server where you can store files in a folder; and (5) A website or a blog that users can access to download the podcast. The entire podcast cycle is shown Figure 12.7.

The hard part is creating a podcast that is interesting and relevant to the target audience. A podcast is not an infomercial, nor is it simply reading a news release or an executive's speech into the microphone. Like radio, a podcast must be informal and conversational. Here are some other tips about podcast content:

- Keep it short. The ideal length is 10 to 20 minutes. Anything longer begins to lose audience.
- Use several stories or segments. A 3- or 4-minute interview with an executive is better than a 20-minute one. Also, no one wants to hear an announcer or host talk for 20 minutes.
- Don't use a script. A podcast should be informal and conversational. It loses vitality if it comes across as a scripted presentation.
- Select an announcer or host with a strong, animated voice that won't put the audience to sleep.
- Select a name for your podcast that matches the content. Remember that users and online podcast directories usually search for a topic, not a brand name.
- Be sure to include an e-mail address or website in every podcast so listeners respond to the content.
- Create an RSS feed for your podcast. News feeds are automatically generated if you use blog software, which also facilitates comments and feedback.
- Establish a regular schedule of producing podcasts so dedicated listeners have new material. Most experts say a podcast should be produced at least once a week.
- Drive traffic to your podcast by using other communication vehicles, such as your website, newsletters, flyers, direct mail, and advertising. Get listed on various podcast directories, including Apple's iTunes.

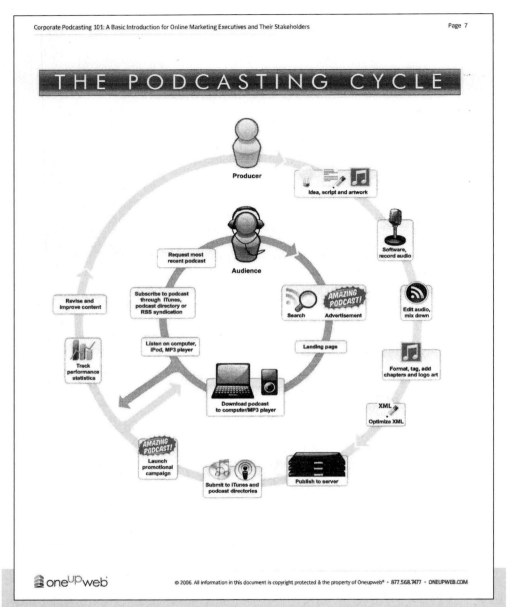

THE PODCASTING CYCLE

Producer

Idea, script and artwork

Software, record audio

Audience

Request most recent podcast

Subscribe to podcast through iTunes, podcast directory or RSS syndication

Search   Advertisement

AMAZING PODCAST!

Edit audio, mix down

Revise and improve content

Listen on computer, iPod, MP3 player

Landing page

Track performance statistics

Format, tag, add chapters and logo art

Download podcast to computer/MP3 player

XML

Optimize XML

AMAZING PODCAST!

Launch promotional campaign

Submit to iTunes and podcast directories

Publish to server

▶ **FIGURE 12.7** The process of producing a podcast has several components which are outlined in this chart prepared by OneUpWeb, an integrated online marketing firm.

The evidence suggests that podcasting will continue to grow as a major communication tool for public relations professionals. The total U.S. podcast audience was 18.5 million in 2007, but *eMarketer* predicts that it will grow to 65 million by 2012. And, of those listeners, 25 million will be "active" users who tune in at least once a week.

The Next Generation: Web 3.0

Two major factors are fueling the growth of podcasting and other social media: (1) the continuing evolution of smart phones and (2) affordable mobile data plans. Indeed, it's now widely predicted that smart phones and extensive mobile-enabled content will be the next major development in the evolution of the Internet. The price of entry will go down, which will allow almost everyone to afford the advanced technology of Web 3.0. Mobile phone users will be able to easily download videos, surf the Internet at will, receive e-mail and RSS feeds, post comments on blogs, and receive an extensive array of mobile-enabled content.

The Wall Street Journal, in mid-2008, made the following predictions for the next generation of mobile phones:

- The ability to dictate text messages and surf the Web just by speaking commands instead of tapping and clicking.
- The transformation of the cell phone as a minicomputer packed with the same amount of power of a laptop.
- Improved browsers that will allow users to rapidly download complete Web pages, including photos and videos. One expert says, "It will be like carrying around a laptop."
- The ability to call up your stored online videos, photos, and even PowerPoint presentations from your mobile phone.
- The ability to send a live video feed from your phone to another phone or the Web.
- Complete map navigation features in a 3-D format of any location on the planet.
- More accessibility and interaction with social network sites such as Facebook, allowing you to tell your friends exactly where you are at any given moment.

The Continuing Role of Traditional Media

There is no doubt that the continuing explosion of Internet services has radically changed the way public relations professionals distribute information. It offers many new distribution and placement opportunities, but the public relations writer should always remember that the Internet hasn't yet replaced—if it ever will—traditional media.

Indeed, the traditional media is very much alive despite the impressive numbers of people who are online. The Nielsen Company, for example, reported in July 2008 that an estimated 220 million Americans have Internet access at home or work, and 162 million of them (73 percent) went

> **❝ It's easy to get drawn into the hype. Yes, it's important to remember that the Net is just another tool in your arsenal. It may be the latest— but it's not necessarily the greatest distribution vehicle for every publicity opportunity. ❞**
>
> ■ Carole Howard, former vice president of public relations for *Reader's Digest*

online during the month of May. It also reported, however, that television viewing was up. The "screen time" spent per user was more than 127 hours for the month, or about 4.30 hours a day. In contrast, using the Internet (including watching videos) was about 29 hours a month, or about an hour a day.

Daniel Eisenberg, writing in *Time* magazine, noting the irony of all this, commented, "Although network television loses viewers every year, ABC can still produce an audience of 18 million in a prime-time hour. Try to get that many visitors to your website in a day or a week." It's also worth noting the following statistics for other "traditional" media:

- Daily newspaper readership, although declining, still has a circulation of about 55 million during the week and 58 million on Sunday, according to statistics compiled by *Editor & Publisher* magazine.
- Weekly papers in the United States have a circulation of about 130 million, according to *Editor & Publisher*.
- Consumer magazines, according to the Audit Bureau of Circulation (ABC), have a monthly circulation of almost 300 million copies.
- Radio reaches 95 percent of the American public every day of the week, and the average person listens to radio 2.6 hours daily, according to the U.S. Census Bureau.

In other words, traditional media continue to reach large audiences for public relations professionals, and they have various audience characteristics that are worth noting. For example, a 2007 media usage study by Ketchum found that U.S. consumers were using more media channels than ever before, but traditional media still ranked the highest in terms of usage. According to the study, 65 percent of consumers surveyed continued to use major network news as a source of information, followed by 62 percent who used local newspapers. Search engines, however, were also used by 60 percent, but business news websites were accessed by only 8 percent of the respondents.

In another study, it was found that newspaper readers were more engaged with print than with a website. According to a report by the Readership Institute at Northwestern University, people who read newspapers spend 27 minutes with them on weekdays and 57 minutes on Sunday. On average, they read about 60 percent of the paper. It's also notable that the Ketchum survey found that the general population still finds traditional media to be more credible and trustworthy than Internet sites.

Even publicity materials in the mass media have increased credibility, because media gatekeepers, a third party, have already decided that the information is newsworthy. Two media researchers, Robert Merton and Robert Lazarsfeld, termed this the "status conferral role" of the press. Other researchers say media coverage of your organization represents an implied third-party endorsement by the press. No such status conferral occurs when anyone can post anything and everything on the Internet.

Although the Internet has no time or space constraints, this is a double-edged sword. Publicists are thrilled that the public can now access the full text of news releases instead of being presented with shortened versions (or no mention) in the news media. However, the flip side is that millions of documents are added daily to the Internet and no one has the time or ability to cope with absorbing this mountain of information.

The traditional media, in such an information glut, perform the valuable function of distilling and synthesizing information so people can easily access it at home, on a bus, or even on a Stairmaster in a health club.

W. Russell Neumann, writing in *The Future of the Mass Audience* (Cambridge University Press) adds:

> People will continue to rely on the editorial judgment of established news media to relay what are deemed to be the significant headlines of the world and the nation. Packaging, formatting, filtering and interpreting complex flows of information represent the valued-added components of public communications. In a more competitive, complex and intense communication environment, that value-added component will be equally important to the individual citizen, if not more so.

Another value-added aspect of traditional media content is that it drives people to the Internet. BIGresearch, for example, found that the top three media for triggering online searches were (1) magazines, (2) reading an article on the product, and (3) TV. Even bloggers seem to rely on traditional media for information and ideas. The Center for Media Research, for example, found that conventional forms of media often triggered bloggers Internet searches, with magazines (51 percent of respondents) ranked the highest. Other sources of ideas, in descending order of influence, were (1) broadcast TV, (2) cable TV, (3) face-to-face communication, and (4) newspapers.

Similar surveys also indicate that ads in traditional media tend to trigger additional Internet searches. Research conducted by Clark, Martire & Bartolomeo and commissioned by Google, for example, found that 67 percent of consumers used the Internet to research products and services after first seeing them advertised in traditional media such as newspapers. And 56 percent researched or purchased at least one product they saw advertised in the newspaper in the previous month. Almost 50 percent responding to a newspaper ad by going directly online to a URL they saw in the advertisement.

In addition, newspaper ads seemed to reinforce consumer confidence. Almost 50 percent of Internet-using newspaper readers in the survey said they trusted the product more and were more likely to make a purchase if they also saw an ad in the newspaper after seeing it online. Spencer Spinnell, head of Google's print ads program sums it up: "Newspaper advertisements drive readers to the Web, where they search, find, and obtain products."

Traditional media, of course, has more usage and influence with older age groups, so the choice of media often depends on the target audience. If the primary audience is seniors, for example, there is ample evidence that they are better reached through television and newspapers than websites, blogs, and social networks.

The Nielson Company survey regarding television viewing, for example, found that individuals aged 65+ watched 178 hours of television each month, whereas 18- to 24-year-olds watched only 103 hours per month. A Northwestern University survey of newspaper readership also noted that readership among 18- to 24-year-olds was declining, whereas readership among the 45+ age group was fairly stable. Within this age group, the report noted, "the penetration of newspaper websites is still quite low." The report concluded, "The very youngest adults have media and news habits very different from their parents."

Public relations professionals need to understand that "traditional" media and "new" media are not mutually exclusive categories. Most public relations programs include both in the media mix. Michael Lissauer, executive vice president of marketing for Business Wire, says it best in an op-ed for *PRWeek*. He writes, "Traditional media is alive and well and, frankly, it goes hand-in-hand with the online community." He also quotes a study from the Online Publishers Association, which found "The power of the Web is strong, especially when combined with other media."

Summary

- The worldwide adoption of the Internet and the World Wide Web has taken less time than the adoption of any other mass medium in history.

- The World Wide Web is the first medium that allows organizations to send controlled messages to a mass audience without the message being filtered by journalists and editors. Before the Web, the placement of advertising in the mass media was the only method by which the organization controlled the message.

- Public relations practitioners are heavy users of the Internet and the Web. They disseminate information to a variety of audiences and also use the Internet for research.

- The new media, including the Web, has unique characteristics. This includes (1) easy updating of material, (2) instant distribution of information, (3) an infinite amount of space for information, and (4) the ability to interact with the audience.

- Writing for the Web requires nonlinear organization. Topics should be in index-card format instead of a long, linear narrative. This allows viewers to click on the information most interesting to them.

- Written material for the Web should be in short, digestible chunks. Two or three paragraphs (or about one screen) should be the ideal length of a news item. Long pieces of information require too much scrolling and turn off viewers.

- Publicizing and promoting a website are necessary to generate traffic. Print and Internet advertising, e-mail, hyperlinks, and putting the URL on all printed material are some ways to promote a site.

- Webcasting, the streaming of audio and video in real time over a website, is now used by the majority of organizations for everything from news conferences to employee training.

- The second generation of the Internet, called Web 2.0, has given rise to "social media" in which most of the Internet content is consumer generated. It provides public relations professionals with the opportunity to participate in social networking sites to get feedback and to also build relationships.

- Usenet is basically a bulletin board where users post notes and make comments. Listservs are used by organizations to send information to subscribers on a regular basis.

- RSS stands for *Real Simple Syndication*. A user may sign up for any number of RSS feeds from various organizations and news outlets. RSS also allows organizations to monitor blogs and other websites that may mention the organization's products or services.

- Blogs have become mainstream in terms of numbers and influence. From a public relations standpoint, there are three kinds of blogs: (1) corporate, (2) employee, and (3) third-party.

- MySpace and Facebook are the most popular social networking sites. Increasingly, organizations are establishing a presence on these sites. Public relations materials, however, need to be low-key and creative to engage the audience.

- YouTube is the premier social networking site for posting and viewing videos. Organizations are also heavily involved in posting video clips. The clips, however, must be creative, interesting, and somewhat humorous to attract an audience.

- Flickr is the major photo sharing site.

- Virtual worlds are part of social media. A major site is Second Life.

- Texting, Twitter, and wikis are used extensively in public relations work.

- Podcasts are gaining in popularity. They can be either audio or video, but they must provide useful and relevant information in a conversational way.

- The next generation of the Internet (Web 3.0) will see the further development of smart phones as minicomputers. The cost of mobile-enabled content will go down, which will enable consumers to send and receive vast amounts of information.

- The traditional media is still alive and well. Despite the advent of new media, people still use traditional media in great numbers. Content in traditional media often makes people aware of new products and services, and drives them to the Internet for more information.

Skill Building Activities

1. Visit the websites of five major corporations or organizations. Do an analysis and assign a grade to each of them, using the guidelines mentioned in the chapter. Some criteria might be (1) design and layout of the home page, (2) the ability to easily navigate the site and find information of interest to you, (3) the ability to easily read text items and download materials, and (4) the ability to contact the company via e-mail to ask a question or give feedback.

2. Find three websites that allow you to e-mail the organization with questions or comments. How long did it take for you to get a response? From a customer relations standpoint, what is your assessment of the response?

3. A maker and distributor of yogurt wants to include the new media in its public relations efforts. What would you recommend in terms of how they might use (1) blogs, (2) RSS feeds, (3) MySpace and Facebook, (4) YouTube, (5) Flickr, (6) Second Life, (7) Twitter, (8) wikis, and (9) podcasts.

4. RSS feeds can help you manage and digest information from a variety of sources. Install an RSS reader on your computer using one of the vendors suggested on pages 325–326. Once you do this, do a "search and browse" to select feeds that would help you in your academic major or in a particular course.

Suggested Readings

Allen, Justin. "Avoid These Mistakes Before Launching a Blog." Ragan.com (www.ragan.com), February 27, 2008.

Allen, Justin. "IBM's Blogging Policy Increases Engagement." Ragan.com (www.ragan.com), February 20, 2008.

Duhe, Sandra C., editor. New Media and Public Relations. New York: Lang Publishing, 2007.

EEI Press Editors. The Elements of Internet Style: The New Rules of Creating Valuable Content for Today's Readers. EEI Press, 2007.

Elliott, Stuart. "For Coors Light, a Night Out That Begins on Facebook." New York Times, May 28, 2008, www.nytimes.com.

Flandez, Raymund. "Lights, Camera, Sales: How to Use Video to Expand Your Business in a YouTube

World." *Wall Street Journal*, November 26, 2007, pp. R1, R3.

Flores, Natalia, and Johnson, Katherine. "Setting Sites on the Hispanic Market: Social Networking Services Aimed at U.S. Hispanics Surge." *PR Tactics*, November 2007, p. 20.

Gingerich, Jon. "Pros Discuss New Media's Impact on PR." *O'Dwyer's PR Report*, March 2008, p. 41.

Greenberg, Karl. "General Motors Launches Wiki to Celebrate Centennial." MediaPost (http://publications.mediapost.com), February 11, 2008.

"How to Subscribe to an RSS Reader." *PR News*, August 4, 2008, p. 2.

Kent, Christine. "The Dos and Don'ts of Using Flickr for PR." Ragan.com (www.ragan.com), April 25, 2008.

Kramer, Farrell. "Enhance Your Communications Program with Podcasting." *PR Tactics*, November 2006, p. 39.

Li, Charlene. "Why Your Company Needs to be on Facebook." *The Strategist*, Winter 2008, pp. 22–24.

Murray, David. "Rules for Blogging at Sun: Don't Do Anything Stupid." Ragan.com (www.ragan.com), May 1, 2008.

Pogue, David. "Are You Taking Advantage of Web 2.0?" *New York Times*, March 27, 2008, www.nytimes.com.

Schmelzer, Randi. "Texting Helps PR Pros Maintain a Message's Impact." *PRWeek*, April 30, 2007, p. 11.

Sebastian, Michael. "Text Messages Help Communicators Reach New Audience." Ragan.com (www.ragan.com), January 15, 2008.

Spors, Kelly. "In Search of Traffic: A Website is Only As Valuable as the Number of People Who See It." *Wall Street Journal*, April 30, 2007, pp. R1, R4.

Vascellaro, Jessica. "Coming Soon to a Phone Near You." *Wall Street Journal*, March 31, 2008, pp. R1, R3.

Vranica, Suzanne. "Can Dove Promote a Cause and Sell Soap? Website is Devoted to 'Real Beauty' and Product Placement." *Wall Street Journal*, April 10, 2008, p. B6.

Walton, Susan Balcom. "Balance in the Blogosphere: Managing Responsiveness and Responsibility." *PR Tactics*, November 2007, p. 15.

Ward, David. "Live, from a Computer Near You. Webcasting Builds Brands and Thought Leadership." *PRWeek*, May 8, 2006, p. 18.

Worthen, Ben. "Dell, by Going Click for Click with Web Posters, Ensured Bloggers Saw Its New Red Mini Laptop." *Wall Street Journal*, June 3, 2008, p. B6.

Wright, Donald, and Hinson, Michelle. "Examining the Increased Impact of Social Media on the Public Relations Practice." Institute for Public Relations (www.instituteforpr.org), March 9, 2008.

Producing Newsletters and Brochures

13

TOPICS covered in this chapter include:

The Value of Print Publications   351

The Balancing Act of Editors   353

Newsletters and Magazines   358

Online Newsletters   368

Brochures   369

Annual Reports   378

Desktop Publishing   382

The Value of Print Publications

Several years ago, *The Wall Street Journal* announced in a page-1 headline that "Employee Newsletters Are Rapidly Becoming Obsolete." The article pointed out that organizations were switching to other communication tools—internal TV, e-mail, and Web pages—to inform employees and even external audiences.

Although organizations frequently use these communication vehicles, most professional communicators agree with Mark Twain who once said, "The reports of my death are highly exaggerated." Indeed, newsletters and magazines in print form—as well as brochures in countless formats—are still alive and well in the age of cyberspace. In fact, the highest circulation magazine in the United States—*AARP Magazine*—a bimonthly produced by the American Association of Retired People (AARP) for its members has a circulation of 23 million.

Printed publications will continue to be produced in vast quantities for several reasons. Many organizations, for example, still find them to be the most efficient method of reaching their entire workforce. This is particularly true of many companies that have field staff and plant workers who have limited access to electronic communications via computer. Walgreen's *World* magazine, for example, must be in print form, because about 150,000 of the company's 226,000 employees work in the stores and have limited access to computers on a daily basis. Readership studies have shown that 65 percent of these employees read the magazine during their 15-minute breaks or on their 30-minute lunch hour.

Gary Grates, now a top executive at Edelman Worldwide, offers a second reason why print newsletters and magazines continue to thrive. He says, "A print publication is unique; employees can hold it, touch it, mark it up, pass it around, take it home, and refer back to it." He quotes another senior communication executive who says, "There's just something about a well-written newsletter or magazine that gives you a real feel for an organization—it's not a feeling you get with e-mail or a fax or any of the more immediate types of communication."

Echoing this thought is Karen White, corporate communications specialist for Alpha Therapeutic Corporation. She told *PR Tactics*:

> There's something about a well-designed newsletter printed on quality paper that gives you a feel for an organization. It has a personality. This is something you can't communicate as easily on a computer. It's a way to recognize employees. Whether it's an employee anniversary, an award ceremony, or the winning softball team, people like to see their names and photos in print. When people appear in the employee newsletter, they want to take them home to their families and post them on bulletin boards at work. It's not as permanent with a video or computer message.

Indeed, one advantage of a print publication is its portability. Employees can easily pass the publication around to their family and friends in almost any situation, and a magazine often has a shelf life for long periods of time as it sits on the family coffee table or in the doctor's waiting room. The look and feel of print publications, coupled with the content, also make a powerful, positive impression on clients, prospective customers, and opinion leaders. In other words, a well-designed and well-written publication conveys the image that the organization is highly successful, well managed, and a market leader.

Accenture, for example, launched a new magazine for its employees when it began a campaign to reinforce its new brand positioning and personality. New typography, photos, and stories reflected and reinforced the idea that the company was composed of professionals who brought "insights, practical know-how, and integrated capabilities to help clients achieve success."

Although it is clear that print publications are not "obsolete," or doomed to extinction anytime soon, they are changing to accommodate the realities of the digital revolution. E-mail and the company **intranet** are excellent channels for giving late-breaking news and daily updates, but newsletters and magazines are better vehicles for in-depth analysis and feature articles. Gary Grates, quoted previously, says, "Today's employee publications are less about immediacy and more about providing analysis, rationale, and specifics. And the content reflects this; instead of news briefs and time-sensitive announcements, included are stories in depth, profiles and lighter feature articles."

Adding to this thought is Mary Hettinger, a communications specialist for Staples, Inc. She is quoted in *PR Tactics* as saying, "The role for printed publications should be to expand on news with more feature-oriented articles—describing the company's goals and direction; educating employees on the business they are in so they can excel; recognizing and profiling model employees; conveying the leader's personalities; showcasing how the company is a good corporate citizen. . . ."

It should also be recognized that print publications play an important role in driving readers to content on the Web. A print story might give the highlights of the

CEO's speech, but the story can also direct readers to the website where interested individuals can view the entire speech or selected video excerpts. In the same vein, a story on employee benefits can provide links to more detailed information. Thus, the "traditional" media and the "new" media continue to complement each other and have an interactive relationship. This means that the editors of these publications have several roles to play.

The Balancing Act of Editors

Editing a sponsored publication has been described as something of a high-wire act. You must produce a newsletter or brochure that advances and promotes management's organizational objectives and, at the same time, provides information that isn't boring to the audience. In addition, you have a responsibility to serve the interests of the employees or other constituents.

There is also the issue of editorial freedom. Many editors, particularly former journalists, think that they should have the right to decide what stories will be covered and in what context. They resent anything that smacks of editorial interference, including story ideas that support organizational objectives.

At the same time, management wants to exercise its rights as "publisher" of the newsletter; that is, the organization pays all the bills, including your salary. Charlotte Forbes, senior vice president of Stromberg Consulting, sums up the management perspective. She told *PRWeek*, "Corporations need to think of a newsletter as something that can inform, educate, and hopefully drive action, as opposed to being a reporter of facts, after the fact."

Indeed, editors need to balance the needs of management, the interests of readers, and their own journalistic standards. Some never do solve the dilemma and stick to folksy stories that please many and offend none. Actually, the balancing act can be done if the editor is able to understand that all three are interrelated.

Take company strategies and goals. These are usually based on broad concepts such as human resources, corporate image, business expansion, competitiveness, productivity, marketing, and economic development. Communication goals should be based on corporate goals, so the editor may decide to support the goal of increased competitiveness by publishing at least six stories during the year about the organization's market share and what factors are involved in making the organization more competitive.

These stories, if done well, should also interest employees, because they are concerned about job security and making sure that the company remains competitive. If the company is successful, it could also mean bonuses and higher pay scales.

Even if management has set broad or specific goals for the year, it is usually the editor who decides how the periodical can support each goal. In this case, the editor can choose any number of journalistic treatments, including the angle of what's in it for employees. Stories about competitiveness don't have to be propaganda. They can be written with the same degree of objectivity as any article in an independent publication.

A Mission Statement Gives Purpose

The best editors, the ones who regularly win awards, seem to understand the purpose of their publication and the interests of their readers. One technique is to develop a concise, simple mission statement of approximately 25 words that helps both editors and management understand the purpose of the publication. The statement should cover the publication's general content, its audience, and its strategic role.

The mission of *Saudi Aramco World*, a quarterly magazine published by oil company Saudi Aramco, is to increase cross-cultural understanding. The editors also place the following statement in the magazine's masthead: "The magazine's goal is to broaden knowledge of the cultures, history and geography of the Arab and Muslim worlds and their connections with the West." The high quality, four-color magazine is distributed free, upon request to interested readers. A cover from the magazine is shown Figure 13.1.

Another example is the goal of *Going for Great!*, published by GuideOne Insurance. The goal of the magazine is to "provide all targeted audiences with in-depth information about current business initiatives, strategic planning, industry changes and education, and other key data that contribute to GuideOne's success, while building trust throughout the organization."

Another premier publication is *Promise*, published by St. Jude's Chil-

FIGURE 13.1 *Saudi Aramco World* is a high-quality company publication that is sent to opinion leaders, libraries, and educators around the world. The well-designed, four-color magazine focuses on in-depth articles about the culture and history of the Muslim world. This edition, for example, featured articles about the Silk Road cities of Almaty and Tashkent; the background of a 17th-century French author who translated popular stories from the Islamic world; and the origin of black pepper along the Malabar coast of India, which was the most profitable seaborne cargo of the late Middle Ages. Aramco is an international consortium of oil companies that operates in the Middle East. The magazine's headquarters are in Houston, Texas.

dren's Research Hospital in Memphis, Tennessee. According to Elizabeth Jane Walker, publications manager:

> The magazine serves as the hospital's external platform to educate the public about the innovative research and excellent medical care happening at St. Jude. The publication tells the public who we are—a world-class biomedical research institution as well as children's hospital that treats patients regardless of their families' ability to pay. Promise puts a 'face' to our work—introducing readers to individual patients who benefit directly from the research and clinical care at St. Jude.

The PR Casebook on pages 356–358 shows the magazine's cover and the text of a feature story about a child whose life was saved.

Editorial Plans

It is also a good idea to prepare an annual editorial plan. Bobby Minter, of Publication Productions in New York, says you need to map out what kind of articles and other material you will prepare for the entire year. This will enable you to develop story ideas that complement the organization's objectives for the year. Bell Atlantic and NYNEX, for example, merged and faced the daunting problem of integrating a combined workforce of 140,000 employees. To energize and rally their support for the new company, corporate communications identified several key needs that could be addressed in various employee publications:

- The need to explain the strategies of the new Bell Atlantic and to illustrate how the company is using these strategies to be a leader in an industry undergoing constant, dramatic change.
- The need to communicate the ways in which Bell Atlantic is positioning itself against our competitors, and to point out how individual employees can support our efforts.
- The need to create a corporate source of information that could be the primary vehicle for news about the company and the industry—supplanting the external media and union sources that had become a principal source for some employees during the merge process.
- The need to quickly foster teamwork and enthusiasm about the new company among employees, many of whom had strong loyalties to their former company and harbored suspicions of being "taken over" by their merger partner.

The primary vehicle chosen for communicating these core strategies was *The Wave*, a four-page weekly tabloid, mailed to all employees. According to Ken Terrell, director of employee media for Bell Atlantic, "Virtually all of the material in *The Wave* is based on our core strategies. Our approach is to depict various groups and individuals that are successfully putting these strategies into action. We use devices such as highlight boxes, bullet points, special column headings, graphics, and **pull quotes** to emphasize key strategic information."

Magazine Puts a "Face" on Saving Children's Lives

The basic mission of *Promise* magazine, published by St. Jude Children's Research Hospital in Memphis, Tennessee, is to educate the public about the facility's research and medical care. Donors and prospective donors are an important audience for the magazine, so it develops feature articles showing how such support has helped save the life of a particular child. This puts a human face on the hospital's work, which helps generate financial support for the facility.

The following is a well-written, compelling feature about Anna Grace Davis that appeared in *Promise* magazine (see Fig. 13.2). One reader was so touched by the story that she donated $100,000 to the hospital. Anna's story was also used in general hospital fund-raising activities, which raised about $41 million in a single year.

Amazing Grace

From a roadside in rural China to the heart of a Mississippi family, the journey of Anna Grace Davis is just beginning.

By Ruth Ann Hensley

Draped in a luxurious feather boa, crowned with a silver jeweled tiara and daintily sipping tea as if the Queen Mother herself had instructed her, a young girl charms her admiring subjects. With a dramatic sweep of her hand and a prim toss of her head, she brushes back the regal, dark locks that cascade to her waist and instructs her court to "Drink more tea!" Her guests might assume that they're in the company of the heir apparent to a throne. Except that the boa is made from chicken feathers dyed purple, the crown is plastic, and the 5-year-old sipping imaginary tea has already won more battles than most royals have fought in a lifetime.

Anna Grace Davis was abandoned on the roadside of a rural community in southern China when she was only a day old. What may seem like a cruel deed may in fact have been the very act of kindness that set off a miracu-

▶ **FIGURE 13.2** A feature story on the care of Anna Grace Davis was featured on the cover of *Promise*, the quarterly magazine of St. Jude's Children's Research Hospital in Memphis, Tennessee. The compelling story, written by Ruth Ann Hensley, illustrates how a print publication can "humanize" and give a "fact" to an organization. It received a Bronze Anvil from the Public Relations Society of American (PRSA) in the feature writing category.

lous chain of events that has inspired, delighted, and amazed people from Memphis to Malaysia. The kindness, divine coincidence and incredible family support that have guided her life are proof that true princesses are made, not born. Anna Grace doesn't require sovereign rights to a kingdom, because her feisty charm has free reign over the hearts of everyone she meets.

The Long and Winding Road

"We bonded immediately," says her dad, Greg Davis, as he recalls holding Anna Grace in his arms the evening he and his wife, Nancy, stood in the Chinese consulate's office to finalize the adoption that had taken 22 months to complete. "There were seven couples with seven new babies in that office; six of the seven babies were screaming at the top of their lungs, and Anna had her head nuzzled right here in my neck," he says, tilting his head to the side.

A rare blood disease that nearly took Nancy's life in 1994 had led the couple to consider adoption when they decided to enlarge their family. Their biological son, Colton, was 8 years old when Anna Grace was adopted from an orphanage in Le Chang, China, where she was taken after being found on the roadside. In addition to dealing with the blood disorder, the family has dealt with a heart disease that has subjected Colton to four open-heart surgeries.

After weathering life-threatening storms of poor health and enduring months of frustrating international adoption delays, Greg and Nancy were ready to begin a new chapter in their lives the day they walked out of the consulate's office.

But less than a week after their arrival home, the couple began to notice a change in Anna Grace. "We thought she had an ear infection," Greg says. It turns out she did have an infection in both ears. But Anna was also losing the ability to sit up on her own, and one of her eyes had begun wandering inward. "Even though her ears were getting better, she was not," Nancy says. A pediatric ophthalmologist who examined Anna Grace indicated the eye problem might correct itself. But when the baby became less steady and began vomiting, the couple rushed her back to the pediatrician. This time the pediatrician ordered a CAT scan. By that point, Anna Grace couldn't sit up at all.

"We were driving home after the CAT scan and the pediatrician called us," Nancy recalls. "The pediatrician said, 'Where are you right now?' Greg said, 'We're driving down the interstate.' And he said, 'Well, you'd better pull over.' "

The Faith Factor

The CAT scan had revealed an orange-sized medulloblastoma tumor on Anna Grace's brain stem. The Davis family didn't go home that day; they immediately turned around and went back to the hospital, where Anna Grace underwent surgery to remove the malignant brain tumor.

"The first words out of the neurosurgeon's mouth were, 'This is every parent's worst nightmare,' " Nancy says. It wasn't a line they expected to read in the new chapter of their life, but the family pulled together.

"We've faced challenges before, and we've learned that what happens inside of you is far more important than what happens to you," Greg says. "The greatest expression of faith is to keep on going when you don't have all the answers, when you don't understand God's plan."

"We have a saying in our family," Nancy says. "You can get bitter, or you can get better." So the Davises decided they were going to get better.

(continues)

Anna Grace survived the complex, life-threatening brain surgery and was referred to St. Jude Children's Research Hospital, where the 13-month-old began 16 months of chemotherapy and a procedure called conformal radiation. This form of radiation is a precise treatment that sends radiation beams from several directions directly onto the brain tumor, killing it and sparing the rest of the brain from most of the harmful effects of radiation. St. Jude pioneered the use of this therapy in protocols for children with brain tumors.

"There were pages, typewritten pages, of the possible negative side effects of the treatment," Greg says, "ranging from mild to don't-even-talk-about-it."

Saving Grace

Not only did Anna Grace survive, but she thrived. She gained 12 pounds while she was in treatment. And most amazing of all, outside of hair loss, she suffered no ill side effects.

"And she did bald really well," Nancy says of her fashion-conscious daughter.

"Yeah, she had about a hundred hats," Greg says with a laugh.

For an infant to survive brain surgery and such an aggressive round of treatments with virtually no side effects such as loss of motor skills, hearing loss, and speech impediments is extremely rare.

"She really is the poster child for our treatment efforts," says Maryam Fouladi, MD, of St. Jude Hematology-Oncology, who monitored Anna's case throughout her treatments and sees her every 6 months for checkups.

■ Newsletters and Magazines

The content of periodicals, in broad terms, is news and information. That is why many of these publications are called *newsletters*—they essentially are messages from the organization to various publics who want news and information.

Civic and professional groups use newsletters to inform their members of upcoming meetings and events. Nonprofit organizations send donors and prospective contributors information about the agency's programs and needs and recognize the efforts of current volunteers.

Muse, the four-color magazine of the Health Museum (www.thehealthmuseum .org) in Houston, Texas, is an example of the multi-audience publication. *Muse* is sent to key groups who can influence the attendance and financial support of the museum, which include educators, families with children, donors, scouts, homeschoolers, corporations, health professionals, and anyone interested in the health and medical sciences.

Such a broad audience requires the publication to have creative design elements that have wide appeal. Consequently, the publication uses bright colors and interesting covers, such as the one shown in Figure 13.3. In this instance, the cover photo and headline referred to a story about a new exhibit regarding the human genome and the amazing world of human genes. Other brief stories gave information on

"Anna is the best of both worlds—she is cured of her disease, and she's functionally normal," Fouladi says. "Not only does that give faith and hope to other families, but it gives us, as doctors, hope that we're making some strides in moving toward that goal."

"It's been a joy to watch her grow up," says Jana Freeman, a clinical research associate in Hematology-Oncology. Freeman and the Davis family maintain a friendship that formed during Anna's treatments. "We are so grateful for stories like this," Freeman says.

The Davises are grateful, too, for the support of the St. Jude staff. "I can't imagine going through what we went through with our daughter anywhere else," Nancy says. "It's an amazing place."

Greg agrees. "These doctors are here for way more than a paycheck," he says. "It's a life mission. It's a calling for them to be here."

Greg would know about that sort of thing, since he's the pastor of a church. He says prayers from around the world, the decision to take things one day at a time and faith in God's plan brought their family together and made them stronger.

"I don't know what Anna Grace is going to do in life. But I do know that God went to an extreme amount of trouble to get her out of China, to get her here and to get her well," he says. Anna Grace's physician says that if the child had not been left on the roadside and adopted by the Davis family, she would not have survived her cancer.

"She wouldn't have lasted another month," says Fouladi, who describes the Davis family as phenomenal.

"It's interesting that her middle name should be Grace," Fouladi continues, "because that's what she is." ■

(1) upcoming summer camps, (2) membership benefits, (3) a calendar of upcoming exhibits, (4) a list of recent donors, and (5) a back page listing hours of operation and the current board of directors and advisors. The museum's outreach and innovative approach won it a PRSA Bronze Anvil award in 2008.

Meeting Audience Interests

Every sponsored periodical is unique, but there are some general guidelines that can be applied. The

FIGURE 13.3 Newsletters to multiple audiences must be creatively designed and highly graphic to attract readership and awareness. *Muse News,* published by the John P. McGovern Museum of Health and Medical Science in Houston, used the firm of Herring Design in Houston to come up with a new design that helped the museum launch a new brand identity and increase public awareness. The publication received a Bronze Anvil from the Public Relations Society of America in the newsletter category.

International Association of Business Communicators (IABC) and Towers, Perrin, Forster & Crosby, a consulting firm, surveyed 40 companies and 45,000 employees to determine what topics employees were most interested in. The top five choices were (1) the organization's future plans, (2) personnel policies and procedures, (3) productivity improvement, (4) job-related information, and (5) job advancement information. The last five choices on the 17-topic list were (1) personnel changes and promotions, (2) financial results, (3) advertising and promotion plans, (4) stories about other employees, and (5) personal news, such as birthdays and anniversaries.

Note, however, that the range of high to low interest was from 95 percent to 57 percent—still more than half for the last choice. The study does indicate, however, that today's employees are more concerned about the health and direction of their companies than they are about the fact that someone in the accounting department just celebrated a wedding anniversary or won a bowling tournament.

Michael C. Brandon, director of internal communication for Northern Telecom in Nashville, Tennessee, puts it more bluntly. He writes in IABC's *Communication World* that today's employee communications need to do more than make employees feel good. He continues:

> Communicators can no longer permit bowling leagues, birthdays and babies to dominate the pages of the company newsletter. Instead, employee communication must deliver business information critical to the organization's success. The most critical information employees need is about the organization's objectives. If employees are to maximize effectiveness, management must strive for alignment between the organization's goals and the individual objectives of the employees.

A survey of employees at one corporation by Dallas consultant Tom Geddie indicates that editors should always start with the assumption that employees want answers to the "what's-in-it-for-me" questions. The number one information concern for 30 percent of employees was the internal work environment and how their work was important to the company. Another 22 percent wanted to know about the company's financial health and the prospects for continued employment. Another 17 percent each were interested in information about improving the day-to-day work process and hearing about annual priorities and goals. It is clear that a publication's content should not only address management's objectives, but that the information must be relevant to the needs of the readers. The Tips for Success on page 361 gives some additional ideas for newsletter stories. How to package this content in an attractive, eye-appealing form is discussed next.

Design

More than one communications expert has pointed out that a publication's design should reinforce the content and also reflect the organization's personality. The idea is that content and design should work together to achieve a complete message.

Consequently, periodicals have distinct "personalities" that reflect their organizations. Reebok International has an employee tabloid that features modern typefaces, cutaway photos of athletes in action, and brown as a dominant second color. Stories are set in large type, ragged right, surrounded by a lot of white space. The publication, in sum, projects ruggedness and the great outdoors.

In contrast, *One Lime Street*, published by Lloyd's of London, is a 24-page newsletter with simple headlines, pages jam-packed with small type, and mug shots. It is a rather conservative publication, again reflecting the nature of the financial and insurance business.

Format

Newsletters are easy to produce, are cost-effective, and can reach any number of small, specialized audiences. Word processing programs such as MacWrite and Microsoft Word make it possible for almost anyone to produce a simple newsletter with mastheads, a two- or three-column format, and clip art or scanned photos. The use of desktop publishing software such as Microsoft Publisher, Illustrator, and InDesign is discussed shortly.

The most popular format for a newsletter is letter-size, 8.5 by 11 inches. Organizations from large corporations to the local garden club use two- to four-page newsletters to reach employees, customers, and members. A good example of such a newsletter is one from the National Wildlife Federation, which is shown in Figure 13.4. Although this format is workable, it has greater design limitations than the larger tabloid format, which is 11 by 17 inches. This format, often called a **magapaper**, allows a great deal of flexibility in design and can incorporate more graphic elements.

The magazine, usually in an 8.5- by 11-inch format, often is an organization's top-tier publication. Magazines are the most expensive to produce because they are printed on glossy paper, have up to 56 pages, and include multiple displays of computer graphics and full-color photographs. Accenture's magazine, mentioned previously, has an annual budget of $700,000. Boeing Co. spends $500,000 annually on its quarterly *Aero* magazine.

Magazines concentrate on in-depth stories about people and industry trends. Stories, unlike the shorter articles found in newsletters and newspapers, are much longer and tend to be more thoroughly researched.

In sum, you have the option of the standard newsletter, the magapaper, or the magazine. It all depends on the purpose of the publication, the kind of messages you want to send, and the target audience. Budget is a major consideration.

FIGURE 13.4 Organizations continue to prepare printed newsletters in the standard 8½- by 11-inch format that uses a two- or three-column format to display headlines, pictures, and text. In addition, organizations such as the National Wildlife Federation (NWF) also publish a print and online version of its monthly magazine. The NWF newsletter and the online magazine, shown above, are attractively designed to maximize readability and colorful graphics.

Layout

Layout is a plan showing the arrangement of the material in the publication—the size and location of such items as stories, regularly appearing columns, headlines, photographs, and artwork.

There is no exact rule for any of these items. The most important stories, of course, should be placed on the front page. If a story is fairly long, it can be continued on a later page. This offers two advantages. First, you can give several stories visibility on the cover if you continue stories on other pages. Second, continuing a story on an inside page encourages the reader to go beyond the first page. Another rule of thumb is to place important stories on the inside right page of a publication, because this is where people look first when they turn the page.

Most periodicals have a layout that is somewhat standardized, so that each issue of the publication has the same look and feel. This is called a **template**. A template starts with the **masthead**, or the name of the publication. It is always in the same type font and has the same graphics. Other items that may remain the same in every issue are the location of the major story on the front page, boxes giving a list of stories inside the issue, or the placement of a standard column or update of late-breaking news items.

The idea behind a template is that the readers rapidly learn where to find specific kinds of information in the publication. Readers of *Time* magazine, for example, know that the "People" section is now in the front of the publication, and the page has a highly recognized format that does not vary. Although the basic layout of a periodical should be the same from issue to issue, each issue will vary, depending on the length of the articles, the availability of good illustrations, and the relative importance of the stories.

Keep the following ideas in mind as you do the layout for a newsletter or magazine:

- Use white space. Don't think you need stories or illustrations covering every single part of the page.

- Vary paragraph length. If your copy looks as dense and forbidding as the Great Wall of China, your readers will be intimidated. Make paragraphs seven lines long or less to create even more white space.

- Break up longer stories with boldface subheads.

- Create bulleted lists. Any sentence containing a sequence of three or more items is a good list candidate. Listing also frees up more white space.

- Use only two or three typefaces, to give consistency to your periodical. The variety comes in using different type sizes, not a different type family.

- Keep articles relatively short for maximum interest. If *USA Today* can summarize a world crisis in four paragraphs, you can cover the company picnic in the same amount of space.

- Inside pages should balance one another. If you use a strong graphic on one page, you should balance it with a large headline or a graphic on the facing page.

- Use headlines that give information, not just labels such as "Company Picnic" or "New Vice President." (See the section on headline writing.)

A summary of how to create great publications is offered in the following Tips for Success.

The traditional method of layout, which is still helpful in this age of computers, is to work with a blank template and sketch out where stories, headlines, and artwork will be placed. This method helps you conceptualize the entire issue and how the various stories you have planned might be incorporated. This can be done with a sheet of paper and a pencil, or you can call up the template on the computer and sketch out the contents electronically. After the section on brochures, we will discuss the whole concept of desktop publishing—and all that it entails.

Photos and Illustrations

Photos and artwork were discussed extensively in Chapter 8. Many of the concepts presented there also apply to sponsored periodicals.

All publications need strong graphic elements to attract the television generation of readers. Photos must be tightly composed or cropped for impact, and a good photo should be used in as large a format as possible. A common criticism of organizational periodicals is that they use tiny photos awash in a sea of type. Another major criticism is dull and boring pictures. *Communication Briefs* gives a list of photos to avoid:

- "Look here!" Someone pointing to something somewhere in the distance.
- "Grip and Grin." Two people shaking hands, jointly holding a giant check or trophy and grinning at the camera.
- "Firing Squad!" Several people standing in a line and staring at the camera while holding their arms straight at their sides or even worse, using them as a fig leaf to cover their crotch.
- "Work!" A group of people gathered around a computer, pretending they are working on something while trying not to smile at the camera.

In addition, *Communication Briefs* says the best order is photo, headline, and text. Never place a photo at the bottom of the story. Justin Allen, writing for Ragan.com, makes another suggestion: "for every photo of execs shaking hands at expensive dinners and parties, include three photos of 'regular' workers hard at work."

Computer-generated graphics and imported clip art are commonly used in periodicals. Clip art is available in Microsoft Office, on CD-ROMs, or through Google Images (http://images.google.com) or other websites, such as iStockphoto (www.istockphoto.com). In addition, if you see something in another publication or book, you can use a scanner to import it into your computer. (Be certain not to violate copyright laws, which were discussed in Chapter 3.) A better use of scanners is to import graphic designs commissioned by the organization.

Headlines

Writing good headlines takes practice. The headline is an important component of any story for two reasons: (1) it attracts a reader to the article and (2) it's often the only thing they will read. According to *Communication Briefs*, 70 to 90 percent of readers look at headlines. Subheads attract 60 to 90 percent of the readers, and photos also rank high with the same percentage. About 40 to 70 percent will read a lead paragraph, but only 5 to 10 percent of the potential readers read the text of a story. In today's culture of information overload, headlines are the real workhorses of effective communication.

There are several rules or guidelines for writing a good headline. Mark Ragan, writing for *Ragan.com*, lists five basic rules:

- Use strong, active verbs.
- Readers want to know "What's in it for me?" so use that angle in the headline.
- Avoid acronyms; they slow down the readers and tax their brains.
- Use how-to headlines to help readers remember the key points.
- When appropriate, speak to readers informally by using "we" or "you."

The major mistake headline writers make is using headlines that are labels and don't say anything. Ragan gives the example of a headline from a major insurance company newsletter. It said, "Regional Structure and Focus Strengthened." Ragan, after reading the story and finding out what was actually being said, changed the headline to:

How restructuring will change our lives

We're hiring more workers and

delivering better customer service

Here are several other revised headlines from Ragan's story. The rewritten headline appears in boldface type:

UNICARE educates Kmart employees about insurance options

How We Matter: Our lower premiums helped Kmart's laid-off workers

E-Learning providing benefits on several Xcel Energy fronts

Online learning can cut your training time in half

Figure 13.5 gives some headlines from various newsletters and magazines. Notice the variety of styles, the use of smaller explanatory heads, and the active voice. You should also note that there are two styles of formatting. One format is known as **downstyle**, because the only the first word and proper nouns are capitalized, just as in a sentence. The second, which is more traditional, is capitalizing all major words in the headline. For example, "GM to Build Diesel Engines in Thailand." In the downstyle format, this would be, "GM to build diesel engines in Thailand."

In writing headlines that require two or more lines, you should avoid splitting ideas between lines. Here is one humorous example:

Pastor Leaves for Good

Friday Services at Prison

FIGURE 13.5 Most people read headlines, but rarely entire articles. Therefore, it is crucial for headlines to convey a key message. Here are some sample headlines from various publications. Notice that kicker heads and secondary headlines combine to give the essence of the story. They also are written in active, present tense.

New Faces, Bright Ideas

These talented Generation Xers were recruited for the ingenuity and initiative they bring to the company

HISTORY

Keep on truckin'

By Cornelia Bayley

A traveling museum-on-wheels celebrates the development of HP's inkjet printing technology.

A Bright Future

1,500 girls look ahead by joining their parents at work

Fast Response On Short Runs
Boscobel Opens To Serve Changing Marketplace

You should also avoid ending lines with a preposition. Here is a sample of a poor headline and how it can be changed:

POOR: Fredericks plans to take 6-month leave

BETTER: Fredericks to take 6-month sabbatical

After writing a headline, it is always a good idea to review it for context, use of the correct word, and whether it conveys the right impression. Here are several somewhat humorous headlines found in the nation's newspapers by the *Columbia Journalism Review*:

Students Recover from Fatal Crash

Survey: Seniors Having More Sex Than Thought

Luxury Models Do Poorly in Bump Tests

Local High School Dropouts Cut in Half

Red Tape Holds Up New Bridge

Panda Mating Fails; Veterinarian Takes Over

Writing headlines requires that you know the width of the space allocated for each headline. In a word processing software program, you simply set the margins and keystroke the headline you want. If it doesn't fit the space allocated to it in your mock-up or in the desktop publishing layout, you can easily enlarge or reduce it until it fits. Selection of type fonts will be discussed shortly.

Lead Sentences

The most important element, after the headline, is the lead sentence or paragraph. All too often, they turn off readers by being vague, mundane, and a tired old cliché.

Examples are "It's spring—a time of renewal—when the snow melts and the flowers bloom," or "A handful of member cooperatives are conducting public hearings that comply with provisions of the Energy Policy Act of 2005."

Contrast these leads with stories that are found in the mainstream press where the leads either arouse reader interest or state the essence of the story. A curiosity or human-interest lead from *The Wall Street Journal* about the cost of operating an RV, for example, was "At a fuel stop where drivers pay before pumping, Ted LeBaron recently surprised others in line when he asked the attendant for $300 worth of fuel. The guy behind me about came unglued," LeBaron says. Other stories require a straight news lead that tells readers the crux of the story without having to read much further. An example, again from *The Wall Street Journal*, was "General Motors said it will invest $445 million to build a diesel engine plant in Thailand and upgrade an existing assembly facility."

Bill Sweetland, writing for *Ragan.com*, believes that leads should do one or more of the following:

- Establish suspense by sparking curiosity
- Tell a story with strong human interest
- Avoid abstraction and vague, general terms, buzzwords, and clichés
- Establish the possibility of conflict or drama
- Use narrative to draw readers into the rest of the story
- Answer the what, why, when, where, who, and how with imagination
- Quickly establish the idea or theme that the writer wants to convey

For more information on writing leads, see Chapters 5 and 7.

Online Newsletters

Many organizations supplement their print publications with online newsletters. These are also known as **e-zines** (the hyphen is optional), and their primary advantage is the instant dissemination of information.

Unlike print publications that go through a number of production steps, editors of an e-zine do everything on the computer. With one mouse click, the newsletter is instantly sent via e-mail or an organization's intranet to everyone on the "subscriber" list.

The second advantage is cost. The cost of paper, printing, and postage is eliminated. An average printed newsletter might cost up to 50 cents per individual copy, whereas an e-zine typically costs less than 5 cents per "copy."

In sum, online newsletters are fast, efficient, and inexpensive. However, they do have limitations. Most rely on a simple format—text only, limited use of color, limited graphics, no photos or fancy design effects. This is because e-zines, especially those using e-mail as a distribution method, are received on a variety of e-mail systems around the world, many with limited graphic capabilities. Extensive graphics and color make the download time much longer.

According to *PRNews*, rule number one for online publications is to keep them short. It adds, "The whole document should be between three and five pages. Articles within them should be news-driven, not feature-y, and should only run a few paragraphs. Think bullet points that can link to a more in-depth article on your website."

Nabisco E, the weekly online newsletter of Nabisco Corporation, follows this advice. The maximum length of any story is 10 to 12 lines. The editor, Vic DePalo, says, "You do lose readers if you put in a long, complex story." According to the experts, readers rapidly tune out if they have to scroll through a long story or a multiple-page newsletter.

Because you have only about 10 lines, the writing style is more informal than in regular print publications. You can be more conversational and use less formal English than is expected in a print publication. This is not to say, however, that you don't need to craft well-written sentences. Every word counts, and it's important to keep sentences short and to the point.

Many corporations, however, have intranets for communicating with their employees. Essentially, an **intranet** works on the same principles as the Internet, but it is a private network within an organization for the exclusive use of employees and perhaps some other audiences, such as suppliers. Intranets, because they are closed systems and the technical standards are set by the organization, are able to produce much more sophisticated electronic newsletters.

A good example of what is possible on an intranet is the daily online publication of Hewlett-Packard Company (HP). *hpNow* is an attractive newsletter that includes (1) color, (2) graphics, (3) photos, and (4) links to thousands of archived pages that contain everything from past issues to news releases, speeches, organizational charts, and employee awards.

American Electric Power also operates a daily intranet newsletter for its 20,000 employees in 11 states. Stories are short and primarily text, but *AEP Now* is well designed

> **" Design is absolutely critical to making your intranet alluring, enticing, and successful. "**
> ■ William Amurgis, manager of intranet strategy for American Electric Power, as reported in *Ragan.com*

with minimum clutter and effective use of color. Its template also includes a photo of the day at the top of the home page that shows employees in various work situations. Increasingly, employee editors are also incorporating videos and podcasts into the company intranet.

Brochures

Writing brochures, like producing newsletters and magazines, requires the coordination of several elements. These include message content, selection of type, graphics, layout, and design. It also requires working with designers and printers.

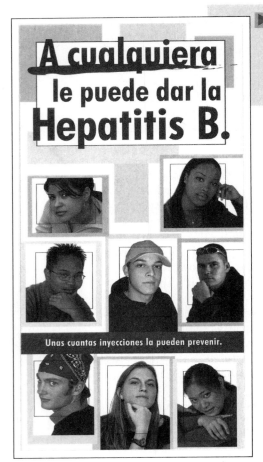

A cualquiera le puede dar la Hepatitis B.

Unas cuantas inyecciones la pueden prevenir.

▶ **FIGURE 13.6** The California Health and Human Services Agency uses simple but attractive brochures to reach Spanish-speaking populations in the state. This brochure, about Hepatitis B and why young people should get vaccine shots to prevent it, supplemented a campaign that also used movie ads, radio and television PSAs, and posters.

Brochures are often called *booklets*, *pamphlets*, or *leaflets*, depending on their size and content. A pamphlet or booklet, for example, is characterized by a booklike format and multiple pages. An example is the corporate annual report, required by the Securities and Exchange Commission (SEC), which is discussed shortly. A leaflet, however, is often described as a single sheet of paper printed on both sides and folded into three panels. A typical leaflet or brochure is shown in Figure 13.6. There are also handbills and flyers, which are printed on one side only and are often found on bulletin boards and a surprising number of telephone poles. For the purposes of this section, however, the term *brochure* will be used.

Brochures are used primarily to give basic information about an organization, a product, or a service. Organizations mail them or hand them out to potential customers, place them in information racks, hand them out at conferences, and generally distribute them to anyone who might be interested. Whenever an organization needs to explain something to a large number of people—be they employees, constituents, or customers—a brochure is the way to do it.

Planning

The first step in planning a brochure is to determine its objective. Such items are always prepared to reach a specific audience and to accomplish a definite purpose, so the following questions should be asked:

- Who are you trying to influence and why? Be as specific as possible in identifying the people you must reach.
- What do you want the piece to do? Be clear about the desired effect. Do you want to impress, entertain, sell, inform, or educate?
- What kind of piece do you need to get your message across? Should it be a simple flier, a pocket-size brochure, a cheaply produced leaflet for widespread public distribution, or a fancy four-color brochure for only key customers or opinion leaders?

Factors such as budget, number of copies needed, and distribution method must be considered. In addition, you should think about the method of printing. There are various levels of printing quality that you can use, depending on the answers to the above three questions. Authors Beach, Shepro, and Russom refer to four levels in their book, *Getting It Printed*:

- **Basic:** This is quick copy, such as fliers, simple business forms, and one-color leaflets. Copy shops such as Kinko's and PIP are commonly used.
- **Good:** This is material that requires strong colors, black-and-white photos, and exact alignment or registration of graphic elements.
- **Premium:** This requires a full-service printer, expensive paper, and high-end graphic elements.
- **Showcase:** Everything from design to paper and specialty inks is first class. Best for portraying an organization as well managed and successful.

Writing

Once you have a general idea of what format you will use to communicate with your audience, you need to think about how that format will shape your writing. If you decide that a simple flier is needed, you will have to be concise and to the point. Fliers, for example, contain the basic five Ws and H—and not much more, because the type must be large and the space (usually an 8.5- by 11-inch piece of paper) is limited. However, a simple brochure that has three to six panels folded to a pocket-sized format (4 by 9 inches) or that will be mailed in a standard business envelope (#10) can contain more detailed information. See the Tips for Success on page 372 for information on how to format a basic brochure.

Whatever the format, you should keep it in mind as you write copy. The most common mistake of novice public relations writers is to write more than the proposed format can accommodate. A second major mistake is to try to cram everything in by reducing type size or margins instead of editing, thus creating a mass of dense type that nobody wants to read. Indeed, the most difficult concept to learn is that less is best. Copy should be short and should have plenty of white space around it. This means ample margins, space between major subsections, and room for appropriate graphics.

The concepts of good writing, elaborated in previous chapters, are the same for brochures. Short, declarative sentences are better than compound sentences. Short paragraphs are better than long ones. Major points should be placed in bulleted lists or under subheads. It is always a good idea to pretest brochure copy on members of the target audience to be sure that it is understandable and that you have included all the necessary information.

> **Keep it (the brochure) short and sweet. The reader should be able to grasp the main points by simply glancing through the piece. If you bury your messages in a lot of heavy text, the reader may decide that it's too much work to read your brochure and throw it away.**
>
> - Christa Hartsook, communications specialist at Agricultural Marketing Resource Center, Iowa State University

Basic Brochure Design 101

The most common brochure format is the basic bi-fold brochure constructed by folding an 8.5-by-11 sheet of paper twice to create three panels on each side. Christa Hartsook, communications specialist for the Agricultural Marketing Resource Center at Iowa State University, offers the following basic brochure guidelines.

Front Cover

Don't just name your product on the front cover, or your logo. Instead, develop a theme that captures attention and interest. Use your theme as a headline for your front cover and repeat it throughout the brochure. Include a customer or reader benefit, clearly stated or implied.

Back Cover

Don't put anything on the back cover other than contact information. This is the panel that people are least likely to read, so if you put an important message there, it will be lost.

Inside Front Panel: First Panel You See When the Brochure Is Opened

This is the most important panel. Use it to summarize why the customer should choose you. It is a good location for a glowing testimonial. Although this is the most important panel, write it last. If you craft the inside spread first, you will have a better idea of what you want to summarize on the inside front page. The inside front panel is also a great place for your phone number, e-mail, or website URL.

Inside Three Panels

When the brochure is fully open, there are three full panels to write a description of your business and what it does. Carry the brochure theme over into your inside panels. Use images, subheads, captions, and body copy that continue your front cover theme throughout the brochure.

Hartsook also recommends that you edit and condense your original copy to make it more succinct and descriptive. A good brochure, she says, is like a conversation, not a manuscript. ■

Research ■ Gathering information for use in a leaflet or brochure may involve anything from asking a few questions to conducting a major survey. In most cases, the needed information can be found within the organization.

Keeping in mind the subject and purpose of the proposed publication, start by talking to the people in the organization who know the most about the subject. Tell them what you want to accomplish, and ask for information that will enable you to prepare a clear explanation of the subject. Often, all the information needed can be obtained from one source.

A good way to decide what to include in a brochure is to put yourself in the position of a member of the prospective audience. Ask every question that this person might have about the subject. The answers can constitute sections of the publication. You can even use the questions as subheads. Many successful brochures have consisted entirely of questions and answers.

Putting It Together ■ Brochures vary so widely that no general guide is applicable. Each has a different audience, a different purpose, and a different format. It is imperative to use words that your readers will understand. If you have to explain a technical topic, check with the experts once you have put the story into everyday English to be sure you've got it right. For any but the briefest publications, you will need to prepare an outline. This should cover all the main points to be included, and it should list the illustrations to be used.

As you write and plan the layout of the publication, remember to include visual variety in your pages. Illustrations, blocks of copy, and headlines not only serve the direct purpose of communication, but can also make the pages attractive and interesting. Some writers recommend preparing a complete layout before starting to write. Others prefer to develop the layout after the writing is finished. A practical compromise is to prepare a rough layout before writing and then to revise it as the writing progresses.

Format

Before deciding on the format of print materials, get samples of items like those you want to produce. Note how they were done and be guided by them. There are several basic formats, which have already been mentioned. The most basic brochure is six or eight panels folded, which is illustrated in Figure 13.7. Brochures with multiple pages, however, need to be bound. The binding may be **saddle-stitched**, which means the pages are stapled together on the centerfold. Magazines, for example, are usually bound in this way. If the booklet is large, it may be stapled on the side (**side-stitched**) or spiral-bound.

Preparing a Layout ▪ The layout is the plan for the finished piece. It may be rough or comprehensive, but it must be accurate enough for the person who assembles the parts to do exactly what you want. The first step in making a layout is to prepare a **dummy**—a blank-paper mock-up of the finished product. It should be made of the paper to be used in the printed piece and should be the same size. If the piece is to be a booklet, the dummy should be stapled just as the finished booklet will be. If it is to be a brochure, the dummy should be folded the same way.

With the dummy in hand, you can now plan where everything is to go. For a leaflet, the layout will be complete—it will indicate what is to go on each page. For a small booklet, the layout will also be complete, but if there are many pages you will need to design only the cover and sample pages of the body.

The layout indicates both type and illustrations. Thus, a page layout might show various blocks of copy, headlines, and the location of illustrations for that page. For very simple jobs, you may make the layout yourself; however, most printers are able and willing to do this for you, especially on big jobs.

Paper

The weight of the paper may range from very light (such as bond) to very heavy (such as cover stock). There is also a range of weights within these classes. Usually, the heavier the paper within a class, the more it costs. Thus a 100-pound cover is more expensive than a 50-pound cover. These weights are based on the

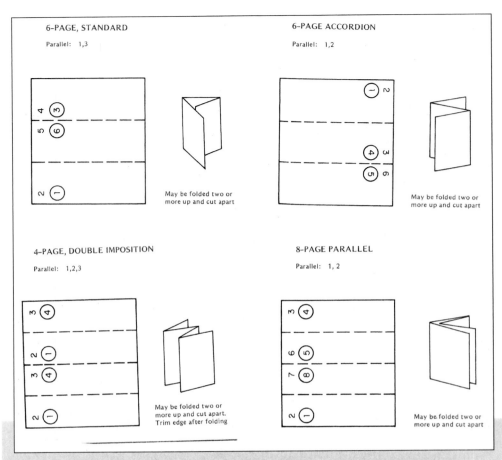

FIGURE 13.7 These diagrams show how a single piece of paper, printed on both sides, can be folded into four, six, or eight panels (or pages). Each panel has its own number. The circled "1" is the cover, and the "2" is the reverse panel. The illustration is from Baum Folder Company in Sidney, Ohio.

actual weight of 500 sheets of that paper in the standard sheet size. For your purposes, you need only remember that heavier paper is bulkier, stronger, and more expensive.

The intended use will guide you in selecting the weight of paper. A simple one-page flier might be printed on 20- or 24-pound bond. If you want it to be more substantial, you could use a 65-pound paper. Brochures are usually printed on fairly substantial paper. This makes them look more impressive and last longer. Another thing to consider is the total bulk of the item. If you choose a heavy paper for a booklet that is to be mailed, you may have to pay more for postage. Still another thing to bear in mind is folding; for example, heavy paper does not fold as readily as lighter paper.

There are seven types of paper, according to Media Distribution Services (MDS), that you are most likely to use. They are

- **Bond** for lightweight directories, letters, business forms, newsletters, and quick printing.
- **Text** for a textured look on annual reports, announcements, books, and calendars.
- **Coated** for a smooth, high-quality look on brochures, magazines, and posters. Coated, or glossy, paper is ideal for photographs and color printing. (See Figure 13.7 for a brochure printed on coated paper.)
- **Book** for an antique or smooth finish on trade and textbooks. Less expensive than text paper.
- **Cover** for a stable, durable quality to complement text and coated papers for covers and booklets.
- **Tag** for good bending and folding qualities. Good for pamphlets that have several folds.
- **Bristol** for a softer surface than tag or index paper. Good for high-speed folding, embossing, or stamping.

There are a number of variations on these basic types, and printers have entire shelves of paper samples from a wide range of manufacturers. Printers are experienced in what papers work best for various jobs, and you should ask them for their recommendations. Paper usually represents 35 to 50 percent of the printing cost for most jobs, so you should take care in selecting paper that is appropriate to your budget and needs. Prices for coated or textured paper, as indicated, are higher than prices for standard stocks of bond or Bristol papers.

Another option is recycled paper. Increasingly, organizations are using such paper for newsletters, stationery, office forms, and brochures. In fact, one survey of public relations people indicated that 90 percent of them had selected recycled paper for printing documents. The main reason for selecting recycled paper was concern for the environment. A large percentage of respondents also thought that it benefited the organization's image.

Type Fonts

There are several ways in which to classify type, but the simplest is to organize the various faces into three groups: serif, sans serif, and decorative.

- **Serif types,** such as Times Roman, Caslon, or Century Schoolbook, are the most readable because the serifs help guide the eye along the lines of type.
- **Sans serif types,** such as Helvetica, are popular. Some of the earlier types in this group were hard to read in body copy but quite satisfactory in headlines. The newer designs seem to work well for text copy, too.
- **Decorative typefaces,** such as Script and Old English, should be used with great care. They look elegant on certificates and invitations, but they should not be used for large blocks of text.

Type Families ■ Thanks to computer graphics, laser printer postscript cartridges, and desktop publishing programs, any number of typefaces are available in countless variations. Among the possibilities are Times Roman, Helvetica, New Century Schoolbook, Avant Garde, and Palatino. A large number of decorative typefaces are available that have shading, stripes, and ultramodern designs.

One note of caution: People are so impressed with the variety of type styles available that they try to use too many in a given publication. Novice desktop publishing enthusiasts tend to go overboard, and the result is a mishmash of conflicting styles that almost guarantees reader confusion.

Printers' Measurements ■ The beauty of word processing programs such as Microsoft Word is that they offer a variety of type fonts that are scalable to any size. In desktop publishing, you can select one type style and size for the headline and another type and size for the body text. If a headline or text copy doesn't quite fit the layout, a few clicks of the mouse will reduce it until it fits. Of course, you have to consider readability, which is discussed shortly.

We are so used to just clicking on a type size such as 14, 16, 24, 36, etc., that some historical background is needed. Printers have always measured type size in **points**; long ago, the standard was 72 points to the inch. In other words, a 72-point headline is 1-inch high. A 36-point headline is ½-inch high. And, of course, copy set in 18-point is ¼-inch high.

Many printers still measure the length of a typeset line by **picas**. There are 6 picas to an inch, so a 24-pica line is 4 inches wide. Note, however, that many experts say column widths should be no more than 12 to 14 picas and no fewer than 8 picas. Picas are also used to measure the depth of a block of copy. Thus, a story that is 42 picas deep will measure 7 inches.

Desktop publishing software has eliminated the need to be totally conversant in points and picas, but you should be familiar with the terms and what they mean when you are talking with a printer.

Readability ■ Legibility is affected by the typeface. Times Roman is more legible than Old English. Readability is affected by the legibility of the type and by letter spacing, line spacing, the length of the lines, the color of paper and ink, the kind of paper, and the total amount of reading matter involved. A brochure could be effective with headlines in 18- or 24-point Times Roman, but using this size type for body text in a 16-page booklet would not work.

The only purpose for printing anything is to get it read. Accordingly, any print material should be planned with readability in mind. Select a legible type and, if necessary, use letter spacing to spread headlines. Use line spacing to improve the readability of lowercase body copy. Keep the length of lines short enough that each can be read as one unit. As a general rule, try to use type no smaller than 10 point for text copy. If your target audience is over 50 years old, you might want to use 12-point, or even 14-point, type.

Ink and Color

Technological advances in printing now make it easy and economical to use color in all kinds of publications. The use of color, either by choosing colored paper or various inks, not only makes the publications more attractive, but studies show that it improves reader comprehension and a willingness to read the material.

Mario Garcia, a nationally known graphic designer, told *PR Tactics*, "The color is the first thing people notice when a publication lands on their desk. People attach meaning to the publication based on the colors they see."

In many respects, color also conveys the image and values of the organization. If the organization is somewhat conservative and traditional, it's best to stick with soft pastels and earth colors. Garcia, for example, used champagne and sky blue shades when he redesigned *The Wall Street Journal*. This approach also is more pleasing to an older and more traditional audience, which the newspaper serves. In contrast, *USA Today*, with a younger audience and considerable reliance on newsstand sales, uses a lot of bright colors throughout its pages to attract readers.

Color is used in photos, graphics, headlines, background screens (text boxes), and even body type. A good example of effective color is the magazine of GuideOne Insurance, *Going for Great!* A two-page article about drunk driving and underage drinking, for example, used light pink as a background screen with the body text in dark blue. The headline and subheads were in red ink, so the light pink was simply a 10- or 20-percent screen of this basic color. A one-line kicker headline was in white reversed through a screen of dark blue, which matched the body text.

Having used this example of color, it is important to note that black continues to be the most often used color for body text in newsletters, magazines, and brochures. There are two reasons for this. First, black provides the strongest and clearest contrast on white or pastel paper. In other words, black type is much easier to read than text in hot pink or another vivid color. Second, printers typically have presses set up for black ink, so the cost is less than that for using multiple colors.

With any ink, however, you must consider the color of the paper on which it will be printed. No color will read well against a dark-colored stock. Black ink on dark green paper, for example, makes the copy almost impossible to read and causes eye strain. Consequently, the best choice is white paper or something in a pastel or neutral shade.

Listen to the advice of your designer and printer. They are much more knowledgeable about how inks and paper go together for maximum effectiveness and readability. A printer's input is particularly important if you plan to use full-color photography.

Finding a Printer

A variety of printers and printing processes are found in every city. In even the smallest town, there is likely to be at least one printer who does offset printing.

Having located some prospects, you should meet with them to discuss your particular needs and their capabilities. Look at samples of their work. Find out what various services cost. It is particularly important to find out what software publishing programs they use and what format is preferred for submission of copy and artwork.

Most printers today are computerized, and the most common software programs used are InDesign, Quark Xpress, and PhotoShop. Therefore, if you are submitting digital files to them via e-mail or CD-ROM, they should be compatible with the printer's system. The computers of most commercial printers, for example, can't

How Much Will It Cost?

Printers need detailed specifications before they can tell you how much your publication will cost. Media Distribution Services in New York says you should be prepared to provide the following information when you contact a printer:

- Size of piece
- Print quantity
- Number of colors
- Type and quantity of photos and illustrations
- Number of folds
- Whether there are "bleeds"
- Type of binding
- Quality and weight of paper
- Whether there will be die cuts or embossing
- Delivery deadlines

It's also a good idea to show printers a "dummy" or sample of what your piece will look like, so they can see what you require. This preliminary "look-see" will help the printer spot potential problems. ■

read files created on programs such as Microsoft Publisher or PrintShop. You also have to ask whether a printer's system is PC- or Mac-based.

You should get bids from several printers to get the most value for your money. Printers, in order to give you a cost estimate, will ask you to give them all the specifications of the publication you are planning. See the Tips for Success on this page for a list of specs that printers will need.

Annual Reports

The most expensive and time-consuming publication prepared by an organization is the annual report. Although it is called a "report," it really is a major brochure complete with photos, charts, text, and color that can run up to a hundred pages.

Much of the information in such a report is mandated by the Securities and Exchange Commission (SEC) as a way to ensure corporate accountability to shareholders. All this legal and financial material, of course, is a fairly dry accounting of how the company did in a previous year, so corporate annual reports often use bar graphs, pie charts, and color to make the report readable and interesting to the average reader.

Many companies also use the annual report as a marketing tool to build stockholder loyalty, attract new investors, recruit employees, recognize current employees, and even increase their customer base. As Bob Butter, associate director of Ketchum's global practice told *PRWeek*, "The annual report is still a company's most rounded corporate capability presentation."

If you work on an annual report, you'll primarily be involved with the nonfinancial part. The report may consist largely of tables, but it is more interesting if it contains items such as a letter from the CEO or details about the products or services and the people who make or perform them. The report might also include information on new product innovations, expansion into new markets, and how the corporation is engaging in social responsibility and environmental matters.

> " *Annual reports—when done right—provide a single document for companies to present their investment case to investors, offering a company's strategy and mission.* "
>
> ■ Fred Bratman, president of Hyde Park Financial Communication, as quoted in *PRWeek*

Another approach is what might be called "storytelling," incorporating short features about employees and their work or customers who have benefited from the organization's products and services. The first half of Johnson & Johnson's 2007 report, for example, was a series of short stories and photographs of people who have benefited from J&J's products and community involvement. FedEx took a similar approach with its 2007 annual report. One entry, with a large photo, simply said "With freight delivery options that match speed to need, FedEx keeps Borders employees selling books rather than waiting for trucks."

Most annual reports are still prepared in print form and mailed to investors and stockholders. Traditionally, companies were required by the SEC to automatically mail the annual report to all stockholders, which may be several million for some corporations, such as GM. A new SEC rule in 2008, however, now allows corporations to mail reports only to those stockholders who request one. The change in requirements was, in part, due to the widespread availability of the annual report on an organization's website.

The readers of annual reports are of two sorts: the nonexpert individual and the sophisticated financial analyst. The amateur is interested mainly in the quality of the management, earnings, dividends, stock appreciation, and the outlook for the industry. The experts—who advise investors or manage large holdings—want much more information, which they feed into their computers. This difference in information needs presents the organization with a problem. A few hundred people want great masses of data, whereas thousands don't want the detail.

A common solution is to design an annual report that gives the financial highlights in easy-to-read charts and graphs at the beginning of the report. This section is often labeled "Financial Highlights." Abbott, a pharmaceutical firm, took this approach in its 2007 report, which is shown in Figure 13.8. The first half of its 80-page report contains simple charts, large type, and plenty of photos of satisfied customers to highlight the "Year in Review." The

FIGURE 13.8 A public company's annual report is the most time-consuming and expensive single publication that is produced during the year. The Securities and Exchange Commission (SEC) requires basic financial data, but many companies, such as Abbott, a pharmaceutical firm, also use the annual report to showcase how their products and services are making a difference in people's lives. The cover photo emphasizes the human dimension of featuring a child helped with a drug developed by the company. The inside cover gives the story: "Swimming is a big part of 5-year-old Arden Cantwell's life. Unfortunately, so is cancer. As part of Arden's ongoing treatment, she needs regular blood transfusions. With its unique automated processing technology, Abbott Prism ensures the safety of her donated blood, allowing Arden to enjoy her swimming lessons."

second half, however, is a mass of small type and many financial tables, which meets the requirements of the SEC and Wall Street analysts.

Planning and Writing

An annual report usually covers every aspect of the organization. Consequently, every department head may want input, and each may have different ideas. The task of the public relations people involved is to coordinate, plan, consult, write, design, and produce the report. Tact, perseverance, and determination to get the job done are essential. In fact, Ragan Research notes that "The majority of editors, with the most crucial print document that their organizations put out, dread annual report time like the flu season."

Work on the report may start 6 months before the date of issue. A first step is to establish a budget. Glossy, four-color reports can run $3 to $5 a copy, so it is important to know how many copies you will need. With a budget established, you can start planning the report. First, you should look at the last report; compare it with those of other organizations; criticize it; think of ways to make it more informative, more understandable, and more useful. One useful tool is focus groups with analysts and stockholders to find out what they want to see in your upcoming annual report.

There are many sources of information that should be tapped for possible use in writing the report. Especially critical are internal reports, planning documents, market research findings, and capital budgets. You should also review the 10-K (annual) and 10-Q (quarterly) reports filed with the SEC.

When you have enough information, you can start consulting with key executives and establishing a theme for the report. Basically, the objective is to inform, but a theme makes the report more interesting and focused. Usually, it focuses on some aspect of the business that the company wants to showcase that particular year. The theme of many corporate annual reports, after the Enron scandal and intense public scrutiny of executive misdoing, was corporate responsibility and accountability. Other examples of themes were "Toward a Healthier World" (Pfizer) "A Promise for Life" (Abbott), "Caring Transforms" (Johnson & Johnson), and "Creating New Value" (Coca-Cola).

When the theme is established, it is time to think of design—how the report will look, what will be included, how the various elements will be treated. You can get some useful ideas by studying the reports that are cited each year by the Financial Analysts Federation.

Design, to a large degree, depends on what the corporation wants to communicate. If it wants to project an image of success and dominance in the marketplace, the report may be a dazzling display of glossy paper, color, and state-of-the-art graphics. However, if the company did not do so well the previous year, there is a tendency to use only one or two colors, simple graphics, and plain paper, so stockholders don't think the company is wasting money. Beth Haiken, vice president at the PMI Group, says it best. In a *PRWeek* interview, she said, "In a good year, more color, photos, or unique design features won't seem out of place. In a bad year, lean and clean is best."

Trends in Content and Delivery

Annual reports change with the times. They are considered the most important single document a public company can produce, so a great amount of attention is given to content, graphics, and overall design. The objective is to ensure that the annual report reflects corporate culture and external economic conditions.

Several key themes in corporate annual reports are apparent:

- **Candor and frankness.** Global competition has caused the shrinkage of corporate profits and major dislocations in many industries. Consequently, many corporations are more candid in their annual reports. St. Paul Insurance Company, for example, told annual report readers, "The relentless parade of storms and floods produced the second-worst total catastrophe loss in our 144-year history."

- **Corporate governance and accountability.** All corporations are under intense public scrutiny because of major scandals in financial reporting and executives receiving benefits in the millions of dollars. Consequently, many companies are being more transparent in their annual reports. Pittsburgh-based utility, DQE, even had a code of ethics in its report signed by the senior executives.

- **Websites.** Most companies now make their annual reports, often with video excerpts from the annual meeting, available online. One advantage is savings on postage and paper costs, but this doesn't mean that the print version is going out of fashion. There are several reasons for this. First, financial analysts and portfolio managers still request a printed annual report to review prior to meeting with the company's management. Second, a printed report has a beginning, middle, and an end that makes it an easy-to-follow narrative that avoids the disjointed pages and links of a website. Third, a printed report represents a tangible item that often projects the human side of an organization better than looking at the same material in digital form.

- **More emphasis on marketing.** Today, the annual report is also used as a marketing tool to increase consumer loyalty and build the company's image. HP, for example, spent most of one report showing how various businesses and individuals benefited from using HP products.

- **Readability.** Annual reports are becoming more magazine-like, with summary headlines, easy-to-understand charts and graphs, simple question-and-answer sections, and more conversational prose. This reflects the growing trend of distributing the annual report to a variety of publics—customers, current and prospective employees, suppliers, community opinion leaders, and others.

- **Environmental sensitivity.** In an effort to portray themselves as environmentally conscious, many organizations use recycled paper and soy-based inks for annual reports. In addition, annual reports are becoming shorter, saving more trees. RPM's annual report, for example, made a major point that 30 percent of the paper used came from recycled material.

- **Corporate social responsibility (CSR).** The public now expects corporations to be good citizens and to make a contribution to society. Consequently,

Pakistan
Corporate Social
Responsibility
Report 2007
www.siemens.com.pk
SIEMENS

FIGURE 13.9 Many corporations are now publishing extensive brochures about their corporate social responsibility (CSR) activities as a complement to their traditional annual reports. This is the cover of the CSR report for Siemens Corporation, which has operations in Pakistan. The 30-page report gives a summary of the corporation's contributions to such projects as earthquake relief, the volunteer work of employees, equipment donated by Siemens, and how the company is ensuring environmental health and safety in its Pakistan manufacturing plants.

corporations now include a summary of their CSR activities in their annual reports, or even take the step of producing another major brochure that exclusively focuses on CSR. A good example is Siemens Corporation's description of CSR activities in Pakistan (Figure 13.9).

- **Global approach.** Corporations now have global operations, and the annual report functions as a capabilities brochure that markets a company on a worldwide scale. Some companies even translate parts of their annual report into several languages. The chairman's letter in Nike's annual report was translated into French, Spanish, and Chinese.

Desktop Publishing

The term "layout" is more accurate than "publishing," because desktop software programs don't "publish" anything; what they do is allow a person to provide a commercial printer with electronic files that, when linked together, provide the text, artwork, photos, and design of your publication.

Today, practically all newsletters, magazines, and brochures are produced through desktop software programs. The biggest advantage of desktop publishing, according to most surveys, is keeping control over the stages of publication preparation, from the writing of copy to camera-ready output.

Desktop software allows you to manipulate text and artwork in a number of ways. You can (1) draw an illustration and then reduce or enlarge it, (2) use different type fonts and sizes, (3) vary column widths, (4) shade or screen backgrounds, (5) add borders around copy, (6) import graphics and photos from other sources, and (7) print out camera-ready pages that can be photocopied or printed on an offset press.

Several levels of desktop publishing software are available. At the very basic level, Microsoft Word or Apple's word processing program has templates for creating basic newsletters and fliers. With a scanner and some creativity, you can create simple documents that are quite adequate for the local garden club or a campus club.

The second level is programs such as Microsoft Publisher or Apple Pages, which give you increased capability to design newsletters, brochures, and banners using an extensive library of layout templates and clip art. Small businesses and real estate agents who might need a neighborhood newsletter or a flier announcing an event often use these user-friendly software programs to create materials that can be produced in limited quantities on a personal printer or at the local photocopy shop.

The third, and most sophisticated, level are programs such as Adobe's InDesign and PageMaker. Another is Quark Xpress. They often are used in conjunction with high-level illustration programs such as Adobe Illustrator, Freehand, and Photo-Shop. Most commercial printers and professional designers use these programs. If you are submitting electronic files to a printer, you need to make sure you are using compatible software.

Although desktop publishing has made it possible for public relations writers to do their own layouts and to prepare materials in a more attractive manner, experts caution that you need more than writing skills. You also need design and layout skills to come up with a camera-ready layout that meets professional standards. As one public relations practitioner observed, "These skills are not necessarily found in a single person under normal circumstances."

In other words, having access to sophisticated software and computer hardware is not a substitute for well-trained technicians and graphic designers who know what to do with the technology. Not everyone is a good designer, and one of the by-products of desktop publishing is the "garbage dump document," put out by people who know nothing about design. In many cases, they are so bedazzled by the technology at their fingertips that they commit the sin of using a dozen typefaces in a single newsletter.

There's also the question of how you want to spend your time. You can write and edit the copy, take all the photos, design the periodical, and prepare the camera-ready artwork—but that doesn't leave much time for other public relations duties.

Consequently, public relations writers often work closely with professional designers who are responsible for putting all the components of a publication together. Good communication and understanding between an editor or writer and the designer are important. Heather Burns, a communications consultant, gave several suggestions in an interview with *Ragan.com*:

- Include the designer at the beginning of the content development process so there is an understanding of the entire production process and what kinds of stories are being planned.

- Discuss the publication's purpose, strategy, and target audience so the designer has a framework in which to work.

- Write creative and interesting copy. Burns says, "If the writer gives the designer something fun to read, it's a lot easier for the designer to design something fun to look at."

- Don't confuse effective design with creative design. A design may be very creative from an artistic standpoint but not very effective if words get lost and readers can't easily find the information they want.

Summary

- Printed materials, such as newsletters, magazines, and brochures, are still important communication channels in the Internet age.

- Two strengths of print publications are that they can feature in-depth stories and they can reflect the "face" of the organization. Other strengths include portability and an extended shelf-life.

- An editor must balance management expectations, employee needs, and journalistic standards.

- A publication's format and content should reflect the organization's culture, goals, and objectives.

- Today's employees want periodicals that address their concerns about the economic health of the organization and their job security.

- Every publication should have an overall mission statement. An annual editorial plan outlines the kind of stories and features that will support the organization's priorities.

- The newsletter is the most common organizational publication. Magazines usually are the most expensive publication and are often sent to both internal and external audiences.

- Headlines should be written in active voice and provide key messages.

- Online newsletters sent on an organization's intranet system often contain more color, graphics, and photos. Newsletters sent via e-mail tend to use fewer graphics and have stories 10 to 12 lines long.

- Brochures vary in format and size from a single sheet of paper folded into panels to multiple-page pamphlets and booklets.

- Writing and designing a brochure requires you to know its purpose, the target audience, and the most cost-effective format.

- A brochure requires simple sentence construction, informative headlines, liberal use of subheads, and short paragraphs.

- The most common mistake of novice writers is to write too much copy for the space available. A brochure page crammed with type is a turnoff.

- Factors such as cost, distribution, and estimated life span of the brochure help determine the format of the printed piece and the kind of writing required.

- It pays to prepare a dummy or mock layout of the brochure before you begin writing.

- Offset lithography is the most versatile and popular form of printing today.

- A printer needs to know all the specifications of a planned piece before he or she can give you a cost estimate.

- There are various grades of paper, each designed for specific kinds of jobs.

- There are various type classes and families. Stick to fonts that are highly readable. Use decorative type and italics sparingly.

- Black ink is the most popular and readable color. Use spot color to make your publication more attractive.

- Although you may be able to write and design a simple flier or brochure, experts recommend hiring a professional graphic designer for bigger jobs.

- Annual reports require considerable planning, resources, and design expertise. It is probably the single most expensive document that an organization produces.

- Desktop publishing is now widely used for preparing newsletters, magazines, and brochures. Desktop publishing requires the preparation of extensive electronic files that show the links between copy, graphics, photos, headlines, and layout.

Skill Building Activities

1. Collect three or four copies of an organization's employee newsletter or magazine. Write a critique of the publication regarding its content and design, using the guidelines and advice given in this chapter. If you were the editor, what changes would you make in the content or design?

2. You have just been hired as the editor of a new monthly magazine for the local hospital. The magazine will be mailed to potential donors, doctors, community leaders, and employees. Write a 25-word mission statement for this publication. Then prepare a 12-month editorial plan, giving your ideas about the type and content of stories that you would publish each month

3. Your manufacturing company has just received a $750,000 contract to produce and install solar panels for a new office building being built in your city. This contract ensures full employment at your plant and the recruitment of another 50 workers. What headline would you write for the employee newsletter?

4. Collect some brochures produced by various organizations. Based on the guidelines suggested in this chapter, write a critique of each brochure from the standpoint of content, format, and design. Mention what you like about each brochure, and what you would change.

5. Write and design a simple brochure for a campus organization. Use the format of a 4-inch by 9-inch brochure with six panels. See the Tips for Success on page 364 for some guidelines.

Suggested Readings

Allen, Justin. "Six Ways to Improve Your Internal Publication." *Ragan.com* (www.ragan.com), November 30, 2007.

Badeusz, Katie. "Design for Nondesigners: 10 Dos and Don'ts." Ragan.com (www.ragan.com), May 30, 2008.

Jorgensen, Linda B. *Real-World Newsletters to Meet Your Demands.* Alexandria, VA: EEI Press, 1999.

McGuire, Craig. "Looking At More than Just the Numbers: Annual Reports Can Include Some Different Features." *PRWeek*, February 18, 2008, p. 45.

Morton, Linda P. *Strategic Publications: Designing for Target Publics.* Greenwood, AZ: Best Books Plus, 2006.

Ragan, Mark. "How to Write Headlines that Scream Read Me." *Ragan.com* (www.ragan.com), January 28, 2008.

Sweetland, Bill. "Intranet Design Reigns Supreme at American Electric Power." *Ragan.com* (www.ragan.com), February 8, 2008.

Ward, David. "Employee Publications Get Online Boost." *PRWeek*, December 3, 2007, p. 11.

Weiner, Richard. "Everything You Always Wanted to Know About Magazine Lingo." *PR Tactics*, April 2007, p. 7.

Woodward, Cheryl. *Starting and Running a Successful Newsletter or Magazine.* San Francisco: Business Publishing, 5th edition, 2006.

Woolf, Gordon. *How to Start and Produce a Magazine or Newsletter.* Gainesville, FL: FAP Books, 2004.

Writing E-mail, Memos, and Proposals

14

TOPICS covered in this chapter include:

The Challenge of Managing
    Communication Overload   386

E-Mail   387

Memorandums   393

Letters   395

Proposals   398

The Challenge of Managing Communication Overload

The public relations writer doesn't always communicate with a large, impersonal audience. He or she also communicates on a more personal level through e-mail, memos, letters, phone calls, and face-to-face communications.

In fact, public relations personnel spend a large percentage of their working day engaging in interpersonal communications. They are constantly sending, receiving, and replying to e-mail, summarizing the results of client or management meetings, answering voice mail messages, sending memos to colleagues, writing proposals, preparing position papers, and—at certain times of the fiscal year—are heavily involved in preparing the organization's annual report. All this takes organization, efficiency, and communication skills.

It takes a lot of time to just read all the messages that inundate us, but it also takes considerable time to organize, write, and send all those messages. In many cases, public relations writers are major contributors to information clutter, because their jobs involve the writing and dissemination of so many messages. The problem is best expressed by Richard E. Neff, a consultant in Belgium, who writes in *Communication World*, "Writers waste too much time producing texts that waste even more time for readers."

The solution, he says, is to "write smart, simple, and short." Neff continues, "When people write letters and reports that are clear enough and simple enough and accurate enough and short enough—the time it saves the reader is immense." In other words, you should follow the basic guidelines of clarity, completeness, conciseness, correctness, courtesy, and responsibility in all your writing:

- **Completeness.**   Whether you are writing a 10-line memo or a 32-page annual report, you must be certain that it contains the information needed to serve its purpose. Ask yourself why you are writing and what your reader wants or needs to know. If more information will aid the reader's understanding, provide it—but don't give your reader a mass of irrelevant material. An outline will help to ensure that your message is on target and complete.

- **Conciseness.** *Less is better.* Conciseness means brevity. Your objective is to be as brief as possible, because people don't have the time or the patience to read through long messages. This means that you need to carefully select words that convey ideas and thoughts in a concise manner. If *USA Today* can summarize a major news event in four paragraphs, so can you.

- **Correctness.** You must be accurate in everything you write. If an item in the mass media contains an error, the blame may be spread among many people. An error in a personalized communication, however, reflects solely on you and your abilities. Be sure that what you prepare is accurate, and you will get credit for being a professional.

- **Courtesy.** These are *personal* communications. Personal names are used extensively, and both senders and receivers have considerable interest in the material. You might think it advisable to make the messages as personal as possible, but don't go overboard. The writing should be polite, but not effusive, personal, but not overly familiar.

- **Responsibility.** Be prudent and think about how your communication will be perceived by the recipient. A letter or e-mail is a highly visible record of what you say, so be careful about setting the right tone. Do you come across as flippant, arrogant, or defensive? Or do you come across as helpful, sympathetic, and concerned? You are representing your employer or client, so your communications must be in accordance with the organization's policies and procedures.

These general guidelines are helpful in all communications, but now we will discuss the specific techniques of how to write e-mails, memos, letters, and proposals in an efficient and professional manner.

E-Mail

Electronic mail, commonly called e-mail, was invented in 1971 and was widely adopted in the late 1980s. Today, it has become so pervasive in our society that organizations and individuals are becoming completely overwhelmed by it.

Inboxes are getting backed up at an astounding rate. According to research by the Radicati Group, a market research firm, in 2007 the average number of corporate e-mails sent and received per person on a daily basis was 142. By 2012, the volume is expected to increase to 228. According to the firm, workers in 2006 spent 26 percent of their time on e-mail, and that figure is expected to rise to 41 percent in 2009.

Other surveys aren't optimistic. RescueTime, a company that analyzes computer use habits, estimates that a typical information worker turns to their e-mail more than 50 times a day and uses instant messaging 77 times. All these constant interruptions, of course, fracture the workday. The loss in job productivity is estimated at about $650 million annually.

In fact, bulging inboxes are now considered more of a workplace problem than the traditional e-mail spam, which has been somewhat tamed by filtering software. So where is the bulge coming from? Actually, a lot of it is coming from what *The Wall Street Journal* calls "colleague spam." That's when your friends send you—and everyone else in their address book—the latest joke or the really "cool" video link from YouTube. Other social networking sites, such as Facebook, or text messages forwarded from cell phones also contribute to the bulge, including all those people who click "reply to all."

E-mail, despite the concerns of psychologists and productivity experts, no doubt will continue to thrive because of its multiple advantages for cost-effective communication on a global scale. As a professional communicator, however, you need to recognize its limitations and to use it efficiently to get your message through the thick forest of information clutter. In many situations, you should bypass e-mail by using text messaging, Twitter, wikis, and RSS feeds. These were discussed in the last chapter. In addition, voice mail is an attractive alternative, which is discussed in the Tips for Success on page 389.

Purpose

According to a survey of communicators in *Fortune* 500 corporations, e-mail (1) reduces the cost of employee communications, (2) increases the distribution of messages to more employees, (3) flattens the corporate hierarchy, and (4) speeds decision making.

E-mail has other advantages. It is a good way for public relations writers to send media advisories and news releases to the media, disseminate employee newsletters, and even chat with colleagues around the world. E-mail is also effective from the standpoint of (1) keeping up with events, (2) making arrangements and appointments, and (3) reviewing or editing documents. Increasingly, however, organizations are also using wikis for group editing, scheduling, and overall logistics.

E-mail, it should be noted, is not suitable for all person-to-person communications. It is primarily an informal memo system. At times, it is best to send a more formal letter on nice stationery. A job recommendation or a letter to a disgruntled customer makes a better impression on paper than in an e-mail message, which seems less official and permanent. Writing the personal letter will be discussed shortly.

Also, the experts say that e-mail should never be a substitute for face-to-face communication. More than two-thirds of the respondents in the Rogen International survey say that face-to-face is the preferred channel of communication for delivering important information. The study notes, "The good and the bad should be delivered face-to face: 71 percent preferred good news to be delivered that way, as did 81 percent for bad news."

According to *PR Reporter*:

Similarly, face-to-face should be used for discussing issues of workplace performance or personal confrontation. When it comes to job performance, employees need to be able to probe for answers and clarify responses, which is lost in e-mail

Avoid E-Mail Clutter: Use Voice Mail

The telephone is still alive and well as an efficient method of sending and receiving messages. Most, if not all, organizations use sophisticated computerized telephone answering systems that allow a person to send a voice message to one, several, or thousands of persons in the organization. This is called *voice mail*.

Advantages

Voice mail speeds the process of getting information. A call is quicker than a memo delivered by interoffice mail and it avoids the problem of an unopened e-mail sitting in a crowded inbox. It eliminates "phone tag," because you can leave messages in someone's "mailbox" and that person can respond by leaving a message in yours. Another feature of voice mail is the group conference call, which often eliminates the need for meetings.

Disadvantages

Although voice mail has advantages, it often frustrates people from outside the organization who call a general number trying to reach a specific person or department. It's called "telephone tree hell," as an individual is asked to go through a series of prompts by pushing digits on the phone. If you know the name of the individual that you wish to reach, some voice mail systems even require you to punch in their last name in order to connect you. Ideally, a good system will always give the caller the option of pressing "0" for immediate operator assistance.

Setting Up a Voice Mail Greeting

You should set up a personal voice mail greeting that is short and to the point. You should give your name, title, and company in a friendly way that assures the caller that their call is important to you. For example, "Hi, this is Susan Jones, manager of public relations here at Cisco. I'm sorry I'm not available right now, but please leave a short message and I will get back to you as soon as possible." If you are going to be out of the office for an extended time, it's often wise to let the caller know and to give the name/number of your assistant or another person in the office who they can contact if they have an immediate concern or question. Public relations personnel, in particular, should do this as a matter of course, because journalists are often on deadline and can't wait for a call-back. It's also good "PR" to return all phone calls in a timely manner.

Leaving a Voice Mail Message

Your message should be brief and to the point. First, determine the key message before you call so you don't have to spend time collecting your thoughts and leaving a somewhat disjointed message that goes on for several minutes. Remember the axiom for making a story pitch to a reporter—say it in 30 seconds. Second, set the context by immediately identifying yourself and stating the reason for your call. Third, slowly give the telephone number where a person can call you back. All too often, people give the phone number so fast that it forces the recipient to play back the message several times—which just irritates them. Some astute individuals even make it a habit to repeat the phone number at the end of their message. Fourth, let the person know the best times to reach you during the day or in the next several days. ■

dialogue. For other discussions around potential conflicts or misunderstandings, face-to-face is crucial because e-mail messages can be misunderstood; readers can perceive angry tones, abrupt manners, and even humor incorrectly.

In other words, you should think of e-mail as one of your communication tools—just not the only one. E-mail is a somewhat sterile, mechanistic form of interpersonal communication that can convey routine information very well, but you should also make the time to use the telephone and talk face-to-face with colleagues and customers.

Content

Both style and substance are important to effective e-mail. Michael Hattersley, writing in *PR Tactics*, continues, "Although one can be quite informal in a personal conversation or even in a meeting, you never know where an e-mail will end up. Make sure it represents you as you want to be seen. Every written communication should be flawless and represent your best work."

> " *We're highly connected, yet we're connecting in thinner, more faceless ways. We experience fewer visits, fewer telephone calls, and fewer contacts all around—except e-mail. We're subsisting on this diet of snippets and glimpses of each other socially.* "
>
> ■ Maggie Jackson, author of *Distracted: The Erosion of Attention and the Coming Dark Age*

In other words, you can be somewhat informal in an e-mail message, but that does not mean you can be sloppy about grammar, punctuation, spelling, and sentence structure. It also means that you need to think twice about writing something that would be embarrassing to you if the sender decides to forward it to any number of other individuals.

Today's technology means that no e-mail message is secure or confidential. If you are using e-mail at your place of work, be aware that management has the ability and legal right to read your e-mail messages, even if you erase them. More than one employee has been fired for posting messages that have included crude jokes about ethnic minorities, comments about supervisors who were "back-stabbing bastards," and complaints about management's incompetence. Newer kinds of surveillance software can even log all your keystrokes even if you don't send a message or erase that rant about your "stupid" boss.

Even Bill Gates found out the hard way that erased e-mail messages can be easily retrieved. The case against Microsoft by the U.S. Justice Department hinged, in part, on what Gates wrote in e-mail messages about the competition. Justice Department lawyers claimed that Gates lied under oath because they were able, through technology, to reconstruct e-mail messages that he had deleted from his computer.

Here are some other suggestions about the content of an e-mail message. See the Tips for Success on page 391 for more tips about minding your e-mail manners.

- Use language that falls halfway between formal writing and spontaneous conversation.
- Blunt words and statements assume more importance in electronic form than in a telephone conversation. Temper your language.
- Keep messages, including quoted material, brief.
- Send messages without attachments whenever possible. An attachment drastically decreases the odds that your message will be read.

Mind Your E-Mail Manners

Microsoft Office Online has a column authored by the "crabby office lady." In one issue, she listed the top 10 cyber-discourtesies that are "driving all of us nuts."

- **Avoid the "Reply to All" button.** In most cases, your personal reply to an e-mail doesn't require you to share your thoughts with everyone on the mailing list. Greta, in accounting, probably could care less if you are attending the company picnic.

- **Skip the CAPITAL letters.** By using uppercase letters, it essentially means that you are yelling at the recipient. Save the capital letters unless you really want to shout and seek assistance.

- **Save the fancy stationery.** You don't need pastel backgrounds, smiley faces, and a fancy letterhead to send an e-mail. Keep it simple and uncluttered.

- **Give your response first.** When you reply to an e-mail, make sure your reply is the first thing the recipient reads.

- **Keep forwards to a minimum.** Everyone has already heard the joke.

- **Don't be a cyber-coward.** If you have something to say that is highly personal, scary, sad, angry, tragic, vicious, shocking or any combination of the above, say it in person.

- **Keep the 500KB image file to yourself.** Most e-mail accounts have limited capacity. Don't send your vacation photos to everyone in your address book. Use Facebook or MySpace to post your photos.

- **Fill out the subject line.** People get plenty of e-mails every day; if you can't take the time to fill out the subject line, I don't need to take time to open it.

- **Avoid HTML format.** The most easily accessible e-mail format around the globe is plain text.

- **Count to 10 before hitting the Send button.** Think twice, or even wait 24 hours, before sending that clever, scathing message to someone and possibly the rest of the world. A "flaming" e-mail often starts more fires than you can put out. ■

- Use standard English and abbreviations. Don't use a lot of cryptic symbols as shorthand.

- Copy only necessary people when responding to a group message. Avoid the "reply to all" syndrome.

- Double-check who will receive your message before sending it.

- When sending e-mail messages to the media, use blind copy distribution so that the recipients don't know it is a mass mailing.

- Don't be an e-mail junkie. Don't clutter up mailboxes with inane chitchat or forwarding jokes to large groups; it's irritating to receivers.

- Although e-mail is a form of one-to-one communication, it is not a substitute for phone conversations and meetings. They are important for maintaining personal relationships.

- Always reread an e-mail message before sending it. Will the tone or choice of words offend the receiver? Are you coming across as friendly and courteous, or brusque and pompous?

- Have a spellchecker automatically review every outgoing email. Poor spelling reflects on your professionalism and the organization's credibility.
- Respond to relevant, work-related e-mail messages in a timely manner.

Format

Everyone knows how to send an e-mail. All you have to do is sit down in front of the computer, connect to the Internet, and start typing. Right? Although this method may be all right for quick notes among your friends, you should be aware that everyone is getting flooded with e-mails, and your missive is one of many that appear in an inbox that already contains hundreds of other e-mails. Consequently, it is important to know some techniques that can improve the readership of your e-mail.

Subject Line ■ An e-mail format, after the address, includes a subject line. This is the opportunity to say succinctly what the message is about. Think of the subject line as a form of headline, which was discussed in Chapter 11, when sending e-mails to journalists. If you are announcing an event, don't just do a label line such as "Spring Concert." You have up to 42 characters to give more detail. For example, you might say "Tickets Now Available for May 5 Spring Concert."

If you need a decision or response, say so. The subject line, in this case, might say, "Your plans for attending Spring Concert?" or even "You're invited to attend Spring Concert on May 5." By providing context and more description, the recipient knows exactly what is being discussed or requested.

Salutation ■ An e-mail is somewhat informal, so it is unnecessary to include the sender's full name, title, organization, and address as you would in a business letter. It is also unnecessary to say, "Dear . . ." Just begin with the person's first name. There is some debate, however, about using first names of people who you haven't met. Many people are put off by an email that assumes a familiarity that doesn't exist. You need to exercise some judgment; if the e-mail is business-oriented, such as to a customer, you might use a more formal designation, such as "Hello, Ms. Smith." You can also say "Dear Ms. Smith," but that term doesn't quite fit the format of an e-mail, which is more like a memo. If the e-mail is being distributed to a group, use an opener such as "Team" or "Colleagues."

First Sentence or Paragraph ■ Get to the "bottom line" right away, so the recipient knows immediately what the key message is and what you want him or her to do with it. Avoid starting e-mail messages with such phrases as "I wanted to inform you . . ."

Body of Message ■ Think of an e-mail as a memo, which is discussed in the next section. Most experts say the best e-mail messages are short. How short? A good rule of thumb is one screen. That is about 20–25 lines, single-spaced. It is also recommended that there be no more than 65 characters per line. Others recommend that you keep the length of lines even shorter, because people can read material faster in a narrow column (left half of page) than as an entire screen of type.

When appropriate, you can use boldfacing, underlining, and bullets to highlight key pieces of information. The idea, as stated in Chapter 13, is to help the viewer scan the message for the important points. Don't use all CAPITAL letters, however; because it is perceived as a form of shouting. It is also a good idea to include other e-mail addresses or websites so a viewer can easily click on them to get more information.

Closing ■ Sign off with a brief word such as "Regards," "Best," or even "Cheers." You can also use the standard closing "Sincerely" if you're so inclined. Include your name, title, organization, e-mail, phone, and fax numbers in a standard signature. This enables the recipient to contact you directly if he or she wants additional information and feedback. It is also a handy reference for them if they print out the message and file it.

Christopher Dobens, a vice president of Creamer Dickson Basford public relations, gives a final bit of advice about e-mail. He writes in *PR Tactics*, "To ensure that my e-mails get read beyond the first line (or even the subject heading), I make sure they are well written. I keep them brief and succinct, and often use creative flair or humor to differentiate them. The tools may have changed and the speed has definitely increased, but there is no substitute for good writing in public relations."

Memorandums

A memorandum—*memo* for short—is a brief written message, usually a page or less in length. In the past, it was on a piece of paper that was photocopied and distributed to employees through the organization's mail system. Today, the standard method of delivery is e-mail for most routine memos. On occasion, however, memos are still distributed in hard copy if they contain important information about employee benefits, major changes in policy, or other kinds of information that an individual should retain for his or her records.

Purpose

A memo can serve almost any communication purpose. It can ask for information, supply information, confirm a verbal exchange, ask for a meeting, schedule or cancel a meeting, remind, report, praise, caution, state a policy, or perform any other function that requires a written message.

Many public relations firms require staff to write a memo whenever there is a client meeting, or even a telephone conversation, because it creates a record and "paper trail" of what was discussed and what decisions were made. Copies are often distributed via e-mail to all staff involved in the project, including the client. A memo avoids the problem of someone saying, "I don't remember that," which can lead to disagreements and uneven execution of the plan.

It should be noted, however, that hard copies of memos are often distributed even if it was sent via e-mail. The reason for this is that not everyone pays close attention to the multiple e-mails they receive, and they often overlook or unintentionally delete some of them before they are read. Consequently, many organizations continue to distribute and retain hard copies of important memos even if they are sent via e-mail.

Also, e-mail memos tend to be somewhat ephemeral, so printed copies provide a more concrete record of what was said, announced, or decided upon. Printouts of e-mail memos have also been a good back-up when someone says, "I never received that information."

Content

A memo should be specific and to the point. The subject line, as in e-mail messages, should state exactly what the memo is about. If it is about a meeting, the subject line should state: "Department meeting on Thursday at 3 P.M." If it is a summary of decisions made at a meeting, you could use: "Decisions made at last staff meeting."

The first sentence or paragraph of a memo should contain the key message that would be of most interest to the reader. All too often, first sentences don't provide any meaningful information. *Communication Briefings*, in one article, asked the reader to choose the best opening statement for a memo. Which one of the choices below would you choose?

1. "Kevin Donaldson and I recommend that we cancel the Carstairs account."
2. "Kevin Donaldson and I met yesterday to discuss the Carstairs account."
3. "Kevin Donaldson and I recommend that we cancel the Carstairs account for these reasons."
4. "I've been asked to reply to your request for more information on the Carstairs account."
5. "You'll be glad to know that we finally got the results on the Carstairs account."

Both 1 and 3 are better than the other choices because they are specific about a course of action. Number 3 is the preferred choice because it includes "for these reasons"—a phrase that explains "why." All the others are too vague and don't give the reader much useful information.

Format

Every memo should contain five elements: (1) date, (2) to, (3) from, (4) subject, and (5) message. This format should be used in e-mail and hard copy memos. Here is an example of a simple memo:

Monday, November 1
To: Public Relations Committee
From: Susan Parker
Subject: Meeting on Monday, November 15

We will meet in the conference room from 3 to 4 P.M. to discuss how to publicize and promote the company's annual employee picnic. The president wants to encourage the families of all employees to attend, so please come prepared to offer your ideas and suggestions.

Letters

Many college students, used to the informality of e-mail, have no idea how to compose a business letter. A business letter, actually printed on paper and sent via snail mail, requires a more systematic approach to writing and formatting a message. It is written primarily to individuals when a more "official" or formal response is required. Job applicants, for example, make a much better impression with prospective employers by sending a thank you letter instead of an e-mail or text message thanking the employer for the interview.

As a public relations writer, you will write two kinds of letters. One is the single, personal letter to a specific individual. This is the most personal form of letter writing, because a one-to-one dialogue is established between the sender and the recipient. A letter, in legal terms, is more permanent than e-mail and often serves as an official record of a dialogue involving employment, an issue about company policy, or even an answer to a consumer complaint.

The second kind of letter is less personal, because it is often a form letter about a specific situation sent to large numbers of people, such as stockholders, customers, or even residents of a city. These form letters might be considered direct mail (discussed Chapter 16), but they go beyond the common description of direct mail as a form of advertising to sell goods or services, or even to solicit funds for a charitable organization. Form letters, often written by public relations staff and signed by the head of the organization, usually give background or an update on a situation affecting the organization and a particular public.

A good example is a form letter signed by the president of Coca-Cola to stockholders about the recall of some of its products in Belgium and France due to quality concerns. Various negative news reports had caused the stock value to drop, so the president wrote the letter to let the stockholders know what the company was doing to solve the problem. He assured the stockholders that "your company remains totally committed to maintaining the quality of our products, the strength of the brand and the trust of our customers and consumers, as we continue to seize the vast opportunities before us to build value for you."

Whether you are writing a personalized letter or a form letter, here are some general guidelines about their purpose, content, and format. Other guidelines are offered in the Tips for Success on page 396.

Purpose

A letter may be used to give information, to ask for information, to motivate, to answer complaints, to soothe or arouse, to warn, to admit, or to deny. In short, a letter can carry any sort of message that requires a written record. It is a substitute for

How to Write Efficient Letters

A personal letter is a labor-intensive effort. Here are some ways to increase your efficiency and still keep the personal touch.

- Produce courteous and effective printed forms for repetitive correspondence, such as requests for printed material or acknowledgments of inquiries.
- Develop standard replies for often-asked questions or often-solicited advice where this is a part of the organization's routine business.
- Develop standard formats for certain kinds of common correspondence to enable inexperienced writers to handle them easily and effectively.
- Prepare a correspondence guide containing hints and suggestions on keeping verbiage and correspondence volume down to reasonable and effective levels.
- Place a brief heading on the letter after the salutation, indicating the letter's subject. The heading will give the reader an immediate grasp of the letter's substance and will also facilitate filing.
- Use subheads if the letter is more than two pages long, thereby giving the reader a quick grasp of how the subject is treated and where the major topics are discussed.
- To personalize printed materials, attach your card with a brief, warm message.
- If a letter requires a brief response, it is acceptable to pen a note on the original letter and mail it back to the sender. Retain a photocopy for your files. ■

personal conversation, although it is not as friendly as face-to-face conversation. It does have the advantage, however, of allowing the writer to get facts in order, develop a logical and persuasive approach, and phrase the message carefully to accomplish a specific purpose.

Answering a complaint letter is a good example. The specific purpose is to satisfy the customer and retain his or her product loyalty. Although many organizations use standard form letters to answer customer complaints, a more personal approach that specifically deals with the complaint is usually more effective. This is not to say that every letter must be written from scratch. There are often key sentences and paragraphs that can be used or modified that fit the situation. Most letters, for example, will include (1) thanking the customer for writing, (2) apologizing for any inconvenience, and (3) replacing the product or providing a coupon for future purchases.

Content

The most important part of any letter is the first paragraph. It should concisely state the purpose of the letter or tell the reader the "bottom-line" so the reader knows immediately what the letter is about. This is the same principle that was discussed in Chapter 5 for the first paragraph of a news release.

From a writing perspective, a declarative statement is best. Instead of writing, "I am writing you to let you know that our company will be contacting you in the near future about your concerns regarding product reliability," you can simply say, "A company representative will be contacting you about our product reliability."

The second and succeeding paragraphs can elaborate on the details and give relevant information. The final paragraph should summarize the important details, or let the recipient know you will telephone if something needs to be resolved through conversation.

Writing a business letter requires clear thought and thorough editing to reduce wordiness. Every time you use the word "I" to start a thought, think about how to remove it. In most cases, starting a sentence with "I believe," "I feel," or "I think" is unnecessary. At the same time, take every opportunity to use the word "you" in a letter. It places the focus on the receiver and his or her needs instead of those of the sender.

The tone of a letter is an important consideration. Readers don't like to be scolded, chastised, or pacified. Try to write positive statements instead of negative ones. Instead of saying, "You didn't follow up with the client," it is better to say, "You need to improve your follow-up with the client." If you are apologizing for something, say so. Don't just say "I'm sorry . . . ."

Format

As a general rule, letters should be written on standard business stationery. The letterhead should have the name, address, and telephone number of the organization. Additional information can include e-mail address, fax numbers, and even a website.

Letters should always be word processed. Usually they are single-spaced. Each paragraph should be indicated, either by indention or by a line space. One page is the preferred length. A two-page letter is acceptable but, if the letter runs longer than that, consider putting the material in another format, such as a brochure that is included in the letter. *Communication Briefings* notes, "If you can't get your point across in one page, you probably haven't done enough preparatory work."

> **" Letters should be concise and focused. If you can't get your point across in one page, you probably haven't done enough preparatory work. "** ■ *Communication Briefings* newsletter

The full name, title, and complete address of the receiver are at the beginning of the letter. It is formatted in the same way as an address on an envelope. The next element is the salutation or greeting. The usual approach is to write "Dear Mr. —" or "Dear Ms. —." The latter avoids the "Miss" or "Mrs." dilemma and is common in business correspondence. You should not use a first name, such as "Dear Susan," in a greeting unless the person already knows you.

On occasion, you will need to write a letter to an organization on some routine matter and you won't know the name of the person. This often occurs when you are requesting information or inquiring about a billing. You can use the traditional "Dear Sir," but this is increasingly inappropriate now that more than half the workforce is female. A better approach is to put your letter in the form of a memo. For example, a letter about a bill might be addressed, "To: Manager, Accounting Department."

The body of the letter should be about four or five paragraphs. It's wise to use short sentences and keep every paragraph to about four or five sentences. One common problem that inexperienced writers have is writing compound sentences that get quite convoluted and difficult to understand.

Closing a letter is easy: You can write "Yours truly," "Truly yours," "Sincerely," or "Sincerely yours." Then leave a few lines for your signed signature, followed by your word-processed name. You can also add your direct phone line or e-mail address so the recipient can easily contact you.

There is one more crucial step. Once you have the final draft, use a spelling and grammar checker to correct any errors. Sending a letter (or even an e-mail) with obvious mistakes is sloppy and unprofessional. Many employers, for example, automatically discard any letter or resume from a job applicant that has grammar or spelling errors.

Proposals

Public relations firms usually get new business through the preparation of a proposal offering services to an organization. In many cases, a potential client will issue a Request for Proposal, known as an **RFP**, and circulate it to various public relations firms. The organization will outline its needs and ask interested public relations firms to recommend a course of action.

In most situations, the public relations firm will prepare a written proposal that will be part of a presentation to the prospective client. A typical public relations proposal might include sections about (1) the background and capabilities of the firm, (2) the client's situation, (3) goals and objectives of the proposed program, (4) key messages, (5) basic strategies and tactics, (6) general timeline of activities, (7) proposed budget, (8) how success will be measured, and (9) a description of the team that will handle the account, and (10) a summary of why the firm should be selected to implement the program. More information about public relations program planning is given in Chapter 18.

> ❝ Make sure your proposal answers these basic questions: 'Why should my audience members care' and 'What's in it for them? ❞ ■ Communication Briefings

Proposal writing, however, is not unique to public relations firms. Any number of outside suppliers and vendors write proposals to provide goods and services to an organization. The proposal may be as simple as a bid to provide goods and services for X amount of money, or it may be much longer, depending on what information the organization needs to make a decision.

Within an organization, proposals are a management technique to consider new programs and policies. Almost anything can be proposed, but to give you a starting point, here are some possible subjects of proposals: to move the office, to adopt a 10-hour workday or a 4-day workweek, to provide a child-care facility at the plant, or to modify the employee benefit plan.

Purpose

The purpose of a proposal is to get something accomplished—to persuade management to approve and authorize some important action that will have a long-lasting effect on the organization or its people. By putting the proposal in writing, you let management know exactly what is proposed, what decisions are called for, and what the consequences may be. A verbal proposal may be tossed around, discussed briefly, and then discarded. In contrast, when the idea is in writing and presented formally, it forces management to make a decision.

Before writing a proposal, author Randall Majors says you should ask yourself questions like these:

- What is the purpose of the proposal?
- Who will read the proposal?
- What are the pertinent interests and values of the readers?
- What specific action can be taken on the basis of the proposal?
- What situation or problem does the proposal address?
- What is the history of the situation?
- How much information, and what kinds of information, will make the proposal persuasive?
- What format is most effective for the proposal?
- How formal in format, tone, and style should the proposal be?

Organization

A proposal may be presented in a few pages or multiple pages, depending on the size of the organization and the scope of the proposal. *Communication Briefings* suggests that proposals are more compelling if the writer includes four major components:

- **Show a need.** The opening should be tailored to your readers' needs. If you are seeking funds for a special event, for example, tell how such an event will enhance the organization's reputation, improve employee morale, or increase customer loyalty.
- **Satisfy the Need.** Suggest how the event would be organized to meet the needs of the audience and the organization.
- **Show benefits.** Stress how the event would improve employee morale, increase media coverage, or improve reputation among key publics.
- **Call for Action.** Ask for a decision. Be specific about the resources and budget that you require to execute the project.

An informal proposal, one that is project-oriented, might include the four components listed above in the following organizational structure:

- **Introduction:** State the purpose of the proposal.

- **Body:** Provide background to the problem situation, criteria for a solution, the proposed solution, a schedule for implementation, personnel assignments, budget, and some background on the proposal's authors.
- **Conclusion:** Request approval or the signing of a contract.

A template for a major proposal includes the following components:

- **Transmittal:** A memo, letter, or a foreword that summarizes why the proposal is being made.

☑ tips FOR SUCCESS

How to Write a Position Paper

Organizations, on occasion, prepare a report about an issue relating to the organization or the industry. Such reports are called *white papers, briefing papers,* or *position statements*. The three reasons for writing and distributing a position paper are: (1) as background information when executives and public relations personnel talk to the media, (2) as a method of advancing an organization's perspective and point of view on a trend or issue, and (3) as a marketing technique for establishing the organization as a "thought leader" in the industry.

Several vendors in the public relations industry, for example, regularly produce white papers on various trends and issues. One example is Cision, which publishes media databases and provides monitoring services. One of its white papers was titled "Staying Afloat in a Sea of Social Media: An Intelligent Approach to Managing and Monitoring Social Media." BurrellesLuce, a similar firm, issued a paper titled "Gearing Up for Web 3.0: What Public Relations Practitioners Can Expect."

Here are some tips for writing a position paper:

- On a cover page, use a title that tells exactly what the paper is about.
- Keep it short. A position paper should be five pages or less. If the paper is 10 pages or more, use a table of contents or an index.
- Include an "executive summary" at the beginning of the paper, which is a succinct summary of the report's findings or recommendations. It enables busy readers to rapidly understand the crux of the position paper.
- Place any supporting materials or exhibits in an appendix at the end of the report.
- Use subheads, boldface, or underlining throughout the paper to break up blocks of copy.
- Use simple graphs, bar charts, and pie charts to present key statistical information.
- Use pull-out quotes from key executives or experts to highlight key messages.
- Be concise. Don't use excessive words. Check for repetitious information.
- Check for clarity. Is it clear what you want to say or communicate?
- Avoid overt marketing and promotion for the organization's services or products.
- Give appropriate websites and other sources for readers who want more information on the topic.
- Post the position paper on your website and make it printer-friendly. ■

- **Table of contents:** A list of all items in the proposal.

- **Tables and exhibits:** A list of illustrative elements and where they can be found.

- **Summary:** A condensation of the proposal, which gives readers the basic information and enables them to appraise the idea before they go on to the details.

- **Introduction:** Giving the scope, the approach, how information was obtained and evaluated, limitations and problems to help the reader understand the idea and weigh its impact.

- **Body:** A complete, detailed statement of what is proposed.

- **Recommendation:** A clear, concise statement of just what is suggested and how it is to be implemented.

- **Exhibits and bibliography.** Items substantiating the statements in the proposal and assuring the readers that the proposal is based on thorough study of the problem or the opportunity.

Public relations writers, on occasion, also author position papers for organizations. See the guidelines in the Tips for Success on page 400 for how to write a position paper.

Summary

- Information overload is pervasive in our society. You can help reduce clutter by keeping your messages simple, short, and to the point. In addition, limit messages to only those who are in your key audiences. Don't shotgun information to the entire planet.

- E-mail bulge is overwhelming many organizations and individuals. Use wikis, text messaging, RSS, and applications such as Twitter to reduce the flow.

- E-mail (electronic mail) is rapid and cost-efficient. It is not, however, a substitute for personal one-on-one communication.

- E-mail is less formal than a letter, but more formal than a telephone call. You can increase the effectiveness of your e-mail messages by (1) providing key information in the subject line, (2) keeping them to 25 lines or less, and (3) using proper grammar, spelling, and punctuation.

- Business letters are personalized communication that should be well organized, concise, and to the point. They can prevent misunderstandings and provide a record of an agreement or a transaction.

- Memos should be one page or less and state the key message immediately. A memo has five components: (1) date, (2) to, (3) from, (4) subject, and (5) message.

- Proposals must follow a logical, well-organized format. They are prepared to convince management to make a decision about a contract or approve money and resources for a project.

- A position paper, or "white paper" gives the organization's perspective on a particular trend or industry. They should begin with an "executive summary" or an overview, so people can read the highlights in a few seconds.

Skill Building Activities

1. The chapter provided a number of suggestions about how to write and format e-mails. Write a short essay about the guidelines that you find relevant and will incorporate into your future e-mails.

2. It is suggested that wikis can often take the place of sending e-mails back and forth among individuals working on the same project. Do some research on wikis and how you might use this application in classroom group projects or in your work setting. See also the discussion on wikis in Chapter 12.

3. You're the public relations manager for a department store. Write a letter to an irate customer who has complained that the clerks were too busy socializing among themselves to give her any service or assistance.

4. Your student organization needs $5,000 to sponsor a week of activities to focus on the dangers of binge drinking on campus. Write a proposal for presentation the executive board of the student council, which has authority to allocate the funds.

Suggested Readings

Brenner, Leslie. "You've Got too Much E-mail." *Los Angeles Times* (www.latimes.com/technology/la-et-email31-2008jul31,1,7371041.story), July 31, 2008.

Goldsborough, Reid. "Business Casual: Looking Good in E-Mail." *PR Tactics*, February 2008, p. 24.

Goldsborough, Reid. "How do you Begin and End an E-mail? Keeping Your Online Missives in Top Form." *PR Tactics*, February 2006, p. 26.

Hagley, Tom. *Writing Winning Proposals: PR Cases.* Boston: Allyn & Bacon, 2006.

Kousek, Susan. "Beyond E-Mail 101: Tips for Writing More Effective E-Mail." *PR Tactics*, February 2008, p. 24.

Richtel, Matt. "Creators of E-Mail Monsters Now Try to Tame It." *New York Times* (www.nytimes/technology), June 14, 2008.

Totty, Michael. "Letter of the Law: Email is Becoming a Big Factor in Court Cases." *Wall Street Journal*, March 26, 2007, p. R10.

Totty, Michael. "Rethinking the Inbox: We Aren't Going to Give Up Email. But We Can Be a Lot Smarter About the Way We Use It." *Wall Street Journal*, March 26, 2007, p. R8.

Giving Speeches and Presentations

15

TOPICS covered in this chapter include:

The Challenge of the Speaking Circuit   403

The Basics of Speechwriting   403

The Basics of Giving a Speech   409

Visual Aids for Presentations   414

Other Speech Formats   418

Speaker Training and Placement   420

The Challenge of the Speaking Circuit

Speakers and audiences are a fundamental part of human communication around the world. An executive of Ruder Finn, a public relations firm, once estimated that—in the United States alone—companies, organizations, and clubs convene more than a million meetings on a daily basis, all of them focusing on speakers in endless succession.

Indeed, speechwriting and presentations are important tools in public relations to reach key publics on an interpersonal level. Such activities are being given even more emphasis today as organizations strive to enhance their reputations, build brand awareness, convey a commitment to transparency, and portray responsibility to society. Michael Witkoski, writing in *PR Tactics*, notes, "It's easy to understand the demand for good speechwriting. More than ever, we recognize the importance of giving large organizations a human face, desirably a face that is trustworthy, competent, friendly, and coherent."

During your career, you will be asked to write speeches for executives; prepare visual aids, such as PowerPoint presentations; conduct speaker training; get executives on the agenda of important conferences; organize speaker bureaus; publicize speeches. You might even give a few speeches and presentations yourself. This chapter will give you the basics of doing all of these activities.

The Basics of Speechwriting

Researching the Audience and Speaker

If you are given a speechwriting assignment, the first step is to find out everything possible about the audience. Who? Where? When? How many people? What time of day? Purpose of meeting? Length of speech? Purpose of talk? Other speakers on the program? To find answers to these questions, you should talk with the organizers of the event or meeting. Don't accept vague answers; keep asking follow-up questions until you have a complete picture.

A good example of defining the audience is when an EDS corporate executive was asked to give the keynote address for a meeting of the Association of American Chambers of Commerce of Latin America in Lima, Peru. Beth Pedison, executive speechwriter of EDS, analyzed the intended audience the following way:

> **Intended Audience:** 400 top Latin American and Caribbean business executives, government leaders, and Chamber representatives. Because the audience came from diverse industries, countries, and company sizes, their familiarity with information technology varied widely. We didn't want to talk down to those who were technologically savvy, or talk over the heads of those who were not technologically proficient. English was the business language for the conference and the speech, although almost everyone in the audience spoke English as a second language. Therefore, we needed to keep sentence structures simple, and avoid the use of colloquialisms, contractions, or U.S.–centric language.

You also need to learn everything you can about the speaker. Listen to the speaker talk—to other groups, to subordinates, to you. See how his or her mind works, what word phrases are favored, and what kinds of opinions are expressed. In addition to listening, it is also a good idea to go over material that the client has written or, if written by others, that the client admires in terms of style and method of presentation.

Laying the Groundwork

Ideally, a writer should have lengthy conversations with the speaker before beginning to write a rough draft of the talk. In a conversational setting, you and the speaker should discuss the speech in terms of objective, approach, strategy, points to emphasize, scope, and facts or anecdotes the speaker would like to include.

This is how Marie L. Lerch, director of public relations and communication for Booz Allen & Hamilton, described her work with the company's chairman for a diversity awards speech to company employees:

> The central message, "Do the Right Thing," has been Mr. Stasior's core theme throughout his tenure as chairman. I worked with him to adapt that theme to the issue of diversity; researched quotes and other materials that would add color and emphasis to the message; and interviewed him to flesh out his ideas and words on the subject. With notes and research in hand, I developed a first draft of the speech, which Mr. Stasior and I revised together into its final form. . . .

Indeed, before you start writing a speech, you should have a thorough understanding of three aspects of the speech—the objective, the key message, and the strategy/approach. This approach is highlighted in the PR Casebook on page 405 about a speech by the CEO of the Grocery Manufacturers of America.

A Systematic Approach to Speechwriting

Writing a speech for someone requires the writer to understand the intended audience, the objectives of the speech, and the key messages that must be delivered. Melissa Brown, a freelance speechwriter in St. Joseph, Michigan, compiled the following outline in consultation with her client.

The assignment: Write a speech for the president of the Grocery Manufacturers of America (GMA) on the topic, "The Changing Challenges Facing the Food Industry."

The audience: The International Food and Lifestyles Media Conference, Cincinnati.

Speech objectives:

- Give food writers useful, research-based information on the lifestyles of American consumers, thus positioning GMA as a good source of statistics/information.
- Neutralize misinformation presented by opponents of biotechnologically developed food products, presenting the industry's side of the story and exposing the lack of credentials of a major voice in the opposition.
- Provide information on the good work the industry has accomplished in addressing environmental issues, in particular, packaging and solid waste.
- Demonstrate to GMA board that GMA is speaking out on the issues that affect their businesses.
- Frame the arguments other food industry spokespeople can use in other opportunities, within their companies and with the press.

Key messages:

- The profile and purchasing habits of the American consumer have changed significantly.
- We enjoy the safest and most abundant food supply in the world, despite what you hear from a small but vocal group of opponents.
- The grocery industry has surpassed government regulations and everyone's expectations in the rapid progress made on environmental issues. ■

Objective ■ First you must determine the objective. What is the speech supposed to accomplish? What facts, attitude or opinion should the audience have when the speech is concluded?

Everything that goes into the speech should be pertinent to that objective. Material that does not help attain the objective should not be used. Whether the objective is to inform, persuade, activate, or commemorate, that particular objective must be uppermost in the speechwriter's mind. This is a start, but objectives are usually stated in more specific terms.

When the CEO of Novelis, the world's largest rolled aluminum company, gave a major presentation at a industry conference about a new manufacturing process, the speech had three objectives: (1) position Novelis as a technology leader and innovator in the industry; (2) create a demand in the automotive, construction, and electronics industries for the new technology and product; and (3) generate coverage in the trade and mainstream media.

Key Messages ■ Objectives provide the framework of a speech, but they must be supported by key messages that are given emphasis throughout the speech. A speech can have only one key message, but it may also have two or three. The major point is that people hear a speech and can remember only two or three points. Consequently, as a speechwriter, you want to ensure that they remember what you believe is most important in terms of organizational objectives.

Novelis, for example, had three key messages to convey: (1) the new process of casting multiple alloys in the same ingot will be marketed under the Novelis Fusion product line, (2) the new process positions aluminum as a viable alternative to steel with superior functionality, and (3) multiple industries, such as auto, construction, and electronics, will be able to use aluminum in new ways.

Strategy ■ This can be described as the setting and tone of the speech. Novelis, for example, decided to have the CEO make the announcement of the new technology in a major presentation at the 11th World Aluminum Conference in Montreal. The setting was ideal, because the entire aluminum industry was there, and the conference was being covered by the trade and mainstream media. By having the CEO give the speech, the new product announcement received much more attention than a low-level product news release would.

The tone of a speech depends on the audience being addressed. A friendly audience may appreciate a one-sided talk, with no attempt to present both sides of an issue. For example, a politician at a fund-raising dinner of supporters does not bother to give the opposition's views. An executive giving a motivational talk to the company's sales force doesn't need to mention the benefits of a competitor's product.

Many speaking engagements, however, take place before neutral audiences (Rotary, Lions, Kiwanis, and any number of other civic or professional organizations) where the audience may have mixed views or even a lack of knowledge about the topic.

In such a case, it is wise to take a more objective approach and give an overview of the various viewpoints. The speech can still advocate a particular position, but the audience will appreciate the fact that you have included other points of view. From the standpoint of persuasion, you also have more control over how the opposition view is expressed if you say it instead of waiting for an audience member to bring it up. If you have included an opposing viewpoint in your talk—even acknowledging that it's a valid point—it takes the wind out of audience opposition to what you are advocating.

Hostile or unfriendly audiences present the greatest challenge. They are already predisposed against what you say, and they tend to reject anything that does not square with their opinions. Remember the old saying, "Don't confuse me with the facts—my mind is already made up." The best approach is to find some common ground with the audience. This technique lets the audience know that the speaker shares or at least understands some of their concerns.

Writing the Speech

Writing the speech is a multistep process involving a finely honed outline and several drafts.

Outline ■ After gathering the material you need, you must prepare an outline. The outline for a speech has three main parts: the opening, the body, and the closing.

The opening is the part of the speech that must get the audience's attention, establish empathy, and point toward the conclusion. In the opening, it is wise to tell the audience what the topic is, why it is important to them, and the direction you plan to take in addressing it.

The body of the speech presents the evidence that leads to the conclusion. The outline should list all the key points. In this section, you will use quotes from acknowledged experts in the field, facts and figures, and examples that drive home your point of view.

The conclusion summarizes the evidence, pointing out what it means to the audience.

The outline should be submitted to the speaker, and, once it has been approved, you can go on to the next step.

Word Selection ■ A speaker talks *to* listeners, not *at* them. Your choice of words can either electrify an audience or put it to sleep. As someone once said, "The best idea in the world isn't worth a damn if it cannot be expressed well." Here are some tips about wording when you write a speech:

- **Use personal pronouns.** "You" and "we" make the talk more conversational and let your listeners know you are talking to them.
- **Avoid jargon.** Every occupation and industry has its own vocabulary of specialized words. Don't use words and acronyms that are unfamiliar to your audience. You may know what "ROI" means, but many people in the audience may not.
- **Use simple words.** Don't say "print media" when you mean "newspapers." Don't say "possess" when "have" means the same thing.
- **Use round numbers.** Don't say, "253,629,384 Americans"; say "more than 250 million Americans."
- **Use contractions.** Instead of "do not," say "don't." Say "won't" instead of "would not." It makes your speech more conversational.
- **Avoid empty phrases.** Don't say "in spite of the fact" when "since" or "because" works just as well. Another common one is saying "In spite of the fact that" when "though" or "although" is better.
- **Use bold verbs.** Instead of saying "profits went up," use a more descriptive verb such as "exploded" or "skyrocketed."
- **Don't dilute expressions of opinion.** It blunts the crispness of your talk if you start sentences with "Of course, it's only my opinion" or "It seems to me. . . ."
- **Avoid modifiers.** Words such as "very" or "most" should be deleted.
- **Use direct quotes.** You can say, "My colleague, Allen Knight, says. . . ."
- **Vary sentence length.** In general, short sentence are best. However, occasionally break up a series of short sentences with some longer ones.
- **Use questions.** Questions often get the audience more involved. "Does anyone know the average family income in the United States?"

- **Make comparisons and contrasts.** "An extra 3 cents in gasoline taxes would provide enough money to build another 400 miles of four-lane highway next year."
- **Create patterns of thought.** It's all right to restate a phrase to create a pattern of emphasis. Senator Hillary Clinton once used this phrase in one of her speeches: "if women are healthy and educated, their families will flourish. If women are free from violence, their families will flourish. If women have a chance to work . . . their families will flourish."

Drafts ■ The next step is to write a rough draft for the speaker. Keep in mind the time constraints on the speech. If the speech is supposed to be about 20 minutes, your draft should be about 2,500 words—or 10 pages, double-spaced. It takes about 2 minutes to read a page to an audience, so a 10-minute talk would only be about five double-spaced pages.

The speaker should use this draft to add new thoughts, cross out copy that doesn't seem to fit, and rewrite sentences to reflect his or her vocabulary and speaking style.

Don't feel rejected if the first, second, or even third draft comes back in tatters. It is only through this process that the speech becomes a natural expression of the speaker's personality.

This is the ideal process. The most successful speakers take the time to work with their speechwriters. Unfortunately, too many executives fail to understand this simple concept.

A report prepared by Burson-Marsteller public relations gives several reasons why businesspeople have trouble explaining themselves to the public. The report noted:

> All too often the chief executive expects a speech to appear magically on his desk without any contribution on his part. He feels too busy to give the speech the attention it deserves. In the end, he becomes the victim of his own neglect. He stumbles through a speech that, from start to finish, sounds contrived. And then he wonders why nobody listened to what he said.

Coaching ■ In addition to writing the speech to reflect the speaker's thoughts and personality, there may be a need for coaching. Whether the speech is memorized, partially read, or read entirely, it should be rehearsed enough times for the speaker to become familiar with it and to permit improvements in its delivery. Tone of voice, emphasis given to certain words or phrases, pauses, gestures, speed—all are important.

Some speakers prefer to have certain phrases underlined and to have detailed cues in the script, such as "pause," "look at audience," and "pound on lectern." Others don't want such cues. It is a matter of individual preference.

Format is also a matter of personal preference. Some people prefer double-spacing; others want triple-spacing. A few like to have the speech typed entirely in capital letters, but most prefer the normal upper- and lowercase format that is used to present most material that is to be read. Some speakers like to have capital letters used in the words that are to be stressed. All of these formats are acceptable.

The speaker should be sufficiently familiar with the note cards or prepared text to permit abridgment on short notice. Such advance thinking is particularly important for a speaker at a luncheon meeting. All too often, the meal is served late or the group takes an excessive amount of time discussing internal matters or making general announcements, leaving the speaker far less time than originally planned.

The same thing can happen at an evening banquet. The awards ceremony takes longer than expected, and the speaker is introduced at 9:15 P.M., 3 hours after everyone has sat down to dinner. In this instance, the most applause is for the person who realizes the hour and makes a 5-minute speech.

The Basics of Giving a Speech

Writing a speech focuses almost exclusively on content. Giving a speech is all about delivery. You can have a wonderful script, but the words are enriched and become more powerful in the hands of an excellent speaker. Consequently, it is important to know the components of how to give an effective speech. In addition, see the following Tips for Success for guidelines on how to introduce a speaker.

✓ tips FOR SUCCESS

How to Introduce a Speaker

On occasion, you will be asked to be an emcee or to introduce a speaker at a meeting or gathering. This is also a speech, which requires thought and preparation in order to be as brief as possible. A good introduction, for example, should be between 30 seconds and 2 minutes.

Introducing a speaker serves two primary purposes, according to Mitchell Friedman, a San Francisco public relations counselor and speech trainer. "First," he says, "it functions as a transition from one part of the program to another." "Second," he says, "your introduction offers valuable cues to the audience as far as what they should expect from the speaker and the topic."

In order to write an introduction, you should contact the speaker in advance and get a copy of his or her professional background. Second, you should ask the speaker about his or her objectives for the presentation, the value of the topic to the audience, and any other thoughts about the forthcoming talk.

Like any speech, the introduction should have an opening, a body, and a conclusion. Friedman says, "The opening should grab the attention of the audience by establishing the importance of the subject. . . ." The body needs to emphasize the importance of the topic, the relevance of the topic to the audience, and establish the credentials of the speaker to address the topic. The conclusion is a brief comment to make the speaker feel welcome and to lead the applause as the speaker steps up to the podium.

Friedman cautions that a good speech introduction does not summarize the speech and, even more important, it doesn't include every detail of the person's background. Indeed, the biggest mistake made in speech introductions is giving the speaker's background in agonizing detail. A final note from Friedman: "It is not typically an occasion to make a joke at the expense of the speaker or to embarrass him or her."

Again for emphasis: Keep your introduction short—30 seconds to 2 minutes—and everyone, including the speaker, will be grateful. ■

Know Your Objective

Knowing your objective, as previously noted, is the most important requirement of all. There is no point in making a speech unless it accomplishes something. In preparing a speech, the first step is to determine what you want the audience to know or do. In other words, what attitude or opinion do you want the audience to have after listening to the speech?

A speech may inform, persuade, activate, or celebrate. It may also amuse or entertain. That particular kind of speech will not be considered here, but this does not rule out the use of *some* humor in the other kinds of speeches.

An informative speech is one that tells the audience something it does not know or does not understand. An informative speech might tell the audience about how the new local sewage system works, the results of the latest United Way campaign, the expansion plans of a major local corporation, or budget problems facing the state's system of higher education.

An activating speech is designed to get the listener to do something. Direct and specific action is suggested and urged. A basic principle of persuasion is that a speaker should provide an audience with a specific course of action to take: write to a congressional representative, vote for a candidate, purchase a product, or take steps to conserve energy.

A celebratory speech is designed to honor some person or event. Such speeches are often trite and boring, but they don't have to be. If a person is being honored for lifetime professional achievement, why not start out with an anecdote that best exemplifies the feats being honored? This is much better than a chronological account of the person's life as if it were being read from an obituary.

Events such as grand openings, anniversaries, and retirements usually have friendly, receptive audiences. In such cases, you can be more emotional and get away with some platitudes, which will probably be warmly received. When you prepare such a speech, however, keep it brief. Five minutes should be ample, because you are probably one of many speakers.

Structure the Message for the Ear

The average speech has only one brief exposure—the few minutes during which the speaker is presenting it. There is no chance to go back, no time to let it slowly digest, no opportunity for clarification. The message must get across now or never.

You may be an accomplished writer, but you must realize that speaking is something else again. As Louis Nizer once said, "The words may be the same, but the grammar, rhetoric, and phrasing are different. It is a different mode of expression—a different language."

66 *A fundamental aspect of speeches is writing not for the page, but for the ear. It's what we say and how we say it that's important.* 99

■ Rob Friedman, director of executive communications at Eli Lilly and Company, as quoted in *Ragan.com*

One major difference is that you have to build up to a major point and prepare the audience for what is coming. The lead of a written story attempts to say everything in about 15 to 25 words right at the beginning. If a speaker used the same form, most of the audience probably wouldn't hear it. When a speaker begins to talk, the audience is still settling down—so the first few words are often devoted to setting the stage: thanking the host, making a humorous comment, or saying how nice it is to be there. Here's the opening of the EDS speech for the Association of American Chambers of Commerce in Latin America:

> Hello. I am glad to be with you at this important event. I am enthusiastic about the event's theme, "The Transformation of the Americas," as well as the topic for this panel, "Opportunities Created by Advances in Information Technology." Because I truly believe we are in a major transformation, and tremendous opportunities abound. . . .

You should also be aware that people's minds wander. As your speech progresses, you must restate basic points and summarize your general message.

One platitude of the speaking circuit, but still a valid one, is to "tell them what you are going to tell them, tell it to them, and then tell them what you have told them." In this way, an audience is given a series of guideposts as they listen to the talk.

Some concepts used by writers are, of course, transferable to speaking. The words you use should be clear, concise, short, and definite. Use words that specify, explain, and paint pictures for the audience. In addition, avoid delivering a speech in a monotone voice. That puts audiences to sleep.

Tailor Remarks to the Audience

Because every speech is aimed at a specific audience, you must know as much as possible about yours. Who are they? Such factors as age, occupation, gender, religion, race, education, intelligence, vocabulary, residence, interests, attitudes, group memberships, knowledge, politics, and income may bear on what they will find interesting.

A talk before a professional group can also end up being more relevant if you prepare for it by doing some audience analysis and basic research. Talk to members of the profession. Get an idea of the issues or problems they face. If you don't know anyone in the profession, at least read five or six issues of the group's professional journal or visit its website. This will give you some insight and perhaps even provide you with some quotations from leaders in the field.

In summary, most audiences have a core of common interests; this should help you to prepare a speech that will appeal to them. A talk to the stockholders of a corporation should be considerably different from one to employees or to a consumer group. See the Tips for Success on page 412 for more tips on tailoring your message for the audience.

Give Specifics

People remember only a small part of what they hear. You must therefore make sure that they hear things they can remember. A vague generality has little or no chance of being understood, let alone remembered. The speech must be built around specific ideas phrased in clear and memorable language.

> ❝ *A great spokesperson knows that a combination of data and anecdotes is the winning formula.* ❞
>
> ■ Brad Phillips, president of Phillips Media Relations, writing in *PR Tactics*

A vague statement—for example, "We ought to do something about gun control"—has no chance of being effective. If it was more specific—"We should ban all handguns and make it an offense to be in possession of one"—it would offer the audience an idea that is definite and understandable.

In most cases, the person who is asked to speak is perceived as an expert on a given subject. Consequently, the audience wants the benefit of that person's thinking and analysis. They don't want platitudes or statements that are self-evident. An economist should offer more than the flat statement that the economy is in trouble; he or she should explain why it is in trouble and what the solution might be. Beth Haiken, vice president of public relations for PMI Group, says its best. She told *PRWeek*, "Never ever announce a problem without also announcing a solution for it."

Keep It Timely and Short

Regardless of the nature and the objective of a speech, it must be interesting *now*. It must include up-to-date facts and information; don't talk about a situation that is no longer current or has no immediate interest for the audience. If the topic is an old one, it is imperative that you talk about it in a new way. For example, everyone knows that dinosaurs are extinct, but their demise retains current interest as scientists argue over the reasons for it.

If the speech is one of several in a general program, it is wise to learn what others will be talking about. This will provide a context for your talk and add interest by reference to the other topics and speakers. It will also help you avoid saying the same thing as other speakers.

Another dimension of timeliness is the length of the speech. In general, shorter is better. For a luncheon meeting, the talk should be about 20 minutes long. As previously mentioned, this is about 10 pages, double-spaced. It is a typical practice in many organizations to put the speaker on after a half-hour of organizational announcements and committee reports.

The time of day is very important. A morning speech generally finds the audience most alert and receptive. At the end of the afternoon, with the cocktail hour only minutes away, a speaker is at an extreme disadvantage. The latter situation calls for more skill on the part of the speaker; he or she must be more enthusiastic, more forceful, and more attention getting than his or her morning counterpart.

The guidelines generally refer to run-of-the-mill luncheon and dinner meetings. If you are giving a major speech at a conference, you often have 30 to 60 minutes for a presentation.

Gestures and Eye Contact

Gestures, posture, and eye contact can make or break a speech. One classic study by Dr. Albert Mehrabian in the 1960s found that 93 percent of all communication occurs not through words, but through vocal and nonverbal performance, such as gestures, posture, and attire.

In other words, gestures play a major role in establishing credibility. Gestures should agree with the vocal message to be effective. If you are making a major point, you might raise your hand for emphasis. See the photo of Barack Obama in Figure 15.1 for an example of how a successful speaker uses gestures. Other experts say that you can "reach out" to an audience by extending your arms outward with the palms up.

Nervous gestures, however, are distracting to the audience. Don't play with your hair, fiddle with a pen, fondle your necklace or tie, or keep moving your leg or foot. Remember your facial expression; smile at the audience, express interest and attention instead of boredom. Audiences pick up on nonverbal cues and assess the speaker accordingly.

Posture is also a gesture. Speakers should stand straight up, leaning slightly forward. Don't hunch over the podium; it conveys a lack of passion for the subject and infers that you are not completely certain of what you are saying.

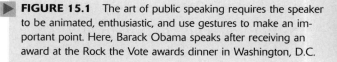

FIGURE 15.1 The art of public speaking requires the speaker to be animated, enthusiastic, and use gestures to make an important point. Here, Barack Obama speaks after receiving an award at the Rock the Vote awards dinner in Washington, D.C.

Eye contact is crucial. Don't read a speech with your eyes glued to the lectern or keep looking at the screen behind you with your PowerPoint slide. It is important to look up at the audience and establish eye contact. Experts recommend that you look at specific people in the audience to keep you from superficially gazing over the heads of the audience. Eye contact, according to research studies, is the major factor that establishes a speaker's rapport and credibility with an audience.

The SPEAK model summarizing the key points of nonverbal communication is provided in the following Tips for Success.

Visual Aids for Presentations

The chapter so far has focused on the techniques of writing and giving a speech or presentation. We now turn our attention to the use of visual aids to enhance and improve the speaker's effectiveness.

First, it is commonly recognized that visual aids can enhance learning, productivity, and message absorption. Consider the following findings:

- Sight accounts for 83 percent of what we learn.
- When a visual is combined with a voice, retention increases by 50 percent.
- Color increases a viewer's tendency to act on the information by 26 percent.

☑ tips FOR SUCCESS

Nonverbal Communication Speaks Volumes

A speaker doesn't communicate to an audience with voice alone. The audience also receives a great deal of nonverbal communication from the speaker. Veteran speaker Jack Pyle, writing in *PR Reporter*, offers the SPEAK method to help you appear confident and become a better communicator:

S = Smile.   It's one of your best communication tools, always helps make a good first impression, and helps make others want to listen to you.

P = Posture.   How you stand or sit makes a big difference. Your physical stance tells others how you feel about yourself. Confident people stand tall and sit straight.

E = Eye contact.   A person who is believable and honest "looks you right in the eye." Don't stare, but look at a person's face for at least 3 seconds before moving on to look at another person. If you are talking to a group, give your message to one person at a time.

A = Animation.   Show your interest in your subject with your energy and animation. Be enthusiastic. Animate your voice by speeding up and slowing down, talking louder and softer at times. Make your face animated. "A" is also for attitude. Make sure you feel good about yourself and what you are doing.

K = Kinetics (motion).   Use your arms to make gestures that support your words. Use two-handed, symmetrical gestures, and hold your hands high when gesturing—at about chest level. ■

- Use of video increases retention by 50 percent and accelerates buying decisions by 72 percent.
- The time required to present a concept can be reduced by up to 40 percent with visuals.

Research at the Wharton School of Business also shows the benefits of visual aids. In its research, it was found that audience members perceived presenters who used visuals as more effective than those who did not. In addition, almost two-thirds of those who were shown visuals were able to make a decision right after the presentation. Using visuals also cut meeting time by 24 percent.

This is not to say that every speech or presentation requires a visual aid. In many cases, such as a banquet or a formal meeting, the speaker uses no visual aids. Nor does the President of the United States need them when presenting the annual State of the Union Address to Congress. More often than not, however, most of us find ourselves giving presentations to a variety of audiences who need visual aids to keep their attention as well as to increase their retention of the information.

It is important to understand the advantages and disadvantages of each visual aid technique to determine what will be the most effective in a given situation. Indeed, visual aids are planned for a specific situation and audience. If you are giving a workshop or seminar where the objective is to inform and educate an audience, a PowerPoint presentation may be the best approach. If, however, you are conducting a brainstorming session where audience interactivity is the objective, perhaps an easel with a blank pad of paper to record ideas is the only visual aid required.

A major speech for a large convention may be more effective if one uses PowerPoint slides and video clips. This was the case when Hector Ruiz, president of AMD, addressed the annual meeting of high-technology manufacturers at Comdex in Las Vegas. He used three short videos in his talk to illustrate how AMD partnered with other companies to solve their particular problems and, along the way, create new products.

PowerPoint

The leading presentation software is Microsoft's PowerPoint. *USA Today* business writer Kevin Maney said it best when he wrote several years ago, "PowerPoint users are inheriting the earth. The software's computer generated, graphic-artsy presentation slides are everywhere—meetings, speeches, sales pitches, websites. They're becoming as essential to getting through the business day as coffee and Post-it notes."

Indeed, Microsoft estimates that there are about 300 million PowerPoint users in the world, and about 30 million presentations are given every day. In fact, about 1 million presentations are going on somewhere in the world as you are reading this. Such a robust market has generated some imitators, such as Google Presentations, which is part of Google Docs, a suite of online applications.

Doug Lowe, author of *PowerPoint for Dummies*, succinctly explains the software program. He says:

Essentially, PowerPoint is similar to a word processor like Word, except that it's geared toward creating presentations rather than documents. Just as a Word document consists of one or more pages, a PowerPoint presentation consists of one or more slides. Each slide can contain text, graphics, and other information. You can easily arrange the slides in a presentation, delete slides you don't need, add new slides, or modify the contents of existing slides.

PowerPoint is a program in Microsoft Office, but it can also be purchased separately. Most users like it because it allows you to make relatively attractive slides of information by simply following the directions and using any number of templates that are offered. By clicking on a variety of options, an individual can write the title and body text in a variety of fonts, select background and text colors, add photos and clip art, and even do multicolored charts and graphs. More sophisticated users also add sound clips, animation, and video files to their slide presentations through the increased use of such creative programs as Photoshop, Illustrator, and Flash.

PowerPoint is a very versatile software program from the standpoint of preparing information that can be used in a variety of ways. Here are some of the ways it can be used:

- **Use your computer monitor.** A desktop or laptop is ideal to show the presentation to one or two individuals. The laptop presentation is popular on media tours when you are talking one-on-one with an editor or a financial analyst.
- **Harness your laptop to a computer projector.** If you are reaching a larger audience, technology has now advanced so you can show a PowerPoint presentation on a large screen in a meeting hall.
- **Post the PowerPoint presentation on the Web.** You can post an entire slide presentation to the organization's website or the company intranet.
- **Make overhead transparencies.** Once you have created a PowerPoint presentation, you can print the slides on clear plastic sheets, called transparencies. Some speakers, for example, carry a set of transparencies just in case the computer projector doesn't work or—even more of a problem—the organization doesn't have a computer projector.
- **Print pages.** You can distribute copies of your entire presentation to the audience. The software also allows you to do thumbnails of each slide on the left column and give a place for individuals to take notes on the right side of the page.
- **Create 35-mm slides.** Your presentation can be printed onto 35-mm slides and then shown using a carousel slide tray. This approach is also a good backup just in case the organization or the meeting room doesn't have a computer projector.
- **Create CDs and DVDs.** Many organizations put PowerPoint presentations on CDs or, increasingly, DVDs so they can be easily sent to media reporters, customers, and field personnel for their viewing and background. A low-tech version of this is to place a spiral-bound copy of a PowerPoint presentation in a media kit as a kind of extended fact sheet giving reporters key points about the organization or product.

Whatever the medium—be it transparencies, 35-mm slides, or paper—there are some rules about the composition of a PowerPoint slide that you should keep in mind.

One key rule is not to make your slide too detailed or cluttered with too much clip art or the use of fancy borders. Another common mistake is to include too much copy. Peter Nolan, writing in *PR Tactics*, says, "The last thing any presenter wants is to have the audience reading a heavy text slide rather than paying attention to what is being said. Presentation slides should support the speaker with a few key words or easily understood graphics."

A good antidote to Nolan's concern is the four-by-four rule. Use no more than four bullets, and no more than four or five words for each bullet. Some experts advise that there should be no more than 10 lines of copy on a slide; others say no more than 20 words. This is not to say that every slide should look like the previous one; that gets boring. Transitional slides, from one topic or major point to another, may only consist of one or two words or perhaps a photo or clip art. In general, remember the motto about text—less is better. Some experts recommend photos; they are more interesting than standard clip art.

A standard rule is a minimum of 24 to 28 point type for all words. Anything smaller will be difficult to see from the back of the room. Also, be aware that you should have at least a 2-inch margin around any copy; this ensures that your copy will fit the configuration of a slide projector or a 35-mm slide if you are using these mediums. PowerPoint has text boxes, which helps the amateur format the right amount of space around the text. Several examples of basic layout, done with PowerPoint, are shown in Figure 15.2.

Color is also an important consideration. PowerPoint has hundreds of colors available in its palette, but that doesn't mean you have to use all of them. Multiple colors for the background and the text only distract the audience and give the impression of an incoherent presentation. It also leads to a common complaint about PowerPoint presentations.

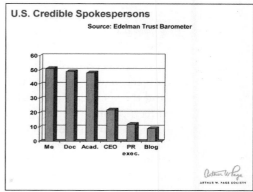

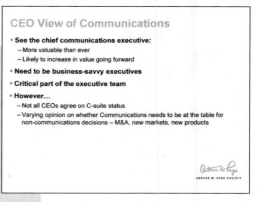

FIGURE 15.2 PowerPoint slides are the workhorse of the speech and presentation circuit. The most effective slides, however, should be simple and relatively uncluttered. These slides, taken from a presentation by the Arthur W. Page Society, a group of senior communication executives, make the point. The first slide (a) shows how basic concepts can be displayed in colorful and graphic terms. The second slide (b) shows how data can be prepared in simple bar chart form for easy readability. The third slide (c) shows how text can be formatted with color and boldfacing.

Manly, from *USA Today*, says, ". . . people spend too much time messing with the PowerPoint and not enough time messing with the message."

In other words, keep it simple. You should use clear, bold fonts for colors that contrast with the background. As for background, dark blues convey a corporate approach, greens work well when feedback is desired, and reds motivate the audience to action. Yellows and purples are not recommended for most business presentations. In general, black is the best color for text, but remember the contrast rule. Black type on a dark blue or red background won't be readable. Other experts simply recommend that you use earth tones and middle-range colors for a slide's background so there is maximum contrast between the color of the text (black or another dark color) and the background.

Art Samansky, president of a public affairs consultancy, makes another comment about the use of PowerPoint in presentations. His advice: "Slides, like a magician's wand, are only a prop. You are the act. If you are merely reciting the material on the slides, you might as well e-mail your audience a copy and save all precious time and travel expenses." Put another way, don't read your slides to the audience; everyone in the audience with a third-grade education can read for themselves. Slides should only provide a track or outline of key points you want to elaborate upon to the audience.

In sum, there are multiple components to giving a speech. The Tips for Success on page 419 summarizes many of the key points.

Other Speech Formats

A speech is controlled by the speaker. He or she knows what is going to be said. The subject matter is complete and well organized. The speech has been well rehearsed, and the speaker has polished his or her remarks to give a solo performance without interruption.

The environment changes, however, when the speaker participates in activities such as panels, debates, and media interviews. Here someone else is directing the action, and a speaker's comments can't always be scripted in advance. Even so, these opportunities are valuable aids to public communication and should be used whenever possible.

Panels

A panel usually consists of a moderator and several people, each of whom makes a brief opening statement 5 to 7 minutes in length. The rest of the time is spent on answering questions from the audience.

The moderator may solicit audience questions in several ways. One common method, if the audience is relatively small, is simply to recognize people who stand up and ask a question. In larger audiences, a portable microphone is brought to the audience member so everyone can hear the question. Another method is to have the audience submit questions on forms distributed to the audience. The moderator, in this case, goes through the written questions and tries to select questions that would be of most interest to the audience.

How to Improve a Speech

Joan Detz, author of *How to Write & Give a Speech*, offers 10 tips on how to improve a speech. In an article for *Communication World*, she makes the following suggestions:

1. **Make it shorter.** A 15-minute speech gets higher ratings from an audience than a 30-minute speech.

2. **Make it sharper.** Give your speech a sharper edge. Use a clever statistic, create a shocking contrast, or articulate your point with vivid language.

3. **Use greater variety in your research.** Don't just use statistics and examples. Also consider customer comments, shareholder letters, witty quotations, professional endorsements, one-liners, surveys, news headlines, references to popular culture, and historical anecdotes. An EDS executive, speaking to a Latin American audience, used a quote from a novel by Vargas Llosa, a famous South American author.

4. **Start strong.** Skip the list of thank-yous and boring generalities. Get to the point with a strong statement.

5. **Use stylistic devices.** Put items in groups of three, use parallel structure, and repeat key phrases throughout the talk. At a diversity awards program, an executive of Booz Allen & Hamilton used the phrase "do the right thing" throughout his speech.

6. **Include rhetorical questions.** Such questions engage the audience because they instinctively start thinking about an answer. Before answering the question, you should pause briefly so the audience has some time to answer the question in their own minds.

7. **Avoid using audiovisual aids as a crutch.** A lot of slides or overheads with meaningless words distract the audience.

8. **Use a light touch of humor.** Use humor to relax the audience and gain rapport, but don't overdo it.

9. **Respect wordsmithing.** Consonants articulate sound, whereas vowels express the musicality of the language.

10. **End strong.** If you say "in conclusion," you have 30 seconds to summarize the key message of your talk. ■

Individual panelists are asked to comment on questions, or the question may be addressed to the entire panel. In either case, it is your responsibility as a panelist to give a short answer (one minute or less) so that other panelists will also have an opportunity to comment. It is unfair for any panelist to monopolize the forum by giving long-winded answers to any question.

Panels are good vehicles for getting audience involvement and participation, and they are a standard feature at most conventions. The key to a good panel, however, is an effective moderator. He or she must control the panel by policing the time that a person takes to give an opening statement, politely cutting off long-winded answers to a single question, and making sure all panelists have an equal opportunity to express their views.

Debates

In high schools and colleges, a debate has teams of several speakers. Most debates in the world of public relations are not team efforts. They pit two opponents against each other, and each carries the burden of making the case of his or her side and re-butting the statements of the opponent. The so-called debates of American political campaigns are not really debates; they are merely presentations during which the rivals offer their answers to the same questions.

The management of political debates is not within the purview of this book. That is best left to the political specialists. But any reader of this volume may at some time have to handle a debate on some public issue.

Aside from the need to know something about debating, there is one special warning worth heeding. This involves the situation in which a moderator may try to split the debate into two parts, with each speaker being allowed a brief period for rebuttal. A toss of the coin determines who will be first. It is advantageous to speak *last* in such a situation, because the last speaker may have 10 minutes or more in which to try to demolish the statements of the opponent. The rebuttal period may be only a minute or two, and this is hardly adequate to overcome the effect of a long windup statement. The audience is left with a much stronger impression of what the last speaker said. To avoid being caught at such a disadvantage, you should insist that the debate be in short segments—5 minutes would be a good length. Then the debate would consist of several 5-minute statements by each speaker and a short summary rebuttal.

Speaker Training and Placement

Giving talks and speeches is an important part of an organization's outreach to its key publics. A talk by an executive or an employee is a highly personal form of communication and adds a human dimension to any organization. It's a form of face-to-face communication, and it offers the chance for interaction between the speaker and the audience.

Speech giving should be an integral part of an organization's overall public relations program. Indeed, public relations personnel are often involved in training speakers and seeking appropriate forums where key publics can be reached.

Executive Training

Today, the public is demanding more open disclosure and accountability from organizations, which is forcing many executives to mount the speaker's platform. Ned Scharff, a longtime speechwriter at Merrill Lynch & Co., says it best in an article for *The Strategist*: "If the . . . CEO is to excel as a leader, he or she cannot avoid giving speeches. People have a deep-seated need to see and hear their leaders actively expressing vision and conviction." *PR Reporter*, in one survey of executives, found that over half spend 10 hours or more each month meeting with outside groups. In addition, the majority average 20 speeches a year, about two-thirds spend time on press conferences, and another third appear on TV.

As a consequence, more executives are taking courses designed to improve their public speaking skills. Cincinnati Gas & Electric holds seminars of this kind for both managers and line employees. Levi Strauss & Company teaches "effective presentation skills" to middle managers. Other companies have also rushed into speech training for executives, creating a major boom for consultants who train employees at all levels to represent their firms in public forums or media interviews.

> ❝ **CEOs clearly recognize that speaking opportunities serve as platforms for senior executives to further amplify corporate messages to key stakeholders and increase mind share and market share.** ❞
>
> ■ Jennifer Risi, executive vice president of Weber Shandwick Global Strategies Media Group, as quoted by *The Strategist*

Because the costs of such training sessions often run into thousands of dollars, organizations with limited budgets may not be able to afford them. Therefore, the public relations department is often given the responsibility of training executives in media interview and speech skills. Videotaping is often done to help an executive see how he or she comes across giving a speech. It's a powerful educational tool that almost always has more impact than telling a person how to give an effective speech.

Speech training can be divided in two parts: what to say and how to say it. Public relations personnel are most effective at helping executives crystallize what they want to say. Both of you should review the context of the speech from the standpoint of location, expected audience, and what information would be interesting to them.

Another consideration is what you want to say that will advance organizational objectives—to position the organization or industry as a leader, to plant the perception that the organization is successful, or simply to show that the organization is environmentally conscious and a good community citizen. All speeches should have one to three key messages.

There are entire courses and many textbooks on how to give a speech. The ideal speaker is one who knows about the subject, whose voice and appearance will make a good impression, and who is comfortable standing in front of an audience. Steve Jobs of Apple is a good communicator because he comes across as an amiable personality with a deep commitment to his company's products.

Speaker's Bureaus

Top executives aren't the only ones who give speeches. Many organizations effectively use technical experts, middle managers, and even rank-and-file employees on a systematic basic to extend the organization's outreach to potential customers, the industry, and the community.

Steve Markman, head of a conference and management firm, makes the case in an article for *PR Tactics*. He writes:

> Companies need to expose their expertise and technologies to prospective customers and clients. What is a proven method of accomplishing this objective? Speaking at public forums produced by other organizations—at conferences, seminars, and forums held by independent event organizations, associations, professional and

industry trade groups, and academic institutions and think tanks. There is much evidence that speaking at public forums often results in the attainment of business, by providing increased awareness of the company in general and specific subjects in particular, to an audience of potential customers or clients.

In every organization, there are individuals who are capable of giving speeches and presentations. In many cases, it is part of their job description. Members of the technical staff, for example, are often asked by professional groups to share their research or talk about the development of a particular product. In other situations, a community group may want a general talk about how the company is dealing with a sluggish economy.

One way of systematically organizing a company's outreach is to set up a **speaker's bureau**. This is more than just a list of employees who are willing to speak. It is also a training center that trains speakers; produces supporting audiovisual aids, such as PowerPoint presentations and videos; and even develops key messages about the organization, product, or service that should be included in any presentation.

Ideally, a speaker's bureau will have a list of employees who are expert on a variety of subjects. A person in finance may be an expert on worker's compensation, and an engineer in product development may have expertise with lasers. Markham warns, however, that a speech or presentation to a group should avoid being a "sales pitch." He says, "A presentation that turns out to be a sales pitch will ensure low evaluations by the audience and a one-way ticket home. . . ."

Placement of Speakers

Once executives and employees have been trained, your job is finding opportunities for them to speak. An organization usually publicizes the existence of a speaker's bureau by preparing a simple pamphlet or brochure and sending it to various clubs and organizations in the community that regularly use speakers. Another method is to place advertisements about the speaker's bureau in local newspapers. The public relations department also encourages calls from various organizations that need speakers on various topics. At other times, you have to be more proactive and contact the organization to offer the services of a speaker on a particular topic. One of the most difficult jobs in any club is that of program director, and they welcome any suggestions that make their lives easier.

Once a speaker has been booked, the manager of a speaker's bureau usually handles all the logistical details. He or she briefs the speaker on (1) the size and composition of the audience, (2) the location, (3) availability of audiovisual equipment, (4) the projected length of the presentation, (5) directions to the meeting, and (6) primary organizational contacts.

The placement of the organization's top executives, however, tends to be more strategic. Top executives often get more requests for speeches than they can ever fulfill, so the problem is selecting a few of the invitations that are extended.

The criteria, at this point, become somewhat pragmatic and cold-hearted. Public relations staff is charged with screening the invitations on the basis of such factors as the venue, the nature of the group, the size of the audience, and whether the audience is an important public to the organization. If most or all of these factors are positive, the executive will most likely consent to give a speech.

Toyota, for example, has even developed a "grading sheet" to screen speech requests. Ron Kirkpatrick, manager of executive communications at the automaker, uses four questions:

1. Will the speaking forum advance the goals/strategies of the company?
2. Will it attract media coverage?
3. Is the audience highly influential?
4. Can we get extended reach through the host group's website, newsletter, etc.?

If a group doesn't make the cut, Kirkpatrick is diplomatic. He writes in Ragan. com, "We usually tell them that our executive's busy travel schedule won't allow them to accept the invitation. And that's pretty much true. Our executives travel so extensively that getting a speech on their calendars is a huge challenge."

At other times, public relations managers are proactive in seeking placement opportunities. If the chief executive officer wants to become a leader in the industry, for example, the public relations staff actively seeks out speech opportunities before prestigious audiences that can help establish the executive as the spokesperson for the industry.

A good example of how strategic executive speech placement works is what Ronald J. McCall, owner of his own executive communication firm, did for the chief executive of Duke Energy, a $15 billion gas and electric utility. He told *Speechwriter's Newsletter*:

> The company was perceived as a local utility, and we wanted more of a national presence, so I placed the chief executive on the *Business Week* symposium for chief executive officers. That was the first time he was able to tell the Duke Energy story, and he did it in front of a very influential audience of other chief executive officers from across the country. Every one of them needed some kind of energy, whether it is gas or electricity. Every one of them was a potential customer.

Another example of strategic thinking is UPS. Several years ago, the company organized an executive communications program that actively promoted its top executives as business leaders through speeches at national and regional business and trade events.

Matthew Arnold, writing in *PRWeek*, quotes Steve Soltis, head of the UPS executive communications unit: "The whole program was created for the express purpose of using senior management as a component of brand building. Using them as leaders, creating the platform for our values and strategies." He continued, "If business as a brand is blemished right now, good companies like us must be out there."

Burson-Marsteller, in a 2008 survey, compiled the 10 top-valued podiums for CEOs. The top five corporate conferences, in descending order, are sponsored by The World Economic Forum, *The Wall Street Journal*, *Forbes*, *Fortune*, and the World Business Forum.

Publicity Opportunities

The number of people a speech or a presentation reaches can be substantially increased through publicity.

Before the Event ■ Whenever anyone from your organization speaks in public, you should make sure that the appropriate media are notified in advance. This often takes the form of a media advisory, discussed in an earlier chapter.

An advisory is simply a short note that gives the speaker's name and title, the speech title, and details about time and place. In a brief sentence or two, describe why the speech is important and of interest to the publication's audience. If it is available and it is a major policy speech, you can also send an advance copy of the speech to selected reporters. Make sure they realize they should not report the speech until after it is given. This request to the media is called an "embargo" and is often invoked in the case of an important speech being delivered at a specific time. Media relations was discussed in Chapter 11. If the speech is a major event, you will also make arrangements with a vendor to do a live Webcast of the speech so reporters and others not attending the event can also view it in "real time." See Chapter 12 for more details on how Webcasts are done. You may also make arrangements for the speech to be videotaped.

Reporters attending the speech should be seated near the podium, and arrangements should be made for accommodating photographers and television camera technicians. Reporters should also be provided with a media kit that gives the background of the organization and the speaker. A copy of the speech is also enclosed. See also Chapter 11 about organizing news conferences.

After the Event ■ After a speech is given, you have more duties. You must prepare news releases about what was said so that the speech can be reported in appropriate publications. The Tips for Success on page 425 offers guidelines for converting a speech into a news release. Video clips must be sent to television stations via the Internet or satellite, and radio stations receive audio clips. Preparing material for broadcast outlets was discussed in Chapter 9.

The speech also can be shortened and excerpted as a possible op-ed article in daily newspapers. (How to write and place op-ed articles was discussed in Chapter 7.) Reprints, or excerpts of the speech, also can be posted on the organization's websites or sent through an organization's intranet to employees.

An example is AMD. Its president, Hector Ruiz, gave the keynote address at Comdex, a major trade show for the high-technology industry. This was a major platform for AMD and Ruiz to establish leadership in the industry, so the company spent considerable time and effort to ensure that the speech got wide coverage and distribution.

The company arranged for a Webcast at the time of the speech, but it also placed the speech on the AMD website for later viewing. The Web page also included a photo of Ruiz giving the speech and a short summary of the key points. In addition, there was a link for "Read a transcript of the keynote address" and "Read what they're saying" in terms of press comments on the speech.

The Speech as News Release

The audience reach of a speech is multiplied many times when a news release is distributed that summarizes the speaker's key message. A speech news release follows many of the same structural guidelines outlined in Chapter 5, but there are some specific concepts that you should keep in mind.

"The key to writing stories about speeches is to summarize the speech or to present one or two key points in the lead sentence," says Douglas Starr, a professor of journalism and public relations at Texas A&M University.

In an article for *PR Tactics*, Starr says a speech news release should follow a particular format. He says, "Answers to the questions—who said what, to whom—must be in the lead of every speech story. Answers to the questions—where, when, how, why—may be placed in the second paragraph."

The most common mistake inexperienced writers make is to tell readers that a *speaker spoke about a topic* instead of saying what the *speaker said about the topic*. An example of the first approach is "Susan Jones, president of XYZ Corporation, spoke about environmental regulations." A better approach would be, "Susan Jones, president of XYZ Corporation, says rigid environmental regulations are strangling the economy." See the difference?

The second sentence or paragraph of a speech news release usually describes the event where the speech was given, the location, the attendance, and the reason for the meeting. It is unnecessary, however, to give the title of a person's speech or even the theme of the convention or meeting. They are meaningless to the reader.

The third and subsequent paragraphs may contain speaker quotes, additional facts or figures, and other relevant information that helps provide context for the speech. When attributing quotes, "said" is the preferred verb. However, some writers vary this by using the terms "stated," or "added." Starr suggests you stay away from such attribution terms as "discussed," "addressed," and "spoke," because they don't say anything. ■

If a speech is particularly important, it can be printed as a brochure and mailed to selected opinion leaders. You can also ask a member of the U.S. House of Representatives or the U.S. Senate to insert the speech into the *Congressional Record*.

■Summary

- Writing and giving speeches are outstanding public relations opportunities for organizations to increase their visibility and reach key publics.

- Speechwriting requires clear objectives, effective organization of relevant key messages, knowledge of the audience, and a close working relationship with the person who will be giving the speech.

- A speech is a powerful communication tool. It must be prepared for listeners, not readers. It must fit the audience, be specific, get a reaction, have a definite objective, and be timely.

- Nonverbal communication is important in a speech. Speakers should be enthusiastic, make eye contact with the audience, and use gestures that support their words.

- The recommended length of a speech at a luncheon or dinner meeting is 20 minutes. Such a speech would be 10 pages, double-spaced.

- Speeches should have one to three key messages.

- Audiovisuals dramatically increase the ability of audiences to retain and understand information.

- PowerPoint can create attractive slides that can be used in a variety of formats—paper copies, computer display, Web pages, overhead transparencies, 35-mm slides, CDs, and DVDs.

- Computer projectors are now widely used by most organizations.

- The key to successful visual aids is brief copy and large type.

- Other presentations—panels, debates, and media interviews—follow the same basic principles as speeches. However, they also involve special preparation for dealing with opposition, interruptions, and hostile questions.

- Executive and staff speech training is often the responsibility of the public relations professional.

- A speaker's bureau is a good way to organize an effective program of community outreach.

- Top executives of an organization must be selective about what speech invitations they accept. Factors such as the sponsoring organization, the size of the audience, and whether the venue advances organizational objectives must be considered.

- Speeches provide opportunities for additional publicity by (1) inviting the press to cover it, (2) preparing news releases, (3) distributing audio and visual clips, (4) converting the speech to an op-ed piece, (5) reprinting it in a brochure, and (6) posting excerpts on a Web page.

Skill Building Activities

1. Interview a fellow classmate or colleague about a current issue or topic that he or she wants to talk about and has some knowledge. Write a 5-minute speech, which is about three pages, double-spaced, for that person on the subject. Get feedback on the first draft and then do a final draft that the person would present to the class.

2. Attend a speech given to a campus or community organization. Write a critique of the speaker and assess his or her effectiveness according to the guidelines for speaking outlined in this chapter.

3. While you are at the speech (see Exercise 2), take notes on what the speaker said and write a news release about what the speaker said. See the guidelines on page 425.

4. Select an organization that regularly has a speaker for its weekly or monthly meeting. Prepare a short memo that would help the president of the university prepare for a talk before the group. Include some brief background on the organization, a profile of the membership, the time and place of the meeting, the format of the entire meeting, and the amount of time that a speaker should talk.

5. Prepare a 10-minute PowerPoint presentation on some topic of interest to you and then present it to your classmates or colleagues. In addition, prepare a handout using a thumbnail of the slide on the left and spaces on the right for the audience to write notes while you are speaking.

Suggested Readings

Beebe, Steven A., and Beebe, Susan. *Public Speaking: An Audience-Centered Approach*, 6th edition. Boston: Allyn & Bacon, 2006.

Fujishin, Randy. *The Natural Speaker*. Boston: Allyn & Bacon, 2005.

Lewis, Tanya. "Finding the Right Words for all Occasions." *PRWeek*, March 10, 2008, p. 14.

Lowe, Doug. *PowerPoint for Dummies*. New York: Hungry Minds, Inc., 2002.

Phillips, Brad. "Don't Alienate Your Audience: Injecting Passion Into Your Information and Anecdotes for a Winning Combination." *PR Tactics*, May 2007, p. 15.

Seitel, Fraser P. "Using PowerPoint." *O'Dwyer's PR Report*, February 2008, pp. 30–31.

Struck, Kevin. "Workin' the Room: 112 Principles for Properly Lecturing Your Audiences." *Communication World*, February–March, 2002, pp. 27–29.

"Study Shows Executive Speaking Engagements on the Rise." *The Strategist*, Winter 2008, p. 4.

"Survey: Top 10 Most Valued Podiums for CEOs and C-Suite Executives." *PR Tactics and The Strategist Online* (www.prsa.org), May 22, 2008.

Witkoski, Michael. "Don't Let Eloquence Derail Your Speech Writing." *PR Tactics*, May 2002, p. 15.

Using Direct Mail and Advertising

16

TOPICS covered in this chapter include:

The Basics of Direct Mail   428

Creating a Direct Mail Package   430

The Basics of Public Relations
   Advertising   436

Types of Public Relations Advertising   438

Creating a Print Ad   444

Working with an Ad Agency   446

Other Advertising Channels   447

The Basics of Direct Mail

Letters and accompanying material mailed to large groups of people is a form of marketing called **direct mail**. Although many consumers and the media often refer to it as **junk mail**, it has a long history. According to Media Distribution Services, one of the first examples of "direct mail" was in 1744, when Benjamin Franklin mailed a list of books for sale to a selected list of prospects. Not exactly Amazon. com, but a start.

Since then, the use of direct mail to sell ideas, goods, and services has skyrocketed. Billions of direct mail pieces are produced each year in the United States, primarily to sell products and services. Indeed, *U.S. News & World Report* says that the average household receives 34 pounds, or more than 550 pieces, of direct mail annually.

Although the major use of direct mail is to sell goods and services, it also has a number of uses as an effective public relations tool. Direct mail, for example, is used by political candidates to inform voters about issues and also to ask for their votes. It is used by charitable groups to educate the public about various social issues and diseases and to solicit contributions.

Corporations often use direct mail to notify consumers about a product recall, inform investors about a merger or acquisition, or make an apology about a poor service or shoddy goods. Community groups use direct mail to let their members and other interested people know about forthcoming events and their stand on important issues. In other words, whenever a number of people can be identified as a key public, it is logical to reach them with direct mail.

Advantages of Direct Mail

Direct mail is a controlled communication medium, just like newsletters, brochures, and websites. It allows you to have total control over the format, wording, and timing of a message to audiences as broad or narrow as you wish. Indeed, the three major advantages of direct mail are (1) targeting your communication to specific individuals, (2) personalization, and (3) cost-effectiveness.

Targeted Audience ■ An appropriate mailing list is the key to using direct mail as an effective public relations tool. At the very basic level, a mailing list may be a compilation of an organization's members, past contributors, employees, or customers. Organizations compile mailing lists on all sorts of audiences. In public relations, for example, you may compile a mailing list of community leaders. People working in investor relations might have a list of analysts, institutional investors, and stockholders.

You can also rent mailing lists from various membership organizations and media outlets. If you want to send a letter to all dentists in your area, you contact the American Dental Association. If your purpose is to reach affluent individuals, you might rent a list of BMW and Mercedes Benz owners from the state department of motor vehicles. You can also rent the subscription lists of various newspapers and magazines if you feel that the demographics of the subscribers fit your particular purpose. For about $150, for example, List Services Corp. will provide 1,000 subscribers to *Forbes* magazine with average incomes of $232,000.

Advances in marketing research, including demographics and psychographics, make it possible to reach almost anyone with scientific precision. Thanks to vast data-collection and data-crunching networks, it is now possible to order mailing lists based on people's spending habits, charitable contributions, and even their favorite beer. Every time you purchase groceries with a store discount card, buy a book from Amazon.com, or order something from a catalog, your name and address goes into a marketing database that is often sold to other organizations.

Personalization ■ Direct mail, more than any other controlled or mass medium, is highly personalized. It comes in an envelope addressed to the recipient (there is no such thing anymore as "occupant"), and the letter often begins with a personalized greeting such as "Dear Jennifer." In addition, through computer software, the name of the person can be inserted throughout the letter. Specialized paragraphs can also be inserted in the direct mail letter to acknowledge past charitable contributions or make reference to localized information or contacts. The technology, which will be discussed shortly, also allows handwritten signatures and notes to make the basic "form" letter as personable as possible.

Cost ■ Direct mail, according to Media Distribution Services, is relatively inexpensive when compared to the cost of magazine ads and broadcast commercials. Typically, a rented list costs about $300 for 1,000 names. You can get these names and addresses on labels or, more commonly, have a software program print them directly on mailing envelopes.

Direct mail is cost-efficient from a production standpoint. In many cases, it is produced in one color (black), with perhaps a second color for emphasis of key points. Graphics are not elaborate, and the whole emphasis is on economical printing. Postage is a consideration. First class is the most expensive, but it is more reliable and timely than the cheaper third class (often called "standard mail"). First class also ensures that mail is forwarded or returned without additional cost to the sender. Nonprofit postage rates, available to qualified organizations, are the cheapest. You can cut postage costs by presorting letters by zip code and mailing at least 200 pieces at one time.

Disadvantages of Direct Mail

The major disadvantage of direct mail is its image as "junk mail." All such mail, whether it is a first-class letter or a flyer from the local pizza parlor, is put into the same category of "useless" information that just clutters up a person's mailbox.

Indeed, *U.S. News & World Report* estimates that nearly half of it goes directly to the garbage without even being opened. Even if it is opened, it is estimated that only 1 or 2 percent of the recipients will act on the message. Despite such odds, however, U.S. consumers purchased $244 billion worth of merchandise in a recent year by responding to direct mail sales pitches. Studies show that, on average, every dollar spent on direct mail advertising brings in $10 in sales—a return more than twice that generated by a television ad. Nonprofit agencies that rely on direct mail for much of their fund-raising efforts also say the ROI (return on investment) makes direct mail a major component of their communication strategy.

Information Overload ■ It has already been noted that the average person receives more than 550 pieces of direct mail annually. Although it is argued that a person reads direct mail in isolation from other messages and distractions, there is the problem of clutter and the inability of people to cope with so many messages on a daily basis. Consequently, it is important to know how to write and format a direct mail piece that gets opened, read, and acted upon.

Creating a Direct Mail Package

The direct mail package has five basic components: (1) mailing envelope, (2) letter, (3) basic brochure, (4) reply card, and (5) return envelope. On occasion, a sixth component is added—"gifts" such as address labels, greeting cards, and even calendars that are designed to entice a person to open the envelope and at least read the message.

Mailing Envelope

The envelope is the headline of a direct mail package, because it is the first thing the recipient sees. If this doesn't attract the reader's interest, a person will not "read on" by opening the envelope.

According to Media Distribution Services, there are several ways to make an envelope attractive and appealing. It can be visually enhanced through the creative use of paper stocks, windows, tabs, teasers, and other design options. Heavy, glossy paper can give the envelope the appearance of value and importance. Windows can provide teasers and other information that cater to the question, "Why should I open this?"

Sometimes, envelopes carry a preview of what's inside. UNICEF, in one of its fund-raising letters, used the envelope teaser, "Enclosed: The Life or Death Seed Catalog." The Sierra Club simply marks its envelopes "Urgent," in big, red letters. UNHCR, the UN Refugee Agency, clearly marks its envelopes. In one mailing about the Darfur crisis, the envelope carried the signage, "U.S. Congress Calls It Genocide: Inside: How You Can Help."

In contrast, some envelopes provide little or no information. They don't even give the name of the organization in the return address. An envelope from Leonardo DiCaprio has his name on it, but it doesn't mention that it's from Natural Resources Defense Council (NRDC). The idea is to arouse the curiosity of the reader so he or she will open the envelope. Other organizations resort to trickery. They make the envelope look like it is an official letter from a government agency or there is the misleading teaser that you are the winner of a large prize.

In general, public relations writers should avoid misleading teasers and envelope designs that mislead readers or cause mistaken impressions. This causes credibility problems, and it often borders on the unethical. Your direct mail envelope should always have the name of the organization and the return address in the upper-left corner. Teasers should provide honest information.

Research has also found that a regular stamp is better than metered postage, and a commemorative stamp is the most effective. Such stamps are attention getting, and it makes the direct mail envelope look more important. Of course, a name and address printed on the envelope is better than an adhesive label.

The Letter

For maximum effectiveness, the cover letter should be addressed to one person and start with a personal greeting, "Dear Ms. Smith." Some letters skip the personal salutation and just use a headline that will grab the reader's attention. A headline or a first paragraph is the most-read part of a letter, so it must be crafted to arouse the reader's interest. Some studies show that it takes a reader about 1 to 3 seconds to decide whether to read on or pitch the letter in the trash.

Headlines and First Paragraphs ■ A sales pitch for a product or service often has a headline that emphasizes a free gift or the promise of saving money. Non-profit groups and public action groups, however, often state the need in a headline. Planned Parenthood, for example, used the headline "Stop Clinic Violence" in an appeal to enlist support for legislation protecting health clinics from pro-life activists.

You can use a straight lead for the beginning paragraph, or a human-interest angle. The straight lead is to the point. The Sierra Club began one letter from the executive director with the following: "I am writing to ask for your immediate help to ensure victory for the most ambitious government plan to protect endangered wilderness in our nation's history—the Wild Forest Protection Plan."

The Care World Hunger Campaign used a human-interest and emotional angle in a recent campaign. The first sentences of the letter were:

Tonight, literally millions of children will go to bed hungry.

Some of them will plead for food, not able to understand that their moms and dads simply have nothing to give them . . .

Others—the little ones—will just cry as the hunger pangs stab through their tiny bodies . . . and some will be too weak to cry.

Can you imagine watching your own child hurting, dying—and being unable to help? It's any parent's nightmare.

Typeface and Length ■ Most direct mail letters are written on the organization's letter-size stationery. There is no rule about length, but experts recommend a maximum of two to four pages. A typewriter-style font for the text makes the letter appear more personal than a fancier typeface. Several devices are used to make the letter easy to use. One is short sentences and paragraphs. Another is putting key words and phrases in boldface or even larger type. Some organizations emphasize key messages with a yellow highlighter, use red ink, or underline them. An example from the Natural Resources Defense Council (NRDC) is shown in Figure 16.1.

Information on how to write a fund-raising letter is found in the accompanying Tips for Success. Other tips for planning a direct mail package are provided in the Tips for Success on page 434.

Postscript ■ The most effective direct mail letters always end with a postscript, or P.S. Many experts say this is the second most-read part of a letter, after the beginning paragraph. It gives the writer an opportunity to restate the benefits or make a final pitch for support. CARE, already mentioned, ended its letter with the postscript "I hope you'll consider sending a gift to support CARE's World Hunger Campaign. Let's show poor children and families we care. May we count on you?"

☑ tips FOR SUCCESS

How to Write a Fund-Raising Letter

A large percentage of fund-raising for charitable institutions is conducted through direct mail. The purpose of the letter, of course, is to elicit a response—a donation. Writers of fund-raising letters have learned to use the following approaches:

- Use an attention-getting headline.
- Follow the headline with an inspirational lead-in on why and how a donation will be of benefit.
- Give a clear definition of the charitable agency's purpose and objectives.
- Humanize the cause by giving an example of a child or family that benefited.
- Include testimonials and endorsements from credible individuals.
- Ask for specific action and provide an easy way for the recipient to respond. Postage-paid envelopes and pledge cards are often included.
- Close with a postscript that gives the strongest reason for the reader to respond. ■

NRDC
THE EARTH'S BEST DEFENSE

POLAR BEAR SOS!

Dear Friend,

The distress signals coming from the Arctic are growing louder and clearer as polar bears suffer the terrible effects of global warming and melting ice.

If you're like me, I'm sure it pains you deeply to imagine . . .

. . . The last gasp of a polar bear before it drowns in the vast waters of the Arctic, unable to reach the increasingly distant ice floes it needs to find food.

Nearly all of the polar bear's summer sea ice could vanish by 2040. Without sea ice, the polar bear cannot survive.

. . . The muffled cries of newborn polar bear cubs as they are buried alive when their snowy den collapses from unseasonable rains.

. . . The exhaustion of a mother polar bear and her young as they succumb to starvation after enduring longer and longer periods without food.

But despite this mounting toll, the Bush Administration stubbornly refused to come to the bear's rescue.

Until now.

You see, the Natural Resources Defense Council (NRDC) and our allies took the Bush Administration to court and forced it to study the plight of the polar bear. As a direct result, the U.S. Fish & Wildlife Service is now considering a proposal to protect the bear under the Endangered Species Act.

But that life-saving proposal won't become reality without an enormous outpouring of public support.

That's where you come in. We need one million Americans like you to speak out right now if we are to overcome the opposition of big polluters and the reluctance of the Bush Administration to cut global warming pollution for the sake of the polar bear.

(over, please)

NATURAL RESOURCES DEFENSE COUNCIL 40 West 20th Street, New York, NY 10011 • www.polarbearSOS.org

100% recycled (30% post-consumer) paper

▶ **FIGURE 16.1** Fund-raising letters require an emotional appeal backed up with facts. This letter, from the Natural Resources Defense Council (NRDC), focuses on the plight of the polar bear in an era of global warming and the disappearance of the arctic ice cap. It asks readers to make a donation and to write members of Congress to protect the arctic environment.

How to Do a Direct Mail Package

Here are several techniques that have proven effective in direct mail over the years.

- **Define the audience.**   Know exactly who you want to reach and why they should respond. The more you know about the demographics of the members of your audience and their motivations, the better you can tailor a letter to them. Don't waste time and money sending your material to people who can't or won't respond.

- **Get the envelope opened.**   There is so much junk mail nowadays that many letters go directly into the trash without ever being opened. Put a teaser headline on the outside of the envelope that makes the recipient want to know what's inside. The opposite approach, which also raises curiosity, is to use a sender's address but not the name of the organization. Using stamps instead of a postal permit number also increases envelope opening.

- **Keep the idea clear and pertinent.**   State the offer or request in the first two or three sentences. Tell what the advantages or benefits are—and repeat them throughout the letter. At the end of the letter, summarize the message. You cannot be too clear.

- **Make it easy for people to respond.**   Tell the recipient exactly what to do and how to do it. Include a postage-paid reply card or envelope. Design forms that require only a checkmark to place an order or make a pledge.

- **Pretest the campaign.**   Conduct a pilot campaign on a limited basis. Prepare two or three different appeals and send them to a sampling of the target audience. By doing this, you can find out what appeal generates the greatest response before doing an entire mailing. ■

Brochures

Chapter 13 discussed the writing and production of brochures, and one popular use is their insertion into direct mail packages. Typically, the brochure describes a product, service, organization, or company. It supports the mailing's offer, adding credibility to the overall message. An effective brochure must be brief but at the same time provide useful information. A brochure insert for the Environmental Defense Action Fund, for example, gave "20 Simple Steps to Fight Global Warming."

Media Distribution Services offers the following elements that can increase a brochure's interest:

- **Testimonials.**   List them in one place or sprinkle them throughout the text.
- **Questions and answers.**   A good format. Your questions should address motivations, not just product features. They should seem natural, not contrived.
- **List of benefits.**   Lists, when highlighted by large numerals or bullet points, make attractive visual reference.
- **Guarantee.**   A guarantee seems even stronger when printed in more elaborate type or framed in a box.
- **Models, colors, options.**   Customer product choices can be pictured or described with words.

- **Benefit tables, comparisons.** These help readers identify your offer's advantages quickly.
- **Call-outs.** These are free-floating captions arranged around a picture or text. Short sentences emphasize key points.

Most brochures used in direct mail are designed to fit into a standard #10 business envelope. This means that it should be about 4 by 9 inches in overall dimension. It may be two or three panels. See page 372 in Chapter 13 about various brochure layouts.

Reply Card

If you want a response from the reader, the best way to get it is to provide a reply card. The card, printed on index-card stock so it is more rigid, should contain all the information you and the reader require to process an acceptance to attend an event, a pledge to the organization, or to order merchandise.

Additional care should be used to prepare the reply form. Exactly what information do you need to process it? Typical reply cards give a space for the respondent to give his or her name, address, city, and zip code. In addition, you may want the person's telephone number, e-mail address, and fax number. This information is valuable for updating lists in future mailings to the same people.

If the person is making a charitable donation or buying a product, you need to provide categories for payment by either check or credit card. The credit card information you need is (1) name of credit card, (2) name of person listed on the credit card, (3) the card number, and (4) expiration date.

It is important to ensure that the space allowed for writing information is large enough to accommodate information. A short line may not be sufficient for a person to write his or her complete address clearly. In general, reply cards should be at least 4 by 6 inches, and many of them are 4 by 8 inches.

Return Envelope

Although reply cards can offer a self-addressed return address on the reverse side, an envelope with a return address is usually provided. This ensures privacy, and an envelope is definitely needed if you are requesting a check or credit card information. Commercial operations often provide a postage-paid envelope, but nonprofits generally ask respondents to provide their own postage. This reduces the cost, and more money can be spent on the cause itself.

Gifts

Many nonprofit and charitable organizations use direct mail packages that include a gift of some kind. Most common are address labels, greeting cards, and calendars. The theory is that the inclusion of such material cuts through all the competing solicitations and gives the person a "reward" for opening the envelope.

The inclusion of such items, however, considerably raises the cost of direct mail, and it's no guarantee that people will make a contribution out of "guilt" or even "gratitude." Indeed, there is some evidence that such "gifts" can increase the ire of individuals, because they don't like charitable causes spending so much money on direct mail—money that could go to the cause itself.

Oxfam, the humanitarian aid agency, took this tact on one mailing. The beginning of the letter announced in big, bold letters the following: "Enclosed: No address labels to use, No calendars to look at, No petitions to sign, and No pictures of starving children. What you will find is a straightforward case for one of the most effective humanitarian aid agencies anywhere in the world."

The Basics of Public Relations Advertising

The American Marketing Association defines advertising as "any paid form of non-personal presentation of ideas, goods, or services by an identified sponsor." Melvin DeFleur and Everett Dennis, authors of *Understanding Mass Media*, go even further and state, "Advertising tries to inform consumers about a *particular* product and to persuade them to make a *particular decision*—usually the decision to buy the product."

They are describing the most common forms of advertising—national consumer advertising (the ad in *Time* magazine about a new car model) and retail advertising (the ad in the local paper telling you where to buy it).

However, advertising can serve other purposes besides just persuading people to buy a product or service. Todd Hunt and Brent Ruben, authors of *Mass Communication: Producers and Consumers*, say other purposes of advertising might be to build consumer trust in an organization (institutional advertising), to create favorable opinions and attitudes (goodwill or public service advertising), or to motivate people to support a cause or a political candidate (issue or political advertising).

These kinds of advertising can be placed under the umbrella of public relations advertising. In fact, the American National Advertisers and Publishers Information Bureau suggests several characteristics that distinguish public relations advertising. The following list uses the word "company," but the concept is applicable to any organization, including nonprofits, trade groups, and special-interest groups:

- It must educate or inform the public regarding the company's policies, functions, facilities, objectives, ideals, and standards.
- It must create a climate of favorable opinion about the company by stressing the competence of the company's management, accumulated scientific knowledge, manufacturing skills, technological progress, and contribution to social advancement and public welfare.
- It must build up the investment qualities of the company's securities or improve the financial structure of the company.
- It must sell the company as a good place in which to work, often in a way designed to appeal to recent college graduates or people with certain skills.

In other words, public relations advertising does not sell goods or services directly. Instead, its primary purpose is to inform, educate, and create a favorable climate of public support that allows an organization to succeed in its organizational objectives. Of course, an indirect by-product of this may be the selling of goods and services.

Advantages of Advertising

Advertising, like direct mail, is paid and controlled mass communication. This means that the organization completely bypasses the newsroom gatekeepers and places its messages, exactly as written and formatted, with the medium's advertising department. Thus a primary reason for advertising as a communications tool is that control of the message remains with the sender.

Some other advantages of advertising are its selectivity and the advertiser's control of the impact and timing.

Audience Selection ▪ Specific audiences can be reached with advertising messages on the basis of such variables as location, age, income, and lifestyle. This is done by closely studying the audience demographics of newspapers, magazines, and broadcast shows. BMW, for example, advertises in magazines such as the *New Yorker* and *National Geographic*, which have highly educated and affluent readers. The neighborhood deli, however, might advertise only in the local weekly that serves the immediate area.

Message Control ▪ Gatekeepers frequently alter or truncate the news or features they receive. Sometimes the changes do little harm, but occasionally the changes ruin an idea or eliminate an important point. Your communications plan may involve informing the public about subject A before you say anything about subject B, but if a gatekeeper changes the order or eliminates one story, the sequence is destroyed. With advertising, however, you can be sure that your message is reproduced in the exact words you choose and in the sequence you have planned.

Impact ▪ With advertising, you can make your messages as big, frequent, and powerful as you choose. Media gatekeepers, by definition, are looking for newsworthy, timely material. An organization, however, might want to send a message to a large audience that doesn't meet the standards of traditional news values. The editor may discard your information or run it in a brief story on page 9. With advertising, however, you can have a much larger impact by simply buying the entire page.

Timing ▪ If timing is an important factor, advertising can guarantee that your message will be timely. Prompt response to a public issue, a fixed sequence of messages, continuity of communication—all can be maintained through advertising. To the gatekeeper, your message may be just as usable on Tuesday as on Friday; but for your purpose, Tuesday may be a day too early and Friday is too late. You can't be sure about the timing unless you pay for it.

Disadvantages of Advertising

Although institutional advertising can be effective in getting key messages to specific audiences, there are some disadvantages.

Cost ▪ Paid space is expensive. Ads in multiple media, which are necessary for message penetration, can cost thousands of dollars in the trade press and millions in the consumer press. The most extreme example is the Super Bowl. A 30-second TV commercial cost $3 million in 2009. Compared to that, a similar commercial on the Academy Awards costs about $1.7 million. Likewise, a 1-minute commercial on a prime TV entertainment show can run $250,000 to $500,000. A national publication such as *The Wall Street Journal* charges about $165,000 for a one-page black-and-white ad and $220,000 for a color ad.

The high cost of buying space for advertising has led many companies to shift more of their marketing communications budgets to the Internet, product publicity, and direct mail.

Credibility ▪ Public relations executives are fond of saying, "Advertising raises awareness, but publicity published as news stories creates credibility."

Because they are controlled messages, advertisements are generally less believable than publicity that appears in the news columns or on broadcast news shows. The public perceives that news reports have more credibility because journalists, who are independent of the organization, have evaluated the information on the basis of truth and accuracy.

Indeed, a widely perceived value of publicity is the concept that a third party, the medium, has endorsed the information by printing or broadcasting it. Advertisements have no such third-party endorsement, because anyone with enough money can place an advertisement, provided it meets the acceptance standards of the medium.

Types of Public Relations Advertising

The majority of public relations advertising is done in magazines, with television and newspapers in second and third place, respectively. The advantage of magazines is a highly defined readership in terms of income, education, occupation, and specific interests.

There are several types of public relations advertising. At times, the distinctions between categories can become blurred; however, for the purposes of this discussion, we will deal with five basic types: (1) image building, (2) investor and financial relations programs, (3) public service messages, (4) advocacy, and (5) announcements.

Image Building

The purpose of image-building advertising is to strengthen an organization's reputation, change or reinforce public perceptions, and create a favorable climate for selling the organization's goods and services.

A good example of an image-building campaign is one by Toyota, which wants to project its image as an integral part of the American economy. One magazine ad, showing an assembly plant, was headlined "Our blue-sky scenario: more U.S. manufacturing jobs, cleaner U.S. manufacturing plants." The copy was as follows:

> Since 1986, Toyota has been building vehicles and creating manufacturing jobs in the U.S. Today, with our eight manufacturing plants, sales and marketing operations, research and design facilities, and through our dealers and suppliers. Toyota's U.S. operations account for more than 190,000 jobs. And with two new state-of-the-art manufacturing facilities being built to strict environmental standards, we're continuing our commitment to responsible growth as an employer, and a neighbor.

The environment and energy conservation are popular topics for image building. BP, a British/Dutch oil company, placed an ad titled "Investing in America's most diverse energy portfolio," which is shown in Figure 16.2. The copy was as follows:

> Oil in the Gulf. Natural gas in the Rockies. Solar in Maryland. Wind in Texas. Biofuels research in California and Illinois. Diversity starts right here. BP is the largest investor in new U.S. energy development. In fact, over the last five years we've invested more than $28 billion in U.S. energy supplies. bp.com.us

Even garbage collectors need to build image. Waste Management (WM) placed a magazine ad showing one of its trucks with the sign "The waste we collect helps power over one million homes." The text was:

> With energy costs and oil dependence on the rise, the need for renewable power is greater than ever. That's why Waste Management is using its resources at our disposal to create the

Investing 💧 in 🔥 America's most 🌀 diverse energy ✳ portfolio.

Oil in the Gulf. Natural gas in the Rockies. Solar in Maryland. Wind in Texas. Biofuels research in California and Illinois. Diversity starts right here. BP is the largest investor in new U.S. energy development. In fact, over the last five years we've invested more than $28 billion in U.S. energy supplies.
bp.com/us

bp

beyond petroleum®

© 2008 BP Products North America Inc.

FIGURE 16.2 Many corporations use public relations advertising to enhance their reputations and inform the public what they are doing to solve various problems, such as global warming and finding new sources of energy. BP, an oil company, makes the point in this ad that it's a major investor in U.S. energy development.

energy equivalent of saving over 14 million barrels of oil per year. It's a powerful idea we're proud to drive forward.

Nonprofits and civic membership groups also engage in image advertising. See Figure 16.3 for an ad prepared by Rotary International.

Professor.
Mother.
Poverty Fighter.

Rotary is 1.2 million ordinary men and women working together to accomplish extraordinary things. Rotary clubs are dedicated to fighting hunger and poverty around the world.

Learn more at rotary.org.

Rotary.
Humanity in motion.

FIGURE 16.3 National and international civic organizations engage in image advertising to inform the public about their scope and mission. This ad is from Rotary International.

Investor and Financial Relations

A different type of public relations advertising is targeted to the financial community—individual and institutional investors, stock analysts, investment bankers, and stockholders. Such advertising often has the objective of informing and reassuring investors that the company is well managed, worthy of investment, and has bright prospects for the future.

Such advertising is used extensively during proxy fights for control of companies, when a company is undergoing some major reorganization, or when a company believes it is being unfairly attacked by consumer groups or regulatory agencies. A variety of these ads appear in financial publications, notably *The Wall Street Journal*.

In one instance, Honeywell placed a full-page ad in *The Wall Street Journal* to announce that it had won a major lawsuit against the Minolta Camera Company for infringing on its patents. The winning of the suit and the protection of its patents assured the financial community that Honeywell would continue to make profits on its technology.

Putnam Investments also had to reassure the financial community and individual investors after its top management was found to have overcharged individual investors and engaged in manipulation of mutual fund administrative fees. In a full-page *New York Times* ad, Putnam announced that it had replaced its top executives and was doing everything possible to cooperate with the SEC and other state regulatory agencies in its investigations.

Other forms of financial advertising are somewhat routine. You can use an ad to announce a new corporate name, the acquisition of another company, or a new CEO. Such ads help fulfill SEC requirements, discussed in Chapter 3, for full and timely disclosure. Releasing news to the media may be adequate, but many corporations also use advertising to ensure wide distribution.

Public Service

Public service advertisements provide information, raise awareness about social issues, and give how-to suggestions. A number of nonprofit and charitable organizations, as well as governmental agencies, use such advertising for public education.

Here are some other examples of public service campaigns by public service agencies and nonprofits:

- The American Cancer Society gives information about vegetables and fruits that can reduce the risk of cancer.
- The American Heart Association informs people about the warning signs of a heart attack.
- The American Red Cross gives encourages people to know CPR and gives an 800 number where they can sign up for courses.
- The American Lung Association warns people about the dangers of smoking.
- The Partnership for a Drug-Free America, a consortium of nonprofit and governmental agencies, informs youth about the dangers of drug abuse.
- Women in Communications raises awareness about sexual harassment in the workplace.

In many instances, the Ad Council prepares public service ads for national non-profit groups. The Council, in cooperation with volunteer advertising agencies, does this as a public service. A good example of an Ad Council campaign is about childhood obesity prevention, which is shown in Figure 16.4. Ads were prepared for newspapers and magazines, TV stations, radio stations, and online social networking sites. Go to www.adcouncil.org to see a full list of current campaigns.

Corporations also do public service kinds of advertising to generate goodwill. In most cases, it is related to their products and services. For example:

- The Pacific Gas & Electric Company provides helpful hints on how to reduce energy costs during the winter months.
- The Shell Oil Company gives motorists hints on how to get better gasoline mileage.
- Microsoft gives tips about easy-to-use parental controls on its Vista and Xbox products.

Advocacy/Issues

Although it can be argued that advocacy is an element in all public relations advertising—whether it's the American Cancer Society telling you to stop smoking or a company telling you it's all right to buy its stock—the term "advocacy advertising" has a more exact meaning.

It usually means advertising to motivate voters, to influence government policy, or to put pressure on elected officials. A good example is the campaign by the Humane Society of the United States to put public and legislative pressure on the Canadian government to stop the killing of baby seals for their fur.

Allstate Insurance has also run a series of advocacy ads that call for more legislation to curb the dangerous driving habits of teenagers. The company would like to see legislation banning anyone under the age of 18 from using cell phones or any text-messaging device while driving. In addition, the insurance company advocates graduated driver licensing laws that place limitations on new drivers.

The headline for one Allstate ad was, "Nearly One-Third of Teens Admit to Texting While Driving: Some of Them Will Never Be Heard From Again." The lead sentence in the text continues, "Car crashes are the leading cause of death among American teens. Is any text message worth the risk?" The ad concludes, "It's time to make the world a safer place to drive. That's Allstate's stand."

GlaxoSmithKline, a pharmaceutical company, took a more subtle advocacy approach to the problem of many Americans ordering drugs from Canada because they were cheaper. Its ad pointed out that the drugs may not be coming from reputable Canadian companies but are probably being made by anonymous companies in China using fake addresses, some out of Caribbean islands. The ad concludes, "Where did all these medicines really come from? And what exactly is in them? Getting drugs from 'Canada' isn't the answer. But it does raise a lot of questions."

The issue of health care reform generates any number of advocacy ads from diverse organizations. Consumer groups advocate for more affordable health benefits,

FIGURE 16.4 This public service ad, sponsored by the U.S. Department of Health & Human Services, was prepared by the Ad Council, which consists of advertising agencies that volunteer their services to write and design public service messages. The Childhood Obesity Prevention campaign was launched to encourage both parents and their children to get more exercise. One fact: About 9 million children over the age of 6 are considered over-weight in the United States.

insurance companies argue that the individuals should have the right to select their own private health plan, and doctors want to cap liability lawsuits. Indeed, such ads are an integral part of the marketplace of public opinion.

Announcements

Announcements can be used for any number of situations. The primary purpose is to inform the public promptly about something that might interest them. This might be the recalling of a product, apologizing for a failure of service, announcing a community event, or even expressing sympathy to the families who lost loved ones in a plane crash. Here are some other examples of announcement ads:

- Jack In The Box reassures customers that it is taking precautions to make sure its restaurants meet new health standards after an outbreak of food poisoning at several locations in the Seattle area.
- State Farm Insurance tells residents of a disaster area how to file claims.
- Santa Clara Valley Transit Authority sets a series of community meetings to get public feedback on new transit proposals.
- The Asian Art Museum of San Francisco announces a speaker series.
- Children's Hospital of New York-Presbyterian announces the opening of a new center of excellence for children's health, the Morgan-Stanley Children's Hospital, which "will enable some of the world's leading healthcare experts to provide the best care possible."
- Rolex announces the completion of the inaugural year of the Rolex Mentor and Protégé Arts Initiative, which will be held at New York State Theatre.

Creating a Print Ad

Print advertisements have several key elements. They are headline, text, artwork, and layout. Although broadcast advertising is not covered here, the basic format follows guidelines that were given for VNRs and PSAs in Chapter 9. You have to write copy for the ear, keep it short, and adopt a conversational style. For television, you need strong graphic elements.

Headline

Advertising expert John Caplets says, "The headline is the most important element in most ads—and the best headlines appeal to the reader's self-interest or give news."

Headlines should be specific about a benefit, or they can be teasers that arouse interest. Here is a headline about a specific program: "The Phoenix Mutual Insurance Retirement Income Plan." Caplets thought this was all right, but he created a headline that sold much more successfully: "To Men Who Want to Quit Work Some Day." This was accompanied by an illustration of a smiling senior citizen fishing in a mountain stream.

Caplets offers the following suggestions for writing an advertising headline:

- Include the interests of the audience.
- Use words such as "introducing," "announcing," "new," or "now" to give the headline a newsworthy appeal.
- Avoid witty or cute headlines unless they include reader interest and appear newsy.
- Present the headline positively. Don't say "Our competitors can't match our service" when you can say, "Our service surpasses that of our competitors."

Text

The headline is followed by one or several copy blocks. These are sentences and short paragraphs that inform and persuade. In general, copy should be limited to one or two major points. Sentences should be short and punchy and use active voice. A declarative sentence is much better than one that includes a dependent or an independent clause.

The copy should evoke emotion, provide information of value to the reader, and suggest a way that the reader can act on the information. You might include a toll-free telephone number, an e-mail address, or the URL of the organization's website. A review of the ads featured in this chapter will give you some idea about copywriting.

Artwork

An ad can consist of just a headline and copy, but the most effective ones usually have a strong graphic element. This may be a striking photo, a line drawing, or a computer-generated design. Visual elements play a crucial role in motivating a reader to even look at the ad.

Artwork and graphics are doubly important if the ad is on the Internet. In this case, text is secondary and graphics are primary. Websites were discussed in Chapter 12, but the guidelines also apply to advertising. The graphics can't be too complex because of possible downloading problems, but the ad does need to be interactive, with buttons to click that allow the viewer to "self-tailor" the message.

Layout

The headline, copy, and graphic elements need to be integrated into an attractive, easy-to-read advertisement. A layout can be a mock-up of the planned ad, or it can be a detailed comprehensive that includes the actual type and artwork that will be used.

A number of tips about layout were given Chapter 13. Many of them are also applicable to preparing an advertisement. In general, avoid all-capital letters or large blocks of copy. Use serif type for body copy, avoid large blocks of reverse type (white on dark color), and use plenty of white space. See the Tips for Success features on pages 446 and 447 for more tips on creating an effective ad.

Effective Ad Elements

The following six elements of an effective ad are provided by the Newspaper Association of America in its annual planbook:

- **Visuals draw readers.** Visuals that occupy about half the total ad space are almost 30 percent more likely to attract readers. When a visual makes up nearly 75 percent of the ad space, readers are 48 percent more likely to take note than if the ad has no illustrations or visuals. Photos and illustrations of models are 20 to 25 percent more likely to get noticed than using simple line art. Show your product in use by a consumer, and 26 percent are more likely to notice than if the product is shown by itself.

- **Reverse type and white space.** Reversed copy or type is all right as long as it is legible. The extensive use of white space, as part of the design in proportion to type elements, increases readability.

- **Size does matter.** Full-page ads get noticed 39 percent more often than quarter-page ads. In fact, larger ads result in greater in-depth reading.

- **Color attracts reader attention.** Color ads get significantly more readership than black-and-white ads. Full color is better than two-color in terms of audience readership.

- **Know your place.** The position of an ad on a newspaper page doesn't seem to affect readership. However, if your ad is the first large ad in a section—or the back page of a section—it gets more readership.

- **Price information.** Readers respond more favorably and pay more attention to the ad if prices are given. ■

Working with an Ad Agency

Most public relations advertising is prepared with the assistance of an advertising agency. The agency has employees who are experts in all phases of creating the ads and purchasing space in the selected media.

In an integrated marketing communications campaign, personnel from a public relations firm and an advertising agency often work together on a campaign. Fleishman-Hillard public relations, for example, works with BBDO on anti-tobacco campaigns for the New Jersey Department of Health and Senior Services. In addition, BBDO has also worked on integrated campaigns with Golin/Harris (for Visa), Edelman Worldwide (for KFC), and Porter Novelli (for Gillette and M&Ms).

The key to a successful relationship is keeping the communication channels as open as possible. Kate Childress, senior vice president of Fleishman-Hillard, told *PRWeek*: "If there is mutual respect and everyone has the same end goals in mind, the two complement each other."

Sara Calabro, a writer for *PRWeek*, gives some pointers for working with an ad agency:

- Do clarify the respective responsibilities of each agency from the outset and communicate openly and frequently throughout the campaign.

Getting the Most from Your Ads

A successful advertisement grabs the reader's attention. *Communication Briefings* offers the following suggestions provided by Direct Response in Torrance, California:

- **Busy layouts often pull better than neat ones.**   One split-run test showed busy layouts out-pull neat ones by 14 percent.

- **Vary shapes, sizes, and colors.**   People will get bored, and turn the page, if there is no variety.

- **Color will attract attention.**   But it may not be cost-effective. Consider using color when the product itself demands it.

- **Putting something odd into a picture will attract attention.**   David Ogilvy's Hathaway Shirts campaign used a model with an eye patch. That odd little detail made the campaign a classic.

- **Too many extraneous props divert attention.**   A curtain material company ran an ad with a cute teddy bear in it. The company got more calls asking about the bear than it did about its product.

- **Photographs are more convincing than drawn illustrations.**   Photos can increase responses by over 50 percent.

- **Before-and-after pictures are very persuasive.**   The technique is a great way to show the benefit of your product. ■

- Do always view an integrated account from the perspective of how public relations can complement advertising and vice versa.

- Do consider the compatibility of team member's personalities when selecting a partner agency.

■ Other Advertising Channels

Other forms of advertising that can be used as a tactic in a public relations program are (1) billboards, (2) transit panels, (3) buttons and bumper stickers, (4) posters, (5) sponsored books, (6) T-shirts, and (7) promotional items.

Billboards

Most outdoor advertising consists of paper sheets pasted on a wooden or metal background. The 24-sheet poster is standard, but there are also painted billboards, which use no paper. Outdoor advertising reaches large audiences in brief exposures. Accordingly, advertising for this medium must be eye-catching and use few words. Ten words is a rule-of-thumb limit for outdoor copy. When design and copy are approved, the individual sheets that make up the whole advertisement are printed and then pasted to the billboard.

Location is vital in this medium—and prices are based on the traffic that is exposed to the site. Occasionally, nonprofit organizations can obtain free or heavily discounted usage of outdoor space that is temporarily unsold. Displays are usually scheduled in monthly units, and occasionally there are gaps in the schedules, so it may pay to keep in touch with local outdoor companies.

Transit Panels

This category includes both the small posters placed in subway and commuter rail stations and the cards used in buses and rail cars. Both types of transit advertising require eye-catching graphics, but the copy can be longer than for outdoor posters. The person waiting for a train or holding a strap or a bar on a bus or rail car has some time to absorb a message. Cards in transit vehicles often carry coupons or tear-off notes allowing readers to ask for more information or respond to some sort of offer.

Buttons and Bumper Stickers

Akin to T-shirts are buttons. They are widely used in political campaigns and at special events. They are also useful in fund-raising, when they are distributed to people who make donations. In San Francisco one year, money was raised for the ballet by selling "SOB" ("Save Our Ballet") buttons to pedestrians in the downtown area.

In general, buttons have a short life span. They are worn by convention delegates or by sales representatives during a trade show. Outside of these areas, people don't generally wear buttons unless they are highly committed to a particular cause.

Bumper stickers are another specialty item. They are often used to support political candidates and various political causes, but they can also be used to promote a special event or a scenic attraction or membership in an organization. In recent years, magnetic bumper stickers have started to replace adhesive ones because they don't mar the finish on a car.

Posters

Posters are used in a variety of settings to create awareness and remind people of something. Many companies use posters on bulletin boards to remind employees about basic company policies, benefits, and safety precautions.

A good example is the Nissan Motor Company's poster campaign to remind employees at various U.S. offices to buckle up when driving. Nissan used a series of posters with a lighthearted touch, using famous artworks and personalities. One poster draped a seat belt over a stock movie photo of Sherlock Holmes with the caption, "It's Elementary, Buckle Up Now."

Government agencies often use posters as part of public information campaigns about preventing AIDS, getting flu shots, or having pets neutered. The PR Casebook on page 449 discusses the use of posters to educate young men about date rape.

Museum exhibits and art shows lend themselves to poster treatments. The poster, often a piece of art itself, can promote attendance and can also be sold as a souvenir of the show.

To be effective, a poster must be attractively designed and have strong visual elements. It should be relatively large, convey only one basic idea, and use only a few words to relate basic information. A poster is a small billboard.

A PR/Advertising Campaign Fights Rape

Rape is a high-incidence crime. One in four U.S. women will be raped in their lifetime. On average, a woman is raped every 54 minutes in California. This shocking statistic led the California Coalition Against Sexual Assault (CALCASA) to launch a public service campaign primarily directed at teenage males. "Our goal was to engage young men to stand up and speak out against sexual violence," according to Chris Kuchenmeister of Paine Public Relations in Los Angeles.

The centerpiece of the joint advertising and public relations campaign was the theme, "My Strength is Not for Hurting." Posters and PSAs, for example, showed close-ups of young couples with the message, "So when she said NO, I said OK," and "So when I wanted to and she didn't, we didn't: Men can stop rape." A typical poster is shown on this page.

In addition, buttons, brochures, and radio public service announcements were used to deliver the message to the somewhat elusive audience of young males. Both English and Spanish versions of the material were used. Parents, counselors, and educators could download the materials at www.mys-trength.org. CALCASA (www.calcasa.org) also made available ring tones for cell phones, screen savers, links to rape crisis centers throughout the state, and other resource materials about such topics as date rape and rape prevention strategies.

Paine Public Relations and CALCASA didn't just rely on publicity materials, but hired a "MyStrength" team of "cool" young bilingual men to be the campaign's face and voice. Actor Dorian Gregory (from *Charmed*) was the celebrity spokesperson, but other "cool" young men went on the road to deliver the message to local media and schools. They distributed about 200,000 brochures at student assemblies in high schools throughout the state.

PRWeek, in critiquing the campaign, noted "The statewide outreach program met its goal and got the MyStrength message out to a multicultural audience. It also managed to open dialogue about a topic that can be controversial as well as uncomfortable for a variety of people." ■

▶ This is one of 12 posters/ads produced, in both English and Spanish, for the MyStrength campaign. For more information about the campaign, visit www.mystrength.com.

Posters, if done properly, can be expensive to design and produce. Therefore, you need to assess how the posters will be used and displayed. Costs can be controlled, often by buying ready-to-use posters from printers and having the organization's name or logo printed on them. Local chapters of national organizations, such as the American Cancer Society, also get posters from the national organization that can easily be localized.

Sponsored Books

Organizations often commission books to be written that highlight their history or products. A history, for example, is often done as part of a company's centennial celebration. A book titled *From Three Cents a Week* is the official history of the Prudential Insurance Company. Air New Zealand has commissioned travel books on the country to generate visitors. More tourists, of course, would no doubt increase the airline's bookings.

Books that relate directly to a company's product are also often underwritten by the company. General Mills has long been producing Betty Crocker cookbooks for Random House. *Creative Cooking with Aluminum Foil* was published for Reynolds Aluminum, and *Protect Yourself* is from Master Lock and Dell Publishing. In addition, coffee table books showing beautiful photographs of the fall colors in New England are often sponsored by state tourism departments in the region.

On occasion, an organization will commission a book to buff up its image or refute criticism. *The New Arabians* is a book that was underwritten by the Bechtel Corporation. It is no coincidence that the company has extensive engineering contracts in the Middle East. The radio and billboard giant Clear Channel took the unusual step of commissioning its own book to refute another book about the company being written by an independent author. According to *The Wall Street Journal*, the company paid a freelance writer more than $100,000 to write a book that would portray Clear Channel in a more favorable light. Both books hit the bookstores at the same time but, if one looks closely, Clear Channel owns the copyright on its version of corporate history.

There are two ways to publish a sponsored book. In most cases, the organization will have public relations staff or a freelancer write the book and then contract with a printer to publish it. The books are then given to customers, vendors, employees, and community opinion leaders. With the second method, the book is produced by an established book publisher, if the book's subject matter has general public interest. The usual procedure is to guarantee the purchase of a sufficient number of books to give the publisher a profit. After the sponsor buys the guaranteed number, the publisher is free to market the book through its regular channels.

T-Shirts

T-shirts have been described as "walking billboards," and some people, including sociologists, lament the fact that people are so materialistic that they willingly become walking ads for products, services, and social or political issues. Why people do this remains unresolved, but the fact is that they do spend their own money to advertise things with which they may or may not have any direct connection.

Because so many people are willing to serve as billboards, you may find an opportunity to use this medium, which is particularly convenient for causes such as environmental protection. Often such groups make sizable incomes from the sale of T-shirts.

Corporations don't usually sell T-shirts, but they do distribute them to attendees at conferences, sales meetings, picnics, and other events. In these situations, the T-shirts contribute to a feeling of belonging to a team.

Almost every town and city in America has at least one shop where you can order T-shirts. You can specify just about anything you can imagine—slogans, corporate logos, symbols, and so on. The process is simple and fast, and the costs are low. At some time, almost any organization may find T-shirts useful.

Promotional Items

An inexpensive item with the organization's logo or name on it often accompanies public relations events. Angela West, public relations manager for the Promotional Products Association International, writes in *PR Tactics*, "Whether you're conducting a media relations program, staging a press conference, or hosting a special event, promotional products are a valuable public relations tool."

Promotional items such as pens, coffee mugs, key chains, paperweights, mouse pads, vinyl briefcases, plaques, and even T-shirts constitute a billion-dollar industry in what some people call "trash and trinkets." An organization may include such an item in a media kit, although most reporters complain they have enough pens and coffee mugs to last a lifetime. At other times, they are made available at press parties and trade shows.

The main consideration, says West, is choosing products that bear a natural relationship to the product, service, or message being promoted. Sybase, for example, included a bright yellow tennis ball with its invitation to a press conference about its sponsorship of a tennis tournament. Donor Network of Arizona promoted its National Organ and Tissue Donor Awareness Week with the theme "Get in the game" and sent a golf putting cup to members of the media.

■ Summary

- Direct mail, used primarily in marketing to sell goods and services, also can be an effective public relations tool to inform, educate, and motivate individuals.

- The three major advantages of direct mail are (1) ability to reach specific audiences, (2) personalization of message, and (3) cost.

- A major disadvantage of direct mail is the perception that it is "junk mail," which reduces its acceptance as a credible tool of communication.

- The direct mail package has five components: (1) envelope, (2) letter, (3) brochure, (4) reply card, and (5) return envelope.

- Advances in technology and market research allow you to rent or buy a mailing list that is compiled with scientific precision.

- Nonprofit and advocacy groups often use a compelling human-interest angle to start direct mail letters.

- Direct mail envelopes, experts say, attract more attention if they use commemorative stamps instead of metered postage.

- The headline and first paragraph, as well as the postscript, get the most readership in a direct mail letter.

- Advertising, the purchase of paid space and time in a mass medium, can be a useful tool in a public relations program.

- Public relations advertising does not sell products directly, but it can create a supportive environment for the selling of products and services by enhancing public perception of an organization.

- The major advantages of advertising are (1) ability to reach specified audiences, (2) control of the message, (3) frequency of the message, and (4) control of the timing and context.

- Advertising has the disadvantages of (1) high cost and (2) lower credibility than publicity that appears in news columns.

- There are five kinds of public relations advertising: (1) image building, (2) financial, (3) public service, (4) advocacy/issues, and (5) announcements.

- Writing an effective ad requires considerable skill and imagination. You must think about the headline, text, artwork, and layout, and how they all relate to each other.

- Effective advertising copy is short and punchy. Copy must be oriented to the self-interest of the reader, viewer, or listener.

- Other channels of public relations advertising include (1) billboards, (2) transit panels, (3) buttons and bumper stickers, (4) posters, (5) sponsored books, (6) T-shirts, and (7) promotional items.

Skill Building Activities

1. Collect five or six fund-raising letters that you have received from various organizations. Critique the contents. What elements did you like? Dislike?

2. Based on your review of these fund-raising letters and the guidelines mentioned in this chapter, write and design a fund-raising letter packet (envelope, letter, and reply card) for a nonprofit in your community.

3. Find at least three samples of ads illustrating the five areas of public relations advertising: image building, investor/financial relations, advocacy, public service, and announcements. Critique the ads from the standpoint of what you liked or disliked.

4. The local utility wants to produce a public service advertisement that would encourage people to conserve water during the summer months. Do some research and thinking. Write the copy for a print ad that would be published in the local daily. In addition, make a rough sketch, showing the visual element or graphics that would be part of the ad.

Suggested Readings

Calabro, Sara. "Firm Relationships: Working with an Ad Agency." *PRWeek*, June 23, 2003, p. 18.

Demetriou, Greg. "The Mailing List Maze: How to Find Your Way Out." *PR Tactics*, October 2002, p. 8.

Fitzgerald, Suzanne Sparks. "Tips for Using Advertising in Public Relations." *Public Relations Quarterly*, Fall 2001, pp. 43–45.

Jewler, Jerome, and Drewniany, Bonnie L. *Creative Strategy in Advertising*, 7th edition. Belmont, CA: Wadsworth, 2001.

Ries, Al and Laura. *The Fall of Advertising and the Rise of PR*. New York: Harper Business, 2002.

Wells, William, Burnett, John, and Moriarty, Sandra. *Advertising Principles & Practice*, 7th edition. Upper Saddle River, New Jersey: Prentice Hall, 2006.

Organizing Meetings and Events

17

TOPICS covered in this chapter include:

A World Filled with Meetings
and Events   453

Staff and Committee Meetings   454

Group Meetings   456

Banquets   461

Receptions and Cocktail Parties   465

Open Houses and Plant Tours   466

Conventions   470

Trade Shows   473

Promotional Events   477

A World Filled with Meetings and Events

Meetings and events are vital public relations tools. Their greatest value is that they let the audience participate, face-to-face, in real time. In this era of digital communication and information overload, there is still a basic human need to gather, socialize, and be part of a group activity.

Individuals attending a meeting or event use all five of their senses—hearing, sight, touch, smell, and taste—so they become more emotionally involved in the process. Marketing and public relations professionals, for example, often use events to foster more brand awareness and loyalty. Procter & Gamble's Charmin toilet tissue event in New York's Times Square, highlighted in the PR Casebook on page 479, illustrates the point. Sheron Bates, an expert on experiential marketing, told *Corporate Events* magazine, "The Charmin event was a true testament of a successful event, as it reflected the brand in a positive manner, was memorable, and allowed participants to interact with the brand on various levels."

Meetings and events, of course, come in all shapes and sizes. A committee meeting of a civic club or an office staff may only include four or five people. Corporate seminars may be for 50 to 250 people. At the other end of the scale is a trade show, such as the Consumer Electronics Show (CES) in Las Vegas, which attracts 130,000 attendees over a 3-day period. MacWorld held in San Francisco every year has 50,000 attendees. In 2008, travel research firm PhoCus Wright estimated that spending on U.S. corporate meetings was about $76 billion.

    ❝ *Events deliver face time between consumers and brands. They also introduce consumers to new products.* ❞

■ Yung Moon, associate publisher of *Self* magazine, as reported in *PRWeek*

However, effective meetings and events don't just happen. Detailed planning and logistics are essential to ensure that defined objectives are achieved whether you're organizing a committee meeting or a national conference. This chapter discusses various types of meetings and events that require attention to detail and good communication skills.

You will learn how to conduct an effective staff or committee meeting, organize a monthly club meeting, put together a banquet, host a cocktail party, sponsor an open house, juggle all the logistics of a national convention, organize an exhibit and do media contact work at a trade show, and conduct promotional events.

Staff and Committee Meetings

Staff and committee meetings are part of any organization, from the local garden club to the multinational corporation. Indeed, through such meetings, employees or group members have a chance to express their views and participate in decision making.

There are two major complaints about meetings: they are time-consuming and they are often ineffective. A survey of office workers by PolyVision Corporation, for example, found that men spend 4.3 hours a week and women spend 2.26 hours a week in meetings. The study also found that 75 percent of the respondents said their meetings could be more effective.

In another study of senior managers, the Wharton Center for Applied Research found that senior managers spend an average of 23 hours a week in meetings, whereas middle managers spend 11 hours. The study also concluded that about 30 percent of the meetings held could be handled better through one-on-one talks, by phone, or via e-mail. Another study concluded that executives spend an average of 288 hours a year—5 full weeks—attending unnecessary meetings.

This is not to say that meetings should be banned. It does say, however, that meetings should be held only if other methods, such as e-mail or wikis, are not appropriate for accomplishing the purpose of the meeting. One question that should always be asked is "What would happen if the meeting isn't held?" If the answer is nothing, then cancel the meeting. Others simply ask the basic question, "Is this meeting really necessary?" If the answer is "yes," consider the following guidelines for having an effective staff or committee meeting:

- **Limit attendance.**   Only those who are directly involved should be invited.
- **Distribute the agenda in advance.**   Let people know what will be discussed or decided, so they can think about the issues before the meeting. Experts recommend that you prioritize the agenda and plan to cover only two or three items.
- **Use a round table.**   Everyone has equal positional status and equal access to each other. The next best alternative is a square table.
- **Set a time limit.**   The agenda should clearly state the beginning and ending time of the meeting, so people can plan their day. A meeting should run a maximum of 60 to 90 minutes. The longer the meeting runs, the less effective it is.

- **Manage the meeting.** The chairperson must make sure the meeting stays on track. Do not allow an individual or the group to go off on tangents.

- **Budget time.** Set a time limit for discussion of a specific agenda item. Do not spend an excessive amount of time on an item that shortchanges other items on the agenda.

- **Know Robert's Rules of Order.** It may be unnecessary in an informal, friendly meeting, but knowledge of parliamentary procedure is helpful if the debate gets heated.

- **Close with a brief overview.** At the end of the meeting, summarize what has been accomplished, what will be done, and who will do it. Remember that meetings are held to make decisions, not just to discuss things.

- **Distribute a summary memo.** The chair or secretary should distribute a summary of the meeting within a day after the meeting. This helps remind people what was decided.

Given these guidelines, how well was your last committee meeting organized? A rating scale is provided in the following Tips for Success.

☑ tips FOR SUCCESS

How Good Are Your Meetings?

Meetings are a way of life in all organizations, including all those committee meetings to brainstorm and plan a public relations campaign. Cliff Shaffran, writing in IABC's *Communication World*, suggests that the effectiveness of a meeting can be determined by rating the meeting from 1 (rarely) to 5 (always) on a number of criteria. How would you rate your last committee meeting based on the following criteria?

- There is a clearly defined, results-focused theme and agenda.
- We make decisions and move forward; it isn't just a debating society.
- The meetings are friendly and don't generate conflict.
- Everyone contributes.
- No one dominates the discussion.
- Communication is open and positive.
- We generate many creative ideas.
- We challenge the status quo to explore alternative ideas and solutions.
- Everyone is energized and focused.
- We fully maximize the knowledge and expertise of all participants.
- We keep on time.
- We always achieve our desired results.
- We have good return on time invested.
- Everyone enjoys the process. ■

Group Meetings

Having meetings seems to be part of human nature. There are literally thousands of civic clubs, professional societies, trade associations, and hobby groups that have meetings that attract millions of people every year. In addition, many of these organizations sponsor workshops, seminars, and symposia on a regular basis.

Planning

The size and purpose of the meeting dictate the plan. Every plan must consider these questions: How many will attend? Who will attend? When and where will it be held? How long will it last? Who will speak? What topics will be covered? What facilities will be needed? Who will run it? What is its purpose? How do we get peo-

---

✓ tips FOR SUCCESS

How to Plan a Meeting

Every meeting requires its own specialized checklist, but here is a general "to do" list for a local dinner meeting of a service club or a professional association.

In Advance

- What is the purpose of the meeting? Business? Social? Continuing education? Combination?
- What date and time are best for maximum attendance?
- What size audience do you realistically expect?
- Select the restaurant facility at least 4 to 6 weeks in advance.
- Confirm the following in writing: date, time, menu, cocktails, seating plan, number of guaranteed reservations, and projected costs.
- Enlist the speaker 4 to 6 weeks in advance. If the speaker is in high demand, make arrangements several months in advance. Discuss the nature of talk, its projected length, and whether audiovisual aids will be used that requires special equipment.
- Publicize the meeting to the membership and other interested parties. This should be done a minimum of 3 weeks in advance. Provide complete information on speaker, date, time, location, meal costs, and reservation procedure.
- Organize a phone committee to call members 72 hours before the event if reservations are lagging. A reminder phone call is often helpful in gaining last-minute reservations.

On the Meeting Day

- Get a final count on reservations, and make an educated guess as to how many people might arrive at the door without a reservation.
- Check the speaker's travel plans and last-minute questions or requirements.

---

ple to attend? A checklist for planning a club meeting is provided in the accompanying Tips for Success.

Location ■ If the meeting is to be held on the premises of the organization, the room can be reserved by contacting whoever is responsible for such arrangements.

If the meeting is to be held at some outside location, you will have to talk to the person in charge. In a hotel or restaurant that person is the catering manager. In a school, it may be the principal; in a church, the minister or priest. Many firms have rooms that are made available to nonprofit groups, so consider this possibility if your organization is eligible.

The meeting room must be the right size for the expected audience. If it is too large, the audience will feel that the meeting has failed to draw the expected attendance. If it is too small, the audience will be uncomfortable. Most hotels have a number of meeting rooms ranging in size from small to very large.

■ Give the catering manager a revised final count for meal service. In many instances, this might have to be done 24 to 72 hours in advance of the meeting day.

■ Check room arrangements 1 to 2 hours in advance of the meeting. Have enough tables been set up? Are tables arranged correctly for the meeting? Does the microphone system work?

■ Prepare a timetable for the evening's events. For example, cocktails may be scheduled from 6:15 to 7 P.M., with registration going on at the same time. Dinner from 7 to 8 P.M., followed by 10 minutes of announcements. At 8:10 P.M., the speaker will have 20 minutes to talk, followed by an additional 10 minutes for questions. Your organizational leaders, as well as the serving staff, should be aware of this schedule.

■ Set up a registration table just inside or outside the door. A typed list of reservations should be available, as well as name tags, meal tickets, and a cash box for making change. Personnel at the registration table should be briefed and in place at least 30 minutes before the announced time.

■ Decide on a seating plan for the head table, organize place cards, and tell VIPs as they arrive where they will be sitting.

■ Designate three or four members of the organization as a hospitality committee to meet and greet newcomers and guests.

After the Meeting

■ Settle accounts with the restaurant, or indicate where an itemized bill should be mailed.

■ Check the room to make sure no one forgot briefcases, handbags, eyeglasses, or other belongings.

■ Send thank-you notes to the speaker and any committee members who helped plan or host the meeting.

■ Prepare a summary of the speaker's comments for the organization's newsletter and, if appropriate, send a news release to local media. ■

FIGURE 17.1 Corporate meetings and conferences are a way of life. The typical setup is an auditorium where attendees sit in theater-style seats and a speaker uses a podium on the stage. Large video monitors project PowerPoint slides. This conference, hosted by Cisco Systems, was held in Nottingham, United Kingdom.

Having selected a room, make sure that the audience can find it. The name of the meeting and the name of the room should be registered on the hotel or restaurant's schedule of events for a particular day.

Seating ■ A variety of seating arrangements can be used, depending on the purpose of the meeting. A monthly club meeting, for example, often features a luncheon or dinner. In this case, attendees are usually seated at round tables of six or eight, where they first have a meal and then listen to a speaker.

Seminars, designed primarily for listening, usually have what is called "theater" seating. Rows of seats are set up, all facing the speakers. Such meetings may be held in theaters or auditoriums (Figure 17.1).

A workshop or a small seminar may use what is called "lunchroom" seating. This uses long tables with chairs on one side so that attendees can take notes or set up laptop computers.

Occasionally, large meetings are broken into discussion groups. Typically, the audience starts in one large room, where a speaker gives information and states a problem. The audience then moves into another room, or set of rooms, where round tables seating 8 or 10 people are available. A discussion leader is designated for each table. After the problem has been discussed, the leaders gather the opinions and the audience returns to the first room, where reports from each group are given to the entire assembly.

Facilities ■ A small meeting may not need much in the way of facilities, whereas a large and formal one may require a considerable amount of equipment and furnishings. Following are things that should be considered—and supplied if needed. You should check everything 1 or 2 hours before the meeting:

- **Meeting identification.** Is it posted on the bulletin board near the building entrance? Are directional signs needed?
- **Lighting.** Is it adequate? Can it be controlled? Where are the controls? Who will handle them?
- **Charts.** Are they readable? Is the easel adequate? Who will handle the charts?
- **Screen or monitors.** Are they large enough for the size of the audience?
- **Projectors and video equipment.** Are they hooked up and working? Who do you contact at the facility if you have technical difficulties?

- **Seating and tables.** Are there enough seats for the audience you are expecting? Are they arranged properly?
- **Telephone.** Where is it? If it is in the meeting room, who will answer?
- **Wiring.** For all electrical equipment, can wires be kicked loose or trip someone?
- **Speaker's podium.** Is it positioned properly? What about a reading light? Is there a PA system? Is it working?
- **Water and glasses.** For speakers? For audience?
- **Audience and speaker aids.** Are there programs or agendas? Will there be notepaper, pencils, and handout materials?
- **Name tags.** For speakers? For all attendees?

Invitations ■ For clubs, an announcement in the newsletter, a flyer, or an e-mail should be adequate. For external groups—people who are not required to attend but whose presence is desired—invitations via the mail or e-mail are necessary. They should go out early enough for people to fit the meeting into their schedules—3 to 6 weeks is a common lead time. See Figure 17.2 for an example of an invitation reply card to an event.

The invitation should tell the time, day, date, place (including the name of the room), purpose, highlights of the program (including names of speakers), and a way for the person to RSVP. This may be a telephone number, an e-mail address, a reply card mailed back to the event's organizers, or even an online registration service that handles everything from making the reservation to processing the credit card information to pay for the event. Using an online reservation service for conferences and conventions is discussed later in the section. A map showing the location and parking facilities is advisable if the facility is not widely known.

Registration

If everyone knows everyone else, registration and identification are highly informal, but if the group is large it is customary to have a registration desk or table at the entrance. Here the names of arrivals are checked against lists of individuals who said they would attend. If there is no invitation list and the presence or absence of any of the people who were invited is not important (as at a regular meeting of a club or association), the arrivals generally sign in on a plain sheet of paper and no one checks the membership roster.

FIGURE 17.2 Invitations to events require reply cards that collect such vital information as names, mailing addresses, e-mail addresses, and credit card information. This reply card, by Hakone Gardens in Saratoga, California, is well organized and gives enough space for an individual to provide all the information requested.

Greeting ▪ A representative of the sponsoring organization should be at the entrance of the room. If the number attending is not too large, a personal welcome is in order. When hundreds of people are expected, this isn't possible, but the chairperson should greet the audience in his or her opening remarks.

Name Tags ▪ Name tags are a good idea at almost any meeting. You should use label-making software to prepare name tags for everyone with advance reservations. Names should be printed in bold, large block letters so that they can be read easily from a distance of 4 feet. If the person's affiliation is used, this can be in smaller bold letters.

For people showing up without advance registration, you can have felt-tip pens available for on-the-spot name tags. However, a nice touch is to designate one person at the registration desk to make these tags so that they look neat and consistent. Another approach is to use a laptop and print out name tags. Most tags are self-adhesive. Plastic badges with clamps or a chain are popular for large meetings such as conventions.

Program

At any meeting, the word "program" has two meanings. It is what goes on at the meeting, and it is the printed listing of what goes on.

The meeting must have a purpose. To serve that purpose, it is necessary to have a chairperson who controls and directs the meeting, introduces the speakers, and keeps discussions from wandering. It is necessary to have speakers who will inform, persuade, or activate the listeners.

The printed program that is handed out to the audience in a workshop or seminar tells them what is going to happen, when, and where. It lists all the speakers, the time they will speak, coffee breaks, lunch breaks, and any other facts attendees should know about the meeting. Because speakers may have last-minute changes in their plans, the programs should not be printed until the last possible moment.

Speakers ▪ Speakers should be selected early—several months in advance, if possible. They should be chosen because of their expertise, their crowd-drawing capacity, and their speaking ability. It is a good idea to listen to any prospective speaker before tendering an invitation, or at least to discuss your intention with someone who has heard the person speak before. Many prominent people are not effective speakers.

When a speaker has agreed to give a talk, it is essential to make sure that the speaker has all the information he or she needs to prepare remarks and get to the meeting. This was also discussed in Chapter 15. Barbara Nichols, owner of a hospitality management firm in New York City, gave this comprehensive checklist to *Meeting News* regarding what speakers need to know about your meeting:

- Information about the meeting sponsor and attendees
- Meeting purpose and objectives
- Presentation location, including meeting room, date, and hour

- Topic and length of presentation
- Anticipated size of the audience
- Session format, including length of time allowed for audience questions
- Names of those sharing the platform, if any, and their topics
- Name of person who will make the introductions
- Speaker fee or honorarium
- Travel and housing arrangements
- Meeting room setup and staging information
- Audiovisual equipment needed
- Dress code (business attire, resort wear, black tie)
- Request to speaker for presentation outline, handout material
- Signed release to tape or videotape the remarks
- Arrangements for spouse, if invited

Meals ■ Club meetings and workshops often occur at a meal time. In fact, many meetings include breakfast, lunch, or dinner.

Early morning breakfast meetings have the advantage of attracting people who cannot take the time during the day to attend such functions. A full breakfast, served buffet style, is a popular choice, because it allows everyone to select what they normally eat for breakfast. People attending a half-day or full-day workshop often partake of a self-served continental breakfast—rolls, juice, and coffee—during the registration period just prior to the start of the meeting.

Luncheons are either sit-down affairs with a fixed menu or a buffet. A 30- to 45-minute cocktail period may precede a luncheon, usually during registration as guests arrive. A good schedule for a typical luncheon is registration, 11:30; luncheon, noon; adjournment, 1:30. In rare instances, the adjournment can be as late as 2 P.M., but it should never be later than that.

Dinner meetings are handled in much the same way as luncheons. A typical schedule is registration and cocktails, 6 P.M.; dinner, 7 P.M.; speaker, 8 P.M.; adjournment, between 8:30 and 9 P.M. Speakers, as mentioned in Chapter 15, should talk about 20 minutes.

You will need to have an accurate count of people who will attend a meal function. The hotel or restaurant facility will need a count at least 24 hours in advance to prepare the food and set up table service. The standard practice is for the organization to guarantee a certain number of meals, plus or minus 10 percent. If fewer than what is guaranteed show up, you still pay for the meals.

■ Banquets

Banquets, by definition, are fairly large and formal functions. They are held to honor an individual, raise money for a charitable organization, or celebrate an event, such as an organization's anniversary.

A banquet or even a reception may have 100 or 1,000 people in attendance, and staging a successful one takes a great deal of planning. The budget, in particular, needs close attention. A banquet coordinator has to consider such costs as (1) food, (2) room rental, (3) bartenders, (4) decorations and table centerpieces, (5) audiovisual requirements, (6) speaker fees, (7) entertainment, (8) photographers, (9) invitations, (10) tickets, and (11) marketing and promotion.

All of these components, of course, must be factored into establishing the per-ticket cost of the event. You are not just paying $50 to $100 for the traditional rubber chicken dinner, but for the total cost of staging the event. If the purpose is to raise money for a worthy charitable organization or a political candidate, tickets might go for $100 to $250. The actual price, of course, depends on how fancy the banquet is and how much you are paying for a speaker. See the Tips for Success on page 463 for a checklist on how to prepare a budget for a special event.

Featuring a well-known personality as a banquet speaker usually helps ticket sales, but it also is a major expense in your budget. Karen Kendig, president of the Speaker's Network, told *PR Tactics* that the going rate is $3,000 to $10,000 for "bread and butter" business-type talks, $15,000 and up for entertainment celebrities, and $50,000 to $60,000 for well-known politicians. A number of firms, such as the Washington Speaker's Bureau in Alexandria, Virginia, and the Harry Walker Agency in New York, represent celebrity speakers.

Such fees cannot be fully absorbed in the cost of an individual ticket so, in addition to sending out individual invitations, there usually is a committee that personally asks corporations and other businesses to sponsor the event or buy a table for employees, clients, or friends. A corporate table of eight, for example, may go for $25,000 or more, depending on the prestige and purpose of the event.

Working with Catering Managers

When organizing a banquet, you usually contact the catering or banquet manager of the restaurant or hotel at least 3 or 4 months before your event. He or she will discuss menus, room facilities, availability of space, and a host of other items with you to determine exactly what you need.

Hotels and restaurants have special menus for banquets, which are often subject to some negotiation. If you plan a banquet during the week, for example, the restaurant or hotel might be willing to give you more favorable rates because week nights aren't ordinarily booked. However, if you insist on having a banquet on Friday or Saturday night—which is the most popular time—you can expect to pay full rates.

A banquet usually has a fixed menu, but you must also make a vegetarian dish available to those who request it. In general, a popular choice for a meat entree is chicken or fish. Pork may be objectionable on religious grounds, and many people refrain from red meats such as beef. Offering two entrees requires the extra work of providing coded tickets for the waiters, and the hotel or restaurant may charge more for the meal. Get the catering manager's advice before ordering multiple entrees.

When figuring food costs, many amateur planners often forget about tax and gratuity, which can add 25 percent or more to any final bill. That $25 chicken dinner on the menu is really $30.75 if tax and gratuity add up to 23 percent. In addition, there

Making a Budget for a Special Event

All events have two sides of the ledger: costs and revenues. It is important to prepare a detailed budget so you know exactly how much an event will cost. This will enable you to also figure out how much you will need to charge so you at least break even. The following are some of the items that you need to consider.

Facilities

Rental of meeting or reception rooms.

Set up of podiums, microphones, audio-visual equipment

Food Service

Number of meals to be served

Cost per person

Gratuities

Refreshments for breaks

Bartenders for cocktail hours

Wine, liquor, soft drinks

Decorations

Table decorations

Direction signs

Design and Printing

Invitations

Programs

Tickets

Name tags

Promotional flyers

Postage

Postage for invitations

Mailing house charges

Recognition Items

Awards, plaques, trophies

Engraving

Framing

Calligraphy

Miscellaneous

VIP travel and expenses

Speaker fees

Security

Transportation

Buses

Vans

Parking

Entertainment

Fees

Publicity

Advertising

News releases

Banners

Postage

Office Expenses

Phones

Supplies

Complimentary tickets

Staff travel and expenses

Data processing ■

are corkage fees if you provide your own liquor or wine. In many establishments, corkage fees are set rather high to discourage you from bringing your own refreshment. At one banquet, for example, the organizers thought it was a great coup to have the wine donated, only to find out that the hotel charged a corkage fee of $20 per bottle.

Logistics and Timing

Organizing a banquet requires considerable logistics, timing, and teamwork. First, you have to establish a timeline for the entire process—from the contacting of catering managers to the sending out of invitations and lining up a speaker. Second, you need a detailed timeline for the several days or day of the event to ensure that everything is in place. Third, you should have a timeline for the event itself, so that it begins and ends at a reasonable time. Good examples of timelines are those of Chevron's Conservation Awards banquet, which are shown in Figures 17.3 and 17.4.

In addition, you need to work out the logistics to ensure that registration lines are kept to a minimum and that everyone is assigned to a table. Table numbers must be highly visible. If the group is particularly large (1,000 or more), you should provide a large seating chart so people can locate where they are sitting. Another more personalized approach is to have staff inside the hall directing people to their seats.

CHEVRON CONSERVATION AWARDS PROGRAM BANQUET

	Event Schedule	Staff Member
9:00 a.m.	Meet with hotel catering manager/staff Confirm event arrangements	Bill/Lauren/Deb
	5:00-6:00 VIP reception & photos 6:30-7:30 general reception 7:30-8:30 dinner (see attached schedule) 8:30-10:00 program-speaker & award presentation	
12:00-3:00	Coordinate ballroom set up Staging & A/V equipment	Deb/Bob
12:00-3:00	Media interviews-award honorees	B.J.
1:00	Complete seating arrangements	Bill/Mary
2:00	Complete and organize nametags	Lauren/Gail
2:00-3:00	Rehearsal/AV run through	Bill/Deb/Bob/Clair
4:00	Award booklets/program each place setting	Gail
4:30	Lobby signs	Gail
5:00-6:00	VIP reception-coordinate honoree photos (see attached)	Lauren/Gail
6:00	Brief hotel staff re reception table staffing	Gail

▶ **FIGURE 17.3** Banquets require coordination of logistics on the day of the event. This is a list of activities that had to be completed before the actual banquet scheduled in the evening.

```
                    CHEVRON CONSERVATION AWARDS BANQUET
                             JW MARRIOTT HOTEL
                             WASHINGTON, DC
                             WEDNESDAY, MAY 13

                                   Crew Agenda

3:30 – 5:00 p.m.        Program agenda review – participants and staff only.  Live run-through
                        of C. Ghylin's remarks.  (Grand Ballroom)

5:00 – 6:00             Private pre-reception for honorees, judges, Chevron staff.  Honoree
                        photo session including E. Zern and J. Sullivan.  (Suite 1231)

6:30 – 7:15             Greetings and reception, open bar.  Photo opportunities available.
                        (Grand Ballroom Foyer)

7:15 – 7:30             Close bar,  enter Grand Ballroom.

7:30 – 7:35             C. Ghylin:  Welcome and opening remarks.

7:30 – 8:20             Dinner served.

8:20 – 8:25             C. Ghylin:  Introduces special guests at head table, introduces E. Zern.

8:25 – 8:30             E. Zern:  Welcome, honoree toast, introduces judges, completes
                        remarks.

8:30 – 8:35             C. Ghylin:  Introduces J. Sullivan.

8:35 – 8:45             J. Sullivan:  Remarks.

8:45 – 8:50             C. Ghylin:  Introduces slide presentation.

8:50 – 9:25             Slide presentation.  (C. Ghylin remains at podium)
                        (a) Introduces/explains honoree category;
                        (b) Comments on professionals.  Introduces/explains honoree
                        category.
                        (c) Comments on citizens.  Introduces/explains organizations' honoree
                        category.

9:25 – 9:40             C. Ghylin:  Comments on organizations.  Invites J. Sullivan and
                        E. Zern for plaque presentation.  Plaque presentation.

9:40 – 9:45             C. Ghylin:  Final remarks.

9:45 p.m.               America the Beautiful.
```

FIGURE 17.4 This is the timeline for Chevron's Conservation Awards Banquet. The compilation of a timeline, and going over it with the master of ceremonies, helps keep the event on schedule.

Receptions and Cocktail Parties

A short cocktail party, as mentioned previously, can precede the start of a club's luncheon or dinner. It can also be part of a reception. The purpose is to have people socialize; it also is a cost-effective way to celebrate an organization's or individual's achievement, to introduce a new chief executive to the employees and the community, or simply to allow college alumni to get together.

In any event, the focus is on interaction, not speeches. If there is a ceremony or speech, it should last a maximum of 5 to 10 minutes.

A reception lasts up to 2 hours, and the typical format is a large room where most people will stand instead of sit. This facilitates social interaction and allows people to move freely around the room. Such gatherings, like any other event, require advance planning and logistics.

> " *Don't make a lengthy presentation part of an event. You'll lose the attendees' attention.* "
>
> ■ Erica Iacono, reporter for *PRWeek*

It is important, for example, that food be served in the form of appetizers, sandwiches, cheese trays, nuts, and chips. People get hungry, and food helps offset some of the effects of drinking. The bar is the centerpiece of any reception, but you should make sure there are plenty of nonalcoholic beverages available, too. Urns of coffee, punch, and tea should be readily available in other locations around the room.

Such precautions will limit your liability if someone does get drunk and has an accident on the way home. You can also limit your liability if you have a **no-host bar**, which means that guests buy their own drinks.

Most receptions, however, have a **hosted bar**, meaning that drinks are free. This is particularly true when a corporation is hosting the cocktail party or reception for journalists, customers, or community leaders. In every case, it is important that bartenders be trained to spot individuals who appear to be under the influence of alcohol and politely suggest a nonalcoholic alternative.

Organizations also try to control the level of drinking by offering only beer or wine instead of hard liquor. Still others issue one or two free drink tickets to arriving guests, with the understanding that there will be a charge for any additional drinks.

A reception, like a meal function, requires you to talk with the catering manager to order finger food and decide how many bartenders are needed. As a rule of thumb, there should be one bartender per 75 people. For large events, bars are situated in several locations around the room to disperse the crowd and shorten lines.

It is also important to find out how the facility will bill you for beverages consumed. If the arrangement is by the bottle, this often leads to the problems of bartenders being very generous in pouring drinks, because more empty bottles mean higher profits for the caterer.

Starting a cocktail party is easy—just open the bar at the announced time. Closing a party is not so easy. The only practical way is to close the bar. The invitation may indicate a definite time for the reception to end, but don't rely on this. A vocal announcement will do the job. The smoothest way is to say, "The bar will close in 10 minutes." This gives guests a chance to get one more drink.

■ Open Houses and Plant Tours

Open houses and plant tours are conducted primarily to develop favorable public opinion about an organization. Generally, they are planned to show the facilities where the organization does its work and, in plant tours, how the work is done. A factory might have a plant tour to show how it turns raw materials into finished products. A hospital open house could show its emergency facilities, diagnostic equipment, operating rooms, and patient rooms.

Open houses are customarily one-day affairs. However, if large numbers of people are to attend, the event may be extended to more than one day. Attendance is usually by invitation, but in other instances, the event is announced in the general media, and anyone who chooses to attend may do so. See Figure 17.5 for a flyer announcing a community open house for a city/university library. If you're having a community open house, you also have to think about entertainment and activities for the attendees.

Many plants offer tours daily or regularly while the plant is in operation. These tours are most common among producers of consumer goods such as beer, wine, food products, clothing, and small appliances. These daily tours are geared to handle only a few people at any one time, whereas open houses generally have a large number of guests and normal operations are not feasible during the tour.

Because the purpose of an open house or a plant tour is to create favorable opinion about the organization, it must be carefully planned, thoroughly explained, and smoothly conducted. The visitors must understand what they are seeing. This requires careful routing, control to prevent congestion, signs, and guides. All employees who will be present should understand the purpose of the event and be coached in their duties.

A detailed checklist for planning an open house is provided in the Tips for Success on page 469, but the following are the major factors to consider in planning an open house:

- **Day and hour.** The time must be convenient for both the organization and the guests.
- **Guests.** These may be families of employees, customers, representatives of the community, suppliers and competitors, reporters, or others whose goodwill is desirable.
- **Publicity and invitations.** These materials should be distributed at least a month before the event.

If a plant tour is a continuing daily event, the availability of the tour should be announced by signs near the plant and possibly by advertising or publicity. For any open house or plant tour, consider the following points:

- **Vehicles.** Parking must be available, and there should be a map on the invitation showing how to get there and where to park.
- **Reception.** A representative of the organization should meet and greet all arriving guests. If guests are important people, they should meet the top officials of the organization.
- **Restrooms.** If you are expecting a large crowd, arrange for portable toilets to supplement the regular facilities.

Dr. Martin Luther King, Jr. Library –
Check It Out!

FREE

FREE

FREE

Grand Opening Celebration
Saturday, August 16
10 a.m. – 4 p.m.
4th & San Fernando, downtown San José

- *Entertainment on 2 stages for the whole family*
- *Games, crafts, children's activities, story times*
- *Book bingo*
- *Mystery tea*
- *Formal dedication ceremony at 10 a.m.*
- *Commemorative gifts*
- *Contests with prizes*
- *Tours and demonstrations*
- *A day of fun and surprises*

You've never seen a library like this one!

(408) 277-4000
www.newkinglibrary.org

Lots of free parking in downtown City garages
Metered on-street parking is free on Saturday

To arrange for an accommodation under the Americans with Disabilities Act, please call (408) 277-4000 or (408) 998-5299 (TTY) at least 48 hours prior to the event.

The Bay Area's **NBC11**

FIRST 5 SANTA CLARA COUNTY

T48 TELEMUNDO

The Mercury News
The Newspaper of Silicon Valley
MercuryNews.com

Printing Donated to the King Library

Dr. Martin Luther King, Jr. Library

A collaboration between the City of San José and San José State University

▶ **FIGURE 17.5** This flyer, in multiple colors, was distributed to various community groups to promote the grand opening of a new city/university library on the grounds of San Jose State University. It gives the basic five Ws and also entices the public with a list of activities for the day. The reverse side of the flyer gave the basic information in Spanish and Vietnamese to reflect the multicultural nature of the city. The outstanding programs and materials received an American Library Association (ALA) award.

How to Plan an Open House

Preplanning

Initial Planning
- Select and research the date.
- Set up your committees or areas of responsibility.
- Determine your budget.

Open House Announcement
- Notify employees and recruit their assistance.
- Invite staff and families, if appropriate.
- Develop your mailing list.
- Design and print invitations.
- Arrange advertising.
- Prepare and distribute press releases/posters.
- Create radio/TV spots.

Food and Beverages
- Decide on the menu.
- Arrange for catering or volunteer servers.
- Arrange for cleanup.

Equipment/Decorations
- Determine the equipment available from your organization.
- Arrange for necessary rentals, such as tables, chairs, or an outdoor tent.
- Arrange for table linens, plates, and silverware.
- Plan flowers in strategic locations.

Specialty Advertising
- Arrange for giveaways that increase your organization's visibility, such as balloons, T-shirts, and mugs.

Media Relations
- Invite the media personally and by mail.
- Develop and distribute press releases announcing the event.
- Arrange for media coverage on the day of the open house.

- Arrange for a photographer to cover the event (photos can be used for publicity or internal communications).

Day of Event

Reception
- Set up a staffed reception table with a sign-in book.
- Distribute information on your organization and giveaways.
- Have staff explain the activities to guests.

Tours
(Some preparation required in planning process)
- Develop a floor plan for tours to ensure consistency.
- Arrange a regular tour schedule, such as every 30 minutes.
- Offer an incentive (such as a T-shirt) to those who complete the tour.
- Brief tour guides on the key points to cover and how to field questions.
- Arrange for visuals such as a display or demonstrations during the tour.

Activities/Entertainment
This depends on the nature of your event but could include:
- Health education displays or screenings.
- A road race.
- Games, a magician, or a storyteller for the children.
- A local band.
- A short questionnaire to evaluate community response to the event and issues related to your organization.

Ceremony
- Arrange a focal point for your open house, such as a ribbon cutting, awards ceremony, music/dance performance, or brief message from the company president. ■

- **Safety.**   Hazards should be conspicuously marked and well lighted. Dangerous equipment should be barricaded.
- **Routing.**   Routes should be well marked and logical (in a factory, the route should go from raw materials through production steps to the finished product). A map should be given to each visitor if the route is long or complicated.
- **Guides.**   Tours should be led by trained guides who have a thorough knowledge of the organization and can explain in detail what visitors are seeing on the tour.
- **Explanation.**   Signs, charts, and diagrams may be necessary at any point to supplement the words of the guides. The guides must be coached to say exactly what the public should be told. Many experts can't explain what they do, so a prepared explanation is necessary.
- **Housekeeping and attire.**   The premises should be as clean as possible. Attire should be clean and appropriate. A punch press operator doesn't wear a necktie, but his overalls need not be greasy.
- **Emergencies.**   Accidents or illness may occur. All employees should know what to do and how to request appropriate medical assistance.

Conventions

A convention is a series of meetings, usually spread over two or more days. The purpose is to gather and exchange information, meet other people with similar interests, discuss and act on common problems, and enjoy recreation and social interchange.

Most conventions are held by national membership groups and trade associations. Because the membership is widespread, a convention is nearly always "out of town" to many attendees, so convention arrangements must give consideration to this.

Planning

It is necessary to begin planning far in advance of the actual event. Planning for even the smallest convention should start months before the scheduled date; for large national conventions, it may begin several years ahead and require hundreds or thousands of hours of work. The main components in planning a convention are (1) timing, (2) location, (3) facilities, (4) exhibits, (5) program, (6) recreation, (7) attendance, and (8) administration.

Timing ■ Timing must be convenient for the people who are expected to attend. Avoid peak work periods. Summer vacation is appropriate for educators, and after harvest is suitable for farmers. Preholiday periods are bad for retailers, and midwinter is probably a poor time in the northern United States but may be very good in the South. Here, as in every area dealing with the public, it is imperative to know your audience and to plan for their convenience.

Location ■ As real estate agents say, "it's location, location, location." A national convention can be anywhere in the country, but one in Fairbanks, Alaska, would probably not be well attended. A convention in Las Vegas or New Orleans could be a great success because the glamour of the location might outweigh the cost and time of travel. Many organizations rotate their conventions from one part of the state, region, or country to another to equalize travel burdens.

Another factor in choosing a location is availability of accommodations. A suitable number of rooms must be available to house the attendees. In addition, enough meeting rooms of the right size must also be available. Timing enters into this, because many such accommodations are booked months, or even years, in advance. Large cities usually have large convention facilities and numerous hotels, but early reservations are necessary for such popular cities as San Francisco, New York, New Orleans, Las Vegas, and San Diego. Once a tentative location has been selected, you must find out if the convention can be handled at the time chosen. Early action on this can forestall later changes. Be sure to get a definite price on guest rooms as well as meeting rooms.

Small conventions are often held in resorts, but accessibility is a factor. If the visitors have to change airlines several times or if the location is hard to get to by automobile, the glamour may fail to compensate for the inconvenience.

Facilities ■ For every meeting or session of the convention, it is necessary to have a room of the right size and the equipment needed for whatever is to occur in that room. The convention might start with a general meeting in a large ballroom, where seating is theater fashion and the equipment consists of a public address system and a speaker's platform with large video monitors. After opening remarks, the convention might break into smaller groups that meet in different rooms with widely varying facilities.

One room may require a computer projector; another may need a whiteboard or an easel for charts; still another may need a VCR and monitor. In one room the seating may be around conference tables; another may have theater seating. To get everything right, you must know exactly what is to happen, who is going to participate, and when.

Exhibits ■ The makers and sellers of supplies that are used by people attending conventions frequently want to show their wares. This means that the convention manager must provide space suitable for that purpose. Most large convention centers have facilities that can accommodate anything from books to bulldozers. There is a charge for the use of these rooms, and the exhibitors pay for the space they use.

The exhibit hall may be in the hotel where the convention is being held or in a separate building. For example, McCormick Place is an enormous building on the Chicago lakefront. It is an easy taxi trip from the Loop, where conventions are usually based and where the visitors sleep. Eating facilities, ranging from hotdog stands to elaborate dining rooms, are to be found in almost any such building. Exhibits are covered in more detail when trade shows are discussed.

Program

A convention program usually has a basic theme. Aside from transacting the necessary organizational business, most of the speeches and other sessions will be devoted to various aspects of the theme. Themes can range from the specific "New Developments in AIDS Research" to the more general "Quality Management and Productivity." Some groups use an even broader theme such as "Connections" or "At the Crossroads."

With a theme chosen, the developer of the program looks for prominent speakers who have something significant to say on a particular topic. In addition, there may be a need for discussions, workshops, and other sessions focusing on particular aspects of the general theme.

The printed program for the convention is a schedule. It tells exactly when every session will be, what room it will be in, and who will speak on what subject. Large conventions often schedule different sessions at the same time. Attendees then choose which session they prefer.

Ideally, the program schedule should be small enough to fit in a pocket or a handbag. Large programs may look impressive, but they are cumbersome to carry and easy to misplace. One compromise is to give attendees the large program, which contains paid advertising, at registration, but also include a tear-out "crib" sheet that summarizes the time and location of the major presentations. If the convention is on multiple floors of a hotel or convention center, it's also a good idea to provide a floor plan so attendees can easily find the various meeting rooms. Printing of the program should be delayed until the last possible moment. Last-minute changes and speaker defaults are common.

Recreation ■ Recreation is a feature of practically all conventions. This may range from informal get-togethers to formal dances, cocktail parties, golf tournaments, sightseeing tours, and free time are among the possibilities. Sometimes recreational events are planned to coincide with regular program sessions. These are patronized by spouses and by delegates who would rather relax than listen to a speaker. Evening receptions and dinners at interesting venues such as an art gallery or museum are often planned for both attendees and their significant others.

Attendance ■ Getting people to attend a convention requires two things: (1) an appealing program and (2) a concerted effort to persuade members to attend. Announcements and invitations should go out several months in advance to allow attendees to make their individual arrangements. A second and even a third mailing often are done in the weeks preceding the convention. Reply cards should be provided, accompanied by hotel reservation forms. Many corporations and organizations now use specialty firms such as cvent (www.cvent.com) that prepare digital invitations and provide event management tools. The Tips for Success on page 473 for more on the use of software programs for event planning.

Administration ■ Managing a convention is a strenuous job. The organization staff is likely to see very little of the program and many delegates with problems. Among the things that must be done are arranging for buses to convey delegates from the airport to the convention (if it is in a remote location) and to carry them on tours. Meeting speakers and getting them to the right place at the right time is another task.

Making Reservations on the Web

The digital age has made event planning more precise. A number of companies now offer event planners the ability to send invitations via the Internet and to track response rates.

E-mail invitations are used for any number of organizational meetings and corporate events, including a college student having a party to celebrate his or her 21st birthday. E-mail invitations, according to cvent (www.cvent.com), a firm offering such services, should have eye-catching graphics, an effective subject line, and relevant content, such as the five Ws and H.

Most individuals just concern themselves in generating a list of yes, no, and maybe responses, but professional and trade groups bundle the e-mail invitation with software that enables attendees to pay registration fees online. According to cvent, event planners can achieve up to three times the standard response rate by integrating e-mail, direct mail, and phone campaigns.

Meeting planners like the capabilities of software programs and online systems that allow them to manage an entire event online. StarCite and cvent, for example, offer a variety of meeting management services—from gathering hotel bids to sending electronic invitations and tracking registrations online. Software can even compile data on why individuals aren't coming to the event, which may help in planning future meetings. Once someone does register, the site also allows them to book hotel, airline, and car reservations at the same time.

Electronic tracking is also helpful for figuring out exactly how many hotel rooms are needed; bad estimates, cancellations, and no-shows can add up to substantial hotel cancellation fees. Other management tools allow groups to track the flow of registrations. If registrations are lagging, it's a signal to do another round of e-mails and direct mail to bolster attendance. You can even track attendance at various sessions. If breakfast sessions, for example, aren't well attended, it might be wise to plan fewer early morning meetings next year.

Although e-mail invitations are economical and efficient, they are most appropriate for business-related meetings and events. It's still considered tacky to send an e-mail invitation to your wedding or to a major fund-raising dinner for a community cause. In these instances, mailed invitations and replies are the norm. If you use a mailed invitation, you can still provide an e-mail address or phone number for people to respond if they don't want to fill out the reply card. ■

People arriving at the convention headquarters must be met, registered, and provided with all the essentials (name tags, programs, and any other needed materials). A message center should be set up so that people can be informed of phone calls or other messages. Special arrangements should be made for the media. A small convention may interest only a few people from trade publications, but larger conventions may draw attention from the major media. In this case, a newsroom should be set up with telephones, computers, tables, and other needed equipment.

Trade Shows

Trade shows are the ultimate marketing event. According to *Tradeshow Week* magazine, about 6,000 trade shows are held annually in the United States. They

FIGURE 17.6 Trade shows attract millions of people annually. They provide an opportunity to see new products from a number of companies, generate sales leads, and attract media coverage. Sony displayed its Blu-ray disc technology at the 2008 Consumer Electronics Show (CES) in Las Vegas, which attracted 130,000 industry professionals. Almost 3,000 companies filled about 2 million square feet of exhibit space.

range in size from more than 100,000 attendees to those in very specialized industries that attract only several thousand people. It is estimated that about 65 million people attend trade shows on an annual basis.

The Consumer Electronics Show (CES), sponsored by the Consumer Electronics Association, illustrates the power and influence of a trade show. The show, open only to industry professionals, attracts 130, 000 attendees to the Las Vegas Convention Center every January. Almost 3,000 companies show their new consumer products, taking up about 2 million square feet of exhibit space. Bill Gates was the keynote speaker in 2008 and gave his farewell as CEO of Microsoft. Panasonic also introduced its new 150-inch plasma TV screen at CES, which caused considerable buzz in the industry and in the media. A photo of the giant television is shown Figure 8.3 on page 193. Sony also showed off its new Blu-ray technology at CES (Figure 17.6).

Exhibit Booths

Although food and entertainment costs are high, the major expense at a trade show is the exhibit booth. At national trade shows, it is not unusual for a basic booth to start at $50,000, including design, construction, transportation, and space rental fees. Larger, more elaborate booths can easily cost between $500,000 and $1 million.

Any booth or exhibit should be designed for maximum visibility. Experts say you have about 10 seconds to attract a visitor as he or she walks down an aisle of booths. Consequently, companies try to out dazzle each other in booth designs. Here is how Karen Chan of Dow Jones International News described one booth at the Telecoms trade show in Geneva:

> Hewlett-Packard Co.'s stand features a huge, upside-down glass pyramid with ever ascending pink neon lights rising from its tip. The 3-floor stand took 30 men 3 months to build and contains 56 tons of steel, 20 tons of glass, 7 truckloads of lumber, 1,000 meters of neon, and 5 miles of cable. Let's not forget the 5,000 bolts holding it all together.

Not every company has the resources of HP, but here are some points to keep in mind if you get involved in planning an exhibit booth:

- Select the appropriate trade shows that have the best potential for developing contacts and generating future sales.
- Start planning and developing your exhibit 6 to 12 months in advance. Exhibit designers and builders need time to develop a booth.
- Make the display or booth visually attractive. Use bright colors, large signs, and working models of products.
- Think about putting action in your display. Have a video or slide presentation running all the time.
- Use involvement techniques. Have a contest or raffle in which visitors can win a prize. An exhibitor at one show even offered free foot massages.
- Give people an opportunity to operate equipment or do something.
- Have knowledgeable, personable representatives on duty to answer questions and collect visitor business cards for follow-up.
- Offer useful souvenirs. A key chain, a shopping bag, a luggage tag, or even a copy of a popular newspaper or magazine will attract traffic.
- Promote your exhibit in advance. Send announcements to potential customers and media kits to selected journalists 4 to 6 weeks before the trade show.

Most organizations feel that the large investment in a booth at a trade show is worthwhile for two reasons. First, a trade show facilitates one-on-one communication with potential customers and helps generate sales leads. It also attracts many journalists, so it is easier and more efficient to provide press materials, arrange one-on-one interviews, and demonstrate what makes the product worth a story. Second, a booth allows an exhibitor to demonstrate how its products differ from the competition. This is more effective than just sending prospects a color brochure. It also is more cost-effective than making individual sales calls.

Hospitality Suites ■ Hospitality suites are an adjunct to the exhibit booth. Organizations use them to entertain key prospects, give more in-depth presentations, and talk about business deals.

The idea is that serious customers will stay in a hospitality suite long enough to hear an entire presentation, whereas they are likely to stop at an exhibit hall booth for only a few minutes. Although goodwill can be gained from free concerts and cocktail parties, the primary purpose of a hospitality suite is to generate leads that ultimately result in product sales.

Press Rooms and Media Relations

Trade shows such as CES and MacWorld attract many journalists. About a thousand reporters, for example, descend on MacWorld every year. Consequently, every trade show has a press room where the various exhibitors distribute media kits and other information to journalists. Press rooms typically have phone, fax, and Internet facilities for reporters to file stories back to their employers.

As a public relations writer, you are often responsible for preparing an organization's media kit. Remember the rules about media kits discussed in Chapter 6; keep them short and relevant, and offer newsworthy information. A common complaint of reporters at a trade show is that media kits are too thick and only a compilation of sales brochures.

> **" For people to pay attention at a trade show, you need real news. "**
>
> ■ David Rich, senior vice president of the George P. Johnson marketing company, as reported in *PRWeek*

An important part of your job is to personally contact reporters several weeks before a trade show to offer product briefings and one-on-one interviews with key executives. The competition is intense, so you have to be creative in pitching your ideas and showing why your company's products or services merit the journalist's time when multiple other companies are also pitching them. If you can arrange as many preshow interviews and briefings as possible, you are more likely to be effective and successful.

A survey by Access Communications, for example, found that more than 90 percent of journalists assigned to a trade show want to hear about the company and product news before the show even starts. Michael Young, senior vice president of Access told *PRWeek*, "Journalists have limited bandwidth at the show. They can only do so much, so they want to know what the news is before getting there." In other words, your media relations work starts before the show; it continues throughout the show, and then you have to do follow-up with reporters to provide additional information.

Sarah Skerik, director of trade show markets for *PR Newswire*, provides some additional tips for working with the media during a trade show:

- Plan major product announcements to coincide with the show.
- Include the name of the trade show in your news releases, so journalists searching databases can log on using the show as a keyword.
- Include your booth number in all releases and announcements.
- Make it easy for journalists to track down key spokespeople and experts connected with your product by including cell phone, pager, and e-mail addresses in your materials.
- Have your spokespeople trained to make brief presentations and equip them with answers to the most-likely-asked questions.
- Consider a looped videotape to run in the booth with copies available to the media.
- Provide photos that show the product in use, in production, or in development.
- Provide online corporate logos, product photos, executive profiles, media kits, and PowerPoint presentations to those journalists who cannot attend or who prefer to lighten their suitcase by having everything in digital format.
- Keep hard copies of news releases, fact sheets, and brochures at the booth and in the press room.

Promotional Events

Promotional events are planned primarily to promote product sales, increase organizational visibility, make friends, and raise money for a charitable cause. It also includes the category of corporate event sponsorship, which is discussed in the following Tips for Success.

The one essential skill for organizing promotional events is creativity. Multiple "ho hum" events compete for media attention, and even attendance, in every city, so it behooves you to come up with something "different" that creates buzz and interest.

Grand openings of stores or hotels, for example, can be pretty dull and generate a collective yawn from almost every journalist in town, let alone all the chamber of commerce types that attend such functions. So how do you come up with something new and different for the same old thing? First, you throw out the old idea of having a ribbon cutting. Second, you start thinking about a theme or idea that fits the situation and is out of the ordinary. A good example is the PR Casebook on page 479 about Procter & Gamble's "event" in New York's Times Square that literally scored a "royal flush."

The reopening of the Morgan Hotel in San Antonio is another good example. The hotel featured a new restaurant Oro (meaning "gold" in Spanish), so the theme for the opening night reception was gold—complete with gold flowers, gold curtains, and even bikini-clad women who were coated with gold paint and served as living mannequins.

Using Celebrities to Attract Attendance

You can also increase attendance at a promotional event by using a television or film personality. The creative part is figuring out what "personality" fits the particular product or situation. A national conference on aging for policy makers, government officials, and health care experts attracted attendees because former senator and astronaut John Glenn was a major speaker. Unilever wanted to reach a Hispanic audience through a series of events promoting its Suave and Caress brands, so it tapped famous stylists Leonardo Rocco and Fernando Navarro, who gave hair and beauty advice to women attending the events. The Avon Walk for Breast Cancer, shown in Figure 17.7, enlisted actress Reese Witherspoon to lead off its 2008 run in Washington, D.C.

A celebrity, or "personality" as they are called in the trade, is not exactly the most creative solution to every situation, but it's a time-honored way to increase the odds that the media will cover your event, because "prominence" is considered a basic news value.

A personality, however, can be a major budget item. Stars such as Oprah Winfrey, Jennifer Lopez, and Jon Stewart typically charge $100,000 for an appearance. If you don't have that kind of budget, you'll have to make do with what the business calls the "up and coming" or the "down and going." Claire Atkinson, writing in *PRWeek*, explains:

> For $5,000 to $10,000, you'll get young TV stars. For $10,000, you can get Ivana Trump to open your restaurant. The cost of a personal appearance by Shirley Maclaine is $50,000. Members of the cast of *Friends* charge $25,000. Super models Claudia Shiffer and Naomi Campbell command between $10,000 and $15,000 per appearance. And soap opera stars tend to get between $5,000 and $10,000 as do lesser TV stars. . . .

On occasion, if the event is for a charity that the celebrity supports as a personal cause, he or she will reduce or waive an appearance fee. You should note,

PR casebook

When Going to the Restroom Is an Event

Toilet tissue isn't exactly an item that generates a lot of consumer interest, or even brand loyalty. Procter & Gamble, however, organized a creative "event" that was literally a "royal flush" for its brand, Charmin. The idea was to install 20 luxury restrooms in New York's Times Square during the Christmas season for harried shoppers on the go and who had to "go."

This was not just a bunch of fancy portable potties. As visitors entered a room with plush carpeting and framed portraits of Charmin bears, hosts in attractive uniforms greeted them and directed them to a reception desk and a Flush-O-Meter chart that tracked visitors' hometowns. In addition to residential-style restrooms, a handful of special New York-themed stalls were created, including a Broadway stall decorated like a theatre dressing room. Another stall had a Wall Street theme with an actual working stock ticker that scrolled Charmin messages.

> **“ *I was dying to pee and headed for McDonald's and saw you here. Charmin, you are my hero.* ”**
>
> ■ A visitor to New York City

The restrooms were only part of the experience. More than 20 TV monitors played an instructional Potty Dance video and there was even a dance floor to practice. Visitors could also get their pictures taken with a giant stuffed Charmin bear riding a toboggan. They could also relax on white couches in a room with a working fireplace.

From November 20 through December 31, more than 400,000 families from all 50 states and more than 100 nations visited the luxury Charmin bathrooms. The average family visit was 22 minutes, which *Corporate Event* magazine called "an impressive amount of time for consumers to interact with any brand, but especially one whose product normally doesn't generate much thought." One visitor was so impressed that she wrote, "I took more pictures at the Charmin restrooms than my whole trip in New York." More than 400 visitors posted video clips of the restrooms on YouTube.

There was extensive coverage in the traditional media. The "Disneyland of Bathrooms," as *The New York Times* dubbed it, generated about 200 million impressions (circulation and broadcast audience numbers). The bathrooms and Charmin even got coverage on the major morning television programs such as *Good Morning America*, *Today*, and *Fox and Friends*.

Adam Lisook, a brand manager for Charmin, makes the case for events. He told *Corporate Events*, "We will always do advertising, but this kind of event can directly interface with hundreds of thousands of consumers, and bring an element of understanding as to what it is they need." ■

however, that the organization is often expected to pay for the celebrity's transportation (first-class, of course), the hotel suite, and room service. In addition, an organization also pays the cost of assistants, hair stylists, valets, and other personnel accompanying them. Such arrangements can greatly increase your costs, even if the celebrity is "free."

One source for finding celebrities for promotional events is the Celebrity Source (www.celebritysource.com). It matches requests with the 4,500 names in its database and handles all the details of negotiating fees, expenses, and transportation logistics

FIGURE 17.7 Participants celebrate their accomplishments as they complete the Avon Walk for Breast Cancer. Avon sponsors walks in major cities to raise money for finding a cure for breast cancer, which is a topic of high concern for its customer base. In San Francisco, for example, 3,200 participants raised $7.5 million in 2008.

for your organization. The value of a firm such as Celebrity Source or Celebrity Access (www.celebrityaccess.com) is that it has regular contact with a celebrity's business agent and publicist. An organization trying to figure out who to contact for a particular celebrity, let alone contacting them, may have less success.

On its website, Celebrity Source gives some tips on what the firm needs to know in order to select the right celebrity for your event. The following is a good checklist for you if you are thinking about using a celebrity:

- What exactly do you want the celebrity to do?
- Who do you want to appeal to by having a celebrity? Is it the public, the media, or the sponsors?
- What do you want to accomplish by having a celebrity participate? Sell tickets or add glamour?
- What are the demographics of your audience or attendees?
- What is your budget?
- What is the maximum that you're willing to spend for the right celebrity?
- Are you prepared to pay for first-class expenses for the celebrity and at least one staff person?
- Do you have access to any perks or gifts that will help motivate the celebrity to say "yes"?

Planning and Logistics

Events that attract large crowds require the same planning as an open house. You should be concerned about traffic flow, adequate restroom facilities, signage, and security. Professionally trained security personnel should also be arranged to handle crowd control, protect celebrities or government officials from being hassled, and make sure no other disruptions occur that would mar the event.

Liability insurance is a necessity, too. Any public event sponsored by an organization should be insured, just in case there is an accident and a subsequent lawsuit charging negligence. If your organization doesn't already have a blanket liability policy, you should get one for the event.

Charitable organizations also need liability insurance if they are running an event to raise money. This is particularly relevant if your organization is sponsoring an event that requires physical exertion, such as a 10K run, a bicycle race, or even a hot-air balloon race.

Participants should sign a release form that protects the organization if someone suffers a heart attack or another kind of accident. One organization, which was sponsoring a 5K "fun run," had the participants sign a statement that read, in part: "I know that a road race is a potentially hazardous activity. . . . I assume all risk associated with running in this event, including, but not limited to, falls, contact with other participants, the effects of the weather, including high heat/or humidity, traffic and the conditions of the road."

Promotional events that use public streets and parks also need permits from various city departments. If you are sponsoring a run, you need to get a permit from the police or public safety department to block off streets, and you need to hire off-duty police to handle traffic control. Permits for the Avon Walk for Breast Cancer, for example, are arranged months in advance, because there are many requests for "runs" and cities have imposed a limit on how many will be permitted each year.

A food event, such as a chili cook-off or a German fest, requires permits from the public health department and, if liquor is served, a permit from the state alcohol board. If the event is held inside a building, a permit is often required from the fire inspector.

You must also deal with the logistics of arranging cleanup, providing basic services such as water and medical aid, registering craft and food vendors, and posting signs. Promotion of an event can often be accomplished by having a radio station or local newspaper cosponsor the event.

■ Summary

- Events and meetings don't just happen. They must be planned with attention to every detail. Nothing can be left to chance.
- Before scheduling a staff or committee meeting, ask, "Is this meeting really necessary?" You can make meetings more effective if you distribute an agenda in advance, adhere to a schedule, and keep people from going off on tangents.
- Club meetings and workshops require you to consider such factors as time, location, seating,

- facilities, invitations, name tags, menu, speakers, registration, and costs.
- Banquets are elaborate affairs that require extensive advance planning. In additional to the factors necessary for a club meeting, you have to consider decorations, entertainment, audiovisual facilities, speaker fees, and seating charts.
- Cocktail parties and receptions require precautions about the amount of alcohol consumed

and the availability of food and nonalcoholic drinks. Possible liability is an important consideration.

- Open houses and plant tours require meticulous planning and routing, careful handling of visitors, and thorough training of all personnel who will be in contact with the visitors.

- Conventions require the skills of professional managers who can juggle multiple events and meetings over a period of several days. A convention may include large meetings, cocktail parties, receptions, tours, and banquets.

- Trade shows are the ultimate marketing events and attract millions of attendees annually. Exhibit booths may cost from $50,000 to $1 million.

- A celebrity at your promotional event will attract crowds and media attention, but appearance fees can be costly.

- A promotional event may be a "grand opening" of a facility or a 10K run sponsored by a charitable organization. It is important to consider such factors as city permits, security, and liability insurance.

Skill Building Activities

1. Select a community group that has just completed a conference, an annual awards banquet, or a convention. Interview the organizers with the intent of analyzing the steps that were taken in planning and organizing the event. You should consider timelines, budget, contracts with hotels and other vendors, speaker arrangements, invitations, registration packets that were prepared, publicity tools, and problems that occurred that should be considered in planning future events.

2. The School of Business at your university has scheduled its annual awards banquet. It will be held in 6 months. It usually attracts about 500 alumni and members of the local business community. Traditionally, a speaker with a national reputation is asked to give the major address at the banquet. In addition, outstanding students will be recognized. Prepare a detailed outline of what must be done to plan the banquet, including a timeline or calendar of what must be done by specific dates.

3. The local coffee shop in your neighborhood wants to celebrate its 10th anniversary with an event at the store that would attract a crowd and get media attention. Do some brainstorming. What would you recommend for a promotional event?

Suggested Readings

Iacono, Erica. "Events Can be Key to a Dazzling Debut." *PRWeek*, September 28, 2007, p. 18.

Janes, Erika Rasmussen. "Charmin Scores a Royal Flush." *Corporate Event*, Fall 2007, pp. 54–57.

Kent, Christine. "How to Make the Most of Your Time at a Trade Show." *Ragan.com* (www.ragan.com), March 14, 2008.

Kilkenny, Shannon. *The Complete Guide to Successful Event Planning*. Ocala, FL: Atlantic Publishing, 2006.

Lewis, Tanya. "McCormack Stays Calm Amid MacWorld Clamor." *PRWeek*, February 4, 2008, p. 4.

Lewis, Tanya. "Improving Connections with Consumers." *PRWeek*, November 19, 2007, p. 14.

Neuman, William. "How Many in Times Sq.? Let's Just Say a Lot." *New York Times*, January 2, 2008, p. A9.

Parker, Glenn, and Hoffman, Robert. *Meeting Excellence: 33 Tools to Lead Meetings That Get Results*. San Francisco: Jossey-Bass, 2006.

Skinner, Bruce, and Rukavina, Vladimir. *Event Sponsorships*. New York: John Wiley & Sons, 2002.

Trottman, Melanie. "In Search of the Cheaper Meeting: Planning Corporate Gatherings Is Getting a Lot Easier—and a Lot Less Expensive." *New York Times*, March 31, 2008, p. R1, R6.

Ward. David. "Taking Full Advantage of Trade Shows." *PRWeek*, December 10, 2007, p. 18.

Planning Programs and Campaigns

18

TOPICS covered in this chapter include:

The Value of a Written Plan   483

Developing a Plan   484

Elements of a Plan   486

Submitting a Plan for Approval   499

The Value of a Written Plan

The primary focus of this book has been on the tactical aspects of public relations—news releases, feature placements, publicity photos, video news releases, satellite media tours, media relations, newsletters, speeches, and so on—that require considerable writing skill and creativity.

Now that you have mastered multiple "media techniques," it is important to devote a chapter to the key concepts of campaign management and public relations programming. Basically, we are now talking about the coordination of multiple "tactics" as part of an overall program to achieve organizational objectives.

A written plan is imperative for any public relations campaign. It improves the campaign's effectiveness. By using multiple communication tools together, you ensure a greater overall impact. Put another way, a plan is a blueprint. It explains the situation, analyzes what can be done about it, outlines strategies and tactics, and tells how the results will be evaluated.

Laurie Wilson, author of *Strategic Program Planning for Effective Public Relations Campaigns*, offers some insight about the relationship of a program plan to the actual process of writing and distributing materials to key audiences. She says:

> Each communication tactic is planned before it is created. The copy outline requires for each communication tactic the identification of the key public, the desired action by the public to contribute to the accomplishment of the plan's objectives, and the message to be sent to that public to motivate its action. Each of these elements draws the information as it is specified in the strategic plan.

This chapter provides a brief overview of how to write a comprehensive public relations program. With this skill, you will become much more than a public relations writer—you will also become a public relations manager.

Developing a Plan

The first step in developing a plan is to consult with the client or your management. This serves two purposes. First, it gets these people involved. Second, it is likely to give you the basic information you need to start making a plan.

In talking with the people who will pay for the campaign, you strive to identify the problems and opportunities confronting the organization. In some cases, these will be apparent to all. At other times, one party will have ideas that have not occurred to the other. Out of this discussion should come an agreement as to the general nature of the problems or opportunities and a preliminary establishment of the campaign's objectives. All of this, of course, is subject to change when more information is gathered.

A good example is the California Avocado Commission. It faced the problem of selling Haas avocados on the East Coast. Sales were not good, and, with a bumper crop of 600 million avocados, the California growers realized that they had a problem. Some informal research found that New Yorkers were not acquainted with avocados that turned jet black when ripe; they thought the fruit was rotten. The objective, then, was to inform consumers that Haas avocados are supposed to have black skins and that they have excellent flavor. The campaign succeeded because it was based on sound information and analysis.

Gathering Information

You cannot know too much about the subject you intend to promote. Don't be satisfied with a cursory investigation—dig and keep on digging until you have the whole story. There are several sources from which you can get the facts and figures that will enable you to plan an effective campaign:

- **Organization.** Much basic information should be available within the organization. Ask for marketing research that has been conducted about the product or service. Talk to sales representatives who deal with customers. Get an overall picture of the organization's successes and failures. Find out why things have happened or how they have been done.

- **References.** Go through all the information in your files. Consult other files. Use libraries and online databases. Read Chapter 1; many sources of information are cited there.

- **Questions.** Ask colleagues for their ideas. Review the experiences of others in similar situations. Read any case histories you can find. The trade press is a good source.

- **Analysis of communications.** Field reports from representatives of the organization, inquiries on telephone hotlines, and consumer complaints should be checked and studied.

- **Brainstorming.** Get a group of colleagues together kick around ideas and suggestions. Many of the ideas won't be practical or realistic, but some may contain the kernel of a creative idea that can be further developed into a strategy. A typical brainstorming session among colleagues is shown in Figure 18.1.

FIGURE 18.1 Planning a public relations program requires brainstorming sessions like this one, at which participants discuss the characteristics of the audience and work to come up with innovative and creative tactics that will accomplish the organization's objectives.

- **Focus group interviews.** Assemble a group of people who are representative of the audience you want to reach. These interviews are not quantitative research, but they may point to a need for detailed research in a specific area.

- **Surveys.** In many situations, you will need to conduct a formal survey to ascertain the attitudes and perceptions of target audiences. Doing a survey takes a lot of time and money. If the organization does not have the relevant data on hand, you must either do the survey yourself or hire someone to do it for you.

- **Media databases.** To plan your tactics, you need to know which channels of communication will be most efficient. A number of media directories, including *Bacon's* and *BurrellesLuce*, provide profiles of various media outlets and their audiences.

- **Demographics.** The *Statistical Abstracts of the United States, American Demographics*, and the comprehensive *Simmons Index* provide insights into the characteristics of an audience. *Simmons*, in particular, will give you detailed information on consumer buying habits and consumers' major sources of information. Another good resource is surveys by various organizations about lifestyles, public opinion, and consumer behavior. Many of these survey results are posted on websites and reported in the media.

Analyzing the Information

Having gathered all pertinent information and conducted one or more surveys (if they are needed), your job is to analyze all the facts and ideas. You must consider the reliability of what you have found. If there are contradictions, you must eliminate erroneous elements and confirm the credibility of what remains.

Now, with reliable information in hand, you can start to draw conclusions. The situation, with its problems and opportunities, and the reason for it should be apparent. The objectives should be obvious, and the strategy, after careful thought, should start to take form.

At this point, you should prepare an outline of your findings and discuss them with management or the client. You can say, "These are the facts that I have, this is the situation as I see it, these are the objectives I think we should select, and this is the strategy I suggest."

This discussion may result in an approval in principle. If it does, you can start writing a program or campaign plan that will outline the strategies and tactics required to address the problem or opportunity.

Elements of a Plan

There is some variation regarding the elements of a basic program or campaign plan. Organizations designate these elements in different ways, combining or dividing them as seems appropriate. Nevertheless, any good plan will cover eight elements: (1) situation, (2) objectives, (3) audience, (4) strategy, (5) tactics, (6) timing, (7) budget, and (8) evaluation. These elements are described in the following sections and summarized in the Tips for Success on page 487.

66 *A PR campaign or program is a series of coordinated, unified activities and messages, driven by a single strategy, delivered to relevant publics by a variety of means.* 99

■ Doug Newsom and Jim Haynes, authors of *Public Relations Writing*

Situation

An organization's situation can be determined by summarizing the organization's relations with its public or publics. This tells why the program is needed and points out the need or the opportunity. This may be the most important part of the plan. Unless a client or management is convinced that a campaign is necessary, it is not likely to approve spending money on it.

A need often is a remedial situation. For example:

- Mattel, after recalling almost 20 million toys, had to restore public confidence in the quality of its toys and its commitment to child safety.

- Wal-Mart, under attack from labor unions about employee benefits and community groups that didn't like "big box" stores, was forced to change policies and begin new "green" initiatives to improve its corporate image and reputation.

Components of a Public Relations Plan

A basic public relations plan is a blueprint of what you want to do and how you will accomplish your task. Such a plan, be it a brief outline or a comprehensive document, will enable you and your client or employer to make sure that all elements have been properly considered, evaluated, and coordinated for maximum effectiveness:

- **Situation.** You cannot set valid objectives without understanding the problem. To understand the problem, (a) discuss it with the client to find out what he or she expects the publicity to accomplish, (b) do your own research, and (c) evaluate your ideas in the broader perspective of the client's long-term goals.

- **Objectives.** Once you understand the situation, it should be easy to define the objectives. To determine if your stated objectives are the right ones, ask yourself: (a) Does it really solve or help to solve the problem? (b) Is it realistic and achievable? (c) Can success be measured in terms meaningful to the client?

- **Audience.** Identify, as precisely as possible, the group of people to whom you are going to direct your communications. Is this the right group to approach in order to solve the problem? If there are several groups, prioritize them according to which are most important for your particular objectives.

- **Strategies.** The strategy describes how, in concept, the objective is to be achieved. Strategy is a plan of action that provides guidelines for selecting the communications activity you will employ. There are usually one or more strategies for each target audience. Strategies may be broad or narrow, depending on the objective and the audience.

- **Tactics.** This is the body of the plan, which describes, in sequence, the specific communications activities proposed to achieve each objective. Discuss each activity as a separate thought, but relate each to the unifying strategy and theme. In selecting communication tools—news releases, brochures, radio announcements, and so on—ask yourself if the use of each will really reach your priority audiences and help you accomplish your stated objectives.

- **Calendar.** It is important to have a timetable, usually outlined in chart form, that shows the start and completion of each project within the framework of the total program. A calendar makes sure that you begin projects—such as brochures, slide presentations, newsletters, or special events—early enough that they are ready when they are needed. A program brochure that reaches its target after the event is not an effective publicity tool.

- **Budget.** How much will implementation of the plan cost? Outline, in sequence, the exact costs of all activities. Make sure that you include such things as postage, car mileage, and labor to stuff envelopes. In addition, about 10 percent of the total budget should be allocated for contingencies.

- **Evaluation.** Before you begin, you and the client or management must agree on the criteria you will use to evaluate your success in achieving the objective. Evaluation criteria should be (a) realistic, (b) credible, (c) specific, and (d) appropriate to the client's expectations. Don't show stacks of press clippings if only sales results are important. ■

- Odwalla had to regain the confidence of its customers after a recall of its apple-based products because of contamination with *E. coli.*

Most public relations situations, however, are not problems that must be solved in a hurry. Instead, they are opportunities for an organization to increase public awareness, advance its reputation, or attract new customers or clients. Here are some examples:

- Dole Food Company conducted a major public relations campaign to inform children and parents about the importance of fruit and vegetables in a balanced diet.
- Friskies PetCare Company increased brand awareness by sponsoring a national canine Frisbee competition.
- The New York State Canal System launched a campaign to make citizens more aware of the historic canal system as a first-class tourist destination.
- Sunkist Growers conducted a cause-related campaign to raise funds for charitable organizations and to increase brand loyalty to Sunkist lemons. This campaign is featured in the PR Casebook on page 490.

Objectives

Neither employers nor clients are likely to approve a campaign without clear objectives. Furthermore, even if a campaign is approved, it will surely fail without objectives.

A campaign may have multiple objectives. Smaller campaigns might have only one target and one objective, but in any planning you must be sure that you thoroughly understand what you are trying to accomplish.

> **Before goals and tactics are drafted, PR Directors must thoroughly understand their organization's business plan.**
>
> - David B. Oates, principal at Stalwart Communications, San Diego

It is also important that you not confuse objectives with the "means" rather than the "end." Novices, for example, often set an objective such as "Generate publicity for the new product." Publicity, however, is not an end in itself. The real objective is to create awareness among consumers about the availability of the new product and to motivate them to purchase it.

There are basically two kinds of objectives: informational and motivational.

Informational Objectives ■ A large percentage of public relations plans are designed primarily to increase awareness of an issue, an event, or a product. Here are some informational objectives:

- To inform people about the kinds of food needed for good nutrition
- To tell people that cigarette smoking is a major cause of cancer
- To proclaim the virtues of raisins
- To inform the public that water conservation is needed

Although informational objectives are legitimate and are used by virtually every public relations firm and department, it is extremely difficult to measure how much "awareness" was attained unless before-and-after surveys are done; these are expensive and time-consuming. In addition, awareness doesn't equal action. Consumers may have been made aware of your new product, but that doesn't necessarily mean that they will buy it.

Motivational Objectives ■ Motivational objectives are more ambitious, and also more difficult to achieve. However, they are easier to measure. Basically, you want to change attitudes and opinions with the idea of modifying behavior.

Some motivational objectives might be:

- To increase the consumption of "healthy" foods, such a spinach and multigrain bakery products
- To reduce cigarette smoking
- To increase the consumption of raisins
- To reduce the amount of water used in a household

Notice that motivational objectives are more "bottom-line oriented." The effectiveness of the public relations plan is based on making something happen, whether increasing sales or changing public support for some issue.

By contrast, informational objectives merely inform or educate people. Take the informational objective of making people aware of cigarette smoking as a major cause of cancer. This might be achieved, but people who are "informed" and "aware" often continue to smoke. A better gauge of the American Cancer Society's success in its efforts would be an actual increase in the number of people who have stopped smoking or a decline in cigarette sales.

In setting objectives, you must be sure that they are realistic and achievable. Furthermore, they must be within the power of the campaign alone to attain. Sometimes the unwary set objectives such as "to increase sales," without realizing that sales may be affected by such things as product quality, packaging, pricing, merchandising, advertising, sales promotion, display, and competitive activity.

In establishing objectives, you must state exactly what you want the audience to know (a new product is now on the market), to believe (it will cut utility bills), and to do (ask for a demonstration). Objectives must be measurable. At some point the people who pay for the campaign are likely to ask, "What did you accomplish?" Many practitioners rely on general feedback—random comments and isolated examples that indicate public reaction. True professionals give facts and figures.

Evaluation is covered in detail in Chapter 19; at this point, however, you must start thinking about setting objectives that can be measured with figures. In an informational campaign, it is easy to state an objective such as: "To increase the number of people who believe that carpooling is a good way to save energy."

A motivational objective in this situation could be "To increase the number of people who use carpooling." However, it would be far better to put it this way: "To increase carpooling by 50 percent."

As you think about these numerical goals, you should realize that there must be a base point for such measurements. To know how many people have been convinced by your campaign, you must know how many people believed in carpooling

Sunkist Turns Lemons into Lemonade for a Cause

A public relations plan contains eight basic elements. The following is an outline of a plan that marketing cooperative Sunkist Growers and its public relations firm, Manning Selvage & Lee (MS&L), developed for a campaign that has raised $800,000 for charitable organizations in the past several years. The campaign also received recognition as *PRWeek's* 2007 Cause-Related Campaign of the Year.

Situation

For many years, Sunkist provided American households with 80 percent of its lemons. In recent years, however, foreign competition has somewhat soured the market. Sunkist wanted to revitalize its brand identity and decided to expand an already established program in cause marketing. The program was "Take a Stand," which provided lemonade stands and Sunkist juicers to 7- to 12-year-olds who pledged to sell lemonade and contribute their proceeds to a charity of their choice.

Objectives

- Extend reach of "Take a Stand" program from 2,000 pledges in the previous 2 years to 10,000.
- Increase lemon sales by 10 percent in key markets to strengthen relationships with major retailers
- Leverage media to tell the Sunkist story on a national scale and reach 10 million consumer impressions (combined circulation and broadcast audience exposed to stories).
- Increase www.sunkist.com page views by 50 percent.

Target Audience

Women ages 25 to 35 with families. Previous research indicated that 65 percent of Sunkist purchasers are married, educated, employed, and have annual household incomes of $50,000+. Research also showed that they make about 80 percent of household purchasing decisions. In addition, other research studies had found that 82 percent of women said they considered an organization's support of charities and the community in forming brand decisions.

Strategies

- Leverage Sunkist "Take a Stand" spokesperson and Grammy-winning country artist Billy Dean to generate awareness about the program with moms in target markets.
- Build relationships with key retailers.
- Leverage key partners to bring additional visibility to the program as well as reach the target audience of parents in general.
- Develop a strategic media outreach campaign that uses the national spokesperson and also focuses on stories why kids set up lemonade stands in their local communities.

Tactics

- Kick-off concert in Nashville featuring spokesperson Billy Dean (see Fig. 18.2). Partners in the concert were community groups working with kids: Big Brothers/Big Sisters, the Nashville Humane Society, and the National Kidney Foundation.
- Placement of heart-warming stories in the local media about kids and their lemonade stands raising money for charity. Feature stories in such periodicals as *Parenting* magazine.

- Distribution of an attractive media kit to food editors that included news releases and background on the "Take a Stand" program.

- Distribution of a matte feature story to media about the "Take a Stand" program and tips on how kids should set up their stand and promote it in the neighborhood.

- Coordination of a Billy Dean concert, barbecue, and lemonade sales during the Little League Baseball (LLB) World Series. Billy Dean also sang the national anthem to begin the series, and the concert raised money to benefit a Little League charity that builds ballparks in disadvantaged urban areas.

- Partnered with Harris Teeter, which has about 150 stories in the Southeast United States, to do a 4-week "Take a Stand" promotion in all of stores.

Calendar

The program was researched and planned during the first four months of the year. The kick-off (concert by Billy Dean) was in early May, and the promotion/publicity aspects of the program continued through the summer months.

Budget

$200,000 for staffing and collateral materials.

Evaluation

All objectives were met or exceeded:

- Instead of 10,000, 11,000 stands were produced and distributed.

- Lemon sales increased in key markets. In the promotion with Harris Teeter stores, there was a 38 percent increase in lemon sales. A side effect was that other store chains not carrying Sunkist lemons asked to be part of the program.

- Media coverage was extensive. Coverage in national outlets included *Parenting* magazine, Fox News Channel, and Radio Disney. Local print and broadcast coverage covered local success stories by interviewing kids on why they took Sunkist up on the offer to take a stand for charity. More than 17 million media impressions were tabulated.

- Page views of www.sunkist.com increased 200 percent over the previous year. ■

FIGURE 18.2 Singer Billy Dean, celebrity spokesperson for Sunkist, poses for a photo op at a child's lemonade stand.

before you began your campaign. With this figure in hand, you can prove that your efforts have increased awareness. When you then get figures on current carpooling, you will be able to prove that the campaign has increased utilization and by how much. Finding these base points requires research.

Audience

Public relations programs should be directed toward specific and defined audiences or publics. If you define the audience as the "general public," you are not doing your homework.

In most cases, you are looking for specific audiences within a "general public." Take, for example, the Ohio vaccination program for children under the age of 2. The primary audience for the message is parents with young children. A secondary audience is pregnant women. This knowledge should provide guidance on the selection of strategies and tactics that would primarily reach these defined audiences.

Increasing the use of carpooling is another example of an objective for which you can define the audience more precisely than saying "the general public." The primary audience for the message on carpooling is people who drive to work. A secondary audience might be parents who drive their children to school.

A third example might be a company that wants to increase the sale of a CD-ROM program on home improvement for do-it-yourselfers. Again, the primary audience is not the "general public," but only those who actually use CD-ROM players and do their own home repairs. Such criteria exclude a large percentage of the American population. See the Tips for Success on page 493 on how public relations can help to fulfill marketing objectives.

Another common mistake is defining the mass media as an audience. In 9 out of 10 cases, selected mass media serve as channels to reach the audiences that you want to inform, persuade, or motivate. On occasion, in programs that seek to change how mass media reports an organization or an issue, editors and reporters can become a primary "public" or audience.

Gaining a thorough understanding of your primary and secondary audiences, which are directly related to accomplishing your objectives, is the only way that you can formulate successful strategies and tactics.

Strategy

Strategy is the broad concept on which the campaign will be based. Strategy must be keyed directly to the objective, and it must be formed with a thorough knowledge of what the primary audiences perceive as relevant and in their self-interest.

The vaccination program for children, for example, was based on the idea that parents love their children and want them to be healthy. Thus, the strategy was to tell parents how important vaccinations are in keeping their children out of danger. In fact, the theme of the campaign became "Project L.O.V.E." with the subhead "Love Our Kids Vaccination Project."

The program to increase carpooling was based on research showing that commuters were interested in saving time and money. Thus, the strategy was to show

How Public Relations Helps Fulfill Marketing Objectives

Public relations programs, particularly product publicity, can make a substantial contribution to fulfilling an organization's marketing objectives:

- It can develop new prospects for new markets, such as inquiries from people who saw or heard a product release in the news media.

- It can provide third-party endorsements—via newspapers, magazines, radio, and television—through news releases about a company's products or services, community involvement, inventions, and new plans.

- It can generate sales leads, usually through articles in the trade press about new products and services.

- It can pave the way for sales calls.

- It can stretch the organization's advertising and promotional dollars through timely and supportive releases about it and its products.

- It can provide inexpensive sales literature for the company, because articles about it and its products can be reprinted as informative pieces for prospective clients.

- It can establish the organization as an authoritative source of information on a given subject.

- It can help sell minor products. Some products are too minor for large advertising expenditures, so exposure to the market is more cost-effective if product publicity is utilized. ■

how people using designated carpool lanes could cut the time of their commute. A second strategy was to show how much money a carpooler would save annually in gasoline, insurance, and maintenance costs.

The strategy for the CD-ROM home improvement product was to let people know that multimedia visual instruction would help do-it-yourselfers complete their jobs more competently and with fewer hassles. The 2,200 full-color illustrations and 50 how-to narrated videos also appealed to those who wanted to do home improvements but didn't have much experience.

These examples illustrate two basic concepts about strategy. First, the strategy must reflect the audience's self-interests. Second, the strategy must be expressed in simple terms as a *key selling proposition*.

The key statement is the message of the communication process. It must be reiterated throughout the campaign in various ways, but the concept should remain clear and simple. Every campaign has one to three key messages, which are expressed in every activity—whether a news release, a feature article, a media interview, or even a VNR.

Indeed, one of the criteria for an effective public relations program is whether the audience was exposed to your key copy points and absorbed them. One way of determining this is a content analysis of media mentions, which will be discussed under evaluation and in the next chapter.

Tactics

This is the "how to do it" portion of the plan. In public relations, it often is called the "execution" part of the plan. Tactics are the actual materials that are produced in a public relations campaign by one or several public relations writers.

The children's vaccination project, for example, used a variety of tactics, including:

- Posters in child-care centers and doctors' offices
- PSAs on radio stations that had audiences of childbearing age
- Articles in newspapers and magazines catering to parents
- Pamphlets sent to child-care service providers
- Booklets mailed to every new mother explaining vaccination and the schedule of shots
- Letters to doctors reminding them to ask about vaccinations when a child has a checkup
- Corporate and hospital sponsorship of two week-long "Shots for Tots" promotional events
- Endorsements by government leaders and child-care experts
- Information advertisements in community newspapers
- Stories about the L.O.V.E. Project on television and in the city's daily newspaper

> **" A tactic is a public relations action designed to have a particular effect on an organization's relationship with a particular public. "** ◦
> ■ David Guth and Charles Marsh, authors of *Public Relations: A Values-Driven Approach*

The campaign on carpooling also used a variety of tactics. One tactic was to enlist the support of drive-time DJs on popular radio stations, who promoted carpooling as part of their early-morning and late-afternoon banter between songs. Billboards along major highways were also used. There was also a concentrated effort to distribute posters and pamphlets that businesses could post and distribute to employees. Editors of employee newsletters and magazines were given background information on carpooling for possible stories. Another successful tactic was the compilation of a kit for employers telling them how to organize carpools for their employees.

The CD-ROM program, because of budget, was primarily a media campaign. The public relations firm worked to place articles and product reviews in (1) publications that reached relatively affluent households that would most likely have a CD-ROM player, (2) publications that catered to home improvement do-it-yourselfers, and (3) publications that covered new titles on CD-ROM.

Calendar

Three aspects of timing must be considered: (1) when the campaign is to be conducted, (2) the sequence of activities, and (3) the reach and frequency of the message.

A campaign must be timely; it must be conducted when the key messages mean the most to the intended audience. Some subjects are seasonal; hence publicists release information on strawberries in May and June, when a crop comes to market. A software program on doing your own taxes attracts the most audience interest in February and March, just before the April 15th deadline.

At times, the environmental context is important. A campaign on carpooling might be more successful if it follows a price increase in gasoline or a government agency report that traffic congestion has reached gridlock proportions. A charitable campaign to provide for the homeless is more effective if the local newspaper has just run a five-part series on the human dimensions of the problem.

Other kinds of campaigns are less dependent on seasonal or environmental context. The L.O.V.E. vaccination program, a Red Cross drive for blood donations, and even the selling of a CD-ROM on home improvements could be done almost anytime during the year. The Christmas season, however, would be great for selling the CD-ROM, but a bad time for running a vaccination project.

The second aspect of timing is the scheduling of activities during a campaign. A typical pattern is to have a concentrated effort at the beginning of a campaign when a number of activities are implemented. This is the launch phase of an idea or concept and, much like a rocket, takes a concentration of power just to break the awareness barrier. After the campaign has achieved orbit, however, it takes less energy, and fewer activities are needed to maintain momentum. A good example of this is the product life cycle shown in Figure 18.3.

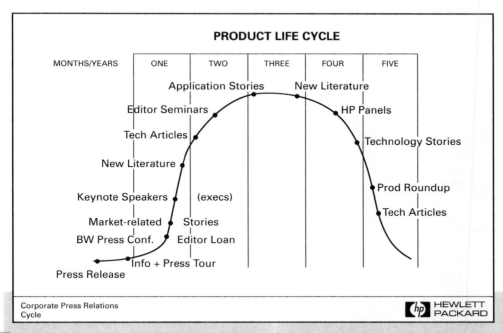

FIGURE 18.3 Planning requires strategies and tactics. This bell curve shows a product's life cycle and the kinds of public relations tools used by organizations, such as HP, at each stage. Note that the emphasis is on using numerous tools to launch a product. After the product is established, fewer tools are needed to sustain visibility and sales.

You must also think about advance planning. Monthly publications, for example, often need information at least 6 to 8 weeks before an issue. If you want something in the August issue, you have to think about placing it in May or June. A popular talk show may work on a schedule that books guests 3 or 4 months in advance. The main idea is that you must constantly think ahead to make things happen in the appropriate sequence.

A brochure may be needed on March 29, but you must start the brochure long before that date. To determine the starting date, you must know every step in the production process and how long it will take.

This activity, as well as the scheduling of other public relations tactics, should not be trusted to your memory or to jottings on your desk calendar. It is important that the entire public relations team working on the program has a single source of information, such as a wiki, for the schedule of the entire campaign.

The easiest way to keep everything on schedule is to prepare a working calendar for detailed planning and internal use. The brochure example, cited earlier, might look like this:

Activity	Date Due	Responsibility
Outline brochure	January 11	J. Ross, G. Jones
Write copy	January 18	J. Ross
Photos and artwork	January 25	A. Peck and N. Lopez
Design and layout	February 8	A. Peck and N. Lopez
Final client approval	February 15	B. Boss
Printer prep and proofs	February 28	Ace Printers. G. Jones, supervising
Printing and binding	March 10	Ace Printers. G. Jones, supervising
Delivery	March 15	United Parcel Service. G. Jones, supervising

Other entries planned using this kind of format might be preparing news releases, drafting speeches, writing pitch letters, scheduling spokespeople on radio talk shows, arranging media tours, and commissioning a camera-ready feature article.

You can also map activities by listing the activities at the left of a chart, with days or weeks across the top. Lines or bars show graphically when various steps are being worked on. This is often called a *Gantt chart*; an example is shown in Figure 18.4.

The main idea is that you should have a systematic means of tracking activities throughout the public relations program so everything stays on schedule. If a brochure or a media kit is delayed, it can delay other activities, such as a media tour or a news conference, that are dependent on having the materials available. All activities in a public relations program are interrelated for maximum effectiveness.

The third element of calendaring is a timeline that ensures that the message reaches every possible audience and the message is repeated frequently. *Reach* is the number of different people exposed to a single message. *Frequency* is the number and pattern of messages presented to a particular public in a given amount of time. In a Gantt chart, for example, multiple news releases about the same subject, but perhaps different angles, will be done throughout the campaign.

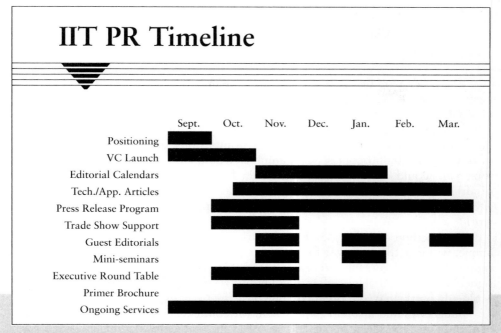

IIT PR Timeline

	Sept.	Oct.	Nov.	Dec.	Jan.	Feb.	Mar.
Positioning	■						
VC Launch	■						
Editorial Calendars			■	■			
Tech./App. Articles		■	■	■	■	■	
Press Release Program		■	■	■	■	■	■
Trade Show Support		■					
Guest Editorials			■		■		■
Mini-seminars			■		■		
Executive Round Table		■	■				
Primer Brochure		■	■	■			
Ongoing Services		■	■	■	■	■	■

FIGURE 18.4 Planning requires precision scheduling. This is a simplified Gantt chart showing the various activities and tactics in a public relations program. Some tactics, such as news releases, are ongoing; others are phased in during the campaign.

Budget

A budget can be divided into two categories: staff time and out-of-pocket (OOP) expenses. Staff and administrative time usually takes the lion's share of any public relations budget. In a $100,000 campaign done by a public relations firm, for example, 70 percent or more will go to salaries and administrative fees.

A public relations firm has different hourly rates for the level of personnel involved. The head of the agency, who would oversee the account, might bill at $200 per hour. The account supervisor might bill at $120 per hour, and the account executive at $100 per hour. Account coordinators, those who do a lot of the clerical work, might bill at $55 per hour.

A public relations firm, when submitting a plan, has usually constructed a budget based on the number of estimated staff hours it will take to implement a plan. Let's say that the plan calls for a media kit, the development of five news releases, the writing of a slide script, and a news conference. The public relations firm might estimate that all this work will take at least 150 hours of staff time, divided as follows:

President, 20 hours @ $200 = $4,000

Vice president, 40 hours @ $180 = $7,200

Account executive, 50 hours @ $100 = $5,000

Account coordinator, 40 hours @ $55 = $2,200

TOTAL STAFF COSTS: $18,400

The other part of the budget is out-of-pocket expenses, which includes payments to various vendors for such things as printing, postage, graphics, production of VNRs, travel, phone, fax, photocopying, and so on.

You can do a reasonable job of estimating out-of-pocket expenses by making a few phone calls. You would call a printer, for example, to get an estimate of how much 10,000 copies of a pamphlet would cost. If you are doing a media tour, you would decide what cities would be visited and then find out the cost of airline fares, hotels, meals, and ground transportation costs. The Internal Revenue Service even has a guide to daily living expenses in major cities around the world.

One method of doing a budget is to use two columns. The left column, for example, will give the staff cost for writing a pamphlet or compiling a media kit. The right column will give the actual OOP for having the pamphlet or the media kit designed, printed, and delivered. Internal public relations departments, where the staff is already on the payroll, often compile only the OOP expenses.

Budgets should also have a line item for contingencies; that is, unexpected expenses. In general, allow about 10 percent of the budget for contingencies.

Evaluation

Evaluation refers directly back to your stated objectives: it is the process by which you determine whether you have met your objectives.

If you have an informational objective, such as increasing awareness, a common procedure is to show placements in key publications and broadcast stations that reached the intended audience. Related to this is a content analysis of whether the news coverage included your key messages. A more scientific approach is to do a benchmark study of audience knowledge and perceptions before and after the campaign. In many cases, "before" activity has already been documented through marketing studies, so all you have to do is a postcampaign survey.

Motivational objectives, such as increased market share or sales, are much easier to determine. The Ohio campaign had the objective of increasing vaccinations—and it succeeded by raising the vaccination rate by 117 percent in public clinics over a 2-year period. A campaign by Ketchum on behalf of prune producers caused a 4 percent increase in sales after several years of decline.

Increased sales, however, may be the result of other factors, such as the economy, the additional use of advertising, or a reduction in prices. Because of this, it is often wise to limit your objectives to something that can be related directly to your activities. For example, you might get feature placements in various magazines that also give an address for a free brochure. Success could then be declared when there have been 10,000 requests for the brochure.

Chapter 19 expands on methods of evaluation in public relations.

Submitting a Plan for Approval

The eight elements of a plan, which have just been discussed, become the sections in a written plan submitted to management or a client for approval. How to write proposals is covered in Chapter 14, but here's the general organization of a public relations plan:

- Title page (date, program name, client or organization, and team members)
- Executive summary (overview of the plan)
- Table of contents (name and page number of each section)
- Statement of principles (the planner's approach to the situation, i.e., integrated with marketing, alignment of campaign with overall organizational goals, etc.)
- Capabilities of the team or public relations firm submitting the plan
- The eight sections of the program plan, from situation to evaluation
- Conclusion (summary of why this is the best plan and asking for approval)

Before you submit your written plan to a client or management for final approval, you should review it with a critical eye. You might even ask some knowledgeable person whose opinion you respect to read the plan and then discuss it with you. Check these points:

- Is the situation clearly stated?
- Is the audience the right one? Is it clearly defined?
- Are the objectives attainable and measurable?
- Is the strategy logical and effective?
- Is the message persuasive and memorable?
- Are the tactics sound and effective?
- Is the timing right?
- Are the costs reasonable and justified?
- Will the proposed evaluation really measure the results?
- Is the plan practical, and appropriate?
- Is the plan logical, strong, and clearly written?
- Should any additions or deletions be made?

In addition to these suggestions, the Tips for Success on page 500 provides a thumbnail of what makes a winning campaign.

Your responsibility is to make the proposed plan as sound as you can make it, based on your professional expertise. You should remember, however, that any plan is a work in progress, and your client or management may suggest changes. They may not think a particular idea is very good, or they may decide to reduce the cost by eliminating a component.

Do You Have a Winning Campaign?

There are thousands of public relations campaigns every year. Some fail, some are moderately successful, and some achieve outstanding success. Each year, about 650 of these campaigns are submitted for the Public Relations Society of America's Silver Anvil award, which recognizes the very best in public relations planning and implementation. Of this number, about 45 are chosen for excellence.

Catherine Ahles and Courtney Botsworth of Florida International University analyzed the campaigns that have received Silver Anvil awards and identified some common characteristics of outstanding public relations campaigns:

- **Budgets.** There's no question that big budgets help a winning campaign, but it's more important to have a budget that is efficiently used. Most winning campaigns are in the $100,000 to $199,000 range and use innovative tactics to stretch dollars over large geographic regions.

- **Research.** According to Jennifer Acord, regional manager for public relations for Avon Products, "The best campaigns use research to develop the objectives, create the strategy, and provide clear benchmarks for evaluation." In terms of Silver Anvil award entries, the most popular form of primary research was face-to-face personal interviews. Telephone surveys ranked second, focus groups ranked third, and impersonal mail surveys ranked fourth. Internet surveys are also used, although respondents are self-selected. In terms of secondary research, literature searches and competitive analysis were the most frequently used techniques. About half of the campaigns used demographic profiles of audiences. About 40 percent of the campaigns pretested messages on the target audience before launching a full campaign.

- **Benchmarking.** A campaign's outcome must be measured against some benchmark so you know if the campaign "moved the needle" in terms of creating awareness, increasing sales, or even changing attitudes and perceptions. However, this needs improvement even in award-winning campaigns. Less than half failed to establish a benchmark in terms of public attitudes about the product or service before launching the campaign.

In many cases, such feedback from the client or management sharpens and improves the plan. At other times, if you think the proposed changes would seriously impact the effectiveness of the plan, you have to express your rationale in a diplomatic manner and persuade them that your initial idea is the better one.

▪ Summary

- Most public relations activities occur within the framework of a program or program plan.

- A program plan has the elements of situation (problem statement), objectives, audience, strategies, tactics, calendar, budget, and evaluation.

- Objectives can be informational or motivational, depending on the desired results.

- Creating publicity is not a valid objective; it is a means to an end.

- For public relations purposes, audiences must be clearly defined. In most cases, a specific audience is defined by income, interest, geography, lifestyle, and a host of other variables.

- A strategy is a broad conceptualization that gives direction to a public relations program. A good strategy is based on research and reflects audience self-interests. It can also be expressed as the program's key selling proposition.

- **Objectives.** "The most important aspect of a campaign is the objective," says Gerard F. Corbett, former vice president of Hitachi America Ltd. "You need to identify where you want to be at the end of the day and what needs to be accomplished when all is said and done." Four out of five Silver Anvil campaigns sought to change behavior in some way, and almost that percentage had awareness- and visibility-based objectives. There are four elements to writing a good objective, says Ahles. They are (1) a clear tie to the organization's mission and goals, (2) specifying the nature of the desired change, (3) the time frame for the change, and (4) specifying the amount of change sought.

- **Measuring results.** It is important, in a winning campaign, to evaluate the impact of a program and the actions taken by the target audience. Too many Silver Anvil entries fail to do this. Instead, they emphasize press clips and the number of meetings held. There is nothing wrong with press clips as one index of success, but Silver Anvil judges say the winning campaigns also devote attention to documenting behavior change.

- **The X factor.** There are many good, solid campaigns, but the X factor is that ounce of daring and creativity that lifts the campaign to the extraordinary level. According to Corbett, "It's the chemistry that makes the program gel. It could be an out-of-the-box idea; it could be the people involved or the manner in which the campaign was implemented. Or it could be many factors woven together like a resilient fabric."

So what is successful campaign planning? Ahles, writing in *The Strategist*, concludes:

> The bottom line for campaign planning? Focus on those aspects of campaign planning that will help you achieve your goal. Do good, solid research that benchmarks your starting point; use that research to build your strategy; set complete objectives that specify type, amount and time frame for change; and document your outcomes. Sprinkle in a heavy dose of creativity, both in problem solving and tactical execution, and efficient use of funding, and you are well on your way to producing an outstanding PR campaign.

- Tactics are the "how to do it" part of the program plan. They list the communication tools and activities that will be used to support the strategy.

- Timing of activities and messages is important. They must occur within a broader context of public interests and must be scheduled in advance.

- A detailed budget is an integral part of a public relations plan. Staff and administrative expenses usually consume more of the budget than out-of-pocket expenses.

- Working a plan means that you must have a detailed calendar of activities and who is responsible for carrying them out.

- A program is evaluated as a success if it meets the set objectives of the campaign. Objectives must be measurable for evaluation methods to be effective.

Skill Building Activities

1. The Almond Advisory Board, a trade group of almond growers, is gearing up for a major marketing effort to increase almond consumption by the American public. Write two informational and two motivational objectives for this campaign.

2. A new social networking site, StarGate, has been launched and is primarily targeted to college

students. This start-up company doesn't have much money for advertising and traditional marketing, so it wants to implement a public relations campaign to get media attention, generate "buzz" among college students, and increase subscribers. Prepare a public relations plan for StarGate that would take place over a period of 6 months. Your plan should include (1) background of the situation, (2) objective(s), (3) publics to be reached, (4) strategies, (5) tactics, (6) timeline, (7) budget, and (8) evaluation method. You should use the media techniques and tools that you have learned throughout this book.

■ Suggested Readings

Ahles, Catherine B. "Campaign Excellence: A Survey of Silver Anvil Award Winners Compares Current PR Practice with Planning, Campaign Theory." *The Strategist*, Summer 2003, pp. 46–53.

Austin, Erica W., and Pinkleton, Bruce E. *Strategic Public Relations Management*. Mahwah, NJ: Lawrence Erlbaum Associates, 2001.

Bobbitt, Randy, and Sullivan, Ruth. *Developing the Public Relations Campaign*. Boston: Allyn & Bacon, 2005.

Daughtery, Emma. "Strategic Planning in Public Relations: A Matrix That Ensures Tactical Soundness." *Public Relations Quarterly*, Spring 2003, pp. 21–26.

Hegley, Tom. *Writing Winning Proposals: PR Cases*. Boston, Allyn & Bacon, 2006.

LaMotta, Lisa. "Launches Must Be Products of Creativity." *PRWeek*, May 22, 2006, p. 30.

Newsom, Doug, and Haynes, Jim. "Writing the PR Plan: Defining Success for Your Organization." *PR Tactics*, February 2008, pp. 16–17.

Samansky, Arthur W. "Successful Strategic Communication Plans Are Realistic, Achievable, and Flexible." *Public Relations Quarterly*, Summer 2003, pp. 24–26.

Smith, Ronald D. *Strategic Planning for Public Relations*, 2nd edition. Mahwah, NJ: Lawrence Erlbaum Associates, 2005.

Wilcox, Dennis L., and Cameron, Glen T. *Public Relations: Strategies and Tactics*, 9th edition. Boston: Allyn & Bacon, 2009.

Wilson, Laurie J., and Ogden, Joseph. *Strategic Program Planning for Effective Public Relations Campaigns*, 4th edition. Dubuque: Kendall-Hunt, 2004.

Measuring Success

19

TOPICS covered in this chapter include:

The Importance of Measurement   503

Program Objectives   506

Measurement of Production/
Distribution   507

Measurement of Message Exposure   507

Measurement of Audience
Awareness   516

Measurement of Audience Attitudes   517

Measurement of Audience Action   518

Evaluation of Newsletters and
Brochures   519

Writing a Measurement Report   522

The Importance of Measurement

The final step in any public relations program or campaign, as the last chapter indicated, is measurement and evaluation.

Bill Margaritis, senior vice president of worldwide communications for FedEx, told *PRWeek*, "Measurement helps us prioritize and execute our programs; it's a road map to our activities. It also helps build alignment with business objectives, and gives executive management a sense of confidence that we are using a quantifiable process in which to invest our money and time."

You Mon Tsang, CEO of Biz360, a measurement firm, is more blunt about the need for evaluation. He is quoted in *PRWeek*, saying, "It's almost inconceivable to invest money in a significant program like communications without understanding the results. How would any other department justify its investments without understanding what they are getting out of it?"

Andy Beaupre of Delahaye/MediaLink, a media measurement firm, says public relations efforts should be measured for the following reasons:

- To document that public relations efforts have actually achieved specified objectives
- To apply lessons learned to future public relations efforts
- To erase a frequent premise that public relations is magic and too intangible to measure
- To prove that practitioners are doing their jobs
- To illustrate concern for PR quality and its impact on the organization

Another important reason for conducting measurement and evaluation, and perhaps the most compelling argument, is that clients and management are demanding more accountability. Today's public relations programs are highly sophisticated and expensive, so organizations want to be sure that they are getting good value for their money. In addition, public relations personnel often compete with advertising and marketing for budget, so it is important to document how public relations activity is a cost-effective use of funds.

Consequently, here are some general questions that you should honestly ask yourself upon completion of a public relations program:

- Was the program or activity adequately planned?
- Did recipients of the message understand it?
- How could the program strategy have been more effective?
- Were all primary and secondary audiences reached?
- Was the desired organizational objective achieved?
- What unforeseen circumstances affected the success of the program or activity?
- Did the program or activity stay within the budget?
- What steps can be taken to improve the success of similar future activities?

Answering these questions requires a mix of measurement methods, many borrowed from advertising and marketing, to provide complete evaluations. To evaluate a public relations program fully, you must use formal and more systematic research methods to document message exposure, accurate dissemination of the message, acceptance of the message, attitude change, and changes in overt behavior.

> **" PR measurement has changed over the years, becoming more sophisticated, efficient, and accurate. "** ■ Tonya Garcia, reporter for *PRWeek*

You can track message exposure and dissemination by noting media mentions and blog postings. You should also perform a content analysis to determine if key messages were included. Indeed, the most common factor in judging the success of a campaign is whether there is an increase in public "awareness" about the key message being disseminated. See the Tips for Success on page 505 for some other factors to consider in judging the effectiveness of a campaign.

These methods, however, emphasize the output of public relations staffs instead of the outcomes that result from their work. Tudor Williams, writing in the online newsletter *NetGain*, explains:

> For many years, organizations were content to measure the outputs of communication, how many newsletters were published, how many 'impressions' or column inches were created, or the size of the audience reached. But in a world where accountability matters, it is the outcomes that are important, the extent to which we were successful in achieving our goal. The output is but the means to achieve successful outcomes, not success itself.

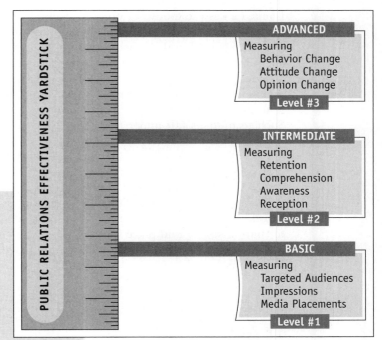

tips FOR SUCCESS

Factors in Program Evaluation

What factors are important in judging the effectiveness of a public relations program? A survey of corporate communicators and marketers conducted by CDB Research & Consulting and Thomas L. Harris & Associates found that 99 percent of the respondents rated "increase in awareness" as the most important factor. Other factors included the following:

- Delivery of message points (95%)
- Enhancement of company image (88%)
- Placement in key publications (87%)
- Increase in awareness of company or issue (85%)
- Change in attitudes (84%)
- Response to program (83%)

- Overall audience reach (72%)
- Increase in reported purchasing (59%)
- Bottom-line sales increase (58%)
- Number of placements (47%)
- Number of gross impressions (40%)
- Advertising equivalents (24%) ■

Williams, when he discusses outcomes, is talking about a higher level of measurement that focuses on the effects of all our news releases, brochures, newsletters, and online efforts. Changes in audience awareness and understanding, as well as changes in attitudes and preferences and even behavior, are all "outcomes" that are more difficult to measure, but are more meaningful to the "bottom line." The chart in Figure 19.1 shows the three levels of measurement and evaluation.

Increasingly, public relations departments and firms are using various research tools to measure

FIGURE 19.1 There are three levels of public relations measurement. The most basic is measuring media placements. At the second level, there is more concern about comprehension and retention of the message on the part of the audience. At the advanced level, the emphasis is on opinion and behavior change. Each level requires different measurement tools.

PUBLIC RELATIONS EFFECTIVENESS YARDSTICK

ADVANCED
Measuring
Behavior Change
Attitude Change
Opinion Change
Level #3

INTERMEDIATE
Measuring
Retention
Comprehension
Awareness
Reception
Level #2

BASIC
Measuring
Targeted Audiences
Impressions
Media Placements
Level #1

outcomes. Indeed, in one *PRWeek* survey more than half of the respondents said they used "outcomes" measurement. Interestingly, they also rated change in attitudes, behavior as the most important form of measurement, but still used media mentions more frequently as a measurement method.

The following pages discuss the measurement and evaluation of "outputs," as well as "outcomes." The first step, however, is how you determine and write your program objectives.

■ Program Objectives

Before any public relations program can be properly evaluated, it is important to have a clearly established set of measurable objectives. These should be part of the program plan, discussed in the last chapter, but some points need reviewing.

First, public relations personnel and management should agree on the criteria that will be used to evaluate success in attaining the objectives. Does the client or management want to evaluate the program on the number of media mentions, or do they want you to show that you actually increased sales or market share? A frank discussion about objectives and client or management expectations—before a program is launched—can make a big difference in how you structure your campaign to achieve specific outcomes.

Second, don't wait until the end of a public relations program to determine how it will be evaluated. Albert L. Schweitzer, of Fleishman-Hillard public relations in St. Louis, makes the following point: "Evaluating impact/results starts in the planning stage. You break down the problems into measurable goals and objectives, then after implementing the program, you measure the results against goals."

In other words, it is not wise to have vague, nonspecific objectives that you will be unable to measure at the end of your program. If the objective is to inform or make people aware of a product or service, you must use measurement techniques that show how successfully information was communicated to target audiences. Such techniques fall under the rubric of "audience exposure," which will be discussed shortly.

In an example of measurement reflecting program objectives, the Illinois Department of Public Health conducted a campaign among teenagers with two objectives: (1) increase adolescents' personal perception of risk for HIV/AIDS, sexually transmitted diseases, and unintended pregnancy resulting from unprotected sex and substance abuse and (2) generate adolescent calls to the department hotline as an information source and place for HIV referral information.

Golin/Harris International, which conducted the program, reported the following results:

- One million Illinois residents were informed about the campaign through stories in print and broadcast media and radio PSAs.
- Adolescent calls to the hotline increased by nearly 50 percent during the 3-month campaign.

- A survey of Illinois teenagers found that 91 percent enjoyed the radio PSAs; 90 percent thought the situations presented in the PSAs could happen in real life; and 69 percent said the ads taught them ways to handle risky situations.

Measurement of Production/Distribution

One elementary form of evaluation is simply to give your client or employer a count of how many news releases, feature stories, photos, and such were produced in a given time period.

This kind of evaluation is supposed to give management an idea of your productivity. However, this approach is not very meaningful, because it emphasizes quantity instead of quality. It also encourages the public relations writer to send out more news releases than necessary, many worthless as news, in an attempt to meet some arbitrary quota.

It may be more cost-effective to write fewer news releases and spend more time preparing truly newsworthy stories tailored to specific publications. Is it better to do 15 routine news releases in a week or to spend the same amount of time pitching one story to the prestigious *Wall Street Journal*?

Closely aligned to the production of materials is their dissemination. Thus, it may be reported that a news release was sent to "977 daily newspapers, 700 weekly newspapers, and 111 trade publications." Such figures are useful in terms of evaluating how widely a news release or feature is distributed, but sending out vast quantities of news releases just to impress management with big numbers is futile. For example, a large media mailing may be a waste of time and money if the news release in question has news value only to the 50 daily newspapers in a region or if the release is so technical that only five trade publications would be interested in it.

Large mailings are not just the fault of publicists. Many organizations, including far too many public relations firms, think sending a news release is a relatively cheap proposition involving only postage or a group e-mail. Why not do a blanket mailing to increase the odds that the material will be used? Such mass mailings, as discussed in Chapter 11, really irritate journalists, who then form the impression that public relations people are basically incompetent.

As a professional public relations practitioner, you should document distribution but not succumb to sending out reams of news releases just to impress the boss or the client. A better approach is to use targeted mailings that generate a high percentage of media placements.

Measurement of Message Exposure

The most common way of evaluating public relations programs is the compilation of print stories, broadcast mentions, and the number of visitors to your website. In fact, *PRWeek* surveyed public relations firms and found that 81 percent of them primarily used media mentions as their major tool to evaluate program success.

Monitoring services can be hired to review large numbers of print and online publications. They digitally "clip" all the articles/mentions about your client or employer. Major firms that offer such services include Cision (*Bacon's*), BurrellesLuce, Vocus, and Factiva. The major electronic newswires also offer monitoring services. PR Newswire, for example, offers a subscription service—eWatch—which can monitor print media, online publications, and thousands of blogs. Business Wire has a similar service called NewsTrak. VMS, a video monitoring service, covers all 210 U.S. television markets. Clients can be notified within minutes of a television news story and even view the video clip.

Most major services offer customers any number of ways to slice, dice, and compile media mentions according to their needs and budget. They can provide clients tabulations giving the name of the publication/program, date, frequency, and circulation/viewership. Clients can also have the monitoring service evaluate clips on such variables as article size, advertising cost equivalent, audience, editorial slant of the article, subject, number of keyword mentions, type of article, byline, and how an organization's overall mentions compares with major competitors. Factiva, which creates pie charts showing such data, calls this "share of voice" in the marketplace. Other aspect of media analysis will be discussed shortly.

The main purpose of compiling media mentions is to find out if your news releases have been used by the media. It gives the organization a way to determine if the public was exposed to its message. The success of a campaign by ESAB Welding Products, for example, was evaluated by its public relations firm, Sawyer Riley Compton, as follows:

- Coverage for ESAB in 532 newspaper outlets in 26 states, representing a total readership of more than 54 million.
- Trade media relations efforts resulted in 167 clips, including by-lined article and feature stories, an increase of 26 percent over last year's figures.

Another purpose of press clippings is to monitor trends and the competition. AT&T may ask its clipping service to clip any articles pertaining to keywords such as "telephone," "fiber optics," and "information technology" to keep track of industry trends and developments. It may also have the clipping service send clips on Verizon, Sprint, and even Comcast, just to see what the competition is doing and saying.

The volume of media mentions is still popular among public relations firms and clients, but their importance and value are declining as a meaningful measurement of campaign effectiveness. Today, public relations managers and senior management are placing more emphasis on who is reached and what they do with the message.

Matthew Creamer, a reporter for *PRWeek*, adds, "The clipbook, that old symbol of PR measurement, has been replaced by the more sophisticated evaluations of the quantity and quality of media placements which in more ambitious PR operations have been links to bottom-line results that resonate outside the corporate communications silo to those doling out the money." We will get to "bottom-line" outcomes shortly, but let's first discuss some up-to-date variations on the "old" clipbook.

Media Impressions

Another popular way of measuring output is to compile the circulation of the publications where your news release, feature story, interview, or product mention appeared. In the case of a broadcast mention on a radio program or television show, you use the audited average of listeners or viewers for that particular show.

This is known as compiling **gross impressions**, **media impressions**, or just **impressions**. Geri Mazur, director of research for Porter Novelli International, told *PRWeek*, "At a most basic level, clients expected to know how many impressions or how many bodies their message touched."

For example, if a story about an organization appears in a local daily with a circulation of 130,000, the number of media impressions is 130,000. If the story appears in a number of publications, you simply add up the circulation of all the publications to get the total impressions.

A story appearing in 15 or 20 publications can easily generate several million media impressions. Korbel Champagne Cellars, for example, generated a lot of media coverage with its "perfect marriage proposal" contest. In fact, Edelman Worldwide had set a goal of 70 million media impressions. The final result, after a year, was almost 90 million media impressions as a result of about 1,000 media placements. The breakdown was as follows:

National print	11, 037,244
Daily and weekly print	37,906,106
National broadcast	9,872,620
Local TV broadcast	1,320,279
Local radio broadcast	6,941,050
Online	22,539,597
Total impressions:	**89,616,896**

Total media impressions are used in advertising and publicity to illustrate the penetration of a particular message. However, high numbers of media impressions only report total circulation and potential audience size, not how many people actually read, heard, or viewed that particular story.

Advertising Value Equivalency

The numbers game is also played by converting stories in the news columns or on broadcast news and talk shows into the equivalent of advertising costs. For example, the public relations department of a major corporation might give top management the following report: "When print inches are calculated as advertising space, the company received exposure worth $158,644 this year—a 27.5 percent increase over last year."

Some practitioners like the concept of advertising value equivalency (AVE) because it is a form of return on investment (ROI). It shows management that the public relations staff is earning its salary by generating much more "income" (even if it is virtual) than it costs to pay the staff's salary.

Mark Scott of HomeBanc Mortgage Company told *PRWeek*, for example, that AVE helps him "justify his PR budget to the CEO and head of marketing." The ad equivalency of HomeBanc's news coverage one year was $810,000, using a metric supplied by Burrelle's Information Services. According to Scott, "When you consider that I make considerably less than that, it's OK. For what they paid me and the expenses incurred, I don't think it exceeded $150,000 to $200,000. In other words, the ROI is about four times the expense—and that's looks pretty good to the corporate bean counters."

Some public relations practitioners even multiply the AVE figures by factoring in the idea that publicity is worth more than advertising because it is more credible and influential. Cision, for example, even has a calculator that allows for a flexible multiplier scale. This means that the software will compute the publicity value of a news clip in terms of cost per inch multiplied by a value between 1 and 10 that is arbitrarily assigned by the account executive. In general, three is the most common multiplier. If such a multiple was applied to HomeBanc's $810,000, that means the news coverage was worth about $2.4 million.

Such exercises in multiplication are criticized by the Institute for Public Relations Research (www.instituteforpr.com). In a white paper on measuring and evaluating public relations effectiveness, the Institute called the use of multipliers "unethical, dishonest, and not at all supported by the research literature."

Indeed, the whole idea of advertising equivalency is highly suspect, because you are comparing apples and oranges. First of all, in advertising, you control the exact wording, graphics, and placement of your message. By contrast, news releases and features are subject to the whims of media gatekeepers who decide what is published and in what context. There is no guarantee, as there is in advertising, that your message will be communicated in the way you wish.

Second, a mystery remains as to what is actually being counted. If a 10-inch article in the local daily mentions your company along with several competitors, is this equivalent to 10 inches of advertising space? Does the university football team reap "millions of dollars of comparable advertising" if its losing season gets extensive media coverage?

Third, the practice of equating news stories and publicity with advertising is not particularly beneficial for promoting effective media relations. Editors often suspect that all that publicists seek is "free advertising," and this impression is reinforced when public relations people take great pains to convert story placements to comparable advertising costs.

Although many public relations departments and public relations firms still measure print and broadcast clips by converting them to advertising rates, the practice is fading among professionals. The winning campaigns in the Silver Anvil awards competition sponsored by the Public Relations Society of America (PRSA), for example, rarely use AVE as a major criterion to demonstrate the success of their programs. Instead, they use outcomes such as increased sales, awareness, change in attitudes or behavior, and contributions to overall organizational objectives. These measurements will be discussed shortly.

Systematic Tracking

Measuring the volume of media mentions is a start, but a more systematic content analysis can now be done thanks to the computer and various software programs.

In addition to getting the traditional information about a publication's name, date, frequency, and circulation, it is now possible to do a more complete analysis of news coverage. BurrellesLuce, for example, offers media analysis that includes (1) article size compared to available space in the publication; (2) whether the article was positive, negative, or neutral; (3) mention of key messages, products, brands, and competitors; (4) the number of keyword mentions; (5) the type of article; (6) the byline of the article's author; (7) degree of coverage in top markets; and (8) coverage by region. Other services, such as Factiva, Vocus, Biz360, Delehaye/MediaLink, and CARMA, offer similar media analysis capabilities.

> **The capability to comprehensively monitor global media coverage is a strategy large companies need to protect reputation and shareholder value.**
> ■ Ad copy from Factiva (Dow Jones & Reuters), a media monitoring company

Such detailed analysis is a good diagnostic tool to tabulate details about the coverage and what audiences were exposed to it. You might find out, for example, that your new product or policy is getting a lot of negative news coverage. See Figure 19.2 for a chart summarizing editorial slant. Or you may find out that only newspapers in the West are using the information, leaving other key markets without any penetration.

Such an analysis may also show that 45 percent of your company's news releases are management and personnel stories, but that these releases account for only 5 percent of the stories published about the company. By contrast, stories about new product developments may constitute only 10 percent of the news releases but account for 90 percent of the press coverage. Given these data, a logical step might be to send out fewer personnel stories and more product development articles.

A systematic tracking system also identifies which publications receiving the news releases are using them. Your mailing list may include 500 different periodicals, but by the end of a 12-month period you may find that only half of these used your releases in any way. Given this information, you would be wise to prune your mailing list.

Computer analysis of press clippings also is a valuable way to make sure that key messages are being included in the published stories. For example, a company may wish to emphasize in all its press coverage that it is a manufacturer of high-quality professional audio and video-recording systems or that it is a well-managed company. Analysis may show that 87 percent of the stories mention the high-quality products but that only 35 percent mention or imply that the company is well managed. Such feedback can help you structure your news releases so that the more important points receive greater emphasis.

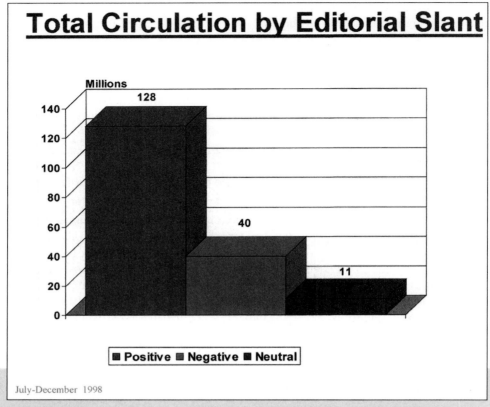

FIGURE 19.2 Thanks to the computer, media mentions can be analyzed on multiple levels—by region, page, mention of key messages, type of article, etc. This chart, originally in color, summarizes the news slant of all your coverage by the total circulation of the publications where stories appeared. As the chart shows, a large percentage of the stories were positive.

Monitoring the Internet

Measuring the reach and effectiveness of your messages on the Internet is getting more sophisticated by the month. One standard method is the cyberspace version of media impressions, used for some years, which is the number of people reached via the organization's Web page. Each instance of a person accessing a site is called a **hit** or a **visit**.

In a national campaign to increase awareness of autism, for example, the Centers for Disease Control and Prevention reported 540,000 unique visitors and more than 50,000 materials downloaded from its website. Even a campaign by the National Potato Board did pretty well. Its Mr. Potato Head site attracted almost 10,000 visitors who spent an average of 5.5 minutes at the site, reviewing an average of 6.6 pages about the health benefits of potatoes.

You can get additional information about users by asking them to answer some demographic questions before they use the site or as they leave it. For best results, offer free software or something similar that must be mailed to users; this entices people to give their names and addresses. Marketers, for example, use this technique to compile databases of potential customers.

Blogs, chat groups, and online publications can also be monitored using the metric of site visits, but such data is less valuable than knowing about the content and tone of what is being said. Consequently, public relations professionals use free online sites such as Technorati, Blogpulse, and Google Alerts to compile mentions regarding your organization or client. You then receive all this information on a daily basis via RSS feeds, which were discussed in Chapter 12. You can also pay companies such as Converseon, Visible Technologies, or Kalivo to monitor the Internet for you and give you a daily report. Kalivo, for example, combines a variety of search techniques, such as RSS, search engine optimization (SEO), and blog interfaces to track everything said anywhere in the blogosphere or on websites. Rod Amis, writing in *PR Tactics*, says, "Think of it as a digital clipping service that runs on autopilot."

Monitoring blogs and chat groups is increasingly important in issues management. It gives you direct feedback about what people are thinking and alerts you to any rumors that are circulating about the organization. Although the people expressing their views may not represent the majority public opinion, their comments often give organizations a "wake-up call" about potential problems and issues.

The metrics of measurement are now available and improving by the month at social networking sites. MySpace, for example, is now compiling data on visits to community pages, the amount of time spent there, whether visitors watched a video, or if a user embedded a piece of content in his or her personal page. It is even tracking the pass-along rate for materials and the demographic and psychological information for "friends" of an organization or brand.

YouTube also has improved its ability to provide data beyond just the number of viewers and how many times a video was downloaded. A feature called YouTube Insight gives account holders who have uploaded videos to the site a range of statistics, charts, and maps about their audience. The data available through Insight include age, gender and geographic location, as well as the identities of the Internet sites that viewers came from and where they went after watching the video. Insight product manager Tracy Chan told the *Los Angeles Times*, "Marketers and advertisers use the data to decide how to target their next round of ads or where bands should tour." She was referring to Weezer, an alternative rock band, which found out that 2.2 million people watched its YouTube video and that 65 percent of the audience was men under age 18 and between the ages of 35 and 45.

Other metrics on the Internet are more difficult to quantify. Social networking sites, for example, are all about listening, participating, and engaging the audience, not necessarily delivering key messages. Ed Terpening, vice president of social media at Wells Fargo, told a Dow Jones seminar, "We care a lot about participation and engagement. That's our number one metric."

One dimension is called the "conversation index," which is the ratio between blog posts and comments. It helps measure whether a blogger is doing a lot of writing with very little response on the part of readers or whether the audience is engaged and contributing to the conversation. Obviously, blogs that generate a lot of "conversation" are more important to organizations in terms of feedback and dialogue.

Another metric that is somewhat difficult to quantify is the tone of the conversation; is it positive, hostile, or neutral? Some experts say this is too simplistic, because it doesn't take into account whether someone is being sarcastic and can be misconstrued by analysis that evaluates language too literally. Nevertheless, such information generally helps you and your organization respond to concerns raised by consumers and other publics. Other forms of measurement are (1) engagement, such as time spent with the site and whether visitors downloaded materials; (2) word-of-mouth impact; and (3) search engine visibility.

In sum, the ability to measure the effectiveness of social media is continuing to evolve. Tonya Garcia, writing in *PRWeek*, highlights four challenges in measuring social media:

1. **The human factor.** Metrics such as tone require a human touch, which is slower than computers and sometimes prone to error.
2. **The language barrier.** The Internet is international and engagement occurs cross-border, creating a need for multilingual analysts.
3. **The need for a new model.** Many try to measure social media using traditional media metrics, which can provide little value.
4. **The blogger effect.** It's tough to decipher the strong feeling and sarcasm usually projected by this group.

Requests and 800 Numbers

Another measure of media exposure is to compile the number of requests for more information. A story in a newspaper or an appearance of a spokesperson on a broadcast show often provides the impetus for driving people to a website to download more information, requesting a brochure, or even ordering the product.

In many cases, a toll-free 800 number is provided. The American Association of Clinical Endocrinologists, through Fleischman-Hillard, conducted a public information campaign about thyroid disorders and got 10,000 requests for its "Thyroid Neck Check" brochures. In addition, the organization's website increased its "hits" from 4,000 to 12,000 immediately after the launch of the information campaign.

The Washington Hospital Center, located in Washington, D.C., with the help of Crofton Communications, also did a public information campaign to make women aware of heart disease risks. Nearly 10,000 women called to request a Women's Heart Health Kit.

The readership of product publicity features, discussed in Chapter 7, is often monitored by offering readers an opportunity to call or go online to get more information. In this way, for example, Air New Zealand has measured the value of sending travel features to daily newspapers throughout the United States. Such monitoring often shows top management that product publicity generates more sales leads than straight advertising.

Cost per Person

The cost of reaching each person in the audience often is calculated as part of the evaluation process. The technique is commonly used in advertising in order to place costs in perspective. Although a 30-second commercial during the Super Bowl costs about $2.7 million ($90,000 per second), most advertisers believe it is worth the price, because an audience of more than 90 million households is reached for about three cents per household. This is a relatively good bargain, even if several million viewers probably visited the bathroom while the commercial played.

Cost-effectiveness, as this technique is known, also is used in public relations. Cost per thousand (CPM) is calculated by taking the total of media impressions (discussed earlier) and dividing it by the cost of the publicity program. Skytel, for example, spent $400,000 to publicize its new two-way paging and messaging system and obtained 52 million impressions, about seven-tenths of a cent per impression. You can do the same thing for events, brochures, and newsletters. Nike produced a sports video for $50,000 but reached 150,000 high school students, for a per-person cost of 33 cents.

Event Attendance

Speeches, meetings, presentations, tours, grand openings, and other such activities have one important thing in common: they all involve audiences who are exposed to a message.

A first step in evaluating these activities is to count the number of people who come to an event. Port Discovery, a new children's museum in Baltimore, conducted a public relations program to let citizens know about its grand opening. Thanks to the efforts of its public relations firm, Trahan, Burden & Charles, Inc., almost 9,000 visited the museum in its first week—double the number expected.

Although numbers are impressive, you also can measure audience attitudes by observation and surveys. A standing ovation at the end of a speech, spontaneous applause, and complimentary remarks as people leave, even the "feel" of the audience as expressed in smiles and the intangible air of satisfaction that can permeate a group of people will give you an idea as to the success of an event.

A more scientific method is the survey. People leaving an event can be asked what they think in a 30-second interview. Another way, for a meeting, is to have attendees fill out a short questionnaire. A simple form might look like this:

Your Evaluation of This Meeting (Please check each item)

	Excellent	Good	Average	Could Be Better
1. Location	☐	☐	☐	☐
2. Costs	☐	☐	☐	☐
3. Facilities	☐	☐	☐	☐
4. Program	☐	☐	☐	☐
5. Speakers (These should be listed by name.)	_____	_____	_____	_____

Why did you attend?

_____

_____

How did you learn about it?

_____

_____

Suggestions for future events:

_____

_____

■ Measurement of Audience Awareness

The meeting survey is one form of determining whether the audience actually became aware of the message and understood it. Recall that the problem with audience exposure is primarily whether the media distributed the message with some degree of accuracy. This really does not answer the question, "How many people actually read or heard the message?"

The tools of survey research are needed to answer such a question. Members of the target audience must be asked about the message and what they remember about it. Such research, for example, found that Apple achieved a phenomenal 99 percent public awareness that its iPhone was coming to an Apple and AT&T store near you.

A good case study of measuring audience awareness is a public relations program conducted by Washington Mutual, a Seattle-based financial services institution. It had become one of the largest banks in California through acquisitions, but was entering the market with virtually no name recognition. It hired Rogers & Associates, a public relations firm, to conduct a program using the introduction of the newly designed $20 bill as the centerpiece. The idea was to give 20 consumers in seven major markets a chance to enter a wind cube filled with the new $20 bills and have 20 seconds to grab as many of the swirling bills as they could.

Shortly after this event, which was called "WaMoola Madness," a survey was conducted that showed that 80 percent of consumers surveyed in new markets were familiar with the Washington Mutual name. This percentage was up from virtually zero name recognition a month before the promotional event.

Another way of measuring audience awareness and comprehension is the day-after recall. Under this method, participants are asked to view a specific television program or read a particular news story, then they are interviewed to learn what messages they remembered.

Ketchum, on behalf of the California Prune Board, used this technique to determine if a 15-city media tour was conveying the key message that prunes are a high-fiber food source. Forty women in Detroit were asked to watch a program on which a prune board spokesperson would appear. The next day, they were asked what they remembered about the program. Ninety-three percent remembered the spokesperson and 65 percent, on an unaided basis, named prunes as a source of high fiber.

Measurement of Audience Attitudes

Closely related to audience awareness and understanding of a message is whether the audience actually changes its attitudes and opinions about the product, service, or idea.

One way to measure changes in attitude is to sample the opinions of the target audience before and after the campaign. This means conducting **benchmark studies**—studies that graphically show percentage differences in attitudes as a result of increased information and persuasion. Of course, a number of possible intervening variables may also account for changes in attitudes, but a statistical analysis of variance can help pinpoint to what degree the attitude change is attributable to your efforts.

Sears, for example, used a benchmark study to prove that its efforts at getting a positive story about the company on *The Oprah Winfrey Show* actually increased sales and influenced consumer attitudes. With the help of Delahaye/Medialink, Sears gauged the attitudes of consumers before and after they saw Oprah Winfrey announce the retailer's donation of $20,000 worth of Christmas gifts to families in need.

Following the show, according to a monograph published by Lawrence Ragan Communications, "a measurement survey

66 *You want to gauge audience or customer response.* 99 ◦■ Katie Paine, president of KD Paine & Partners

showed a fivefold increase in perceptions that Sears does good things for the community and the environment. The respondents who said they agreed with the statement, 'Sears is a quality company' increased from 58 to 65 percent." In addition, consumers expressing intent to shop at Sears increased from 59 to 70 percent, and estimated spending levels rose 39 percent per shopper, or about $13 million in incremental sales.

Such companies as ExxonMobil, General Electric, and Wal-Mart regularly use benchmark surveys to measure their reputation on a continuing basis. Surveys showed, for example, that Microsoft's corporate reputation dropped after the U.S.

Justice Department filed an antitrust suit against the company. As a result, Microsoft considerably beefed up its public relations efforts and Bill Gates announced the formation of the Gates Foundation, now the largest foundation in the world. Benchmarking showed that the image of Microsoft improved among the public despite the antitrust case against it.

Benchmark surveys are only one way to measure attitudes and opinions. You can also do evaluations on a less sophisticated level by keeping complete and thorough tabs on telephone calls logged and letters received and by conducting focus group interviews with cross sections of the publics being reached. Analysis of telephone calls, e-mails, and letters is very important in the area of consumer affairs. If a pattern can be ascertained, it often tells the company that a particular product or service is not up to standard.

Measurement of Audience Action

The ultimate objective of any public relations effort, as has been pointed out, is to accomplish organizational objectives. David Dozier, of San Diego State University, says it succinctly: "The outcome of a successful public relations program is not a hefty stack of news stories. . . . Communication is important only in the effects it achieves among publics."

In other words, you should never say that the objective is to generate publicity. This is simply a tactic to achieve a specific outcome. Greenpeace's objective, for example, is not to get publicity, but to motivate the public to (1) become aware of environmental problems, (2) understand the consequences of not doing anything about it, (3) form attitude and opinions favorable to conservation, and (4) take some action such as writing elected officials or even sending a donation to Greenpeace.

A change in audience behavior or motivating them to purchase a product or service is difficult to accomplish through public relations efforts, because people are complex and make decisions on the basis of many factors. At the same time, however, measurement of audience action is relatively easy to measure. All you have to do is look at sales figures or increase in market share.

A campaign that measured audience action was one for Hungry Jack instant potatoes, pancake mixes, and syrups. The objective of the public relations firm, Carmichael Lynch Spong, was to increase the brand equity of Hungry Jack by sponsoring a national contest, "Who is Your Hungry Jack," to find hard-working, dependable and adventurous "Hungry Jacks."

The program, mostly through radio promotions, had a goal of 10,000 entries and received 22,000 entries. In addition, the contest promotion helped increase market share between 10 and 20 points in targeted markets. Following the campaign launch, there was a 23 percent sales increase in instant potatoes and a 9 percent sales increase for pancake mixes. The campaign received a Bronze Anvil award from PRSA.

The ballot box also can provide convincing proof. Beaufort County in South Carolina had a bond referendum providing for a 1 percent sales tax to raise $40 million over 2 years to improve a local highway. There was strong opposition to the sales tax, so the local citizens committee supporting the measure hired a public relations firm to conduct a campaign to persuade the voters. The theme "Vote Yes, Highway 170, the Wait Is Killing Us," was used and a series of activities were organized. This included a grassroots coalition with speaker events and letter writing, recruiting third-party endorsements, and getting media support. The result: The bond issue passed with 58 percent of the vote.

Evaluation of Newsletters and Brochures

If you are an editor of a newsletter or an employee magazine, it is wise to evaluate its readership on an annual basis. This will help you ascertain reader perceptions of layout and design, the balance of stories, kinds of stories that have high reader interest, additional topics that could be covered, the publication's credibility, and whether the publication is actually meeting organizational objectives.

Systematic evaluation, it should be emphasized, is not based on whether all the copies are distributed or picked up. This is much like saying that the news release was published in the newspaper. Neither observation tells you anything about what the audience actually read, retained, or acted on. If all newsletters or printed materials disappear from the racks in a few days, it may simply mean that the janitorial staff is efficient.

The following discussion focuses on periodical publications, but the same methods can be used to evaluate leaflets, booklets, and brochures. Because many of these may be used externally, you also need to study the reactions and opinions of people who are not employees. Informal questioning of readers, monitoring of mail, and requests for additional information can all show whether the material is being read and whether it is doing its job or needs improvement.

There are a number of ways in which a newsletter, newspaper, or magazine can be audited. These include content analysis, readership interest surveys, readership recall of articles actually read, application of readability formulas, and use of advisory boards or focus interview groups.

Content Analysis

Select a representative sample of past issues and categorize the stories under general headings. You may wish to cover such subjects as management announcements, new product developments, new personnel and retirements, employee hobbies and interests, corporate finances, news of departments and divisions, and job-related information.

A systematic analysis will quickly tell you if you are devoting too much space, perhaps unintentionally, to management or even to news of a particular division at the expense of other organizational aspects. For example, you may think that you have a lot of articles about employee personnel policies and job advancement opportunities, only to find, on analysis, that less than 10 percent of the publication is devoted to such information.

By analyzing organizational objectives and coupling the results of a content analysis with a survey of reader interests, you may come to the conclusion that the publication's content requires some revision.

Readership Surveys

The purpose of readership surveys is to obtain employee feedback on the types of stories they read, and what they think of the publication. The Figure 19.3, for example, shows a sample "feedback" form that could be faxed to the company. Such surveys are also done online, but it depends on the organization and whether its employees have regular access to the Web. Retail stores, for example, have a large percentage of sales clerks who don't use a computer as part of their job.

These are relatively simple surveys. You can provide a list of topics or statements and have employees mark each one as "very important," "somewhat important," or "not important." Another way is to have them circle numbers 1 through

---

FAX YOUR FEEDBACK!

Please take a few moments to fill out this questionnaire, and fax it to us by Oct. 9. Your answers will help guide Corporate Communications efforts to continually improve the usefulness to you of the company's varied communications publications and other media. Results will be published in an upcoming issue of Praxair News. *Thanks for your time, and we look forward to hearing from you!*

1. My primary sources of information about Praxair's business and strategies are (check 3):

_____ Praxair News	_____ "The Grapevine"
_____ Electronic Bulletins	_____ Telephone Conferences
_____ Immediate Supervisor	_____ Bulletin Board Postings
_____ Group Meetings	_____ Local Publications
_____ Other (specify)_____	

2. Please indicate how strongly you agree or disagree with the following statements:

	Strongly Disagree	Disagree	No Opinion	Agree	Strongly Agree
Praxair communicates clear company goals.	_____	_____	_____	_____	_____
Praxair communicates clear strategies to achieve its goals.	_____	_____	_____	_____	_____
Praxair communications are believable.	_____	_____	_____	_____	_____
The information I receive helps me do my job better.	_____	_____	_____	_____	_____
My supervisor does a good job of communicating useful information.	_____	_____	_____	_____	_____

3. Please circle the number for each phrase that best describes your opinion of *Praxair News*. You may circle any number from 1 to 5:

It's all old news to me	1	2	3	4	5	I learn a lot
The articles are boring	1	2	3	4	5	It has interesting articles
The stories are trivial	1	2	3	4	5	The stories have substance
The design is unappealing	1	2	3	4	5	The design is attractive
It is poorly written	1	2	3	4	5	It is well-written
It's too management-oriented	1	2	3	4	5	There's something for everyone

Additional comments:_____

▶ **FIGURE 19.3** Employee publications need reader feedback to evaluate effectiveness. This is part of a questionnaire that was included as an insert in an issue of a company newspaper.

5 to show the degree of agreement with a statement. In such a survey, you may be surprised to find employees expressing limited interest in personals (anniversaries and birthdays), but great interest in the organization's future plans.

A readership interest survey becomes even more valuable if you can compare it to the content analysis of what your publication has been covering. If there are substantial differences, it is a signal to change the editorial content of your publication.

Article Recall

The best kind of readership survey is done when you or other interviewers sit down with a sampling of employees to find out what they have actually read in the latest issue of the publication.

Employees are shown the publication page by page and asked to indicate the articles they have read. As a check on the tendency for employees to tell you that they have read the publication from cover to cover (often called a "courtesy bias"), you also ask them how much of the article they read and what the article was about. The resulting marked copies of the publication are then content-analyzed to determine what kinds of articles have the most readership.

The method just described is much more accurate than a questionnaire asking employees to tell you how much of the publication they read. You do not get accurate data when you ask questions such as "What percentage of the newsletter do you read? All of it? Most of it? Some of it?" In this case, employees know that the company expects them to read the publication, so you get a preponderance of answers at the high end of the scale. Very few people will want to admit that they don't read it at all.

It is also somewhat fruitless to ask rank-and-file employees to evaluate the graphic design or the quality of the photographs. Most employees don't have the expertise to make such judgments. It would be much wiser to ask these questions of individuals who are versed in graphic design and printing quality.

Readability

Every publication should be evaluated for readability at least once a year. This can be done in several ways. An informal method is to ask people during a reader recall survey if they think the articles are clear and understandable. Comments such as "I don't know what they're talking about" and "I don't get anything out of some articles" might indicate that there is a readability problem.

Also available are various readability formulas that quantify reading level. Rudolf Flesch was one of the first educational researchers to develop a formula, now commonly called the Flesch formula. Others tools include the Gunning formula, the Dale-Chall formula, the Fry formula, and the Cloze procedure.

Basically, these techniques allow you to determine how difficult a given piece of writing might be to read. Most rely on mean sentence length and the average number of multisyllabic words. Some also include the number of personal pronouns used. In general, writing is easier to read (is accessible to readers at a lower educational level) if the sentences are simple and there are many one- and two-syllable words.

If a randomly selected sample of 100 words contains 4.2 sentences and 142 syllables, it is ranked at about the ninth-grade level. If you are writing for an employee publication, ninth-grade level is usually a good starting point. However, if a large percentage of the employees are high school graduates or English is their second language, you might want to strive for six or seven sentences and 120 syllables per 100 words.

For news releases to the general media and publications geared to all employees, you should write at a ninth-grade level. News releases to trade publications with a primary audience of scientists and engineers as well as publications geared to managers can be written at a higher level. For example, readability formulas show that a college-educated audience can readily cope with 3.8 sentences and 166 syllables per 100 words.

Advisory Boards and Focus Groups

Periodic feedback and evaluation can be provided by organizing an employee advisory board that meets several times a year to discuss the direction and content of your publication. Between meetings, members of the advisory board would also be able to relay employee comments and concerns to the editor. This is a useful technique in that it expands the editor's network of feedback and solicits comments that employees may be hesitant to offer the editor face to face.

A variation of the advisory board is to periodically invite a sampling of employees to participate in a general discussion of the publication and its contents. It is important that all segments of the organization's employees be represented and that these sessions not become forums for charges and countercharges. The purpose is to share information, generate new ideas, and work to make the publication more valuable as an instrument for obtaining organizational objectives.

Writing a Measurement Report

When you have finished evaluating a campaign, you must report the results to the people who paid for it. In some cases, it may be necessary to report on individual events or activities immediately after they have occurred. Even if an immediate report is unnecessary, an overall report on the entire program must be made—usually annually. Budgets and programs are generally reviewed at least once a year, and this is the time when you must convince management or the client that what you have done is worthwhile and that the program should be continued and improved.

To prepare the report, you should refer to the original plan and state what you accomplished under each heading. Answer the following questions:

- **Situation.** Was the situation properly appraised? While the program was underway, did you learn anything that forced changes? What happened, and what did you do?
- **Audience.** Was it properly identified? Did you reach it? How effectively did you reach it (numbers reached, response, feedback)?

- **Objectives.** Did you achieve what you planned to achieve? Provide figures. You should have set numerical goals; now tell how well you did in reaching them.

- **Strategy.** Did it work? Did you have to modify it? Should it be continued or changed?

- **Tactics.** Did all the tools accomplish what they were supposed to accomplish? Were changes made? Why? Here again you can give numbers: news items published, feature stories published, printed items distributed, response of readers or viewers, TV and radio appearances, and so on.

- **Timing.** Was everything done at the right time? Should changes be made next year?

- **Costs.** Did you stay within the budget? If not, why not? This is the point at which you set the stage for the next budget and perhaps explain why more money would have permitted greater accomplishment.

■ Summary

- Measurement is absolutely essential. You must tell what was done, how well it was done, and what good it did. Quantify your results.

- Evaluation and measurement starts with having a set of program objectives that are realistic, credible, and measurable.

- Public relations staff and the client or employer should mutually agree on objectives and how they will be measured at the end of the program.

- Measuring the production and distribution of news releases and features puts an emphasis on quantify instead of quality.

- The most common form of measurement in public relations is the compilation of media mentions. It is an indication that an audience was exposed to the message.

- Monitoring services can be hired to monitor print, broadcast, and online mentions of your client or employer's name, products, and services.

- Today's software can give metrics such as message reach, tone of coverage, and how many times a key message is mentioned.

- Impressions are the total circulation of a publication or the audience of a broadcast outlet. It does not tell you how many people actually read or heard your story.

- Advertising equivalency, the idea of converting publicity in the news columns to comparative advertising rates, is highly suspect as a legitimate form of measurement.

- It is important to monitor the Internet to find out what bloggers, chat groups, and online publications are saying about your organization, products, and services.

- The metrics of measuring the effects and impact of social media on brands and organizations are still evolving. It's important, however, to consider participation and engagement as a criterion.

- Social networking sites such as MySpace and YouTube are now providing statistics about the gender, age group, geographic location, and other demographics of individuals who sign up as "friends" of a company or a brand.

- Requests for brochures and calls to 800 numbers give you an indication of people's exposure to a message.

- Cost per person is a way to analyze the cost of reaching your audience.

- Attendance at an event is a form of measurement because it shows audience exposure to the message. You, through surveys at a meeting, can also ascertain attitudes and opinions about the meeting.

- Surveys are needed to tell whether an audience actually got the message and understood it.

- Benchmark surveys done before and after a campaign can help you to ascertain whether audience attitudes and opinions have changed.

- Measurement of action, although difficult to accomplish, is relatively easy to measure. You can use sales figures, market share, or even voting results.

- Newsletters and brochures should be evaluated on a frequent basis. Some techniques include content analysis, readership surveys, article recall, and readability formulas.

- After a campaign is over, it is important to write up the results for the client or employer. This report becomes a record of accomplishment and a source of ideas for future programs.

Skill Building Activities

1. Over the course of several weeks, clip all the articles about your college or another organization of choice that appear in the local daily newspaper. Find out the cost of advertising per column inch and multiply it by the number of column inches found. Given the dollar value of the publicity, do you think the coverage was worth this amount? Why or why not?

2. Over the course of several weeks, clip all the articles about your college or another organization of choice that appear in the local daily newspaper. Perform a content analysis of the clippings. What percentage of mentions, in terms of information provided, probably originated with the organization? What percentage of space was devoted to such things as (1) the size of the company, (2) its services or product lines, and (3) the attributes of a particular product or service?

3. Use Technorati or Blogsphere to subscribe to an RSS feed (see Chapter 12) that will track mentions of a company or a national nonprofit group. Perform a content analysis of what you receive over a period of several weeks. What aspects can be quantified? What aspects of the coverage are difficult to quantify, such as tone and level of conversation?

4. Perform a content analysis of a company or organizational newsletter. Place articles, including the number of column inches, into the following general categories: messages from management, employee features, news of departments and divisions, recreational activities, retirements, and so on. Given your findings, do you think the organization is accomplishing such objectives as (1) building employee loyalty and morale, (2) informing employees of opportunities for advancement, and (3) informing employees about policies and procedures?

Suggested Readings

Amis, Rod. "You Can't Ignore Social Media: How to Measure Internet Efforts to Your Organization's Best Advantage." *PR Tactics*, May 2007, p. 10.

Council of Public Relations Firms. "Measuring the Impact of Public Relations on Sales." White paper, 2005.

Garcia, Tonya. "The New Rules of Evaluation: As Social Media's Role in the PR Mix Becomes Greater, It Becomes More Important to Figure Out the Best Way to Measure It." *PRWeek*, March 24, 2008, p. 12.

Garcia, Tonya. "Making the Case for Measurement." *PRWeek*, November 26, 2007, p. 15.

Hazley, Craig. "Blog Tracking Advances; Whether PR Is Ready or Not." *O'Dwyer's PR Report*, June 2006, pp. 25, 33.

Iacona, Erica. "A Measured Response." *PRWeek*, November 13, 2006, pp. 12–13.

McGuire, Craig. "Monitoring Conversation Is a Good Start: A Product Launch Is a Prime Opportunity to Track Online Dialogue." *PRWeek*, March 3, 2008, p. 18.

McGuire, Craig. "Going Beyond Press Release Distribution: Newswires Today Also Offer a Wide Range of Measurement Solutions." *PRWeek*, November 26, 2007, p. 22.

Morrissey, Brian. "Conversation Quotient: Social Media Metrics Are Still a Work in Progress." *AdWeek,* March 24, 2008.

Paine, Katie Delahaye. *Measuring Public Relationships: The Data-Driven Communicator's Guide to Success.* Berlin, NH: KD Paine & Partners, 2007.

Weiner, Mark. "PR Outshines Advertising in Return on Investment." *O'Dwyer's PR Report*, September 2007, p. 16.

Glossary

Actuality   A recorded statement by an identified person used in a radio newscast. See *Soundbite*.

Advertising equivalency   Converting news articles to how much it would cost to advertise in the same space.

Advertorial   A paid advertisement expressing an organization's views on issues of public concern.

ANR (audio news release)   Distributed to radio stations via CD or telephone.

Application story   In feature writing, a story that tells how to use a new product or how to use a familiar product in a new way. Similar to a *case study*.

Backgrounder   A compilation of information about an organization, a problem, a situation, an event, or a major development. It is given to media to provide a factual basis for news to be published or broadcast.

Benchmark studies   Surveying public attitudes and opinions before and after a public relations campaign.

Bio   Biography. A brief summary of someone's background, often supplied in a media kit or as part of a printed program or event.

Blog   A website maintained by an individual to post comments, link to other sites, and engage in dialogue with readers.

Boilerplate   Standard news release copy, usually in paragraph form, that provides basic information about a company, including stock symbols and URLs.

Booker   The contact person for a broadcast talk show who is responsible for arranging guests.

Brainstorming   Sessions designed to generate creative ideas in which the participants are encouraged to express any idea that comes to mind.

Branding   The use of symbols to market organizations or products.

B-roll   Only the video portion of a tape, without an announcer. It may include additional soundbites that broadcast editors may include in a newscast.

Browsers   Software programs that allow users to navigate the Internet, access URLs, and employ Web resources. Popular examples include Mozilla's FireFox and Microsoft's Internet Explorer.

Bulk fax   The faxing of materials to multiple receivers simultaneously.

Bureau of Alcohol, Tobacco, and Firearms (BATF)   A federal regulatory agency that oversees advertising and promotion of alcohol, tobacco, and guns.

Camera-ready   News releases and features already formatted in column format. Editors insert the material into the layout and prepare the page for offset printing. Camera-ready copy also is called a *repro proof*.

Caption   The brief text under a photo that informs the reader about the picture and its source.

Case study   In feature writing, a story that demonstrates the value of a product or service by detailing how it works and by providing specific examples that are often supported with statistics or customer testimonials.

Channeling   The use of a group's attitudes and values in order to create a meaningful message.

Clip art   Line art and other graphic designs that can be used in public relations materials. Clip art is available on CD and online.

Corporate profile(s)   A fact sheet that focuses exclusively on an organization's identity, particularly its nature and objectives, main business activity, size, market position, revenues, products, and key executives.

Cropping   The editing of photographs by cutting off portions of the original.

Cyber media tour A media event that involves interviewing a spokesperson via the Internet or videoconferencing.

Desktop tour A series of meetings at the desks of editors and reporters at various media outlets for the purpose of building a relationship.

Editorial calendar A listing of topics and special issues that a periodical will feature throughout the year.

E-mail Electronic mail. Personal messages to individual receivers transmitted on the Internet.

EPKs (electronic press kits) Press kits distributed via CD, e-mail, and online newsrooms.

Evergreen A news release or feature that has no particular time element. The subject matter can be used by media outlets at almost any time.

E-zines Electronic newsletters distributed via the Internet or organizational intranets. Sometimes called *E-pubs*.

Fact sheet A brief outline of who, what, when, where, why, and how. Sent to journalists so they have a quick review of basic information.

Fair comment privilege A legal concept derived from the First Amendment right to freedom of speech that allows for the public airing of opinion. To protect against libel, however, experts suggest that (1) opinion statements be accompanied by the facts on which the opinions are based; (2) opinion statements be clearly labeled as such; and (3) the context of the language surrounding the expressions of opinion be reviewed for possible libel implications.

Fam trip Familiarization trip. Refers to journalists who go on a trip at the invitation of an organization to become acquainted with a situation, product, or service.

FAQ (frequently asked question) A variation on the traditional fact sheet in which information is presented in a question question-and-answer format. Often used on the Internet.

Fax on demand Individuals can order specific materials via the telephone or e-mail, and a fax including the information is sent automatically.

Feature story A story, generally longer than a news release, that focuses on a human interest or provides background about a service or product in an entertaining way.

Federal Trade Commission (FTC) A federal regulatory agency that scrutinizes advertising and publicity products for fairness and accuracy.

Filler Video materials from an organization that are used to fill gaps in programming on a television station or a cable outlet.

Food and Drug Administration (FDA) A federal regulatory agency that oversees the advertising and promotion of prescription drugs, over-the-counter medicines, and cosmetics.

Historical piece In feature writing, a story that stresses the continuity between past and present to garner reader interest.

Hits A term used in relationship to the number of people that click on a particular page on the World Wide Web.

Hometowners Stories custom tailored to a particular newspaper or broadcast station by focusing on the local angle in the first paragraph of the news release.

Hype Exaggerated publicity about a product, service, or a celebrity. Often characterized by flowery adjectives and inflated claims.

Implied consent The unwritten and unstated consent employees give their employers to use their photographs in such items as the employee newsmagazine and newsletters. Implied consent does not extend to advertising or promotion, which requires *written* consent.

Impressions Relates to the circulation of a publication or the audience size of a particular radio or television program. If a story or ad appears in a newspaper with 100,000 circulation, this constitutes 100,000 impressions

Infographics Computer-generated artwork used to display statistics in the form of tables and charts.

Intranet A private network within an organization for the exclusive use of employees. Intranets are based on the same principles as the Internet.

IT An acronym for *information technology*, which encompasses hardware, software, and how computers systems operate.

JPEG An acronym for Joint Photographic Experts Group, which deals with a common method to compress photos and send them via the Internet.

Letters-to-the-editor (LTE) A concise letter designed intended to rebut an editorial, clarify information mentioned in a news story or column, or add information that might not have been included in an original story.

Listserv An Internet site that automatically e-mails messages to individuals who subscribe to the service.

Magapaper An organizational publication that has a newspaper-type layout but incorporates the design elements of a magazine.

Mailing house A commercial firm that prepares and mails materials on behalf of its clients.

Masthead The place on the layout of a newsletter, newspaper, or magazine where the name of the publication appears. This is usually at the top of the first page.

Mechanical Type, photos, line art, and copy assembled on a single board used for offset printing.

Media alert A notification to assignment editors informing them of a newsworthy event that could lend itself to photo or video coverage.

Media gatekeepers The people within media who decide what information is newsworthy and what is not. Factors that influence the final decisions of media gatekeepers include timeliness, prominence, proximity, significance, unusualness, human interest, conflict, and newness.

Media kit A packet of materials distributed by mail, CD, or online to media outlets that contains news releases, photos, backgrounders, and fact sheets about a new product or service.

Misappropriation of personality The use of a person's image, particularly a popular personality, without permission.

Mug shot A slang term for a head-and-shoulders photo of an individual.

News release A news story prepared by an organization and sent to media outlets. Also called a press release.

No-host bar Guests buy their own drinks. A hosted bar means that the drinks are free to guests.

Op-ed Opposite the editorial page. A page that contains the views and opinions of individuals who are not on the staff of the newspaper.

Page impression The number of times a Web page is pulled up by individuals. The term is used in relation to tracking "traffic" on the Internet.

Personality profile In feature writing, a story that focuses on a person of public interest to stimulate reader awareness of that person and/or the organization, product, or service the person represents.

Photo news release (PNR) A photograph with a long caption beneath it that tells an entire story.

Pica A printer's term for measuring the length of typeset lines. There are 6 picas to the inch.

Pitch Jargon for making an appeal to an editor or journalist to do a story on your product or service.

Plagiarism A form of theft in which an author appropriates the writing or ideas of another author and claims them as his own.

Podcast An audio or video program that can be downloaded from the Internet via an iPod, MP3 player, or RSS feed.

Plugs Refers to mentions of organizations, products, and services in movies and broadcast entertainment shows.

Press kit See *media kit*.

Press release See *news release*.

Product positioning The contextual background used to market a product to the public.

Product tie-in The appearance of a branded product or service in a movie or TV series as part of a contracted agreement between the organization and the producers. Such a contract may call for the organization to actively promote the movie or TV series in its product advertising.

PSA (public service announcement) These short messages, usually by a nonprofit agency or governmental agency, are used on radio and television stations as a public service at no charge.

Pseudoevent   A term coined by historian Daniel Boorstin to describe events and situations staged primarily for the sake of generating press coverage and media interest.

Public service announcement   See *PSA*.

Publics   The potential or actual audiences for any given public relations message. Often defined by income, age, gender, race, geography, or psychographic characteristics.

Research study   In feature writing, a story that uses information derived from surveys, polls, or scientific studies to garner reader interest and to demonstrate the value of a product or service.

Retouching   The alteration of a photograph by the traditional means of airbrushing or, more frequently now, by the electronic manipulation of a digital image.

RFP (request for proposal)   Organizations seeking public relations assistance often issue a RFP requesting public relations firms to prepare a proposal outlining their recommendations and capabilities.

RMT (radio media tour)   A spokesperson conducting a series of interviews with various broadcast outlets from a central location.

ROI (return on investment)   A comparison of total costs to reach an audience divided by the amount of business that is generated.

RSS   Acronym for *Real Simple Syndication*. Materials are aggregated according to subscriber interests and sent directly to their computers.

Saddle-stitched   Refers to the binding of a magazine, where the pages are stapled together at the centerfold.

Satellite media tour   See *SMT*.

Search engines   Software programs that allow users to search for topically identified resources and information on the Internet. Popular examples include Google, Yahoo!, and MSN.

Securities and Exchange Commission (SEC)   A federal regulatory agency that requires that any information affecting the value of a security be made known to the owners and to themselves.

Service journalism   The practice of publishing "news you can use," for example, stories featuring consumer tips, professional advice, etc.

SMT (satellite media tour)   A media event that involves arranging for news anchors around the country to interview a spokesperson in a television studio via satellite.

Snail mail   First-class mail delivered by the U.S. Postal Service.

Social media   Online technologies that allow people to share opinions and perspectives with each other.

Soundbite   A statement or quote from an individual, which is inserted into audio and video news releases.

Speaker's bureau   An organization's effort to provide spokespersons to civic clubs and other organizations at no cost. Commercial speaker's bureaus serve as agents to book celebrity speakers who charge for an appearance.

Spin doctor   A pejorative term for a public relations person or political consultant who presents ("puts spin on") negative or potentially damaging information in such a way as to minimize or completely dispel its effect.

Sponsored communication   Refers to newsletters, magazines, brochures, and other materials that are prepared and distributed by organizations without the intervention of gatekeepers in traditional mass media.

Stakeholders   The groups impacted by an organization's decisions. These potentially include employees, consumers, neighbors, suppliers, environmental groups, and investors.

Stock footage   Standard video shots of an organization's production line, headquarters, and activities that a television station can store until the company is in the news.

Storyboard   A written outline of an audio or video news release. For video, a description of scenes, plus dialogue, is prepared.

Talking head   Refers to a television broadcast or a video news release in which the screen is dominated by a person who is talking.

Template   The standardized format of a newsletter or magazine, so each issue has the same look and feel.

Usenet A network of Internet-based *newsgroups* that uses a bulletin board system to post and read messages.

VNR (video news release) A short publicity piece formatted for immediate use by a television station.

Webcasting The delivery of a broadcast (live or delayed) over the Internet. When it is done in real time, it is also called *streaming*.

White paper An organization's analysis of a particular issue or the potential of a market for a specific product or service. Other terms used are *briefing paper* and *position statement*.

Wiki An interactive website that allows multiple persons to access content, make changes, and edit each other's input.

World Wide Web The location on the Internet where thousands of organizations display their own pages.

Index

A-roll, defined, 229
A4S Security, 230–231
AARP Magazine, 351
Abbott Labs, 237
  annual report of, 379, 380
ABC, defamation suit against, 65
Abundant Forests Alliance, 171, 179
Academic Search Premier, 18
Academy Awards, 44, 52, 103–104, 437
Accenture, magazine of, 352
Achievers, 37
Acronyms, 47
Action verbs, 24
Activating speech, 410
Active audiences, 43
Active voice, 23–24
Actualities, 212, 526
Ad Council, 234, 442, 443
Adobe Illustrator, 383
Adoption process, 40–41
Advance planning, 496
Adventures by Disney, 147, 201
  media kits of, 148, 149
Advertisements
  graphic elements in, 445
  headline of, 444
  layout of, 445
  text of, 445
  tips for creating, 446, 447
Advertising
  advantages and disadvantages of, 437–438
  audience for, 437
  billboards, 447-448
  buttons and bumper stickers, 448
  cost of, 438
  credibility of, 438
  defined, 436
  impact of, 437
  influence of, 281
  message of, 437
  posters, 448, 450
  privacy issues in, 68
  promotional products, 451
  purposes of, 436–437
  sponsored books, 450
  on t-shirts, 450–451
  timing of, 437
  transit panels, 448

types of, 438–444
  of websites, 318
Advertising Age, 15
Advertising agency, working with, 446–447
Advertising equivalency, 526
Advertising value equivalency, 509–511
Advertorial, 526
Advisory boards, editorial, 522
Advocacy, advertising for, 442
AEP Now, 369
Aetna, news release format of, 121
Afghanistan, U.S. intervention in, 56
Agnes, Brian, 264
Ahles, Catherine, 500
AIDS (acquired immunodeficiency syndrome), 47
Air New Zealand, 515
  sponsored books by, 450
AirTran, YouTube promotions of, 335
Akron Children's Hospital, 5
Alaska Division of Tourism, 174–175
Allstate Insurance, advertising by, 442
Allure magazine, 51-52
Amato, Melanie, 99
American Academy of Ophthalmology, 93
American Association of Clinical Endocrinologists, 514
American Association of Kidney Patients, 96
American Association of Orthodontists, 93
American Cancer Society, 50, 441, 489
American College of Gastroenterologists, 94
American Dental Association, 52
American Fly Fishing Trade Association, 115
American Heart Association, 441
American Heritage Dictionary, 9–10
American Heritage Electronic Dictionary, 10
American Idol, 243
American Journalism Review, 15
American Kennel Club, 111
American Lung Association, 441
American Medical Association, 110

American Optometric Association, 93
American Petroleum Institute, 276
American Psychological Association, 213
American Red Cross, 441
American Revolution, 47
American Society for the Prevention of Cruelty to Animals (ASPCA), 52, 53, 54
Amis, Rod, 513
Amurgis, William, 369
Anderson, Chris, 276
Anheuser-Busch, 80
Anniversaries, 106–107
  historical pieces for, 173–175
Announcements, 122
  advertisements as, 444
Annual reports, 370
  audience of, 379
  key themes in, 380–381
  planning and writing of, 380
  purpose of, 378
  storytelling by, 379
  on the Web, 381
Appeal to self-interest, 45
Apple Computer, 7, 43, 101, 287, 516
Apple Pages, 383
Application stories, 169–170, 526
April Fool's Day, 93
Arbesu, Christiane, 221
Arbitron ratings, 214
Architectural Digest, 281
Aristotle, 4, 34
Arizona Highways, Flickr presence of, 338
Arnold, Matthew, 423
Arth, Marvin, 128
Arthur W. Page Society, 57
Article recall, 521
Artworks
  copyright issues of, 72–73
  distribution of, 205–206
  keeping files of, 205
Asahi beer, 52
Associated Press Stylebook (AP Style), 10–11, 122
Atkins, Charles, 38
Atkinson, Claire, 478
Atlantic City Chamber of Commerce, 103

Attitude change, 504
  measurement of, 517–518
Audience analysis
  benchmark surveys, 517–518
  meeting survey as, 516–517
  for persuasive writing, 42–43
Audio news releases (ANRs), 526
  delivery of, 214
  format of, 212–213
  production of, 214
  types of, 212–213
  use of, 214–215
Aurora Foods, 238
Australian Tourist Commission, 246,
  294
Avon Walk for Breast Cancer, 478,
  480
Awards, as source for publicity, 116

B-rolls, 230, 237–238
  defined, 229, 526
  notification about, 232
  placement of, 230–231
Backgrounders, 171–172, 526
Bacon's Media Directories, 10-11,
  209, 250–251
Baer, Sheri, 230, 231
Bahr, Tim, 225
Baidu, 17
Bandwagon, 50, 55
Banquets
  catering of, 462–464
  cost of, 462–463
  logistics and timing of, 464
  purpose of, 461
Bar charts, 203
Barrie, John, 71
Baskin-Robbins, 113
Bates, Sheron, 453
Baudisch, Paul, 318
Baum Folder Co., 374
BBC, Twitter use by, 341
BBDO, 446
Beardsley, John, 19
Beaufort County (SC), 518–519
Beaupre, Andy, 503
Becca cosmetics, 52
Bechtel, sponsored books by, 450
Behavior change, 504
Beijing Olympics, 40, 55, 81, 106,
  477
Bell Atlantic, 355
Belongers, 37
Benchmark studies, 526
Benchmark surveys, 517–518
Best Buy, 236

Bias, avoiding, 30
Billboards, 447–448
Bios, 526
Blendtec, 112
Blogger.com, 323, 327
Bloglines, 325
Blogosphere, 305, 327
Blogpulse, 332
Blogs, 51, 322
  advantages of, 326, 327
  corporate, 327–328
  defined, 526
  employee, 330
  monitoring content of, 513, 514
  pitching to, 155, 276
  privacy issues of, 68–69
  responding to, 332–333
  rise of, 326
  third-party, 330–332
  tips for writing, 327
Blogster.com, 327
Bloom, Orlando, 52
Blue Rhino, 109
Boatfield, Jane, 107
Body
  of advertisement, 445
  of feature, 178–179
  of news release, 131–133
Boggiato Produce, 170
Boggs, Rich, 289
Boilerplate, 133, 526
Bond paper, 375
Bonner & Associates, 61
Book paper, 375
Bookers, 241, 526
Booklets, 370
Books, sponsored, 450
Boorstin, Daniel, 103
Booths, exhibit, 474–475
Borders Books, 106
Boston Beer Company, 146, 173
Bosworth, Kate, 52
Botsworth, Courtney, 500
Bowen, David, 322
Bowling Green State University, 173
BP, advertising by, 439
Bragg, Lynn, 321
Brainstorming, 105, 526
Branching, 310
Branding, 47, 526
Brandon, Michael, 360
Bratman, Fred, 378
Breast Cancer Awareness Week, 95
Briefing book, 290, 291
Briefing papers, 400
Briggs & Stratton, 111

Bristol paper, 375
Britannica Ultimate Reference Suite,
  9
Broadcast fax, 270
Broadcasting & Cable, 15
Brochures, 369–370
  cost of, 378
  design of, 372
  in direct mailing, 434–435
  editing of, 353
  evaluation of, 519–522
  format of, 373
  ink and color choice for, 376–377
  layout for, 373
  paper choice for, 373–375
  planning for, 370–371
  printing of, 377–378
  research for, 372
  tips for putting together, 372–373
  typefaces for, 375–376
  writing for, 371
Brookings Institution, 182
Brooks, Kelly, 150
Broom, Glen, 2
Broward County Public Schools, web-
  site of, 315
Brown, Adam, 276
Brown, Janelle, 300
Brown, Melissa, 405
Browsers, Web, 17, 526
  future of, 345
Bucktold, Tom, 149
Budget, compiling, 497–498
Buffett, Jimmy, 110
Buick, 52
Bulk fax, 270, 526
Bulldog Reporter, 12, 13
Bulletin boards, 324
Bumper stickers, 448
Bureau of Alcohol, Tobacco, and
  Firearms, 87, 526
Bureau of Engraving and Printing,
  Webcast of, 321
Burger King, 245
Burke, Sbonali, 512
Burns, Heather, 383
BurrellesLuce, 12, 251, 508, 511
Burson, Harold, 4
Business, knowledge of, 3
Business letters, 397
Business Wire, 224, 260, 263
  news releases of, 136
Butter, Bob, 378
Butterball Turkey, 94
Buttons, advertising, 448
Butzgy, Michael, 22, 310

Calabro, Sara, 446
CALCUSSA, 449
California Association of Winegrowers, 111
California Avocado Commission, 484
California Pharmacists Association, 116
California Prune Board, 517
California Strawberry Advisory Board, 44
Camera-ready
    art, 264
    defined, 526
    layout, 165
Campbell, Naomi, 478
Campbell Soup, 83
Canadian Tourist Commission, 113
Cantelmo, Daniel, 150, 269
Cantwell, Arden, 379
Caplets, John, 444, 445
Captions
    defined, 526
    photo, 200–202
Card stacking, 55
CARE World Hunger Campaign, 432
Carliner, Kathy, 113
Cartier, MySpace profile of, 334
Carver, Benedict, 277
Case studies, 168–169
    defined, 526
    writing, 169
    technique of, 49
Cash, Johnny, 110
Catering
    of banquets, 462–464
    of meetings, 461
CBS, 276
Celebratory speech, 410
Celebrities
    hiring for event, 479–480
    and source credibility, 44, 52
Celebrity Access, 480
Celebrity Source, 479, 480
Cell phones
    future of, 345
    proliferation of, 306
    text messages on, 340
Centers for Disease Control and Prevention, 512
Chabria, Anita, 57, 107
Champagne Wine Information Bureau, 292
Chan, Karen, 474
Chan, Tract, 513
Channel, of communication, 36
Channeling, 42, 526

Charisma, as factor in credibility, 43
Charmin tissue event, 453, 478, 479
Charts, creating, 203–204
Chase, Chevy, 109
Cheapflights.com, 109
Chemical Bank of New York, privacy suit against, 67
Chevron, 39
    conservation awards of, 464, 465
Chiagouris, Larry, 109
Child and Family Services of New Hampshire, 103
Children's Defense Fund, 222
Children's Hospital of New York-Presbyterian, advertising by, 444
Childress, Kate, 446
China
    attitudes toward, 39, 40, 55
    Internet use in, 17
Chocolate Manufacturers Association, Webcast of, 321
Christie's, 239
Christmas, 94
Cincinnati Gas & Electric, 420
Cingular, 243
Cisco, 259, 458
    backgrounder use by, 172–173
    blogging policy of, 330
    privacy policy of, 69
    trademark suit of, 80
    Twitter use by, 340
    website ROI of, 319
Cision, 209, 210, 250–251, 508, 510
Clapper, Bill, 252
Clarity, of writing, 21, 24
    importance of, 46
Clark, Roy Peter, 278
Clarkson University, Webcast of, 321
Clear Channel, sponsored books by, 450
Clinton, Hillary, 40
Clip art, 204, 365, 526
Clippings, 75, 102, 299
    computer analysis of, 511
Closed-circuit television, 322
Cloze procedure, 521
CNN, Twitter use by, 341
Coated paper, 375
Coca-Cola, 47, 98
    annual report of, 380
    product placement of, 243
Cocktail parties, 465–466
Cody, Steve, 330
Cognitive dissonance, 38–39
Cohen, Susan, 76
Coleman camping equipment, 243

Colgan, Terry, 319
Colleague spam, 388
College of American Pathologists, 226, 228
Collins, Jennifer, 478
Collins, Thomas, 56–57
Color
    tips for using, 364
    use in brochures, 376–377
Columbia Journalism Review, 15
Comcast, Twitter use by, 340
Committee meetings, 454
    assessment of, 455
    complaints about, 454
    guidelines for, 454
Communication
    elements of, 35–37
    in public relations, 1
    theories of, 37–41
Communication facilitators, 2
Communication technicians, 2
Communication World, 13
Communications Briefings, 13
Community calendars, 245–246
Community for Creative Nonviolence v. Reid, 73
Comparison, in writing, 29
Computer
    choosing, 7–8
    components of, 8
    cost of, 8
    importance of, 6–7
Condon, George, 270
Conflict, creating news, 100–101
Consolino, Ron, 128
Conspiracy, 62
Consumer Electronics Show (CES), 453, 474, 475
Contact information, in news release, 126
Content analysis, 504, 519–520
Contests, 108–109
Context, of communication, 46
Conti, Donna St. Jean, 170
Contract, with photographer, 198
Conventions, 470
    administration of, 472
    attendance at, 472
    exhibits at, 471
    e-mail invitations and reservations for, 473
    facilities and equipment for, 471
    location of, 470–471
    program for, 471–473
    recreation during, 472
    timing of, 470

Conversation index, 514
Cook, Dan, 342
Cookies, 319
Coors, social networking promotions of, 334
Copyright
    of art and photography, 72–73, 200
    definitions of, 69–70
    guidelines on, 74
    Internet and, 75
    issues in, 69
    notice and registration of, 70
    and work for hire, 73–74
Copyright Clearance Center, 71
Corbis Corporation, 75
Corley, Carol Anne, 115
Corporate blogs, 327–328
Corporate profiles, 143, 526
Corporate sponsorships, 477
Corporate social responsibility (CSR) reports, 381–382
Cosmetic Executive Women, 52
Cost-effectiveness analysis, 515
Covenant House, 48
Cover paper, 375
Crayola, media kits of, 147, 148
Creamer, Matthew, 508
Credibility, of sources, 43–45
Crisis communication
    news release, 123
    media relations, 300–302
CRO, 116
Cropping, of photos, 199, 526
Cruise Lines International Association, fact sheets of, 143
Crutzen, Paul, 321
CSI: Miami, 243
CU, defined, 229
Cunningham, Ward, 341
A Current Affair, 280
Current events, 3, 15–16
Cury, James, 101
Cut-and-paste, 264
cvent.com, 473
CyberAlert, 332
Cyber media tour, 527
Cytryn v. Cook, 85

Dale-Chall formula, 521
Dallas Museum of Art, centennial of, 107
Danskin, 157–158
Darden, Michael, 93
Darfur, 49
Databases, electronic, 18–19, 20
Dateline, of news release, 127–128

Dateline NBC, 63, 280
Davis, Anna Grace, and family, 356–359
Dawson's Creek, 244
Dean, Billy, 490, 491
Debates, 420
Deckers Outdoor Corporation, 77
Decorative typefaces, 375
Defamation, 62-63
    avoiding action for, 65
    basis for awards for, 63
    defenses against, 64
    against public figures, 63
Defense Department, news releases of, 124
Definition, in writing, 29
DeFleur, Melvin, 436
del.icio.us, 317, 323
Dell
    blog entries about, 331
    blogging policy of, 330
Dell Japan, 8, 202
Della Femina, Jerry, 67
DeLorme, Denise, 274
Dennis, Everett, 436
DePalo, Vic, 369
Derelian, Doris, 19
Design
    for brochures, 372
    of print publications, 360–361
Desktop publishing, 382–383
Desktop tours, 289, 527
Desperate Housewives, 243
Detroit, 300th birthday of, 107
Diagrams, creating, 203
DiCaprio, Leonardo, 431
Diffusion and adoption, 40–41
Digg.com, 317, 323
Digital Millennium Copyright Act, 75
Direct mail
    advantages and disadvantages of, 429–430
    audience of, 429
    brochures in, 434–435
    cost of, 429–430
    creating packages for, 430–436
    gifts in, 435–436
    information overload from, 430
    personalization of, 429
    purposes of, 427
    reply card in, 435
    return envelope in, 435
    tips on, 434
    volume of, 428
Direct mail letter
    envelope for, 430–431

    headline and lead paragraph of, 431–432
    postscript of, 432
    tips for writing, 432
    typeface and length of, 432
Disclosure, timeliness of, 85
Discussion groups, 458
Disney, copyright activities of, 70
Disneyland, podcasts of, 342
District of Columbia Housing Authority, 111
Ditka, Mike, 93
Dobens, Christopher, 393
Dr. Seuss, 73, 98
Documentary videos, 246–247
Dodge, 242
Dole Food Company, 488
Dollywood, 292
Domino's, 260
Donahue, Phil, 240
Donor Network of Arizona, 451
Donovan, Ryan, 205
Dow Jones, reprint service of, 72
Dowler, Helen, 188
Dozier, David, 2, 518
DQE, annual report of, 381
Drama, in persuasive writing, 48–49
Dremel, 177
Dub, defined, 229
Dugan, Kevin, 19, 155
Duke Energy, 423
Dummy, 373
Dunst, Kirsten, 52
Duracell, 94
Dutton Children's Books, 75
The Dynamics of Persuasion, 34
Dysart, Joe, 316

E-mail (electronic mail), 527
    advantages and disadvantages of, 256–257
    attitudes towards, 254
    colleague spam, 388
    content of, 390–391
    convention invitations and reservations by, 473
    etiquette of, 391
    format of, 382–383
    for news, 352
    news releases by, 134, 136, 254–257
    origin of, 387
    pervasiveness of, 387
    purpose of, 388
    spam, 256–257, 388
    subject line of, 136, 158

tips for using, 255–256
voice mail as alternative to, 389
E-zines, 368, 527
Early Show, 240
Eckert, Robert, 301
Edelman Trust Barometer, 43
Edelman Worldwide, 446
Edelstein, Jonathan, 86
Editor, role of, 353
Editor & Publisher, 15
Editorial boards, meetings with, 294
  reasons for, 295
  tips for, 295
  value of, 296
Editorial calendars, 252–253, 527
Editorial plan, 355
Editorial slant, 511, 512
Einstein, Albert, 82
Eisenberg, Daniel, 346
Elasser, John, 68
Electronic databases, 18–19, 20
Electronic media kits (EPKs, e-kits),
    149–150, 527
  advantages of, 150
  example of, 150–151
Electronic wire services, 259–261
  sample news release on, 262
Electronic Arts (EA), 152
Elements of Style, 10
Eli Lilly, 87
Embargo, 125, 126, 424
Emotional appeals, 52–54
Employee blogs, 330
  privacy issues of, 68–69
Employee newsletters, 4
  placement of features in, 180
  privacy issues of, 66–67
  story ideas for, 361
  subjects of, 360
Employees, media inquiries regarding,
    67–68
Encarta, 9
Endorsements, in persuasive writing,
    50-52
Energy Department, U.S., 246
Enron, 62
  SEC action against, 84
Entrepreneur magazine, 80
Entropia, 69
ER, 244
ESAB Welding Products, 508
ET, product placement in, 243
Ethical considerations
  in persuasion, 56–58
  in photography retouching, 199–200
  on press tours, 294

Ethos, 34
Evaluation. *See* Measurement
Events
  banquets, 461–465
  characteristics of, 453
  cocktail parties, 465–466
  conventions, 470–473
  corporate sponsorships, 477
  monitoring attendance of, 515–516
  open houses, 466–468
  planning for, 454
  plant tours, 466, 467, 470
  promotional, 477–481
  receptions, 466
  trade shows, 473–476
Evergreens, 232, 264, 527
eWatch, 325
Examples
  in persuasive writing, 50
  in writing, 29
Excel (Microsoft), 7
Exhibits, trade show, 474–475
Expert prescribers, 2
Expertise, as factor in credibility, 43,
    44
ExxonMobil, 55, 86, 517
Eye contact, 414

Facebook, 322, 323
  using, 333–334
Fact sheets
  defined, 141, 527
  types and examples of, 142–144
Factiva, 508
Fair comment
  defense, 64
  privilege, 527
Fair Disclosure Regulation (Reg FD),
    85–86
Fair use, 71
Fam (familiarization) trips, 293, 527
Family Features, 267
FAQ (frequently asked questions),
    527
Fax
  bulk, 279, 526
  on demand (FOD), 270, 527
  news distribution via, 269–270
Fear arousal, 54
Fearn-Banks, 300
Feature lead, 131
Feature Photo Service, 190, 268
Feature story
  asking questions for, 164–165
  body, 177–178
  components of, 265

contrasted with news release,
    163–164
  cost of distributing, 267
  defined, 527
  example of, 167
  headline of, 175–177
  lead of, 177–178
  parts of, 175–179
  photos and graphics in, 179
  placement of, 180-181, 264–267
  planning of, 164–165
  sample of, 266
  skills required for writing, 164
  summary of, 178
  tips for writing, 176
  types of, 168-175
  writing and releasing, 165–166
Feder, Barnaby, 204
Federal Communications Commis-
    sion, 86–87
Federal Express, website of, 308
Federal Trade Commission, 82–84,
    527
FedEx®, 78, 269
  annual report of, 379
Fedler, Fred, 274
FeedShow, 326
Festinger, Leon, 38
Field Museum, 142, 172, 175,
    245–246
Filler, 527
Filoli Estate, 177
Financial relations advertising, 441
Fireman's Fund, 246
First Act, 93
First Amendment, 64
  scope of, 82
Fisher Nuts, 174
Fleishman-Hillard, 446
Flickr.com., 323
  corporate use of, 338
Flyers, 370
Focus groups, 522
Fonts, 375–376
Food blogs, 333
Food and Drug Administration
    (FDA), 87, 527
Food & Wine, 110
Forbes, Charlotte, 353
Ford, Henry, 243
Ford & Harrison, blog of, 328, 329
Ford Motor Company, 214, 294
Form letters, 395
Format
  of news release, 120–121
  of print publications, 361–362

Forrester Research, 315
Fouladi, Maryam, 358
Fox News, 80
FPG International, 72
Framing, 39
Franken, Al, 80
Franklin, Benjamin, 428
Freedom of speech, 64, 82
Freehand, 383
Freeman, Jana, 359
Friedman, Marsha, 241
Friedman, Michael, 241
Friedman, Rob, 410
Friskies PetCare Company, 488
Frito-Lay, 44
Fry formula, 521
Fujitsu, Wiki use by, 341
The Future of the Mass Audience, 347
Fund-raising letter, 432

Gallina, Emil, 232
Gandy, O. H., 274
Gantt charts, 496–497
Gap stores, 300
Garcia, Mario, 377
Garcia, Tonya, 504, 514
Gates, Bill, 390, 474
Gates Foundation, 518
Gatorade, 52
Gay, semantics of, 47
Gebbie Press All-in-One Directory,
    12
Geddie, Tom, 360
Gender-neutral language, 30
General Electric, 517
General Mills, sponsored books by,
    450
General Motors
    defamation suit by, 63, 281
    FastLane blog of, 328
    Wiki use by, 341
Genesis One Computer Corporation,
    defamation suit against, 64
Genkin, Larry, 327
German National Tourist Office, 234
Gerstner, John, 259
Gestures, in speechmaking, 413
Getting It Printed, 371
Geyser Peak, 87
    in direct mail, 435–436
    to journalists, 299
Gillette, 52, 116
Gilman Ciocia, 92
Gimmicks, in news releases, 277–278
Gladwell, Malcolm, 16
Glass, Matt, 481

Glaxo, 87
    advertising by, 442
Glenn, John, 478
Glittering generalities, 56
Globe tabloid, 280
Glossary, 526–530
GM FastLane blog, 328
Gobbledygook, 26–27
Godwin, Peter, 109
Going for Great!, 354, 377
Gold's Gym, 170
Goldberg, Betsy, 283
Goldsborough, Julie Story, 19
Golin/Harris, 446
Good Morning America, 240
Goodman, Wanda, 340
Goodyear Tire & Rubber Co, 338
Google, 17, 108, 133, 306, 317, 332
Google Presentations, 415
Google Reader, 325
Gossett, Steven, 175
Graham, Andrea, 294
Graham, Karen, 115
Graphs, 203
Grates, Gary, 351, 352
Great Date, 168
Greenpeace, 48, 518
Gregory, Dorian, 449
Grey's Anatomy, 244
Greyhound Friends, Inc., 144, 145
Gross impressions, 509
Grosse Pointe News, 124
Group meetings
    advance planning for, 456
    catering of, 461
    facilities and equipment for,
        458–459
    greeter for, 460
    invitations for, 459
    location of, 457–458
    name tags for, 460
    post-event tasks for, 457
    program for, 460–461
    registration for, 459–460
    same-day planning for, 456
    seating for, 458
    speeches at, 460
Grove, Teri, 294
Grunig, James, 43
GuideOne Insurance, 377
Guinness Book of World Records,
    107, 112, 113
Gunderson, Amy, 159
Gunderson, Glen, 80
Gunning formula, 521
Guth, David, 494

H&R Block
    Second Life presence of, 339
    YouTube promotions of, 335
Hacker, Diana, 10
Haddix, Carol, 166
Haiken, Beth, 380, 412
Hakone Gardens, 459
Hall, Eric, 252
Hall, Julie, 108
Hallahan, Kirk, 39, 43
Hallowe'en, 93
Hammons, Rich, 93
Handbills, 370
Handspring, Inc., 290
Hard Copy, 280
Harding, Ralph, 157
Harlequin Books, 277
Harrington, Ed, 96
Harris, Joshua, 93
Harry Potter books, 106
Harry Walker Agency, 462
Hatch, Eric, 23
Hattersley, Michael, 390
Hauss, Deborah, 200
Hawaii Tourism Board, 238
Hawking, Stephen, 261
Hayek, Selma, 52
Haynes, Jim, 486
Hazelton, Vincent, 6
Headline
    of advertisement, 444–445
    caveats about, 366–367
    of direct mail letter, 431
    of feature, 175–177
    of news release, 126–127
    tips for writing, 365–366
Health care reform, 442, 444
Health & Human Services Depart-
    ment, advertising by, 443
Health Museum (Houston), 358, 359
Heath, Robert, 4, 34, 56, 58
Heckel Consumer Adhesives, 99
Heinrich, Aaron, 276
Helitzer, Melvin, 160
Helm, Janet, 333
Henry, Reg, 95
Hensley, Ruth Ann, 356
Hernandez, Nick, 312
Herrington, Jeff, 311
Hershey's
    centennial of, 107, 113, 174
    product placement by, 243
Hettinger, Mary, 352
Hewlett-Packard, 144
    annual report of, 381
    exhibit booths of, 474

online newsroom of, 166–167,
168–169, 258
website ROI of, 319
Hicks, Nancy, 110
Hidden Valley Ranch, 113, 145, 213
Hierarchy of needs, 41
Higbee, Ann, 296
Hill, Eric, 253
Hill, Michael, 238
Himler, Peter, 275
Hirsch, Alan, 125
Historical pieces, 173–175, 527
History Channel, 246
Hit, defined, 318, 527
Hoffman, Barbara, 241
Hollywood Walk of Fame, 116
Holtz, Shel, 152, 311–312, 319, 320,
340
Home Depot, 94
Homeownership Preservation Founda-
tion, 92, 216–217
Hometowners, 96, 527
Homewood Suites, 170, 171
Honeywell, 49
advertising by, 441
Hong Kong Tourist Board, 94
Hoover Institution, 182
Hospitality suites, at trade shows, 475
Hovland, Carl, 55
Howard, Carole, 345
HpNow, 369
Huffy, 178
Human interest stories, 99–100
Humane Society of the United States,
advertising by, 442
Hungry Jack, 518
Hunt, Todd, 436
Hype, 275–276
avoiding, 29
defined, 527
Hyperlinks, 316–317

Iacono, Erica, 466
IBM, 194, 196, 259
blogging policy of, 331
Second Life presence of, 69, 339
website of, 308
ICI Pharmaceuticals, 95
Illinois Department of Public Health,
506
Illustrations, in publications, 365
Illustrator software, 204, 361
Image building, 438–439
Imagery, 25–26
Implied consent, 527
Impressions, 527

In-Flight Phone, 292
Inactive public, 43
InDesign, 204, 361, 377, 383
*Indiana Jones and the Kingdom of the
Crystal Skull*, 334
Infographics, 179, 527
creating, 203–204
Informal lead, 130–131
Information Technology (IT) depart-
ments, 320, 527
Informational headline, 175
Informative speech, 410
Ink, choice of, 377
Inside Children, 5
Inside Edition, 280
Insider trading, 61, 85
Institute for Public Relations Re-
search, 510
Insurance Institute for Highway
Safety, 233
Intel, 116, 133–134
news releases of, 134
website of, 314
Intel Science Talent Search, 108, 191,
202
International Association of Business
Communicators (IABC), 13
International Olympic Committee, 40
International Public Relations Associ-
ation (IPRA), 15
International Trademark Association,
79
Internet, 14
browsers for, 17
components of, 305
history of, 305–306
monitoring of, 512–514
prevalence of, 7, 306, 345
and public relations, 6
search engines for, 17–18
See also Websites; World Wide
Web (Web)
Internet Explorer (Microsoft), 17
Internet Media Directory, 11, 274
Interpersonal communications, 386
guidelines for, 386–387
Interviews, press
preparation for, 282
tips for, 283–285
Into the Fire, 246
Intranet, 527
characteristics of, 369
for news, 352
Invasion of privacy, 62, 65
circumstances of, 66–69
Inverted pyramid structure, 132

Investor relations advertising, 441
iPhone, 80
Iraq, U.S. intervention in, 56
Issue placement, 244
Iwata, Satoru, 182

J. Walter Thompson, defamation suit
against, 63
Jack In The Box, 302
advertising by, 444
Jack O'Dwyer's Newsletter, 13
Jackson, Amy, 319
Jackson, Maggie, 390
Jargon, avoiding, 24, 26–27
Jenkins, Carri, 199
JetBlue, 80, 300
Jewett, Sally, 237
Jobs, Steve, 43, 421
Joe Boxer Corporation, 293
Johannesen, Richard, 57
Johnson, George P., 476
Johnson & Johnson, annual report of,
379, 380
Journal of Public Relations Research,
13
Journalism
attitudes towards, 279
audience of, 5
channels for, 5
correcting errors in, 280
function of, 3
relations with public relations,
272–275
tabloid, 279–280
Jowett, Garth, 55
JPEGs, 528
July 4, 93
Junk mail. *See* Direct mail
Junkets, 293–294
ethical issues of, 294

Kalivo, 513
Kalm, Nick, 158, 159
Kansas City Health Department, 45
Katonah, 80
Katz, Darren, 331
Kay, John, 109
Keller, Scot, 341
Kelly, J. Ronald, 19
Kendall, Robert, 101
Kendig, Karen, 462
Keogh, Scott, 51
Kerin, Ray, 272
Kidman, Nicole, 52
Kimberly-Clark, 49, 93, 108
King, Ben, 326, 328

Kirkpatrick, Ron, 423
Klepper, Michael, 102, 157
Knightley, Keira, 44
Knoth, Audrey, 95
Knutsson, Kurt, 230
Koch, Jim, 146, 173
Kodak, 44
Koenig, Mark, 84
Koop, Everett, 95
Korbel Champagne Cellars, 145–146,
    170, 239, 509
Kournikova, Anna, 287
Kronholz, June, 278
Kryptonite Company, blog entries
    about, 330–331
Kuchenmeister, Chris, 449

L. L. Bean, website of, 308
L.O.V.E. project, 493, 494
Labor Day, 93
Lafayette College, privacy suit
    against, 67
Lake, Matt, 278
Lancaster, Hal, 104
Langert, Bob, 328
Larry King Live, 115
Lasky, Michael, 83
Late Show with David Letterman,
    115
Law & Order, 244
Lawry's Seasoned Salt, 44
Layout, 363, 382
    for brochure, 373
    tips for, 363–364
    traditional, 365
Lazarsfeld, Robert, 346
Lead paragraph
    of direct mail letter, 431–432
    errors in, 129
    of feature, 177–178
    of news release, 128
    types of, 130–131
Lead sentence, of article, 367–368
Leaflets, 370
LeBaron, Ted, 368
Legal issues
    conspiracy, 62
    copyright, 69–75
    defamation 62–65
    examples of, 61–62
    invasion of privacy, 65–69
    regulatory agencies, 82–87
    trademark infringement, 76–82
    working with lawyers, 88
Lennon, John, 82
Leopard operating system, 7–8

Lerch, Marie, 404
Lesly, Philip, 42
Letterhead, of news release, 125
Letters
    content of, 396–397
    format of, 397–398
    purpose of, 395–396
    tips for writing, 396
    types of, 395
Letters to the editor (LTEs), 184–186,
    528
Levi Strauss, 420
Levine, Lori, 95
Levy, Ron, 175, 176, 283
Lexis/Nexis, 18
Libel, 62–63
Lies and Lying Liars Who Tell Them,
    80
Line drawings, 204
Linear writing, 310
LinkedIn, 333
Lipinski, Lynn, 154–155
Lisook, Adam, 479
Lissauer, Michael, 137, 263, 348
List Services Corp., 428
Listservs, 15, 324, 325, 528
Lloyd's of London, employee newslet-
    ter of, 361
Local interest, 96–97
Log Cabin Syrup, 238
Logitech, 174
Logos, 34
Lokey, Lorry, 122, 133
Lopez, Jennifer, 108, 478
Lord of the Rings, 93
Los Angeles Fire Department, Twitter
    use by, 341
Lowe, Doug, 415
Lowery, Joan, 26, 27
Lunch dates, with journalists, 299
Lunchroom seating, 458
Lynn, Janet, 260

M&Ms, 243
MacDonald, Gordon, 313
MacLaine, Shirley, 478
Macworld, 453, 475
MacWrite, 7, 361
Madonna, 52
Magapapers, 361, 528
Magazine shows, 242
Magazines
    circulation of, 346, 351
    described, 361
    placement of features in, 180–181
    role of, 352

Mailing houses, 269, 528
Management
    knowledge of, 3
    role in public relations, 2
Maney, Kevin, 415
March of Dimes, 226, 227
Marchini, Fredrick, 317
Margaritis, Bill, 503
Margins, 120–121
Marie, Constance, 98
Marine Mammal Center, 52, 54
Marketwire, 138, 260
Markman, Steve, 420
Marsh, Charles, 45, 494
Martin, Jennifer, 257
Martinique, 108
Maslow, Abraham, 41
Master Lock, sponsored books by,
    450
MasterCard, 47
Masthead, 363, 528
Mat releases, 264
Mateas, Margo, 158
Mattel, 39, 301, 486
Mazur, Geri, 509
McCafferty Interests, 182
McCall, Ronald, 423
McCormick Place, 471
McDonalds, 47
    blog of, 328
    social networking promotions of,
    334
McFarland, Ruth, 252
McGruff, 234
McGuire, Craig, 119, 137, 152, 261
McQuillian, Larry, 299
MCU, defined, 229
Measurement, 1
    advertising value equivalency,
    509–511
    advisory boards and focus groups
    for, 522
    of article recall, 521
    of audience action, 517–518
    of audience attitudes, 517–518
    of audience awareness, 516-517
    content analysis, 519–520
    of cost per person, 515
    establishing objectives, 506–507
    of event attendance, 515–516
    importance of, 503–504
    of Internet exposure, 512–514
    levels of, 505
    of media impressions, 509
    of message exposure, 507–509
    methods of, 504

of newsletters and brochures, 519–522
of production and distribution, 507
purposes of, 504
readability, 521–522
readership surveys, 520–521
reporting on, 522–523
research methods, 505–506
systematic tracking, 511
Mechanical, defined, 528
Media
choice of, 36
uses of, 37–38
See also Internet; New media; Traditional media
Media advisory (media alert), 141, 224, 528
examples of, 145–146
Media databases, 249–251
online, 251–252
updating of, 252
Media gatekeepers, 91, 92, 275, 528
and local interest stories, 96–97
Media impressions, measurement of, 509
Media kits
compiling, 147–149
defined, 141, 146, 528
electronic, 149–151
examples of, 146–147
See also Press kits
Media mentions, 506
measurement of, 507–509
Media placement specialists, 2
Media relations
areas of friction, 275–281
checklist for, 297–288
in crisis situation, 300–302
editorial board meetings, 294–296
etiquette for, 298–300
fam trips, 293
importance of, 272–273
junkets, 293–294
media tours, 289–290
as mutual dependency, 273–275
news conferences, 285–289
press interviews, 282–285
previews and parties, 291–293
at trade shows, 475–476
Media tours
briefing book for, 290, 291
case study of, 290
described, 289
to generate coverage, 289
as relationship builder, 289–290
PR role in, 290

satellite, 115, 223, 235–239
Media Week, 15
Mediasphere, 305
Medicare, 47
Medtronic, 143
Meet the Press, 115
Meetings
characteristics of, 453
group, 456–461
planning for, 454, 456–457
shortcomings of, 454
staff and committee, 454–455
Mega Linkage List, 317
Memoranda
content of, 394
format of, 394–395
purpose of, 393–394
Merton, Robert, 346
Message, of communication, 35–36
Message acceptance, 504
Message dissemination, 504
measures of, 516–517
Message exposure, 504, 506
measurement of, 507–509
Metro California Media Directory, 11
Metro Editorial Services, 267
Meyers, Peter, 17
Mickey Mouse Law, 70
Microsoft, 442, 474, 517–518
Microsoft Office, 7, 202, 416
Microsoft Publisher, 383
Microsoft search engine (MSN), 17, 317
Middleman, Ann, 109
Milana, Paolina, 137
Miller, Henry, 181
Miller, Michael, 29
Miller, Stephen, 156
Mindbridge Software, 277
Minkalis, Annette, 238
Minnis, John, 124
Minolta, 441
Minter, Bobby, 355
Misappropriation of personality, 67, 81–82, 528
Miss America pageant, 103
Miss Universe, 94
Mission statement, 354
Mitternight, Helen, L., 311
Modu, 113
Monitoring services, 508
Montaigne, Fen, 281
Monterey Aquarium, Flickr presence of, 338
Moon, Thom, 215
Moon, Yung, 453

Morgan Hotel (San Antonio), 4
Morgan-Stanley Children's Hosp 444
Moroney, Phyllis, 158
Morton, Linda, 96
Mossberg, Walt, 101
Mother's Day, 95
Mothers Against Drunk Driving (MADD), 50
Moultrie News Generation, 215
Mourning, Alonzo, 96
Mug shots, 193, 528
Multimedia news releases, 136–137
example of, 138
future of, 137, 139
tips for creating, 137
Muse News, 358, 359
MyEdcals, 253
MySpace, 306, 322, 323, 513
using, 333–334
Mystrength.org, 449

Nabisco E, 369
Naked Juice Company, 195
National Asparagus Month, 95
National Association of Engine and Boat Manufacturers, 247
National Association of Potato Growers, 164
National Campaign to Prevent Teen Pregnancy, 244
National Cattlemen's Beef Association, 266, 267
National Education Association, 98, 192
National Enquirer, 280
National Football League, 104
National Foundation for Infectious Diseases, 218–219, 221
National Heart Lung and Blood Institute, 219–220, 221
National Onion Association, 266, 267
National Organization on Fetal Alcohol Syndrome, 234
National Paint Month, 95
National Pitch Book, 12
National Pork Producers Council, 238
National Potato Board, 512
National Resource Defense Council (NRDC), 39
National Safety Council, 52
National Turkey Federation, 37, 41
National Wildlife Federation, magpaper of, 361, 362
Natural Resources Defense Council, 97–98, 431, 432, 433

against, 63,

...14
...ussell, 347
...epartment of Health and
Services, 446
...ia
...rasted with traditional media,
307
See also Internet; World Wide Web
(Web)
New York Fashion Week, 276
*New York Publicity Outlets
Directory*, 11
New York State Canal System, 488
New York Times Stylebook, 11
New York Times v. Tasini, 73
New York Yankees, defamation suit
against, 64
Newman, Andrew, 278
Newman, Marc, 305–306
Newness, and publicity, 101
News
external sources of, 102–103
internal sources of, 101–102
making, 103–107. *See also* Publicity
News conferences, 285
followup after, 288
indications for, 285–286
invitations to, 287
location for, 286–287
running of, 287–288
scheduling of, 286
teleconferences and Webcasts,
288–289
News distribution, 249
choosing a channel for, 255
costs of, 263–264
via e-mail, 254–257
editorial calendars and, 252–253
via electronic wire service,
259–261, 262
via fax, 269–270
via feature placement firms,
264–265, 267
via mail, 268–269
maximizing, 261
media choice, 249
media databases, 249–252
via online newsroom, 257–259
tip sheets and, 253–254
News feature. *See* Feature story

News feeds, 239
News release, 1, 2, 528
audio, 212–215
of bad news, 123
body of, 131–133
contact information on, 126
danger of hype and gimmicks in,
275–278
dateline of, 127–128
don'ts of, 129
electronic dissemination of,
134–136, 254–266
headline of, 126–127
importance of, 118
lead paragraph of, 128–131
letterhead of, 125
of local news, 124
multimedia, 136–139
organization description in,
133–134
paper for, 120
parts of, 124–134
physical presentation of, 120–121
planning, 119–120
on radio, 209–212
for speaking engagement, 424–425
speech as, 425
for television, 224
timing of, 125
tips for writing, 135
types of, 122–124
value of, 119
video (VNR), 224, 225–233
NewsCom, 190, 206, 267–268
Newsday, 72
NewsGator, 326
Newsgroups, 15, 324
monitoring content of, 513
Newsletters
constituencies of, 353
consumer, 5
design elements of, 358–359
editing of, 353
electronic, 368–369
employee, 4, 360, 361
evaluation of, 519–522
privacy issues of, 66–67
Newsmagazines, as source, 16
Newsom, Doug, 486
Newspaper/Magazine Directory, 11
Newspapers
circulation of, 346
placement of features in, 180,
264–267
as source for current events, 16
NewsTrak, 508

NewsUSA, 267
Nichols, Barbara, 460
Nielsen, Jakob, 314
Nike, 515
annual report of, 382
blog entries about, 332
endorsements of, 52
slogans of, 47
Swoosh of, 46
trademark issues of, 79
Nintendo, 182
Nissan, advertising of, 448
Nizer, Louis, 410
No-host bar, 528
Noah Was an Amateur, 247
Nolan, Peter, 417
Nonfiction best sellers, as source for
current events, 16
Nonlinear writing, 310, 311
North American Precis Syndicate, 267
Novartis, 44
Novelis, 405, 406
NOW (National Organization for
Women), 47
Numbers, guidelines for using, 29
NYNEX, 355

Oakland Raiders, 61
Oates, David, 154, 488
Obama, Barack, 40, 413
presidential campaign of, 341
Obici, Amedeo, 174
Occidental Petroleum, 247
Ochman, B. L., 136
O'Donnell, Victoria, 55
Odwalla, 487
O'Dwyer's PR Report, 13
Ogilvy PR Worldwide, 61
Oil over the Andes, 247
Olympic Paints and Stains, 44
Olympic rings, 81
Olympics
Beijing, 40, 55, 81, 106
corporate sponsorships of, 477
On cam, defined, 229
One A Day Weight Smart, 62
One Lime Street, 361
Online
monitoring of content, 513
newsletters, 368–369
Online newsroom, 257–259
example of, 166–167, 168–169,
258
Op-ed columns, 102, 528
characteristics of, 184
format of, 184

placement of, 183
purposes and motivations of
   181–182
tips for writing, 183
Open houses, 466
   planning for, 467, 469
Opening paragraph, crafting, 25
Oprah Winfrey Show, 115, 240
Oregon state lottery, 98
Osman, Jack, 157
Outcomes measurement, 506
Outlook (Microsoft), 7
Outputs measurement, 506
Oxfam, 436
Oxford English Dictionary (OED), 9
*Oxford Pocket Dictionary and The-
saurus*, 9

Pacific Gas & Electric, 442
Page impression, 318, 528
Page view, defined, 318
PageMaker, 383
Paine, Katie, 517
Pamphlets, 370
Pan, defined, 229
Panasonic, 193, 194, 474
Panel discussions, 418–419
Paper
   colors of, 120
   folds of, 374
   types of, 375
   weights of, 120, 373–374
Paragraphs, guidelines for writing, 22
Paramount Pictures, 75
   promotions by, 334
Parties, for the press, 292–293
Partnership for a Drug-Free America,
   441
PartyLine, 253–254
Passive audiences, 43
Passive voice, 23
Pathos, 34
Pay for inclusion, 317
Pay-for-position, 317
PC computers, 7
Peachpit Press, Flickr presence of, 338
Pearson, Bob, 69
Pedison, Beth, 404
Pepsi, news releases of, 226
Perloff, Richard, 34
Personal appearances, 115, 239–247
Personal letters, 395
Personality profiles, 173
   defined, 528
   tips for writing, 174
Persuasion

communication and, 35–41
   ethics of, 56–58
   and propaganda, 55–56
   research on, 38
   rhetoric, 34
   techniques of, 54–55
Persuasive speech, 410
Persuasive writing
   audience analysis for, 42–43
   barriers to, 51
   contents and structure of, 48–54
   as spur to action, 48
   tips for, 42, 51
   tools for, 44–47
PETA, 277
PETCO, 105
Peterson, Ken, 338
PetSmart, 112
Pexton, Laura, 338
Pfanner, Eric, 334
Pfizer, annual report of, 380
Pharmaceutical Research and Manufacturers of America, 61
Philip Morris, defamation suit by, 65
Philips Norelco, 177
   fact sheets of, 143, 144
   research studies of, 171
Philips Roving Reporter, 4
Phipps, Jennie, 184
Photo news releases (PNRs), 200,
   201, 528
Photo session, planning, 198
Photography
   copyright issues of, 72–73
   distribution of, 205–206
   in feature articles, 179
   keeping files of, 205
   outdoor, 195
   privacy issues of, 66–67
   in publications, 365
   See also Publicity photos
PhotoShop, 377, 383
Picas, 376, 528
Pie charts, 203
Pitchmaking, 141, 528
   to bloggers, 155
   by e-mail, 158–159
   followup to, 160
   importance of, 152–154
   opening lines in, 156–157
   preparing the pitch, 156–157
   researching for, 154–156
   by telephone, 158–160
   to television station, 224
   tips for, 157
Pitt, Brad, 94

Plagiarism, 71, 528
Plain folks, propaganda techniqu[e]
Plan, in public relations
   advance, 496
   audience and, 492
   budget, 497–498, 500
   components of, 487
   evaluation of, 498, 500
   importance of, 1
   information analysis, 486
   information gathering, 484–486,
      500
   informational objectives of,
      488–489
   motivational objectives of, 489, 492
   situation of, 486–488
   strategy in, 492–493
   submission of, 499
   tactics in, 494
   timing in, 494–495
   written, 483
Planned Parenthood, 431
Plant tours, 466
   planning for, 467, 470
Planters Peanuts
   centennial of, 107, 174
   media kits of, 147, 148
Plast World, 177
Please Don't Do That, 10
Plugs, 242, 528
A Pocket Style Manual, 10
Podcasts, 306, 323, 528
   corporate use of, 342–343
   cycle of, 344
   growth of, 344
   tips for producing, 343
Pogue, David, 153, 156, 324
Points, 376
Political correctness, 30–31
   semantics of, 47
Polls, 109–110
   persuasive use of, 49–50
Porsche, 243
Port Discovery, 515
Porter Novelli, 446
Position papers, 400
Post-It® Notes, 77
Posters, advertising, 448, 450
Postman, Joel, 341
Posture, in speechmaking, 413
PowerPoint (Microsoft), 7, 415
   tips for using, 416–418
PR News, 13
PR Newswire, 260, 263–264
PR/Newswire Ewatch, 332
PR Reporter, 13

sample article from, 356–359
Promotional events, 477–478
  celebrities at, 478–480
  liability insurance for, 480–481
  permits for, 481
  planning and logistics for, 480
Promotional items, 451
Propaganda, techniques of, 55–56
Propaganda and Persuasion, 55
Proposals, 398
  components of, 399–401
  purpose of, 399
ProQuest Newsstand, 18
Protests, as source of publicity, 114–115
Proximity, and publicity, 97
Prudential, sponsored books by, 450
Pseudoevent, defined, 103, 529
Public domain, 70
Public figures, defamation laws regarding, 63
Public relations
  and marketing, 493
  attitudes towards, 278–279
  channels of, 5–6
  components of, 1–2
  definitions of, 4
  dissemination of, 507
  evaluation of, 503–523
  Internet and, 6, 305–350 *passim*
  knowledge of, 3
  legal issues in, 61–88
  media relations, 272–301
  multicultural issues in, 36–37
  news distribution, 249–270
  planning for, 486–500
  production of, 507
  purpose of, 35
  reliance of media on, 273–274
  reliance on media of, 274–275
  roles in, 2
Public Relations Quarterly, 13
Public Relations Review, 13
Public Relations Society of America (PRSA), 13, 15, 315
Public Relations Strategist, 13
Public service advertising, 441–442
Public service announcements (PSAs)
  characteristics of, 217–218
  defined, 215–216, 528
  distribution of, 221
  effectiveness of, 216–217
  format of, 218–219
  production of, 220–221
  sounds added to, 219–220
  for television, 233–234
  tips for producing, 222

  use of, 221
Publicist
  audience of, 5
  defined, 91
  objectives of, 3–4
  persuasive role of, 34–35
  role of, 2
  skills of, 91
  tools of, 6-16
Publicity
  brainstorming for, 105
  celebrities aiding in, 94–95
  conflict in, 100–101
  contests, 108–109
  creating news, 103–107
  defined, 91
  finding news, 101–103
  human interest in, 99–100
  local appeal in, 96–97
  newness in, 101
  obstacles to, 91–92
  privacy issues in, 67–68
  significance of, 97–98
  special events in, 105–116
  timeliness of, 92–93
  tips for creating, 104
  unusualness of, 98
Publicity photos
  action in, 192–193
  camera angle for, 193–194
  captions for, 200–202
  color in, 196
  composition of, 191–192
  cost of, 196
  cropping and retouching of, 199
  desirable characteristics of, 188–196
  distribution of, 267–268
  ethical considerations regarding, 199–200
  finding a photographer for, 197–198
  importance of, 188–189
  lighting and timing of, 194–196
  photo session for, 199
  scale of, 193
  subject matter of, 190–191
  technical quality of, 189–190
  tips for shooting, 189, 197
Publics, 36, 529
Publisher (Microsoft), 7, 361
Pull concept, 315
Purina, podcasts of, 342, 343
Purpose, for writing, 19, 21
Putka, Gary, 273
Putnam Investments, advertising by, 441

  ion for, 282
  283–285
  ts, 141, 146, 528
  npiling, 147–149
  electronic, 149–151
  examples of, 146–147
  See also Media kits
Press release. *See* News release
Press rooms, 475–476
Previews, press, 291–293
The Price is Right, 243
Priest, Joseph, 28
Print publications
  advantages of, 352
  design of, 360–361
  editorial plan for, 355
  as feeder to Web, 352–353
  format of, 361–362
  headlines of, 365–367
  layout of, 363–365
  lead sentences of, 367–368
  mission statement for, 354
  tips for producing, 364
  value of, 351–352
  visuals in, 365
  See also Brochures; Magazines; Newsletters; Newspapers
Printers, choosing, 377
Printers' measurements, 376
Privacy, invasion of, 65–69
Pro-choice, semantics of, 47
Pro-life, semantics of, 47
Problem-solving facilitators, 2
Procter & Gamble, 108, 112, 453, 478, 479
Product demonstrations, 112–113
Product placement, 242
  history of, 243
Product positioning, 528
Product tie-in, defined, 528
Production staff, 2
Professional Photographers of America, 72
Program evaluation. *See* Measurement
Program objectives, 506–507
Program planning. *See* Plan
Promise, 354–355
  mission of, 356

³ 55
  ions, 3

Quark Xpress, 377, 383
Query, for feature story, 166
Quizno's, defamation suit against, 65
Quotes, guidelines for using, 25

Rabin, Phil, 222
Radio
   audio news releases for (ANRs),
      212–215
   audience of, 208, 346
   community calendars on, 245–246
   importance of, 209
   news releases for (RNRs), 209–212
   promotions on, 244–245
   public service announcements on,
      215–222
   tips for using, 215
*Radio Marketing Guide and Fact
   Book for Advertisers*, 209
Radio media tours (RMTs), 222–223,
   529
Radio/TV/Cable Directory, 11
Rafe, Stephen, 284
Ragan, Mark, 366
Ragan Report, 13
Rallies, as source of publicity,
   114–115
Ramapough Lenape Indian Nation,
   80
Rampton, Sheldon, 273, 277
Rand, Paul, 322
Rand McNally, 109, 203
Rape, advertising against, 449
Rayburn, Jay, 6
Reaction releases, 123
Readability, 46
   of newsletters and brochures,
      521–522
   of typeface, 376
Readership surveys, 520–521
Reading, on screen vs. of hard copy,
   310
Receiver, of communication, 36
Receptions, 466
Red Crescent, 46
Red Cross, 46
Redundancy, avoiding and eschewing,
   28
Reebok, employee newsletter of,
   360–361
Reese's Pieces, 243

References, 8–9
   dictionaries, 9–10
   encyclopedias, 9
   Internet Groups and blogs, 15
   media directories, 11–12

professional publications, 13
   stylebooks, 10–11
   websites, 14
Regan, Tim, 327
Regulatory agencies, 82
   Bureau of Alcohol, Tobacco, and
      Firearms, 87
   Federal Communications Commis-
      sion, 86–87
   Federal Trade Commission, 82–84
   Food and Drug Administration, 87
   Securities and Exchange Commis-
      sion, 84–86
Reid, Eric, 338
Reid case, 73
Relief organizations, persuasive writ-
   ing by, 49
Renderings, 203
Reply card, 435
Reporting, distinguished from public
   relations, 3
Requests, monitoring, 514–515
Rescigno, Richard, 153, 156
Research, 1
   for brochures, 372
   sources for, 17–19
   studies, 170–171, 529
   types of, 16–17
Residence Inns, 170–171
Restatement, in writing, 29
Rethinking Tomorrow, 246
Retouching, of photos, 199, 529
Return envelope, 435
Return on investment (ROI)
   defined, 529
   of websites, 319–320
Rewriting, 25
Rex Health Care, 242
Reynolds Aluminum, sponsored
   books by, 450
RFPs (Requests for Proposal), 398,
   529
Rhetoric, 4, 34, 56
*Rhetorical and Critical Approaches to
   Public Relations*, 4
Rice, Ronald, 38
Rich, Frank, 278
Rich, Judith, 104
Risi, Jennifer, 420
Rivera, Zuleyka, 98
Robert's Rules of Order, 455
Robertie, Renee, 103
Rocca, Mo, 236
Rocco, Leonardo, 478
Rock and Roll Hall of Fame, 73
Roddy, Kevin, 335
Rogers, Everett, 40

Rogue websites, 332
Rojo, 326
Rolex, advertising by, 444
Roman Catholic Church, 55
Ronald McDonald House Charities
   233–234
Rosenblum, Mort, 97
Rotary International, 234, 235, 296
   advertising by, 449
Rowling, J. K., 106
RPM, annual report of, 381
RSS (Real Simple Syndication),
   325–326, 528
Ruben, Brent, 436
Rubin, Maureen, 85
Rudman, Rick, 310
Ruiz, Hector, 415, 424
Ruiz, Manny, 137
Rutherford Hill Winery, website of,
   308
Ryan, Michael, 132

Safeway Select Bank, 99
Saddle stitching, 529
St. Hillaire, Karen, 321
St. John, Burton, III, 185
St. Louis Convention & Visitors
   Commission, 126
St. Paul Insurance Company, annual
   report of, 381
Salvation Army, 234
Samansky, Art, 418
San Diego Convention Center, website
   of, 314
San Diego Zoo, 98
San Giacomo, Laura, 234
San Jose State University, 468
Sans serif types, 375
Santa Clara Valley Transit Authority,
   advertising by, 444
Saperstein, Larry, 219
SARS epidemic, 94
Satellite media tours (SMTs), 115,
   223, 529
   content of, 237–238
   cost of, 238–239
   format of, 236–237
   function of, 236
   mechanics of, 236
   origin of, 235
   tips for producing, 237, 238
Saudi Aramco World, 354
Save Darfur Coalition, 114
Scale models, 203
Scharff, Ned, 420
Schmelzer, Randi, 340
Schoengold, Samantha, 157

ptimization (SEO),
ᵕes, 17–18
, 529
ᵕcizing websites on, 317
ᵕ for using, 18
ᵕrchenginewatch.com, 317
ᵕears, 214, 517
Seating, for meetings, 458
Second Life, 323
    corporate presences on, 339–340
    privacy issues of, 69
Securian Dental, 109
Securities and Exchange Commission
    (SEC), 84–86, 529
Seitel, Fraser, 3
Self-interest, appeal to, 45
Semantics, 47
Seminars, 458
Sender, of communication, 35
Sentences
    guidelines for writing, 21
    length of, 45
    structure of, 27
Serif types, 375
Service journalism, 164, 529
Service marks, 76
Sex in the City, 243
SGI, 287
Shaffran, Cliff, 455
Shankman, Peter, 277
Shedd Aquarium
    electronic media kit of, 150–151
    fact sheets of, 142
    news release of, 125
Shell, Adam, 226
Shell Oil, 442
Sheng, Ellen, 290
Shiffer, Claudia, 478
Shipley, David, 183
Shortman, Melanie, 332
Siemens, CSR report of, 382
Sierra Club, 55, 431
Sigal, L. V., 273
Silver Anvil awards, 500, 510–511
*Simmons Study of Media and
    Markets*, 18
Simon, Morton, 66
Sincerity, as factor in credibility, 43

60 Minutes, 280
Skerik, Sarah, 476
Skilling, Jeffrey, 84
Skytel, 515
Slander, 63
Slocan Forest Products, 324
Slogans, 47
Smart media releases (SMRs),
    136–137
    example of, 138
    future of, 137, 139
    tips for creating, 137
Smart phones, 345
Smead Corporation, 170
Smirnoff, YouTube promotions of,
    335
Smokey the Bear, 46
Snail mail, 529
Snell, David, 26
Social media, 254, 322, 529
    aspects of, 323–324
    rise of, 324
    types of, 322–323
Social networking, 334
    monitoring of content, 514
Solberg, Ron, 256
Sony, 230–231
    Blu-ray technology of, 474
Sony Pictures, 83
Sopranos, 243
SOT, defined, 229
Soundbites, 36, 115, 212, 529
Source credibility, 43–45
South Dakota Office of Tourism, text
    message use by, 340
Spacing, 120–121
Spam, 256–257, 388
    news release, 275–278
Spataro, Mike, 333
SPEAK model, 414
Speaker
    introducing, 409
    placement of, 422–423
    researching, 403–404
    training of, 420–421
Speakers' bureaus, 420–421, 529
Special-interest publications, 5
Specialty magazines, 180–181
Speech, freedom of, 64, 82
Speeches
    audience of, 403–404, 406
    brevity of, 412–413
    coaching and rehearsal of, 408–409
    drafting of, 408
    introducing speaker of, 409
    message of, 406

news release about, 424–425
    objective of, 405
    outline of, 407
    publicity before, 424
    settings for, 403
    strategy of, 406
    timeliness of, 412–413
    types of, 410
    visual aids for, 414–418
    word choice for, 407–408
Speechmaking
    focusing on audience in, 410–411,
        412
    focusing on objective in, 410
    focusing on specifics in, 411–412
    gestures and eye contact in,
        413–414
    SPEAK model for, 414
    tips for, 419
Speechwriting
    demand for, 403
    groundwork for, 404–406
    process of, 406–408
    researching the audience and
        speaker, 403–404
    tips for, 419
Spelling, 26
    computer checking of, 28
Spielberg, Steven, 287
Spin doctors, 56, 529
Spinnell, Spencer, 347
Spinning the Web, 312, 314
Spitzer, Eliot, 92–93
Sponsored books, 450
Sponsored communication, 529
Sports Step, 289
Spot announcements, 122-123
Sproul, Tim, 334
Staff meetings, 454
    assessment of, 455
    complaints about, 454
    guidelines for, 454
Stakeholders, 36, 529
Standard Rate and Data Services, 209
Stanton, Edward M., 4
Star tabloid, 280
Starbucks, 193
    website of, 308
StarCite, 473
Starr, Douglas, 425
State Farm Insurance, advertising by,
    444
Statistics, 49
    guidelines for using, 29
Step Reebok, 289
Stereotypes, avoiding, 29–30

Stewart, Joan, 295
Stewart, Jon, 478
Stewart, Martha, 80
Stock footage, 232, 529
Stone, Glen, 151
Story Corps, 80
Storyboard
  defined, 529
  for public service announcement,
    234, 235
  for VNR, 226-227
Straight summary lead, 130
Strategies, defined, 1
Strauss Radio Strategies, 214
Strigel, Gresham, 242
Structure, of news release, 131–132
Strunk, William, 10
Stunts, publicity, 112–113
Sturaitis, Laura, 261
Styli-Style, 112
Subject line, of e-mail news release,
  136, 158
Subway, defamation suit by, 65
Sun Microsystems
  employee blogs of, 330
  privacy policy of, 68
Sun tabloid, 280
Sunkist, 153, 488
  Take a Stand campaign of, 490
Super, defined, 229
Super Bowl, 93, 104, 438, 515
Surveys, 109–110
  to monitor event attendance,
    515–516
  persuasive use of, 49–50
  tips for creating, 111
Survivors, 37
Sustainers, 37
Swatch, 287
Sweetland, Bill, 368
Systematic tracking, 511

T-shirts, 450–451
Tactics, defined, 1–2
Tag paper, 375
Talk shows
  guests on, 241, 242
  product placement on, 240
  radio, 115
  television, 240–241
  tips for appearances on, 241
Talking heads, 237, 529
TCS Daily Science Roundtable, 86
Technorati.com, 15, 323, 332
Telecoms show, 474
Teleconferences, 288–289

Telephone pitch, 158–160
  excessive use of, 298–299
Television
  audience of, 208
  closed-circuit, 322
  documentary videos on, 246–247
  jargon of, 229
  magazine shows on, 242
  pervasiveness of, 223
  public service announcements on,
    233–234
  satellite media tours on, 115, 223,
    234–235
  soundbites for, 36
  as source for trends, 16
  talk shows on, 240–242
  video news releases (VNRs) for,
    224, 225–233
  viewing trends for, 346, 347–348
Television station, organization of,
  223–224
Templates, 363, 529
Tense, present, 24
Terpening, Ed, 514
Terrell, Ken, 355
Testimonials
  in persuasive writing, 50
  in propaganda, 55
Texas Gulf Sulphur, 85
Text paper, 375
Texting, 340
Thalberg, David, 222
Thanksgiving, 94
Theater seating, 458
There.com, 69
Third-party endorsements, 50
3M, 77
Time magazine, 363
Timeliness
  of communication, 46
  of publicity, 92
Tip sheets, 253–254
The Tipping Point, 16
Today, 115, 240
Todorova, Aleksandra, 317
Toll-free numbers, 514
Tommy Hilfiger, 108
Top Ten lists, 110–111
Toyota, 49, 423
  advertising by, 439
  Prius, 52
Tracking, of Website visitors,
  318–319
Trade shows, 473–474
  booths for, 474–475
  hospitality suites at, 475

  press rooms and media relat[.]
    475–476
Trademarks, 76
  capitalization of, 79
  genericization of, 79
  infringement of, 79–80
  protection of, 76–78
  of sports teams, 80–81
Trade-outs, 243
Traditional media
  changing role of, 305–306
  contrasted with new media, 307
  and flow of information, 305
  role of, 346–347
  value of, 351–353
Trammell, Jack, 215
Transfer, 44
  propaganda technique, 55
Transit panels, 448
Trends, 15–16
Triggering event, 105
Trojan, promotions of, 335, 336–337
Trump, Ivana, 478
Tsang, You Mon, 503
Tucker, Kerry, 19
Turnitin.com, 71
Twain, Mark, 351
Twentieth Century Fox, 83
20/20, 280
Twitter.com, 323
  corporate use of, 340–341
Type families, 376
Typefaces, 375–376
  for brochures, 375–376
  for direct mail letter, 432
  tips for using, 364
Tyson Foods, 61

UNHCR, 431
UNICEF, 431
Unilever, 478
Unique visitor, defined, 318
United Airlines, 242
U.S. Potato Board, 39
United Steelworkers, YouTube use by,
  338
United Way of America, 62
Universe (virtual community), 69
UPS, blog of, 327–328
UPS Store, 165
Usenet
  defined, 529–530
  groups, 15, 324
Uses and gratification theory, 37–38

V/O, defined, 229

Webcasting, 288–289
  defined, 530
  of news conference, 321–322
Weber, Thomas, 315
Weber Grills, 112
Weber-Stephens Products, 294
Weberg, Don, 253
Weblogs. *See* Blogs
Websites
  audience for, 314
  control over, 320
  design elements for, 314–315
  effective building of, 311, 313–314
  effective use of, 36
  interactive elements of, 315–316
  marketing through, 313
  organizational use of, 308
  planning of, 313–314
  publicizing, 316–318
  rogue, 332
  ROI of, 319–320
  tips for, 312
  tracking visitors to, 318–319
  writing for, 310–313
Webster's Electronic Dictionary, 10
Webster's New World Dictionary, 9
Weezer, 513
Weidlich, Thom, 188
Weight loss claims, 62
Wells, Linda, 281
Wendy's, 300
West, Angela, 451
Westchester Medical Center, website
  of, 308, 309
WestGlen Communications, 225
Wharton School, podcasts of, 343
Whetsell, Tripp, 154
Whirlpool, podcasts of, 342
White, E. B., 10
White, Karen, 352
White papers, 400, 530
Whole Foods, Twitter use by, 340
The Wiki Way, 341
Wikipedia, 9, 323
Wikis, 323
  corporate use of, 341
  defined, 530
Wiley, Michael, 328
Williams, Bob, 273–274
Williams, Tudor, 504
Wilson, Laurie, 483
Wilson, Ralph, 313
Winfrey, Oprah, 478
Witherspoon, Reese, 478
Witkoski, Michael, 403
Witmer, Diane, 312, 314, 316

Wolfe, Catherine, 168
Women in Communications, 441
Woods, Tiger, 52
Word choice, 22–23
Word (Microsoft), 7, 361
Words
  choice of, 27–28
  sound-alike, 28
Work for hire, 73–74
Workshops, 458
World (Walgreen), 351
World Wide Web (Web), 14
  annual reports on, 381
  browsers for, 17
  characteristics of, 306, 308
  convention registration via, 473
  defined, 530
  as journalistic tool, 308, 310
  organizational use of, 308
  print publications and, 352–353
  search engines for, 17–18
  size of, 306
  See also Internet; Websites
World Wildlife Fund, 106
Wreden, Nick, 332
Wright, Tony, 332
Writing
  avoiding errors in, 26–31
  clarity of, 29
  as creative process, 25
  focus of, 24
  function of, 3
  guidelines for, 19–26, 386–387
  linear vs. nonlinear, 310–311
  for publication, 364
  purpose for, 19, 21
  tips for, 24
  for websites, 310–313

Xenadrine EFX, 62

Yahoo!, 17, 18, 300, 317
Yahoo! Groups, 324
Yamomoto, Mike, 164
Yehuda, Bev, 238
YMCA, 116
Young, Michael, 476
YouTube, 75, 322, 323, 513
  demographics of, 335
  importance of, 334–335
  promotions using, 335–336

Zazza, Frank, 243
Zero Gravity, 260–261
Zimmerman, Jan, 316
Zoom, defined, 229

eases (VNRs), 224, 530
  .ts of, 224
  , 225
  .y of, 229–230
  .nat of, 226
  .otification about, 232
  production of, 226–227
  samples of, 227, 228
  tips for producing, 228–229
  use of, 232–233
Video parodies, 335
Virtual online communities, 323,
    339–340
  privacy issues of, 69
Virtual reality, 323
Visa, 106, 133
Vista operating system, 7
Visual aids, for speeches, 414
  benefits of, 415
  software for, 415–418
VMS, 508
Vocus, 12, 508
Vogel, David, 302
Voice mail, 389
Voiceover, defined, 229

Wal-Mart, 486, 517
  copyright actions by, 73–74
Walker, Elizabeth Jane, 355
Walker, Jerry, 197
Wall Street Journal, 279
Wall Street Journal Stylebook, 11
Wallace, Michelle, 209
Wallenstein, Andrew, 253
Walton, Susan Balcom, 158, 159, 327
Waltzing Matilda, 246
Wanta, Wayne, 189
Ward, David, 108
Washington Hospital Center, 514
Washington Mutual, 516–517
Washington Speaker's Bureau, 462
Washington University, 184
Waste Management, advertising by,
    439
Watlington, Amanda, 189
The Wave, 355
Web 1.0, 322
Web 3.0, 345

Photo Credits

Chapter 1, p. 8, © AFPPhoto/Toru Yamanaka/ Newscom; p. 12, Courtesy of Andree Beckham, Cision US, Inc.; p. 13, top left, Courtesy of Julia Hood, *PRWeek,* New York; p. 13, top right, Courtesy of John Elsässer, Public Relations Tactics, Public Relations Society of America (PRSA); p. 13, bottom, Courtesy of Jack O'Dwyer, *O'Dwyers Newsletter,* New York.

Chapter 2, p. 52, Courtesy of Gatorade and PRNewsFoto/Newscom.

Chapter 3, p. 77, Courtesy of 3M Corporation; p. 78, Courtesy of Federal Express Corporation; p. 81, © Daniel Berehulak/Getty Images.

Chapter 4, p. 96, Courtesy of OrthoBioTech (OBT) and its distributor, Feature Photo Service/Newscom; p. 98, © Bryan Bedder/Getty Images; p. 100, © Bill Pugliano/Getty Images; p. 107, Courtesy of Cheryl Georges, The Hershey Company, and Whitney Miller, JSH&A Public Relations; p. 113, Courtesy of Feature Photo Service/Newscom; p. 114, © Bryan Smith/Zuma Press/Newscom.

Chapter 5, p. 121, Courtesy of Aetna and Ketchum communications; p. 125, Courtesy of Roger Germann, Shedd Aquarium, Chicago, IL; p. 134, Courtesy of Intel Corporation/Business Wire; p. 136, Courtesy of Business Wire; p. 138, Courtesy of Lisa Davis, Marketwire.

Chapter 6, p. 142, Courtesy of Roger Germann, Shedd Aquarium, Chicago, IL; p. 143, Courtesy of Cruise Lines International Association (CLIA)/ Business Wire; p. 144, Courtesy of Philips Norelco and Manning, Selvage & Lee public relations; p. 145, Courtesy of Greyhound Friends/ Feature Photo Service; p. 148, left, Courtesy of Laurie Guzzinati, Planters Peanuts and Mike Gehrig, Weber Shandwick; p. 148, right, Courtesy of Laurie Guzzinati, Planters Peanuts and Mike Gehrig, Weber Shandwick; p. 149, Courtesy of Adventures by Disney; p. 150, Courtesy of Roger Germann, Shedd Aquarium, Chicago, IL; p. 151, Courtesy of Roger Germann, Shedd Aquarium, Chicago, IL.

Chapter 7, p. 165, Courtesy of The UPS Store, Brian Agnes of Family Features Editorial Syndicate, and Marisa Giller, Fleishman-Hillard; p. 167, Courtesy of Gary Rainville, HP news department, Hewlett Packard, Palo Alto, CA; p. 170, Courtesy of Boggiato Produce, Inc. and Cindy Railing, Railing & Associates; p. 171, Courtesy of Homewood Suites/Business Wire; p. 172 , Courtesy of The Field Museum, Chicago, IL.

Chapter 8, p. 191, Courtesy of Intel Corporation/ Newscom; p. 193, top, Courtesy of Business Wire; p. 193, bottom, Courtesy of Panasonic/Newscom; p. 194, Courtesy of Panasonic and Feature Photo Service/Newscom; p. 195, Courtesy of Naked Juice Company and Feature Photo Service/Newscom; p. 196, Courtesy of IBM and Feature Photo Service/ Newscom; p. 201, Courtesy of Adventures by Disney vacations; p. 203, Courtesy of Rand McNally.

Chapter 9, p. 210, Courtesy of Andree Beckham, Cision US, Inc.; p. 221, Courtesy of American Veterinary Medical Association; p. 224, Courtesy of Business Wire; p. 227, Courtesy of March of Dimes and DS Simon Productions; p. 228, Courtesy of Julie Monzo, the American College of Pathologists; p. 231, Courtesy of Sheri Baer, The Hoffman Agency, San Jose, CA; p. 235, Courtesy of Jane Lawicki, director of public relations, Rotary International; p. 236, Illustration copyright © MediaLink, New York.

Chapter 10, pp. 250–251, Courtesy of Andree Beckham, Cision US, Inc.; p. 258, Courtesy of Gary Rainville, HP news department, Hewlett Packard, Palo Alto, CA; p. 262, Courtesy of Janet Evans, vice president, and Phil Dennison, graphic designer, Business Wire; p. 266, Courtesy of Brian Agnes, Family Features, and the National Cattlemen's Beef Association and Northwest Cherry Growers; p. 268, Courtesy of Feature Photo Service (FPS). Daniel Berehwlak, Getty Images.

Chapter 11, p. 287, Courtesy of Newscom. Gene Young, Splash News; p. 292, Courtesy of Dollywood, Pigeon Forge, Tennessee; p. 293, Courtesy of Lake Tahoe Visitor's Center and Switchback public relations; p. 296, Courtesy of Jane Lawicki, director of public relations, Rotary International.

Chapter 12, p. 309, Courtesy of David Billig, director of media relations, Westchester Medical Center, Valhalla, New York; p. 329, Courtesy of Linda Donaghy, Ford and Harrison, and Vincent Skyers, designer for M. Lee Smith Publishers, LLC; p. 336, Courtesy of David Johnson, group product manager, Trojan Brand Condoms; p. 337, Courtesy of David Johnson, group product manager, Trojan Brand Condoms; p. 339, Courtesy of Radley Moss, Text100; p. 343, Courtesy of Purina/Arc Worldwide © Mogan/Greenpeace; p. 344, Courtesy of Maureen Michaels, manager of public relations for OneUpWeb, Traverse City, Michigan. Copyright 2006 OneUpWeb.

Chapter 13, p.354, Courtesy of Robert Arndt, editor, *Saudi Aramco World*; p. 356, Courtesy of Elizabeth Walker, publications manager, St. Jude's Children's Research Hospital, Memphis, TN; p. 359, Courtesy of Anna M. Hawley, director of public relations, The Health Museum, Houston, Texas; p. 362, Courtesy of Mary Burnette, Associate Director of Communications, National Wildlife Federation; p. 370, Courtesy of the California Health and Human Services Agency; p. 374, Illustration courtesy of Baum Folder Company, Sidney, Ohio; p. 379, Courtesy of Catherine Babington, vice president for public affairs, Abbott Corporation; p. 382, Courtesy of Zia Zuberi, director of corporate communications, Siemens Pakistsan.

Chapter 15, p. 413 , Courtesy of Matthew Cavanaugh/epa/Corbis; p. 417, Illustrations courtesy of Tom Nicholson, executive director of the Arthur W. Page Society.

Chapter 16, p. 433, Courtesy of Amy Greer, the Natural Resources Defense Council (NRDC). Copyright © nrdc.org; p. 439, Courtesy of Mukta Tandon, corporate advertising group, and Patricia Wright, vice president of communications, BP Corporation; p. 440, Courtesy of Jane Lawicki, director of public relations, 0Rotary International; p. 443, Courtesy of Ad Council, U.S. Department of Health and Human Services; p. 449, Used with permission. Copyright © 2005 Men Can Stop Rape, Inc. Photography by Lottie Hansen.

Chapter 17, p. 458, Courtesy of Cisco Systems, Inc.; p. 459, Courtesy of Hakone Gardens, Saratoga, California; p. 468, Courtesy of the Dr. Martin Luther King, Jr. Library of the City of San Jose and San Jose State University; p. 474, Courtesy of Newscom/Sony Corporation. Ethan Miller/Getty Images; p. 480, Courtesy of the Avon Walk for Breast Cancer, Avon Corporation.

Chapter 18, p. 485, Photo courtesy of LWA/Stone/ Getty Images; p. 491, Courtesy of Claire H. Smith, director of corporate communications, Sunkist Growers, Inc. All Rights Reserved; p. 495, Illustration courtesy of Hewlett Packard Corporation.